Y0-CAP-448

WORLD ATLAS OF NATIONS

Rand McNally

WORLD ATLAS OF NATIONS

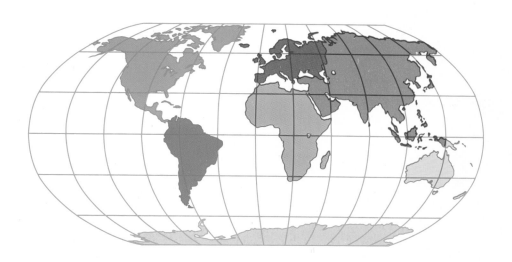

Rand McNally & Company

Chicago • New York • San Francisco

CONTENTS

WORLD ATLAS OF NATIONS
Rand McNally Editorial
and Cartographic Staff
Photo Credits
Photographs appearing on the pages listed are reproduced from these Rand McNally publications: *Images of the World* © 1983: viii (middle right). *Atlas of Mankind* © 1982: 2, 3 (left and right), 23, 40 (top and bottom), 46 (right), 78 (left), 79, 80 (left and right), 81 (left), 83, 93, 112 (bottom left), 117, 119, 121, 190, 191 (left and right). *Pictorial World Atlas* © 1980 (Colour Library International Limited): 4, 7, 8, 9, 15, 25, 32, 33, 34, 37, 39, 42, 46 (left), 47, 50, 54, 57 (right), 59 (top and bottom), 63, 66 (all photos), 67, 76, 78 (bottom right), 85, 86, 87, 88 (top and bottom), 89, 92, 94, 96, 103, 106, 112 (top right), 115, 116 (bottom), 118, 121, 122, 127, 129, 135, 136, 153 (bottom), 159, 163, 164, 168, 171 (top and bottom), 172 (all photos), 173 (all photos), 175, 176 (all photos), 177, 178 (all photos), 179 (all photos), 180, 181, 184. *Our Magnificent Earth* © 1979: 40, 78 (top right), 81 (right), 108, 147, 148.

Acknowledgment is made to these additional sources for use of the photographs on the following pages: 6, Hutchison Picture Library; 10, R. Phillips/The Image Bank; 12, Annie Price/Survival Anglia; 13 (top), J.N.B. Richardson/Telegraph Colour Library; 13 (bottom), E. Streichan/The Photo Source; 17, 18, Hutchison Picture Library; 19, S. B. Burman/Hutchison Picture Library; 27, J. Miles/Telegraph Colour Library; 29, J. Pate/Hutchison Picture Library; 30, Hutchison Picture Library; 31, Val and Alan Wilkins/Hutchison Picture Library; 35, S. Errington/Hutchison Picture Library; 45, P. Barker/The Photo Source; 56, Nick Meers/The Photo Source; 57 (left), Eric Wilkins/Telegraph Colour Library; 62, J. Ullal/The Image Bank; 65, Anna Tully/Hutchison Picture Library; 70, Joya Haars/Telegraph Colour Library; 72, 73, Hutchison Picture Library; 74, John Madere/The Image Bank; 75, Hong Kong Tourist Bureau; 77, Patrick Thurston/Telegraph Colour Library; 90, C. O. Rentmeester/The Image Bank; 91, N. Sutherland/The Photo Source; 95, P. Teuscher/FPG; 98, Graham Harrison/Telegraph Colour Library; 99, Tim Mollon/Hutchison Picture Library; 100, Hutchison Picture Library; 101, L.L. Rhodes/Telegraph Colour Library; 116 (top), Hutchison Picture Library; 118 (bottom), Hutchison Picture Library; 125, Allan S. Stone/FPG; 126, Hutchison Picture Library; 131, Helen Cole/Telegraph Colour Library; 134, Peter Keen/Telegraph Colour Library; 137, Ed Nowak/FPG; 140 (top and bottom), Commonwealth of Puerto Rico Tourism Co.; 142, Tom Tracy/FPG; 150, Jean Kugler/FPG; 152, 153 (top), Nic van Oudtshoorn/Telegraph Colour Library; 155, Hutchison Picture Library; 156, Jenny Pate/Hutchison Picture Library; 157, R. Phillips/The Image Bank; 158, Nick Meers/The Photo Source; 160, C. Silvestris/Telegraph Colour Library; 161, Mike Hardy/Telegraph Colour Library; 162, Christine Pemberton/Hutchison Picture Library; 167, R. G. Williamson/Telegraph Colour Library; 170, E. L. Wheater/The Image Bank; 183, Venezuelan International Airways; 188, T. E. Clark/Hutchison Picture Library; 192, C. de Jaeger/Telegraph Colour Library.

Copyright © 1988 by Rand McNally
All rights reserved. No part of this publication may be reproduced, stored in a retrieval system, or transmitted, in any form or by any means — electronic, mechanical, photocopying, recording, or otherwise — without the prior written permission of Rand McNally & Company

Printed in Italy
Library of Congress Catalog Card Number: 88-060112
ISBN 0-528-83315-4

USING THE ATLAS

Evidence suggests that mapmaking had its origins in humankind's earliest ages. Artifacts clearly show that ancient peoples possessed the skills necessary to draw maps, and it is a known fact that almost anyone can sketch simple directions with ease. Thus it seems likely that for hundreds of years maps have been playing their unique and important role, presenting information about routes, territories, and the lay of the land.

Some of the earliest known maps are those defining territory and ownership. Dating from the second and first millenia B.C., the rock-carving map in Figure 1 shows stepped square fields, paths, rivers, and houses of the Val Comonica in Italy. But as many cultures have demonstrated, maps can be elegant as well as useful. In Figure 2, the Mexican map of the Tepetlaoztoc Valley, drawn in 1583, depicts the land with colorful artistry. Hills are shown with wavy lines, and footprints between parallel lines indicate roads.

Although these early maps served the immediate purpose of the mapmaker, their accuracy suffered considerably, dependent upon the methods and materials of the then-available technology. Today's highly accurate maps stand in sharp contrast to their predecessors, and modern-day mapmakers benefit from the world's ever-increasing technological knowledge. Satellite imagery, shown in Figures 3 and 4, now furnish current, highly precise material from which maps such as those in Figures 5 and 6 can be created and updated.

A map is unique in that nowhere else can the countries, cities, roads, rivers, and lakes that cover a vast area be simultaneously viewed — each in its location relative to the other. In the 1500s Gerardus Mercator, a Flemish cartographer, coined the word *atlas* to describe a collection of maps. The atlas is unique among reference works because, with its maps, it actually shows where things are located in the world. As a dictionary defines words, as an encyclopedia defines people and things, so an atlas graphically defines the world. Only on the maps of an atlas can routes between places be traced, trips planned, boundaries examined, distances measured, meandering rivers and streams visualized, large and small lakes compared — and faraway places imagined.

RAND MᶜNALLY'S
WORLD ATLAS OF NATIONS

A nation is often described as a community of people of one or more nationalities inhabiting a defined territory and possessing a specific government. Nations are generally thought of as being relatively large and having independent status.

But the world comprises many lands that do not fit neatly into this definition. Semi-independent areas, regions struggling to gain independence, colonies, commonwealths, and possessions — each has a population, history, and geography that cannot be fully appreciated when included with its administering nations.

Therefore, this atlas uses a much broader definition, considering a nation to be any politically organized entity. The atlas not only features the 168 independent countries, but also gives details on the remote, romantic, interesting, and relatively unknown places that are often looked for, but seldom found, in other world atlases.

Rand McNally's *World Atlas of Nations* is also unique in its combination of map and nonmap material to describe each nation. The atlas features
□ Reference maps for each nation presented in alphabetical order — find the place you're looking for quickly and easily.
□ Complete nation-by-nation description . . . map index, fact block, article, and photos accompany each reference map — no back-and-forth paging to find the information you need.
□ Quick-reference index alongside the map lists major cities, lakes, rivers, and other features . . . Universal Index at the back of the book lists *all* the places on *all* the maps in alphabetical order.
□ Locator maps show each nation in relation to its neighbors and give an idea of strategic importance.
□ Fact block for each nation — an at-a-glance description of people, economy, land, and politics.
□ Articles on each nation describe what maps cannot — trends, economic problems, political climates, people and culture, history.
□ Photographs, captions, and flags bring the land and culture of each nation to life.
□ Mini-atlas shows all the world's places in relation to one another in vivid color — 16 pages.

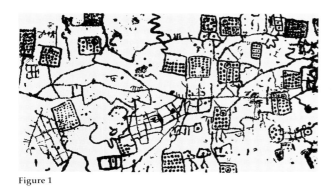

Figure 1

Figure 2

Figure 3

Figure 4

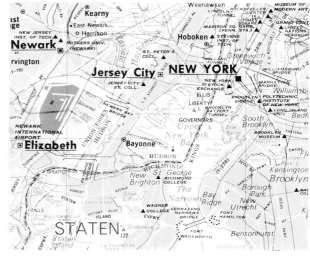

Figure 5

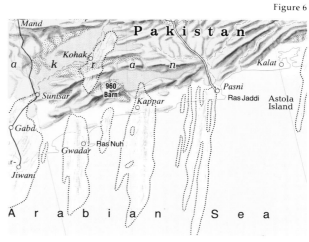

Figure 6

With its maps, articles, statistics, photos, and flags, Rand McNally's *World Atlas of Nations* presents the 216 nations as no atlas has done before. The innovative alphabetical presentation of nations, rather than a traditional geographic arrangement, is new to atlas organization and makes this a truly unique reference work patterned to quickly and easily provide answers to your questions about "where"—and a lot more. Rand McNally's *World Atlas of Nations* is a standard reference work for the home, office, school, and university.

GETTING THE MOST INFORMATION FROM THE MAPS

You can use this atlas for many purposes—to plan a trip, to find hot spots in the news, to supplement your knowledge of the world and its events. All the information you need can be found quickly and easily because of the atlas's unique alphabetical organization.

But to realize the full potential of the atlas, and to get the most from the maps, the user must be able to
1. Find places on the maps
2. Measure distances
3. Determine directions
4. Understand map symbols

Finding Places

One of the most common and important tasks facilitated by an atlas is finding the location of a place in the world. A river's name in a book, a city mentioned in the news, or a vacation spot in a travel guide may prompt your need to know *where* a place is located. The following illustrations explain how to find Benguela, a place in the African country of Angola.

1. If you know that Benguela is in Angola, you can easily find the map of Angola, which appears in its alphabetical position on page 6. If you don't know which country Benguela is in, refer to the Universal Index on page 193. This index lists the maps' place-names alphabetically and will direct you to the map of Angola.

2. On page 6, find the Angola Map Index, an alphabetical listing of the major places and features on the map (Figure 7). In the index, city names appear in regular roman type, whereas physical feature names, such as rivers, mountains, and lakes, are shown in slanted, or italic, type. Locate Benguela in the alphabetical list.

3. Look in the two columns to the right of the place-name of Benguela and find the city's latitude (Lat.) and longitude (Long.). The degrees (°) and minutes (') of latitude and longitude measure distance and indicate the location of a place on the earth and its position on the map. The index shows that Benguela is found at 12°35's latitude and 13°25'E longitude (Figure 7).

The degrees of latitude, found near the right and left edges of the map, identify the blue lines of latitude that run horizontally across the map. Latitude tells how far north (N) or south (S) of the equator a place is located. The degrees of longitude, found near the map's top and bottom edges, identify the vertical lines of longitude, also shown in blue. Longitude indicates how far east (E) or west (W) of the prime meridian a place is located. Only certain lines of latitude and longitude are identified and numbered on the maps (Figure 8).

4. Looking along the left edge of the map, locate Benguela's latitude, 12°35'S, which lies between the 10° and the 15° lines of latitude. Benguela's longitude, 13°25'E, lies between the 10° and 15° lines of longitude, and these numbers appear near the top of the map (Figure 8).

5. To find Benguela, place your left index finger near the approximate location of 12°S latitude, between 10°S and 15°S, and place your right index finger between 10°E and 15°E, about where 12°E would lie. Move your left finger across the map horizontally and your right finger down the map vertically. Benguela is found in the area in which your fingers meet (Figure 8).

Measuring Distances

In planning a trip, it is essential to know the distance between places, and the maps in this atlas can help in this, as well as other, aspects of travel preparation. For example, to determine the distance between Benguela and Caconda, Angola, you would follow these steps:

1. Lay a slip of paper on the map of Angola so that its edge touches the two cities (Figure 8). Adjust the paper so one corner touches Benguela. Mark the paper directly at the spot where Caconda is situated.

2. Now place the paper along the scale of miles (mi) found in the map's legend area. Position the corner at 0 and line up the edge of the paper along the scale. (Figure 9 shows how the piece of paper should line up with the scale.) The pencil mark on the paper indicates Caconda is about 125 miles (200 kilometers) from Benguela.

The scale relationship of the map to the earth may also be expressed as a ratio. For example, 1:10,570,000 is the scale of the map of Angola (Figure 8). The map unit in the ratio is always given as 1, and the number of similar units the map unit represents on the earth's surface is written after the colon. Thus, for the map of Angola, 1 inch on the map represents 10,570,000 inches on the earth's surface. To convert the inches to miles, divide 63,360 (the number of inches in 1 mile) into 10,570,000, and you will find that 1 inch on the map of Angola represents approximately 167 miles on the earth.

Figure 7

Angola Map Index

	Lat.	Long.		Lat.	Long.
Benguela	12°35'S	13°25'E	*Longa*	10°15'S	13°30'E
Cabinda	5°33'S	12°12'E	Luanda	8°48'S	13°14'E
Cassai (Kasai)	7°15'S	21°48'E	*Luangue*	7°00'S	19°33'E
Chilengue			Lubango	14°55'S	13°30'E
Mountains	13°10'S	15°18'E	Luena	11°47'S	19°52'E
Congo	6°04'S	12°24'E	*Lungué-Bungo*	13°27'S	22°00'E
Cuando	17°38'S	23°22'E	Malanje	9°32'S	16°20'E
Cuango	5°50'S	16°35'E	*Marca Point*	16°31'S	11°42'E
Cuanza	9°19'S	13°08'E	M'banza Congo	6°16'S	14°15'E
Cubango	18°00'S	21°27'E	*M'Bridge*	7°14'S	12°52'E
Cuilo (Kwilu)	7°38'S	19°25'E	Menongue	14°36'S	17°48'E
Cuito	18°01'S	20°48'E	*Môco, Mount*	12°28'S	15°10'E
Cunene	17°20'S	11°50'E	N'dalatando	9°18'S	14°54'E
Cuvo	10°50'S	13°47'E	*Neve Mountains*	13°52'S	13°26'E
Huambo	12°30'S	15°40'E	*Santa Maria,*		
Humbe			*Cape*	13°25'S	12°32'E
Mountains	12°13'S	15°25'E	Saurimo	9°39'S	20°24'E
Kuito	12°22'S	16°56'E	Uige	7°37'S	15°03'E
Lobito	12°20'S	13°34'E	*Zambezi*	13°00'S	22°42'E

Figure 8

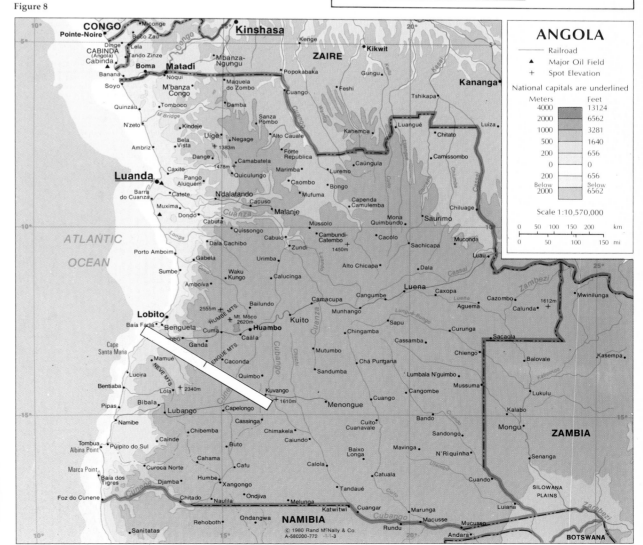

Figure 9

Determining Directions

Most of the maps in this atlas are drawn so that when oriented for normal reading, north is at the top of the map, south is at the bottom, west is at the left, and east is at the right. Most maps have a gridwork of lines drawn across them—the lines of latitude and longitude. Lines of latitude, or parallels of latitude, are drawn east and west. Lines of longitude, or meridians of longitude, are drawn north and south (Figure 10).

Parallels and meridians appear as either curved or straight lines. For example, in the section of the map of France in Figure 10 the parallels of latitude appear as curved lines. The meridians of longitude are straight lines that come together toward the top of the map.

Not only do latitude and longitude lines help in locating places on a map, they also aid in determining direction. Parallels of latitude are numbered in degrees north and south of the equator. Meridians of longitude are numbered in degrees east and west of the prime meridian, an imaginary line that runs through Greenwich, England, near London (Figure 11). As previously illustrated, latitude and longitude lines can help you locate any place on earth.

Parallels and meridians are also used to determine directions. For example, suppose you want to know which city is farther north, Paris or Nantes, France. The map in Figure 10 shows that Nantes is south of the 48° parallel of latitude, and Paris lies north of it. This means that Paris is farther north than Nantes. The meridians of longitude help determine which city is farther east. Nantes is approximately 2° west of the 0° meridian, or prime meridian, and Paris is almost 3° east of it. This means that Paris is farther east than Nantes.

Figure 11

Understanding Map Symbols

In a very real sense, a whole map is a symbol, representing parts of the world or the world itself. A map is a reduced representation of the earth; and each of the world's features—its cities, rivers, mountains—is represented on the map by a symbol. Map symbols may appear as points, lines, or areas.

Point symbols, such as dots or stars, are often used for cities, capital cities, or points of interest. Line symbols generally represent roads, rivers, and railroads. Area symbols are used for features that cover a large area, such as states, forests, and deserts. Area symbols can also indicate elevation. Most of the maps in this atlas, for example, show the different elevations of the land and the depths of the water by differently colored tints. The lighter tints indicate lower land elevations and shallower water depths; darker tints represent higher elevations and lower depths.

Symbols seldom look like the feature they represent and, therefore, must be identified and interpreted. The map legend, found either on the map itself or on a separate legend page identifies the symbols used on the maps. In this atlas, the map legend on page I•1 pertains to the maps on pages I•2 to I•16. The map legend on page 1 identifies symbols used on pages 2 to 192.

GETTING THE MOST FROM THE LOCATOR MAPS, THE FACT BLOCKS, AND THE ARTICLES

In this atlas, each of the world's major political entities is described in a half-page, full-page, two-page, or three-page unit, depending on the entity's size and importance. For each unit there is a locator map, a fact block (printed in blue type), and a brief article (printed in black). The geographic, political, and population-related information presented in each unit is derived from the most current Rand McNally data available. Foreign census information, United Nations publications, and United States documents about foreign places are the major sources for the material.

Fact Block

This statistical list gives a quick overview of the nation's people, politics, economy, and land. **Ethnic groups, Religions, Trade Partners, Exports,** and **Imports** are listed in order of decreasing size and/or importance. **Languages** are similarly organized, with official language(s) listed first. **Political parties** are cited alphabetically, as are **Memberships,** which represent member nations of the following organizations:

Arab League (AL)
Association of South East Asian Nations (ASEAN)
Commonwealth of Nations (CW)
Council for Mutual Economic Assistance (CEMA)
European Communities (Common Market) (EC)
North Atlantic Treaty Organization (NATO)
Organization for Economic Cooperation and Development (OECD)
Organization of African Unity (OAU)
Organization of American States (OAS)
Organization of Petroleum Exporting Countries (OPEC)
United Nations (UN)
Warsaw Pact

For certain political entities, reliable facts are not available and, therefore, are not included.

Articles

The articles that describe the places in the atlas are segmented in a consistent fashion to allow quick access to the information you need.

PEOPLE. This section describes a place's population, often touching on ethnicity, religion, language, social problems, and other important factors.

ECONOMY AND THE LAND. The strengths and weaknesses of each nation's economy, as well as the terrain and climate, are covered in this section.

HISTORY AND POLITICS. The significant events that have shaped each nation are related here.

Figure 10

MAPS OF THE WORLD, OCEANS, AND CONTINENTS

This section of the atlas opens with a map of the world that shows the nations as they are linked together to make up the total world community. The political boundaries are emphasized to show the intricate way in which all countries are interrelated. The brown shading indicates the land surface and how it is related to the earth's political scene.

The portrait maps that follow the map of the world are included to show the large ocean expanses and the individual continents in detail. The continent maps are all drawn to a consistent scale of 1:24,000,000 to show a global view of the earth as it would appear from about 4,000 miles in space. The consistent scale enables comparison of the sizes, shapes, and relationships of the world's features. The scale is approximately that of a globe 20 inches in diameter.

The colors and shading on the continent and ocean maps portray the surface of the land, its broad terrain and vegetative environments, as if viewed from space during the growing season. Underwater features and varying water depths are represented by shading and different color tones. The result is a dramatic portrait of the earth's major land and submarine forms.

The form of the land, major vegetative environments, and submarine features portrayed on the maps are identified in the legend below.

World, Ocean, and Continent Map Legend

Land's Vegetative Environments

Ice and Snow

High and Barren

Tundra and Alpine

Needleleaf Tree

Broadleaf Tree

Tropical Rainforest

Grassland

Dry Scrub

Desert

Water Features

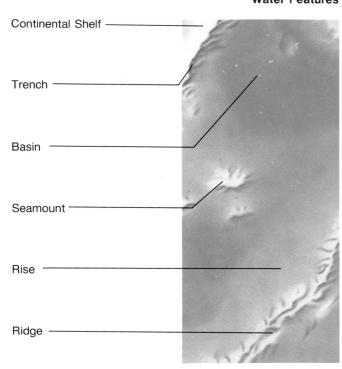

Continental Shelf
Trench
Basin
Seamount
Rise
Ridge

Other Land Features

Matterhorn 4478 △   Elevation Above Sea Level

76 ▽   Elevation Below Sea Level

Mount Cook 3764 ▲   Highest Elevation in Country

133 ▼   Lowest Elevation in Country

Elevations and depths are given in meters

Highest elevation and lowest elevation of a continent are underlined.

A N D E S   Mountain Range

BAFFIN ISLAND   Island

POLUOSTROV KAMČATKA   Peninsula, Cape, Point, etc.

Other Water Features

Shoreline

Undefined or Fluctuating Shoreline

Amur   River, Stream

Intermittent Stream

764 ▽   Depth of Water

8428 ▼   Greatest Depth (Atlantic, Pacific, and Indian oceans)

L. Victoria   Lake, Reservoir

Intermittent Lake, Reservoir

Tuz Gölü   Salt Lake

Inhabited Localities

. 0—100,000
⊙ 100,000—1,500,000
■ >1,500,000

The symbol size represents the approximate number of inhabitants within the locality.

Kiruna
Bordeaux
Frankfurt
BARCELONA

The size of the type indicates the relative economic and political importance of the locality.

LONDON   Capitals of political entities are underlined.

International Political Boundaries

Demarcated, Undemarcated, and Administrative

These colored boundaries are shown only on the world map.

Disputed De Facto

Disputed De Jure

Indefinite or Undefined

Demarcation Line

FAEROE ISLANDS (Den.)   Administering country is shown in parentheses.

MOSKVA MOSCOW   Unless a feature is international in scope, the name form used on the map is the country's local official name for the feature. For certain unfamiliar names the English form is also printed with the local form.

Kilometers
0   1000   2000   3000 Km.

Statute Miles
0   1000   2000   3000 Mi.

One centimeter represents 750 kilometers.
One inch represents approximately 1200 miles.
Robinson Projection
Scale 1:75,000,000

Copyright © by Rand McNally & Co.
Map prepared by Rand McNally & Co.
A-510000-264   -9 -11. -25

Scale 1:48,000,000
at 35° latitude
One centimeter represents 480 kilometers.
One inch represents approximately 760 miles.
Modified Cylindrical Projection

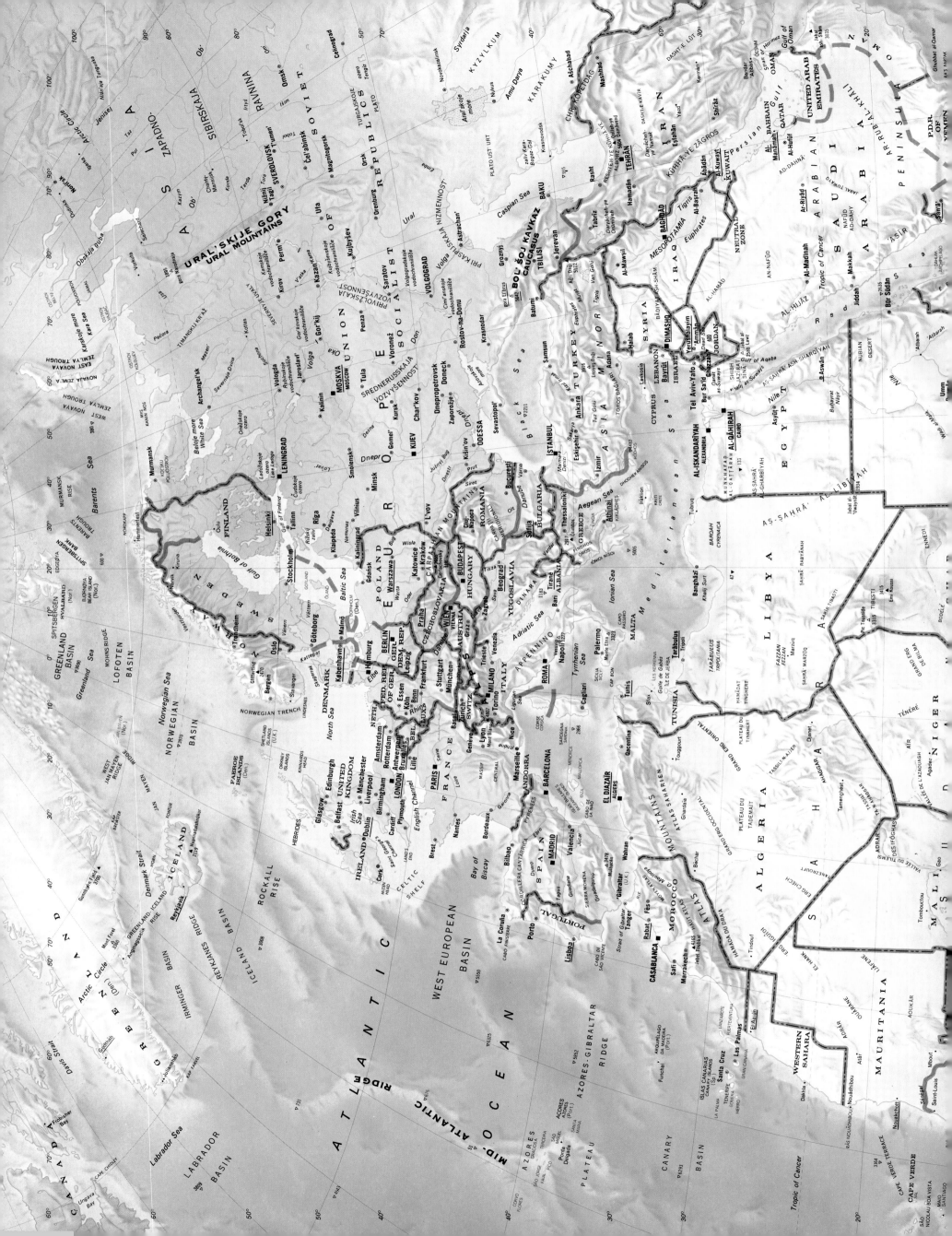

PHILIPPINE Sea

PHILIPPINE TRENCH

SAMAR

MINDANAO

LUZON

Luzon Strait

TAIWAN

Xiamen

PHILIPPINES

MANILA
Quezon City

VICTORIA
HONG KONG
Macau
GUANGZHOU
CANTON

Haikou
HAINAN DAO

SOUTH CHINA SEA

Sulu Sea

Celebes Sea

SULAWESI
CELEBES

Ujung Pandang

Banjarmasin

BORNEO
KALIMANTAN

BRUNEI

MALAYSIA

Kuching

SUNDA ISLANDS

INDONESIA

JAKARTA
Bandung

Surabaya

JAWA

JAVA

Palembang

SUMATRA
SUMATERA

SINGAPORE

Kuala Lumpur

George Town

Medan

MALAY PENINSULA

MALAYSIA

ISTHMUS OF KRA

Gulf of Thailand

THAILAND

KRUNG THEP
BANGKOK

KAMPUCHEA
Phnum Pénh

VIETNAM

LAOS

Vientiane

HO CHI MINH
(SAIGON)
THANH-PHO

Da-nang

Hai-phong
Gulf of Tonkin
Ha-nôi

INDOCHINA

Mekong

BURMA

Mandalay

Rangoon

Moulmein

Irrawaddy

Andaman Sea

ANDAMAN ISLANDS (India)

COCO ISLANDS

PREPARIS ISLAND

Ten Degree Channel

NICOBAR ISLANDS (India)

Bay of Bengal

SRI LANKA

Colombo

CAPE COMORIN

MADRAS

COROMANDEL COAST

Hyderābād

Bangalore

Cochin

MALABAR COAST

Pune

BOMBAY

Ahmadābād

INDIA

DELHI
New Delhi

Kānpur

Vārānasi

Patna

CALCUTTA

Dhaka

BANGLADESH

Chittagong

Kathmandu

NEPAL

BHUTAN

HIMALAYAS

Lhasa

Ganges

Brahmaputra

PAKISTAN

KARACHI

Hyderābād

Sukkur

Gulf of Kutch

Gulf of Khambhat

LAKSHADWEEP (India)

LACCADIVE Sea

MALDIVES

Male

EIGHT DEGREE CHANNEL

NINE DEGREE CHANNEL

CHAGOS ARCHIPELAGO (B.I.O.T.)

DIEGO GARCIA

LACCADIVE PLATEAU

CHAGOS LACCADIVE RIDGE

INDIAN OCEAN

MID-INDIAN BASIN

WHARTON BASIN

COCOS ISLANDS (Austl.)

CHRISTMAS ISLAND (Austl.)

JAVA TRENCH

NINETYEAST RIDGE

BROKEN RIDGE

AUSTRALIA

Perth

PERTH BASIN

NORTH AUSTRALIAN BASIN

GIBSON DESERT

GREAT SANDY DESERT

Broome

EXMOUTH

DARLING RANGE

Tropic of Capricorn

ARABIAN SEA

ARABIAN BASIN

CARLSBERG RIDGE

OWEN FRACTURE ZONE

OMAN

Gulf of Oman

Strait of Hormuz

UNITED ARAB EMIRATES

QATAR

AR-RUB'-AL-KHĀLĪ

ARABIAN PENINSULA

P.D.R. OF YEMEN

YEMEN

Gulf of Aden

Aden

DJIBOUTI

ETHIOPIA

SOMALIA

Muqdisho

Shabeelle

SOMALI BASIN

Equator

SEYCHELLES

SEYCHELLES BANK

SAYA DE MALHA BANK

NAZARETH BANK

CARGADOS CARAJOS (Maur.)

MASCARENE PLATEAU

MASCARENE BASIN

MAURITIUS

RÉUNION (Fr.)

MASCARENE ISLANDS

RODRIGUES (Maur.)

SOUTHWEST INDIAN RIDGE

MID-INDIAN RIDGE

MADAGASCAR

Antananarivo

MADAGASCAR BASIN

Tropic of Capricorn

Scale 1:24,000,000

One centimeter represents 240 kilometers.
One inch represents approximately 380 miles.
Lambert Azimuthal Equal-Area Projection

Statute Miles
Kilometers

Mi.
Km.

Copyright © by Rand McNally & Co.
Map prepared by Rand McNally & Co.
A-855200-784

160° 170° 180° KURE MIDWAY PEARL AND 170° HAWAIIAN 160° 150° ZONE
ISLAND ISLANDS HERMES REEF Tropic of Cancer
Guadalupe KURE (U.S.) LISIANSKI ISLANDS FRACTURE
Seamount ISLAND LAYSAN (U.S.)
ISLAND
HAWAIIAN GARDNER
PINNACLES
PAUL NECKER NIHOA
▽ 6890 Seamount FRENCH
FRIGATE
SHOALS KAUAI
NECKER RIDGE RIDGE NIIHAU OAHU MOLOKAI Honolulu MAUI
▽ 1477 LANAI
HORIZON Hilo
▽ 1316 Tablemount Swordfish MAUNA KEA HAWAII
PACIFIC WAKE ISLAND MOUNTAINS HESS Seamount 4205
(U.S.) Tablemount KARIN Seamount MAUNA KEA KA LAE
▽ 859 JOHNSTON ATOLL ▽ 1057 Pensacola
CAPE (U.S.) Seamount
JOHNSON
Tablemount 4809 ▽
MARSHALL SCHJETMAN
ISLANDS TAONGI REEF
(T.T.P.I.) 20°
P
BIKINI RIKAR A
ENEWETAK RONGELAP UTIRIK 6519 ▽ CENTRAL C
AILUK I
WOTHO MARSHALL F
UJAE LAE LIB NAMU WOTJE MALOELAP PACIFIC I
KWAJALEIN RATAK CHAIN
RALIK ISLANDS C
KOSRAE NAMORIK ARNO MAJURO BASIN 10°
PINGELAP KILI MILI
JALUIT
EBON O
BUTARITARI C
MELANESIAN TARAWA GILBERT E
▽ 4462 KURIA ABEMAMA A
NAURU N
BANABA NONOUTI BERU NIKUNAU Equator
BASIN TABITEUEA ONOTOA WINSLOW 0°
TAMANA REEF
▽ 1737 ARORAE HOWLAND ISLAND (U.S.)
BAKER ISLAND (U.S.)
SOLOMON NANUMEA KIRIBATI PHOENIX KANTON
ISLANDS NIUTAO ENDERBURY
TUVALU NANUMANGA ISLANDS BIRNIE RAWAKI
NUI ORONA MANRA
VAITUPU NIKUMARORO
10°

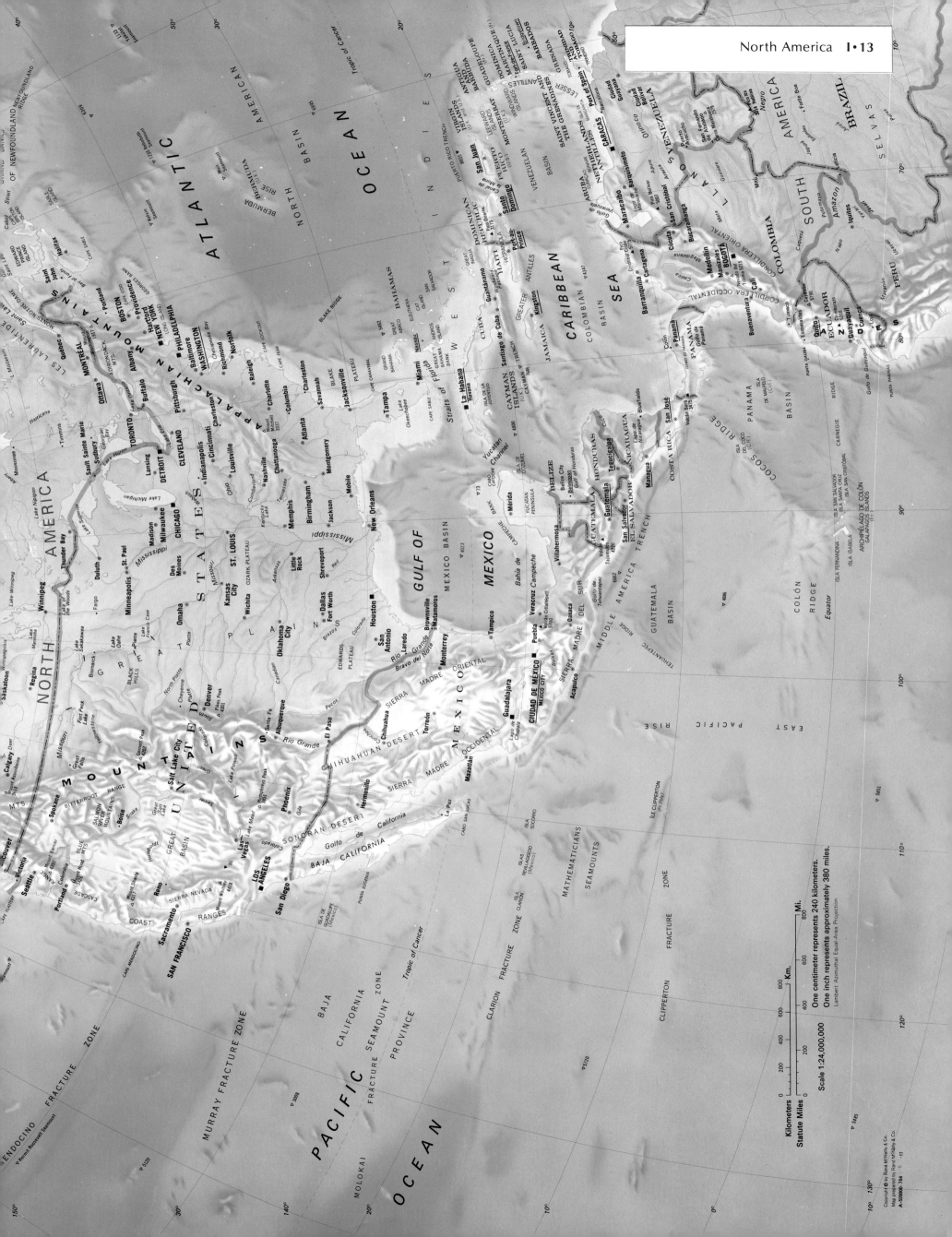

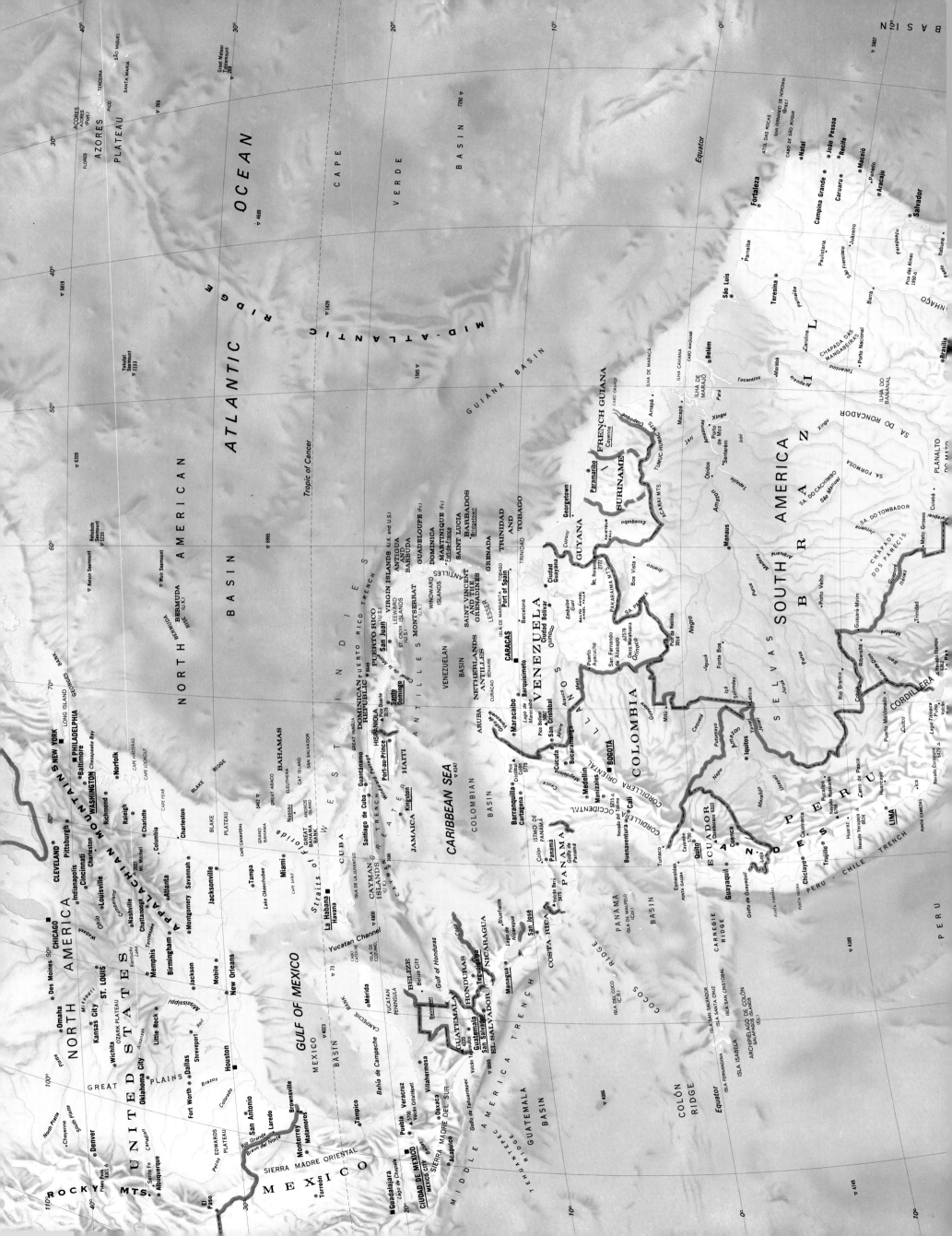

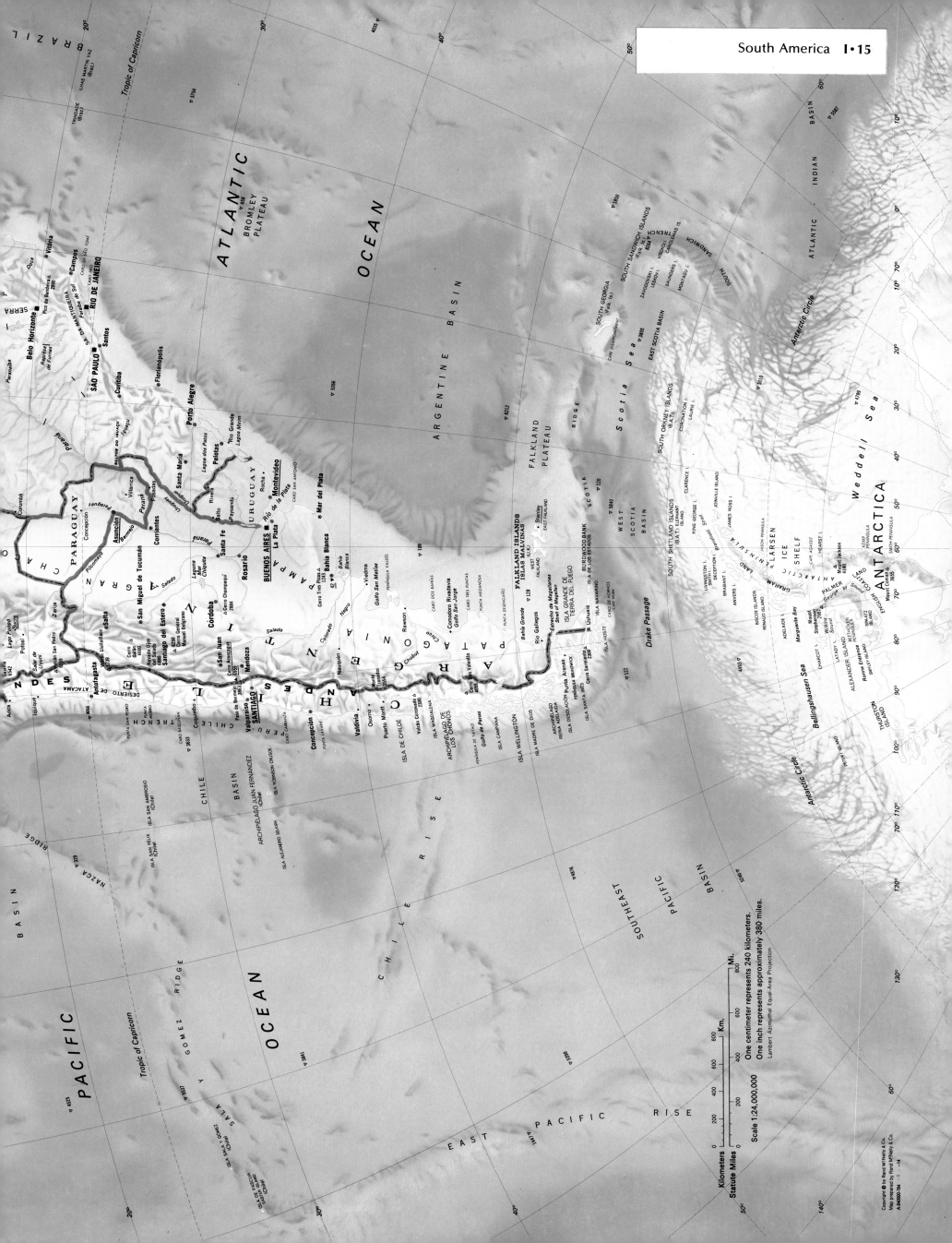

ATLANTIC

OCEAN

BROMLEY
PLATEAU

A R G E N T I N E   B A S I N

FALKLAND
PLATEAU

FALKLAND
RIDGE

SOUTH GEORGIA (FALK. IS.)

SOUTH SANDWICH ISLANDS (U.K.)

SANDWICH TRENCH

Scotia
Sea

Scotia
Sea

SOUTH ORKNEY ISLANDS (B.A.T.)

CORONATION I.
LAURIE I.

WEST
SCOTIA
BASIN

EAST SCOTIA BASIN

Antarctic Circle

ATLANTIC

INDIAN

Weddell Sea

ANTARCTICA

SOUTH SHETLAND ISLANDS (B.A.T.)

ELEPHANT I.
CLARENCE I.
KING GEORGE I.

LIVINGSTON I.
DECEPTION I.

LARSEN
ICE
SHELF

PALMER LAND

GRAHAM LAND

ANTARCTIC PENINSULA

KEMP
LAND

ENGLISH COAST

THURSTON
ISLAND

Bellingshausen Sea

ALEXANDER ISLAND

Marguerite Bay

ADELAIDE I.

BISCOE ISLANDS

ANVERS I.
BRABANT I.

RENAUD ISLAND

BISCOE ISLANDS

LATADY ISLAND

CHARCOT I.

PETER I ISLAND

Antarctic Circle

PACIFIC

OCEAN

BRAZIL

Tropic of Capricorn

Vitória
Campos
RIO DE JANEIRO
Santos
Curitiba
Florianópolis
Porto Alegre
Rio Grande
Pelotas
SÃO PAULO
Belo Horizonte
Paraná

PARAGUAY

ASUNCIÓN

URUGUAY

Montevideo
BUENOS AIRES
La Plata
Rosario
Santa Fe
Paraná
Corrientes
Posadas
Santa Maria
Rivera

Córdoba
Santiago del Estero
San Miguel de Tucumán
Salta
Mendoza
San Juan
SANTIAGO
Valparaíso
Concepción
Valdivia
Osorno
Puerto Montt

ANDES

P A M P A

Bahía Blanca
Mar del Plata

Viedma
PENÍNSULA VALDÉS
Golfo San Matías
Neuquén
Rawson
Comodoro Rivadavia
Golfo San Jorge

P A T A G O N I A

ISLA DE CHILOÉ

ARCHIPIÉLAGO DE LOS CHONOS

Golfo de Penas

ISLA WELLINGTON

ISLA GRANDE DE
TIERRA DEL FUEGO

Estrecho de Magallanes
Strait of Magellan

Punta Arenas
Río Gallegos
Ushuaia

CABO DE HORNOS

Drake Passage

BURDWOOD BANK

FALKLAND ISLANDS
ISLAS MALVINAS (U.K.)

Stanley
EAST FALKLAND
WEST FALKLAND

CHILE BASIN

NAZCA RIDGE

GOMEZ RIDGE

CHILE RISE

ARCHIPIÉLAGO JUAN FERNÁNDEZ
(Chile)

ISLA SAN FÉLIX
ISLA SAN AMBROSIO
(Chile)

ISLA DE PASCUA
EASTER ISLAND (Chile)

ISLA SALA Y GOMEZ
(Chile)

SOUTHEAST
PACIFIC
BASIN

EAST PACIFIC RISE

Tropic of Capricorn

DESIERTO DE ATACAMA

ATACAMA TRENCH

PERÚ - CHILE TRENCH

Kilometers
Statute Miles

0   200   400   600   800   Km.
                              Mi.
0   200   400   800

One centimeter represents 240 kilometers.
One inch represents approximately 380 miles.
Lambert Azimuthal Equal-Area Projection

Scale 1:24,000,000

Copyright © by Rand McNally & Co.
Map prepared by Rand McNally & Co.
A-640000-784 –5. –14

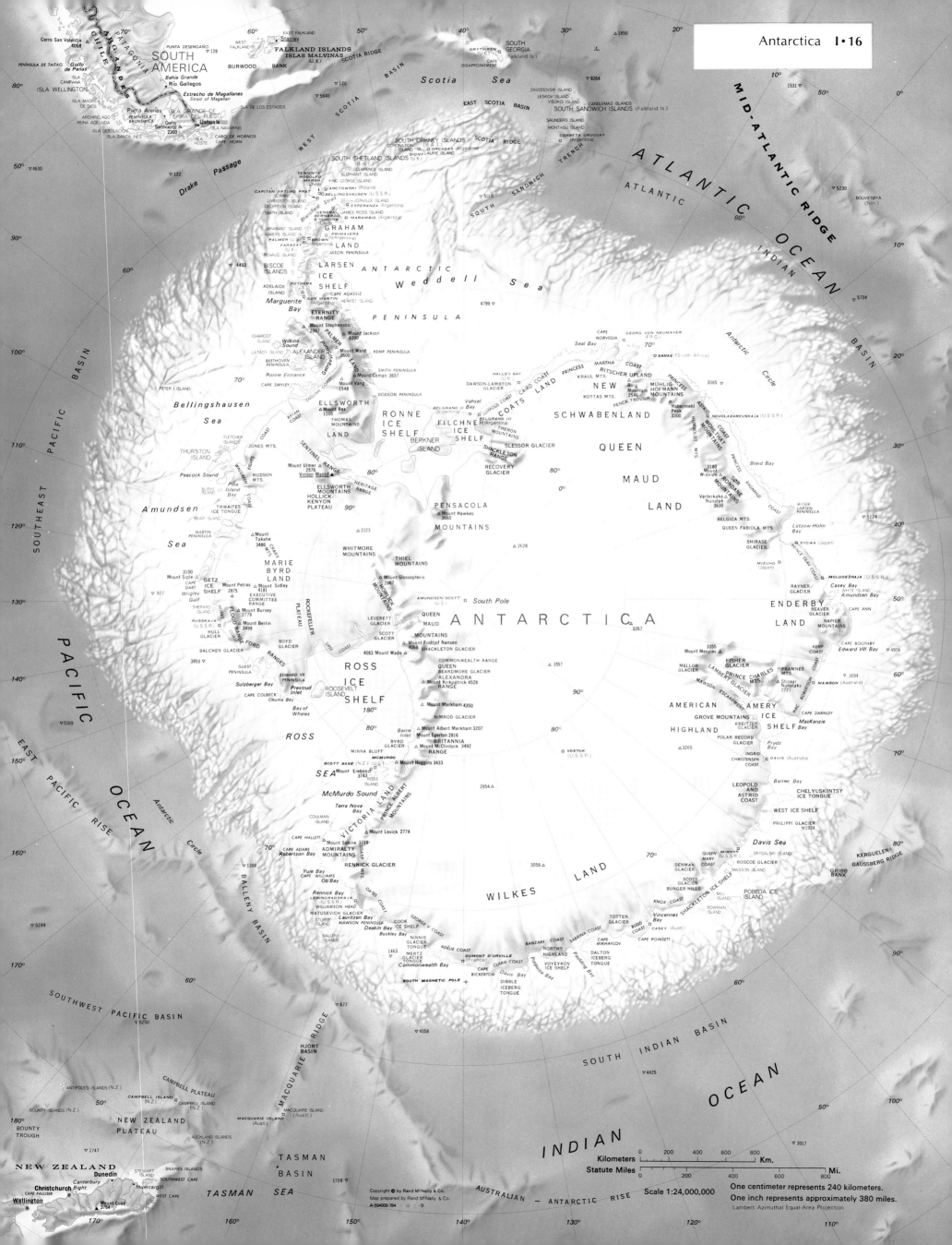

Scale 1:24,000,000

One centimeter represents 240 kilometers.
One inch represents approximately 380 miles.
Lambert Azimuthal Equal-Area Projection

Copyright © by Rand McNally & Co.
Map prepared by Rand McNally & Co.
A-594000-764

MAPS OF WORLD NATIONS

Map Legend

The following symbols are found on the reference maps that follow.
In addition to this master legend, most maps have an individual legend.

Major Urban Area

Clayton
Evansville
Oakland
Seattle
Pittsburgh
New York

City type size indicates the relative importance of the places.

<u>Washington</u> National Capital (underlined)

International Boundary

Secondary Boundary (states, provinces, etc.)

Autonomous Region Boundary

Occupied Territory

Lake Keban Lake

Huallaga River

Twente Canal Canal or Waterway

Dike

Glacier

Ice Cap

Ice Shelf

+ Mt. Wade
  4083M Spot Elevation or Depth

Railroad

Major Oil Pipeline

▲ Major Oil Field

Elevations and Depths.

Elevations and depths can be determined by referring to the color bar on each map. The different colors represent areas of different elevations. The darker the color, the higher the elevation and the lower the depth. From the colors you can get an idea of terrain and depth.

The diagram below illustrates the relationship between the earth's terrain and depths, the color bar legend, and the map.

Map Legend
Elevations above and depths below Sea Level

Profile of Land / Water Surface

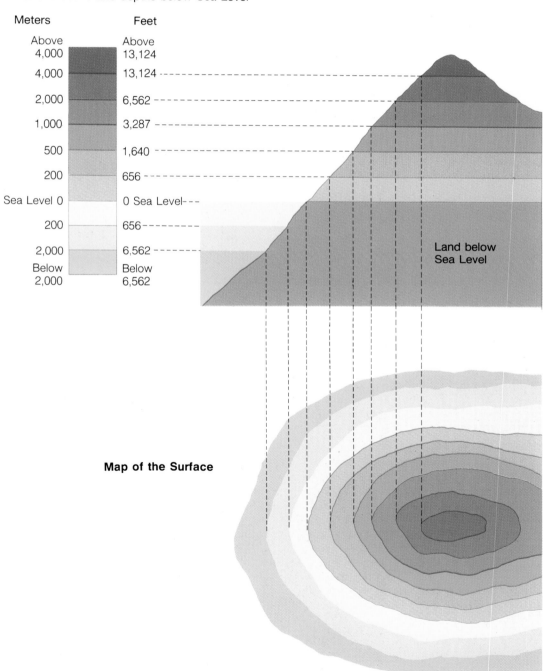

Meters	Feet
Above 4,000	Above 13,124
4,000	13,124
2,000	6,562
1,000	3,287
500	1,640
200	656
Sea Level 0	0 Sea Level
200	656
2,000	6,562
Below 2,000	Below 6,562

Land below Sea Level

Map of the Surface

AFGHANISTAN

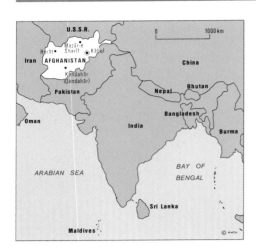

OFFICIAL NAME Democratic Republic of Afghanistan

PEOPLE
Population 14,650,000.
Density 59/mi² (23/km²).
Urban 16%.
Capital Kābul, 913,164.
Ethnic groups Pushtun 50%, Tajik 25%, Uzbek 9%, Hazara 9%.
Languages Dari, Pushtu.
Religions Sunni Muslim 87%, Shiite Muslim 12%.
Life expectancy 40 female, 41 male.
Literacy 12%.

POLITICS
Government Socialist republic.
Parties People's Democratic.
Suffrage Universal, over 18.
Memberships UN.
Subdivisions 29 provinces.

ECONOMY
GNP $2,800,000,000.
Per capita $200.
Monetary unit Afgháni.
Trade partners U.S.S.R., Eastern European countries.
Exports Fruits, nuts, natural gas, carpets.
Imports Food, petroleum.

LAND
Description Southern Asia, landlocked.
Area 250,000 mi² (647,497 km²).
Highest point Nowshak, 24,557 ft (7,485 m).
Lowest point Amu Darya River valley, 837 ft (255 m).

PEOPLE. Afghanistan shares borders with the Soviet Union, China, India, Pakistan, and Iran, and this crossroads position has resulted in a population that is both ethnically and linguistically diverse. Religion, however, plays a strong unifying role. Most Afghans are Muslim, and Islamic laws and customs determine life-styles and beliefs both religious and secular. The population is mainly rural, most are farmers, and there is a small nomad population.

ECONOMY AND THE LAND. The main force of Afghanistan's underdeveloped economy is agriculture, with subsistence farming and animal husbandry accounting for much activity. Crop production has been greatly aided by irrigation systems. A terrain of mountains and valleys, including the Hindu Kush, separates the desert region of the southwest from the more fertile north, an area of higher population density and the site of natural gas deposits. Increased development has made natural gas an important export. Winters are generally cold, and summers hot and dry.

HISTORY AND POLITICS. Once part of the Persian Empire, the area of present-day Afghanistan saw invasions by Persians, Macedonians and Greeks, Turks, Arabs, Mongols, and other peoples. An Arab invasion in 652 introduced Islam. In 1747 Afghan tribes led by Ahmad Shah

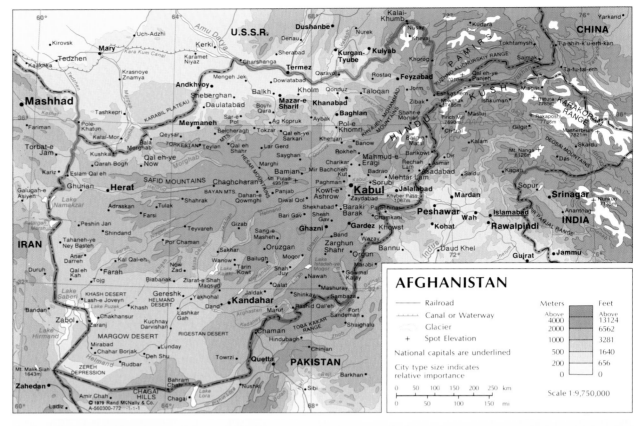

Afghanistan Map Index

	Lat.	Long.		Lat.	Long.		Lat.	Long.		Lat.	Long.
Amu Darya	37°33′N	65°45′E	Gereshk	31°48′N	64°34′E	Kholm	36°42′N	67°41′E	Orgun	32°51′N	69°07′E
Andkhvoy	36°56′N	65°08′E	Ghazni	33°33′N	68°26′E	Khowst	33°22′N	69°57′E	Oruzgan	32°56′N	66°38′E
Arghandab	31°27′N	64°23′E	Ghurian	34°21′N	61°30′E	*Khyber Pass*	34°05′N	71°10′E	*Panj*	37°06′N	68°20′E
Asadabad	34°52′N	71°09′E	*Harirud (Tedzhen)*	35°35′N	61°15′E	Kowt-e Ashrow	34°27′N	68°48′E	Pol-e Khomri	35°56′N	68°43′E
Baghlan	36°13′N	68°46′E	*Helmand*	31°12′N	61°34′E	*Lora, Lake*	29°20′N	64°50′E	Qal'eh-ye Now	34°59′N	63°08′E
Balkh	36°46′N	66°54′E	Herat	34°20′N	62°12′E	Mahmud-e Eragi	35°01′N	69°20′E	*Rigestan Desert*	31°00′N	65°00′E
Bamian	34°50′N	67°50′E	*Hindu Kush*	36°00′N	71°30′E	Mazar-e Sharif	36°42′N	67°06′E	*Safid Mountains*	34°30′N	63°30′E
Baraki Barak	33°56′N	68°55′E	Jalalabad	34°26′N	70°28′E	Mehtar Lam	34°39′N	70°10′E	Sheberghan	36°41′N	65°45′E
Chaghcharan	34°32′N	65°15′E	Kabul	34°31′N	69°12′E	Meymaneh	35°55′N	64°47′E	Sorubi	34°36′N	69°43′E
Daulatabad	36°26′N	64°55′E	*Kabul*	34°20′N	71°10′E	*Morghab*			Taloqan	36°44′N	69°33′E
Farah	32°22′N	62°07′E	*Kajaki, Lake*	32°22′N	65°16′E	*(Murgab)*	35°50′N	63°05′E	Zarghun Shahr	32°51′N	68°25′E
Feyzabad	37°06′N	70°34′E	Kandahar	31°32′N	65°30′E	*Nowshak*	36°26′N	71°50′E	*Zereh Depression*	29°45′N	61°50′E
Gardez	33°37′N	69°07′E	Khanabad	36°41′N	69°07′E						

Durrani united the area and established today's Afghanistan. Power remained with the Durrani tribe for more than two centuries. In the nineteenth and early twentieth centuries, Britain controlled Afghanistan's foreign affairs. A Durrani tribe member and former prime minister led a military coup in 1973 and set up a republic, ending the country's monarchical tradition. This new government's failure to improve economic and social conditions led to a 1978 revolution that established a Marxist government and brought Soviet aid. Intraparty differences and citizenry dissent resulted in a Soviet invasion in 1979. Fighting between government forces and the *mujaheddin,* "holy warrior," guerrillas continues, and the government has failed to gain complete control. In foreign affairs, the country's policy has been nonalignment and neutrality. ■

Mountainous, rocky terrain, as shown in this stretch of troubled border with the U.S.S.R., is characteristic of most of the landlocked nation of Afghanistan.

ALBANIA

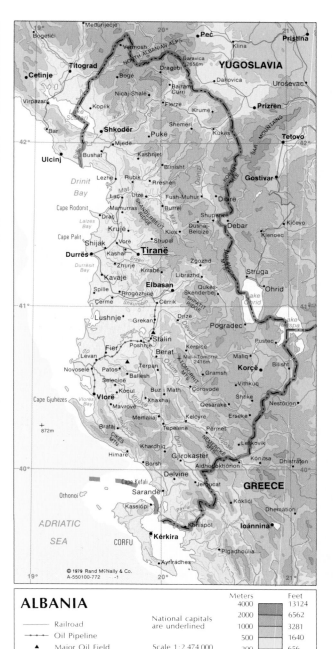

OFFICIAL NAME People's
Socialist Republic of Albania

PEOPLE
Population 2,935,000.
Density 264/mi² (102/km²).
Urban 33%.
Capital Tiranë 198,000.
Ethnic groups Albanian 96%.
Languages Albanian, Greek.
Religions Muslim 70%, Albanian Orthodox 20%,
Roman Catholic 10%.
Life expectancy 72 female, 68 male.
Literacy 75%.

POLITICS
Government Socialist republic.
Parties Workers'.
Suffrage Universal, over 18.
Memberships UN.
Subdivisions 26 districts.

ECONOMY
GNP $2,150,000,000.
Per capita $820.
Monetary unit Lek.
Trade partners Yugoslavia, Czechoslovakia, Italy.
Exports Asphalt, bitumen, petroleum products.
Imports Machinery, machine tools, iron and steel
products.

LAND
Description Southeastern Europe.
Area 11,100 mi² (28,748 km²).
Highest point Korabit 9,026 ft (2,751 m).
Lowest point Sea level.

PEOPLE. A homogeneous native population characterizes Albania, with Greeks the main minority. Five centuries of Turkish rule shaped much of the culture and led many Albanians to adopt Islam. Since 1944, when the current Communist regime was established, an increased emphasis on education has more than tripled the literacy rate. In 1967 religious institutions were banned, and Albania claims to be the world's first atheist state.

ECONOMY AND THE LAND. Reputedly one of the poorest countries in Europe, Albania has tried to shift its economy from agriculture to industry. Farms employed about 50 percent of the work force in the early 1980s, a significant decrease from more than 90 percent before World War II. Mineral resources make mining the chief industrial activity. The terrain consists of forested hills and mountains, and the climate is mild.

HISTORY AND POLITICS. Early invaders and rulers included Greeks, Romans, Goths, and others. In 1468 the Ottoman Turks conquered the area, and it remained part of their empire until the First Balkan War in 1912. Invaded by Italy and occupied by Germany during World War II, Albania set up a Communist government in 1944, following the German retreat. A strict approach to communism caused the country to sever ties with its onetime allies—Yugoslavia, the Soviet Union, and most recently China—and today the country remains unallied. Relations with some nations have improved. ∎

ALBANIA

		Meters	Feet
—— Railroad	National capitals are underlined	4000	13124
┅ Oil Pipeline		2000	6562
▲ Major Oil Field	Scale 1:2,474,000	1000	3281
+ Spot Elevation or Depth		500	1640
		200	656
		0	0
		200	656
		2000	6562

© 1979 Rand McNally & Co.
A-550100-772   -1

As the seasons change in the mountain regions, farmers herd livestock to pastures at different elevations. Called transhumance, this seasonal movement takes advantage of the best grazing lands.

About half the Albanian population is involved in agriculture, working on collective and state farms to produce corn, potatoes, sugar beets, and wheat and raise livestock. As elsewhere in southern Europe, traditional and modern agricultural practices exist side by side, as shown in this scene of the ox-drawn cart and the tractor-driven threshing machine. The government continues its attempts to modernize farming methods, and state aid and collectivization have led to increased use of power equipment where possible. But in many areas the land is worked much the same way today as it has been for generations. Despite outmoded methods and the lowest amount of arable land per capita in Europe, Albania claims to be self-sufficient in food production.

ALGERIA

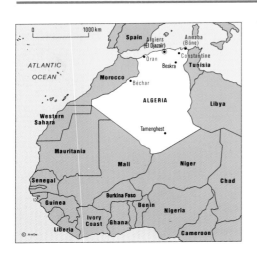

OFFICIAL NAME Democratic and Popular Republic of Algeria

PEOPLE
Population 21,695,000.
Density 24/mi² (9.1/km²).
Urban 52%.
Capital Algiers, 1,523,000.
Ethnic groups Arab-Berber.
Languages Arabic, Berber, French.
Religions Sunni Muslim 99%.
Life expectancy 58 female, 55 male.
Literacy 46%.

POLITICS
Government Socialist republic.
Parties National Liberation Front.
Suffrage Universal, over 19.
Memberships AL, OAU, OPEC, UN.
Subdivisions 48 departments.

ECONOMY
GDP $42,900,000,000.
Per capita $2,142.
Monetary unit Dinar.
Trade partners U.S., West Germany, France.
Exports Petroleum, natural gas.
Imports Capital equipment, semifinished goods, food.

LAND
Description Northern Africa.
Area 919,595 mi² (2,381,741 km²).
Highest point Tahat, 9,541 ft (2,908 m).
Lowest point Melrhir Shatt, 131 ft (40 m) below sea level.

PEOPLE. Indigenous Berbers and invading Arabs shaped modern Algeria's culture, and today most of the population is Muslim, of Arab-Berber, Arab, or Berber descent. European cultural influences, evidence of over a century of French control, exist in urban areas, however. Since independence in 1962, free medical care has been instituted and the educational system has been greatly improved.

ECONOMY AND THE LAND. A member of the Organization of Petroleum Exporting Countries (OPEC), Algeria produces oil and natural gas. Agriculture is divided between state and privately owned farms. The government continues to emphasize gas production and exportation while it maintains a socialistic economy and promotes development of private business. Algeria's terrain is varied. The Tell, Arabic for "hill," is a narrow Mediterranean coastal region that contains the country's most fertile land and highest population. South of this lie high plateaus and the Atlas Mountains, which give way to the Sahara Desert. The climate is temperate along the coast and dry and cool in the plateau region.

HISTORY AND POLITICS. In the eighth and eleventh centuries invading Arabs brought their language and religion to the native Berbers. The Berbers and Arabs together became known as

Moors, and conflicts between Moors, Turks, and Spaniards erupted periodically over several centuries. France began conquering Algeria in 1830, and by 1902 the entire country was under French control. The revolution against French rule began in 1954, but it was not until 1962 that the country was declared independent. Since a bloodless coup in 1965, the political situation has been relatively stable. The centralized government follows a policy of independence and nonalignment, but it is influenced by other Third World countries. ■

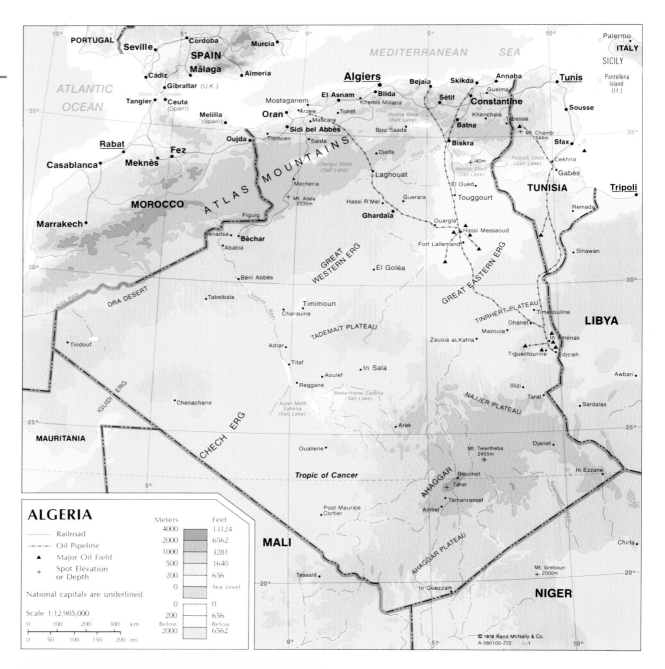

ALGERIA

	Meters	Feet
Railroad	4000	13124
Oil Pipeline	2000	6562
▲ Major Oil Field	1000	3281
+ Spot Elevation or Depth	500	1640
	200	656
	0	Sea Level

National capitals are underlined

Scale 1:12,985,000

© 1979 Rand McNally & Co.
A-580100-772

Algeria Map Index

Though oil and gas fields beneath the Sahara have been a major source of income for Algeria, much of the desert region is typified by nomadic herding. This photo shows flocks and date palms near the oasis town of Béchar in the Atlas Mountain foothills.

AMERICAN SAMOA

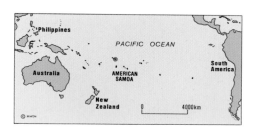

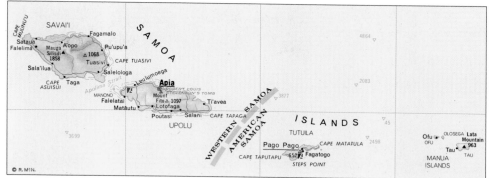

OFFICIAL NAME Territory of
American Samoa

PEOPLE
Population 35,000.
Density 455/mi² (176/km²).
Urban 18%.
Capital Pago Pago, Tutuila I., 3,075.
Ethnic groups Samoan, Euronesian.
Languages English, Samoan.
Religions Christian 94%.
Life expectancy 69 female, 65 male.

POLITICS
Government Unincorporated territory (U.S.).
Suffrage Universal adult.
Subdivisions 3 districts.

ECONOMY
GNP $140,000,000.
Per capita $4,100.
Monetary unit U.S. dollar.
Trade partners U.S., Japan, New Zealand, Australia.
Exports Canned tuna, pet food, fish meal.
Imports Fuel, food, jewelry.

LAND
Description South Pacific islands.

Area 77 mi² (199 km²).
Highest point Lata Mtn. Tav I., 3,160 ft (963 m).
Lowest point Sea level.

PEOPLE. Ethnically and linguistically, the people of American Samoa are the same as those of Western Samoa: mainly Samoan-speaking Polynesians, with a minority of Samoan-European descent. The majority of American Samoans are bilingual, speaking English in addition to Samoan. Most live in rural villages on Tutuila, the main island and location of the capital of Pago Pago, but more American Samoans live on the United States mainland and in Hawaii than live on the islands themselves.

ECONOMY AND THE LAND. American Samoa's industry is based on fishing, and activities include tuna canning and producing fish products. Most farming is on the subsistence level. In the 1960s an economic expansion program, funded by the United States, improved transportation systems, medical and educational facilities, and the tourist and fish industries. Many benefits were short-lived, however. The seven islands are part of the South Pacific island chain that includes Western Samoa. Tutuila, Aunuu, and the Manua group—Tau, Ofu, and Olosega—are volcanic in origin, and Rose and Swain islands are coral atolls. The terrain is mostly mountainous, and the climate is tropical.

HISTORY AND POLITICS. More than two thousand years ago, the first inhabitants of the Samoan Islands probably migrated from eastern Melanesia. The first Europeans arrived at the islands in the early 1700s. Foreign competition for influence resulted in the division of the islands between the United States and Germany in 1900, with the United States receiving the eastern islands of Tutuila, Aunuu, and the Manua group. Swain Island was annexed in 1925. In 1976 American Samoans voted to elect their own governor, who had previously been appointed by the secretary of the interior. ■

ANDORRA

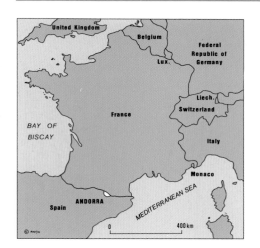

OFFICIAL NAME Principality
of Andorra

PEOPLE
Population 39,000.
Density 223/mi² (86/km²).
Capital Andorra, 14,928.
Ethnic groups Spanish 61%, Andorran 30%, French 6%.
Languages Catalan, Spanish, French.
Religions Roman Catholic.
Literacy 100%.

POLITICS
Government Coprincipality (France, Spain).
Parties None.
Suffrage Third-generation Andorrans, over 21.
Memberships None.
Subdivisions 7 districts.

ECONOMY
Monetary unit Spanish peseta, French franc.
Trade partners Spain, France.

LAND
Description Southwestern Europe, landlocked.
Area 175 mi² (453 km²).
Highest point Coma Pedrosa Pk., 9,665 ft (2,946 m).
Lowest point Valira River valley, 2,756 ft (840 m).

PEOPLE. Much of Andorran life and culture has been shaped by its mountainous terrain and governing countries, France and Spain. Population is concentrated in the valleys, and despite a tourism boom in the past decades, the peaks and valleys of the Pyrenees have isolated the small country from many twentieth-century changes. Catalan is the official language, and cultural and historic ties exist with the Catalonian region of northern Spain. The majority of the population is Spanish; Andorran citizens are a minority.

ECONOMY AND THE LAND. The terrain has established Andorra's economy as well as its lifestyle. Improved transportation routes together with other factors have resulted in a thriving tourist industry—a dramatic shift from traditional sheepherding and tobacco growing. In addition, duty-free status has made the country a European shopping mecca. Tobacco is still the main agricultural product, though only about 4 percent of the land is arable. Climate varies with altitude; winters are cold, and summers cool.

HISTORY AND POLITICS. Tradition indicates that Charlemagne freed the area from the Moors in A.D. 806. A French count and the Spanish bishop of Seo de Urgel signed an agreement in the 1200s to act as coprinces, establishing the political status and boundaries that exist today. The coprincipality is governed by the president of France and the bishop of Seo de Urgel. The country has no formal constitution, no armed forces other than a small police force, and no political parties. ■

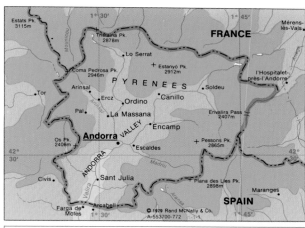

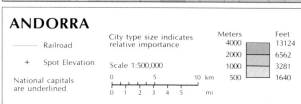

ANDORRA

City type size indicates relative importance

— Railroad
+ Spot Elevation
National capitals are underlined

Scale 1:500,000

Meters	Feet
4000	13124
2000	6562
1000	3281
500	1640

ANGOLA

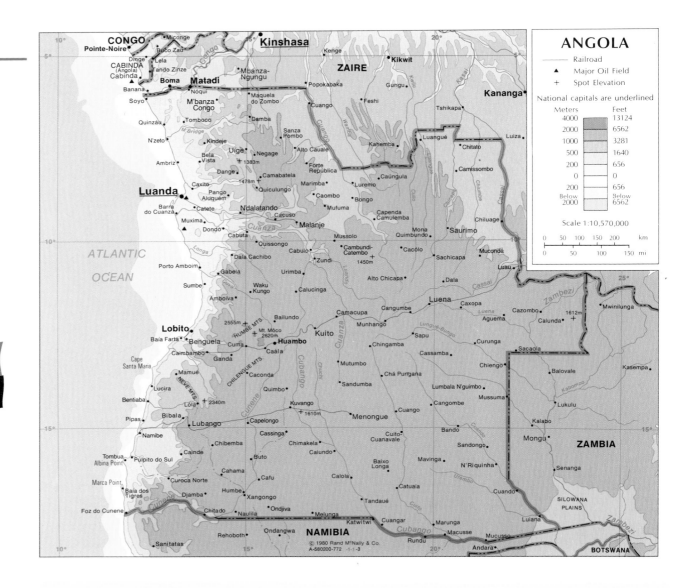

OFFICIAL NAME People's Republic of Angola

PEOPLE
Population 7,875,000.
Density 16/mi² (6.3/km²).
Urban 21%.
Capital Luanda, 475,328.
Ethnic groups Ovimbundu 38%, Kimbundu 23%, Kongo 13%.
Languages Portuguese, indigenous.
Religions Animist, Roman Catholic, Protestant.
Life expectancy 43 female, 41 male.
Literacy 20%.

POLITICS
Government Socialist republic.
Parties Popular Movement for Liberation–Labor.
Suffrage Universal adult.
Memberships OAU, UN.
Subdivisions 18 provinces.

ECONOMY
GDP $3,900,000,000.
Per capita $591.
Monetary unit Kwanza.
Trade partners Cuba, U.S.S.R., Portugal, U.S.
Exports Petroleum, coffee, diamonds.
Imports Capital equipment, wines, iron and steel.

LAND
Description Southern Africa.
Area 481,353 mi² (1,246,700 km²).
Highest point Mt. Môco, 8,596 ft (2,620 m).
Lowest point Sea level.

Angola Map Index

	Lat.	Long.		Lat.	Long.		Lat.	Long.		Lat.	Long.
Benguela	12°35'S	13°25'E	Cuilo (Kwilu)	7°38'S	19°25'E	Luanda	8°48'S	13°14'E	Môco, Mount	12°28'S	15°10'E
Cabinda	5°33'S	12°12'E	Cuito	18°01'S	20°48'E	Luangue	7°00'S	19°33'E	N'dalatando	9°18'S	14°54'E
Cassai (Kasai)	7°15'S	21°48'E	Cunene	17°20'S	11°50'E	Lubango	14°55'S	13°30'E	Neve Mountains	13°52'S	13°26'E
Chilengue			Cuvo	10°50'S	13°47'E	Luena	11°47'S	19°52'E	Santa Maria,		
Mountains	13°10'S	15°18'E	Huambo	12°30'S	15°40'E	Lungué-Bungo	13°27'S	22°00'E	Cape	13°25'S	12°32'E
Congo	6°04'S	12°24'E	Humbe			Malanje	9°32'S	16°20'E	Saurimo	9°39'S	20°24'E
Cuando	17°38'S	23°22'E	Mountains	12°13'S	15°25'E	Marca Point	16°31'S	11°42'E	Uige	7°37'S	15°03'E
Cuango	5°50'S	16°35'E	Kuito	12°22'S	16°56'E	M'banza Congo	6°16'S	14°15'E	Zambezi	13°00'S	22°42'E
Cuanza	9°19'S	13°08'E	Lobito	12°20'S	13°34'E	M'Bridge	7°14'S	12°52'E			
Cubango	18°00'S	21°27'E	Longa	10°15'S	13°30'E	Menongue	14°36'S	17°48'E			

PEOPLE. Angola today is made up mostly of various Bantu peoples—mainly Ovimbundu, Kimbundu, Kongo, and Chokwe. Despite influences resulting from a half-century of Portuguese rule, Angolan traditions remain strong, especially in rural areas. Each group has its own language, and although Portuguese is the official language, it is spoken by a minority. Many Angolans, retaining traditional animist beliefs, worship ancestral spirits.

ECONOMY AND THE LAND. A 1975 civil war, the resultant departure of skilled European labor, and continuing guerrilla activity have taken their toll on Angola's economy. The country has been working toward recovery, however, encouraging development of private industries and foreign trade. Although not a member of the Organization of Petroleum Exporting Countries (OPEC), Angola is a large oil producer. Cabinda, an enclave separated from the rest of the country by Zaire and the Zaire River, is the main site of oil production. Diamond mining remains an important activity, as does agriculture. Much of the land is forested, however, and is therefore not suited for commercial farming. The flat coastal area gives way to inland plateaus and uplands. The climate varies from tropical to subtropical.

HISTORY AND POLITICS. Bantu groups settled in the area prior to the first century A.D. In 1483 a Portuguese explorer became the first European to arrive in Angola, and slave trade soon became a major activity. Portuguese control expanded and continued almost uninterrupted for several centuries. In the 1960s ignored demands led to two wars for independence. Three nationalist groups emerged, each with its own ideology and supporters. In 1974 a coup in Portugal resulted in independence for all Portuguese territories in Africa, and Angola became independent in 1975. A civil war ensued, with the three liberation groups fighting for power. By 1976, with the assistance of Cuban military personnel, the Popular Movement for the Liberation of Angola had established control. Unrest continues, with occasional guerrilla activity, an independence movement in Cabinda, and controversy over South African influence. Nonalignment is a government policy, and the country is attempting to expand its Western relationships, having already established ties with Cuba and the Soviet Union. ■

Angola's coast is a narrow strip of flat land that rises abruptly to the plateau region of southern Africa. This is one of Africa's great watershed areas. The Tundavala Gorge, shown here, is typical of the many spectacular landforms found in southwest Angola. Here the rivers break over the edge of the plateau, flowing down to the coastland and on into the Atlantic Ocean.

ANGUILLA

OFFICIAL NAME Anguilla

PEOPLE
Population 7,000.
Density 200/mi² (77/km²).
Capital The Valley, 760.
Ethnic groups Black.
Languages English.
Religions Angelican, Methodist.
Literacy 80%.

POLITICS
Government Associated state (U.K.).
Parties Anguilla National Alliance, Anguillan People's.

ECONOMY
GDP $6,000,000.
Per Capita $6,000.
Monetary unit East Caribbean dollar.
Trade partners U.K.
Exports Fish, lobsters.

LAND
Description Caribbean island.
Area 35 mi² (91 km²).
Highest point Crocus Hill, 225 ft (70 m).
Lowest point Sea level.

PEOPLE. Most of the inhabitants of Anguilla are descendants of black Africans, who were brought to the region to work as plantation slaves during the early colonial period. A dependency of the United Kingdom, Anguilla has a majority language of English, and the main religion is Anglican. The Valley, a village area, serves as capital, and most Anguillans live in rural communities scattered over the island. Many people are poor, and fewer than one-tenth of the population has a telephone.

ECONOMY AND THE LAND. Many Anguillans work as subsistence farmers, although only 5 percent of the land is cultivatable; soils are poor and rainfall low and unpredictable. Some people raise livestock such as cattle and goats, which they trade with inhabitants of nearby islands. Other activities include fishing, lobstering, producing sea salt, and boat building. Jobs have been scarce, however, and this has led to a high rate of emigration. A large portion of the population's income comes from money former inhabitants send home. Tourism is an economic contributor and offers potential for expansion. Amenities include a warm climate, tempered by trade winds, and more than thirty white-coral beaches, but hotel facilities and air transportation need to be expanded. In the late 1970s the government established a plan to build new hotels, and despite setbacks, the plan is beginning to come to fruition. Some development has taken place along Rendezvous Bay on the southern coast. Other sectors with potential for economic expansion include light industry and offshore banking, with the island's lack of income tax as

incentive. But growth in these areas as well as tourism will continue to depend upon economic aid. Anguilla is a low-lying coral island, with a mostly flat, scrub-covered terrain. Uninhabited Dogs Island lies off the east coast, Scrub Island off the northeast, and tiny Anguillita off the southwestern tip. Anguilla has a tropical climate, subject to occasional hurricanes.

HISTORY AND POLITICS. Artifacts of an Indian culture dating back to around 100 B.C. and petroglyphs in the Fountain, a cave currently under excavation, are reminders of Anguilla's ancient history. The island's early inhabitants were probably the Arawak Indians, who were most likely conquered by the more aggressive Caribs. In 1493 Christopher Columbus arrived on the island, naming it *anguila*, Spanish for "eel," because of its long, narrow shape. Anguilla became a British colony in 1650, and in 1796 the French landed at Rendezvous Bay in an unsuccessful attempt to take the island from Britain. In 1882 Britain united Anguilla with St. Christopher and Nevis, and subsequent years saw St. Christopher, Nevis, and Anguilla administered as a single colony. Many Anguillans rebelled against this status, and dissatisfaction led to unilateral secession from the state in 1967 and British military intervention in 1969. The Anguilla Act of 1980 formally established Anguilla as a separate dependency of Britain, although the de facto separation had been in effect for some time. A new constitution became effective in 1982, and Anguilla continues to be governed by an appointee of the Crown. ∎

ANTARCTICA

Antarctic Peninsula, Antarctica

ANTARCTICA

PEOPLE
Population No permanent population.
Capital None.

LAND
Description Continent in Southern Hemisphere.
Area 5,400,000 mi² (14,000,000 km²).
Highest point Vinson Massif, 16,067 ft (4,897 m).
Lowest point Sea level.

PEOPLE. Antarctica, which surrounds the South Pole, is the southernmost continent, the coldest place on earth, and one of the last frontiers. There are no native inhabitants, and its temporary population is made up mainly of scientists from various countries operating research stations.

ECONOMY AND THE LAND. Harsh climate and terrain inhibit both resource exploration and exploitation. Antarctica's natural resources include coal, various ores, iron, and offshore oil and natural gas. Fishing for krill, a marine protein source, is currently being conducted. Crossed by several ranges collectively known as the Transantarctic Mountains, Antarctica can be roughly divided into a mountainous western region and a larger eastern sector consisting of an icy plain rimmed by mountains. With its tip about 700 miles (1,127 kilometers) from southern South America, the mountainous Antarctic Peninsula and its offshore islands jut northward. Nearly all Antarctica is ice covered; precipitation is minimal, and the continent is actually a desert.

HISTORY AND POLITICS. In the 1770s Captain James Cook of Britain set out in search of the southernmost continent and sailed completely around Antarctica without sighting land. Explorations beginning in 1820 resulted in sightings of the mainland or offshore islands by the British, Russians, and Americans. British explorer Sir James C. Ross conducted the first extensive explorations. After a lull of several decades, interest in Antarctica was renewed in the late nineteenth and early twentieth centuries. The main figures were Captain Robert F. Scott and Ernest Shackleton of Britain and Roald Amundsen of Norway. The race to the South Pole was won by Amundsen in 1911. According to the Antarctic Treaty of 1959, only peaceful scientific research can be conducted in the region. The treaty also delays the settlement of overlapping territorial claims for thirty years. Claims to Antarctica are held by Norway, Australia, France, New Zealand, Chile, Britain, and Argentina. ∎

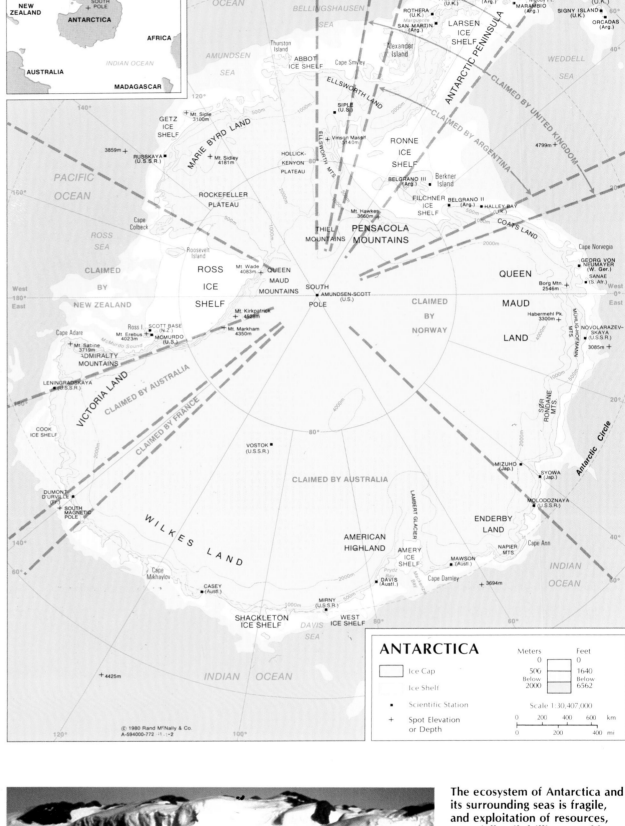

Antarctica Map Index

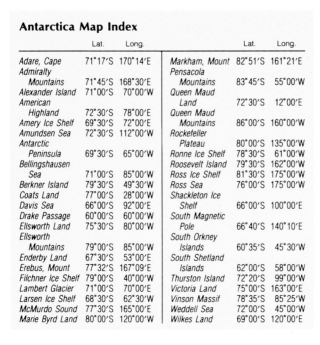

The ecosystem of Antarctica and its surrounding seas is fragile, and exploitation of resources, especially oil drilling, would almost certainly disturb existing life forms. The ocean supplies food for most Antarctic species, but onshore, insects, spiders, and microscopic organisms obtain their nourishment from the land. Among the ocean-dependent creatures are whales, seals, and several types of birds, including the Adélie penguins shown here.

ANTIGUA AND BARBUDA

OFFICIAL NAME Antigua and Barbuda

PEOPLE
Population 78,000.
Density 459/mi² (177/km²).
Urban 34%.
Capital St. Johns, Antigua I., 24,359.

Ethnic groups Black.
Languages English.
Religions Anglican.
Life expectancy 64 female, 60 male.
Literacy 88%.

POLITICS
Government Parliamentary state.
Parties Labor, Progressive Labor Movement, United People's Movement.
Suffrage Universal, over 18.
Memberships CW, OAS, UN.
Subdivisions 6 parishes, 2 islands.

ECONOMY
GDP $125,600,000.
Per capita $1,650.
Monetary unit East Caribbean dollar.
Trade partners U.K., U.S., Caribbean countries.
Exports Clothing, rum, lobsters.
Imports Fuels, food, machinery.

LAND
Description Caribbean islands.
Area 170 mi² (440 km²).
Highest point Boggy Pk., Antigua I., 1,319 ft (402 m).
Lowest point Sea level.

PEOPLE. Most Antiguans are descendants of black African slaves brought by the British to work sugarcane plantations. The largest urban area is St. Johns, but Antiguans generally live in rural areas. Just as elsewhere in the Caribbean, British rule has left its imprint on these islands. The people are mostly Protestant, especially Anglican, and speak English.

ECONOMY AND THE LAND. A dry tropical climate and sandy beaches attract many visitors, making tourism Antigua and Barbuda's economic mainstay and major employer. Once completely dependent on sugar cultivation, the nation has shifted to a multiple-crop system of agriculture. One impetus for this change was the drop in sugar prices in the 1960s. However, the government is attempting to revive the sugar industry, and cotton growing, a traditional activity, continues to play an economic role. Drought sometimes threatens agriculture, possibly caused by overcultivation of the land during the colonial period when settlers were eager to exploit the sugar crop. The government is also interested in expanding the nation's industrial base; economic advantages and access to American and European transportation routes have already attracted foreign investment in manufacturing. Three islands make up the nation. Antigua is the largest island, composed of volcanic rock, coral, and limestone; Barbuda is a flat coral island, with pink-and-white sand beaches; and the rocky islet of Redondo is uninhabited.

HISTORY AND POLITICS. The original inhabitants of Antigua and Barbuda were the peace-loving Arawak Indians. When the warlike Caribs invaded the region, driving out the Arawaks, it seems they did not settle on either Antigua or Barbuda. Christopher Columbus arrived in 1493 on his second voyage to the West Indies, giving Antigua the name Santa Maria de la Antigua. Early European settlement attempts met with the problems of hostilities from the Carib population in the region and lack of water. The Spanish came in the 1500s but soon departed for more hospitable lands. In the 1600s the French gave up their attempt at settlement, prefering the agricultural potential of St. Kitts. Later in that century the British arrived, and in time the island became a British colony. After initial attempts at tobacco cultivation, in the latter half of the seventeenth century the British found that sugar had more potential. The labor-intensive sugar industry was fueled by members of armies defeated in British wars in other colonies. Unused to the tropical climate, however, these slaves and indentured workers were not as productive as the British would have liked. Here as elsewhere, African slave trade began, reaching its peak in the eighteenth century, and the sugar industry was soon booming. Although the French made an attempt to take the island during wars with Britain, they were unsuccessful, and the island remained under British influence. Britain freed its Antiguan slaves in 1834. Antigua and Barbuda joined the Federation of the West Indies as an independent member in 1958, remaining a member until the organization disbanded in 1962. Negotiations on a new constitution took place in 1966, and in 1967 the British colony became an associated state of the United Kingdom. Antigua gained independence in 1981. ■

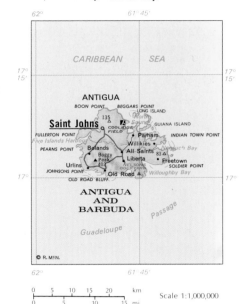

Map shows major islands only.

Scale 1:1,000,000

Antigua and Barbuda Map Index

	Lat.	Long.		Lat.	Long.
All Saints	17°03'N	61°48'W	Old Road	17°01'N	61°50'W
Boggy Peak	17°03'N	61°51'W	Saint Johns	17°06'N	61°51'W
Bolands	17°02'N	61°53'W	Urlins	17°02'N	61°52'W

Despite Antigua and Barbuda's successful tourist industry, many Antiguans are poor and continue to rely on small-scale farming. In open-air markets, Antiguans buy, sell, and trade produce and other items.

ARGENTINA

OFFICIAL NAME Argentine Republic

PEOPLE
Population 30,340,000.
Density 28/mi² (11/km²).
Urban 82%.
Capital Buenos Aires, 2,908,001.
Ethnic groups White 85%; mestizo, Indian, and others 15%.
Languages Spanish.
Religions Roman Catholic 90%, Jewish 2%, Protestant 2%.
Life expectancy 73 female, 69 male.
Literacy 94%.

POLITICS
Government Republic.
Parties Justicialist, Movement for Industrial Development, Radical Civic Union.
Suffrage Universal, over 18.
Memberships OAS, UN.
Subdivisions 22 provinces, 1 district, 1 territory.

ECONOMY
GNP $130,000,000,000.
Per capita $4,610.
Monetary unit Peso.

Trade partners Western European countries, U.S., Brazil, U.S.S.R.
Exports Meat, corn, wheat.
Imports Machinery, lubricating oils, iron and steel.

LAND
Description Southern South America.
Area 1,068,301 mi² (2,766,889 km²).
Highest point Cerro Aconcagua, 22,831 ft (6,959 m).
Lowest point Salinas Chicas, 138 ft (42 m) below sea level.

PEOPLE. An indigenous Indian population, Spanish settlement, and a turn-of-the-century influx of immigrants have made Argentina an ethnically diverse nation. Today, most Argentines are descendants of Spanish and Italian immigrants. Other Europeans, mestizos of mixed Indian-Spanish blood, Indians, Middle Easterners, and Latin American immigrants diversify the population still further. Those of European descent are concentrated in the Buenos Aires area, while mestizos constitute half the population in the far northern provinces. Spanish influence is evidenced by the major religion, Roman Catholicism; the official language, Spanish; and many aspects of Argentine cultural life. Buenos Aires is the nation's commercial and cultural center and one of the largest cities in the world.

ECONOMY AND THE LAND. Political difficulties beginning in the 1930s have resulted in economic problems and have kept this onetime economic giant from realizing its potential. The most valuable natural resource is the rich soil of the pampas, fertile plains in the east-central region. Crops and livestock from this area provide for domestic consumption plus exports. The greatest contributors to the economy, however, are manufacturing and services. The second largest country in South America, Argentina has a varied terrain, with northern lowlands, the east-central pampas, the Andes Mountains in the west, and the southern Patagonian steppe. The climate likewise varies, from subtropical in the north to subarctic in the south.

HISTORY AND POLITICS. The earliest inhabitants of the area were Indians. In the 1500s silver-seeking Spaniards arrived, and by 1580 they had established a colony on the site of present-day Buenos Aires. In the eighteenth century the Spanish holdings in South America were consolidated into a single colony, with Buenos Aires the capital and trade center. In 1816 Argentina officially announced its independence from Spain, and Jose de San Martin led the successful fight for independence. In 1853 a constitution was adopted and a president elected. Advances in agricultural technology, foreign interest that resulted in improved transportation routes, and the immigration of farm laborers led to economic strength in the late 1800s. The country continued to prosper through World War I, and immigration and foreign investment increased. Unsatisfactory power distribution and concern over foreign investment resulted in a military coup in 1930. Thus began a series of civil and military governments; coups; the election, overthrow, and reelection of Juan Perón; and controversial human rights violations. In 1982 Argentina lost a war with Britain over the Falkland Islands. Elections in 1983 resulted in a new government that is trying to resolve continued economic problems, deal with human rights transgressions, and institute other reforms. ∎

Argentina's spectacular scenery offers potential for expanding tourism to the international level. Currently, hotels such as this one in the Andes serve mostly Latin American visitors.

Argentina Map Index

	Lat.	Long.		Lat.	Long.
Acevedo	33°45'S	60°27'W	General Roca	39°02'S	67°35'W
Aconcagua	32°39'S	70°01'W	Godoy Cruz	32°55'S	68°50'W
Aguada de			Goya	29°08'S	59°16'W
Guerra	41°04'S	68°25'W	Gran Chaco	23°00'S	60°00'W
Alemania	25°36'S	65°38'W	Grand Bay	50°45'S	68°45'W
Alta Gracia	31°40'S	64°26'W	Gualeguay	33°09'S	59°20'W
Andalgalá	27°36'S	66°19'W	Gualeguaychú	33°01'S	58°31'W
Andes	31°00'S	71°00'W	Holdich	45°57'S	68°13'W
Antofalla Volcano	25°34'S	67°55'W	Huanguelén	37°02'S	61°57'W
Arequito	33°09'S	61°28'W	Humahuaca	23°12'S	65°21'W
Argentino, Lake	50°13'S	72°25'W	Ibicuy	33°44'S	59°10'W
Astra	45°44'S	67°30'W	Jáchal	30°14'S	68°45'W
Avellaneda	34°39'S	58°23'W	Joaquín Y.		
Ayacucho	37°09'S	58°29'W	González	25°05'S	64°11'W
Azucena	37°29'S	59°18'W	Juárez	37°40'S	59°48'W
Azul	36°47'S	59°51'W	Jujuy	23°00'S	66°00'W
Bahía Blanca	38°43'S	62°17'W	Junín	34°35'S	60°57'W
Bahía Laura	48°24'S	66°29'W	La Banda	27°44'S	64°15'W
Balcarce	37°50'S	58°15'W	La Pampa	38°30'S	65°00'W
Banda del Río			La Paz	30°45'S	59°39'W
Salí	26°50'S	65°10'W	La Plata	34°55'S	57°57'W
Barranqueras	27°29'S	58°56'W	La Rioja	29°26'S	66°51'W
Bella Vista	28°30'S	59°03'W	La Rioja	30°00'S	67°30'W
Bell Ville	32°37'S	62°42'W	Las Flores	36°03'S	59°07'W
Bermejo	26°51'S	58°23'W	Las Lajas	38°31'S	70°22'W
Blanca Bay	38°55'S	62°10'W	Las Lomitas	24°42'S	60°36'W
Bolívar	36°15'S	61°06'W	Las Ovejas	37°01'S	70°45'W
Bragado	35°08'S	60°30'W	Las Plumas	43°43'S	67°15'W
Buenos Aires	34°36'S	58°27'W	Las Rosas	32°28'S	61°34'W
Buenos Aires	38°45'N	61°45'W	Lincoln	34°52'S	61°32'W
Buenos Aires,			Lobería	38°09'S	58°47'W
Lake	46°35'S	72°00'W	Los Antiguos	46°33'S	71°37'W
Buta Ranquil	37°03'S	69°50'W	Los Blancos	23°36'S	62°36'W
Cabildo	38°29'S	61°54'W	Los Frentones	26°25'S	61°25'W
Cabo Raso	44°21'S	65°14'W	Magellan, Strait		
Calafate	50°20'S	72°18'W	of	54°00'S	71°00'W
Camarones	44°48'S	65°42'W	Maipú	36°52'S	57°52'W
Campana	34°10'S	58°57'W	Malargüe	35°28'S	69°35'W
Campo Gallo	26°35'S	62°51'W	Mar Chiquita,		
Canada de			Lake	30°42'S	62°36'W
Gomez	32°49'S	61°24'W	Marcos Juárez	32°42'S	62°06'W
Capitan			Marcos Paz	34°46'S	58°50'W
Bermúdez	32°49'S	60°43'W	Mar del Plata	38°00'S	57°33'W
Carmen de			María Grande	31°39'S	59°54'W
Patagones	40°48'S	62°59'W	Médanos	38°50'S	62°41'W
Casilda	33°03'S	61°10'W	Melincue	33°39'S	61°27'W
Castillo, Mount	43°03'S	71°57'W	Mendoza	32°53'S	68°49'W
Catamarca	28°28'S	65°47'W	Mendoza	34°30'S	68°30'W
Catamarca	27°00'S	67°00'W	Mercedes	34°39'S	59°27'W
Chacabuco	34°38'S	60°29'W	Mercedes	29°12'S	58°05'W
Chaco	26°25'S	60°30'W	Metán	25°29'S	64°57'W
Chico	43°48'S	66°25'W	Miramar	38°16'S	57°51'W
Chilecito	29°10'S	67°30'W	Misiones	27°00'S	55°00'W
Chivilcoy	34°53'S	60°01'W	Monte Caseros	30°15'S	57°39'W
Choele-Choel	39°16'S	65°41'W	Morón	34°39'S	58°37'W
Chubut	44°00'S	69°00'W	Navia	34°47'S	66°35'W
Chubut	43°20'S	65°03'W	Necochea	38°33'S	58°45'W
Cipolletti	38°56'S	67°59'W	Negro	41°02'S	62°47'W
Colonia Las			Neuquén	38°57'S	68°04'W
Heras	46°33'S	68°57'W	Neuquén	39°00'S	70°00'W
Colorado	39°50'S	62°08'W	Nogoyá	32°24'S	59°48'W
Comodoro			Nueve de Julio	35°27'S	60°52'W
Rivadavia	45°52'S	67°30'W	Oberá	27°29'S	55°08'W
Concepción	27°20'S	65°35'W	Olavarría	36°54'S	60°17'W
Concepción del			Orense	38°40'S	59°47'W
Uruguay	32°29'S	58°14'W	Palo Santo	25°34'S	59°21'W
Concordia	31°24'S	58°02'W	Pampas	35°00'S	63°00'W
Córdoba	31°24'S	64°11'W	Paraguay	27°18'S	58°38'W
Córdoba	32°00'S	64°00'W	Paraná	31°44'S	60°32'W
Coronel Brandsen	35°10'S	58°14'W	Paraná	33°43'S	59°15'W
Coronel Dorrego	38°42'S	61°17'W	Paso de los		
Coronel Pringles	37°58'S	61°22'W	Libres	29°43'S	57°05'W
Coronel Vidal	37°27'S	57°43'W	Patagonia	44°00'S	68°00'W
Corrientes	27°28'S	58°50'W	Pedernales	35°15'S	59°39'W
Corrientes	29°00'S	58°00'W	Pehuajó	35°48'S	61°53'W
Cruz Alta	33°01'S	61°49'W	Pergamino	33°53'S	60°35'W
Cruz del Eje	30°44'S	64°48'W	Pila	36°01'S	58°08'W
Curuzú-Cuatiá	29°47'S	58°03'W	Pilcomayo	25°21'S	57°42'W
Daireaux	36°36'S	61°45'W	Pirovano	36°30'S	61°34'W
Deán Funes	30°26'S	64°21'W	Plata, Río de la	35°00'S	57°00'W
Diamante	32°04'S	60°39'W	Posadas	27°23'S	55°53'W
Dolores	36°20'S	57°40'W	Puerto Deseado	47°45'S	65°54'W
Dos Bahías,			Puerto Libertad	25°55'S	54°36'W
Cape	44°55'S	65°32'W	Puerto Madryn	42°46'S	65°03'W
Eduardo Castex	35°54'S	64°18'W	Punta Alta	38°53'S	62°05'W
El Colorado	26°18'S	59°22'W	Punta Delgada	42°46'S	63°38'W
El Cuy	39°56'S	68°20'W	Rafaela	31°16'S	61°29'W
El Mayoco	42°39'S	70°59'W	Rawson	34°36'S	60°04'W
Elortondo	33°42'S	61°37'W	Resistencia	27°27'S	58°59'W
El Turbio	51°41'S	72°05'W	Rinconada	22°26'S	66°10'W
Elvira	35°14'S	59°29'W	Río Colorado	39°01'S	64°05'W
Ensenada	34°51'S	57°55'W	Río Cuarto	33°08'S	64°20'W
Entre Ríos	32°00'S	59°00'W	Río Gallegos	51°38'S	69°13'W
Esquel	42°54'S	71°19'W	Río Grande	53°47'S	67°42'W
Fernández	27°55'S	63°54'W	Río Negro	40°00'S	67°00'W
Fiambalá	27°41'S	67°38'W	Rojas	34°12'S	60°44'W
Fitzroy, Mount	49°17'S	73°05'W	Roque Perez	35°25'S	59°20'W
Formosa	26°11'S	58°11'W	Rosario	32°57'S	60°40'W
Formosa	25°00'S	60°00'W	Rosario del Tala	32°18'S	59°09'W
Galán, Mount	25°55'S	66°52'W	Rufino	34°16'S	62°42'W
Gálvez	32°02'S	61°13'W	Saavedra	37°45'S	62°22'W
General Juan			Saladillo	35°38'S	59°46'W
Madariaga	37°00'S	57°09'W	Salado	31°42'S	60°44'W
General Lavalle	36°24'S	56°58'W	Salado	35°44'S	57°21'W
General Paz	35°31'S	58°19'W	Saldungaray	38°12'S	61°47'W
General Pico	35°40'S	63°44'W			

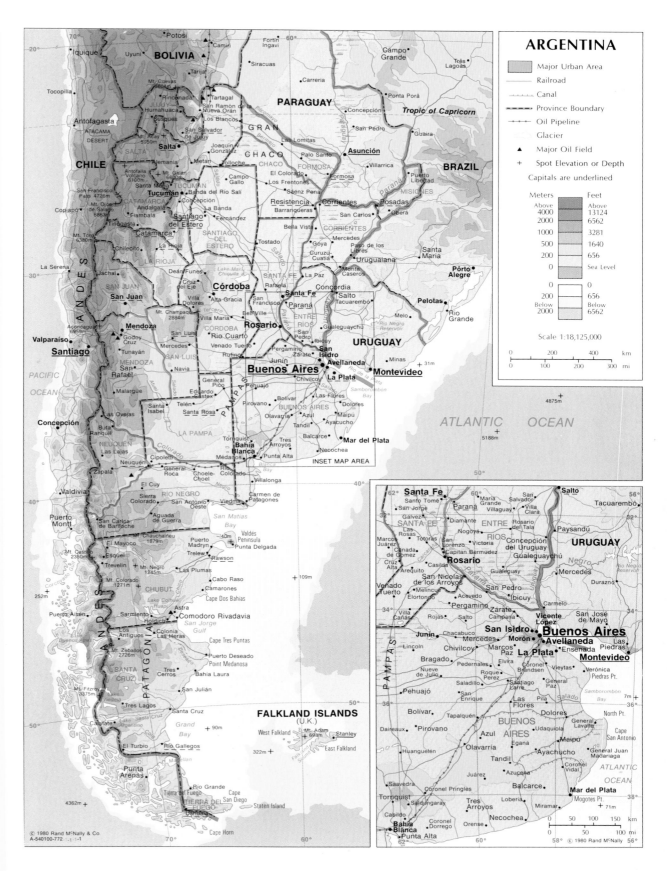

ARGENTINA

Meters		Feet
Above 4000		Above 13124
2000		6562
1000		3281
500		1640
200		656
0	Sea Level	0
0		0
200		656
Below 2000		Below 6562

Scale 1:18,125,000

INSET MAP AREA

	Lat.	Long.		Lat.	Long.		Lat.	Long.		Lat.	Long.
Salta	24°47'S	65°25'W	San Luis	34°00'S	66°00'W	Sarmiento	45°36'S	69°05'W	Tucumán	27°00'S	65°30'W
Salta	25°00'S	64°30'W	San Matías Bay	41°30'S	64°15'W	Sierra Colorada	40°35'S	67°48'W	Tunuyán	33°34'S	69°01'W
Salto	34°17'S	60°15'W	San Nicolas de			Susques	23°25'S	66°29'W	Udaquiola	36°34'S	58°31'W
Samborombón			los Arroyos	33°20'S	60°13'W	Tandil	37°19'S	59°09'W	Uruguay	34°12'S	58°18'W
Bay	36°00'S	57°12'W	San Pedro	33°40'S	59°40'W	Tapalquén	36°21'S	60°01'W	Ushuaia	54°48'S	68°18'W
San Antonio,			San Rafael	34°36'S	68°20'W	Tartagal	28°40'S	59°52'W	Valdés Peninsula	42°30'S	64°00'W
Cape	36°40'S	56°42'W	San Ramón de la			Telén	36°16'S	65°30'W	Venado Tuerto	33°45'S	61°58'W
San Antonio			Nueva Orán	23°08'S	64°20'W	Tierra del Fuego	54°00'S	67°00'W	Verónica	35°22'S	57°20'W
Oeste	40°44'S	64°56'W	San Salvador	31°37'S	58°30'W	Tinogasta	28°04'S	67°34'W	Vicente López	34°32'S	58°28'W
San Carlos	27°45'S	55°54'W	San Salvador de			Tolloche	25°30'S	63°32'W	Victoria	32°37'S	60°10'W
San Carlos de			Jujuy	24°11'S	65°18'W	Tornquist	38°06'S	62°14'W	Viedma	40°48'S	63°00'W
Bariloche	41°09'S	71°18'W	Santa Cruz	50°01'S	68°31'W	Toro, Mount	29°08'S	69°48'W	Viedma, Lake	49°35'S	72°35'W
San Enrique	35°47'S	60°22'W	Santa Cruz	49°00'S	70°00'W	Tostado	29°14'S	61°46'W	Vieytes	35°16'S	57°35'W
San Francisco	31°26'S	62°05'W	Santa Fe	31°38'S	60°42'W	Totoras	32°35'S	61°11'W	Villa Cañás	34°00'S	61°36'W
San Isidro	34°27'S	58°30'W	Santa Fe	31°00'S	61°00'W	Trelew	43°15'S	65°18'W	Villa Clara	31°50'S	58°49'W
San Jorge	31°54'S	61°52'W	Santa Isabel	36°15'S	66°56'W	Tres Arroyos	38°23'S	60°17'W	Villa Dolores	31°56'S	65°12'W
San Jorge Gulf	46°00'S	67°00'W	Santa María	26°41'S	66°02'W	Tres Cerros	48°13'S	67°33'W	Villaguay	31°51'S	59°01'W
San Juan	31°32'S	68°31'W	Santa Rosa	36°37'S	64°17'W	Tres Lagos	49°37'S	71°30'W	Villalonga	39°53'S	62°35'W
San Juan	31°00'S	69°00'W	Santiago del			Tres Puntas,			Villa María	32°25'S	63°15'W
San Julián	49°18'S	67°43'W	Estero	28°00'S	63°30'W	Cape	47°06'S	65°53'W	Zapala	38°54'S	70°04'W
San Lorenzo	32°45'S	60°44'W	Santiago Larre	35°34'S	59°10'W	Trevelin	43°04'S	71°28'W	Zárate	34°06'S	59°02'W
San Luis	33°18'S	66°21'W	Santo Tomé	31°40'S	60°46'W	Tucumán	26°49'S	65°13'W	Zeballos, Mount	47°01'S	71°42'W

© 1980 Rand McNally & Co.
A-540100-772

ARUBA

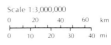

Aruba Map Index

	Lat.	Long.
Basora, Punt	12°25'N	69°52'W
Bushiribana	12°33'N	69°58'W
Oranjestad	12°33'N	70°06'W
Sint Nicolaas	12°27'N	69°52'W

OFFICIAL NAME Aruba

PEOPLE
Population 65,000.
Density 867/mi² (337/km²).
Capital Oranjestad, 14,700.
Ethnic groups Carib Indian, black, European.
Languages Dutch, English, Papiamento, Spanish.
Religions Roman Catholic 82%, Protestant 8%.
Literacy 95%.

POLITICS
Government Self-governing territory (Netherlands).
Parties Aruban People's, People's Electoral
  Movement.
Suffrage Universal, over 18.

ECONOMY
GNP $461,000,000.
Per capita $6,900.
Monetary unit Florin.

LAND
Description Caribbean island.
Area 75 mi² (193 km²).

PEOPLE.   Aruba's population combines descendants of the original Indian population, black Africans, Spanish invaders, and Dutch settlers. Spoken and understood almost universally here are Dutch, English, Spanish, and Papiamento—a language that combines elements of Spanish, Portuguese, English, and Dutch with Indian words.

ECONOMY AND THE LAND.   Aruba is dry with soils unsuited for agriculture, and for many years the economy did not show much potential for development. In the twentieth century, however, nearby Venezuela began producing crude oil, and companies were attracted to Aruba as an economical and stable site to establish a refinery center. The refinery complex is now a major employer. Tourism, too, has grown, with visitors attracted by the coral reefs, white-sand beaches, and tropical climate moderated by trade winds. Aruba's land is dry and rocky, and scattered over the island are giant boulders and monoliths.

HISTORY AND POLITICS.   Early in Aruba's history, the Caribs replaced the peaceful Arawak Indians, and caves on the island are marked with signs and symbols of these early peoples. In 1499, some time after the first arrival of the Spanish, the island was claimed for the Spanish Crown. Aruba was a center of activity for pirates until the 1600s, when the Netherlands obtained possession after long years of war with the Spanish. For a brief time during the Napoleonic Wars, the British occupied Aruba, but the island remained in Dutch hands. Until the 1980s Aruba was part of the Netherlands Antilles, two groups of West Indies islands that belong to the Netherlands. A current plan calls for complete independence in 1996. ∎

ASCENSION

OFFICIAL NAME Ascension

PEOPLE
Population 1,400.
Density 41/mi² (16/km²).
Capital Georgetown.
Languages English.

POLITICS
Government Dependency
  (St. Helena).

ECONOMY
Monetary unit
  St. Helena pound.

LAND
Description South
  Atlantic island.
Area 34 mi² (88 km²).

During a typical week this runway handles two or three flights, but during the 1982 British-Argentine conflict over the Falkland Islands, it became one of the world's busiest airstrips. The runway is situated near Green Mountain, Ascension's extinct crater.

PEOPLE.   Despite Ascension's sparse vegetation, subsistence farming is practiced by many people on this small island in the southern Atlantic. A dependency of the British colony of St. Helena, Ascension is also home to a number of immigrants from that island, which lies about 700 miles (1,126 kilometers) to the southeast.

ECONOMY AND THE LAND.   Agricultural activity includes raising livestock and growing vegetables and fruit. Ascension is the site of a British communications relay station and a United States satellite tracking station; thus the communications industry is a major employer. In addition, the island is known for its wildlife: the sea turtles that come ashore to lay their eggs and the sooty terns that use Ascension as their breeding grounds. The climate of this volcanic island is mild.

HISTORY AND POLITICS.   A Portuguese explorer arrived on the island in 1501. He was followed by the British in 1701, and in 1815 Britain took possession of Ascension. In 1922 administration of Ascension was transferred to St. Helena, and along with Tristan da Cunha, Ascension remains a dependency of that colony. Mainly of strategic importance, Ascension served as a United States refueling station during World War II and played a role in the British battle with Argentina over the Falkland Islands in 1982. ∎

AUSTRALIA

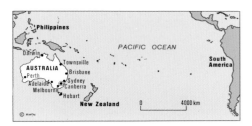

OFFICIAL NAME Commonwealth
of Australia

PEOPLE
Population 15,565,000.
Density 5.2/mi² (2/k n²).
Urban 86%.
Capital Canberra, 219,323.
Ethnic groups White 99%, Asian and aborigine 1%.
Languages English.
Religions Anglican 28%, Roman Catholic 26%, other
Protestant 25%.
Life expectancy 77 female, 72 male.
Literacy 99%.

POLITICS
Government Parliamentary state.
Parties Democratic, Labor, Liberal, National.
Suffrage Universal, over 18.
Memberships CW, OECD, UN.
Subdivisions 6 states, 2 territories.

ECONOMY
GNP $153,000,000,000.
Per capita $10,087.
Monetary unit Dollar.
Trade partners Japan, U.S., Western European
countries.
Exports Coal, wool, wheat.
Imports Capital equipment, consumer goods,
transportation equipment.

LAND
Description Continent between South Pacific and
Indian oceans.
Area 2,967,909 mi² (7,686,850 km²).
Highest point Mt. Kosciusko, 7,310 ft (2,228 m).
Lowest point Lake Eyre (north), 52 ft (16 m) below sea
level.

Formed during the Cambrian period, Ayers Rock is a huge sandstone outcrop rising from the desert scrub. Small caves within the rock carry traces of Australia's **past in paintings done by the aboriginal people. Ayers Rock is found in Australia's plateau region and is geologically related to nearby Mount Olga.**

PEOPLE. Australia's culture reflects a unique combination of British, other European, and ab original influences. Settlement and rule by the United Kingdom gave the country a distinctly British flavor, and many Australians trace their roots to early British settlers. Planned immigration also played a major role in Australia's development, bringing more than three million Europeans since World War II. Refugees, most recently from Indochina, make up another group of incoming peoples. The country is also home to a small number of aborigines. The nation's

size and a relatively dry terrain have resulted in uneven settlement patterns, with people concentrated in the rainier southeastern coastal area. Because of this, the population is mainly urban, though overall population density remains low.

ECONOMY AND THE LAND. Australia's economy is similar to economies in other developed nations, characterized by problems of inflation and unemployment and a postwar shift from agriculture to industry and services. Wool is a major export, and livestock raising takes place on relatively flat, wide grazing lands surrounding an arid central region. Commercial crop raising is concentrated on a fertile southeastern plain. Plentiful mineral resources provide for a strong mining industry. Australia is the world's smallest continent but one of its largest countries. The climate is varied, and part of the country lies within the tropics. Because it is south of the equator, Australia has seasons the reverse of those in the Northern Hemisphere.

HISTORY AND POLITICS. Aboriginal peoples probably arrived about forty thousand years ago and established a hunter-gatherer society. The Dutch explored the area in the seventeenth century, but no claims were made until the eighteenth century, when British captain James Cook found his way to the fertile east and annexed the land to Britain. The first colony, New South Wales, was founded in 1788, and many of the early settlers were British convicts. During the 1800s a squatter movement spread the popula-

In 1788 the British founded New South Wales, Australia's first colony, on the site of present-day Sydney. New South Wales was to assume the role formerly played by British colonies in the United States—repository for convicts from overcrowded English jails. But an independent spirit, one of the world's best natural harbors, and successful development turned the one-time penal colony into a cosmopolitan leader. Today, Sydney's reputation as Australia's cultural and commercial center is reflected in its modern skyline.

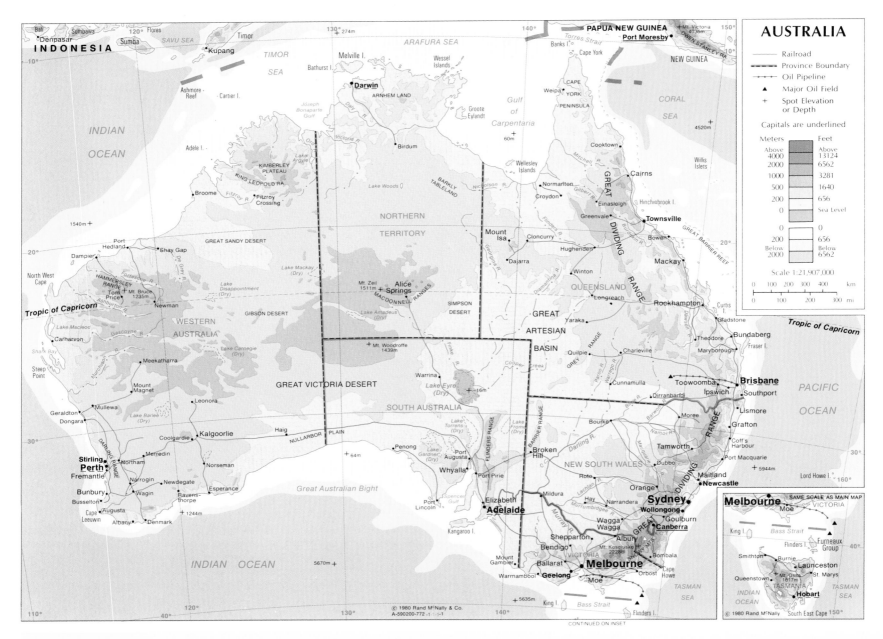

Australia Map Index

	Lat.	Long.		Lat.	Long.		Lat.	Long.		Lat.	Long.		Lat.	Long.
Adelaide	34°55′S	138°35′E	Cape York			Flinders Range	31°00′S	139°00′E	Howe, Cape	37°31′S	149°59′E	Mount Isa	20°44′S	139°30′E	South East Cape	43°39′S	146°50′E
Albury	36°05′S	146°55′E	Peninsula	14°00′S	142°30′E	Fortescue	21°00′S	116°06′E	Ipswich	27°36′S	152°46′E	Murchison	27°42′S	114°09′E	Southport	27°58′S	153°25′E
Alice Springs	23°42′S	133°53′E	Carnarvon	24°53′S	113°40′E	Fraser Island	25°15′S	153°10′E	Joseph			Murray	35°22′S	139°22′E	Spencer Gulf	34°00′S	137°00′E
Arafura Sea	11°00′S	135°00′E	Carnegie, Lake	26°10′S	122°30′E	Fremantle	32°03′S	115°45′E	Bonaparte Gulf	14°15′S	128°30′E	Murrumbidgee	34°43′S	143°12′E	Steep Point	26°08′S	113°08′E
Argyle, Lake	16°15′S	128°45′E	Carpentaria, Gulf			Frome, Lake	30°48′S	139°48′E	Kalgoorlie	30°45′S	121°28′E	Namoi	30°00′S	148°07′E	Stirling	31°54′S	115°47′E
Arnhem Land	13°10′S	134°30′E	of	14°00′S	139°00′E	Furneaux Group	40°10′S	148°05′E	Kangaroo Island	35°50′S	137°06′E	Newcastle	32°56′S	151°46′E	Sydney	33°52′S	151°13′E
Ashburton	21°40′S	114°56′E	Cooktown	15°28′S	145°15′E	Gairdner, Lake	31°35′S	136°00′E	Kimberley			New South Wales	33°00′S	146°00′E	Tamworth	31°05′S	150°55′E
Ashmore Reef	12°14′S	123°05′E	Cooper Creek	28°29′S	137°46′E	Gascoyne	24°52′S	113°37′E	Plateau	17°00′S	127°00′E	Nicholson	17°31′S	139°36′E	Tasmania	43°00′S	147°00′E
Australian Capital			Coral Sea	13°00′S	150°00′E	Geelong	38°08′S	144°21′E	King Island	39°50′S	144°00′E	Northern Territory	20°00′S	134°00′E	Timor Sea	11°00′S	128°00′E
Territory	35°30′S	149°00′E	Curtis Island	23°38′S	151°09′E	Georgina	23°30′S	139°47′E	Kosciusko, Mount	36°27′S	148°16′E	North West Cape	21°45′S	114°10′E	Toowoomba	27°33′S	151°57′E
Ballarat	37°34′S	143°52′E	Dajarra	21°41′S	139°31′E	Geraldton	28°46′S	114°36′E	Lachlan	34°21′S	143°57′E	Nullarbor Plain	31°00′S	129°00′E	Torrens, Lake	31°00′S	137°50′E
Banks Island	10°12′S	142°16′E	Daly	13°20′S	130°19′E	Gibson Desert	24°30′S	126°00′E	Launceston	41°26′S	147°08′E	Orange	33°17′S	149°06′E	Torres Strait	10°25′S	142°10′E
Barkly Tableland	18°00′S	136°00′E	Dampier	20°39′S	116°45′E	Gladstone	23°51′S	151°16′E	Leeuwin, Cape	34°22′S	115°08′E	Ord	15°30′S	128°21′E	Townsville	19°16′S	146°48′E
Barlee, Lake	29°10′S	119°30′E	Darling	34°07′S	141°55′E	Goulburn	34°45′S	149°43′E	Leonora	28°53′S	121°20′E	Ossa, Mount	41°54′S	146°01′E	Victoria	38°00′S	145°00′E
Barwon	30°00′S	148°05′E	Darling Range	32°00′S	116°30′E	Grafton	29°41′S	152°56′E	Lismore	28°48′S	153°17′E	Paroo	31°28′S	143°32′E	Victoria	15°12′S	129°43′E
Bass Strait	39°20′S	145°30′E	Darwin	12°28′S	130°50′E	Great Artesian			Longreach	23°26′S	144°15′E	Penong	31°55′S	133°01′E	Wagga Wagga	35°07′S	147°22′E
Bathurst Island	11°37′S	130°27′E	De Grey	20°12′S	119°11′E	Basin	25°00′S	143°00′E	Lord Howe Island	31°33′S	159°05′E	Perth	31°56′S	115°50′E	Warrina	28°12′S	135°50′E
Bendigo	36°46′S	144°17′E	Denmark	34°57′S	117°21′E	Great Australian			Macdonnell			Port Hedland	20°19′S	118°34′E	Weipa	12°41′S	141°52′E
Birdum	15°39′S	133°13′E	Diamantina	26°45′S	139°10′E	Bight	35°00′S	130°00′E	Ranges	23°45′S	133°20′E	Port Lincoln	34°44′S	135°52′E	Wellesley Islands	16°42′S	139°30′E
Bourke	30°05′S	145°56′E	Disappointment,			Great Barrier Reef	18°00′S	145°50′E	Mackay	21°09′S	149°11′E	Queensland	22°00′S	145°00′E	Wessel Islands	11°30′S	136°25′E
Brisbane	27°28′S	153°02′E	Lake	23°30′S	122°50′E	Great Dividing			Macleod, Lake	24°00′S	113°35′E	Ravensthorpe	33°35′S	120°02′E	Western Australia	25°00′S	122°00′E
Broken Hill	31°57′S	141°27′E	Dubbo	32°15′S	148°36′E	Range	25°00′S	147°00′E	Macquarie	30°07′S	147°24′E	Rockhampton	23°23′S	150°31′E	Whyalla	33°02′S	137°35′E
Broome	17°58′S	122°14′E	Elizabeth	34°43′S	138°40′E	Great Sandy			Maitland	32°44′S	151°33′E	Shark Bay	25°30′S	113°30′E	Wollongong	34°25′S	150°54′E
Bruce, Mount	22°36′S	118°08′E	Eyre, Lake	28°30′S	137°20′E	Desert	21°30′S	125°00′E	Meekatharra	26°36′S	118°29′E	Shepparton	36°23′S	145°25′E	Woodroffe, Mount	26°20′S	131°45′E
Bunbury	33°19′S	115°38′E	Finke	27°00′S	136°10′E	Great Victoria			Melbourne	37°49′S	144°58′E	Simpson Desert	25°00′S	137°00′E	Woods, Lake	17°50′S	133°30′E
Bundaberg	24°52′S	152°21′E	Fitzroy	17°31′S	123°35′E	Desert	28°30′S	127°45′E	Melville Island	11°40′S	131°00′E	Snowy			York, Cape	10°42′S	142°31′E
Busselton	33°39′S	115°20′E	Fitzroy Crossing	18°11′S	125°35′E	Groote Eylandt	14°00′S	136°40′E	Merredin	31°29′S	118°16′E	Mountains	36°30′S	148°20′E	Zeil, Mount	23°24′S	132°23′E
Cairns	16°55′S	145°46′E	Flinders	17°36′S	140°36′E	Hamersley Range	21°53′S	116°46′E	Moe	38°10′S	146°15′E	South Australia	30°00′S	135°00′E			
Canberra	35°17′S	149°08′E	Flinders Island	40°00′S	148°00′E	Hobart	42°53′S	147°19′E	Mount Gambier	37°50′S	140°46′E						

tion to other parts of the island, and the discovery of gold led to a population boom. Demands for self-government soon began, and by the 1890s all the colonies were self-governing, with Britain maintaining control of foreign affairs and defense. Nationalism continued to increase, and a new nation, the Commonwealth of Australia, was created in 1901. During both world wars, Australia fought on the side of the British, and postwar years saw increased attention to the rights of the much-declined aboriginal population. Since World War II, participation in international affairs has expanded, with attention being turned to Asian countries. ■

Places and Possessions of Australia

Entity	Status	Area	Population	Capital / Population
Ashmore and Cartier Islands (north of Australia)	External territory	1.9 mi² (5 km²)	*None*	None
Christmas Island (Indian Ocean)	External territory	52 mi² (135 km²)	3,300	None
Cocos (Keeling) Islands (Indian Ocean)	Part of Australia	5.4 mi² (14 km²)	600	None
Coral Sea Islands Territory (South Pacific)	External territory	1 mi² (2.6 km²)	*No permanent population*	None
Heard and McDonald Islands (Indian Ocean)	External territory	113 mi² (293 km²)	*No permanent population*	None
Norfolk Island (South Pacific)	External territory	14 mi² (36 km²)	1,700	Kingston
Tasmania (island south of Australia)	State	26,383 mi² (68,332 km²)	440,000	Hobart / 47,920

AUSTRIA

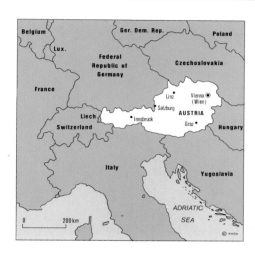

OFFICIAL NAME Republic of Austria

PEOPLE
Population 7,580,000.
Density 234/mi² (90/km²).
Urban 55%.
Capital Vienna, 1,515,666.
Ethnic groups German 98%.
Languages German.
Religions Roman Catholic 85%, Protestant 7%.
Life expectancy 76 female, 71 male.
Literacy 98%.

POLITICS
Government Republic.
Parties Communist, Liberal, People's, Socialist.
Suffrage Universal, over 19.
Memberships OECD, UN.
Subdivisions 9 states.

ECONOMY
GNP $66,890,000,000.
Per capita $10,995.
Monetary unit Schilling.
Trade partners West Germany, Italy, Eastern European countries.
Exports Iron and steel products, machinery, wood.
Imports Machinery, chemicals, textiles, clothing.

LAND
Description Central Europe, landlocked.
Area 32,377 mi² (83,855 km²).
Highest point Grossglockner, 12,457 ft (3,797 m).
Lowest point Neusiedler See, 377 ft (115 m).

PEOPLE. Nearly all Austrians are native born, German speaking, and most are Roman Catholic, a homogeneity belying a history of invasions by diverse peoples. With a long cultural tradition, the country has contributed greatly to music and the arts; and Vienna, the capital, is one of the great cultural centers of Europe.

ECONOMY AND THE LAND. Austria's economy is a blend of state and privately owned industry. After World War II the government began nationalizing industries, returning many to the private sector as the economy stabilized. Unemployment is low, and the economy remains relatively strong. The economic mainstays are services and manufacturing. Agriculture is limited because of the overall mountainous terrain, with the Danube River basin in the east containing the most productive soils. The alpine landscape also attracts many tourists, as does the country's cultural heritage. The climate is generally moderate.

HISTORY AND POLITICS. Early in its history, Austria was settled by Celts, ruled by Romans, and invaded by Germans, Slavs, Magyars, and others. Long rule by the Hapsburg family began in the thirteenth century, and in time Austria became the center of a vast empire. In 1867 Hungarian pressure resulted in the formation of the dual monarchy of Austria-Hungary. Nationalist movements against Austria culminated in the 1914 assassination of the heir to the throne,

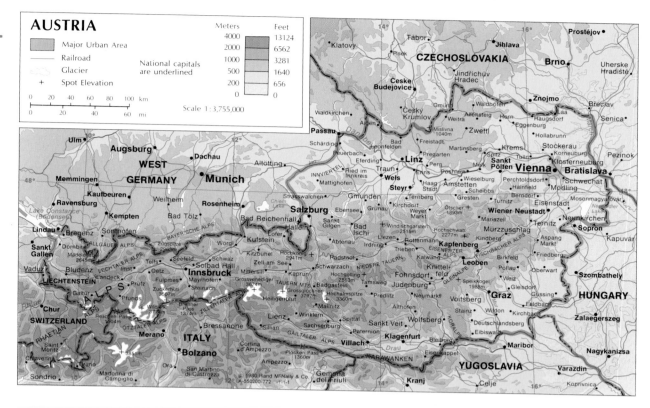

Austria Map Index

	Lat.	Long.		Lat.	Long.		Lat.	Long.		Lat.	Long.
Alps	47°00'N	10°30'E	Grossvenediger	47°06'N	12°21'E	Lechtaler Alps	47°15'N	10°30'E	Schwechat	48°08'N	16°29'E
Amstetten	48°07'N	14°53'E	Hallein	47°41'N	13°06'E	Leoben	47°23'N	15°06'E	Solbad Hall	47°17'N	11°31'E
Bad Ischl	47°43'N	13°37'E	Hochalmspitze	47°01'N	13°19'E	Lienz	46°50'N	12°47'E	Steyr	48°03'N	14°25'E
Bludenz	47°09'N	9°49'E	Hochgolling	47°16'N	13°45'E	Linz	48°18'N	14°18'E	Stockerau	48°23'N	16°13'E
Bregenz	47°30'N	9°46'E	Hochkönig	47°25'N	13°04'E	Madelegabel	47°18'N	10°18'E	Tauern		
Brenner Pass	47°00'N	11°30'E	Hochschwab	47°37'N	15°09'E	March	48°10'N	16°59'E	Mountains	47°10'N	12°30'E
Danube	48°09'N	17°03'E	Inn	48°35'N	13°28'E	Mödling	48°05'N	16°17'E	Ternitz	47°44'N	16°03'E
Drau	46°36'N	14°59'E	Innsbruck	47°16'N	11°24'E	Mur	46°38'N	16°02'E	Traun	48°13'N	14°14'E
Eisenerzer Alps	47°28'N	14°45'E	Innviertel	48°10'N	13°15'E	Mürzzuschlag	47°36'N	15°41'E	Vienna	48°13'N	16°20'E
Eisenstadt	47°51'N	16°32'E	Judenburg	47°10'N	14°40'E	Neunkirchen	47°43'N	16°05'E	Villach	46°36'N	13°50'E
Enns	48°14'N	14°32'E	Kapfenberg	47°26'N	15°18'E	Neusiedler Lake	47°50'N	16°46'E	Voitsberg	47°03'N	15°10'E
Fischbacher Alps	47°28'N	15°30'E	Karawanken	46°30'N	14°25'E	Niedere Tauern	47°18'N	14°00'E	Wels	48°10'N	14°02'E
Fohnsdorf	47°13'N	14°41'E	Klagenfurt	46°38'N	14°18'E	Nindischgarsten	47°44'N	14°04'E	Wiener Neustadt	47°49'N	16°15'E
Gaillaler Alps	46°42'N	13°00'E	Klosterneuburg	48°18'N	16°20'E	Ötscher	47°52'N	15°12'E	Wild Peak	46°53'N	10°52'E
Gleinalpe	47°15'N	15°03'E	Knittelfeld	47°14'N	14°50'E	Rhine	47°30'N	9°34'E	Wolfsberg	46°51'N	14°51'E
Gmunden	47°55'N	13°48'E	Koralpe	46°50'N	14°58'E	Salzburg	47°48'N	13°02'E	Zillertaler Alps	47°00'N	11°55'E
Graz	47°05'N	15°27'E	Krems	48°25'N	15°36'E	Sankt Pölten	48°12'N	15°37'E	Zuckerhütl	46°58'N	11°09'E
Grossglockner	47°04'N	12°42'E	Kufstein	47°35'N	12°10'E	Sankt Veit	47°20'N	13°09'E	Zwettl	48°37'N	15°10'E

Archduke Francis Ferdinand, and set off the conflict that became World War I. In 1918 the war ended, the Hapsburg emperor was overthrown, Austria became a republic, and present-day boundaries were established. Political unrest and instability followed. In 1938 Adolf Hitler incorporated Austria into the German Reich. A period of occupation after World War II was followed by Austria's declaration of neutrality and ongoing political stability. Austria today frequently serves as a bridge for exchanges between Communist and non-Communist countries. ■

As the photo of this castle near Salzburg demonstrates, what once provided protection now provides an incentive for tourism. Early rulers and landholders erected castles and fortresses in locations that afforded a panoramic view. Intruders could be seen, and access was difficult. Villages grew up in surrounding valleys.

BAHAMAS

OFFICIAL NAME The Commonwealth of the Bahamas

PEOPLE
Population 230,000.
Density 43/mi² (17/km²).
Urban 65%.
Capital Nassau, New Providence I., 135,000.
Ethnic groups Black 85%, white 15%.
Languages English.
Religions Baptist 29%, Anglican 23%, Roman Catholic 22%.
Life expectancy 67 female, 64 male.
Literacy 89%.

POLITICS
Government Parliamentary state.
Parties Free National Movement, Progressive Liberal.
Suffrage Universal, over 18.

Memberships CW, OAS, UN.
Subdivisions 17 island groups.

ECONOMY
GNP $1,400,000,000.
Per capita $6,000.
Monetary unit Dollar.
Trade partners U.S., U.K.
Exports Pharmaceuticals, rum, cement.
Imports Food, manufactured goods, fuels.

LAND
Description Caribbean islands.
Area 5,382 mi² (13,939 km²).
Highest point Mt. Alvernia, Cat I., 206 ft (63 m).
Lowest point Sea level.

PEOPLE. Only about twenty-nine of the seven hundred Bahamian islands are inhabited, and most of the people live on Grand Bahama and New Providence. Blacks are a majority, mainly descendants of slaves routed through the area or brought by British Loyalists fleeing the American colonies during the revolutionary war.

ECONOMY AND THE LAND. The thin soils of these flat coral islands are not suited for agriculture, and for years the country struggled to develop a strong economic base. The solution was tourism, which capitalizes on the islands' most valuable resource—a semitropical climate. Because it is a tax haven, the country is also an international finance center.

HISTORY AND POLITICS. Christopher Columbus's first stop on his way to America in 1492, the Bahamas were originally the home of the Lucayo Indians, whom the Spaniards took for slave trade. The British arrived in the 1600s, and the islands became a British colony in 1717. Independence was achieved in 1973. ∎

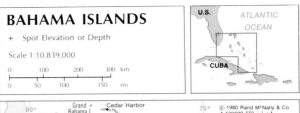

Bahamas Map Index

	Lat.	Long.		Lat.	Long.
Abrahams Bay	22°21′N	72°55′W	Great Abaco	26°28′N	77°05′W
Adelaide	25°00′N	77°31′W	Great Exuma	23°32′N	75°50′W
Alice Town	25°44′N	79°17′W	Great Inagua	21°05′N	73°18′W
Andros Island	24°26′N	77°57′W	Kemps Bay	24°02′N	77°33′W
Andros Town	24°43′N	77°47′W	Killarney, Lake	25°03′N	77°27′W
Bimini Islands	25°44′N	79°15′W	Marsh Harbour	26°33′N	77°03′W
Burnt Ground	23°09′N	75°17′W	Matthew Town	20°57′N	73°40′W
Cat Island	24°27′N	75°30′W	Nassau	25°05′N	77°21′W
Cedar Harbor	26°52′N	77°38′W	New Providence	25°02′N	77°24′W
Crooked Island	22°45′N	74°13′W	Nicolls Town	25°08′N	78°00′W
Deadmans Cay	23°14′N	75°14′W	Paradise Island	25°05′N	77°19′W
Eleuthera	25°10′N	76°14′W	Rum Cay	23°40′N	74°53′W
Exuma Sound	24°15′N	76°00′W	San Salvador		
Freeport	26°30′N	78°45′W	(Watling I.)	24°02′N	74°28′W
George Town	23°30′N	75°46′W	The Bight	24°19′N	75°24′W
Grand Bahama	26°38′N	78°25′W	West End	26°41′N	78°58′W

BAHRAIN

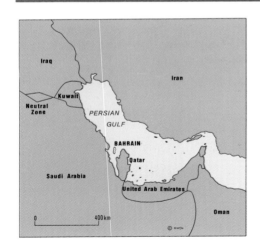

OFFICIAL NAME State of Bahrain

PEOPLE
Population 415,000.
Density 1,621/mi² (627/km²).
Urban 81%.
Capital Manama, Bahrain I., 108,684.
Ethnic groups Bahraini 63%, Asian 13%, other Arab 10%, Iranian 8%.
Languages Arabic, English.
Religions Shiite Muslim 60%, Sunni Muslim 40%.
Life expectancy 69 female, 65 male.
Literacy 47%.

POLITICS
Government Constitutional monarchy.
Parties None.
Suffrage None.

Memberships AL, UN.
Subdivisions 6 municipalities.

ECONOMY
GDP $4,000,000,000.
Per capita $10,000.
Monetary unit Dinar.
Trade partners Japan, U.K., U.S., Saudi Arabia.
Exports Petroleum, aluminum, fish.
Imports Machinery, motor vehicles, manufactured goods, food.

LAND
Description Persian Gulf islands.
Area 256 mi² (662 km²).
Highest point Mt. al-Dukhan, Bahrain I., 440 ft (134 m).
Lowest point Sea level.

PEOPLE. Most residents of Bahrain are native-born Muslims, with the Sunni sect predominating in urban areas and Shiites in the countryside. Many of the country's thirty-three islands are barren, and population is concentrated in the capital city—Manama, on Bahrain Island—and on the smaller island of Muharraq. The oil economy has resulted in an influx of foreign workers and considerable westernization.

ECONOMY AND THE LAND. The onetime pearl-and-fish economy was reshaped by exploitation of oil and natural gas, careful management, and diversification. A major refinery processes crude oil piped from Saudi Arabia as well as the country's own oil, and Bahrain's aluminum industry is the Gulf's largest nonoil activity. Because of its location, Bahrain is able to provide Gulf countries with services such as dry docking, and the country has also become a Middle Eastern banking center. Agriculture exists on northern Bahrain Island, where natural springs provide an irrigation source. But much of the state is desert; summers are hot and dry, and winters mild.

HISTORY AND POLITICS. From around 2000 to 1800 B.C. the area of Bahrain flourished as a center for trade. After early periods of Portuguese and Iranian rule, the al-Khalifa family came to power in the eighteenth century, and it has governed ever since. Bahrain became a British protectorate in the nineteenth century, and independence was gained in 1971. Political allegiance to the Arab League characterizes the current government. ∎

Bahrain Map Index

	Lat.	Long.		Lat.	Long.
al-Hadd	26°15′N	50°39′E	Hawar	25°40′N	50°45′E
al-Muharraq	26°16′N	50°37′E	Jidd Hafs	26°13′N	50°32′E
al-Rifa al-Gharbi	26°07′N	50°33′E	Madinat Isa	26°10′N	50°33′E
Awali	26°05′N	50°33′E	Manama	26°13′N	50°35′E
Bahrain, Gulf of	25°45′N	50°40′E	Muharraq Island	26°16′N	50°37′E
Barr, Cape al-	25°47′N	50°34′E	Persian Gulf	26°20′N	50°30′E
Dukhan, Mount al-	26°02′N	50°32′E	Sitra	26°09′N	50°38′E

BANGLADESH

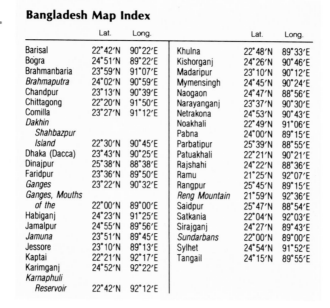

Bangladesh Map Index

	Lat.	Long.		Lat.	Long.
Barisal	22°42'N	90°22'E	Khulna	22°48'N	89°33'E
Bogra	24°51'N	89°22'E	Kishorganj	24°26'N	90°46'E
Brahmanbaria	23°59'N	91°07'E	Madaripur	23°10'N	90°12'E
Brahmaputra	24°02'N	90°59'E	Mymensingh	24°45'N	90°24'E
Chandpur	23°13'N	90°39'E	Naogaon	24°47'N	88°56'E
Chittagong	22°20'N	91°50'E	Narayanganj	23°37'N	90°30'E
Comilla	23°27'N	91°12'E	Netrakona	24°53'N	90°43'E
Dakhin			Noakhali	22°49'N	91°06'E
Shahbazpur			Pabna	24°00'N	89°15'E
Island	22°30'N	90°45'E	Parbatipur	25°39'N	88°55'E
Dhaka (Dacca)	23°43'N	90°25'E	Patuakhali	22°21'N	90°21'E
Dinajpur	25°38'N	88°38'E	Rajshahi	24°22'N	88°36'E
Faridpur	23°36'N	89°50'E	Ramu	21°25'N	92°07'E
Ganges	23°22'N	90°32'E	Rangpur	25°45'N	89°15'E
Ganges, Mouths			*Reng Mountain*	21°59'N	92°36'E
of the	22°00'N	89°00'E	Saidpur	25°47'N	88°54'E
Habiganj	24°23'N	91°25'E	Satkania	22°04'N	92°03'E
Jamalpur	24°55'N	89°56'E	Sirajganj	24°27'N	89°43'E
Jamuna	23°51'N	89°45'E	*Sundarbans*	22°00'N	89°00'E
Jessore	23°10'N	89°13'E	Sylhet	24°54'N	91°52'E
Kaptai	22°21'N	92°17'E	Tangail	24°15'N	89°55'E
Karimganj	24°52'N	92°22'E			
Karnaphuli					
Reservoir	22°42'N	92°12'E			

BANGLADESH

	Meters	Feet
Major Urban Area	4000	13124
	2000	6562
Railroad	1000	3281
	500	1640
Scale 1:6,000,000	200	656
0 50 100 150 km	0	0
0 50 100 mi	200	656

OFFICIAL NAME People's
Republic of Bangladesh

PEOPLE
Population 101,130,000.
Density 1,819/mi² (702/km²).
Urban 11%.
Capital Dhaka, 1,850,000.
Ethnic groups Bengali 98%.
Languages Bangla, English.
Religions Muslim, 83%, Hindu 16%.
Life expectancy 48 female, 47 male.
Literacy 25%.

POLITICS
Government Republic.
Parties None (banned).
Suffrage Universal, over 18.
Memberships CW, UN.
Subdivisions 21 districts.

ECONOMY
GNP $11,000,000,000.
Per capita $117.
Monetary unit Taka.
Trade partners Western European countries, Japan, U.S.
Exports Jute, leather, tea.
Imports Grain, fuels, cotton, fertilizer.

LAND
Description Southern Asia.
Area 55,598 mi² (143,998 km²).
Highest point Reng Mtn., 3,141 ft (957 m).
Lowest point Sea level.

PEOPLE. Bangladesh's population is characterized by extremes. The people, mostly peasant farmers, are among Asia's poorest and most rural. With a relatively small area and a high birthrate, the country is also one of the world's most densely populated. The areas around Dhaka, the capital, and Comilla, southeast of Dhaka near the Indian border, are the country's most densely settled regions. The lowest population density lies in the Chittagong Hill Tracts in the southeast and the Sundarbans jungle area in the southwest. Life expectancy is relatively low, and the average age of the citizenry is only 16. Nearly all Bangladeshis are Bengali. Minority groups include Urdu-speaking immigrants from India, sometimes called Biharis, and various tribal groups. Many residents are victims of disease, floods, and ongoing medical and food shortages. Islam, the major religion, has influenced almost every aspect of life—from culture to politics. However, there is a sizable Hindu minority and also a number of Christians, Buddhists, and animists, who practice traditional beliefs. Bangla is the official language, but English is widely spoken, especially among the educated in urban regions.

ECONOMY AND THE LAND. The country has yet to recover economically from damage sustained in a 1971 civil war and a 1985 tidal wave, but efforts to eliminate poverty and achieve self-sufficiency continue. Fertile floodplain soil is the chief resource of this mostly flat, river-crossed country, and farming is the main activity. Temperature, soil, and precipitation are suited for rice production, and some areas of the country are able to harvest rice three times a year. Jute is another important crop, much of which is exported, and livestock raising provides for a leather industry. Farm output fluctuates greatly, however, subject to the frequent monsoons, floods, and droughts of a semitropical climate. The nation has few mineral resources, although natural gas deposits have been found. Inexpensive, unskilled labor may attract future foreign investment, but instability continues as a drawback, along with a poorly developed infrastructure. Transportation is improving, but waterways still provide the main source of access. Roads are expensive to build and frequently flooded during the rainy seasons. Because of these and other factors, foreign aid, imports, and an emphasis on agriculture have not assuaged the continuing food shortage, and Bangladesh remains one of the world's poorest countries.

HISTORY AND POLITICS. Most of Bangladesh lies in eastern Bengal, an Asian region whose western sector encompasses India's Bengal province. Early religious influences in Bengal included Buddhist rulers in the eighth century and Hindus in the eleventh. In 1200 Muslim rule introduced the religion to which the majority of eastern Bengalis eventually converted, while most western Bengalis retained their Hindu beliefs. British control in India, beginning in the seventeenth century, expanded until all Bengal was part of British India by the 1850s. When British India gained independence in 1947, Muslim population centers were united into the single nation of Pakistan in an attempt to end Hindu-Muslim hostilities. More than 1,000 miles (1,600 km) separated West Pakistan, formed from northwest India, from East Pakistan, composed mostly of eastern Bengal. The bulk of Pakistan's population resided in the eastern province and felt the west wielded political and economic power at its expense. A civil war began in 1971, and the eastern province declared itself an independent nation called Bangladesh, or "Bengal nation." That same year West Pakistan surrendered to eastern guerrillas joined with Indian troops. The state has seen many political crises since independence, including two leader assassinations, several coups, and the establishment of a martial law government in 1982. Protests continue, with occasional outbreaks of violence. A moderate, nonaligned foreign policy is maintained. ∎

Abundant rivers and excessive precipitation combine for flooding in Bangladesh so that much of the land area is underwater, especially during the summer rainy season. A densely settled people uses even the flooded areas to grow and harvest reeds, as seen in this photo, and to raise different varieties of rice suited to varying water depths.

BARBADOS

OFFICIAL NAME Barbados

PEOPLE
Population 250,000.
Density 1,506/mi² (581/km²).
Urban 41%.
Capital Bridgetown, 7,552.

Ethnic groups Black 80%,
 mixed 16%, European 4%.
Languages English.
Religions Anglican 70%, Methodist 9%, Roman
 Catholic 4%.
Life expectancy 72 female, 67 male.
Literacy 99%.

POLITICS
Government Parliamentary state.
Parties Democratic Labor, Labor.
Suffrage Universal, over 18.
Memberships CW, OAS, UN.
Subdivisions 11 parishes, 1 independent city.

ECONOMY
GDP $997,500,000.
Per capita $3,977.
Monetary unit Dollar.
Trade partners U.S., Caribbean countries, U.K.
Exports Sugar and sugarcane by-products, clothing,
 electrical equipment.
Imports Food, machinery, consumer goods, fuels.

LAND
Description Caribbean island.
Area 166 mi² (430 km²).
Highest point Mt. Hillaby, 1,115 ft (340 m).
Lowest point Sea level.

PEOPLE. A history of British rule is reflected in the Anglican religion and English language of this easternmost West Indian island. Most citizens are black descendants of African slaves. Slightly more people live in rural than in urban areas, but Barbados is one of the world's most densely populated countries. To deal with this problem, the government funds and promotes family-planning programs

ECONOMY AND THE LAND. Barbados's pleasant tropical climate and its land have determined its economic mainstays: tourism and sugar. Sunshine and year-round warmth attract thousands of visitors and, in conjunction with the soil, provide an excellent environment for sugarcane cultivation. It was not until the late 1960s, however, that tourism replaced traditional sugar as Barbados's largest industry. Manufacturing consists mainly of sugar processing and the government is trying to attract more industry to the island. Other economic plans include promoting cotton and crops other than sugar. The coral island's terrain is mostly flat, rising to a central ridge and cliffs along the east coast.

HISTORY AND POLITICS. Arawak Indians were the island's original inhabitants, driven out by the Caribs in the sixteenth century. It is believed the Caribs later abandoned Barbados, and when the British arrived in the 1620s, they found the island uninhabited. An influx of British settlers followed, and soon an agricultural economy based on sugar was established. The land was divided into large estates, and slaves were brought from Africa to work on these plantations

until the British Empire abolished slavery in 1834. For many years a small group of powerful landowners and tradespeople dominated the politics of Barbados, and this led to a movement for political rights, begun in the 1930s by descendants of the slaves. In 1951 universal adult suffrage was introduced, followed by steps toward increasing self-government, culminating with Barbados's independence in 1966. ■

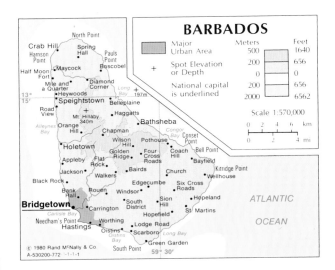

Barbados Map Index

	Lat.	Long.		Lat.	Long.
Bathsheba	13°13'N	59°31'W	Hillaby, Mount	13°12'N	59°35'W
Bridgetown	13°06'N	59°37'W	Holetown	13°11'N	59°39'W
Carlisle Bay	13°05'N	59°37'W	Kitridge Point	13°10'N	59°25'W
Chapman	13°12'N	59°33'W	Rouen	13°05'N	59°34'W
Church	13°08'N	59°29'W	Scarboro	13°04'N	59°33'W
Crab Hill	13°19'N	59°38'W	Sion Hill	13°05'N	59°30'W
Diamond Corner	13°17'N	59°35'W	Speightstown	13°15'N	59°39'W
Four Cross			Spring Hall	13°19'N	59°37'W
Roads	13°10'N	59°32'W	Wellhouse	13°08'N	59°28'W
Hastings	13°04'N	59°35'W	Windsor	13°08'N	59°32'W

Barbados's rugged east coast, shown here, stands in contrast to the beaches and calm water found along the western shore.

BELGIUM

OFFICIAL NAME Kingdom of Belgium

PEOPLE
Population 9,875,000.
Density 838/mi² (324/km²).
Urban 95%.
Capital Brussels, 137,738.
Ethnic groups Fleming 55%, Walloon 33%, mixed and others 12%.
Languages Dutch (Flemish), French, German.
Religions Roman Catholic 75%.
Life expectancy 75 female, 69 male.
Literacy 98%.

POLITICS
Government Constitutional monarchy.
Parties Flemish: Liberal, Social Christian, Socialist. Walloon: Liberal, Socialist.
Suffrage Universal, over 18.
Memberships EC, NATO, OECD, UN.
Subdivisions 9 provinces.

ECONOMY
GNP $85,420,000,000.
Per capita $8,628.
Monetary unit Franc.
Trade partners West Germany, France, Netherlands.
Exports Machinery, chemicals, food, livestock.
Imports Machinery, fuels, food, motor vehicles.

LAND
Description Western Europe.
Area 11,783 mi² (30,518 km²).
Highest point Botrange, 2,277 ft (694 m).
Lowest point Sea level.

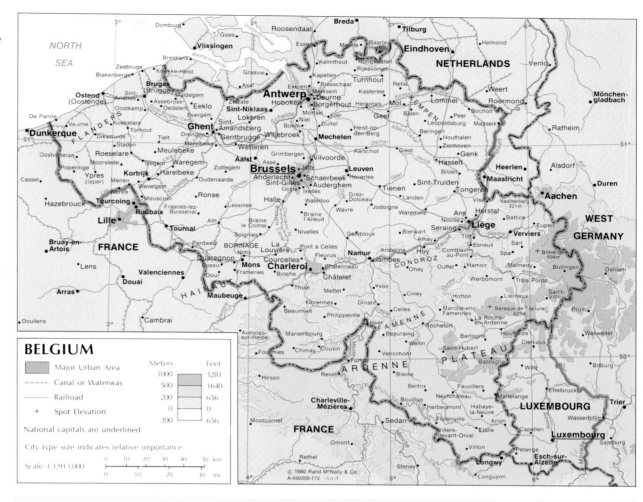

BELGIUM

	Meters	Feet
Major Urban Area	1000	3,281
Canal or Waterway	500	1640
Railroad	200	656
+ Spot Elevation	0	0
	200	656

National capitals are underlined

City type size indicates relative importance

Scale 1:1,913,000

© 1980 Rand McNally & Co.
A-550300-772 -1-1-1

Belgium Map Index

	Lat.	Long.		Lat.	Long.		Lat.	Long.		Lat.	Long.
Aalst	50°56′N	4°02′E	Geel	51°10′N	5°00′E	Lokeren	51°06′N	4°00′E	Seraing	50°36′N	5°29′E
Albert Canal	50°39′N	5°37′E	Genk	50°58′N	5°30′E	Lommel	51°14′N	5°18′E	Sint-Amandsberg	51°04′N	3°45′E
Anderlecht	50°50′N	4°18′E	Gent-Bruges			Maas (Meuse)	51°08′N	5°52′E	Sint-Gilles	50°49′N	4°20′E
Ans	50°39′N	5°32′E	Canal	51°03′N	3°43′E	Mechelen	51°02′N	4°28′E	Sint-Niklaas	51°10′N	4°08′E
Antwerp	51°13′N	4°25′E	Gentbrugge	51°03′N	3°45′E	Meulebeke	50°57′N	3°17′E	Sint-Truiden	50°48′N	5°12′E
Ardenne Plateau	50°10′N	5°45′E	Ghent	51°03′N	3°43′E	Meuse (Maas)	51°08′N	5°52′E	Tienen	50°48′N	4°57′E
Auderghem	50°49′N	4°26′E	Halle	50°44′N	4°13′E	Mol	51°11′N	5°06′E	Tongeren	50°47′N	5°28′E
Borgerhout	51°13′N	4°26′E	Harelbeke	50°51′N	3°18′E	Mons	50°27′N	3°56′E	Tournai	50°36′N	3°23′E
Botrange	50°30′N	6°08′E	Hasselt	50°56′N	5°20′E	Namur	50°28′N	4°52′E	Turnhout	51°19′N	4°57′E
Bruges (Brugge)	51°13′N	3°14′E	Herstal	50°40′N	5°38′E	Ostend			Verviers	50°35′N	5°52′E
Brussels	50°50′N	4°20′E	Hoboken	51°10′N	4°21′E	(Oostende)	51°13′N	2°55′E	Vilvoorde	50°56′N	4°26′E
Charleroi	50°25′N	4°26′E	Huy	50°31′N	5°14′E	Quaregnon	50°26′N	3°51′E	Waregem	50°53′N	3°25′E
Charleroi to			Ieper → Ypres	50°51′N	2°53′E	Roeselare	50°57′N	3°08′E	Wetteren	51°00′N	3°53′E
Brussels Canal	50°51′N	4°19′E	Jambes	50°28′N	4°52′E	Ronse	50°45′N	3°36′E	Willebroek	51°04′N	4°22′E
Châtelet	50°24′N	4°31′E	Kortrijk	50°50′N	3°16′E	Sambre	50°28′N	4°52′E	Ypres (Ieper)	50°51′N	2°53′E
Courcelles	50°28′N	4°22′E	La Louvière	50°28′N	4°11′E	Schaerbeek	50°51′N	4°23′E			
Deurne	51°13′N	4°28′E	Leuven	50°53′N	4°42′E	Schelde	51°22′N	4°15′E			
Flanders	51°00′N	3°00′E	Liège	50°38′N	5°34′E	Semois	49°53′N	4°45′E			

PEOPLE. Language separates Belgium into two main regions. Northern Belgium, known as Flanders, is dominated by Flemings, Flemish-speaking descendants of Germanic Franks. French-speaking Walloons, descendants of the Celts, inhabit southern Belgium, or Wallonia. Both groups are found in centrally located Brussels. In addition, a small German-speaking population is concentrated in the east. Flemish and French divisions often result in discord, but diversity has also been a source of cultural richness. Belgium has often been at the hub of European cultural movements.

ECONOMY AND THE LAND. The economy as well as the population was affected by Belgium's location at the center of European activity. Industry was early established as the economic base, and today the country is heavily industrialized. Although agriculture plays a minor economic role, Belgium is nearly self-sufficient in food production. The north and west are dominated by a flat fertile plain, the central region by rolling hills, and the south by the Ardennes Forest, often a tourist destination. The climate is cool and temperate.

HISTORY AND POLITICS. Belgium's history began with the settlement of the Belgae tribe in the second century B.C. The Romans invaded the area around 50 B.C. and were overthrown by Germanic Franks in the A.D. 400s. Trade, manufacturing, and art prospered as various peoples invaded, passed through, and ruled the area. In 1794 Napoleon annexed Belgium to France. He was defeated at Waterloo in Belgium in 1815, and the country passed into Dutch hands. Dissatis-

faction under Netherland rule led to revolt and, in 1830, the formation of the independent country of Belgium. The country was overrun by Germans during both world wars. Linguistic divisions mark nearly all political activity, from parties split by language to government decisions based on linguistic rivalries. ■

Belgium's transportation system developed to support and encourage industrialization, and in addition to roads and railroads, inland waterways play a vital role in the Belgian economy. Barges transport goods over a network of canals and rivers, including the Schelde and

Meuse, that connect North Sea ports with inland cities and, beyond, with other European countries. The canal shown here runs between the Belgian cities of Brugge and Damme. In turn, Brugge is connected to the port of Zeebrugge by another canal.

BELIZE

OFFICIAL NAME Belize

PEOPLE
Population 160,000.
Density 18/mi² (7/km²).
Urban 52%.
Capital Belmopan, 4,500.
Ethnic groups Black 51%, mestizo 22%, Amerindian 19%.
Languages English, Spanish, indigenous.
Religions Roman Catholic 50%, Anglican, other Protestant.
Literacy 90%.

POLITICS
Government Parliamentary state.
Parties People's United, United Democratic.
Suffrage Universal adult.
Memberships CW, UN.
Subdivisions 6 districts.

ECONOMY
GDP $169,000,000.
Per capita $1,120.
Monetary unit Dollar.
Trade partners U.S., U.K.
Exports Sugar, clothing, fish, citrus fruits.
Imports Food, machinery, consumer goods, transportation equipment.

LAND
Description Central America.
Area 8,866 mi² (22,963 km²).
Highest point Victoria Pk., 3,680 ft (1,122 m).
Lowest point Sea level.

PEOPLE. With the lowest population of any Central American country, Belize has a mixed populace, including descendants of black Africans; mestizos of Spanish-Indian ancestry; and Indians. Population is concentrated in six urban areas along the coast.

ECONOMY AND THE LAND. Belize's economy focuses on agriculture, with sugar the major crop and export. Arable land is the primary resource, but only a small portion has been cultivated. Industrial activity is limited, but Belize hopes to expand tourism. The coastal region consists of swampy lowlands rising to the Maya Mountains inland. The hot, humid climate is offset by sea breezes.

HISTORY AND POLITICS. The Mayan civilization flourished in the area of present-day Belize until about A.D. 1000. In the 1500s Spain claimed the region, and British colonization began in 1638. In 1862 the area officially became the Crown colony of British Honduras. Its name was changed to Belize in 1973, and independence was achieved in 1981. ■

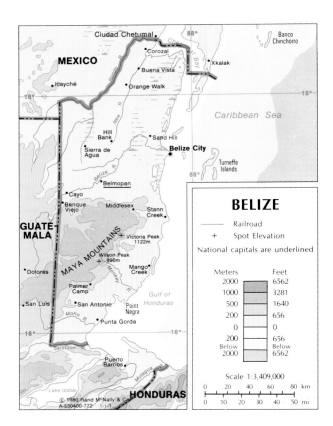

BELIZE

Railroad
+ Spot Elevation
National capitals are underlined

Meters	Feet
2000	6562
1000	3281
500	1640
200	656
0	0
200 Below	656 Below
2000	6562

Scale 1:3,409,000

Belize Map Index

	Lat.	Long.		Lat.	Long.
Belize	17°30'N	88°12'W	Orange Walk	18°06'N	88°33'W
Belmopan	17°15'N	88°46'W	Punta Gorda	16°07'N	88°48'W
Middlesex	17°02'N	88°31'W	Stann Creek	16°58'N	88°13'W

BENIN

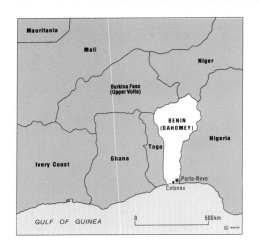

OFFICIAL NAME People's Republic of Benin

PEOPLE
Population 3,970,000.
Density 91/mi² (35/km²).
Urban 26%.
Capital Porto-Novo, 123,000.
Ethnic groups Fon, Adja, Yoruba, Bariba, others.
Languages French, Fon, Adja, indigenous.
Religions Animist 70%, Christian 15%, Muslim 15%.
Life expectancy 52 female, 48 male.
Literacy 20%.

POLITICS
Government Socialist republic.
Parties People's Revolutionary.
Suffrage Universal adult.
Memberships OAU, UN.
Subdivisions 6 provinces.

ECONOMY
GNP $1,100,000,000.
Per capita $294.
Monetary unit CFA franc.
Trade partners France, other Western European countries.
Exports Palm products, cotton.
Imports Clothing, consumer goods, construction materials.

LAND
Description Western Africa.
Area 43,484 mi² (112,622 km²).
Highest point 2,235 ft (681 m).
Lowest point Sea level.

PEOPLE. The mostly black population of Benin is composed of numerous peoples, and the nation's linguistic diversity reflects its ethnic variety. Most Beninese are rural farmers, although urban migration is increasing. Animist beliefs predominate, but there are also Christians, especially in the south, and Muslims in the north.

ECONOMY AND THE LAND. Benin's agricultural economy is largely undeveloped, and palm trees and their by-products provide the chief source of income and activity for both farming and industry. Some economic relief may be found in the exploitation of offshore oil. The predominately flat terrain features coastal lagoons and dense forests, with mountains in the northwest. Heat and humidity characterize the coast, with less humidity and varied temperatures in the north.

HISTORY AND POLITICS. In the 1500s, Dahomey, a Fon kingdom, became the power center of the Benin area. European slave traders came to the coast in the seventeenth and eighteenth centuries, and the area became known as the Slave Coast. In the 1890s France made the area a territory of French West Africa. Independence was gained in 1960. In 1975 the nation's name was changed from Dahomey to Benin. ■

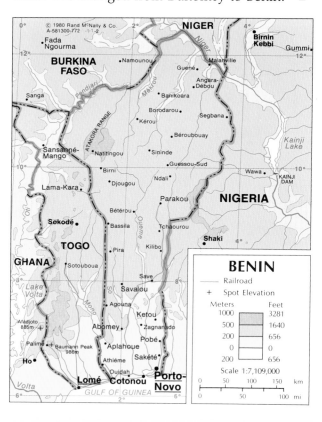

BENIN

Railroad
+ Spot Elevation

Meters	Feet
1000	3281
500	1640
200	656
0	0
200	656

Scale 1:7,109,000

Benin Map Index

	Lat.	Long.		Lat.	Long.
Abomey	7°11'N	1°59'E	*Oueme*	6°29'N	2°32'E
Cotonou	6°21'N	2°26'E	Parakou	9°21'N	2°37'E
Mono	6°17'N	1°51'E	Porto-Novo	6°29'N	2°37'E
Niger	11°40'N	3°38'E	Savalou	7°56'N	1°58'E

BERMUDA

OFFICIAL NAME Bermuda

PEOPLE
Population 70,000.
Density 3,333/mi² (1,321/km²).
Urban 100%.
Capital Hamilton, Bermuda I., 1,600.
Ethnic groups Black 61%, white and others 39%.
Languages English.
Religions Anglican 37%, other Protestant 21%, Roman Catholic 14%, Black Muslim and others 28%.
Life expectancy 72 female, 66 male.
Literacy 98%.

POLITICS
Government Colony (U.K.).
Parties Progressive Labor, United.
Suffrage Universal, over 21.
Memberships None.
Subdivisions 9 parishes, 2 municipalities.

ECONOMY
GDP $598,000,000.
Per capita $16,150.
Monetary unit Dollar.
Trade partners U.S., Caribbean countries, U.K.
Exports Semitropical produce, light manufactures.
Imports Fuels, food, machinery.

LAND
Description North Atlantic islands.
Area 21 mi² (53 km²).
Highest point Town Hill, Bermuda I., 259 ft (79 m).
Lowest point Sea level.

PEOPLE.   The people of this British colony are mainly black descendants of African slaves. Descendants of British settlers and Portuguese indentured workers—plus immigrants from Canada, the West Indies, Asia, and Europe—make up minorities. In addition, there are a number of American military personnel living here.

ECONOMY AND THE LAND.   A mild climate, beautiful beaches, and a scenic, hilly terrain make tourism Bermuda's economic mainstay. Foreign businesses, attracted by tax exemptions, provide additional economic contributions. There is limited light manufacturing, agriculture, and fishing and no heavy industry. Situated about 650 miles (1,046 kilometers) east of the U.S. state of North Carolina, the archipelago consists of many small islands and islets. About twenty are inhabited and collectively known as the Island of Bermuda.

HISTORY AND POLITICS.   The colony received its name from Juan de Bermudez, a Spanish explorer who sailed past the islands in 1503, not landing because of the dangerous coral reefs. Spain showed no real interest in the islands, and Britain seemed likewise apathetic following the

visit of an Englishman in 1593. In 1690 a British ship carrying colonists to Virginia was wrecked upon the islands' reefs. These colonists found the soils fertile and land scenic, and soon Britain had settled the islands. Bermuda continues as a British colony, recognizing Great Britain's queen as the head of state. ■

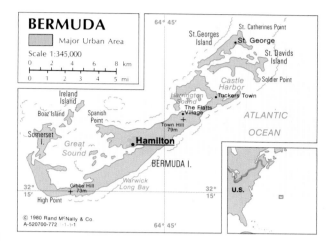

Bermuda Map Index

	Lat.	Long.		Lat.	Long.
Bermuda Island	32°20'N	64°45'W	Saint George's		
Castle Harbor	32°21'N	64°40'W	Island	32°22'N	64°40'W
Great Sound	32°17'N	64°51'W	Somerset Island	32°17'N	64°52'W
Hamilton	32°17'N	64°46'W	Spanish Point	32°18'N	64°48'W
Harrington Sound	32°19'N	64°43'W	The Flatts Village	32°19'N	64°43'W
High Point	32°15'N	64°50'W	Town Hill	32°19'N	64°44'W
Ireland Island	32°19'N	64°50'W	Tuckers Town	32°22'N	64°40'W
Saint David's			Warwick Long		
Island	32°22'N	64°39'W	Bay	32°16'N	64°47'W
Saint George	32°22'N	64°40'W			

BHUTAN

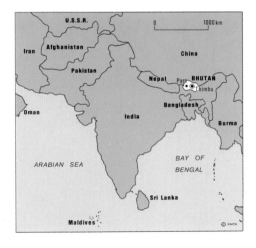

OFFICIAL NAME Kingdom of Bhutan

PEOPLE
Population 1,435,000.
Density 79/mi² (31/km²).
Urban 4%.
Capital Thimbu, 8,982.
Ethnic groups Bhote 60%, Nepalese 25%, others 15%.
Languages Dzongkha, English, Nepalese dialects.
Religions Buddhist 75%, Hindu 25%.
Life expectancy 43 female, 44 male.
Literacy 5%.

POLITICS
Government Monarchy (Indian protection).
Parties None.
Suffrage One vote per family.
Memberships UN.
Subdivisions 18 districts.

ECONOMY
GDP $131,000,000.
Per capita $109.
Monetary unit Ngultrum, Indian rupee.
Trade partners India.
Exports Agricultural products, wood, coal.
Imports Textiles, grain, vehicles, fuels.

LAND
Description Southern Asia, landlocked.
Area 18,147 mi² (47,000 km²).
Highest point Kula Kangri, 24,784 ft (7,554 m).
Lowest point Mans River valley, 318 ft (97 m).

PEOPLE.   A mountainous terrain long isolated Bhutan and limited internal mingling of peoples. The population is ethnically divided into the Bhotes, Nepalese, and various tribes. Of Tibetan ancestry, the Bhotes are a majority and have determined the major religion, Buddhism, and language, Dzongkha, a Tibetan dialect. The Nepalese are mostly Hindu and speak Nepalese; tribal dialects diversify language further.

ECONOMY AND THE LAND.   Partially due to physical isolation, Bhutan has one of the world's least developed economies. Forests cover much of the land, limiting agricultural area but offering opportunity for the expansion of forestry. Farming is concentrated in the more densely populated, fertile valleys of the Himalayas. The climate varies with altitude; the icy Himalayas in the north give way to temperate central valleys and a subtropical south.

HISTORY AND POLITICS.   Bhutan's early history remains mostly unknown, but it is thought that by the early sixteenth century descendants of Tibetan invaders ruled the area. Proximity to and interaction with British India resulted in British control of Bhutan's foreign affairs in the nine-

teenth and early twentieth centuries. In 1907 the current hereditary monarchy was established. Indian ties were strengthened in the late fifties to counter Chinese influence. At the same time, modernization programs were instituted, improving primitive transportation and communication systems and bringing Bhutan further into the twentieth-century mainstream. ■

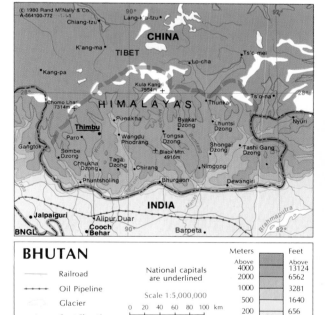

Bhutan Map Index

	Lat.	Long.		Lat.	Long.
Chomo Lhari	27°50'N	89°15'E	Paro	27°26'N	89°25'E
Himalayas	28°00'N	90°30'E	Thimbu	27°28'N	89°39'E
Kula Kangri	28°03'N	90°27'E	Wong	27°10'N	89°30'E

BOLIVIA

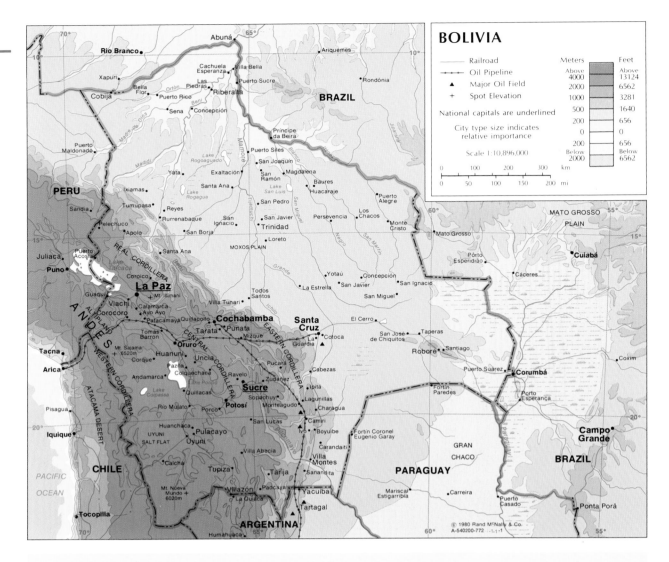

OFFICIAL NAME Republic of Bolivia

PEOPLE
Population 6,115,000.
Density 14/mi² (5.6/km²).
Urban 45%.
Capital La Paz (seat of government), 719,780; Sucre (seat of judiciary), 68,426.
Ethnic groups Quechua 30%, Aymara 25%, mixed, European.
Languages Spanish, Quechua, Aymara.
Religions Roman Catholic 95%.
Life expectancy 53 female, 49 male.
Literacy 68%.

POLITICS
Government Republic.
Parties Movement of the Revolutionary Left, Nationalist Democratic Action, Nationalist Revolutionary Movement of the People, National Revolutionary Movement of the Left.
Suffrage Universal adult (married, 18; single, 21).
Memberships OAS, UN.
Subdivisions 9 departments.

ECONOMY
GNP $5,600,000,000.
Per capita $933.
Monetary unit Peso.
Trade partners Argentina, U.S., Brazil, Western European countries.
Exports Tin, natural gas, silver.
Imports Machinery, consumer goods, food.

LAND
Description Central South America, landlocked.
Area 464,164 mi² (1,098,581 km²).
Highest point Nevado Illimani, 22,579 ft (6,882 m).
Lowest point Paraguay River valley, 325 ft (100 m).

PEOPLE. Indians compose the majority of Bolivia's population. Minorities include mestizos, of Spanish-Indian descent, and Europeans. Although most people are poor, Bolivia has a rich cultural heritage, evidenced by early Aymaran and Quechuan artifacts; Spanish-influenced Indian and mestizo art; and twentieth-century achievements. Roman Catholicism is the major religion, frequently combined with Indian beliefs. Sucre is the judicial seat and constitutional capital, while La Paz is the center of government.

ECONOMY AND THE LAND. Bolivia is underdeveloped and among South America's poorest nations. It is rich in natural resources, however. Farming is the main activity, although mining makes the largest contribution to the gross national product. Population, industry, and major cities are concentrated on the western altiplano, an Andean high plateau, where many Bolivians continue to practice agriculture according to ancestral methods. The eastern llano, or lowland plain, contains fuel deposits and is the site of commercial farming. The yungas, hills and valleys between the altiplano and the llano, form the most developed agricultural region. Successful exploitation of Bolivia's rich resources is partially dependent upon political stability. The cli-

mate varies from tropical to semiarid and cool, depending on altitude.

HISTORY AND POLITICS. The Aymara Indian culture flourished in the area that is now Bolivia between 100 B.C. and A.D. 900. In the mid-1400s the area was absorbed into the expanding empire of the Incas, who controlled the region until ousted by the Spanish in 1535. The discovery of silver increased Spain's interest in this colony. Potosí, the site of much mining activity, became the largest city in the Western Hemisphere. During the Napoleonic Wars, Spain's authority diminished somewhat, and colonists became increasingly dissatisfied with Spanish rule. The colonists claimed independence in 1809, but many years of struggle followed. Simón Bolívar,

the Venezuelan organizer of the South American movement to free the Spanish colonies, helped lead the way to independence, which was finally won in 1825. Bolívar assisted in writing the constitution, and he became the country's namesake. Political instability followed independence, with coups and short-lived constitutions. A brief period of stability occurred in the 1800s with rising silver prices on the world scene. Politics, however, were greatly influenced by the interests of mine owners, and the Indian population remained ensconced in poverty and enjoyed few rights. After years of turmoil, a 1952 revolution installed a government that introduced suffrage, land, and education reforms. Since the regime was ousted in a 1964 coup, instability and social unrest have continued. ■

Bolivia Map Index

	Lat.	Long.		Lat.	Long.		Lat.	Long.		Lat.	Long.
Altiplano	18°00'S	68°00'W	Huanchaca	20°20'S	66°39'W	Pucará	18°43'S	64°11'W	San Pedro	14°20'S	64°50'W
Andamarca	18°49'S	67°31'W	Huanuni	18°16'S	66°51'W	Puerto Acosta	15°32'S	69°15'W	San Ramón	13°17'S	64°43'W
Andes	17°00'S	69°00'W	*Illimani, Mcunt*	16°39'S	67°48'W	Puerto Alegre	13°53'S	61°36'W	Santa Ana	13°45'S	65°35'W
Apolo	14°43'S	68°31'W	Ipitá	19°20'S	63°32'W	Puerto Rico	11°05'S	67°08'W	Santa Ana	15°31'S	67°30'W
Ayo Ayo	17°05'S	68°00'W	*Iténez*	11°54'S	65°01'W	Puerto Siles	12°48'S	65°05'W	Santa Cruz	17°48'S	63°10'W
Baures	13°35'S	63°35'W	Ivo	20°27'S	63°26'W	Puerto Suárez	18°57'S	57°51'W	Santiago	18°19'S	59°34'W
Bella Flor	11°09'S	67°49'W	Ixiamas	13°45'S	68°09'W	Puerto Sucre	10°48'S	65°23'W	Sena	11°32'S	67°11'W
Beni	14°00'S	65°30'W	La Estrella	16°30'S	63°45'W	Pulacayo	20°25'S	66°41'W	Sopachuy	19°29'S	64°31'W
Boyuibe	20°25'S	63°17'W	La Guardia	17°54'S	63°20'W	Punata	17°32'S	65°50'W	Sucre	19°02'S	65°17'W
Cabezas	18°46'S	63°24'W	Lagunillas	19°38'S	63°43'W	Quillacas	19°14'S	66°58'W	Taperas	17°54'S	60°23'W
Cachuela			*La Paz*	16°30'S	68°09'W	Quillacollo	17°26'S	66°17'W	Tarata	17°37'S	66°01'W
Esperanza	10°32'S	65°38'W	Las Piedras	11°06'S	66°10'W	Ravelo	18°48'S	65°32'W	Tarija	21°31'S	64°45'W
Calamarca	16°55'S	68°09'W	Loreto	15°13'S	64°40'W	*Real Cordillera*	17°00'S	67°10'W	*Tijamuchi*	14°10'S	64°58'W
Calcha	21°06'S	67°31'W	Los Chacos	14°33'S	62°11'W	Reyes	14°19'S	67°23'W	*Titicaca, Lake*	15°50'S	69°20'W
Camiri	20°03'S	63°31'W	*Madre de Dios*	10°59'S	66°08'W	Riberalta	10°59'S	66°06'W	Todos Santos	16°48'S	65°08'W
Carandaiti	20°45'S	63°04'W	Magdalena	13°20'S	64°08'W	Río Mulato	19°42'S	66°47'W	Tomás Barron	17°35'S	67°31'W
Central Cordillera	18°30'S	64°55'W	*Mamoré*	10°23'S	65°23'W	Roboré	18°20'S	59°45'W	Trinidad	14°47'S	64°47'W
Charagua	19°48'S	63°13'W	Mizque	17°56'S	65°19'W	*Rogagua, Lake*	13°43'S	66°54'W	Tumupasa	14°09'S	67°55'W
Cobija	11°02'S	68°44'W	Monteagudo	19°49'S	63°59'W	Rurrenabaque	14°28'S	67°34'W	Tupiza	21°27'S	65°43'W
Cochabamba	17°24'S	66°09'W	Monte Cristo	14°43'S	61°14'W	*Sajama, Mount*	18°06'S	68°54'W	Uncia	18°27'S	66°37'W
Coipasa, Lake	19°12'S	68°07'W	*Moxos Plain*	15°00'S	65°00'W	Sanandita	21°40'S	63°35'W	Uyuni	20°28'S	66°50'W
Colquechaca	18°40'S	66°01'W	*Neuvo Mundo,*			San Borja	14°49'S	66°51'W	*Uyuni Salt Flat*	20°20'S	67°42'W
Concepción	11°29'S	66°31'W	*Mount*	21°55'S	66°53'W	San Ignacio	14°53'S	65°36'W	Viachi	16°39'S	68°18'W
Concepción	16°15'S	62°04'W	Oruro	17°59'S	67°09'W	San Ignacio	16°23'S	60°59'W	Villa Abecia	21°00'S	65°23'W
Corocoro	17°12'S	68°29'W	Padcaya	21°52'S	64°48'W	San Javier	14°34'S	64°42'W	Villa Bella	10°23'S	65°24'W
Coroico	16°10'S	67°44'W	*Paraguay*	20°10'S	58°08'W	San Javier	16°20'S	62°38'W	Villa Montes	21°15'S	63°30'W
Corque	18°21'S	67°42'W	Patacamaya	17°14'S	67°55'W	San Joaquín	13°04'S	64°49'W	Villa Tunari	16°55'S	65°25'W
Cotoca	17°49'S	63°03'W	Pazña	18°36'S	66°55'W	San José de			Villazón	22°06'S	65°36'W
Eastern Cordillera	17°30'S	64°30'W	Pelechuco	14°48'S	69°04'W	Chiquitos	17°51'S	60°47'W	Yata	13°20'S	66°35'W
El Cerro	17°31'S	61°34'W	Persevencia	14°44'S	62°48'W	San Lucas	20°06'S	65°07'W	Yotaú	16°03'S	63°03'W
Exaltación	13°16'S	65°15'W	Pilcomayo	22°15'S	62°38'W	*San Luis, Lake*	13°45'S	64°00'W	Zudañez	19°06'S	64°44'W
Grande	15°51'S	64°39'W	*Poopó, Lake*	18°45'S	67°07'W	*San Martín*	13°08'S	63°43'W			
Guaqui	16°35'S	68°51'W	Porco	19°50'S	65°59'W	San Miguel	16°42'S	61°01'W			
Huacaraje	13°33'S	63°45'W	*Potosí*	20°40'S	67°00'W	*San Miguel*	13°52'S	63°56'W			

BOTSWANA

OFFICIAL NAME Republic of
Botswana

PEOPLE
Population 1,055,000.
Density 4.6/mi² (1.8/km²).
Urban 16%.
Capital Gaborone, 59,700.
Ethnic Tswana 94%, Bushmen 5%, European 1%.
Languages English, Setswana.
Religions Indigenous 40%, Christian 15%.
Life expectancy 58 female, 52 male.
Literacy 35%.

POLITICS
Government Republic.
Parties Democratic, Independence, National Front.
Suffrage Universal, over 21.
Memberships CW, OAU, UN.
Subdivisions 11 districts.

ECONOMY
GDP $721,600,000.
Per capita $830.
Monetary unit Pula.
Trade partners Switzerland, U.S., U.K., southern
African countries.
Exports Diamonds, cattle, animal products, copper.
Imports Food, machinery, vehicles, petroleum,
textiles.

LAND
Description Southern Africa, landlocked.
Area 231,805 mi² (600,372 km²).
Highest point 4,969 ft (1,515 m).
Lowest point Confluence of Shashi and Limpopo
rivers, 1,684 ft (513 m).

PEOPLE. The population of this sparsely populated country is composed mostly of Tswana,
Bantu peoples of various groups. The Tswana
are divided into about eight ethnic groups, with
the largest being the Bamangwato, followed by
the Bakwena, Batawana, Bangwaketse, Bakgatla,
Bamalete, Barolong, and Batlokwa. Minorities include the Kalanga, Herero, and Bushmen. Following settlement patterns laid down centuries
ago, Tswana predominate in the more fertile and
more populated eastern region, and Bushmen
are concentrated in the Kalahari Desert. There is
also a minority white population, mainly British
citizens, and people of various other nationalities. Despite its smaller numbers, overall the
white population enjoys a higher standard of living than does the black. Most Batswana live in
small villages in rural areas, but some traditional
villages are quite large, with populations of more
than thirty thousand people. English is the official language, resulting from years of British
rule, but the majority speak Setswana. Religion
follows a similar pattern, with most people following traditional beliefs, and Christianity a minority practice.

ECONOMY AND THE LAND. In the early seventies Botswana's economy began to shift course

with the exploitation of previously untapped natural resources. Diamond mining was the main
impetus behind development, along with the
mining of copper, nickel, and coal, and growth
was rapid. Despite this new economic emphasis,
traditional agricultural activity continues, and although agriculture is limited by the southwestern
Kalahari Desert and a subtropical climate suscep-
tible to drought, most Batswana are dependent
upon farming in some form. Some Batswana
raise crops such as corn, millet, and sorghum,
and many are engaged in subsistence farming,
especially cattle raising. Livestock provides for
commercial earnings as well, with cattle and animal products making up a large portion of Botswana's exports. The most productive farmland
lies in the east and north, where rainfall is greater and grazing lands plentiful. Industry remains
largely undeveloped, and despite ideological differences, the country's economy remains dependent upon South Africa. Together with Lesotho
and Swaziland, Botswana belongs to a customs
union with South Africa, which affords the country economic benefits. In 1976 Botswana made a
step toward economic independence when it
stopped using the South African rand in favor of
its own unit of currency, the pula. The rolling
sand and grassy expanses of the Kalahari cover
southwestern Botswana, and in the north and
northwest the Okavango and Chobe rivers create
an inland delta called the Okavango Swamps.
Eastern hills give way to more level terrain elsewhere in the country. The climate is dry and
subtropical but varies with latitude and altitude.

HISTORY AND POLITICS. In Botswana's early
history, Bushmen, the original inhabitants, re-
treated into the Kalahari region when the
Tswana invaded and established their settlements in the more fertile east. Intertribal wars
were followed by conflicts with the Boers, settlers
of Dutch or Huguenot descent. These conflicts
led the Tswana to seek British assistance, and
the area of present-day Botswana became part of
the British protectorate of Bechuanaland. When
the Union of South Africa was created in 1910,
those living in Bechuanaland, later Botswana; Basutoland, later Lesotho; and Swaziland requested
exclusion from the Union and were granted it.
Despite requests from South Africa that the protectorate be transferred to their domain, British
rule continued. A program that gradually increased the political involvement of the Batswana
led to a constitution in 1965 and independence
the following year. Thus in 1966 the protectorate

of Bechuanaland became the independent Republic of Botswana. The country maintains a policy of nonalignment in foreign affairs and is seeking to expand relations with other nations.
Botswana hopes to reduce its traditional dependence upon South Africa, whose policy of apartheid it opposes. Although Botswana is one of the
few multiparty countries in Africa, tensions are
on the rise, as dissent over policies in neighboring South Africa continue. ∎

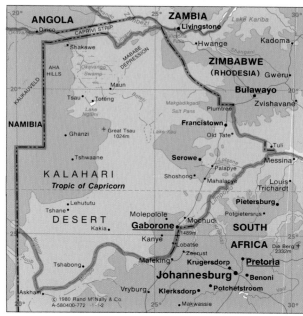

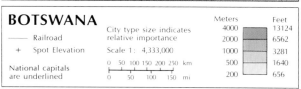

BOTSWANA
— Railroad
+ Spot Elevation

City type size indicates
relative importance

National capitals
are underlined

Scale 1: 4,333,000

Meters	Feet
4000	13124
2000	6562
1000	3281
500	1640
200	656

Botswana Map Index

	Lat.	Long.		Lat.	Long.
Francistown	21°11'S	27°32'E	Mochudi	24°28'S	26°05'E
Gaborone	24°45'S	25°55'E	Molepolole	24°25'S	25°30'E
Great Tsau	21°14'S	22°45'E	Molopo	26°55'S	20°40'E
Kalahari Desert	23°00'S	22°00'E	Ngami, Lake	20°37'S	22°40'E
Kanye	24°59'S	25°19'E	Okavango		
Limpopo	22°12'S	29°20'E	Swamp	18°45'S	22°45'E
Mababe			Serowe	22°25'S	26°44'E
Depression	18°50'S	24°15'E	Xau, Lake	21°15'S	24°38'E
Makgadikgadi			Zambezi	17°50'S	25°18'E
Salt Pans	20°45'S	25°30'E			

Since large numbers of men mi-
grate annually from Botswana to
South Africa in search of work,
a growing proportion of the
households have to be managed
entirely by women. To supplement their income, many
women take up heavy work,
such as bricklaying.

BRAZIL

OFFICIAL NAME Federative Republic of Brazil

PEOPLE

Population 134,340,000.
Density 41/mi² (16/km²).
Urban 68%.
Capital Brasília, 1,177,393.
Ethnic groups White 55%, mixed 38%, black 6%.
Languages Portuguese.
Religions Roman Catholic 89%.
Life expectancy 66 female, 62 male.
Literacy 75%.

POLITICS

Government Republic.
Parties Democratic Movement, Social Democratic.
Suffrage Universal, over 18 (excluding illiterates).
Memberships OAS, UN.
Subdivisions 23 states, 3 territories, 1 federal district.

ECONOMY

GNP $295,000,000,000.
Per capita $2,360.
Monetary unit Cruzeiro.
Trade partners U.S., Saudi Arabia, Japan, West Germany.
Exports Soybeans, coffee, transportation equipment, iron ore.
Imports Petroleum, machinery, chemicals, pharmaceuticals.

LAND

Description Eastern South America.
Area 3,265,075 mi² (8,456,508 km²).
Highest point Neblina Pk., 9,888 ft (3,014 m).
Lowest point Sea level.

PEOPLE. The largest South American nation, Brazil is also the most populous. The mixed population was shaped by indigenous Indians, Portuguese colonists, black African slaves, and European and Japanese immigrants. Today, native Indians compose less than 1 percent of the population, and the group is disappearing rapidly due to contact with modern cultures and other factors. Brazil is the only Portuguese-speaking nation in the Americas, and Roman Catholicism is the major religion.

ECONOMY AND THE LAND. Brazil's prosperous economy stems from a diversified base of agriculture, mining, and industry. Most commercial farms and ranches lie in the southern plateau region, and coffee, cocoa, soybeans, and beef are important products. Mineral resources include iron ore deposits, many found in the central and southern plateau regions. Additional mineral deposits have recently been discovered in the Amazon area. Industrial expansion during and after World War II was focused in the southeast, and the capital was moved from Rio de Janeiro to Brasília in 1960 to redistribute activity. Undeveloped states have been targeted for development, but programs may require displacement of the Indian population. Forests cover about half the country, and the Amazon River basin is the site of the world's largest rain forest. The northeast

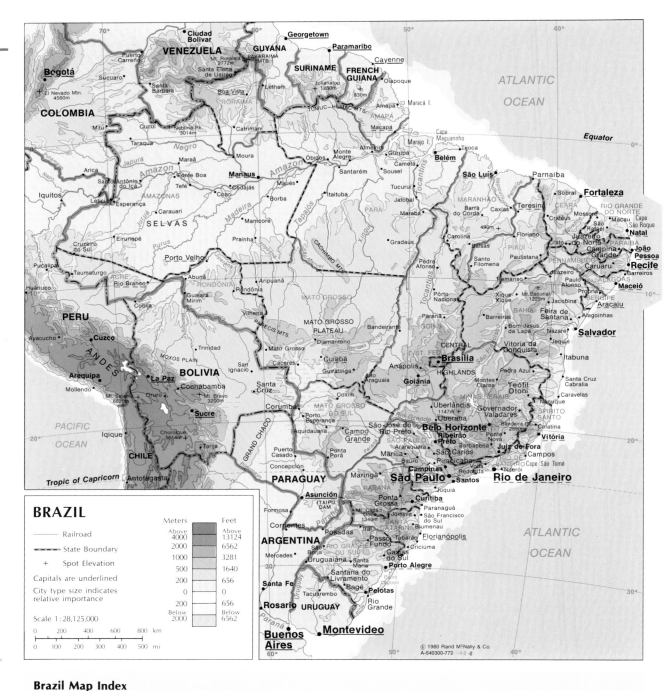

BRAZIL

	Meters	Feet
—— Railroad	Above 4000	Above 13124
---- State Boundary	2000	6562
+ Spot Elevation	1000	3281
	500	1640
Capitals are underlined	200	656
City type size indicates relative importance	0	0
	200	656
Scale 1 : 28,125,000	Below 2000	Below 6562

0   200   400   600   800 km
0   100   200   300   400   500 mi

© 1980 Rand McNally & Co.
A-540300-772

Brazil Map Index

	Lat.	Long.		Lat.	Long.		Lat.	Long.		Lat.	Long.
Acre	9°00'S	70°00'W	Diamantino	14°25'S	56°27'W	Minas Gerais	18°00'S	44°00'W	Rio Grande do		
Alagoas	9°00'S	36°00'W	Distrito Federal	15°45'S	47°45'W	Monte Alegre	2°01'S	54°04'W	Norte	5°45'S	36°00'W
Alagoinhas	12°07'S	38°26'W	Espírito Santo	19°30'S	40°30'W	Montes Claros	16°43'S	43°52'W	Rio Grande du		
Almeirim	1°32'S	52°34'W	Feira de Santana	12°15'S	38°57'W	Mossoró	5°11'S	37°20'W	Sul	30°00'S	54°00'W
Alto Araguaia	17°19'S	53°12'W	Floriano	6°47'S	43°01'W	Moura	1°27'S	61°38'W	Rondônia	10°52'S	61°57'W
Amapá	1°00'N	52°00'W	Florianópolis	27°35'S	48°34'W	Nanuque	17°50'S	40°21'W	Rondônia	11°00'S	63°00'W
Amazon	0°05'S	50°00'W	Fonte Boa	2°32'S	66°01'W	Natal	5°47'S	35°13'W	Roraima	1°00'N	61°00'W
Amazonas	4°00'S	58°00'W	Fortaleza	3°43'S	38°30'W	Nazaré	13°02'S	39°00'W	Salvador	12°59'S	38°31'W
Anápolis	16°20'S	48°58'W	Goiânia	16°40'S	49°16'W	Neblina Peak	0°48'N	66°02'W	Santa Catarina	27°00'S	50°00'W
Aquidauana	20°28'S	55°48'W	Goiás	15°00'S	49°00'W	Negro	3°08'S	59°55'W	Santana do		
Aracaju	10°55'S	37°04'W	Governador			Niterói	22°53'S	43°07'W	Livramento	30°53'S	55°31'W
Araguaia	5°21'S	48°41'W	Valadares	18°51'S	41°56'W	Óbidos	1°55'S	55°31'W	Santarem	2°26'S	54°42'W
Araraquara	21°47'S	48°10'W	Gradaús	7°43'S	51°11'W	Oiapoque	3°50'N	51°50'W	Santo Filomena	9°07'S	45°56'W
Aripuanã	9°10'S	60°38'W	Grande, Rio	19°52'S	50°20'W	Pakaraima			Santos	23°57'S	46°20'W
Bagé	31°20'S	54°06'W	Guajará Mirim	10°48'S	65°22'W	Mountains	5°30'N	60°40'W	São Carlos	22°01'S	47°54'W
Bahia	11°00'S	42°00'W	Guaporé	11°54'S	65°01'W	Pará	4°00'S	53°00'W	São Francisco	10°30'S	36°24'W
Bandeirante	13°41'S	50°48'W	Guiratinga	16°21'S	53°45'W	Paraíba	7°15'S	36°30'W	São José do Rio		
Bandeira Peak	20°26'S	41°47'W	Gurupá	1°25'S	51°39'W	Paraná	12°33'S	47°52'W	Prêto	20°48'S	49°23'W
Barbacena	21°14'S	43°46'W	Iguaçu Falls	25°41'S	54°26'W	Paraná	23°30'S	52°00'W	São Luís	2°31'S	44°16'W
Barreiras	12°08'S	45°00'W	Itabuna	14°48'S	39°16'W	Paraná	33°43'S	59°15'W	São Manuel	7°21'S	58°03'W
Barreiros	8°49'S	35°12'W	Itaituba	4°17'S	55°59'W	Parnaiba	2°54'S	41°47'W	São Paulo	23°32'S	46°37'W
Bauru	22°19'S	49°04'W	Jacobina	11°11'S	40°31'W	Parnaiba	3°00'S	41°50'W	São Paulo	22°00'S	49°00'W
Belém	1°27'S	48°29'W	Japurá	3°08'S	64°46'W	Passo Fundo	28°15'S	52°24'W	São Rafael	5°47'S	36°55'W
Belo Horizonte	19°55'S	43°56'W	Jari	1°09'S	51°54'W	Paulista	8°09'S	41°09'W	São Roque, Cape	5°29'S	35°16'W
Boa Vista	2°49'N	60°40'W	Jequié	13°51'S	40°05'W	Paulo Afonso	9°21'S	38°14'W	Selvas	5°00'S	68°00'W
Branco	1°24'S	61°51'W	João Pessoa	7°07'S	34°52'W	Pedra Azul	16°01'S	41°16'W	Sergipe	10°30'S	37°30'W
Brasília	15°47'S	47°55'W	Juàzeiro	9°25'S	40°30'W	Pedro Afonso	8°59'S	48°11'W	Sobral	3°42'S	40°21'W
Cáceres	16°04'S	57°41'W	Juazeiro do Norte	7°12'S	39°20'W	Pelotas	31°46'S	52°20'W	Tapajós	2°24'S	54°41'W
Cametá	2°15'S	49°30'W	Juiz de Fora	21°45'S	43°20'W	Pernambuco	8°00'S	37°00'W	Taumaturgo	8°57'S	72°48'W
Campina Grande	7°13'S	35°53'W	Juruá	2°37'S	65°44'W	Piauí	7°00'S	43°00'W	Teófilo Otoni	17°51'S	41°30'W
Campinas	22°54'S	47°00'W	Macapá	0°02'N	51°03'W	Piracicaba	22°43'S	47°38'W	Teresina	5°05'S	42°49'W
Campo Grande	20°27'S	54°37'W	Macau	5°07'S	36°38'W	Ponta Grossa	25°05'S	50°09'W	Tocantins	1°45'S	49°10'W
Campos	21°45'S	41°18'W	Maceió	9°40'S	35°43'W	Ponta Porã	22°32'S	55°43'W	Trombetas	1°55'S	55°35'W
Carauari	4°52'S	66°54'W	Madeira	3°22'S	58°45'W	Ponte Nova	20°24'S	42°54'W	Tucuruí	3°42'S	49°27'W
Caravelas	17°45'S	39°15'W	Mamoré	10°23'S	65°23'W	Porto Alegre	30°04'S	51°11'W	Tumuc-Humac		
Carolina	7°20'S	47°28'W	Manaus	3°08'S	60°01'W	Porto Esperança	19°37'S	57°27'W	Mountains	2°20'N	55°00'W
Caruaru	8°17'S	35°58'W	Marajó Island	1°00'S	49°30'W	Porto Nacional	10°42'S	48°25'W	Uberaba	19°45'S	47°55'W
Caxias do Sul	29°10'S	51°11'W	Maranhão	5°00'S	45°00'W	Porto Velho	8°46'S	63°54'W	Uberlândia	18°56'S	48°18'W
Ceará	5°00'S	40°00'W	Marília	22°13'S	49°56'W	Prainha	1°48'S	53°29'W	Uruguaiana	29°45'S	57°05'W
Coari	4°05'S	63°08'W	Maringá	23°25'S	51°55'W	Propriá	10°13'S	36°51'W	Uruguay	34°12'S	58°18'W
Colatina	19°32'S	40°37'W	Mato Grosso	15°00'S	59°57'W	Purus	3°42'S	61°28'W	Vilhena	12°43'S	60°07'W
Corumbá	19°01'S	57°39'W	Mato Grosso	11°00'S	55°00'W	Recife	8°03'S	34°54'W	Vitória	20°19'S	40°21'W
Coxim	18°30'S	54°45'W	Mato Grosso do			Remanso	9°41'S	42°04'W	Vitoria da		
Cratèus	5°10'S	40°40'W	Sul	20°30'S	53°30'W	Ribeirão Prêto	21°10'S	47°48'W	Conquista	14°51'S	40°51'W
Crato	7°14'S	39°23'W	Mato Grosso			Rio Branco	9°58'S	67°48'W	Volta Redonda	22°32'S	44°07'W
Cucuí	1°12'N	66°50'W	Plateau	15°30'S	56°00'W	Rio de Janeiro	22°54'S	43°14'W	Xingu	1°30'S	51°53'W
Cuiabá	15°35'S	56°05'W	Maués	3°24'S	57°42'W	Rio de Janeiro	22°00'S	42°30'W	Xique-Xique	10°50'S	42°44'W
Curitiba	25°25'S	49°15'W				Rio Grande	32°02'S	52°05'W			

consists of semiarid grasslands, and the central-west and south are marked by hills, mountains, and rolling plains. Overall the climate is semi-tropical to tropical, with heavy rains.

HISTORY AND POLITICS. Portugal obtained rights to the region in a 1494 treaty with Spain and claimed Brazil in 1500. As the native Indian population died out, blacks were brought from Africa to work the plantations. In the 1800s, during the Napoleonic Wars, the Portuguese royal family fled to Rio de Janeiro, and in 1815 the colony became a kingdom. In 1821 the Portuguese king departed for Portugal, leaving Brazil's rule to his son, who declared Brazil an independent country and himself emperor in 1822. Economic development in the mid-1800s brought an influx of Europeans. Following a military take-over in 1889, Brazil became a republic. Economic problems resulted in a 1930 military coup and a dictatorship lasting until 1945, plus military take-overs in 1954 and 1964. In 1985 Brazil's electoral college voted civilian Tancredo de Almeida Neves to the presidency, ending twenty-one years of military rule. He died, however, before taking office. Brazil's economic importance has led to greater involvement in global affairs. ■

Brazil's natural resources make it a leading producer of hydroelectric power, with potential for further development. Forming part of the border between Brazil and Argentina, Iguaçu Falls would provide great power if harnessed.

BRITISH INDIAN OCEAN TERRITORY

OFFICIAL NAME British Indian
Ocean Territory

PEOPLE
Population None.
Capital None.

POLITICS
Government Colony (U.K.).

LAND
Description Indian Ocean islands.
Area 23mi² (60 km²).
Lowest point Sea level.

PEOPLE. Up until the late 1960s and early 1970s, the Chagos Islands, which make up the British Indian Ocean Territory, were inhabited by the Ilois, descendants of slaves who had worked the islands' coconut plantations. Between 1967 and 1973, about 3,000 Ilois were removed and resettled in Mauritius and Seychelles to make way for British and United States military development. Therefore, no permanent population currently resides in the British Indian Ocean Territory. There are about 4,500 temporary residents, including about 1,600 military personnel working for a joint British–United States military operation.

ECONOMY AND THE LAND. Because of its proximity to the Persian Gulf, the British Indian Ocean Territory is of strategic importance, and the island of Diego Garcia is the site of a United States naval facility. Diego Garcia, the largest island of the Chagos archipelago, has a lagoon with natural anchorages and a V shape well suited for runway construction. Other major island groups in the archipelago include Peros Banhos and Salomon. In total, the British Indian Ocean Territory comprises about 2,300 islands. The overall terrain is flat and low, and the climate is tropical, with heat and humidity moderated by trade winds.

HISTORY AND POLITICS. European rivalry for the spice trade and routes to India and the Far East centered in the coastal lands and islands of the Indian Ocean in the 1700s. After gaining possession of Mauritius in 1715, in the 1750s France claimed the islands of Seychelles, which included the Chagos. An economy based on the production of copra, or coconut meat, soon developed, and slaves were brought to work the plantations. With the end of slavery in the nineteenth century, the slaves became contract employees, and work on the plantations continued. These former slaves and their descendants became known as the Ilois. Following the Napoleonic Wars, in the 1814 Treaty of Paris, France ceded to Britain the colony of Mauritius and its dependencies, which included Seychelles and the Chagos Islands. These islands were administered from Mauritius until 1903, when Seychelles became a separate colony. The Chagos Islands, however, remained a dependency of Mauritius. In 1965 Britain separated the Chagos Islands, along with the islands of Aldabra, Desroches, and Farquhar, from Mauritius to create the British Indian Ocean Territory. Mauritius received monetary compensation and the promise that the islands would be returned when they ceased to be of military value. The following year the United States and Britain agreed to develop the islands as a joint military project, and a communications facility began operating in 1973. To make way for this and future projects, the copra plantations were dissolved, and the Ilois relocated to Mauritius and Seychelles. When Seychelles gained independence in 1976, Britain ceded Aldabra, Desroches, and Farquhar to the new country. Since 1973, the British Indian Ocean Territory's communications facility has expanded to become a major United States naval operation in the Indian Ocean. Opposition to military development in the region has been nearly unanimous among the islands and coastal nations of the Indian Ocean. The current United States lease on the island of Diego Garcia extends to the year 2025. The now-independent country of Mauritius also claims rights to the island of Diego Garcia. ∎

BRUNEI

OFFICIAL NAME State of
Brunei

PEOPLE
Population 220,000.
Density 99/mi² (38/km²).
Urban 76%.
Capital Bandar Seri Begawan, 63,868.
Ethnic groups Malay 75%, Chinese 20%.
Languages Malay, English, Chinese.
Religions Muslim 60%, Christian 8%, Buddhist and others 32%.
Life expectancy 62 female, 62 male.
Literacy 45%.

POLITICS
Government Constitutional monarchy.
Parties People's Independence Front.
Suffrage Universal, over 21.

Memberships ASEAN, CW, UN.
Subdivisions 4 districts.

ECONOMY
GDP $19,800,000,000.
Per capita $27,000.
Monetary unit Dollar.
Trade partners Japan, U.S., Singapore, U.K.
Exports Petroleum, natural gas.
Imports Machinery, transportation equipment, manufactured goods, food.

LAND
Description Southeastern Asia (island of Borneo).
Area 2,226 mi² (5,765 km²).
Highest point Mt. Pagon, 6,070 ft (1,850 m).
Lowest point Sea level.

PEOPLE. The majority of Brunei's population is Malay, with minorities of Chinese and indigenous peoples. Most Malays are Muslim, and the Chinese are mainly Christian or Buddhist. Many Chinese, although wealthy, are unable to become citizens due to language-proficiency exams and strict residency requirements. The standard of living is high because of Brunei's oil-based economy, yet wealth is not equally distributed.

ECONOMY AND THE LAND. Oil and natural gas are the economic mainstays, giving Brunei a high per capita gross domestic product. Much food is imported, however, and a current goal is diversification. This would allow Brunei to become less dependent upon the fluctuations of the oil market. Situated on northeastern Borneo, Brunei is generally flat and covered with dense rain forests. The climate is tropical.

HISTORY AND POLITICS. Historical records of Brunei date back to the seventh century. The country was an important trading center, and by the sixteenth century the sultan of Brunei ruled Borneo and parts of nearby islands. In 1888 Brunei became a British protectorate. In the 1920s oil was discovered offshore, bringing prosperity and great wealth to the protectorate. Brunei gained independence from Britain in 1984, and the nation is ruled by a sultan. ∎

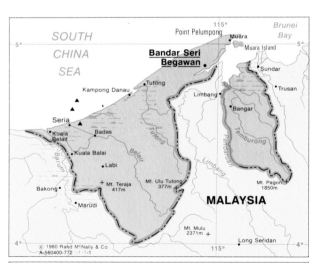

BRUNEI

——	Railroad
▲	Major Oil Field
+	Spot Elevation

National capitals are underlined

Scale 1:2,000,000

Brunei Map Index

	Lat.	Long.		Lat.	Long.
Bandar Seri Begawan	4°56′N	114°55′E	Muara Island	5°00′N	115°06′E
Belait	4°35′N	114°12′E	Pagon, Mount	4°18′N	115°19′E
Brunei Bay	5°05′N	115°18′E	Seria	4°39′N	114°23′E
			Temburong	4°48′N	115°03′E

BULGARIA

OFFICIAL NAME People's
Republic of Bulgaria

PEOPLE
Population 8,980,000.
Density 210/mi² (81/km²).
Urban 64%.
Capital Sofia, 1,056,945.
Ethnic groups Bulgarian 85%, Turkish 9%, Gypsy 3%,
   Macedonian 3%.
Languages Bulgarian.
Religions Bulgarian Orthodox 85%, Muslim 13%.
Life expectancy 75 female, 71 male.
Literacy 95%.

POLITICS
Government Socialist republic.
Parties Communist.
Suffrage Universal, over 18.
Memberships CEMA, UN, Warsaw Pact.
Subdivisions 27 provinces, 1 city.

ECONOMY
GNP $35,300,000,000.
Per capita $3,963.
Monetary unit Lev.
Trade partners U.S.S.R., Eastern European countries,
   West Germany.
Exports Machinery, agricultural products, fuels.
Imports Fuels, machinery, transportation equipment.

LAND
Description Southeastern Europe.
Area 42,823 mi² (110,912 km²).
Highest point Musala, 9,596 ft (2,925 m).
Lowest point Sea level.

PEOPLE. Bulgaria's ethnic composition was determined early in its history when Bulgar tribes
conquered the area's Slavic inhabitants. Bulgarians, descendants of these peoples, are a majority
today, and Turks, Gypsies, and Macedonians
compose the main minority groups. Postwar development is reflected in an agriculture-to-
industry shift in employment and a resultant
rural-to-urban population movement.

ECONOMY AND THE LAND. Following World
War II, the Bulgarian government began a program of expansion, turning the undeveloped agricultural nation into an industrial state modeled
after the Soviet Union. Today the industrial sector is the greatest economic contributor and employer. Farming, however, continues to play an
economic role. A climate similar to that of the
American Midwest and rich soils in river valleys
are suited for raising livestock and growing grain
and other crops. The overall terrain is mountainous.

HISTORY AND POLITICS. The area of modern
Bulgaria had been absorbed by the Roman Empire by A.D. 15 and was subsequently invaded by
the Slavs. In the seventh century Bulgars conquered the region and settled alongside Slavic
inhabitants. Rule by the Ottoman Turks began in
the late fourteenth century and lasted until 1878,
when the Bulgarians defeated the Turks with the

aid of Russia and Romania. The Principality of
Bulgaria emerged in 1885, with boundaries ap-
proximating those of today, and in 1908 Bulgaria
was declared an independent kingdom. A desire
for access to the Aegean Sea and increased territory was partially responsible for Bulgaria's involvement in the Balkan Wars of 1912 and 1913
and alliances with Germany during both world
wars. Following Bulgaria's declaration of war on
the United States and Britain in World War II, the
Soviet Union declared war on Bulgaria. Defeat
came in 1944, the monarchy was overthrown,
and a Communist government established shortly thereafter. Foreign policy is guided by alliance
with the Soviet Union and other Communist nations, but lately more attention has been given to
relations with Western European countries and
developing nations in Africa and the Middle
East. ∎

Bulgaria Map Index

	Lat.	Long.		Lat.	Long.
Asenovgrad	42°01′N	24°52′E	Novi Pazar	43°21′N	27°12′E
Balkan			Pazardzhik	42°12′N	24°20′E
Mountains	43°15′N	25°00′E	Pernik	42°36′N	23°02′E
Blagoevgrad	42°01′N	23°06′E	Pleven	43°25′N	24°37′E
Botev	42°43′N	24°55′E	Plovdiv	42°09′N	24°45′E
Burgas	42°30′N	27°28′E	Razgrad	43°32′N	26°31′E
Burgas Bay	42°30′N	27°33′E	*Rhodope*		
Danube	44°07′N	27°15′E	*Mountains*	41°30′N	24°30′E
Dimitrovgrad	42°03′N	25°36′E	Ruse	43°50′N	25°57′E
Dobrudzhansko			Shumen	43°16′N	26°55′E
Plateau	43°32′N	27°50′E	Silistra	44°07′N	27°16′E
Dobruja	43°50′N	28°00′E	Sliven	42°40′N	26°19′E
Gabrovo	42°52′N	25°19′E	Sofia	42°41′N	23°19′E
Isker	43°44′N	24°27′E	Stanke Dimitrov	42°16′N	23°07′E
Kamchiya	43°02′N	27°53′E	Stara Zagora	42°25′N	25°38′E
Kazanluk	42°37′N	25°24′E	*Struma*	41°20′N	23°20′E
Khaskovo	41°56′N	25°33′E	Tolbukhin	43°34′N	27°50′E
Kurdzhali	41°39′N	25°22′E	Turgovishte	43°15′N	26°34′E
Kyustendil	42°17′N	22°41′E	Varna	43°13′N	27°55′E
Lovech	43°08′N	24°43′E	Vratsa	43°12′N	23°33′E
Maritsa	41°42′N	26°19′E	Yambol	42°29′N	26°30′E
Mikhaylovgrad	43°25′N	23°13′E	*Yantra*	43°38′N	25°34′E
Musala	42°11′N	23°34′E			

Bulgaria's mostly mountainous terrain is marked by
deep river gorges, waterfalls, and wooded slopes. The
village of Momchiovtsi, shown here, lies in the Rhodope
Mountains, which form Bulgaria's southern land region.

BURKINA FASO

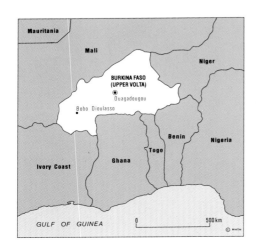

OFFICIAL NAME Burkina Faso

PEOPLE
Population 6,820,000.
Density 64/mi² (25/km²).
Urban 9%.
Capital Ouagadougou, 235,000.
Ethnic groups Mossi, Bobo, Mande, Fulani, others.
Languages French, indigenous.
Religions Animist 65%, Muslim 25%, Christian 10%.
Life expectancy 45 female, 43 male.
Literacy 10%.

POLITICS
Government Provisional military government.
Parties None (banned).
Suffrage Universal adult.
Memberships OAU, UN.
Subdivisions 30 provinces.

ECONOMY
GNP $1,100,000,000.
Per capita $169.
Monetary unit CFA franc.
Trade partners Ivory Coast, Western European countries, Ghana.
Exports Livestock, peanuts, shea-nut products.
Imports Food, fuels, transportation equipment, consumer goods.

LAND
Description Western Africa, landlocked.
Area 105,869 mi² (274,200 km²).
Highest point Téna Kourou, 2,451 ft (747 m).
Lowest point Volta Noire River valley, 650 ft (200 m).

PEOPLE. The agricultural Mossi, descendants of warrior migrants, are Burkina Faso's majority population. Other groups include the Bobo, Mande, and Fulani. Languages vary from group to group, although French is the official language.

ECONOMY AND THE LAND. Burkina Faso's agricultural economy suffers from frequent droughts and an underdeveloped transportation system. Most people engage in subsistence farming or livestock raising, and industrialization is minimal. Resources are limited but include gold and manganese. The country remains dependent on foreign aid, much of it from France. The land is marked by northern desert, central savanna, and southern forests. The climate is generally tropical.

HISTORY AND POLITICS. During the eleventh century the Mossi arrived from central or eastern Africa. The French came in the late nineteenth century and in 1919 created the colony of Upper Volta. The colony was divided among other French colonies in 1932, reinstituted in 1937 as an administrative unit called the Upper Coast, and returned to territorial status as Upper Volta in 1947. Independence was gained in 1960, followed by leadership changes, military rule, and coups. The country's name changed from Upper Volta to Burkina Faso in 1984. ■

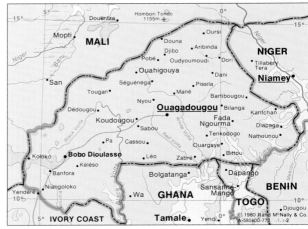

BURKINA FASO

		Meters	Feet
—— Railroad	National capitals are underlined	1000	3281
+ Spot Elevation		500	1640
		200	656
Scale 1:10,839,000		0	0

Burkina Faso Map Index

	Lat.	Long.		Lat.	Long.
Black Volta	9°27′N	2°39′W	Ouahigouya	13°35′N	2°25′W
Bobo Dioulasso	11°12′N	4°18′W	Red Volta	10°55′N	0°35′W
Ouagadougou	12°22′N	1°31′W	White Volta	11°05′N	0°18′W

Changing Africa

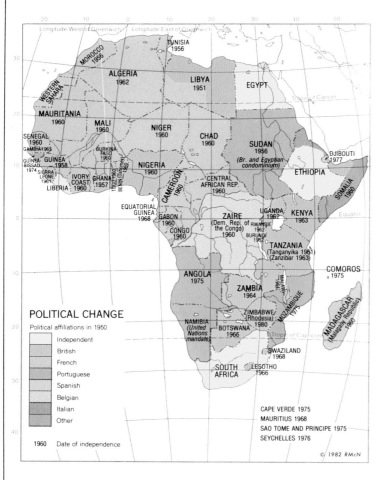

POLITICAL CHANGE
Political affiliations in 1950

- Independent
- British
- French
- Portuguese
- Spanish
- Belgian
- Italian
- Other

1960 Date of independence

CAPE VERDE 1975
MAURITIUS 1968
SAO TOME AND PRINCIPE 1975
SEYCHELLES 1976

© 1982 RMcN

Between 1951 and 1980, forty-seven European colonies on the continent of Africa gained independence. These nations faced not only the problems of leadership and unity that most newly independent countries encounter, but also the challenge of catching up in a global community that had made dramatic economic, social, and technological advances in the postwar years. But achieving self-sufficiency in a complex world after years of foreign rule was just one problem the nations had to overcome.

European interest in Africa began in the 1400s when Portuguese explorers arrived on the west coast. Soon African gold and peoples were being shipped and traded all over the globe, and other European countries came to stake their claim in this profitable land, continually advancing farther into the African interior.

But the real power struggle for possession of African territory began in the 1880s, during a period known as the "Scramble for Africa." As traders convinced their governments that prosperity depended on investment in and exploitation of this continent, European rivalry intensified. Although the peoples of Africa resisted, they could not withstand the greater power of the Europeans. By 1914 most of the continent and its islands were divided among Belgium, France, Germany, Great Britain, Italy, Portugal, and Spain.

In time, however, anticolonial feelings became organized into a movement for independence. Early attempts at resisting the colonial rulers focused on criticizing policies of the governing power and seeking additional rights within the system. But soon the goal became the right to self-determination and total independence. The turning point for the movement was World War II. As nationalist groups gained mass support, the war weakened most of the colonial powers and often changed attitudes at home about policies in far-off lands.

But victory was often hard won. Peaceful demonstrations sometimes gave way to riots and terrorist activities as the colonial powers refused to give in to African demands. The long and bloody struggle between Algeria and France, lasting from 1954 until peace talks began in 1961, is an example of the strength of newfound African nationalism. The country finally won its independence in 1962.

Rhodesia, now Zimbabwe, also fought long and hard for its freedom from British and white Rhodesian rule. In 1965, in the face of pressure for a black-majority government, Rhodesian whites declared independence from Britain. Economic sanctions and antigovernment violence brought white rule to an end in 1979, and Rhodesia gained independence as Zimbabwe in 1980.

In the Portuguese holdings the long fight for independence ended abruptly and unexpectedly when a 1974 coup in Portugal installed a new leadership opposed to the colonial policies of the past. Angola became independent in 1975 in the midst of a three-way struggle for power among rebel groups. After an initial agreement, a civil war broke out. Although the war ended in 1976, unrest continues.

Despite all the continent has experienced in the past few decades, the future promises even more change. To meet the challenges of the twenty-first century, single-product economies are attempting diversification, educational systems are improving, and the Organization of African Unity and the pan-African movement are working for cooperation among nations. But Namibia's ongoing fight for independence remains to be won, and the struggle for black-majority rule and an end to apartheid continues in the nation of South Africa. The first African nations to achieve independence are thus moving toward greater stability, but for others on the continent, the independence movement has not yet come to an end.

BURMA

PEOPLE. The population of Burma is characterized by variety. The many ethnic groups include Tibetan-related Burmans, who compose the majority; Karen, who inhabit mainly the south and east; and Thai-related Shan, found on the eastern plateaus. Diversity results in many languages, although Burmese predominates. Buddhist monasteries and pagodas dot the landscape, and minority religions include Christianity; animism, a traditional belief; and Islam. The primarily rural population is concentrated in the fertile valleys and on the delta of the Irrawaddy River.

ECONOMY AND THE LAND. Fertile soils, dense woodlands, and mineral deposits provide a resource base for agriculture, forestry, and mining. Burma has been beset with economic problems, however, caused mainly by the destruction of World War II and postindependence instability. Today agriculture continues as the economic mainstay, and the hot, wet climate is ideal for rice production. In addition, dense forests provide for a timber industry, and resource deposits include petroleum and various minerals. Burma's economic future most likely depends on political stability and exploitation of natural resources. The terrain is marked by mountains, rivers, and forests, and the climate is tropical.

HISTORY AND POLITICS. Burma's Chinese and Tibetan settlers were first united in the eleventh century. Independence ended with the invasion of Mongols led by Kublai Khan, followed by national unification in the fifteenth and eighteenth centuries. Annexation to British India in the nineteenth century ended Burma's monarchy. During World War II, Japanese occupation and subsequent Allied-Japanese conflicts caused much economic and physical damage. Burma officially became independent in 1948. After initial stability, the government was unable to withstand separatist and political revolts, and military rule alternated with civilian governments. In 1974, a new government was installed and a new constitution adopted. A strongly nationalistic country, Burma maintains a policy of neutrality. Sporadic uprisings continue, often carried out by ethnic minorities. ■

OFFICIAL NAME Socialist Republic of the Union of Burma

PEOPLE
Population 36,795,000.
Density 141/mi² (54/km²).
Urban 29%.
Capital Rangoon, 2,276,000.
Ethnic groups Burman 72%, Karen 7%, Indian 6%, Shan 6%, Chinese 3%.
Languages Burmese, indigenous.
Religions Buddhist 85%; animist, Christian, and others 15%.
Life expectancy 56 female, 53 male.
Literacy 78%.

POLITICS
Government Socialist republic.
Parties Socialist Program.
Suffrage Universal, over 18.
Memberships UN.
Subdivisions 7 divisions, 7 states.

ECONOMY
GDP $5,900,000,000.
Per capita $180.
Monetary unit Kyat.
Trade partners Singapore, Japan, Western European countries.
Exports Rice, teak, hardwoods, base metals.
Imports Machinery, transportation equipment, construction materials.

LAND
Description Southeastern Asia.
Area 261,228 mi² (676,577 km²).
Highest point Hkakabo Mtn., 19,296 ft (5,881 m).
Lowest point Sea level.

From the mid-eleventh century to the Mongol takeover in 1287, the town of Pagan, shown here, served as Burma's capital. The Buddhist rulers introduced today's majority religion to the region, and ancient temples and monuments are found in and near the town.

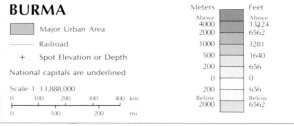

BURMA

	Meters Above	Feet Above
Major Urban Area	4000	13,124
Railroad	2000	6562
	1000	3281
+ Spot Elevation or Depth	500	1640
	200	656
National capitals are underlined	0	0
	200	656
Scale 1: 13,888,000	Below 2000	Below 6562

Scale 1: 13,888,000
0 100 200 300 400 km
0 100 200 mi

Burma Map Index

	Lat.	Long.		Lat.	Long.
Allanmyo	19°22′N	95°13′E	Moulmein	16°30′N	97°38′E
Andaman Sea	10°00′N	95°00′E	Moulmeingyun	16°23′N	95°16′E
Bassein	16°47′N	94°44′E	Myingyan	21°28′N	95°23′E
Bilauktaung			Myitkyina	25°23′N	97°24′E
Range	13°00′N	99°00′E	*Naga Hills*	26°00′N	95°00′E
Bogale	16°17′N	95°24′E	Nyaunglebin	17°57′N	96°44′E
Chawk	20°54′N	94°50′E	Pakokku	21°20′N	95°05′E
Chindwin	21°26′N	95°15′E	*Patkai Range*	27°00′N	96°00′E
Chin Hills	22°30′N	93°30′E	Paungde	18°29′N	95°30′E
Henzada	17°38′N	95°28′E	Pegu	17°20′N	96°29′E
Hkakabo, Mount	28°20′N	97°32′E	Prome	18°49′N	95°13′E
Irrawaddy	15°50′N	95°06′E	Pyinmana	19°44′N	96°13′E
Kra, Isthmus of	10°20′N	99°00′E	Pyu	18°29′N	96°26′E
Kumon Range	26°30′N	97°15′E	Rangoon	16°47′N	96°10′E
Kyaikto	17°18′N	97°01′E	*Salween*	16°31′N	97°37′E
Labutta	16°09′N	94°46′E	*Shan Plateau*	21°30′N	98°30′E
Lashio	22°56′N	97°45′E	Shwebo	22°34′N	95°42′E
Magwe	20°09′N	94°55′E	Sittwe	20°09′N	92°54′E
Mandalay	22°00′N	96°05′E	Taungdwingyi	20°01′N	95°33′E
Martaban, Gulf of	16°30′N	97°00′E	Taunggyi	20°47′N	97°02′E
Mawlaik	23°38′N	94°24′E	Tavoy	14°05′N	98°12′E
Meiktila	20°52′N	95°52′E	Thaton	16°55′N	97°22′E
Mekong	20°27′N	100°06′E	Thayetmyo	19°19′N	95°11′E
Mergui	12°26′N	98°36′E	Thonze	17°38′N	95°47′E
Mergui			Toungoo	18°56′N	96°26′E
Archipelago	12°00′N	98°00′E	*Victoria, Mount*	21°14′N	93°55′E
Mogaung	25°18′N	96°56′E	Ye	15°15′N	97°51′E
Monywa	22°05′N	95°08′E	Yenangyaung	20°28′N	94°52′E

BURUNDI

Burundi Map Index

	Lat.	Long.		Lat.	Long.
Bubanza	3°06′S	29°23′E	Nyanza-Lac	4°21′S	29°36′E
Bujumbura	3°23′S	29°22′E	*Rugwero, Lake*	2°25′S	30°15′E
Bururi	3°57′S	29°37′E	Rutana	3°55′S	30°00′E
Gitega	3°26′S	29°56′E	*Ruvubu*	2°23′S	30°47′E
Kibumbu	3°32′S	29°45′E	Ruyigi	3°29′S	30°15′E
Muramuya	3°16′S	29°37′E	*Ruzizi*	3°16′S	29°14′E
Muyinga	2°51′S	30°20′E	Tshokoha-Sud,		
Ngozi	2°54′S	29°50′E	Lake	2°25′S	30°05′E
Nyamisana	3°03′S	30°33′E			

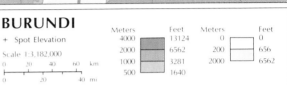

OFFICIAL NAME Republic of Burundi

PEOPLE
Population 4,760,000.
Density 443/mi² (171/km²).
Urban 4%.
Capital Bujumbura, 160,000.
Ethnic groups Hutu 85%, Tutsi 14%, Twa 1%.
Languages Kirundi, French, Swahili.
Religions Roman Catholic 62%, Protestant 5%, indigenous 32%, Muslim 1%.
Life expectancy 46 female, 42 male.
Literacy 25%.

POLITICS
Government Republic.
Parties Unity and Progress.
Suffrage Universal adult.
Memberships OAU, UN.
Subdivisions 15 provinces.

ECONOMY
GDP $1,200,000,000.
Per capita $272.
Monetary unit Franc.
Trade partners U.S., Western European countries.
Exports Coffee, tea, cotton.
Imports Textiles, food, transportation equipment.

LAND
Description Eastern Africa, landlocked.
Area 10,747 mi² (27,834 km²).
Highest point 9,055 ft (2,760 m).
Lowest point Lake Tanganyika, 2,534 ft (772 m).

PEOPLE. One of Africa's most densely populated nations, Burundi has a populace composed mainly of three Bantu groups. The Hutu, whose ancestors arrived about 800 to 1,000 years ago, are a majority. The Tutsi, descendants of invaders from Ethiopia, wield most of the power. The Twa are Pygmy hunters, probably descended from the area's inhabitants prior to the influx of the Hutu. Most Burundians are subsistence farmers living on family farms in the highlands. The majority religion of Roman Catholicism evidences foreign influence and rule.

ECONOMY AND THE LAND. An underdeveloped country, Burundi relies mainly on agriculture, although undependable rainfall, depleted soil, and erosion occasionally combine for famine conditions. Food production per capita has been declining, and solutions to this problem do not seem to be forthcoming. Coffee is the major export item, and government programs for more efficient cultivation should improve output in the long term. The tea crop is increasing in importance, and cotton production is improving after a period of decline. Exploitation of nickel deposits, industrial development through foreign investment, and expansion of tourism offer potential for growth. Although the country is situated near the equator, its high altitude and hilly terrain result in a pleasant climate.

HISTORY AND POLITICS. The ancestors of the Pygmy Twa were most likely the region's aboriginal inhabitants. Some time between the tenth and twelfth centuries the Hutu arrived. In the fourteenth century invading pastoral Tutsi warriors conquered the peasant Hutu and established themselves as the region's power base. They established a feudal society, with a king, or *mwami*, selected from royal dynastic families, called *ganwa*. Under this system of feudalism, the agriculturalist Hutu cared for Tutsi cattle, receiving a share of herd increases in return. Cattle soon became a symbol of wealth, and the Hutu gradually traded away their land for the Tutsi's cattle. The areas of modern Burundi and Rwanda were absorbed into German East Africa in the 1890s. In 1919, following a period of Belgian occupation during World War I, the League of Nations placed present-day Burundi and Rwanda under Belgian rule as part of Ruanda-Urundi. After World War II Ruanda-Urundi was made a United Nations trust territory under Belgian administration. Urundi became independent Burundi in 1962, with the mwami as constitutional monarch. Political turmoil followed, and a Tutsi-dominated government replaced the monarchy in 1966. An unsuccessful Hutu coup attempt in 1972 was followed by the massacre of thousands of Hutu and the flight of thousands more to other countries. A subsequent government has attempted to resolve the problem of rural poverty, enacted reforms to end the feudal landholding system, and sought ethnic unity and redistribution of power. However, Hutu participation in the military and administration remains limited. ∎

Burundi's terrain is high and rolling. The border region between Burundi and Tanzania, shown here, is marked by steep hills and valleys.

CAMEROON

OFFICIAL NAME Republic of Cameroon

PEOPLE
Population 9,640,000.
Density 53/mi² (20/km²).
Urban 36%.
Capital Yaoundé, 313,706.
Ethnic groups Cameroon Highlander 31%, Equatorial Bantu 19%, Kirdi 11%, Fulani 10%, others.
Languages English, French, indigenous.
Religions Animist 50%, Christian 34%, Muslim 16%.
Life expectancy 51 female, 48 male.
Literacy 65%.

POLITICS
Government Republic.
Parties National Union.
Suffrage Universal, over 21.
Memberships OAU, UN.
Subdivisions 10 provinces.

ECONOMY
GNP $7,000,000,000.
Per capita $845.
Monetary unit CFA franc.
Trade partners France, other Western European countries, U.S.
Exports Petroleum, cocoa, coffee, wood.
Imports Machinery, transportation equipment, petroleum products, consumer goods.

LAND
Description Central Africa.
Area 183,569 mi² (475,442 km²).
Highest point Mt. Cameroun, 13,451 ft (4,100 m).
Lowest point Sea level.

PEOPLE. Immigration and foreign rule shaped Cameroon's diverse population, composed of some two hundred groups speaking twenty-four major African languages. Both English and French are official languages, resulting from the merging of former French-ruled eastern and British-ruled western territories. Population is concentrated in the French-speaking eastern region. The majority of people practice animism, a traditional belief often influencing Islamic and Christian practices as well. The Muslim population is concentrated in the north, and most Christians live in the south.

ECONOMY AND THE LAND. A series of five-year plans have focused on agriculture, industry, and the development of oil deposits. Currently, the economic emphasis is on agriculture and further diversification. Agriculture is the primary employer and economic contributor, and farm output is diverse. Cocoa, coffee, and timber are some of Cameroon's major exports, and other crops include bananas, rubber, cotton, peanuts, and palm oil. Crop diversity has helped protect Cameroon from the effects fluctuating prices in the world market. Additional forest areas have been opened to the timber industry, but a lack of transportation routes has slowed expansion. Improvements are underway; however, during the

Cameroon Map Index
	Lat.	Long.		Lat.	Long.
Adamaoua	7°00'N	12°00'E	Logone	12°06'N	15°02'E
Bamenda	5°56'N	10°10'E	Mandara		
Cameroun,			Mountains	10°45'N	13°40'E
Mount	4°12'N	9°11'E	Mbabo, Mount	7°16'N	12°09'E
Chad, Lake	13°20'N	14°00'E	Ngoko	1°40'N	16°03'E
Chari	12°58'N	14°31'E	Nyong	3°17'N	9°54'E
Douala	4°03'N	9°42'E	Sanaga	3°35'N	9°38'E
Foumban	5°43'N	10°55'E	Yaoundé	3°52'N	11°31'E

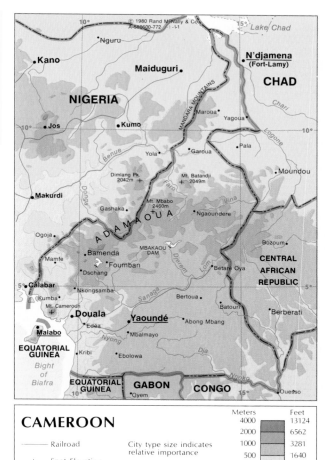

rainy season many roads become impassible. In the manufacturing sector, output is limited, with small assembly and processing plants producing consumer goods. A decline is anticipated in the country's oil industry, but oil currently plays a major role in export income. A varied terrain features southern coastal plains and rain forests, central plateaus, mountainous western forests, and northern savanna and marshes. Climate varies from a hot, humid coastal region to fluctuating temperatures and less humidity northward.

HISTORY AND POLITICS. The Sao people, about whom little is known, reached the Cameroon area in the tenth century. During the 1500s the Portuguese arrived, and the following three centuries saw an influx of European and African peoples and the establishment of slave trade along the coast. In the 1800s Germany, Britain, and France strived for possession of the region, and by 1914 Germany had established a protectorate that included the area of modern Cameroon. During World War I British and French troops occupied the German protectorate, and following the war, in 1919 the League of Nations divided Cameroon into eastern French and western British mandates. The Cameroons became trust territories in 1946, and French Cameroon became an independent republic in 1960. In 1961 the northern region of British Cameroon elected to join Nigeria, and the southern area chose to unite with the eastern Republic of Cameroon. The resulting Federal Republic of Cameroon consisted of two states with separate governments. A 1972 referendum combined the states into the United Republic of Cameroon, and in 1984 the official name was changed to the Republic of Cameroon. The government maintains a foreign policy of nonalignment. ■

Situated near the town of Nkambe, not far from the Nigerian border, these cultivated fields lie in the central Adamaoua plateau region of Cameroon. On the plateau as elsewhere in the country, most Cameroonians are engaged in agriculture, usually growing crops on small farms. Parts of the plateau, however, are inhabited by nomadic pastoralists, who move with the seasons in search of grazing land.

CANADA

OFFICIAL NAME Canada

PEOPLE
Population 25,270,000.
Density 6.6/mi² (2.5/km²).
Urban 76%.
Capital Ottawa, 295,163.
Ethnic groups British Isles origin 45%, French 29%, other European 23%, Indian and Inuit 2%.
Languages English, French.
Religions Roman Catholic 46%, United Church 18%, Anglican 12%.
Life expectancy 77 female, 73 male.
Literacy 99%.

POLITICS
Government Parliamentary state.
Parties Liberal, New Democratic, Progressive Conservative.
Suffrage Universal, over 18.
Memberships CW, NATO, OECD, UN.
Subdivisions 10 provinces, 2 territories.

ECONOMY
GNP $288,800,000,000.
Per capita $11,725.
Monetary unit Dollar.
Trade partners U.S., Western European countries, Japan.
Exports Transportation equipment, wood and paper, petroleum, food, natural gas.
Imports Transportation equipment, machinery, petroleum, communication equipment.

LAND
Description Northern North America.
Area 3,831,033 mi² (9,922,330 km²).
Highest point Mt. Logan, 19,524 ft (5,951 m).
Lowest point Sea level.

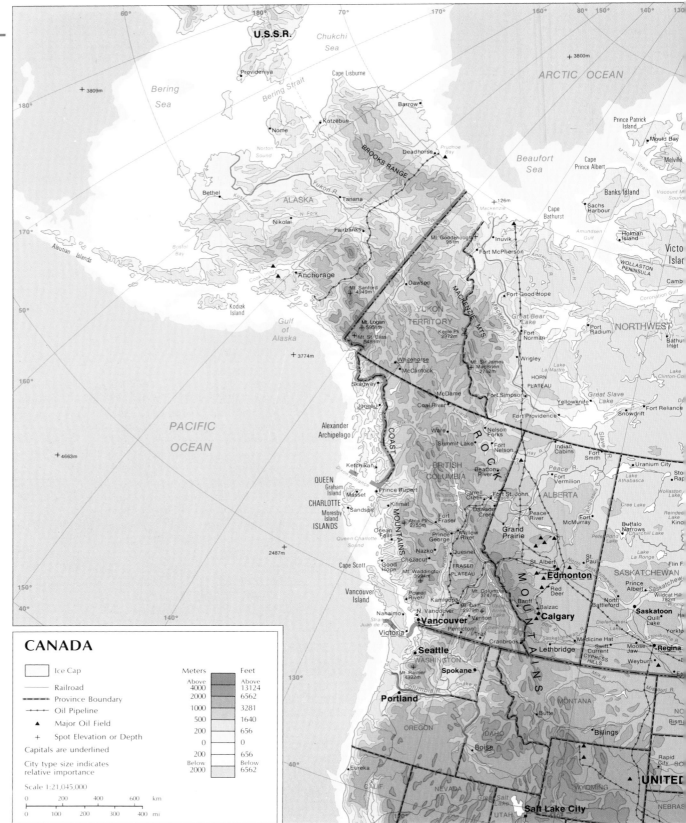

CANADA

		Meters	Feet
Ice Cap			
Railroad		Above 4000	Above 13124
Province Boundary		2000	6562
Oil Pipeline		1000	3281
▲ Major Oil Field		500	1640
+ Spot Elevation or Depth		200	656
		0	0
Capitals are underlined		200	656
City type size indicates relative importance		Below 2000	Below 6562

Scale 1:21,045,000

PEOPLE. Canada was greatly influenced by its years under French and British rule, and its culture reflects this dual nature. Descendants of British and French settlers compose the two main population groups, and languages include both English and French. French-speaking inhabitants, called Quebecois, are concentrated in the Province of Quebec. Minorities include descendants of various European groups, indigenous Indians, and Inuit. Because of the rugged terrain and harsh climate of northern Canada, population is concentrated near the United States border.

ECONOMY AND THE LAND. Rich natural resources—including extensive mineral deposits, fertile land, forests, and lakes—helped shape Canada's diversified economy, which ranks among the world's most prosperous. Economic problems are those common to most modern industrial nations. Agriculture, mining, and industry are highly developed: Canada is a major wheat producer; mineral output includes asbestos, zinc, silver, and nickel; and crude petroleum is an important export. The service sector is also active. Second only to the U.S.S.R. in land area, Canada has a terrain that varies from eastern rolling hills and plains to mountains in the west. The Canadian Shield consists of ancient rock and

extends from Labrador to the Arctic Islands. It is covered by thick forests in the south and tundra in the north. Overall, summers are moderate and winters long and cold.

HISTORY AND POLITICS. Canada's first inhabitants were Asian Indians and Inuit, an Arctic people. Around the year 1000 Vikings became the first Europeans to reach North America, and in 1497 John Cabot claimed the Newfoundland coastal area for Britain. Jacques Cartier established French claim when he landed at the Gaspé Peninsula in the 1500s. Subsequent French and British rivalry culminated in several wars during the late seventeenth and eighteenth centuries. The wars ended with the 1763 Treaty of Paris, by which France lost Canada and other North American territory to Britain. To aid in resolving the continued conflict between French and English residents, the British North America Act of 1867 united the colonies into the Dominion of Canada. During World War I Canada fought on the side of the British. In 1926, along with other

Canada Map Index

	Lat.	Long.		Lat.	Long.
Alberta	54°00'N	113°00'W	Nipigon	49°01'N	88°16'W
Baffin Bay	73°00'N	66°00'W	North Battleford	52°47'N	108°17'W
Baffin Island	68°00'N	70°00'W	North Bay	46°19'N	79°28'W
Baie-Comeau	49°13'N	68°10'W	North Vancouver	49°19'N	123°04'W
Banks Island	73°15'N	121°30'W	Northwest		
Barrie	44°24'N	79°40'W	Territories	70°00'N	100°00'W
Bathurst	47°36'N	65°39'W	Nova Scotia	45°00'N	63°00'W
Beaufort Sea	73°00'N	140°00'W	Ontario	51°00'N	85°00'W
Brandon	49°50'N	99°57'W	Ottawa	45°25'N	75°42'W
British Columbia	54°00'N	125°00'W	Ottawa	45°20'N	73°58'W
Calgary	51°03'N	114°05'W	Owen Sound	44°34'N	80°56'W
Cambridge Bay	69°03'N	105°05'W	Parent	47°55'N	74°37'W
Cape Dorset	64°14'N	76°32'W	Peace	59°00'N	111°25'W
Charlottetown	46°14'N	63°08'W	Penticton	49°30'N	119°35'W
Chatham	47°02'N	65°28'W	Portage la Prairie	49°59'N	98°18'W
Chesterfield Inlet	63°21'N	90°42'W	Povungnituk	60°02'N	77°10'W
Chicoutimi	48°26'N	71°04'W	Powell River	49°52'N	124°33'W
Churchill	58°46'N	94°10'W	Prince Albert	53°12'N	105°46'W
Churchill	58°47'N	94°12'W	Prince Edward		
Cochrane	49°04'N	81°01'W	Island	46°20'N	63°20'W
Corner Brook	48°57'N	57°57'W	Prince George	53°55'N	122°45'W
Cornwall	45°02'N	74°44'W	Prince Rupert	54°19'N	130°19'W
Cranbrook	49°31'N	115°46'W	Quebec	46°49'N	71°14'W
Dartmouth	44°40'N	63°34'W	Quebec	52°00'N	72°00'W
Davis Strait	67°00'N	57°00'W	Queen Charlotte		
Dawson	64°04'N	139°25'W	Islands	53°00'N	132°00'W
Dawson Creek	55°46'N	120°14'W	Queen Elizabeth		
Eastmain	52°15'N	78°30'W	Islands	78°00'N	95°00'W
Edmonton	53°33'N	113°28'W	Red Deer	52°16'N	113°48'W
Ellesmere Island	81°00'N	80°00'W	Regina	50°25'N	104°39'W
Fort Albany	52°15'N	81°37'W	Rivière-du-Loup	47°50'N	69°32'W
Fort Frances	48°36'N	93°24'W	Rouyn	48°15'N	79°01'W
Fort McMurray	56°44'N	111°23'W	Saint Anthony	51°22'N	55°35'W
Fort McPherson	67°27'N	134°53'W	Saint John	45°16'N	66°03'W
Fort Saint John	56°15'N	120°51'W	Saint John's	47°34'N	52°43'W
Fort Severn	56°00'N	87°38'W	Saint Lawrence	49°30'N	67°00'W
Fort Simpson	61°52'N	121°23'W	Saint Lawrence,		
Fraser	49°09'N	123°12'W	Gulf of	48°00'N	62°00'W
Fredericton	45°58'N	66°39'W	Saskatchewan	54°00'N	105°00'W
Fundy, Bay of	45°00'N	66°00'W	Saskatchewan	53°12'N	99°16'W
Gaspé	48°50'N	64°29'W	Saskatoon	52°07'N	106°38'W
Georgian Bay	45°15'N	80°50'W	Sault Sainte		
Glace Bay	46°12'N	59°57'W	Marie	46°31'N	84°20'W
Grande Prairie	55°10'N	118°48'W	Schefferville	54°48'N	66°50'W
Great Bear Lake	66°00'N	120°00'W	Sept-Îles	50°12'N	66°23'W
Halifax	44°39'N	63°36'W	Somerset Island	73°15'N	93°30'W
Hamilton	43°15'N	79°51'W	Southampton		
Hudson Bay	60°00'N	86°00'W	Island	64°20'N	84°40'W
Hull	45°26'N	75°43'W	Sudbury	46°30'N	81°00'W
Inukjuak	58°27'N	78°06'W	Swift Current	50°17'N	107°50'W
Inuvik	68°25'N	133°30'W	Sydney	46°09'N	60°11'W
Iqaluit	63°44'N	68°28'W	Thompson	55°45'N	97°45'W
James Bay	53°30'N	80°30'W	Thunder Bay	48°23'N	89°15'W
Kamloops	50°40'N	120°20'W	Timmins	48°28'N	81°20'W
Kapuskasing	49°25'N	82°26'W	Toronto	43°39'N	79°23'W
Kingston	44°18'N	76°34'W	Trail	49°06'N	117°42'W
Kirkland Lake	48°09'N	80°02'W	Trois-Rivières	46°21'N	72°33'W
Kitimat	54°03'N	128°33'W	Ungava		
Labrador	54°00'N	62°00'W	Peninsula	60°00'N	74°00'W
Labrador Sea	57°00'N	53°00'W	Uranium City	59°34'N	108°36'W
Lethbridge	49°42'N	112°50'W	Val-d'Or	48°07'N	77°47'W
Logan, Mount	60°34'N	140°24'W	Vancouver	49°16'N	123°07'W
London	42°59'N	81°14'W	Vancouver Island	49°45'N	126°00'W
Mackenzie	69°15'N	134°08'W	Vernon	50°16'N	119°16'W
Manitoba	54°00'N	97°00'W	Victoria	48°25'N	123°22'W
Marathon	48°40'N	86°25'W	Victoria Island	71°00'N	114°00'W
Matane	48°51'N	67°32'W	Waddington,		
Medicine Hat	50°03'N	110°40'W	Mount	51°23'N	125°15'W
Melville Island	75°15'N	110°00'W	Whitehorse	60°43'N	135°03'W
Mistassini	50°25'N	73°52'W	Windsor	42°18'N	83°01'W
Montreal	45°31'N	73°34'W	Winisk	55°17'N	85°05'W
Moose Jaw	50°23'N	105°32'W	Winnipeg	49°53'N	97°09'W
Moosonee	51°17'N	80°39'W	Winnipeg, Lake	52°00'N	97°00'W
Nanaimo	49°10'N	123°56'W	Yarmouth	43°50'N	66°07'W
Nelson	57°04'N	92°30'W	Yellowknife	62°27'N	114°21'W
New Brunswick	46°30'N	66°15'W	Yorkton	51°13'N	102°28'W
Newfoundland	52°00'N	56°00'W	Yukon Territory	64°00'N	135°00'W

dominions, Canada declared itself an independent member of the British Commonwealth, and in 1931 Britain recognized the declaration through the Statute of Westminster. Canada once more allied with Britain during World War II, and postwar years saw an improved economy and the domination of two parties: Liberal and Progressive Conservative. The Quebec separatist movement is striving for independent status for French-speaking Quebec. ■

Settled in the 1640s by the French, Montreal today is a cultural, commercial, and industrial center, successfully blending the old with the new. Horse-drawn carriages in Mount Royal Park, shown at the left, recall the city's past and contrast with modern architecture in the streets below.

Niagara Falls is situated on the Niagara River, which flows from Lake Erie to Lake Ontario and forms part of the Canadian–United States border.

CAPE VERDE

OFFICIAL NAME Republic of Cape Verde

PEOPLE
Population 300,000.
Density 193/mi² (74/km²).
Urban 20%.
Capital Praia, São Tiago I., 37,480.
Ethnic groups Mulatto 71%, African 28%, European 1%.
Languages Portuguese, Crioulo.
Religions Roman Catholic.
Life expectancy 64 female, 60 male.
Literacy 37%.

POLITICS
Government Republic.
Parties African Party for the Independence of Cape Verde.
Suffrage Universal, over 15.
Memberships OAU, UN.
Subdivisions 10 islands.

ECONOMY
GNP $142,000,000.
Per capita $473.
Monetary unit Escudo.
Trade partners Portugal, U.K., Japan.
Exports Fish, bananas, salt.
Imports Petroleum products, corn, rice, machinery.

LAND
Description Western African islands.
Area 1,557 mi² (4,033 km²).
Highest point Pico, Fogo I., 9,281 ft (2,829 m).
Lowest point Sea level.

PEOPLE. The Portuguese-African heritage of Cape Verde's population is a result of Portuguese rule and the forced transmigration of Africans for slavery. Although Portuguese is the official language, the majority speaks Crioulo, a creole dialect. Most people are Roman Catholic, but animist practices exist, sometimes in combination with Catholicism. The mainly poor population is largely undernourished and plagued by unemployment. The country consists of five islets and ten main islands, and all but one are inhabited.

ECONOMY AND THE LAND. The volcanic, mountainous islands have few natural resources and low rainfall; thus the country's economy remains underdeveloped. Fishing and agriculture are important for both subsistence and commercial purposes. Much of the land is too dry for farming, and drought is a frequent problem. Cape Verde's location on air and sea routes and its tropical climate offer potential for expansion into services and tourism. However, Cape Verde will most likely continue to rely on foreign aid for some time.

HISTORY AND POLITICS. The islands that make up Cape Verde were uninhabited when the Portuguese arrived around 1460. Settlement began in 1462, and by the sixteenth century Cape Verde had become a shipping center for the African slave trade. Until 1879 Portugal ruled Cape Verde and present-day Guinea-Bissau as a single colony. A movement for the independence of Cape Verde and Guinea-Bissau began in the 1950s, and a 1974 coup in Portugal ultimately resulted in autonomy for both countries, with Cape Verde proclaiming independence in 1975. Plans to unify Cape Verde and Guinea-Bissau were abandoned following a 1980 coup in Guinea-Bissau. Cape Verde follows a foreign policy of nonalignment and takes a special interest in African affairs. ■

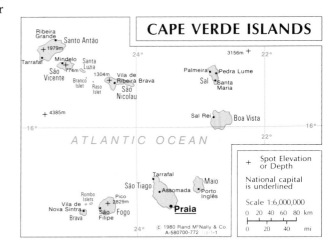

Cape Verde Map Index

	Lat.	Long.		Lat.	Long.
Boa Vista	16°05'N	22°50'W	Sal	16°45'N	22°55'W
Brava	14°52'N	24°43'W	Santo Antão	17°05'N	25°10'W
Fogo	14°55'N	24°25'W	São Nicolau	16°35'N	24°15'W
Maio	15°15'N	23°10'W	São Tiago	15°05'N	23°40'W
Praia	14°55'N	23°31'W	São Vicente	16°50'N	25°00'W

CAYMAN ISLANDS

OFFICIAL NAME Cayman Islands

PEOPLE
Population 22,000.
Density 220/mi² (85/km²).
Urban 100%.
Capital Georgetown, Grand Cayman I., 7,617.
Ethnic groups Black 20%, white 20%, mixed and others 60%.
Languages English.
Religions Presbyterian, Church of God, other Protestant, Roman Catholic.
Literacy 97%.

POLITICS
Government Colony (U.K.).
Suffrage Universal, over 18.
Subdivisions 8 districts.

ECONOMY
GDP $225,000,000.
Per capita $10,227.
Monetary unit Dollar.
Trade partners U.S., Trinidad and Tobago, U.K., Netherlands Antilles.
Exports Turtle products.
Imports Foodstuffs, manufactured goods, textiles.

LAND
Description Caribbean islands.
Area 100 mi² (259 km²).
Highest point 138 ft (42 m).
Lowest point Sea level.

PEOPLE. The population of the Caymans combines descendants of African slaves, Jamaican and North American immigrants, and people of European ancestry. Most live on Grand Cayman Island. The standard of living is relatively high, mainly because of the proliferation of offshore banking.

ECONOMY AND THE LAND. In the 1960s the government created a board of tourism and established tax laws favorable to financial services, and today tourism and banking are the economic leaders. Fishing, especially for turtles, also contributes to the economy. The Caymans consist of the coral islands of Grand Cayman, the largest and most populated; Little Cayman; and Cayman Brac. The climate is tropical, with cooling trade winds.

HISTORY AND POLITICS. Christopher Columbus arrived at the Cayman Islands in 1503. In 1670 Spain ceded the Caymans and Jamaica to Britain. True settlement began in 1734 on Grand Cayman, and Cayman Brac and Little Cayman were settled in 1833. In 1959 administration of the Cayman Islands was separated from that of Jamaica, but the Cayman Islands remained under British rule. A governor appointed by the British Crown is head of government. ■

The climate of the Cayman Islands, along with its white-sand beaches and clear sea waters, attracts thousands of visitors each year. Grand Cayman, shown here, is the largest of the three islands in this British colony where tourism and banking are the main activities.

CENTRAL AFRICAN REPUBLIC

OFFICIAL NAME Central African Republic

PEOPLE
Population 2,620,000.
Density 11/mi² (4.2/km²).
Urban 35%.
Capital Bangui, 387,143.
Ethnic groups Baya 34%, Banda 28%, Sara 10%, others.
Languages French, Sangho.
Religions Protestant 25%, Roman Catholic 25%, indigenous 24%, Muslim 10%.
Life expectancy 48 female, 44 male.
Literacy 33%.

POLITICS
Government Republic.
Parties None (banned).
Suffrage Universal, over 21.
Memberships OAU, UN.
Subdivisions 17 prefectures.

ECONOMY
GDP $658,000,000.
Per capita $273.
Monetary unit CFA franc.
Trade partners France, Belgium, Japan, other Western European countries.
Exports Cotton, coffee, diamonds, wood.
Imports Petroleum products, machinery, textiles, motor vehicles.

LAND
Description Central Africa, landlocked.
Area 240,535 mi² (622,984 km²).
Highest point Mont Ngaoui, 4,626 ft (1,410 m).
Lowest point Ubangi River, 1,100 ft (335 m).

PEOPLE. Lying near Africa's geographic center, the Central African Republic was the stopping point for many precolonial nomadic groups. The resultant multiethnic populace was further diversified by migrations during the slave-trade era. Of the country's many languages, Sangho is most widely used. Overall, the population is rural and suffers from poverty and a low literacy rate.

ECONOMY AND THE LAND. Fertile land, extensive forests, and mineral deposits provide adequate bases for agriculture, forestry, and mining. Economic development remains minimal, however, impeded by poor transportation routes, a landlocked location, lack of skilled labor, and political instability. Subsistence farming continues as the major activity, and agriculture is the chief contributor to the economy. The country consists of a plateau region with southern rain forests and a northeastern semidesert. The climate is temperate, and ample rainfall sometimes results in impassable roads.

HISTORY AND POLITICS. Little is known of the area's early history except that it was the site of many migrations. European slave trade in the nineteenth century led to the 1894 creation of a

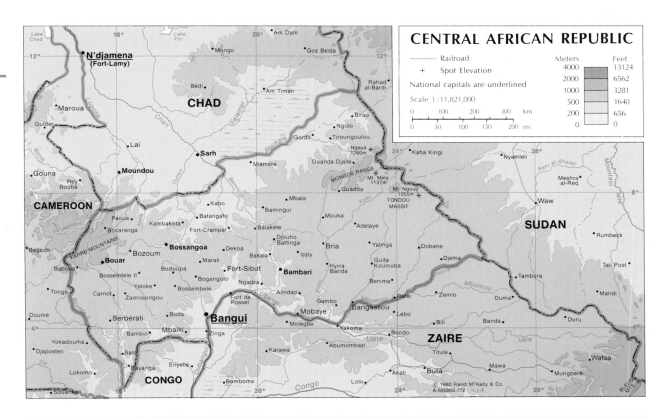

Central African Republic Map Index

	Lat.	Long.		Lat.	Long.		Lat.	Long.		Lat.	Long.
Aoukalé	9°17′N	22°42′E	Berbérati	4°16′N	15°47′E	Fort-Sibut	5°44′N	19°05′E	Mobaye	4°19′N	21°11′E
Bambari	5°45′N	20°40′E	Bossangoa	6°29′N	17°27′E	Karre Mountains	6°33′N	15°40′E	Mongos Range	8°45′N	23°00′E
Bamingui	8°33′N	19°05′E	Bouar	5°57′N	15°36′E	Kotto	4°14′N	22°02′E	Ouham	7°58′N	17°40′E
Bangassou	4°50′N	23°07′E	Bozoum	6°19′N	16°23′E	Mbaiki	3°53′N	18°00′E	Ubangi	3°27′N	18°40′E
Bangui	4°22′N	18°35′E	Bria	6°32′N	21°59′E	Mbomou	4°08′N	22°26′E	Uele	4°09′N	22°26′E

French territory called Ubangi-Chari. This in turn combined with the areas of the present-day Congo, Chad, and Gabon in 1910 to form French Equatorial Africa. The Central African Republic gained independence in 1960. A 1966 military coup installed military chief Jean-Bedel Bokassa, who in 1976 assumed the title of emperor, changed the republic to a monarchy, and renamed the nation the Central African Empire. A 1979 coup ended the monarchy and reinstated the name Central African Republic. Another coup in 1981 deposed this government, proposing to solve the state's economic problems. ■

Markets such as this one in the Central African Republic are common throughout Africa, and they play important cultural and economic roles. Urban areas have daily markets, whereas in rural regions markets occur periodically. People may travel great distances to trade and barter for food and craft items at the marketplace.

CHAD

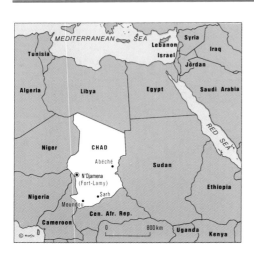

OFFICIAL NAME Republic of
Chad

PEOPLE
Population 5,180,000.
Density 10/mi² (4/km²).
Urban 18%.
Capital N'Djamena, 224,000.
Ethnic groups 200 distinct groups.
Languages French, Arabic, indigenous.
Religions Muslim 52%, indigenous 43%, Christian 5%.
Life expectancy 45 female, 42 male.
Literacy 20%.

POLITICS
Government Republic.
Parties None (banned).
Suffrage Universal, over 18.
Memberships OAU, UN.
Subdivisions 14 prefectures.

ECONOMY
GDP $500,000,000.
Per capita $110.
Monetary unit CFA franc.
Trade partners Nigeria, France, other Western
European countries.
Exports Cotton, meat, fish.
Imports Food, petroleum, machinery, motor
vehicles, textiles.

LAND
Description North-central Africa, landlocked.
Area 495,755 mi² (1,284,000 km²).
Highest point Emi Koussi, 11,204 ft (3,415 m).
Lowest point Bodélé Depression, 525 ft (160 m).

PEOPLE. Centuries ago Islamic Arabs intermixed
with indigenous black Africans and established
Chad's diverse population. This variety has led
to a rich and often divisive culture. Descendants
of Arab invaders mainly inhabit the north, where
Islam is the major religion and nomadic farming
the major activity. In the south—traditionally the
economic and political center—the black Sara
predominate, operating small farms and practicing animist or Christian faiths. Chad's many languages also reflect its ethnic variety.

ECONOMY AND THE LAND. Natural features
and instability arising from ethnic and regional
conflict have combined to prevent Chad from
prospering. Agriculture and fishing are economic
mainstays and are often conducted at subsistence
levels. The Sahara extends into Chad's northern
region, and the southern grasslands with their
heavy rains compose the primary agricultural
area. The relative prosperity of the region, in
conjunction with its predominantly Sara population, has fueled much of the political conflict.
Future growth is greatly dependent on political
equilibrium. Climate varies from the hot, dry
northern desert to the semiarid central region
and rainier south.

HISTORY AND POLITICS. African and Arab so-
cieties began prospering in the Lake Chad region
as early as the eighth century. Subsequent centuries saw the landlocked area become an ethnic
crossroads for Muslim nomads and African
groups. European traders made their way to the
region in the late 1800s, and by 1900 France had
gained control. French Equatorial Africa was created in 1910, its boundaries including modern
Chad, Gabon, the Congo, and the Central African Republic. Following Chad's independence in
1960, the southern Sara gained dominance over
the government. A northern rebel group
emerged, and government-rebel conflict has continued, resulting in shifting governments. ■

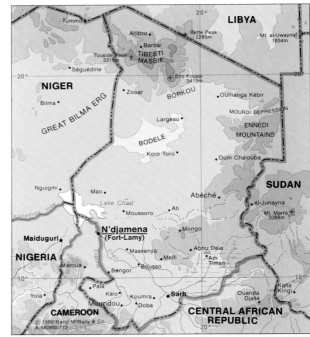

CHAD
— Railroad
+ Spot Elevation
National capitals
are underlined

City type size indicates
relative importance
Scale 1:20,000,000

	Meters	Feet
	4000	13124
	2000	6562
	1000	3281
	500	1640
	200	656
	0	0

Chad Map Index

	Lat.	Long.		Lat.	Long.
Abéché	13°49'N	20°49'E	Logone	12°06'N	15°02'E
Bodele	16°30'N	16°30'E	Moundou	8°34'N	16°05'E
Chad, Lake	13°20'N	14°00'E	N'djamena (Fort-		
Chari	12°58'N	14°31'E	Lamy)	12°07'N	15°03'E
Emi Koussi	19°50'N	18°30'E	Salamat	9°27'N	18°06'E
Ennedi			Sarh	9°09'N	18°23'E
Mountains	17°15'N	22°00'E	Tibesti Massif	21°30'N	17°30'E
Fort-Lamy →			Touside Peak	21°02'N	16°25'E
N'djamena	12°07'N	15°03'E			

CHANNEL ISLANDS

OFFICIAL NAME Channel Islands

PEOPLE
Population 132,000.
Density 1,760/mi² (680/km²).
Urban 35%.
Ethnic groups British, French.
Languages English, French.
Religions Anglican, Roman Catholic.
Life expectancy 74 female, 67 male.

POLITICS
Government Dependency (U.K.).
Suffrage Universal adult.
Subdivisions 2 bailiwicks.

ECONOMY
Monetary unit British pound sterling.
Trade partners U.K.
Exports Vegetables, manufactured goods, textiles.
Imports Fuels, machinery, transportation equipment.

LAND
Description Northwestern European islands.
Area 75 mi² (194 km²).
Highest point 460 ft (140 m).
Lowest point Sea level.

PEOPLE. Most people are French and British,
thus mostly Anglican and Roman Catholic. English is the main language, and a Norman-
French dialect is spoken in some areas.

ECONOMY AND THE LAND. The mild climate
has encouraged tourism and agriculture. The
Channel Islands consist of the main islands of
Jersey, Guernsey, Alderney, and Sark plus several smaller islands.

HISTORY AND POLITICS. In the tenth century,
the Channel Islands came under the duke of
Normandy, and in 1066 the Norman Conquest
tied them to Britain. The islands continue as a
British dependency. ■

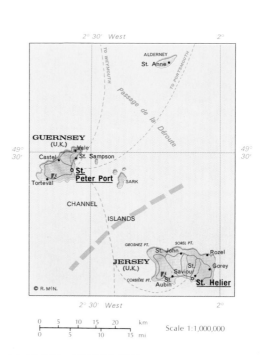

Channel Islands Map Index

	Lat.	Long.		Lat.	Long.
Alderney	49°43'N	2°12'W	Saint John	49°15'N	2°08'W
Castel	49°28'N	2°34'W	Saint Peter Port	49°27'N	2°32'W
Saint Helier	49°12'N	2°37'W	Sark	49°26'N	2°21'W

CHILE

OFFICIAL NAME Republic of Chile

PEOPLE
Population 11,740,000.
Density 40/mi² (16/km²).
Urban 81%.
Capital Santiago, 425,924.
Ethnic groups White and mestizo 91%, Indian 3%.
Language Spanish.
Religions Roman Catholic 89%, Protestant 11%.
Life expectancy 65 male, 70 female.
Literacy 90%.

POLITICS
Government Republic.
Parties None (recessed).
Suffrage None.
Memberships OAS, UN.
Subdivisions 13 regions.

ECONOMY
GDP $23,600,000,000.
Per capita $2,178.
Monetary unit Peso.
Trade partners U.S., Japan, West Germany, Brazil.
Exports Copper, molybdenum, iron ore, paper products.
Imports Petroleum, sugar, wheat, capital equipment, vehicles.

LAND
Description Southern South America.
Area 292,135 mi² (756,626 km²).
Highest point Mt. Ojos del Salado, 22,615 ft (6,893 m).
Lowest point Sea level.

PEOPLE. Chile's land barriers—the eastern Andes, western coastal range, and northern desert—have resulted in a mostly urban population concentrated in a central valley. Mestizos, of Spanish-Indian heritage, and descendants of Spanish immigrants predominate. In addition to an Indian minority, the population includes those who trace their roots to Irish and English colonists or nineteenth-century German immigrants. The country enjoys a relatively high literacy rate, but poverty remains a problem.

ECONOMY AND THE LAND. Chile's land provides the natural resources necessary for a successful economy, but longtime instability has taken its toll. The northern desert region is the site of mineral deposits, and mining is a major component of trade, making Chile vulnerable to outside market forces. An agricultural zone lies in the central valley, and the south contains forests, grazing land, and some petroleum deposits. The climate varies from region to region but is generally mild.

Chile's central valley is the country's most populated region. Here lie fertile soils, rich mineral deposits, and major cities, including Valparaíso, Concepción, and Santiago, which is shown here. Capital and industrial center, Santiago produces most of the nation's industrial goods and processes many of its natural resources. The prospect of industrial jobs has drawn many people to the area, compounding urban problems of housing shortages and poverty.

Chile Map Index

	Lat.	Long.		Lat.	Long.
Ancud	41°52'S	73°50'W	Ollagüe	21°14'S	68°16'W
Andes	27°00'S	69°00'W	Osorno	40°34'S	73°09'W
Angol	37°48'S	72°43'W	Ovalle	30°36'S	71°12'W
Antofagasta	23°39'S	70°24'W	Penas, Gulf of	47°22'S	74°50'W
Arica	18°29'S	70°20'W	Pisagua	19°36'S	70°13'W
Atacama Desert	24°30'S	69°15'W	Puerto Aisen	45°24'S	72°42'W
Bermejo Pass	32°50'S	70°05'W	Puerto Montt	41°28'S	72°57'W
Bio-Bio	36°49'S	73°10'W	Puerto Natales	51°44'S	72°31'W
Calama	22°28'S	68°56'W	Punta Arenas	53°09'S	70°55'W
Castro	42°29'S	73°46'W	Quillota	32°53'S	71°16'W
Cauquenes	35°58'S	72°21'W	Quilpué	33°03'S	71°27'W
Chillán	36°36'S	72°07'W	Rancagua	34°10'S	70°45'W
Chuquicamata	22°19'S	68°56'W	Rengo	34°25'S	70°52'W
Concepción	36°50'S	73°03'W	San Antonio	33°35'S	71°38'W
Copiapo	27°19'S	70°56'W	San Bernardo	33°36'S	70°43'W
Corcovado Gulf	43°30'S	73°30'W	San Carlos	36°25'S	71°58'W
Coronel	37°01'S	73°08'W	San Felipe	32°45'S	70°44'W
Cunco	38°55'S	72°02'W	San Fernando	34°35'S	71°00'W
Horn, Cape	55°59'S	67°16'W	San Martín, Lake	49°00'S	72°40'W
Illapel	31°38'S	71°10'W	Santa Inés Island	53°45'S	72°45'W
Iquique	20°13'S	70°10'W	Santiago	33°27'S	70°40'W
La Calera	32°47'S	71°12'W	Socompa Pass	24°27'S	68°18'W
La Serena	29°54'S	71°16'W	Talagante	33°40'S	70°56'W
Lautaro	38°31'S	72°27'W	Talca	35°26'S	71°40'W
Lebu	37°37'S	73°39'W	Talcahuano	36°43'S	73°07'W
Linares	35°51'S	71°36'W	Temuco	38°44'S	72°36'W
Loa	21°26'S	70°04'W	Tierra del Fuego	54°00'S	69°00'W
Longitudinal			Tocopilla	22°05'S	70°12'W
Valley	36°00'S	72°00'W	Toltén	39°13'S	73°14'W
Los Angeles	37°28'S	72°21'W	Tomé	36°37'S	72°57'W
Los Chonos			Toroni, Mount	19°43'S	68°41'W
Archipelago	45°00'S	74°00'W	Traiguén	38°15'S	72°41'W
Lota	37°05'S	73°10'W	Tronador, Mount	41°10'S	71°54'W
Magellan, Strait			Valdivia	39°48'S	73°14'W
of	54°00'S	71°00'W	Valparaíso	33°02'S	71°38'W
Maipú	33°31'S	70°46'W	Victoria	20°44'S	69°42'W
Melipilla	33°42'S	71°13'W	Viña del Mar	33°02'S	71°34'W
Mulchén	37°43'S	72°14'W			
Ojos del Salado,					
Mount	27°06'S	68°32'W			

HISTORY AND POLITICS. Upon their arrival in the 1500s, the Spanish defeated the northern Inca Indians, but many years were spent in conflict with Araucanian Indians of the central and south regions. From the sixteenth through nineteenth centuries, Chile received little attention from ruling Spain, and colonists established a successful agriculture. In 1818 Bernardo O'Higgins led the way to victory over the Spanish and became ruler of independent Chile. By the 1920s dissent arising from unequal power and land distribution united the middle and working classes, but social-welfare, education, and economic programs were unable to eliminate inequalities rooted in the past. A 1960 earthquake and tidal wave added to the country's problems. Leftist Salvador Allende Gossens was elected to power in 1970, but a 1973 military coup resulted in his death and began a reign marked by human rights violations. Military rule continues, but Chile's foreign relations, damaged by the government's human rights abuses, have improved somewhat. ∎

CHILE
Major Urban Area
Railroad
Glacier
Spot Elevation or Depth

Meters		Feet	
Above 4000		Above 13124	
2000		6562	
1000		3281	
500		1640	
200		656	
0		0	
200		656	
Below 2000		Below 6562	

Scale 1:19,031,000

CHINA

OFFICIAL NAME People's
Republic of China

PEOPLE
Population 1,080,980,000.
Density 291/mi² (112/km²).
Urban 21%.
Capital Peking (Beijing), 5,597,972.
Ethnic groups Han Chinese 93%.
Languages Chinese dialects.
Religions Confucian, Taoist, Buddhist.
Literacy 76%.

POLITICS
Government Socialist republic.
Parties Communist.
Suffrage Universal, over 18.
Memberships UN.
Subdivisions 21 provinces, 3 municipalities, 5
  autonomous regions.

ECONOMY
GNP $313,000,000,000.
Per capita $308.
Monetary unit Yuan.
Trade partners Japan, Hong Kong, U.S.
Exports Manufactured goods, agricultural products,
  petroleum.
Imports Grain, chemical fertilizer, raw materials.

LAND
Description Eastern Asia.
Area 3,718,783 mi² (9,631,600 km²).
Highest point Mt. Everest, 29,028 ft (8,848 m).
Lowest point Turfan Depression, 505 ft (154 m) below
  sea level.
The above information excludes Taiwan.

PEOPLE. Population is concentrated in the
east, and Han Chinese are the majority group.
Uighur, Hui, Mongol, Korean, Manchu, Zhuang,
Yi, Miao, and Tibetan peoples compose minorities. Many Chinese languages are spoken, but
the national language is Putonghua—Standard
Chinese, or Mandarin—based on a northern dialect. Following a Communist revolution in 1949,
religious activity was discouraged. It is now on
the increase, and religions include Confucianism,
Taoism, and Buddhism, plus Islam and Christianity. China ranks first in the world in population, and family-planning programs have been
implemented to aid population control. With a
recorded civilization going back about 3,500
years, China has contributed much to world culture.

ECONOMY AND THE LAND. Most economic
progress dates from 1949, when the new People's
Republic of China was faced with a starving,
war-torn, and unemployed population. Industry
is expanding, but agriculture continues as a
major activity. Natural resources include coal,
oil, natural gas, and minerals, many of which
remain to be exploited. A current economic plan
focuses on growth in agriculture, industry, science and technology, and national defense. Chi-

na's terrain is varied: two-thirds consists of
mountainous or semiarid land, with fertile plains
and deltas in the east. The climate is marked by
hot, humid summers, and the dry winters are
often cold.

HISTORY AND POLITICS. China's civilization
ranks among the world's oldest. The first dynasty, the Shang, began sometime during the second millennium B.C. Kublai Khan's thirteenth-
century invasion brought China the first of its
various foreign rulers. The Shang dynasty was
followed by the Chou, from about the eleventh
to the third century B.C.; the Ch'in, from 221 to
207 B.C.; and the Han, from 202 B.C. to A.D. 220.
The area then divided into three kingdoms, and
the following centuries saw invasions and a lack
of unity. China was reunited under the Sui dynasty, from 581 to 618; and the T'ang dynasty,
from 618 to 906, greatly expanded China's territory. After a period of dissolution, the empire
was again united under the Sung dynasty, from
960 to 1279. Kublai Khan's thirteenth-century invasion brought China under foreign rule until
the establishment of the Ming dynasty in 1368.

In 1644 the Ch'ing dynasty was set up under
Manchu invaders from the north, who had
adopted Chinese culture and philosophy. This
last dynasty remained in power until 1912. In the
nineteenth century, despite government efforts
to the contrary, foreign influence and intervention grew. The government was weakened by
the Opium War with Britain in the 1840s; the
Taiping Rebellion, a civil war; and a war with
Japan from 1894 to 1895. Opposition to foreign
influences erupted in the antiforeign and anti-
Christian Boxer Rebellion of 1900. After China
became a republic in 1912, the death of the president in 1916 triggered the warlord period, in
which conflicts were widespread and power concentrated among military leaders. Attempts to
unite the nation began in the 1920s with Sun
Yat-sen's Nationalist party, initially allied with
the Communist party. Under the leadership of
Chiang Kai-shek, the Nationalist party overcame
the warlords, captured Peking, and executed
many Communists. Remaining Communists re-
organized under Mao Zedong, and the
Communist-Nationalist conflict continued, along
with Japanese invasion and occupation. By 1949

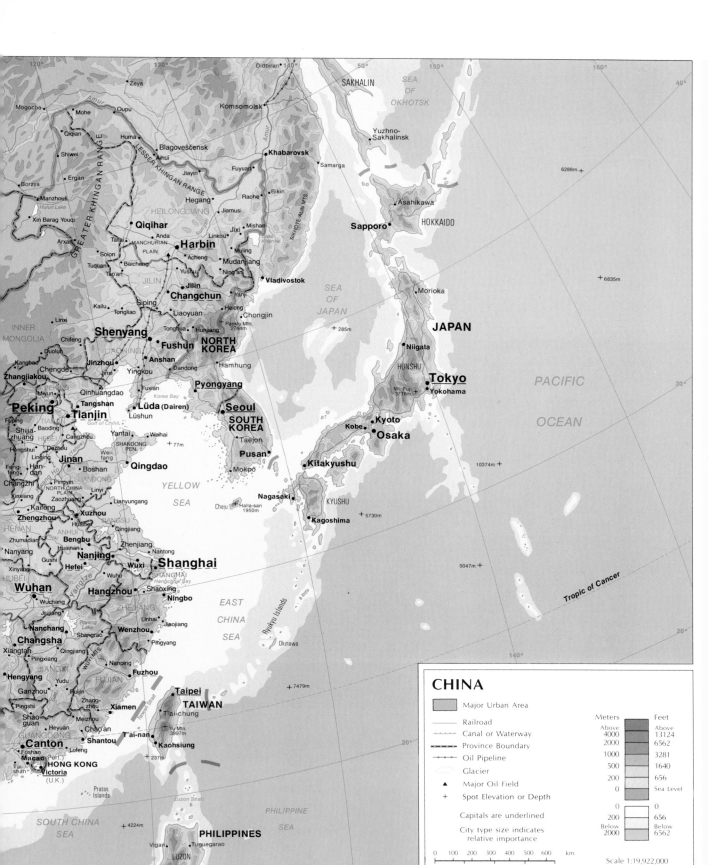

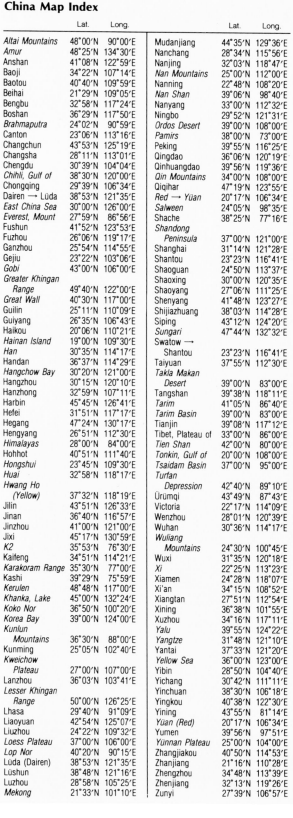

China Map Index

	Lat.	Long.		Lat.	Long.
Altai Mountains	48°00'N	90°00'E	Mudanjiang	44°35'N	129°36'E
Amur	48°25'N	134°30'E	Nanchang	28°34'N	115°56'E
Anshan	41°08'N	122°59'E	Nanjing	32°03'N	118°47'E
Baoji	34°22'N	107°14'E	Nan Mountains	25°00'N	112°00'E
Baotou	40°40'N	109°59'E	Nanning	22°48'N	108°20'E
Beihai	21°29'N	109°05'E	Nan Shan	39°06'N	98°40'E
Bengbu	32°58'N	117°24'E	Nanyang	33°00'N	112°32'E
Boshan	36°29'N	117°50'E	Ningbo	29°52'N	121°31'E
Brahmaputra	24°02'N	90°59'E	Ordos Desert	39°00'N	108°00'E
Canton	23°06'N	113°16'E	Pamirs	38°00'N	73°00'E
Changchun	43°53'N	125°19'E	Peking	39°55'N	116°25'E
Changsha	28°11'N	113°01'E	Qingdao	36°06'N	120°19'E
Chengdu	30°39'N	104°04'E	Qinhuangdao	39°56'N	119°36'E
Chihli, Gulf of	38°30'N	120°00'E	Qin Mountains	34°00'N	108°00'E
Chongqing	29°39'N	106°34'E	Qiqihar	47°19'N	123°55'E
Dairen → Lüda	38°53'N	121°35'E	Red → Yüan	20°17'N	106°34'E
East China Sea	30°00'N	126°00'E	Salween	24°05'N	98°35'E
Everest, Mount	27°59'N	86°56'E	Shache	38°25'N	77°16'E
Fushun	41°52'N	123°53'E	Shandong		
Fuzhou	26°06'N	119°17'E	Peninsula	37°00'N	121°00'E
Ganzhou	25°54'N	114°55'E	Shanghai	31°14'N	121°28'E
Gejiu	23°22'N	103°06'E	Shantou	23°23'N	116°41'E
Gobi	43°00'N	106°00'E	Shaoguan	24°50'N	113°37'E
Greater Khingan			Shaoxing	30°00'N	120°35'E
Range	49°40'N	122°00'E	Shaoyang	27°06'N	111°25'E
Great Wall	40°30'N	117°00'E	Shenyang	41°48'N	123°27'E
Guilin	25°11'N	110°09'E	Shijiazhuang	38°03'N	114°28'E
Guiyang	26°35'N	106°43'E	Siping	43°12'N	124°20'E
Haikou	20°06'N	110°21'E	Sungari	47°44'N	132°32'E
Hainan Island	19°00'N	109°30'E	Swatow →		
Han	30°35'N	114°17'E	Shantou	23°23'N	116°41'E
Handan	36°37'N	114°29'E	Taiyuan	37°55'N	112°30'E
Hangchow Bay	30°20'N	121°00'E	Takla Makan		
Hangzhou	30°15'N	120°10'E	Desert	39°00'N	83°00'E
Hanzhong	32°59'N	107°11'E	Tangshan	39°38'N	118°11'E
Harbin	45°45'N	126°41'E	Tarim	41°05'N	86°40'E
Hefei	31°51'N	117°17'E	Tarim Basin	39°00'N	83°00'E
Hegang	47°24'N	130°17'E	Tianjin	39°08'N	117°12'E
Hengyang	26°51'N	112°30'E	Tibet, Plateau of	33°00'N	86°00'E
Himalayas	28°00'N	84°00'E	Tien Shan	42°00'N	80°00'E
Hohhot	40°51'N	111°40'E	Tonkin, Gulf of	20°00'N	108°00'E
Hongshui	23°45'N	109°30'E	Tsaidam Basin	37°00'N	95°00'E
Huai	32°58'N	118°17'E	Turfan		
Hwang Ho			Depression	42°40'N	89°10'E
(Yellow)	37°32'N	118°19'E	Ürümqi	43°49'N	87°43'E
Jilin	43°51'N	126°33'E	Victoria	22°17'N	114°09'E
Jinan	36°40'N	116°57'E	Wenzhou	28°01'N	120°39'E
Jinzhou	41°00'N	121°00'E	Wuhan	30°36'N	114°17'E
Jixi	45°17'N	130°59'E	Wuliang		
K2	35°53'N	76°30'E	Mountains	24°30'N	100°45'E
Kaifeng	34°51'N	114°21'E	Wuxi	31°35'N	120°18'E
Karakoram Range	35°30'N	77°00'E	Xi	22°25'N	113°23'E
Kashi	39°29'N	75°59'E	Xiamen	24°28'N	118°07'E
Kerulen	48°48'N	117°00'E	Xi'an	34°15'N	108°52'E
Khanka, Lake	45°00'N	132°24'E	Xiangtan	27°51'N	112°54'E
Koko Nor	36°50'N	100°20'E	Xining	36°38'N	101°55'E
Korea Bay	39°00'N	124°00'E	Xuzhou	34°16'N	117°11'E
Kunlun			Yalu	39°55'N	124°22'E
Mountains	36°30'N	88°00'E	Yangtze	31°48'N	121°10'E
Kunming	25°05'N	102°40'E	Yantai	37°33'N	121°20'E
Kweichow			Yellow Sea	36°00'N	123°00'E
Plateau	27°00'N	107°00'E	Yibin	28°50'N	104°40'E
Lanzhou	36°03'N	103°41'E	Yichang	30°42'N	111°11'E
Lesser Khingan			Yinchuan	38°30'N	106°18'E
Range	50°00'N	126°25'E	Yingkou	40°38'N	122°30'E
Lhasa	29°40'N	91°09'E	Yining	43°55'N	81°14'E
Liaoyuan	42°54'N	125°07'E	Yüan (Red)	20°17'N	106°34'E
Liuzhou	24°22'N	109°32'E	Yumen	39°56'N	97°51'E
Loess Plateau	37°00'N	106°00'E	Yünnan Plateau	25°00'N	104°00'E
Lop Nor	40°20'N	90°15'E	Zhangjiakou	40°50'N	114°53'E
Lüda (Dairen)	38°53'N	121°35'E	Zhanjiang	21°16'N	110°28'E
Lüshun	38°48'N	121°16'E	Zhengzhou	34°48'N	113°39'E
Luzhou	28°58'N	105°25'E	Zhenjiang	32°13'N	119°26'E
Mekong	21°33'N	101°10'E	Zunyi	27°39'N	106°57'E

CHINA

Major Urban Area

Railroad
Canal or Waterway
Province Boundary
Oil Pipeline
Glacier
▲ Major Oil Field
+ Spot Elevation or Depth

Capitals are underlined

City type size indicates relative importance

Meters	Feet
Above 4000	Above 13124
2000	6562
1000	3281
500	1640
200	656
0	Sea Level
0	0
200	656
Below 2000	Below 6562

Scale 1:19,922,000

0 100 200 300 400 500 600 km
0 100 200 300 400 mi

the Communists controlled most of the country, and the People's Republic of China was proclaimed. Chiang Kai-shek fled to Taiwan, proclaiming Taipei China's provisional capital. Since Mao's death in 1976 foreign trade and contact have expanded. In 1979 the United States recognized Peking (Beijing), rather than Taipei, as China's capital. Five autonomous regions are included within China's boundaries—Inner Mongolia, Xinjiang Uygur, Guangxi Zhuangzu, Sinkiang, and Tibet. ■

Built to keep out nomadic tribes from the north, the Great Wall winds over northern China from Gansu province to the Yellow Sea. The wall's total length is about 1,500 miles (2,414 kilometers). In the third century B.C., laborers under Emperor Shih Huang Ti constructed the wall, joining shorter walls built during an earlier dynasty. The last major restoration occurred during the fifteenth century Ming dynasty.

China's success in feeding its vast population almost entirely from its own resources is a major achievement of the centrally planned economy instituted by the People's Republic after 1949. Although China has been exceptionally self-sufficient throughout its long history, undernourishment was widespread before the 1950s, and famine was a periodic threat. Communal control of food supplies and intensive agricultural practices now ensure an adequate, if frugal, diet for China's millions of people.

But zeal and manpower were the main elements that transformed the hillsides of Dazhai into the productive terrace shown here, where thousands of tons of rock and earth were moved by hand after floods in 1963. Visitors now file past workers on a commune that has become a model of self-reliance, hard work, and rejection of profit motive.

Mountains and semiarid land cover about two-thirds of China, and 90 percent of the population lives on one-sixth of the total area. These people are concentrated in the eastern fertile plains and deltas, where China has harnessed its rivers for the benefit of agriculture, transportation, and energy needs. Irrigation and flood-control programs have lessened damage from variable rainfall, and navigable waterways provide access to markets. Developing water resources for electricity has resulted in fewer power shortages, but this country with the world's greatest hydroelectric potential has tapped only a portion of its total capacity.

When the Communists came to power in 1949, China's agricultural community was facing many problems. Rich landowners controlled a feudal-style agricultural system, with most rural families working as tenant farmers or laborers, paying excessively high rents, and often living in abject poverty. Under the new government's system of collectivized agriculture, communes were created. Here, crops are grown on jointly owned land, and all families receive a share in the output. The average size of a commune is about five thousand households; communal land ranges from a few hundred to more than 25,000 acres. The commune leaders, who are elected by members, oversee the group's political and economic administration. Each commune is further divided into a production brigade, which may consist of several small villages or one large village, and in turn the brigades are divided into production teams of twenty to forty families. This social reorganization has served to harness China's greatest resource—its people.

In this picture, commune members are carrying stones to shore up the banks of a river. Previously, annual flooding had prevented the commune from fully exploiting the potential of its fertile lands.

CHRISTMAS ISLAND

OFFICIAL NAME Territory of
Christmas Island

PEOPLE
Population 3,300.
Density 63/mi² (24/km²).
Ethnic groups Chinese 61%, Malay 25%, European
11%, others 3%.
Languages English, Chinese, Malay.
Religions Buddhist, Muslim, Christian.

POLITICS
Government External territory (Australia).

ECONOMY
Monetary unit Australian dollar.
Trade partners Australia, New Zealand.
Exports Phosphate rock.
Imports Fuels, building materials, machinery,
vehicles.

LAND
Description Indian Ocean island.
Area 52 mi² (135 km²).
Highest point Murray Hill, 1,184 ft (361 m).
Lowest point Sea level.

PEOPLE. Most of the inhabitants of Christmas Island are Chinese, with minorities including Malays, Europeans, Indians, and Eurasians. Although lying about 1,000 miles (1,609 kilometers) from Australia, Christmas Island is an external territory of that country, and in 1981 Christmas Islanders gained new rights with Australia's Migration Act. Under the provisions of this act, the island's inhabitants can become residents of Australia and are eligible for Australian citizenship. In addition, the government of Australia will assist any Asian islanders who desire to settle elsewhere. Most of these emigrants choose western Australia as their destination.

ECONOMY AND THE LAND. The economy of Christmas Island is dependent upon the phosphate rock deposits found in various locations. Most residents are employed in mining the rock and work for the Phosphate Mining Company of Christmas Island Limited, which is a company of the Australian government. Christmas Island also exports phosphate rock, shipping it to Australia, New Zealand, and Asian nations. Situated in the Indian Ocean, Christmas Island is the top of an underwater mountain, and its terrain is marked by steep slopes that rise from the coast to a central plateau. Tropical rain forest covers much of the island, and the climate is pleasant, with little temperature variation.

HISTORY AND POLITICS. Long before any major powers showed an interest in Christmas Island, sailors and navigators were familiar with this tropical island situated south of Java, Borneo, and their other destinations. The United Kingdom annexed Christmas Island in 1888, and the following year it came under the administration of the governor of the Straits Settlements, a group of British colonies in Southeast Asia. In 1900 Britain made Christmas Island a dependency of Singapore, also a member of the Straits Settlements, and the island remained united with Singapore when the Straits Settlements dissolved in 1946. From 1942 to 1945, during World War II, the Japanese occupied Christmas Island. In 1958 Britain granted Australia sovereignty of Christmas Island. ■

COCOS ISLANDS

OFFICIAL NAME Territory of
Cocos (Keeling) Islands

PEOPLE
Population 600.
Density 111/mi² (43/km²).
Ethnic groups Cocos Malay, Australian.
Languages English, Cocos Malay, Malay
Religions Muslim, Christian.

POLITICS
Government Part of Australia.

ECONOMY
Monetary unit Australian dollar.
Trade partners Australia.
Exports Copra.
Imports Foodstuffs, fuels, manufactured goods.

LAND
Description Indian Ocean islands.
Area 5.4 mi² (14 km²).

PEOPLE. The Cocos Islands' majority group is made up of Cocos Malay, the ancestors of Muslim workers brought from the Netherlands, East Indies, and Malaya in the 1800s. Australians of European descent form a minority. Of the twenty-seven islands that make up the Cocos Islands, only West Island and Home Island are inhabited, and their combined population totals about 600. The Australian population lives on West Island, and the Cocos Malay live on Home Island. Following World War II, the Cocos Malay population underwent a resettlement program because their numbers had grown until the islands' copra plantation could no longer accommodate them. About 1,600 Cocos Malay moved to Christmas Island and the present-day Malaysian state of Sabah. In 1984 the Cocos Malay participated in a referendum to determine the future of their relationship with Australia, and they elected to integrate with that country and thus assume the rights and obligations of Australian citizens.

ECONOMY AND THE LAND. Coconut palms cover the Cocos Islands, and the territory's economy is based on the production of copra, dried coconut meat from which coconut oil is extracted. The islands' copra estate was owned and run by the Clunies-Ross family until 1978, when they sold their interests in the islands to Australia. In 1979 the Cocos Islands Cooperative Society Limited, run by the Cocos Malay community, took over management of the coconut plantation and the production of copra. The Cocos Islands comprise flat, low-lying coral islands in two separate atolls—North Keeling Island and the South Keeling Islands. In the South Keeling island group, the main islands are West Island, which is the site of an airport; Home Island; Direction Island; South Island; and Horsburgh Island. The islands' climate is pleasant, with cooling trade winds.

HISTORY AND POLITICS. In 1609 Captain William Keeling, a seaman employed by the East India Company, discovered the uninhabited islands, but it wasn't until 1826 that the first settlers arrived. These were mostly Malay workers led by Alexander Hare, an Englishman who established a settlement on the South Keeling Islands. A Scottish mariner, John Clunies-Ross, soon founded the islands' second settlement, and when Hare left in 1831, Clunies-Ross took charge of Hare's community, developing a successful coconut economy and bringing in more workers. Britain annexed the islands in 1857 and in 1878 transferred administration of the islands from the colonial office to the government of Ceylon. In 1886 responsibility was passed to the government of the Straits Settlements, and that same year Queen Victoria issued an official document that gave all land above the high-water mark to Clunies-Ross and his heirs and successors in perpetuity. The islands became part of the Settlement of Singapore in 1903, and for about four years in the early 1940s responsibility once again passed temporarily to Ceylon. This situation ended in 1946 when the Cocos Islands again became a dependency of Singapore. The United Kingdom transferred the Territory of the Cocos (Keeling) Islands to Australia in 1955. In 1975 the United Nations Special Committee suggested that Australia assist the Cocos Malay community in becoming more independent of the Clunies-Ross copra estate. The solution came in 1978 when the Clunies-Ross family sold Australia all their interests in the islands, with the exception of the family home, thus ending United Nations and Australian criticism of their handling of workers. In 1979 the Cocos (Keeling) Islands Council was set up, and as a result of the 1984 referendum in which the Cocos Malay community decided to integrate with Australia, the council has been given greater responsibility. The islands' electorate now has full voting rights in the Australian Parliament. ■

COLOMBIA

OFFICIAL NAME Republic of Colombia

PEOPLE
Population 28,545,000.
Density 65/mi² (25/km²).
Urban 64%.
Capital Bogotá, 4,067,000.
Ethnic groups Mestizo 58%, white 20%, mulatto 14%, black 4%.
Languages Spanish.
Religions Roman Catholic 95%.
Life expectancy 64 female, 61 male.
Literacy 81%.

POLITICS
Government Republic.
Parties Conservative, Liberal.
Suffrage Universal, over 18.
Memberships OAS, UN.
Subdivisions 23 departments, 4 *intendencias*, 5 *comisarías*, 1 special district.

ECONOMY
GNP $40,000,000,000.
Per capita $1,435.
Monetary unit Peso.
Trade partners U.S., West Germany, Venezuela, Japan.
Exports Coffee, cotton, fuels, bananas.
Imports Transportation equipment, machinery, metals, chemicals.

LAND
Description Northwestern South America.
Area 439,737 mi² (1,138,914 km²).
Highest point Cristóbal Colón Pk., 19,029 ft (5,800 m).
Lowest point Sea level.

PEOPLE. Colombia's mixed population traces its roots to indigenous Indians, Spanish colonists, and black African slaves. Most numerous today are mestizos, those of Spanish-Indian descent. Roman Catholicism, the Spanish language, and Colombia's overall culture evidence the long-lasting effect of Spanish rule. Over the past decades the population has shifted from mainly rural to urban as the economy has expanded into industry.

ECONOMY AND THE LAND. Industry now keeps pace with traditional agriculture in economic contributions, and mining is also important. Natural resources include oil, coal, natural gas, most of the world's emeralds, plus fertile soils. The traditional coffee crop also remains important, and Colombia is a leading coffee producer. The terrain is characterized by a flat coastal region, central highlands, and wide eastern llanos, or plains. The climate is tropical on the coast and in the east, with cooler temperatures in the highlands.

HISTORY AND POLITICS. In the 1500s Spaniards conquered the native Indian groups and established the area as a Spanish colony. In the early 1700s Bogotá became the capital of the viceroyalty of New Granada, which included modern Colombia, Venezuela, Ecuador, and Panama. Rebellion in Venezuela in 1796 initiated revolt elsewhere in New Granada, including Colombia, and in 1813 independence was declared. In 1819 the Republic of Greater Colombia was formed, which came to include all the former members of the Spanish viceroyalty. Independence leader Simón Bolívar became president, and Francisco de Paula Santander vice-president. By 1830 Venezuela and Ecuador had seceded from the republic, and Panama did the same in 1903. The Conservative and Liberal parties, dominating forces in Colombia's political history, arose from differences between supporters of Bolívar and Santander. Conservative-Liberal conflict led to a violent civil war from 1899 to 1902 and to La Violencia, "The Violence," a civil disorder that continued from the 1940s to the 1960s and resulted in about 200,000 deaths. From the late fifties through the mid-seventies, a government program alternated Conservative and Liberal rule every four years. Political unrest led to a 1980 embassy siege by a group demanding freedom for political prisoners. A pursuit of diplomatic relations with all nations defines Colombian foreign policy. ∎

Colombia Map Index

	Lat.	Long.
Amazon	4°12'S	69°57'W
Andes	2°30'N	76°00'W
Apaporis	1°23'S	69°25'W
Arauca	7°05'N	70°45'W
Arauca	7°00'N	70°05'W
Arica	2°08'S	71°47'W
Armenia	4°31'N	75°41'W
Atrato	8°17'N	76°58'W
Ayapel	8°19'N	75°09'W
Barrancabermeja	7°03'N	73°52'W
Barranquilla	10°59'N	74°48'W
Bello	6°20'N	75°33'W
Bogotá	4°36'N	74°05'W
Bolívar	1°50'N	76°58'W
Bucaramanga	7°08'N	73°09'W
Buenaventura	3°53'N	77°04'W
Buga	3°54'N	76°17'W
Cali	3°27'N	76°31'W
Caquetá (Japurá)	1°35'S	69°25'W
Cartagena	10°25'N	75°32'W
Cauca	8°54'N	74°28'W
Ciénaga	11°01'N	74°15'W
Condoto	5°06'N	76°37'W
Cristóbal Colón Peak	10°50'N	73°41'W
Cúcuta	7°54'N	72°31'W
Cumbal Volcano	0°57'N	77°52'W
Duitama	5°50'N	73°02'W
Eastern Cordillera	6°00'N	73°00'W
El Banco	9°00'N	73°58'W
El Encanto	1°37'S	73°14'W
El Nevado, Mount	3°59'N	74°04'W
Florencia	1°36'N	75°36'W
Gallianas, Point	12°28'N	71°40'W
Girardot	4°18'N	74°48'W
Guajira Peninsula	12°00'N	71°40'W
Guapi	2°36'N	77°54'W
Guaviare	4°03'N	67°44'W
Huila, Mount	3°00'N	76°00'W
Ibagué	4°27'N	75°14'W
Icá (Putumayo)	3°07'S	67°58'W
La Chorrera	0°44'S	73°01'W
La Dorada	5°27'N	74°40'W
Llanos	5°00'N	70°00'W
Magangue	9°14'N	74°45'W
Magdalena	11°06'N	74°51'W
Málaga	6°42'N	72°44'W
Manizales	5°05'N	75°32'W
Medellín	6°15'N	75°35'W
Meta	6°12'N	67°28'W
Mitú	1°08'N	70°03'W
Montería	8°46'N	75°53'W
Mosquera	2°30'N	78°29'W
Negro	1°15'N	66°50'W
Neiva	2°56'N	75°18'W
Ocaña	8°15'N	73°20'W
Orinoco	6°12'N	67°28'W
Orocué	4°48'N	71°20'W
Palmira	3°32'N	76°16'W
Pamplona	7°23'N	72°39'W
Pasto	1°13'N	77°17'W
Pereira	4°49'N	75°43'W
Pitalito	1°51'N	76°02'W
Planeta Rica	8°25'N	75°36'W

	Lat.	Long.
Plato	9°47'N	74°47'W
Popayán	2°27'N	76°36'W
Puerto Asís	0°30'N	76°31'W
Puerto Berrío	6°29'N	74°24'W
Puerto Carreño	6°12'N	67°22'W
Puerto Leguízamo	0°12'S	74°46'W
Putumayo (Icá)	2°55'S	69°40'W
Quibdó	5°42'N	76°40'W
San Felipe	1°55'N	67°06'W
San José del Guaviare	2°35'N	72°38'W

	Lat.	Long.
Santa Marta	11°15'N	74°13'W
San Vicente del Caguán	2°07'N	74°46'W
Simiti	7°58'N	73°57'W
Sincelejo	9°18'N	75°24'W
Sogamoso	5°43'N	72°56'W
Sonsón	5°42'N	75°18'W
Tame	6°28'N	71°44'W
Tolima, Mount	4°40'N	75°19'W
Tres Esquinas	0°43'N	75°16'W
Tuluá	4°06'N	76°11'W

	Lat.	Long.
Tumaco	1°49'N	78°46'W
Tunja	5°31'N	73°22'W
Turbo	8°06'N	76°43'W
Uribia	11°43'N	72°16'W
Valledupar	10°29'N	73°15'W
Vaupés	0°35'N	69°10'W
Vichada	4°55'N	67°50'W
Villavicencio	4°09'N	73°37'W
Western Cordillera	5°00'N	76°00'W
Yarumal	6°58'N	75°24'W

COLOMBIA

— — — Railroad
+ - + - Oil Pipeline
▲ Major Oil Field
+ Spot Elevation or Depth

National capitals are underlined

Scale 1:13,519,000

Meters	Feet
Above 4000	Above 13124
2000	6562
1000	3281
500	1640
200	656

Meters	Feet
0	0
200	656
Below 2000	Below 6562

In Colombia, migration from rural areas to the cities is an ongoing trend. As the city of Bogotá, shown here, absorbs its new residents, modern buildings shoot skyward and urban problems such as crime and housing shortages increase. In some areas, however, Bogotá's Spanish heritage remains evident in its architecture.

COMOROS

OFFICIAL NAME Federal Islamic
Republic of the Comoros

PEOPLE
Population 460,000.
Density 549/mi² (212/km²).
Urban 19%.
Capital Moroni, Grande Comore I., 20,112.
Ethnic groups Antalote, Cafre, Makua, Oimatsaha,
Sakalava.
Languages Arabic, French, Swahili.
Religions Shirazi Muslim 86%, Roman Catholic 14%.
Literacy 15%.

POLITICS
Government Republic.
Parties Union for Progress.

Suffrage Universal adult.
Memberships OAU, UN.
Subdivisions 7 regions.

ECONOMY
GNP $90,000,000.
Per capita $230.
Monetary unit CFA franc.
Trade partners France, Madagascar, Kenya.
Exports Perfume oils, vanilla, copra, cloves.
Imports Rice, fuels, textiles, machinery.

LAND
Description Southeastern African islands.
Area 838 mi² (2,171 km²).
Highest point Kartala, Njazidja I., 7,746 ft (2,361 m).
Lowest point Sea level.

PEOPLE. The ethnic groups of Comoros'
Njazidja, Nzwani, and Mwali islands are mainly
of Arab-African descent, practice the Muslim religion, and speak a Swahili dialect. Arab culture
predominates throughout the island group,
which includes French-ruled Mayotte Island.
Poverty, disease, a shortage of medical care, and
low literacy continue to plague the nation.

ECONOMY AND THE LAND. The economic
mainstay of Comoros is agriculture, and most
Comorans engage in subsistence farming and
fishing. Plantations employ workers to produce
the main cash crops. Of volcanic origin, the islands have soils of varying quality, and some are
unsuited for farming. Terrain varies from the
mountains of Njazidja to the hills and valleys of
Mwali. The climate is cool and dry, with a winter rainy season.

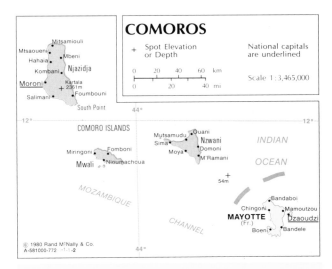

Comoros Map Index

	Lat.	Long.		Lat.	Long.
Kartala	11°45'S	43°22'E	Njazidja	11°35'S	43°20'E
Moroni	11°41'S	43°16'E	Nzwani	12°15'S	44°25'E
Mwali	12°15'S	43°45'E			

HISTORY AND POLITICS. The Comoro Islands
saw invasions by coastal African, Persian Gulf,
Indonesian, and Malagasy peoples. Portuguese
explorers landed in the 1500s, around the same
time Arab Shirazis, most likely from Persia, introduced Islam. The French took Mayotte in 1843 and
by 1912 had extended its rule to include Njazidja,
Nzwani, and Mwali. Comoros declared unilateral
independence in 1975. Mayotte voted to remain
under French administration. ■

CONGO

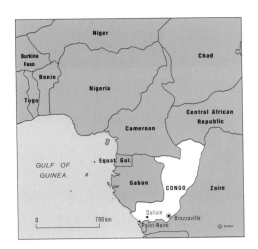

OFFICIAL NAME People's
Republic of the Congo

PEOPLE
Population 1,770,000.
Density 13/mi² (5.2/km²).
Urban 48%.
Capital Brazzaville, 442,400.
Ethnic groups Kongo 48%, Sangha 20%, M'Bochi 12%,
Teke 17%.
Languages French, indigenous.
Religions Animist 48%, Christian 47%, Muslim 2%.
Life expectancy 61 female, 57 male.
Literacy 50%.

POLITICS
Government Republic.
Parties Workers'.
Suffrage Universal, over 18.
Memberships OAU, UN.
Subdivisions 9 regions.

ECONOMY
GDP $1,800,000,000.
Per capita $1,140.

Monetary unit CFA franc.
Trade partners France, other Western European
countries, U.S.
Exports Petroleum, wood, coffee, cocoa.
Imports Machinery, transportation equipment,
consumer goods, food.

LAND
Description Central Africa.
Area 132,047 mi² (342,000 km²).
Highest point 2,963 ft (903 m).
Lowest point Sea level.

PEOPLE. The Congo's four main groups, the
Kongo, Sangha, M'Bochi, and Teke, create an
ethnically and linguistically diverse populace.
The official language, French, is a result of former colonial rule. Population is concentrated in
the south, away from the dense forests, heavy
rainfall, and hot climate of the north. Educational
programs, and thus literacy, have improved, although rural inhabitants remain isolated.

ECONOMY AND THE LAND. Brazzaville was
the commercial center of the former colony called
French Equatorial Africa, and the Congo now
benefits from the early groundwork laid for service and transport industries. Subsistence farming occupies most Congolese, however, as well
as most cultivated land. Low productivity and a
growing populace create a need for foreign aid,
much of it from France. Offshore petroleum is
the most valuable mineral resource and a major
economic contributor. The land is marked by
coastal plains, a south-central valley, a central
plateau, and the Congo River basin in the north.
The climate is tropical, with high temperatures
and humidity.

HISTORY AND POLITICS. Several tribal kingdoms existed in the area during its early history.
The Portuguese arrived on the coast in the 1400s,
and slave trade flourished until it was banned in
the 1800s. Shortly thereafter a Teke king signed a

treaty placing the area, then known as Middle
Congo, under French protection. In 1910 Middle
Congo, the present-day Central African Republic,
Gabon, and Chad were joined to form French
Equatorial Africa. The Republic of the Congo became independent in 1960. Subsequent years saw
unrest, including coups, a presidential assassination, and accusations of corruption and human
rights violations. In 1979 a newly elected president granted amnesty to political prisoners. ■

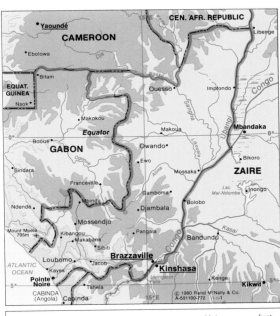

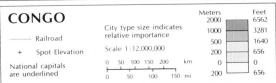

Congo Map Index

	Lat.	Long.		Lat.	Long.
Brazzaville	4°16'S	15°17'E	Owando	0°29'S	15°55'E
Congo	4°50'S	14°30'E	Pointe-Noire	4°48'S	11°51'E
Ouesso	1°37'N	16°04'E	Ubangi	0°30'S	17°42'E

COOK ISLANDS

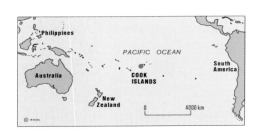

OFFICIAL NAME Cook Islands

PEOPLE
Population 16,000.
Density 176/mi² (68/km²).
Urban 54%.
Capital Avarua, Rarotonga I., 9,525.
Ethnic groups Polynesian 81%, mixed 15%, European 2%, others 2%.
Languages English, Maori.
Religions Christian, Roman Catholic.

POLITICS
Government Self-governing territory (New Zealand).
Parties Cook Islands, Democratic.
Suffrage Universal adult.

ECONOMY
GDP $21,000,000.
Per capita $1,170.
Monetary unit New Zealand dollar.
Trade partners New Zealand, Japan.
Exports Copra, fruit.
Imports Foodstuffs, textiles, fuels.

LAND
Description South Pacific islands.
Area 91 mi² (236 km²).
Highest point Te Manga, Rarotonga I., 2,142 ft (653 m).
Lowest point Sea level.

PEOPLE. Of the fifteen islands, Rarotonga is the largest and most populated. Many of the islands' Polynesians are of Maori ancestry.

ECONOMY AND THE LAND. The economy is agricultural. In the north are coral islands; and in the south, volcanic. The climate is warm, with occasional hurricanes.

HISTORY AND POLITICS. Captain James Cook arrived in the area in 1773. In 1888 the islands came under British protection, and in 1901 they were annexed to New Zealand. The islands can unilaterally declare independence from New Zealand at any time. ■

Map shows major island only.

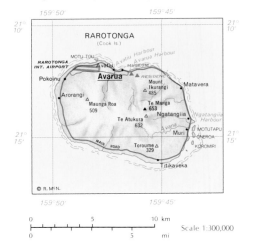

Cook Islands Map Index

	Lat.	Long.		Lat.	Long.
Avarua	21°12′S	159°46′W	Muri	21°14′S	159°43′W
Avatiu	21°12′S	159°47′W	Rarotonga	21°14′S	159°46′W
Matavera	21°13′S	159°44′W	Te Manga	21°13′S	159°45′W

COSTA RICA

OFFICIAL NAME Republic of Costa Rica

PEOPLE
Population 2,725,000.
Density 138/mi² (53/km²).
Urban 48%.
Capital San José, 259,126.
Ethnic groups White and mestizo 96%, black 3%, Indian 1%.
Languages Spanish.
Religions Roman Catholic 95%.
Life expectancy 74 female, 70 male.
Literacy 90%.

POLITICS
Government Republic.
Parties Christian Democratic, National Liberation, Popular Union, Republican Calderonista, Unity Coalition of Democratic Renovation.
Suffrage Universal, over 18.
Memberships OAS, UN.
Subdivisions 7 provinces.

ECONOMY
GDP $3,300,000,000.
Per capita $1,390.
Monetary unit Colón.
Trade partners U.S., Central American countries, West Germany.
Exports Coffee, bananas, beef, sugar.
Imports Manufactured goods, machinery, transportation equipment.

LAND
Description Central America.
Area 19,730 mi² (51,100 km²).
Highest point Mt. Chirripó, 12,530 ft (3,819 m).
Lowest point Sea level.

PEOPLE. Compared with most other Central American countries, Costa Rica has a relatively large population of European descent, mostly Spanish with minorities of German, Dutch, and Swiss ancestry. Together with mestizos, people of Spanish-Indian heritage, they compose the bulk of the population. Descendants of black Jamaican immigrants inhabit mainly the Caribbean coastal region. Indigenous Indians in scattered enclaves continue traditional life-styles; some, however, have been assimilated into the country's majority culture.

ECONOMY AND THE LAND. Costa Rica's economy has long been one of the most prosperous in Central America, but it has not been without problems, some resulting from falling coffee prices and rising oil costs. Agriculture remains important, producing traditional coffee and banana crops, while the country attempts to expand industry. Population and agriculture are concentrated in the central highlands. Much of the country is forested, and the mountainous central area is bordered by coastal plains on the east and west. The climate is semitropical to tropical.

HISTORY AND POLITICS. In 1502 Christopher Columbus arrived and claimed the area for Spain. Spaniards named the region Rich Coast, and settlers soon flocked to the new land to seek their fortune. Rather than riches, they found an Indian population unwilling to surrender its land. But many Spaniards remained, establishing farms in the central area. In 1821 the Central American provinces of Costa Rica, Guatemala, El Salvador, Honduras, and Nicaragua declared themselves independent from Spain, and by 1823 they had formed the Federation of Central America. Despite efforts to sustain it, the federation was in a state of virtual collapse by 1838, and Costa Rica became an independent republic. Since the first free elections in 1889, Costa Rica has experienced a presidential overthrow in 1919 and a civil war in 1948, arising over a disputed election. ■

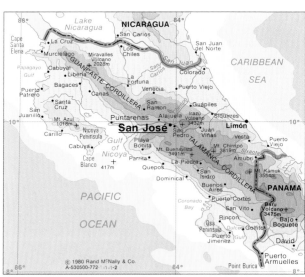

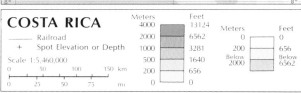

COSTA RICA
Railroad
+ Spot Elevation or Depth
Scale 1:5,460,000

Meters	Feet
4000	13124
2000	6562
1000	3281
500	1640
200	656
0	0

Meters	Feet
0	0
200	656
Below 2000	Below 6562

Costa Rica Map Index

	Lat.	Long.		Lat.	Long.
Alajuela	10°01′N	84°13′W	Miravalles		
Amubri	9°31′N	82°56′W	Volcano	10°45′N	85°10′W
Buenavista,			Nicoya, Gulf of	9°47′N	84°48′W
Mount	9°33′N	83°45′W	Nicoya Peninsula	10°00′N	85°25′W
Buenos Aires	9°10′N	83°20′W	Playa Bonita	9°39′N	84°27′W
Cabuya	9°36′N	85°06′W	Puerto Jiménez	8°33′N	83°19′W
Chirripó	10°41′N	83°41′W	Puerto Viejo	9°39′N	82°45′W
Chirripó, Mount	9°29′N	83°30′W	Puntarenas	9°58′N	84°50′W
Colorado	10°46′N	83°35′W	Quepos	9°27′N	84°09′W
Dominical	9°13′N	83°51′W	San José	9°56′N	84°05′W
Dulce Gulf	8°32′N	83°14′W	San Juan	10°56′N	83°42′W
Golfito	8°38′N	83°11′W	San Juanillo	10°02′N	85°44′W
Guápiles	10°13′N	83°46′W	Santa Cruz	10°16′N	85°36′W
Irazú Volcano	9°58′N	83°53′W	Santa Elena,		
Juan Viñas	9°54′N	83°45′W	Cape	10°54′N	85°57′W
Kámuk, Mount	9°17′N	83°04′W	Talamanca,		
La Cruz	11°04′N	85°39′W	Cordillera	9°30′N	83°40′W
Liberia	10°38′N	85°27′W	Venecia	10°22′N	84°17′W
Limón	10°00′N	83°02′W	Vesta	9°43′N	83°03′W
Los Chiles	11°02′N	84°43′W			

CUBA

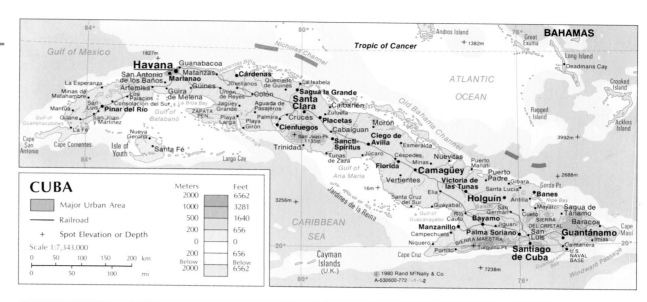

CUBA

☐ Major Urban Area

— Railroad

+ Spot Elevation or Depth

Scale 1:7,343,000

	Meters	Feet
	2000	6562
	1000	3281
	500	1640
	200	656
	0	0
	200 Below 2000	656 Below 6562

© 1980 Rand McNally & Co.
A-530600-772 -1-1-2

OFFICIAL NAME Republic of Cuba

PEOPLE
Population 9,770,000.
Density 221/mi² (85/km²).
Urban 69%.
Capital Havana, 1,924,886.
Ethnic groups Mulatto 51%, white 37%, black 11%, Chinese 1%.
Languages Spanish.
Religions Roman Catholic 85%.
Life expectancy 75 female, 71 male.
Literacy 96%.

POLITICS
Government Socialist republic.
Parties Communist.
Suffrage Universal, over 16.
Memberships CEMA, UN.
Subdivisions 15 provinces.

ECONOMY
GNP $14,900,000,000.
Per capita $1,534.
Monetary unit Peso.
Trade partners U.S.S.R., Eastern European countries.
Exports Sugar, nickel, shellfish, tobacco.
Imports Capital equipment, raw materials, petroleum, food.

LAND
Description Caribbean island.
Area 44,218 mi² (114,524 km²).
Highest point Turquino Pk., 6,476 ft (1,974 m).
Lowest point Sea level.

PEOPLE. Most Cubans are descendants of Spanish colonists, African slaves, or a blend of the two. The government provides free education and health care, and although religious practices are discouraged, most people belong to the Roman Catholic church. Personal income, health, education, and housing have improved since the 1959 revolution, but most food products and consumer goods remain in short supply.

ECONOMY AND THE LAND. Cuba's economy is largely dependent on sugar. Other forms of agriculture are important as well, and the most fertile soils lie in the central region between mountain ranges. The island is also the site of mineral deposits, and nickel is found in the northeast. In addition to agriculture and mining, industry is an economic contributor. Most economic activity is nationalized, and Cuba remains dependent on aid from the Soviet Union. Mountains, plains, and a scenic coastline make Cuba one of the most beautiful islands in the West Indies. The climate is tropical.

HISTORY AND POLITICS. Christopher Columbus claimed Cuba for Spain in 1492, and Spanish settlement began in 1511. Soon the native Indian population died out, and African slaves were brought to work plantations. The United States joined with Cuba against Spain in the Spanish-American War in 1898. Spain surrendered that

Cuba Map Index

	Lat.	Long.		Lat.	Long.		Lat.	Long.		Lat.	Long.
Aguada de Pasajeros	22°23′N	80°51′W	Esmeralda	21°51′N	78°07′W	Mantua	22°17′N	84°17′W	San Antonio, Cape	21°52′N	84°57′W
Ana Maria, Gulf of	21°25′N	78°40′W	Florida	21°32′N	78°14′W	Manzanillo	20°21′N	77°07′W	San Antonio de los Baños	22°53′N	82°30′W
Artemisa	22°49′N	82°46′W	Guacanayabo, Gulf of	20°28′N	77°30′W	Marianao	23°05′N	82°26′W	Sancti-Spíritus	21°56′N	79°27′W
Banes	20°58′N	75°43′W	Guanabacoa	23°07′N	82°18′W	Matanzas	23°03′N	81°35′W	San Luis	20°12′N	75°51′W
Baracoa	20°21′N	74°30′W	Guantánamo	20°08′N	75°12′W	Morón	22°06′N	78°38′W	Santa Clara	22°24′N	79°58′W
Batabanó, Gulf of	22°15′N	82°30′W	Güines	22°50′N	82°02′W	Nueva Gerona	21°53′N	82°48′W	Santa Fé	21°45′N	82°45′W
Bayamo	20°23′N	76°39′W	Güira de Melena	22°48′N	82°30′W	Nuevitas	21°33′N	77°16′W	Santiago de Cuba	20°01′N	75°49′W
Cabaiguan	22°05′N	79°30′W	Havana	23°08′N	82°22′W	Old Bahama Channel	22°30′N	78°50′W	Trinidad	21°48′N	79°59′W
Caibarién	22°31′N	79°28′W	Holguín	20°53′N	76°15′W	Palma Soriano	20°13′N	76°00′W	Turquino Peak	19°59′N	76°50′W
Camagüey	21°23′N	77°55′W	Imías	20°04′N	74°38′W	Pigs, Bay of	22°07′N	81°10′W	Vertientes	21°16′N	78°09′W
Cárdenas	23°02′N	81°12′W	Jagüey Grande	22°32′N	81°08′W	Pinar del Río	22°25′N	83°42′W	Victoria de las Tunas	20°58′N	76°57′W
Ciego de Avila	21°51′N	78°46′W	Jardines de la Reina	20°50′N	78°55′W	Placetas	22°19′N	79°40′W	Windward Passage	20°00′N	73°50′W
Cienfuegos	22°09′N	80°27′W	La Broa Bay	22°35′N	82°00′W	Portillo	19°55′N	77°11′W	Youth, Isle of	21°40′N	82°50′W
Colón	22°43′N	80°54′W	La Isabela	22°57′N	80°01′W	Puerto Padre	21°12′N	76°36′W	Zapata Peninsula	22°20′N	81°35′W
Cruces	22°21′N	80°16′W	Los Palacios	22°35′N	83°15′W	Sagua de Tánamo	20°35′N	75°14′W			
Cruz, Cape	19°51′N	77°44′W	Maestra, Sierra	20°00′N	76°45′W	Sagua la Grande	22°49′N	80°05′W			
Elia	20°59′N	77°26′W	Maisí, Cape	20°15′N	74°09′W						

Havana, shown here from the Castillo del Morro, is a main port of the West Indies. Originally founded in 1515 on Cuba's south coast, the city was rebuilt on the **northwest coast four years later. Havana thrived in its new location, and by 1552 it had become the capital of Cuba and a busy trade center.**

same year, and full independence was gained in 1902. Unrest continued, however, and the United States again intervened from 1906 to 1909 and in 1917. A 1933 coup ousted a nine-year dictatorship, and a subsequent government overthrow in 1934 ushered in an era dominated by Sergeant Fulgencio Batista. After ruling through other presidents and serving an elected term himself, Batista seized power in a 1952 coup that established an unpopular and oppressive regime. Led by lawyer Fidel Castro, a revolutionary group opposed to Batista gained quick support, and

Batista fled the country on January 1, 1959, leaving the government to Castro. Early United States support of Castro soured when nationalization of American businesses began. American aid soon ceased, and Cuba looked to the Soviet Union for assistance. The United States ended diplomatic relations with Cuba in 1961. In 1962 the United States and the Soviet Union became embroiled in a dispute over Soviet missile bases in Cuba, which nearly led to war. The nation maintains ties with the Soviet Union and has sent aid to several Third World countries. ■

CYPRUS

OFFICIAL NAME Republic of Cyprus

PEOPLE
Population 675,000.
Density 189/mi² (73/km²).
Urban 53%.
Capital Nicosia, 48,222.
Ethnic groups Greek 78%, Turkish 18%.
Languages Greek, Turkish.
Religions Greek Orthodox 78%, Muslim 18%.
Life expectancy 76 female, 72 male.
Literacy 90%.

POLITICS
Government Republic.
Parties Greek: Democratic, Democratic Rally, Progressive Party of the Working People. Turkish: Communal Liberation, National Unity.
Suffrage Universal, over 21.
Memberships CW, UN.
Subdivisions 6 districts.

ECONOMY
GNP $2,172,000,000.
Per capita $3,342.
Monetary unit Pound.
Trade partners U.K., other Western European countries, Iraq, Greece, Turkey.
Exports Food and beverages, clothing, cement.
Imports Petroleum, machinery, transportation equipment, manufactured goods, food.

LAND
Description Eastern Mediterranean island.
Area 3,572 mi² (9,251 km²).
Highest point Olympus, 6,401 ft (1,951 m).
Lowest point Sea level.

PEOPLE. Most Cypriots are of Greek ancestry, and the island's religion, language, and general culture reflect this heritage. Muslim, Turkish-speaking descendants of Turks are a minority. Although the two groups have some common customs, ethnicity usually supersedes national allegiance, and a 1974 Turkish invasion resulted in formal segregation. Greek Cypriots now inhabit the island's southern two-thirds, and Turkish Cypriots the northern third. Other minorities include Armenians and Maronites.

ECONOMY AND THE LAND. Relocation of Greek Cypriots in the south and Turkish Cypriots in the north has severely disrupted the economy. With foreign assistance, Greek Cypriots have made progress, expanding traditional southern agriculture to light manufacturing and tourism. Northern Turkish Cypriots lack capital, experience, foreign aid, and official recognition, and they remain agriculturally based and dependent on Turkey for tourism, trade, and assistance. Known for its scenic beauty and tourist appeal, Cyprus is marked by a fertile central plain bordered by mountains in the southwest and north. Sandy beaches dot the coastline. The Mediterranean climate results in hot, dry summers and damp, cool winters.

HISTORY AND POLITICS. In the Late Bronze Age—from 1600 to 1050 B.C.—a Greek culture flourished in Cyprus. Rule by various peoples followed, including Assyrians, Egyptians, Persians, Romans, Byzantines, French, and Venetians. The Ottoman Turks invaded in 1571. In the nineteenth century Turkey ceded the island to the British as security for a loan. Although many Turks remained on Cyprus, the British declared it a Crown colony in 1925. A growing desire for enosis, or union with Greece, led to rioting and guerrilla activity by Greek Cypriots. The Turkish government, opposed to absorption by Greece, desired separation into Greek and Turkish sectors. Cyprus became independent in 1960, with treaties forbidding either enosis or partition, but Greek-Turkish conflicts continued. A 1974 coup

by pro-enosis forces led to an invasion by Turkey and the current partition. In foreign affairs, the Republic of Cyprus follows a policy of nonalignment. The Turkish Republic of Northern Cyprus, which is not recognized internationally, maintains a separate government with a prime minister and a president. ∎

CYPRUS

	Meters	Feet		Meters	Feet
	2000	6562		0	0
+ Spot Elevation or Depth	1000	3281		200	656
Scale 1:3,000,000	500	1640		Below 2000	Below 6562
0 20 40 60 km	200	656			
0 10 20 30 40 mi	0	0			

Cyprus Map Index

	Lat.	Long.		Lat.	Long.
Apostolos			Kyrenia	35°20′N	33°19′E
Andreas, Cape	35°42′N	34°35′E	Larnaca	34°55′N	33°38′E
Arnauti, Cape	35°06′N	32°17′E	Limassol	34°40′N	33°02′E
Famagusta	35°07′N	33°57′E	Mesayitonia	34°42′N	33°03′E
Famagusta Bay	35°15′N	34°10′E	Morphou	35°12′N	32°59′E
Gata, Cape	34°34′N	33°02′E	Morphou Bay	35°10′N	32°50′E
Greco, Cape	34°56′N	34°05′E	Nicosia	35°10′N	33°22′E
Khrysokhou Bay	35°06′N	32°25′E	Olympus	34°56′N	32°52′E
Kormakiti, Cape	35°24′N	32°56′E	Paphos	34°45′N	32°25′E

CZECHOSLOVAKIA

Coal and iron ore reserves made Bohemia one of the leaders of the nineteenth-century industrialization of Austria-Hungary. Czechoslovakia's industrial legacy continues today, as shown in this photo of heavy industry in Plzeň, a city in western Czechoslovakia.

In addition to heavy industry, light industry plays a role in Czechoslovakia's economy, and activities such as textile production and glass manufacturing evidence the ongoing importance of industries rooted in the past. Since the 1600s northern Bohemia has been a leader in the craft of glassmaking, and the traditional art is carried on today in modern settings. Shown here is the Světlá glassworks in Bohemia.

CZECHOSLOVAKIA

OFFICIAL NAME
Czechoslovak
Socialist Republic

PEOPLE
Population 15,490,000.
Density 314/mi² (121/km²).
Urban 67%.
Capital Prague, 1,185,693.
Ethnic groups Czech 65%, Slovak 30%,
Hungarian 3%.
Languages Czech, Slovak, Hungarian.
Religions Roman Catholic 77%, Protestant 20%,
Greek Orthodox 2%.
Life expectancy 74 female, 67 male.
Literacy 99%.

POLITICS
Government Socialist republic.
Parties Communist.
Suffrage Universal, over 18.
Memberships CEMA, UN, Warsaw Pact.
Subdivisions 2 semiautonomous republics.

ECONOMY
GNP $147,100,000,000.
Per capita $9,550.
Monetary unit Koruna.
Trade partners U.S.S.R., East Germany, Poland,
Hungary, West Germany.
Exports Machinery, transportation equipment, iron
and steel, consumer goods.
Imports Fuels, machinery, raw materials,
transportation equipment.

LAND
Description Eastern Europe, landlocked.
Area 49,381 mi² (127,896 km²).
Highest point Gerlachovka, 8,711 ft (2,655 m).
Lowest point Bodrog River, 308 ft (94 m).

PEOPLE. Czechs and Slovaks, descendants of
Slavic tribes, predominate in Czechoslovakia.
Characterized by a German-influenced culture,
Czechs are concentrated in the regions of Bohemia and Moravia. Slovaks, whose culture was
influenced by Hungarian Magyars, reside mainly
in Slovakia. Both Czech and Slovak are official
languages. Minorities include Hungarians, or
Magyars; Ukrainians; Germans; Poles; and Gypsies, a rapidly growing group concentrated in
Slovakia. Most people are Roman Catholic, and
the government licenses and pays clergy.

ECONOMY AND THE LAND. An industrial nation, Czechoslovakia has a centralized economy
and one of the highest standards of living among
Communist countries. Coal deposits in Bohemia
and Moravia provided a base for industrial development, and Bohemia remains an economically
important region. Nearly all agriculture is collectivized, and farm output includes grains, potatoes, sugar beets, and livestock. Farming areas
are found in the river valleys of north-central
Bohemia and central Moravia, and Slovakia remains largely agricultural. Czechoslovakia's terrain is characterized by a rolling western area,
low mountains in the north and south, central

Czechoslovakia Map Index

	Lat.	Long.		Lat.	Long.		Lat.	Long.		Lat.	Long.
Banská Bystrica	48°44′N	19°07′E	Hradec Králové	50°12′N	15°50′E	Nitra	48°20′N	18°05′E	Slovenské		
Berounka	50°00′N	14°24′E	Hron	47°49′N	18°45′E	Nitra	47°46′N	18°10′E	Mountains	48°45′N	20°00′E
Bodrog	48°20′N	21°42′E	Jablonec nad			Nové Zámky	47°59′N	18°11′E	Sudeten		
Bohemian Forest	49°15′N	12°45′E	Nisou	50°44′N	15°10′E	Ohře	50°32′N	14°08′E	Mountains	50°30′N	16°00′E
Bratislava	48°09′N	17°07′E	Javorie	48°27′N	19°18′E	Olomouc	49°36′N	17°16′E	Svitáva	49°10′N	16°38′E
Brno	49°12′N	16°37′E	Jihlava	49°24′N	15°36′E	Opava	49°56′N	17°54′E	Tatry Mountains	49°12′N	20°05′E
Carpathian			Jihlava	48°55′N	16°37′E	Ore Mountains	50°30′N	13°10′E	Teplice	50°39′N	13°48′E
Mountains	49°20′N	21°00′E	Karlovy Vary	50°11′N	12°52′E	Ostrava	49°50′N	18°17′E	Trenčín	48°54′N	18°04′E
Cerna Mountain	48°58′N	13°48′E	Kladno	50°08′N	14°05′E	Pardubice	50°02′N	15°47′E	Trnava	48°23′N	17°35′E
České Budějovice	48°59′N	14°28′E	Klet'	48°52′N	14°17′E	Plzeň	49°45′N	13°23′E	Ústí nad Labem	50°40′N	14°02′E
Cheb	50°01′N	12°25′E	Komárno	47°45′N	18°09′E	Prague	50°05′N	14°26′E	Váh	47°55′N	18°00′E
Chomutov	50°28′N	13°26′E	Košice	48°43′N	21°15′E	Přerov	49°27′N	17°27′E	Vltava	50°21′N	14°30′E
Danube	47°48′N	18°50′E	Labe (Elbe)	50°53′N	14°14′E	Prešov	49°00′N	21°15′E	Žilina	49°14′N	18°46′E
Děčín	50°48′N	14°13′E	Liberec	50°46′N	15°03′E	Příbram	49°42′N	14°01′E	Znojmo	48°52′N	16°02′E
Dyje	48°37′N	16°56′E	Mladá Boleslav	50°23′N	14°59′E	Prievidza	48°47′N	18°37′E	Zvolen	48°35′N	19°08′E
Gerlach Peak	49°12′N	20°08′E	Morava	48°10′N	16°59′E	Prostějov	49°29′N	17°07′E			
Gottwaldov	49°13′N	17°41′E	Most	50°32′N	13°39′E						

hills, and the Carpathian Mountains in the east.
The climate is temperate.

HISTORY AND POLITICS. Slavic tribes were established in the region by the sixth century. By
the tenth century Hungarian Magyars had conquered the Slovaks in the region of Slovakia.
Bohemia and Moravia became part of the Holy
Roman Empire, and by the twelfth century Bohemia had become a strong kingdom that included
Moravia and parts of Austria and Poland. Austria
gained control of the area in 1620, and it later
became part of Austria-Hungary. With the collapse of Austria-Hungary at the end of World
War I, an independent Czechoslovakia consisting
of Bohemia, Moravia, and Slovakia was formed.
Nazi Germany invaded Czechoslovakia in 1939,
and the Soviet Union liberated the nation from
German occupation in the winter and spring of
1944 to 1945. By 1948 Communists controlled the
government, and political purges continued from
1949 to 1952. A 1968 invasion by the Soviet
Union and Bulgaria, Hungary, Poland, and East
Germany resulted when the Czechoslovakian
Communist party leader introduced liberal reforms. Efforts to eliminate dissent continued into
the seventies. Foreign policy closely follows that
of the Soviet Union, and Czechoslovakia maintains economic ties with the Soviet bloc nations. ■

Prague, Czechoslovakia's capital and largest city, lies on the Vltava River in
Bohemia. The city was founded in the ninth century and by the tenth century
was already a renowned center of trade. The section of Prague known as the
Old Town contains many of Czechoslovakia's important architectural structures.
Shown here is the Old Town square.

DENMARK

NORTH SEA
DENMARK
BALTIC SEA
Neth.
Belgium
Lux.
France
Switzerland
Liech.
Federal Republic of Germany
German Democratic Republic
Poland
Czechoslovakia
Austria
Hungary

OFFICIAL NAME Kingdom of Denmark

PEOPLE
Population 5,010,000.
Density 301/mi² (116/km²).
Urban 83%.
Capital Copenhagen, 498,850.
Ethnic groups Scandinavian.
Languages Danish.
Religions Lutheran 97%.
Life expectancy 77 female, 73 male.
Literacy 99%.

POLITICS
Government Constitutional monarchy.
Parties Conservative, Liberal, Social Democratic, Socialist People's.
Suffrage Universal, over 21.
Memberships EC, NATO, OECD, UN.
Subdivisions 14 counties, 2 cities.

ECONOMY
GNP $56,400,000,000.
Per capita $11,016.
Monetary unit Krone.
Trade partners West Germany, U.K., Sweden, U.S., Norway.
Exports Meat and dairy products, machinery, transportation equipment, textiles.
Imports Raw materials, fuels, machinery, transportation equipment.

LAND
Description Northern Europe.
Area 16,633 mi² (43,080 km²).
Highest point Yding Skovhøj, 568 ft (173 m).
Lowest point Lammefjord, 23 ft (7 m) below sea level.
The above information excludes the Faeroe Islands.

PEOPLE. Denmark is made up of the Jutland Peninsula and more than four hundred islands, about one hundred of which are inhabited. Copenhagen, the capital, is situated on Denmark's largest island. But besides these nearby islands, Greenland, lying northeast of Canada, and the Faeroe Islands, between Scotland and Iceland in the North Atlantic, are part of Denmark. Lutheran, Danish-speaking Scandinavians constitute the homogeneous population of the peninsula and surrounding islands, although a German minority is concentrated near the West German border. The government provides extensive social services, including insurance programs covering health and safety, unemployment, the aged, and widows. The literacy rate is high, and Denmark has made significant contributions to science, literature, and the arts.

ECONOMY AND THE LAND. Despite limited natural resources, Denmark has a diversified economy. Agriculture contributes to trade, and dairy products, pork, and bacon are important commodities. Postwar expansion focused on industry, and the country now imports the raw materials it lacks and exports finished products. The North Sea is the site of oil and natural gas deposits. Most of Denmark's terrain is rolling,

DENMARK
Major Urban Area
Railroad
+ Spot Elevation or Depth
National capitals are underlined
City type size indicates relative importance

Meters	Feet
1000	3281
500	1640
200	656
0	0
200	656
2000	6562

Scale 1:2,426,000

Denmark Map Index

	Lat.	Long.		Lat.	Long.		Lat.	Long.		Lat.	Long.
Åbenrå	55°02'N	9°26'E	Gudena	56°29'N	10°13'E	Little Belt, The	55°20'N	9°45'E	Sjællands Point	55°58'N	11°22'E
Ærø	54°53'N	10°20'E	Haderslev	55°15'N	9°30'E	Lolland	54°46'N	11°30'E	Skagen	57°44'N	10°36'E
Ålborg	57°03'N	9°56'E	Helsingør	56°02'N	12°37'E	Middelfart	55°30'N	9°45'E	Skagerrak	57°45'N	9°00'E
Ålborg Bay	56°45'N	10°30'E	Herning	56°08'N	8°59'E	Møn	55°00'N	12°20'E	Skive	56°34'N	9°02'E
Als	54°59'N	9°55'E	Hillerød	55°56'N	12°19'E	Mors	56°50'N	8°45'E	Slagelse	55°24'N	11°22'E
Amager	55°37'N	12°37'E	Hjørring	57°28'N	9°59'E	Næstved	55°14'N	11°46'E	Smålands Sound	55°05'N	11°20'E
Århus	56°09'N	10°13'E	Holstebro	56°21'N	8°38'E	Nakskov	54°50'N	11°09'E	Sønderborg	54°55'N	9°47'E
Birkerød	55°50'N	12°26'E	Horsens	55°52'N	9°52'E	Nørresundby	57°04'N	9°55'E	Stevns Bluff	55°18'N	12°27'E
Bornholm	55°10'N	15°00'E	Hørsholm	55°53'N	12°30'E	Nyborg	55°19'N	10°48'E	Storå	56°19'N	8°19'E
Brønderslev	57°16'N	9°58'E	Ise Bay	52°30'N	10°33'E	Nykøbing	54°46'N	11°53'E	Struer	56°29'N	8°37'E
Copenhagen	55°40'N	12°35'E	Jutland	56°00'N	9°15'E	Nykøbing	56°48'N	8°52'E	Svendborg	55°03'N	10°37'E
Esbjerg	55°28'N	8°27'E	Kalundborg	55°41'N	11°06'E	Odense	55°24'N	10°23'E	Tåsinge	55°00'N	10°36'E
Fakse Bay	55°10'N	12°15'E	Kattegat	57°00'N	11°00'E	Øresund	55°50'N	12°40'E	Thisted	56°57'N	8°42'E
Falster	54°48'N	11°58'E	Køge	55°27'N	12°11'E	Randers	56°28'N	10°03'E	Varde	55°38'N	8°29'E
Frederica	55°35'N	9°46'E	Køge Bay	55°30'N	12°20'E	Ringkøbing Bay	56°00'N	8°15'E	Vejle	55°42'N	9°32'E
Frederikshavn	57°26'N	10°32'E	Kolding	55°31'N	9°29'E	Ringsted	55°27'N	11°49'E	Viborg	56°26'N	9°24'E
Frederikssund	55°50'N	12°04'E	Korsør	55°20'N	11°09'E	Rønne	55°06'N	14°42'E	Vordingborg	55°01'N	11°55'E
Fyn	55°20'N	10°20'E	Læsø	57°16'N	11°01'E	Roskilde	55°39'N	12°05'E	Yding Skovhøj	56°00'N	9°48'E
Great Belt, The	55°30'N	11°00'E	Langeland	54°50'N	10°50'E	Samsø	55°52'N	10°37'E	Zealand	55°30'N	11°45'E
Grenå	56°25'N	10°53'E	Lim Bay	56°55'N	9°10'E	Silkeborg	56°10'N	9°34'E			

Places and Possessions of Denmark

Entity	Status	Area	Population	Capital / Population
Faeroe Islands (North Atlantic)	Part of Danish realm	540 mi² (1,399 km²)	45,000	Tórshaun / 14,443
Greenland (North Atlantic island)	Part of Danish realm	840,004 mi² (2,175, 600 km²)	53,000	Godthåb / 9,717

with hills covering much of the peninsula and the nearby islands. Coastal regions are marked by fjords and sandy beaches, especially in the west. The climate is temperate, with North Sea winds moderating temperatures.

HISTORY AND POLITICS. By the first century access to the sea had brought contact with other civilizations and led to the Viking era, lasting from the ninth to eleventh centuries and resulting in temporary Danish rule of England. In the fourteenth century, Sweden, Norway, Finland, Iceland, the Faeroe Islands, and Greenland were united under Danish rule. Sweden and Finland withdrew from the union in the 1500s, and Den-

mark lost Norway to Sweden in 1814. A constitutional monarchy was instituted in 1849. Late nineteenth-century social reform, reflected in a new constitution in 1915, laid the groundwork for Denmark's current welfare state. The country remained neutral during World War I. Iceland gained independence following the war but maintained its union with Denmark until 1944. Despite declared neutrality during World War II, Denmark was invaded by Germany in 1940 and occupied until 1945. Compromise and gradual change characterize Danish politics, and foreign policy emphasizes relations with developing nations and peaceful solutions to international problems. ■

DJIBOUTI

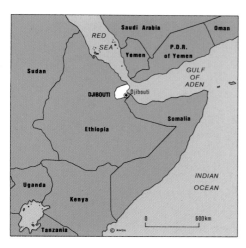

OFFICIAL NAME Republic of
Djibouti

PEOPLE
Population 360,000.
Density 41/mi² (16/km²).
Urban 74%.
Capital Djibouti, 120,000.
Ethnic groups Somali Issa 60%, Afar 35%.
Languages French, Somali, Afar, Arabic.
Religions Muslim 94%, Christian 6%.
Literacy 20%.

POLITICS
Government Republic.
Parties People's Progress Assembly.
Suffrage Universal adult.
Memberships AL, OAU, UN.
Subdivisions 5 districts.

ECONOMY
GDP $116,000,000.

Per capita $400.
Monetary unit Franc.
Trade partners France, U.K., Japan, Ethiopia.
Exports Hides and skins, coffee.
Imports Machinery, food, transportation equipment,
textiles.

LAND
Description Eastern Africa.
Area 8,880 mi² (23,000 km²).
Highest point Moussa Ali, 6,768 ft (2,063 m).
Lowest point Lake Assal, 509 ft (155 m) below sea
level.

PEOPLE. Characterized by strong cultural unity,
Islam, and ethnic ties to Somalia, Somali Issas
compose Djibouti's majority. Afars, who make
up the other main group, are also mostly Muslim
and are linked ethnically with Ethiopia. Rivalry
between the two groups has marked the nation's
history. Because of unproductive land, the population is concentrated in the city of Djibouti.

ECONOMY AND THE LAND. Traditional nomadic herding continues as a way of life for
many Djiboutians, despite heat, aridity, and limited grazing area. Several assets promote Djibouti
as a port and trade center: a strategic position on
the Gulf of Aden, an improved harbor, and a
railway linking the city of Djibouti with Addis
Ababa in Ethiopia. Marked by mountains that
divide a coastal plain from a plateau region, the
terrain is mostly desert. The climate is extremely
hot and dry.

HISTORY AND POLITICS. In the ninth century
Arab missionaries introduced Islam to the population, and by the 1800s a pattern of conflict
between the Issas and Afars had developed. The
French purchased the port of Obcock from Afar
sultans in 1862, and their territorial control ex-

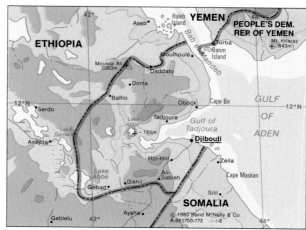

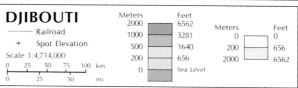

Djibouti Map Index

	Lat.	Long.		Lat.	Long.
Abbé, Lake	11°09'N	41°47'E	Mandeb, Bab el-	12°40'N	43°20'E
Assal, Lake	11°41'N	42°25'E	Moussa Ali	12°28'N	42°24'E
Djibouti	11°36'N	43°09'E	Tadjoura, Gulf of	11°42'N	43°00'E

panded until the region became French Somaliland. The goal of the pro-independence Issas
was defeated in elections in 1958 and 1967, when
the majority voted for continued French control.
The name was changed to the French Territory of
Afars and Issas in 1967, and as the Issa population grew, so did demands for independence. A
1977 referendum resulted in the independent Republic of Djibouti. ■

DOMINICA

OFFICIAL NAME
Commonwealth of
Dominica

PEOPLE
Population 74,000.
Density 255/mi² (98/km²).
Urban 27%.

Capital Roseau, 8,346.
Ethnic groups Black, Carib Indian.
Languages English, French.
Religions Roman Catholic 80%, Anglican, Methodist.
Life expectancy 59 female, 57 male.
Literacy 94%.

POLITICS
Government Republic.
Parties Freedom, Labor, United Labor.
Suffrage Universal, over 18.
Memberships CW, OAS, UN.
Subdivisions 10 parishes.

ECONOMY
GNP $56,400,000.
Per capita $883.
Monetary unit East Caribbean dollar.
Trade partners U.S., U.K., other Western European
countries, Caribbean countries.
Exports Bananas, coconuts, lime juice and oil.

Imports Machinery, food, manufactured goods,
fuels.

LAND
Description Caribbean island.
Area 290 mi² (752 km²).
Highest point Morne Diablotin, 4,747 ft (1,447 m).
Lowest point Sea level.

PEOPLE. Dominica's population consists of descendants of black Africans brought to the island
as slaves and Carib Indians descended from early
inhabitants. The Carib population is concentrated
in the northeastern part of the island, and this
community maintains its own customs and life-
style under a tribal chief. This position, however,
is mainly ceremonial, as the chief wields no political power on the island. English is widely spoken in urban areas, but villagers, who compose a
majority, speak mainly a French-African blend,
resulting from French rule and the importation
of Africans.

ECONOMY AND THE LAND. Volcanic soils
make Dominica's land suitable for farming, but
the mountainous and densely forested terrain
limits cultivation. Nonetheless, the traditional
practice of agriculture continues as the island's
economic mainstay. In 1979 and 1980 Dominica's
crop was wiped out by hurricanes, which also
destroyed roads and communication lines. In addition to agriculture, many Dominicans are employed in construction and road building, and
forestry and fishing offer potential for expansion.
Tourists are drawn to the island by its tropical
climate and scenic landscape.

HISTORY AND POLITICS. In the fourteenth century Caribs conquered the Arawak Indians who
originally inhabited the island. Dominica received its name in 1493 when Christopher Co-

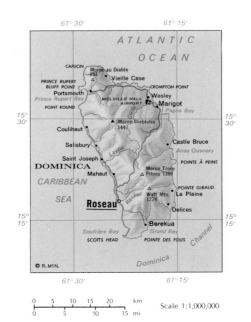

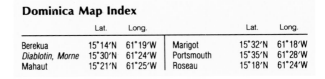

Dominica Map Index

	Lat.	Long.		Lat.	Long.
Berekua	15°14'N	61°19'W	Marigot	15°32'N	61°18'W
Diablotin, Morne	15°30'N	61°24'W	Portsmouth	15°35'N	61°28'W
Mahaut	15°21'N	61°25'W	Roseau	15°18'N	61°24'W

lumbus arrived on a Sunday, *dominica*, but Carib
hostilities and the mountainous terrain kept the
Spanish from settling here. After unsuccessful
British attempts at control, the French established a de facto colony, despite a British-French
agreement not to colonize. A period of French
and British rivalry followed, and the British
gained possession in 1783. Independence was
gained in 1978. ■

DOMINICAN REPUBLIC

OFFICIAL NAME Dominican
Republic

PEOPLE
Population 6,205,000.
Density 332/mi² (128/km²).
Urban 52%.
Capital Santo Domingo, 1,313,172.
Ethnic groups Mixed 73%, white 16%, black 11%.
Languages Spanish.
Religions Roman Catholic 95%.
Life expectancy 64 female, 60 male.
Literacy 68%.

POLITICS
Government Republic.
Parties Liberation, Reformist, Revolutionary.
Suffrage Universal, over 18 or married.
Memberships OAS, UN.
Subdivisions 26 provinces, 1 national district.

ECONOMY
GNP $7,600,000,000.
Per capita $1,400.
Monetary unit Peso.
Trade partners U.S., Puerto Rico, Venezuela.

Exports Sugar, nickel, coffee, tobacco.
Imports Food, petroleum, raw materials, machinery.

LAND
Description Caribbean island (eastern Hispaniola
Island).
Area 18,704 mi² (48,442 km²).
Highest point Duarte Pk., 10,417 ft (3,175 m).
Lowest point Lake Enriquillo, 131 ft (40 m) below sea
level.

PEOPLE. Occupying eastern Hispaniola Island,
the Dominican Republic borders Haiti and has a
population of mixed ancestry. Haitians, other
blacks, Spaniards, and European Jews compose
minority groups. Population growth has resulted
in unemployment and made it difficult for the
government to meet food and service needs.

ECONOMY AND THE LAND. Agriculture remains important, with sugar a main component
of trade, and sugar refining a major manufacturing activity. Farmland is limited, however, by a
northwest-to-southeast mountain range and an
arid region west of the range. Mineral exploitation, especially of nickel, contributes to trade,
and a number of American firms have subsidiar-
ies here. Tourism is growing, aided by the warm,
tropical climate.

HISTORY AND POLITICS. In 1492 Christopher
Columbus arrived at Hispaniola Island. Spanish
colonists followed, and the Indian population
was virtually wiped out, although some inter-
mingling with the Spanish probably occurred. In
1697 the western region of the island, which
would become Haiti, was ceded to France. The
entire island came under Haitian control as the
Republic of Haiti in 1822, and an 1844 revolution
established the independent Dominican Republic. Since independence the country has experienced periods of instability, evidenced by military coups and rule, U.S. military intervention
and occupation, and human rights abuses. United States troops were last sent in 1965. Various
presidents have been installed since 1966. ■

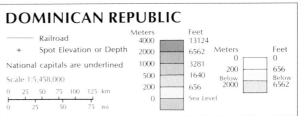

DOMINICAN REPUBLIC

	Meters	Feet
——— Railroad	4000	13124
+ Spot Elevation or Depth	2000	6562
National capitals are underlined	1000	3281
Scale 1:5,458,000	500	1640
0 25 50 75 100 125 km	200	656
0 25 50 75 mi	0	Sea Level

Meters	Feet
0	0
200	656
Below 2000	Below 6562

Dominican Republic Map Index

	Lat.	Long.		Lat.	Long.
Azua	18°27′N	70°44′W	Pedernales	18°02′N	71°45′W
Bandera			Puerto Plata	19°48′N	70°41′W
Mountain	18°49′N	70°37′W	Sabana de la		
Baní	18°17′N	70°20′W	Mar	19°04′N	69°23′W
Bonao	18°56′N	70°25′W	Samaná	19°13′N	69°19′W
Central Cordillera	18°45′N	70°30′W	*Samaná Bay*	19°10′N	69°25′W
Cotuí	19°03′N	70°09′W	Sánchez	19°14′N	69°36′W
Dajabón	19°33′N	71°42′W	San Cristóbal	18°25′N	70°06′W
Duarte Peak	19°02′N	70°59′W	San Francisco de		
Elías Piña	18°53′N	71°42′W	Macorís	19°18′N	70°15′W
El Seibo	18°46′N	69°02′W	San José de		
Enriquillo	17°54′N	71°14′W	Ocoa	18°33′N	70°30′W
Enriquillo, Lake	18°27′N	71°39′W	San Juan	18°40′N	71°05′W
Hato Mayor	18°46′N	69°15′W	San Pedro de		
Higüey	18°37′N	68°42′W	Macorís	18°27′N	69°18′W
La Romana	18°25′N	68°58′W	Santiago de los		
La Vega	19°13′N	70°31′W	Caballeros	19°27′N	70°42′W
Manzanillo Bay	19°45′N	71°46′W	Santo Domingo	18°28′N	69°54′W
Miches	18°59′N	69°03′W	Valverde	19°34′N	71°05′W
Monte Cristi	19°52′N	71°39′W	Vicente Noble	18°23′N	71°11′W
Nagua	19°23′N	69°50′W	Villa Vázquez	19°45′N	71°27′W
Oviedo	17°47′N	71°22′W	Yaque del Norte	19°51′N	71°41′W
Palenque, Point	18°14′N	70°09′W	Yaque del Sur	18°17′N	71°06′W

ECUADOR

Shown here is Quito, the capital
of Ecuador, a city known for its
spectacular setting and cultural,
educational, and political importance. Quito is situated in the
sierra, a highlands region that
runs north and south through
the center of the country. The
town lies on a fertile plateau beneath the Pichincha volcano, not
far from the equator and about
180 miles (290 kilometers) from
the Pacific Coast. Despite
Quito's proximity to the equator, its climate is generally
balmy but comfortable because
of the high elevation—9,300
feet (2,835 meters) above sea
level.

Quito has a long history, extending from pre-Columbian
times to the present. The Quito
Indians first settled the area,
and in 1487 they were overcome by the Incas, who established the site as the capital of
their Quito kingdom. The Inca
capital was in turn captured by
the Spanish in 1534. Ecuador's
independence was won in a battle led by Antonio José de Sucre
at the Pichincha volcano in
1822.

ECUADOR

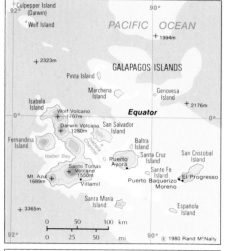

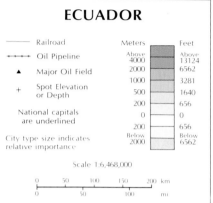

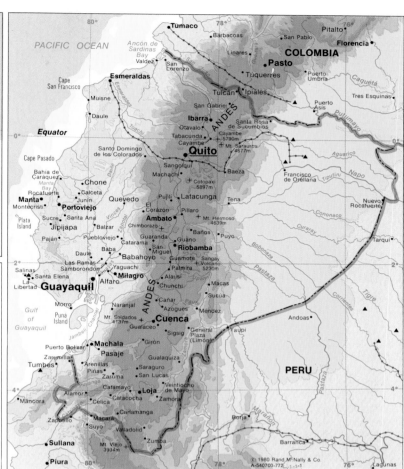

OFFICIAL NAME Republic of
Ecuador

PEOPLE

Population 9,235,000.
Density 84/mi² (33/km²).
Urban 44%.
Capital Quito, 918,884.
Ethnic groups Mestizo 55%, Indian 25%, Spanish 10%,
African 10%.
Languages Spanish, Quechua.
Religions Roman Catholic 95%.
Life expectancy 64 female, 60 male.
Literacy 84%.

POLITICS

Government Republic.
Parties Concentration of Popular Forces, Democratic
Left, Popular Democracy, Social Christian.
Suffrage Universal, over 18.
Memberships OAS, OPEC, UN.
Subdivisions 20 provinces.

ECONOMY

GNP $13,300,000,000.
Per capita $1,507.
Monetary unit Sucre.
Trade partners U.S., Western European countries,
Japan.
Exports Petroleum, bananas, coffee, cocoa, fish
products.
Imports Machinery, raw materials, transportation
equipment, chemical products.

LAND

Description Western South America.
Area 109,483 mi² (283,561 km²).
Highest point Chimborazo, 20,702 ft (6,310 m).
Lowest point Sea level.

PEOPLE. Ecuador's ethnicity was established by
an indigenous Indian population and Spanish
colonists. Minority whites, of Spanish or other
European descent, live mainly in urban areas or
operate large farms called haciendas. Of mixed
Spanish-Indian blood, mestizos compose about
half the population, although economic and political power is concentrated among whites. Minority Indians speak Quechua or other Indian
languages and maintain traditional customs in
Andean villages or nomadic jungle tribes. Blacks
are concentrated on the northern coastal plain.
Recent trends show a movement from the interi-
or highlands to the fertile coastal plain and a
rural-to-urban shift. A history of economic in-
equality has produced a literary and artistic tradition that has focused on social reform.

ECONOMY AND THE LAND. Despite an oil
boom in the 1970s, Ecuador remains underdeveloped. Minor oil production began in 1911, but
since a 1967 petroleum discovery in the *oriente,* a
jungle region east of the Andes, Ecuador has
become an oil exporter and a member of the
Organization of Petroleum Exporting Countries
(OPEC). Agriculture remains important for much
of the population, although primitive, thus inefficient, practices continue among the poor. Rich

soils of the *costa,* extending from the Pacific to
the Andes, support most of the export crops.
Forestry and fishing have growth potential, and
the waters around the Galapagos Islands are rich
in tuna. Manufacturing is mainly devoted to
meeting domestic needs. The oriente and costa
lie on either side of the sierra, a region of highland plateaus between the two Andean chains.
Varied altitudes result in a climate ranging from
tropical in the lowlands to temperate in the plateaus and cold in the high mountains. A variety
of wildlife inhabits the Galapagos Islands, five
large and nine small islands about 600 miles (966
kilometers) off Ecuador's coast in the Pacific
Ocean.

HISTORY AND POLITICS. In the fifteenth century Incas conquered and subsequently united the

area's various tribes. In the 1500s the Spanish
gained control, using Indians and African slaves
to work the plantations. Weakened by the Napoleonic Wars, Spain lost control of Ecuador in
1822, and Simón Bolívar united the independent
state with the Republic of Greater Colombia. Ecuador left the union as a separate republic in
1830, and subsequent years saw instability and
rule by presidents, dictators, and juntas. From
1925 to 1948 no leader was able to complete a
full term in office. A new constitution was established in 1978, and a 1979 election installed a
president who died in a plane crash in 1981.
Subsequent elections have been marked by divisions between the left and right, and power rivalries are complicated by numerous parties and
economic problems. ■

Ecuador Map Index

	Lat.	Long.		Lat.	Long.		Lat.	Long.		Lat.	Long.
Alamor	4°02′S	80°02′W	Esmeraldas	0°59′N	79°42′W	Muisne	0°36′N	80°02′W	San Lucas	3°45′S	79°15′W
Alausí	2°12′S	78°50′W	*Esmeraldas*	0°58′N	79°38′W	*Napo*	1°00′S	75°10′W	San Miguel	1°44′S	79°01′W
Alfaro	2°12′S	79°50′W	Francisco de			Naranjal	2°42′S	79°37′W	*San Salvador*		
Ambato	1°15′S	78°37′W	Orellana	0°28′S	76°58′W	Nuevo Rocafuerte	0°56′S	75°24′W	*Island*	0°14′S	90°45′W
Ancón de			*Galapagos*			Otavalo	0°14′N	78°16′W	Santa Ana	1°13′S	80°23′W
Sardinas Bay	1°30′N	79°00′W	*Islands*	0°30′S	90°30′W	Pajań	1°34′S	80°25′W	*Santa Cruz*		
Andes	2°30′S	79°00′W	General Plaza			Palmira	2°05′S	78°43′W	*Island*	0°38′S	90°23′W
Arenillas	3°33′S	80°04′W	(Limón)	2°58′S	78°25′W	*Pasado, Cape*	0°22′N	80°30′W	Santa Elena	2°14′S	80°51′W
Azogues	2°44′S	78°50′W	Girón	3°10′S	79°08′W	Pasaje	3°20′S	79°49′W	Santa Rosa de		
Baba	1°47′S	79°40′W	Gualaceo	2°54′S	78°47′W	*Pastaza*	2°34′S	76°40′W	Sucumbios	0°22′N	77°10′W
Babahoyo	1°49′S	79°31′W	Gualaquiza	3°24′S	78°33′W	Pillaro	1°10′S	78°32′W	Santo Domingo		
Baeza	0°27′S	77°53′W	Guamote	1°56′S	78°43′W	Piñas	3°42′S	79°42′W	de los		
Bahía de			Guano	1°35′S	78°38′W	Portoviejo	1°03′S	80°27′W	Colorados	0°15′S	79°09′W
Caráquez	0°36′S	80°25′W	Guaranda	1°36′S	79°00′W	Puebloviejo	1°34′S	79°30′W	Saraguro	3°36′S	79°13′W
Balzar	1°22′S	79°54′W	Guayaquil	2°10′S	79°50′W	Puerto Ayora	0°44′S	90°19′W	Sigsig	3°01′S	78°45′W
Baños	1°24′S	78°25′W	*Guayaquil, Gulf*			Puerto Baquerizo			Sucre	1°16′S	80°26′W
Calceta	0°51′S	80°10′W	*of*	3°00′S	80°30′W	Moreno	0°54′S	89°36′W	Sucúa	2°28′S	78°10′W
Cañar	2°33′S	78°56′W	*Guayas*	2°36′S	79°52′W	Pujili	0°57′S	78°41′W	Tabacunda	0°03′N	78°12′W
Carlamanga	4°20′S	79°35′W	Ibarra	0°21′N	78°07′W	*Puná Island*	2°50′S	80°08′W	Tena	0°59′S	77°49′W
Catacocha	4°04′S	79°38′W	*Isabela Island*	0°30′S	91°06′W	*Putumayo*	0°08′S	75°15′W	Tulcán	0°48′N	77°43′W
Catamayo	3°59′S	79°21′W	*Jambeli Channel*	3°00′S	80°00′W	Puyo	1°28′S	77°59′W	Valdez	1°15′N	79°00′W
Catarama	1°35′S	79°28′W	Jipijapa	1°20′S	80°35′W	Quevedo	1°02′S	79°29′W	Valladolid	4°33′S	79°08′W
Cayambe	0°03′N	78°08′W	Junin	0°56′S	80°13′W	Quito	0°13′S	78°30′W	Veintiocho de		
Cayambe	0°02′N	77°59′W	Las Ramas	1°50′S	79°48′W	Riobamba	1°40′S	78°38′W	Mayo	3°50′S	78°52′W
Celica	4°07′S	79°59′W	Latacunga	0°56′S	78°37′W	Rocafuerte	0°55′S	80°28′W	Villamil	0°56′S	91°01′W
Chimborazo	1°28′S	78°48′W	Loja	4°00′S	79°13′W	Salinas	2°13′S	80°58′W	*Wolf Volcano*	0°02′N	91°20′W
Chone	0°41′S	80°06′W	Macará	4°23′S	79°57′W	Samborondón	1°57′S	79°44′W	Yaguachi	2°07′S	79°41′W
Chunchi	2°17′S	78°55′W	Macas	2°19′S	78°07′W	*San Cristobal*			Yaupi	2°59′S	77°50′W
Cotopaxi	0°40′S	78°26′W	Machachi	0°30′S	78°34′W	*Island*	0°50′S	89°26′W	Zamora	4°04′S	78°58′W
Cuenca	2°53′S	78°59′W	Machala	3°16′S	79°58′W	*San Francisco,*			Zapotillo	4°25′S	80°31′W
Daule	0°24′N	80°00′W	Manta	0°57′S	80°44′W	*Cape*	0°40′N	80°05′W	Zaruma	3°41′S	79°37′W
Daule	1°50′S	79°56′W	Méndez	2°43′S	78°19′W	San Gabriel	0°36′N	77°49′W	Zumba	4°52′S	79°09′W
Daule	2°10′S	79°52′W	Milagro	2°07′S	79°36′W	*Sangay Volcano*	2°00′S	78°20′W			
El Corázon	1°12′S	79°06′W	Montecristi	1°03′S	80°40′W	Sangolquí	0°19′S	78°27′W			
El Progreso	0°54′S	89°33′W	Morro	2°39′S	80°19′W	San Lorenzo	1°17′N	78°50′W			

EGYPT

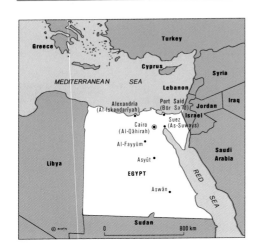

OFFICIAL NAME Arab
Republic of Egypt

PEOPLE
Population 47,755,000.
Density 124/mi² (48/km²).
Urban 44%.
Capital Cairo, 5,278,000.
Ethnic groups Egyptian, Bedouin, Nubian.
Languages Arabic.
Religions Muslim 94%, Coptic Christian
and others 6%.
Life expectancy 59 female, 55 male.
Literacy 40%.

POLITICS
Government Socialist republic.
Parties National Democratic, Socialist Labor,
Socialist Liberal.
Suffrage Universal, over 18.
Memberships OAU, UN.
Subdivisions 26 governorates.

ECONOMY
GNP $30,800,000,000.
Per capita $690.
Monetary unit Pound.
Trade partners U.S., Western European countries,
Japan.
Exports Petroleum, cotton, cotton yarn and fabric.
Imports Food, machinery, transportation
equipment, fertilizer.

LAND
Description Northeastern Africa.
Area 386,643 mi² (1,001,400 km²).
Highest point Mt. Katrina, 8,668 ft (2,642 m).
Lowest point Qattara Depression, 436 ft (133 m)
below sea level.

PEOPLE. Egypt's population is relatively homogeneous, and Egyptians compose the largest
group. Descended from ancient Nile Valley inhabitants, Egyptians have intermixed somewhat
with Mediterranean and Asiatic peoples in the
north and with black Africans in the south. Minorities include Bedouins, Arabic-speaking desert
nomads; Nubians, black descendants of migrants
from the Sudan; and Copts, a Christian group.
Islam, the major religion, is also a cultural force,
and many Christians as well as Muslims follow
Islamic life-styles.

ECONOMY AND THE LAND. Egypt's economy
has suffered from wars, shifting alliances, and
limited natural resources. Government-sponsored
expansion and reform in the 1950s concentrated
on manufacturing, and most industry was nationalized during the 1960s. Agriculture, centered
in the Nile Valley, remains an economic mainstay. Petroleum, found mainly in the Gulf of
Suez, will most likely continue its economic role,
and tourism is a contributor as well. Much of
Egypt is desert, with hills and mountains in the
east and along the Nile River. The climate is
warm and dry.

HISTORY AND POLITICS. Egypt's recorded history began when King Menes united the region

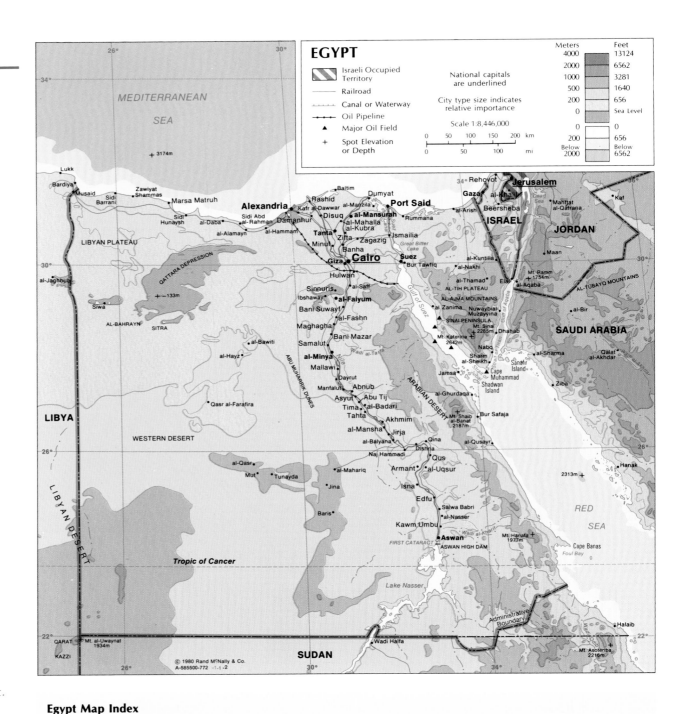

Egypt Map Index

	Lat.	Long.		Lat.	Long.		Lat.	Long.		Lat.	Long.
Abnub	27°16′N	31°09′E	Banas, Cape	23°54′N	35°48′E	Kawn Umbu	24°28′N	32°57′E	Shaib al-Banat,		
Abu Tij	27°02′N	31°19′E	Banha	30°28′N	31°11′E	Libyan Desert	24°00′N	25°00′E	Mount	26°59′N	33°29′E
Akhmim	26°34′N	31°44′E	Bani Mazar	28°30′N	30°48′E	Maghagha	28°39′N	30°50′E	Sinai, Mount	28°32′N	33°59′E
al-Badari	26°59′N	31°25′E	Bani Suwayf	29°05′N	31°05′E	Mallawi	27°44′N	30°50′E	Sinai Peninsula	29°30′N	34°00′E
Alexandria	31°12′N	29°54′E	Cairo	30°03′N	31°15′E	Marsa Matruh	31°21′N	27°14′E	Sinnuris	29°25′N	30°52′E
al-Faiyum	29°19′N	30°50′E	Damanhur	31°02′N	30°28′E	Minuf	30°28′N	30°56′E	Suez	29°58′N	32°33′E
al-Fashn	28°49′N	30°54′E	Disuq	31°08′N	30°39′E	Muhammad,			Suez, Gulf of	29°00′N	32°50′E
al-Mahalla al-			Dumyat	31°25′N	31°48′E	Cape	27°44′N	34°15′E	Suez Canal	29°55′N	32°33′E
Kubra	30°58′N	31°10′E	Edfu	24°58′N	32°52′E	Nasser, Lake	22°40′N	32°00′E	Tahta	26°46′N	31°30′E
al-Mansha	26°28′N	31°48′E	First Cataract	24°01′N	32°52′E	Nile	30°10′N	31°06′E	Tanta	30°47′N	31°00′E
al-Mansurah	31°03′N	31°23′E	Foul Bay	23°30′N	35°39′E	Port Said	31°16′N	32°18′E	Tima	26°54′N	31°26′E
al-Minya	28°06′N	30°45′E	Giza	30°01′N	31°13′E	Qattara			Tiran, Strait of	27°58′N	34°28′E
al-Uqsur	25°41′N	32°39′E	Hulwan	29°51′N	31°20′E	Depression	30°00′N	27°30′E	Uwaynat, Jabal		
Aqaba, Gulf of	29°00′N	34°40′E	Ismailia	30°35′N	32°16′E	Qus	25°55′N	32°45′E	al-	21°54′N	24°58′E
Arabian Desert	28°00′N	32°00′E	Isna	25°18′N	32°33′E	Rashid	31°24′N	30°25′E	Western Desert	27°00′N	27°00′E
Armant	25°37′N	32°32′E	Jirja	26°20′N	31°53′E	Red Sea	25°00′N	36°00′E	Zagazig	30°35′N	31°31′E
Aswan	24°05′N	32°53′E	Jubal, Strait of	27°40′N	33°55′E	Samalut	28°18′N	30°42′E			
Asyut	27°11′N	31°11′E	Katerina, Mount	28°31′N	33°57′E						

in about 3100 B.C., beginning a series of Egyptian
dynasties. Art and architecture flourished during
the Age of the Pyramids, from 2700 to 2200 B.C.
In time native dynasties gave way to foreign conquerors, including Alexander the Great in the
fourth century B.C. The Coptic Christian church
emerged between the fourth and sixth centuries
A.D., but in the 600s Arabs conquered the area
and established Islam as the main religion. Ruling parties changed frequently, and in 1517 the
Ottoman Turks added Egypt to their empire.
Upon completion of the strategically important
Suez Canal in 1869, foreign interest in Egypt
increased. In 1875 Egypt sold its share of the
canal to Britain, and a rebellion against foreign
intervention ended with British occupation in
1882. Turkey sided with Germany in World War
I, and the United Kingdom made Egypt a British
protectorate in 1914. The country became an independent monarchy in 1922, but the British

presence remained. In 1945 Egypt and six other
nations formed the Arab League, and the founding of Israel in 1948 initiated an era of Arab-
Israeli hostilities, including periodic warfare in
which Egypt often had a major role. Dissatisfaction over dealings with Israel and continued British occupation of the Suez Canal led to the overthrow of the king, and Egypt became a republic
in 1953. Following a power struggle, Gamal
Abdel Nasser was elected president in 1956, and
the British agreed to remove their troops. Upon
the death of Nasser in 1970, Vice-President
Anwar Sadat came to power. Negotiations between Egyptian president Sadat and Israeli prime
minister Menachem Begin began in 1977, and in
1979 the leaders signed a peace treaty ending
conflicts between Egypt and Israel. As a result,
Egypt was suspended from the Arab League. In
1981 President Sadat was assassinated. ■

EL SALVADOR

OFFICIAL NAME Republic of
El Salvador

PEOPLE
Population 4,905,000.
Density 604/mi² (233/km²).
Urban 39%.
Capital San Salvador, 397,100.
Ethnic groups Mestizo 89%, Indian 10%, white 1%.
Languages Spanish.
Religions Roman Catholic 97%.
Life expectancy 65 female, 62 male.
Literacy 65%.

POLITICS
Government Republic.
Parties Authentic Institutional, Christian Democratic,
National Republican Alliance.
Suffrage Universal, over 18.
Memberships OAS, UN.
Subdivisions 14 departments.

ECONOMY
GDP $3,600,000,000.
Per capita $700.
Monetary unit Colón.
Trade partners U.S., Central American countries,
Western European countries.
Exports Coffee, cotton, sugar.
Imports Machinery, petroleum, fertilizer, motor
vehicles, food.

LAND
Description Central America.
Area 8,124 mi² (21,041 km²).
Highest point Mt. El Pital, 8,957 ft (2,730 m).
Lowest point Sea level.

PEOPLE. Most Salvadorans are Spanish-
speaking mestizos, and an Indian minority is
mainly descended from the Pipil. El Salvador,
the smallest Central American country in area,
has the highest population density in mainland
Latin America.

ECONOMY AND THE LAND. El Salvador's
economy has been plagued by political instability
and unemployment. Agriculture remains the economic mainstay, and nearly all arable land has
been cultivated. East-to-west mountain ranges divide El Salvador into a southern coastal region,
central valleys and plateaus, and northern mountains. The climate is subtropical.

HISTORY AND POLITICS. Maya and Pipil pre-
dominated prior to the 1500s, when Spaniards
conquered the region. In 1821 the Spanish-
controlled Central American colonies declared independence, and in 1823 they united as the Federation of Central America. By 1838 the federation was in a state of collapse, and El Salvador
became independent. A dictatorship from 1931
to 1944 was followed by various military rulers.

Discontent increased throughout the seventies until a civil war erupted, accompanied
by right-wing death squads and human rights
abuses by the government. Guerrilla activity continues today. ■

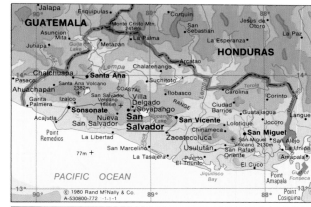

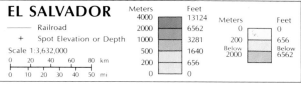

El Salvador Map Index

	Lat.	Long.		Lat.	Long.
Fonseca, Gulf of	13°10′N	87°40′W	San Miguel	13°29′N	88°11′W
Goascoran	13°36′N	87°45′W	San Salvador	13°42′N	89°12′W
Guija Lake	14°17′N	89°31′W	Santa Ana	13°59′N	89°34′W
Ilopango Lake	13°40′N	89°03′W	San Vicente	13°38′N	88°48′W
Jocoro	13°37′N	88°01′W	Sonsonate	13°43′N	89°44′W
La Unión	13°20′N	87°51′W	Soyapango	13°42′N	89°09′W
Lempa	13°14′N	88°49′W	Usulután	13°21′N	88°27′W
Monte Cristo			Villa Delgado	13°43′N	89°10′W
Mountain	14°25′N	89°21′W	Zacatecoluca	13°30′N	88°52′W
Nueva San					
Salvador	13°41′N	89°17′W			

EQUATORIAL GUINEA

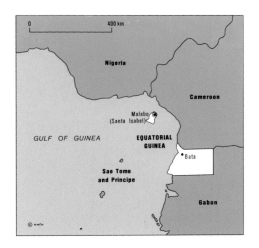

OFFICIAL NAME Republic of
Equatorial Guinea

PEOPLE
Population 280,000.
Density 26/mi² (10/km²).
Urban 54%.
Capital Malabo, Bioko I., 17,500.
Ethnic groups Fang 80%, Bubi 15%.
Languages Spanish, indigenous, English.
Religions Roman Catholic 83%, Protestant, animist.
Life expectancy 48 female, 44 male.
Literacy 20%.

POLITICS
Government Republic.
Parties None (suspended).
Suffrage Universal adult.
Memberships OAU, UN.
Subdivisions 7 provinces.

ECONOMY
GNP $100,000,000.
Per capita $417.
Monetary unit Ekuele.
Trade partners Spain.
Exports Cocoa, wood, coffee.
Imports Food, petroleum, machinery, textiles.

LAND
Description Central Africa.
Area 10,831 mi² (28,051 km²).
Highest point Santa Isabel Pk., Bioko I., 9,868 ft
(3,008 m).
Lowest point Sea level.

PEOPLE. Several ethnic groups inhabit Equatorial Guinea's five islands and the mainland region
of Río Muni. The Fang are concentrated in Río
Muni, but they also inhabit Bioko. Found mainly
on Bioko Island are the Bubi. Coastal groups
known as *playeros* live on both the mainland and
the small islands. The Fernandino are concentrated on Bioko. Equatorial Guinea is the only black
African state with Spanish as its official language.

ECONOMY AND THE LAND. Equatorial Guinea's economy is based on agriculture and forestry. Bioko is of volcanic origin, and Río Muni
consists of a coastal plain and interior hills. The
climate is tropical, with high temperatures and
humidity.

HISTORY AND POLITICS. Pygmies most likely
inhabited the Río Muni area prior to the thirteenth century, when mainland Bubi came to
Bioko. From the seventeenth to the nineteenth
centuries Bantu migrations brought the coastal
tribes and, lastly, the Fang. Portugal claimed
Bioko and part of the mainland in the 1400s,
then ceded them to Spain in 1778. From 1827 to

1843 British antislavery activities were based on
Bioko, which became the home of many former
slaves, the ancestors of the Fernandino population. In 1959 the area became the Spanish Territory of the Gulf of Guinea, and the name was
changed to Equatorial Guinea in 1963. Independence was achieved in 1968. ■

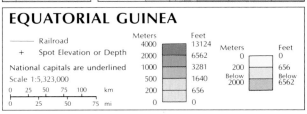

Equatorial Guinea Map Index

	Lat.	Long.		Lat.	Long.
Annobón Island	1°25′S	5°36′E	Malabo	3°45′N	8°47′E
Bata	1°51′N	9°45′E	Mbini	1°35′N	9°37′E
Bioko	3°30′N	8°40′E	San Carlos	3°27′N	8°33′E

ETHIOPIA

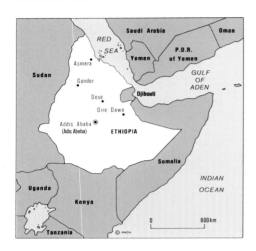

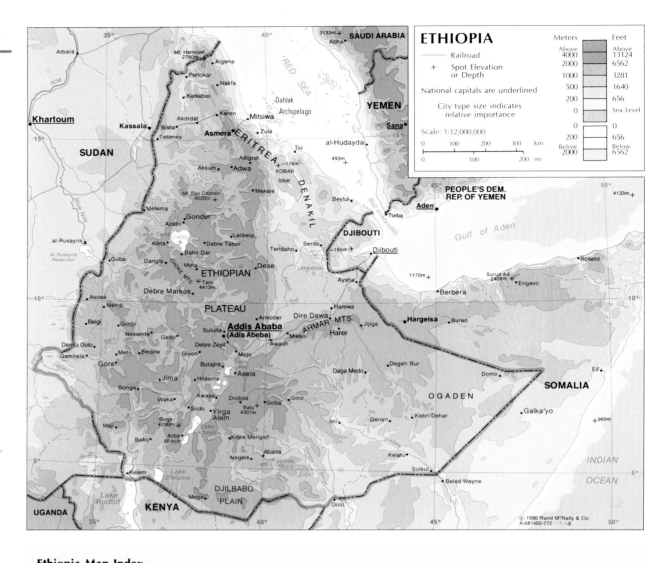

OFFICIAL NAME Ethiopia

PEOPLE
Population 34,050,000.
Density 72/mi² (28/km²).
Urban 14%.
Capital Addis Ababa, 1,408,068.
Ethnic groups Galla 40%, Amhara and Tigrai 32%, Sidamo 9%, Shankella 6%, Somali 6%.
Languages Amharic, Arabic, indigenous.
Religions Muslim 40–45%, Coptic Christian 35–40%, animist 15–20%.
Life expectancy 48 female, 45 male.
Literacy 15%.

POLITICS
Government Provisional military government.
Parties Workers'.
Suffrage Universal, over 21.
Memberships OAU, UN.
Subdivisions 14 provinces.

ECONOMY
GDP $4,800,000,000.
Per capita $141.
Monetary unit Birr.
Trade partners U.S.S.R., Italy, West Germany, Japan, U.S.
Exports Coffee, hides and skins.
Imports Petroleum, machinery, motor vehicles, chemicals.

LAND
Description Eastern Africa.
Area 472,434 mi² (1,223,600 km²).
Highest point Ras Dashen Mtn., 15,158 ft (4,620 m).
Lowest point Lake Asale, 381 ft (116 m) below sea level.

PEOPLE. Ethiopia is ethnically, linguistically, and religiously diverse, but the Galla and the Amhara predominate. The Galla include agricultural Muslims, Christians, and nomadic practitioners of traditional religions. Mainly Christian and also agricultural, the Amhara have dominated the country politically. In all, Ethiopia's boundaries encompass more than forty ethnic groups.

ECONOMY AND THE LAND. Not only has Ethiopia's agricultural economy been plagued by political instability, but existing problems of soil erosion and deforestation resulted in disaster when planting-season rains failed to fall in much of the country in 1982. A severe drought and famine resulted, and massive relief efforts could do little to prevent hundreds of thousands of deaths between 1983 and 1984. Despite the ongoing threat of drought and resulting famine, Ethiopia's soil continues as its most valuable resource. Subsistence farming remains a major activity, and much arable land is uncultivated, offering room for future growth. Mines produce gold, copper, and platinum, and there is potential for expansion here as well. A central plateau is split diagonally by the Great Rift Valley, with lowlands on the west and plains in the southeast. The climate is temperate on the plateau and hot in the lowlands.

Ethiopia Map Index

	Lat.	Long.		Lat.	Long.		Lat.	Long.		Lat.	Long.
Abaya, Lake	6°20′N	37°55′E	Batu	6°55′N	39°46′E	Dire Dawa	9°37′N	41°52′E	Omo	4°51′N	36°55′E
Addis Ababa			Blue Nile	11°12′N	35°00′E	Eritrea	15°20′N	39°00′E	Ras Dashen,		
(Adis Abeba)	9°00′N	38°50′E	Choke Mountains	11°00′N	37°30′E	Ethiopian Plateau	9°00′N	38°00′E	Mount	13°10′N	38°26′E
Adwa	14°10′N	38°55′E	Dahlak			Ganale Dorya	4°10′N	42°07′E	Red Sea	17°00′N	41°00′E
Ahmar Mountains	9°15′N	41°00′E	Archipelago	15°45′N	40°30′E	Gonder	12°40′N	37°30′E	Shebele	5°00′N	45°03′E
Akobo	7°48′N	33°03′E	Dawa	4°11′N	42°06′E	Kobar Sink	14°00′N	40°30′E	Stefanie, Lake	4°40′N	36°50′E
Asmera	15°20′N	38°53′E	Debre Markos	10°20′N	37°45′E	Mandeb, Bab el-	12°40′N	43°20′E	Talo	10°44′N	37°55′E
Awash	11°45′N	41°05′E	Denakil	12°25′N	40°30′E	Mitsiwa	15°38′N	39°28′E	Tana, Lake	12°00′N	37°20′E
Baro	8°26′N	33°13′E	Dese	11°05′N	39°41′E	Ogaden	7°00′N	46°00′E			

HISTORY AND POLITICS. Ethiopia's history is one of the oldest in the world. Its ethnic patterns were established by indigenous Cushites and Semite settlers, who probably arrived from Arabia about three thousand years ago. Christianity was introduced in the early fourth century. During the 1800s modern Ethiopia began to develop under Emperor Menelik II. Ras Tafari Makonnen became emperor in 1930, taking the name Haile Selassie. Italians invaded in the 1930s and occupied the country until 1941, when Haile Selassie returned to the throne. Discontent with the feudal society increased until Haile Selassie was ousted by the military in 1974. Reform programs and the change in leadership have done little to ease political tensions, which have sometimes erupted in governmental and civilian violence. Government troops continue their battle with separatists in Eritrea, a former Italian colony and autonomous province incorporated into Ethiopia in 1962, and Somali separatists are active as well. ■

Known in Ethiopia as the Abay, the Blue Nile River flows from Lake Tana, Ethiopia's largest lake, situated in the highlands of the north. At the city of Khartoum in Sudan, the Blue Nile joins the White Nile and continues as the Nile River. Tisisat Falls, shown here, lies on the Blue Nile near Bahir Dar. Some of Ethiopia's water resources have been tapped for hydroelectric power, yet many of its waterways remain undeveloped.

FAEROE ISLANDS

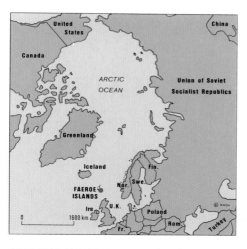

OFFICIAL NAME Faeroe Islands

PEOPLE
Population 45,000.
Density 83/mi² (32/km²).
Urban 32%.
Capital Tórshavn, Streymoy I., 14,443.
Ethnic groups White.
Languages Danish, Faeroese.
Religions Lutheran, Plymouth Brethren.
Life expectancy 79 female, 73 male.

POLITICS
Government Part of Danish realm.
Parties Home Rule, People's, Republican, Social Democratic.
Suffrage Universal, over 21.
Subdivisions 7 districts.

ECONOMY
GDP $369,300,000.

Per capita $8,800.
Monetary unit Danish krone.
Trade partners Denmark, Norway, West Germany, U.S., U.K.
Exports Fish.
Imports Machinery and transportation equipment, petroleum, foodstuffs.

LAND
Description North Atlantic islands.
Area 540 mi² (1,399 km²).
Highest point Slættaratindur, Eysturoy I. 2,894 ft (882 m).
Lowest point Sea level.

PEOPLE. Most of the inhabitants of the Faeroe Islands are of Norse descent. Their language, Faeroese, is related to the Old Norse language, and many islanders feel strongly about preserving their linguistic heritage. Danish is taught in the schools, however. Eighteen of the more than twenty islands are inhabited, and over one-third of the population lives on Streymoy, the largest island of the group.

ECONOMY AND THE LAND. Today as in the past, the Faeroe Islands' economy is dependent upon a fishing industry subsidized by Denmark. Only about 6 percent of the land is cultivated, and besides potatoes and some vegetables, this area provides grass for sheep raising. Coal is mined on the island of Sudhuroy, and throughout the island group people make and sell handicrafts. In addition, some islanders collect and sell the eggs and feathers of the birds that inhabit the cliffs along the coast. The main islands in this volcanic chain are Streymoy, Eysturoy, Vágar, Sudhuroy, and Sandoy. Many islands rise to steep cliffs from a rugged and uneven coastline. Winters are mild, and summers cool.

HISTORY AND POLITICS. Norse settlers arrived in the eighth century, but the islands didn't officially become part of Norway until the eleventh century. In the 1300s, along with Norway, Sweden, Finland, Iceland, and Greenland, the Faeroe Islands came under Danish rule. During World War II, when the Germans invaded Denmark, the British occupied the islands. In 1946 the people participated in a plebiscite, and the result was a declaration of the islands' independence from Denmark. But when the island of Sudero remained in favor of Danish rule, the Danish king announced the result was not conclusive, and the islands continued under Danish control. Two years later, however, the Faeroe Islands became self-governing. ■

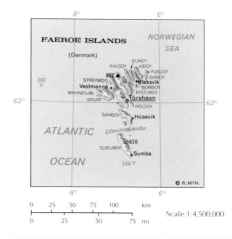

Faeroe Islands Map Index

	Lat.	Long.		Lat.	Long.
Eysturoy	62°13′N	6°52′W	Suduroy	61°32′N	6°50′W
Klaksvik	62°14′N	6°36′W	Sumba	61°24′N	6°42′W
Streymoy	62°08′N	7°00′W	Tórshavn	62°01′N	6°46′W

FALKLAND ISLANDS

OFFICIAL NAME Colony of the Falkland Islands

PEOPLE
Population 2,000.
Density 0.4/mi² (0.2/km²).
Urban 53%.
Capital Stanley, East Falkland I., 1,050.
Ethnic groups British.
Languages English.
Religions Anglican.

POLITICS
Government Colony (U.K.).
Parties None.
Suffrage Universal, over 18.
Memberships None.
Subdivisions None.

ECONOMY
Monetary unit Pound.
Trade partners U.K.
Exports Wool, hides and skins.
Imports Food, clothing, fuels, machinery.

LAND
Description South Atlantic islands.
Area 4,700 mi² (12,173 km²).
Highest point Mt. Usborne, East Falkland I., 2,312 ft (705 m).
Lowest point Sea level.

PEOPLE. Most Falkland Islanders are of British birth or descent. This heritage is reflected in the islands' official language, English, and its majority religion, Anglican. British military also make up a portion of the islands' residents. The only town is Stanley, which is also the capital, situated on East Falkland Island. The countryside outside Stanley, known as the Camp, is the site of the settlement of Goose Green.

ECONOMY AND THE LAND. Sheep raising is the main activity on the Falkland Islands, and dairy farms provide for local needs. Agriculture is supplemented by fishing. In 1982 the government of Britain earmarked funds to be used for economic development of the Falklands, and the Falkland Islands Development Corporation began operating in 1984. Under consideration are plans to expand the dairy industry, fishing, and housing. Situated about 300 miles (482 kilometers) east of southern Argentina, East and West Falkland compose the main and largest islands. South Georgia and the South Sandwich Islands, lying to the southeast, are administered from the Falkland Islands. The climate is cool, damp, and windy.

HISTORY AND POLITICS. There are many conflicting claims as to which country first saw the Falklands, but a Dutch sailor is credited with the original sighting. An Englishman made the first known landing, in 1690. In 1764 the French established the first settlement, on East Falkland, followed by British settlement on West Falkland the next year. Spain, who ruled the Argentine territories to the west, purchased the French area and drove out the British in 1770. When Argentina gained independence from Spain in 1816, it claimed Spain's right to the islands. Britain reasserted its sovereignty over the islands in the 1830s, and the Falklands became a British colony in 1892, with dependencies annexed in 1908. Continued Argentine claim resulted in an April 1982 Argentine invasion and occupation. The British won the subsequent battle and continue to govern the Falklands. ■

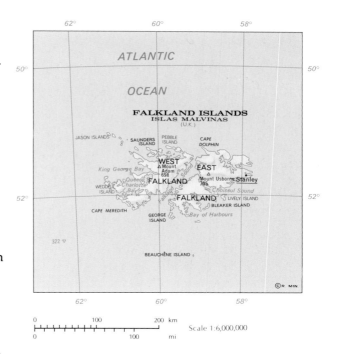

Falkland Islands Map Index

	Lat.	Long.		Lat.	Long.
East Falkland	51°55′S	59°00′W	Usborne, Mount	51°41′S	58°50′W
Falkland Sound	51°45′S	59°25′W	West Falkland	51°50′S	60°00′W
Stanley	51°42′S	57°41′W			

FIJI

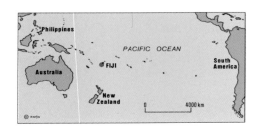

OFFICIAL NAME Fiji

PEOPLE
Population 695,000.
Density 99/mi² (38/km²).
Urban 37%.
Capital Suva, Viti Levu I., 68,178.
Ethnic groups Indian 50%, Fijian 45%.
Languages English, Fijian, Hindustani.
Religions Christian, Hindu, Muslim.
Life expectancy 63 female, 60 male.
Literacy 80%.

POLITICS
Government Parliamentary state.
Parties Alliance, National Federation, Western United Front.
Suffrage Universal adult.
Memberships CW, UN.
Subdivisions 14 provinces.

ECONOMY
GDP $1,850,000,000.
Per capita $1,852.
Monetary unit Dollar.
Trade partners Australia, New Zealand, Japan, U.K.
Exports Sugar, copra. .
Imports Machinery, food, fuels.

LAND
Description South Pacific islands.
Area 7,055 mi² (18,272 km²).
Highest point Tomanivi, Viti Levu I., 4,341 ft (1,323 m).
Lowest point Sea level.

PEOPLE. Fiji's majority population is descended from laborers brought from British India between 1879 and 1916. Most Indians are Hindu, but a Muslim minority exists. Native Fijians are of Melanesian and Polynesian heritage, and most are Christian. English is the official language, a result of British rule, but Indians speak Hindustani, and the main Fijian dialect is Bauan. Tensions between the two groups occasionally arise because plantation owners, who are mainly Indian, must often lease their land from Fijians, the major landowners. About one hundred of the several hundred islands are inhabited.

ECONOMY AND THE LAND. The traditional sugarcane crop continues as the basis of Fiji's economy, and agricultural diversification is a current goal. Tourism is another economic contributor, and expansion of forestry is planned. Terrain varies from island to island and is characterized by mountains, valleys, rain forests, and fertile plains. The tropical islands are cooled by ocean breezes.

HISTORY AND POLITICS. Little is known of Fiji's history prior to the arrival of Europeans. Melanesians probably migrated from Indonesia, followed by Polynesian settlers in the second century. After a Dutch navigator sighted Fiji in 1643, Captain James Cook of Britain visited the island in the eighteenth century. The nineteenth century saw the arrival of European missionaries, traders, and whalers, and several native

wars. In 1874 tribal chiefs ceded Fiji to the British, who established sugar plantations and brought indentured Indian laborers. The country became independent in 1970. Foreign policy is based on regional cooperation. ∎

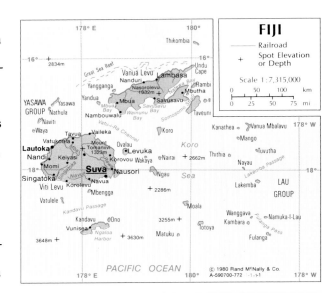

Fiji Map Index

	Lat.	Long.		Lat.	Long.
Kandavu Passage	18°45'S	178°00'E	Nausori	18°02'S	175°32'E
Korolevu	18°13'S	177°44'E	Navua	18°14'S	178°10'E
Koro Sea	18°00'S	179°50'E	Savusavu	16°16'S	179°21'E
Korovou	17°57'S	178°21'E	Singatoka	18°08'S	177°30'E
Lambasa	16°26'S	179°24'E	Suva	18°08'S	178°25'E
Lau Group	18°20'S	178°30'E	Taveuni	16°51'S	179°58'E
Lautoka	17°37'S	177°27'E	Tavua	17°27'S	177°51'E
Levuka	17°41'S	178°50'E	*Tomaniivi, Mount*	17°37'S	178°01'E
Mbua	16°48'S	178°37'E	Vaileka	17°23'S	178°09'E
Mbutha	16°39'S	179°50'E	*Vanua Levu*	16°33'S	179°15'E
Nambouwalu	16°59'S	178°42'E	Vatukoula	17°31'S	177°51'E
Nandi	17°48'S	177°25'E	*Viti Levu*	18°00'S	178°00'E
Nanduri	16°27'S	179°09'E	Vunisea	19°03'S	178°09'E
Natewa Bay	16°35'S	179°40'E	*Yasawa Group*	17°00'S	177°23'E

FINLAND

Helsinki Cathedral, Finland

FINLAND

Finland Map Index

	Lat.	Long.		Lat.	Long.
Ahvenanmaa	60°15'N	20°00'E	Loken tekojärvi	67°55'N	27°40'E
Bothnia, Gulf of	64°00'N	22°00'E	Mikkeli	61°41'N	27°15'E
Cyrön	63°14'N	21°45'E	Näsi Lake	61°37'N	23°42'E
Espoo	60°13'N	24°40'E	Nattas Mountain	68°12'N	27°20'E
Finland, Gulf of	60°00'N	27°00'E	Nokia	61°28'N	23°30'E
Haltia Mountain	69°18'N	21°16'E	Oulu	65°01'N	25°28'E
Hämeenlinna	61°00'N	24°27'E	Oulu Lake	64°20'N	27°15'E
Helsinki	60°10'N	24°58'E	Ounas	66°30'N	25°45'E
Hyvinkää	60°38'N	24°52'E	Päijänne	61°35'N	25°30'E
Imatra	61°10'N	28°46'E	Pallas Mountain	68°06'N	24°00'E
Inari	69°00'N	28°00'E	Pieksämäki	62°18'N	27°08'E
Jakobstad	63°40'N	22°42'E	Pielinen	63°15'N	29°40'E
Joensuu	62°36'N	29°46'E	Pihlaja Lake	61°45'N	28°50'E
Jyväskylä	62°14'N	25°44'E	Pori	61°29'N	21°47'E
Kajaani	64°14'N	27°41'E	Porttipahdan		
Karhula	60°31'N	26°57'E	tekojärvi	68°08'N	26°40'E
Kemi	65°49'N	24°32'E	Puula Lake	61°50'N	26°42'E
Kemi	65°47'N	24°30'E	Pyhä	64°28'N	24°13'E
Kemijärvi	66°40'N	27°25'E	Rauma	61°08'N	21°30'E
Kemijärvi	66°36'N	27°24'E	Rovaniemi	66°34'N	25°48'E
Kokkola	63°50'N	23°07'E	Savitaipale	61°12'N	27°42'E
Könkämä	68°29'N	22°17'E	Seinäjoki	62°47'N	22°50'E
Kotka	60°28'N	26°55'E	Tampere	61°30'N	23°45'E
Kuopio	62°54'N	27°41'E	Turku	60°27'N	22°17'E
Lahti	60°58'N	25°40'E	Vaasa	63°06'N	21°36'E
Lappeenranta	61°04'N	28°11'E	Varkaus	62°19'N	27°55'E
Livo	65°24'N	26°48'E			

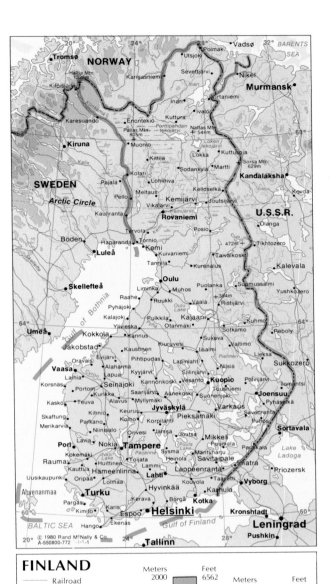

FINLAND

	Meters	Feet		Meters	Feet
Railroad	2000	6562			
+ Spot Elevation	1000	3281		0	0
	500	1640		200	656
Scale 1:8,634,000	200	656		2000	6562
0 50 100 150 km	0	0			
0 50 100 mi					

© 1980 Rand McNally & Co. A-550800-772

OFFICIAL NAME Republic of Finland

PEOPLE
Population 4,885,000.
Density 37/mi² (14/km²).
Urban 60%.
Capital Helsinki, 483,051.
Ethnic groups Finnish, Swedish, Lappish.
Languages Finnish, Swedish.
Religions Lutheran 97%, Greek Orthodox 1%.
Life expectancy 78 female, 69 male.
Literacy 100%.

POLITICS
Government Republic.
Parties Center, National Coalition, People's Democratic League, Social Democratic.
Suffrage Universal, over 18.
Memberships OECD, UN.
Subdivisions 12 provinces.

ECONOMY
GNP $49,100,000,000.
Per capita $10,124.
Monetary unit Markka.
Trade partners U.S.S.R., Sweden, West Germany, U.K.
Exports Wood, paper and wood pulp, machinery.
Imports Fuels, chemicals, machinery, food.

LAND
Description Northern Europe.
Area 130,558 mi² (338,145 km²).
Highest point Haltia Mtn., 4,357 ft (1,328 m).
Lowest point Sea level.

PEOPLE. As a result of past Swedish rule, the mainly Finnish population includes minorities of Swedes, in addition to indigenous Lapps. Because part of northern Finland lies in the Arctic Circle, population is concentrated in the south. Finland's rich cultural tradition has contributed much to the arts, and its highly developed social-welfare programs provide free education through the university level and nationalized health insurance.

ECONOMY AND THE LAND. Much of Finland's economy is based on its rich forests, which support trade and manufacturing activities. The steel industry is also important. Agriculture focuses on dairy farming and livestock raising; hence many fruits and vegetables must be imported. Coastal islands and lowlands, a central lake region, and northern hills mark Finland's scenic terrain. Summers in the south and central regions are warm, and winters long and cold. Northern Finland—located in the Land of the Midnight Sun—has periods of uninterrupted daylight in summer and darkness in winter.

HISTORY AND POLITICS. In the first century the indigenous nomadic Lapps migrated north when the Finns arrived, probably from west-central Russia. A Russian-Swedish struggle for control of the area ended with Swedish rule in the 1100s. Finland was united with Denmark from the fourteenth through the sixteenth centuries, and from the sixteenth through the eighteenth centuries Russia and Sweden fought several wars for control of the country. In 1809 Finland became an autonomous grand duchy within the Russian Empire. The Russian czar was overthrown in the 1917 Bolshevik Revolution, and Finland's declaration of independence was recognized by the new Russian government. During World War II Finland fought against the Soviets and, by the peace treaty signed in 1947, lost a portion of its land to the Soviet Union. During the postwar years Finland and Russia renewed their economic and cultural ties and signed an agreement of friendship and cooperation. Foreign policy emphasizes friendly relations with the U.S.S.R. and Scandinavia. ■

Situated on a peninsula off the Gulf of Finland and protected by offshore islands, Helsinki is a natural port, the capital of Finland, and a cultural and commercial center. Most city residents work in commerce, services, or communications, but today, just as in the past, some people look to the sea for their livelihood, as shown in this scene of Helsinki Harbor.

Olavinlinna, in Savonlinna, Finland, is one of the largest castles in northern Europe. Savonlinna was built around the castle in the seventeenth century and is situated on an island in the Lake Saimaa region of southeast Finland. The town is a popular summer resort, and the castle a well-known tourist destination.

FRANCE

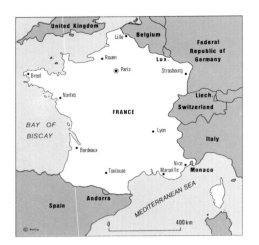

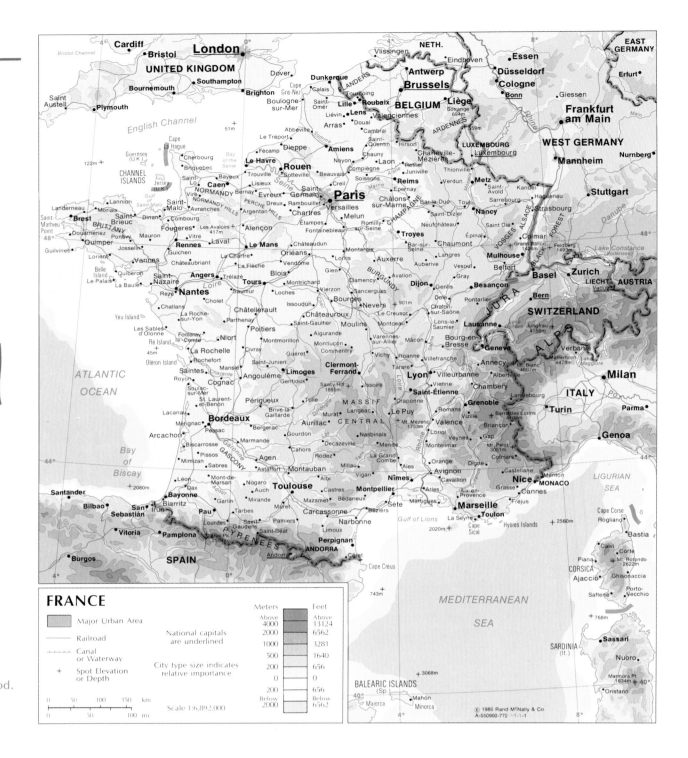

OFFICIAL NAME French
Republic

PEOPLE

Population 55,020,000.
Density 261/mi² (101/km²).
Urban 73%.
Capital Paris, 2,176,243.
Ethnic groups Celtic, Latin.
Languages French.
Religions Roman Catholic 90%, Protestant 2%.
Life expectancy 78 female, 70 male.
Literacy 99%.

POLITICS

Government Republic.
Parties Communist, Rally for the
Republic, Socialist, Union for Democracy.
Suffrage Universal, over 18.
Memberships EC, NATO, OECD, UN.
Subdivisions 96 departments.

ECONOMY

GDP $542,000,000,000.
Per capita $9,996.
Monetary unit Franc.
Trade partners West Germany, Italy, Belgium,
Luxembourg, U.S., U.K.
Exports Machinery, transportation equipment, food.
Imports Petroleum, machinery, chemicals.

LAND

Description Western Europe.
Area 211,208 mi² (547,026 km²).
Highest point Mt. Blanc, 15,771 ft (4,807 m).
Lowest point Lac de Cazaux et de Sanguinet, 10 ft
(3 m) below sea level.
*The above information excludes French overseas
departments.*

PEOPLE. Many centuries ago Celtic tribes, Germanic tribes, and Latins established France's current ethnic patterns. The French language developed from the Latin of invading Romans but includes Celtic and Germanic influences as well. Language and customs vary somewhat from region to region, but most people who speak dialects also speak French. France has long contributed to learning and the arts, and Paris is a world cultural center. In addition to mainland divisions, the country has overseas departments and territories.

ECONOMY AND THE LAND. The French economy is highly developed. The nation is a leader in agriculture and industry, and its problems of inflation and unemployment are common to other modern countries. Soils in the north and northeast are especially productive, and grapes are grown in the south. Minerals include iron ore and bauxite. Industry is diversified, centered in the Paris manufacturing area, and tourism is also important. About two-thirds of the country is flat to rolling, and about one-third is mountainous, including the Pyrenees in the south and the Alps in the east. In the west and north winters are

FRANCE

	Meters	Feet
Major Urban Area	Above 4000	Above 13124
Railroad	2000	6562
Canal or Waterway	1000	3281
Spot Elevation or Depth	500	1640
	200	656
	0	0
	200	656
	Below 2000	Below 6562

National capitals are underlined
City type size indicates relative importance

Scale 1:6,892,000

© 1980 Rand McNally & Co.
A-550900-772-1-1-1

France Map Index

	Lat.	Long.		Lat.	Long.
Agen	44°12'N	0°37'E	Chambery	45°34'N	5°56'E
Aisne	49°26'N	2°50'E	Charleville-		
Ajaccio	41°55'N	8°44'E	Mézières	49°46'N	4°43'E
Alençon	48°26'N	0°05'E	Chartres	48°27'N	1°30'E
Allier	45°05'N	3°35'E	Châteauroux	46°49'N	1°42'E
Alps	46°00'N	8°00'E	Châtellerault	46°49'N	0°33'E
Amiens	49°54'N	2°18'E	Chaumont	48°07'N	5°08'E
Angers	47°28'N	0°33'W	Clermont-Ferrand	45°47'N	3°05'E
Angoulême	45°39'N	0°09'E	Cognac	45°42'N	0°20'W
Anie Peak	42°57'N	0°43'W	Colmar	48°05'N	7°22'E
Annecy	45°54'N	6°07'E	*Corse, Cape*	43°00'N	9°25'E
Arcachon	44°37'N	1°12'W	*Corsica*	42°00'N	9°00'E
Arras	50°17'N	2°47'E	Dieppe	49°56'N	1°05'E
Aurillac	44°56'N	2°26'E	Dijon	47°19'N	5°01'E
Auxerre	47°48'N	3°34'E	*Dordogne*	45°02'N	0°35'W
Avignon	43°57'N	4°49'E	Dunkerque	51°03'N	2°22'E
Barre des Écrins	44°55'N	6°22'E	*English Channel*	50°20'N	1°00'W
Bastia	42°42'N	9°27'E	Evreux	49°01'N	1°09'E
Bayonne	43°29'N	1°29'W	Fougeres	48°21'N	1°12'W
Belfort	47°38'N	6°52'E	*Garonne*	45°02'N	0°36'W
Belle Island	47°20'N	3°10'W	*Geneva, Lake*	46°25'N	6°30'E
Besançon	47°15'N	6°02'E	*Grand Ballon*	47°55'N	7°08'E
Biarritz	43°29'N	1°34'W	*Gris-Nez, Cape*	50°52'N	1°35'E
Biscay, Bay of	44°00'N	4°00'W	*Hyères Islands*	43°00'N	6°20'E
Blanc, Mount	45°50'N	6°52'E	*Jura*	46°45'N	6°30'E
Blois	47°35'N	1°20'E	*La Hague, Cape*	49°43'N	1°57'W
Bordeaux	44°50'N	0°34'W	Laon	49°34'N	3°40'E
Boulogne-sur-Mer	50°43'N	1°37'E	La Rochelle	46°10'N	1°10'W
Bourg-en-Bresse	46°12'N	5°13'E	Laval	48°04'N	0°46'W
Bourges	47°05'N	2°24'E	Le Havre	49°30'N	0°08'E
Brest	48°24'N	4°29'W	Le Mans	48°00'N	0°12'E
Caen	49°11'N	0°21'W	Lens	50°26'N	2°50'E
Cannes	43°33'N	7°01'E	Le Puy	45°02'N	3°53'E
Carcassonne	43°13'N	2°21'E	*Ligurian Sea*	43°30'N	9°00'E
Central, Massif	45°00'N	3°10'E	Lille	50°38'N	3°04'E
Châlons-sur-			Limoges	45°50'N	1°16'E
Marne	48°57'N	4°22'E	*Lions, Gulf of*	43°00'N	4°00'E

	Lat.	Long.		Lat.	Long.
Loire	47°16'N	2°11'E	Rouen	49°26'N	1°05'E
Lot	44°18'N	0°20'E	Saint-Brieuc	48°31'N	2°47'W
Lyon	45°45'N	4°51'E	Saint-Étienne	45°26'N	4°24'E
Marne	48°49'N	2°24'E	Saint-Germain	48°54'N	2°05'E
Marseille	43°18'N	5°24'E	Saint-Malo	48°39'N	2°01'W
Melun	48°32'N	2°40'E	*Saint-Malo, Gulf*		
Metz	49°08'N	6°10'E	*of*	48°45'N	2°00'W
Montauban	44°01'N	1°21'E	*Saint-Mathieu*		
Montpellier	43°36'N	3°53'E	*Point*	48°20'N	4°46'W
Moselle	49°28'N	6°22'E	Saint-Nazaire	47°17'N	2°12'W
Moulins	46°34'N	3°20'E	Saintes	45°45'N	0°52'W
Mulhouse	47°45'N	7°20'E	*Sancy Hill*	45°32'N	2°49'E
Nancy	48°41'N	6°12'E	*Saone*	45°44'N	4°50'E
Nantes	47°13'N	1°33'W	*Seine*	49°26'N	0°26'E
Narbonne	43°11'N	3°00'E	*Seine, Bay of the*	49°30'N	0°30'W
Nevers	47°00'N	3°09'E	Sète	43°24'N	3°41'E
Nice	43°42'N	7°15'E	*Sicié, Cape*	43°03'N	5°51'E
Nîmes	43°50'N	4°21'E	*Somme*	50°11'N	1°39'E
Niort	46°19'N	0°27'W	Strasbourg	48°35'N	7°45'E
Normandy	48°35'N	0°30'W	*Tarn*	44°05'N	1°06'E
Oléron Island	45°56'N	1°15'W	Toulon	43°07'N	5°56'E
Orléans	47°55'N	1°54'E	Toulouse	43°36'N	1°26'E
Paris	48°52'N	2°20'E	Tours	47°23'N	0°41'E
Pau	43°18'N	0°22'W	Troyes	48°18'N	4°05'E
Perche Hills	48°25'N	0°40'E	Valence	44°56'N	4°54'E
Périgueux	45°11'N	0°43'E	Valenciennes	50°21'N	3°32'E
Perpignan	42°41'N	2°53'E	Vannes	47°39'N	2°46'W
Poitiers	46°35'N	0°20'E	Versailles	48°48'N	2°08'E
Pyrenees	42°40'N	1°00'E	Villeurbanne	45°46'N	4°53'E
Quimper	48°00'N	4°06'W	*Vosges*	48°30'N	7°10'E
Reims	49°15'N	4°02'E	*Yeu Island*	46°42'N	2°20'W
Rè Island	46°12'N	1°25'W			
Rennes	48°05'N	1°41'W			
Rhine	48°58'N	8°13'E			
Rhône	43°20'N	4°50'E			
Rotondo, Mount	42°13'N	9°03'E			
Roubaix	50°42'N	3°10'E			

France's Loire Valley is famous for the châteaux built during the fifteenth and sixteenth centuries. Shown here is the Château de Chenonceaux, considered by many to be the Loire's prettiest château.

cool and summers mild. Climate varies with altitude in the mountains. The southern coast has a Mediterranean climate with hot summers and mild winters.

HISTORY AND POLITICS. In ancient times Celtic tribes inhabited the area that encompasses present-day France. The Romans, who called the region Gaul, began to invade about 200 B.C., and by the 50s B.C. the entire region had come under Roman rule. Northern Germanic tribes—including the Franks, Visigoths, and Burgundians—spread throughout the region as Roman control weakened, and the Franks defeated the Romans in A.D. 486. In the 800s Charlemagne greatly expanded Frankish-controlled territory, which was subsequently divided into three kingdoms. The western kingdom and part of the central kingdom included modern France. In 987 the Capetian dynasty began when Hugh Capet came to

the throne, an event which is often considered the start of the French nation. During subsequent centuries the power of the kings increased, and France became a leading world power. Ambitious projects, such as the palace built by Louis XIV at Versailles, and several military campaigns resulted in financial difficulties. The failing economy and divisions between rich and poor led to the French Revolution in 1789 and the First French Republic in 1792. Napoleon Bonaparte, who had gained prominence during the revolution, overthrew the government in 1799 and established the First Empire, which ended in 1815 with his defeat at Waterloo in Belgium. The subsequent monarchy resulted in discontent, and a 1848 revolution established the Second French Republic with an elected president, who in turn proclaimed himself emperor and set up the Second Empire in 1852. Following a war with Prussia in 1870, the emperor was ousted, and

the Third Republic began. This republic endured Germany's invasion in World War I but ended in 1940 when invading Germans defeated the French. By 1942 the Nazis had control of the entire country. The Allies liberated France in 1944, and General Charles de Gaulle headed a provisional government until 1946, when the Fourth Republic was established. Colonial revolts in Africa and French Indochina took their toll on the economy during the fifties, and controversy over a continuing Algerian war for independence brought de Gaulle to power once more and resulted in the Fifth Republic in 1958. Dissension and national strikes erupted during the 1960s, a result of dissatisfaction with the government, and de Gaulle resigned in 1969. France is active in European foreign relations and continues to play a role in its former African colonies, with extensive economic aid programs, commercial enterprises, and military liaisons. ■

Places and Possessions of France

Entity	Status	Area	Population	Capital / Population
Corsica (Mediterranean island)	Part of France	3,352 mi² (8,681 km²)	220,000	None
French Guiana (northeastern South America)	Overseas department	35,135 mi² (91,000 km²)	81,000	Cayenne / 38,091
French Polynesia (central South Pacific islands	Overseas territory	1,544 mi² (4,000 km²)	160,000	Papeete / 23,453
French Southern and Antarctic Territories (Indian Ocean islands)	Overseas territory	3,000 mi² (7,770 km²)	76	None
Guadeloupe and dependencies (Caribbean islands)	Overseas department	687 mi² (1,780 km²)	320,000	Basse-Terre / 13,656
Kerguelen Islands (Indian Ocean)	Part of French Southern and Antarctic Territories	2,700 mi² (6,993 km²)	76	None
Martinique (Caribbean island)	Overseas department	425 mi² (1,100 km²)	320,000	Fort-de-France / 99,844
Mayotte (southeastern African island)	Territorial collectivity	144 mi² (373 km²)	63,000	Dzaoudzi / 4,147
New Caledonia (South Pacific islands)	Overseas territory	7,366 mi² (19,079 km²)	149,000	Nouméa / 56,078
Reunion (Indian Ocean island)	Overseas department	967 mi² (2,504 km²)	545,000	Saint-Denis / 84,400
St. Pierre and Miquelon (North Atlantic islands)	Territorial collectivity	93 mi² (242 km²)	6,200	Saint-Pierre / 5,371
Wallis and Futuna (South Pacific islands)	Overseas territory	98 mi² (255 km²)	12,000	Mata-Utu / 558

The Bordeaux area in southwest France is known worldwide for its wines. This photo depicts the grape harvest at one of the region's many vineyards.

FRENCH GUIANA

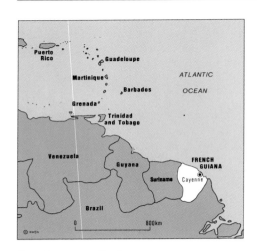

OFFICIAL NAME Department of Guiana

PEOPLE
Population 81,000.
Density 2.3/mi² (0.9/km²).
Urban 61%.
Capital Cayenne, 38,091.
Ethnic groups African and Afro-European 66%; European 12%; East Indian, Chinese, and Amerindian 12%.
Languages French.
Religions Roman Catholic.
Life expectancy 65.
Literacy 74%.

POLITICS
Government Overseas department (France).
Parties Rally for the Republic, Socialist, Union of the People.
Suffrage Universal, over 18.

Memberships None.
Subdivisions 2 arrondissements.

ECONOMY
GNP $120,000,000.
Per capita $1,935.
Monetary unit French franc.
Trade partners France, U.S., Trinidad and Tobago.
Exports Shrimp, wood, rum.
Imports Food, manufactured goods, petroleum.

LAND
Description Northeastern South America.
Area 35,135 mi² (91,000 km²).
Highest point 2,723 ft (830 m).
Lowest point Sea level.

PEOPLE. French Guiana has a majority population of black descendants of African slaves and people of mixed African-European ancestry. Population is concentrated in the more accessible coastal area, but the interior wilderness is home to minority Indians and descendants of slaves who fled to pursue traditional African life-styles.

ECONOMY AND THE LAND. Shrimp production and a growing timber industry are French Guiana's economic mainstays. Agriculture is limited by wilderness, but mineral deposits offer potential for mining. The fertile coastal plains of the north give way to hills and mountains along the Brazilian border. The climate is tropical.

HISTORY AND POLITICS. Indigenous Indians and a hot climate defeated France's attempt at settlement in the early 1600s. The first permanent French settlement was established in 1634, and the area became a French colony in 1667. For almost one hundred years, beginning in the 1850s, penal colonies such as Devils Island brought an influx of prisoners. The region became a French overseas department in 1946. ∎

FRENCH GUIANA

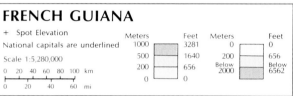

French Guiana Map Index

	Lat.	Long.		Lat.	Long.
Cayenne	4°56'N	52°20'W	Saint-Laurent-du-		
Devil's Island	5°17'N	52°35'W	Maroni	5°30'N	54°02'W
Maroni	5°45'N	53°58'W	Sinnamary	5°23'N	52°57'W
Oyapock	4°08'N	51°40'W			

FRENCH POLYNESIA

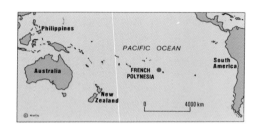

OFFICIAL NAME Territory of French Polynesia

PEOPLE
Population 160,000.
Density 103/mi² (40/km²).
Urban 57%.
Capital Papeete, Tahiti I., 23,453.
Ethnic groups Polynesian 78%, Chinese 12%, French 6%.
Languages French, Tahitian.
Religions Protestant 55%, Catholic 32%, Mormon 6%.
Life expectancy 63 female, 60 male.
Literacy 98%.

POLITICS
Government Overseas territory (France).
Parties Here Ai'a, Tahoeraa Huiraatira.
Suffrage Universal adult.
Memberships None.
Subdivisions 5 districts.

ECONOMY
GDP $1,052,400,000.
Per capita $6,400.
Monetary unit CFP franc.
Trade partners France, U.S.
Exports Coconut products, mother-of-pearl.
Imports Fuels, food.

LAND
Description Central South Pacific islands.
Area 1,544 mi² (4,000 km²).
Highest point Mt. Orohena, Tahiti I., 7,352 ft (2,241 m).
Lowest point Sea level.

PEOPLE. Most inhabitants are Polynesian, with minorities including Chinese and French. More than one hundred islands compose the five archipelagoes, and population and commercial activity is concentrated in Papeete on Tahiti. Although per capita income is relatively high, wealth is not equally distributed. Emigration from the poorer islands to Tahiti is common. Polynesia's reputation as a tropical paradise has attracted European and American writers and artists, including French painter Paul Gauguin.

ECONOMY AND THE LAND. The islands' economy is based on natural resources, and coconut, mother-of-pearl, and tourism are economic contributors. This South Pacific territory, located south of the equator and midway between South America and Australia, is spread over roughly 1.5 million square miles (3.9 million square kilometers) and is made up of the Marquesas Islands, the Society Islands, the Tuamotu Archipelago, the Gambier Islands, and the Austral Islands. The Marquesas, known for their beauty, form the northernmost group. The Society Islands, southwest of the Marquesas, include Tahiti and Bora-Bora, both popular tourist spots. The Tuamotu Archipelago lies south of the Marquesas and east of the Society Islands, the Gambier Islands are situated at the southern tip of the Tuamotu group, and the Austral Islands lie to the southwest. The region includes both volcanic and coral islands, and the climate is tropical, with a rainy season extending from November to April.

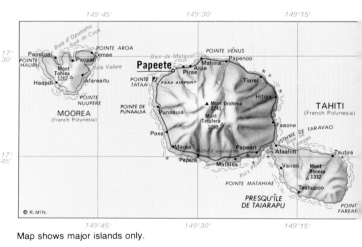

Map shows major islands only.

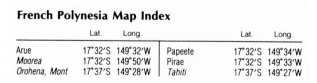

French Polynesia Map Index

	Lat.	Long.		Lat.	Long.
Arue	17°32'S	149°32'W	Papeete	17°32'S	149°34'W
Moorea	17°32'S	149°50'W	Pirae	17°32'S	149°33'W
Orohena, Mont	17°37'S	149°28'W	Tahiti	17°37'S	149°27'W

HISTORY AND POLITICS. The original settlers probably came from Micronesia and Melanesia in the east. Europeans began arriving around the sixteenth century. By the late 1700s they had reached the five major island groups, and visitors to the area included mutineers from the British vessel *Bounty*. By the 1880s the islands had come under French rule, although they did not become an overseas territory until 1946. During European settlement, many Polynesians died as a result of exposure to foreign diseases. The French use several of the islands for nuclear testing. ∎

FRENCH SOUTHERN AND ANTARCTIC TERRITORIES

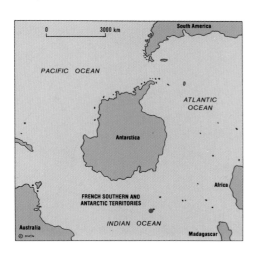

OFFICIAL NAME French Southern and Antarctic Territories

PEOPLE
Population 76.
Density 0.3/mi² (0.01/km²).
Ethnic groups French.
Languages French.

POLITICS
Government Overseas territory (France).

LAND
Description Indian Ocean islands.
Area 3,000 mi² (7,770 km²).
Highest point Mt. Ross, 6,070 ft (1,850 m).
Lowest point Sea level.

PEOPLE. The French Southern and Antarctic Territories consist of the Kerguelen Islands, the Crozet Islands, Amsterdam Island, St. Paul Island, and the Adélie Coast, an area in Antarctica. Scientists working at research and meteorological stations make up the population.

ECONOMY AND THE LAND. France has established research stations throughout the territories, including major bases in Port-aux-Français in the Kerguelen Islands, on Possession Island in the Crozet archipelago, and on the Adélie Coast.

Amsterdam Island is the site of a hospital and administrative offices as well as a scientific station. Coal, peat, and semiprecious stones have been found in the Kerguelen Islands, and cod and lobster are caught off the shores of St. Paul and Amsterdam islands. Throughout the territories seals, sea lions, and whales can be found. The largest island is mountainous Kerguelen Island; the rugged islands of the Crozet group are volcanic in origin; and Amsterdam, a volcanic island, lies near St. Paul, which is the site of hot springs. The climate of St. Paul and Amsterdam is milder than elsewhere in the territories.

HISTORY AND POLITICS. The Portuguese discovered Amsterdam Island in 1522, the Dutch visited it in 1633, and France claimed it in 1843. Captain Marion-Dufresne discovered the islands of the Crozet archipelago in 1772, annexing them to France, and whalers and seal hunters visited the Crozets throughout the nineteenth century. Also in 1772, Frenchman Kerguélen-Trémarec came upon Kerguelen Island, naming it Desolation Island. In 1840 the French arrived on the Adélie Coast. The French Southern and Antarctic Territories are governed from Paris. ■

GABON

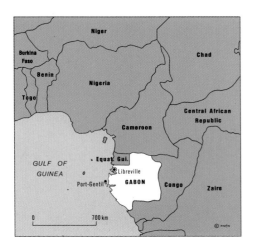

OFFICIAL NAME Gabonese Republic

PEOPLE
Population 975,000.
Density 9.4/mi² (3.6/km²).
Urban 36%.
Capital Libreville, 340,000.
Ethnic groups Fang, Eshira, Bapounou, Teke.
Languages French, indigenous.
Religions Christian 80%, Muslim, animist.
Life expectancy 45 female, 42 male.
Literacy 65%.

POLITICS
Government Republic.
Parties Democratic.
Suffrage Universal, over 18.
Memberships OAU, OPEC, UN.
Subdivisions 9 provinces.

ECONOMY
GDP $3,500,000,000.
Per capita $2,742.
Monetary unit CFA franc.
Trade partners France, U.S., West Germany.
Exports Petroleum, wood and wood products, minerals.
Imports Machinery, electrical equipment, transportation equipment, food.

LAND
Description Central Africa.
Area 103,347 mi² (267,667 km²).
Highest point 3,346 ft (1,020 m).
Lowest point Sea level.

PEOPLE. Of Gabon's more than forty ethnic groups, nearly all are of Bantu descent. The Fang are a majority and inhabit the area north of the Ogooué River. Other major groups include the Eshira, Bapounou, and Teke. The French, who colonized the area, compose a larger group today than during colonial times. Each of the groups has its own distinct language as well as culture, but French remains the official language.

ECONOMY AND THE LAND. Gabon is located astride the equator, and its many resources include petroleum, manganese, uranium, and dense rain forests. The most important activities are oil production, forestry, and mining. The economy depends greatly on foreign investment and imported labor, however, and many native Gabonese continue as subsistence farmers. An existing labor shortage is a hindrance to economic development, but the low population density combined with profits from forestry and mining have given the country a relatively high per capita income. The terrain is marked by a coastal plain, inland forested hills, and savanna in the east and south. The climate is hot and humid.

HISTORY AND POLITICS. First inhabited by Pygmies, Gabon was the site of migrations by numerous Bantu peoples during its early history. The thick rain forests isolated the migrant groups from one another and thus preserved their individual cultures. The Portuguese arrived in the fifteenth century, followed by the Dutch, British, and French in the 1700s. The slave and ivory trades flourished, and the Fang, drawn by the prosperity, migrated to the coast in the 1800s. In 1839 and 1841 the chiefs of the coastal regions signed treaties making France the protector of Gabon. In 1849 a slave ship was captured by the French at the Komo River, and the released slaves founded a settlement called Libreville, or "free town," which later became the capital of the French colony. French influence continued to grow, and by 1885 the region was under French control. In 1910 Gabon was united with present-day Chad, the Congo, and the Central African Republic as French Equatorial Africa. Gabon became independent in 1960, and in 1964 French assistance thwarted a military takeover. Because Gabon's economy relies on foreign investment, foreign policy is often influenced by economic interests. ■

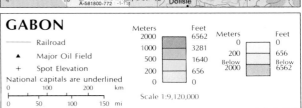

GABON

	Meters	Feet	Meters	Feet
—— Railroad	2000	6562	0	0
▲ Major Oil Field	1000	3281	200	656
+ Spot Elevation	500	1640	Below 2000	Below 6562
National capitals are underlined	200	656		
	0	0		

Scale 1:9,120,000

Gabon Map Index

	Lat.	Long.		Lat.	Long.
Balaquiri, Mount	0°55'N	13°12'E	Mayumba	3°25'S	10°39'E
Birougou Mountains	1°51'S	12°20'E	Mikongo Mountains	0°15'N	10°55'E
Cristal Mountains	0°30'N	10°30'E	Mouila	1°52'S	11°01'E
Djoua	1°13'S	13°12'E	Mvoung	0°04'N	12°18'E
Franceville	1°38'S	13°35'E	Ngounié	0°37'S	10°18'E
Iboundji, Mount	1°08'S	11°48'E	Ogooué	0°49'S	9°00'E
Koula-Moutou	1°08'S	12°29'E	Onanguzze, Lake	0°57'S	10°04'E
Lambaréné	0°42'S	10°13'E	Oyem	1°37'N	11°35'E
Libreville	0°23'N	9°27'E	Port-Gentil	0°43'S	8°47'E
Makokou	0°34'N	12°52'E	Tchibanga	2°51'S	11°02'E

GAMBIA

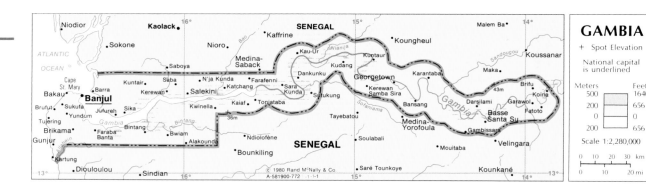

OFFICIAL NAME Republic of
The Gambia

PEOPLE
Population 715,000.
Density 164/mi² (63/km²).
Urban 18%.
Capital Banjul, 49,181.
Ethnic groups Mandingo 38%, Fulani 16%, Wolof 14%, Jola 8%, Serahuli 5%.
Languages English, indigenous.
Religions Muslim 85%, Christian 14%.
Life expectancy 36 female, 32 male.
Literacy 15%.

POLITICS
Government Republic.
Parties National Convention, People's Progressive.
Suffrage Universal, over 21.
Memberships CW, OAU, UN.
Subdivisions 5 divisions, 1 city.

ECONOMY
GNP $240,000,000.
Per capita $370.
Monetary unit Dalasi.
Trade partners U.K., China, Netherlands.
Exports Peanuts and peanut products, fish.
Imports Manufactured goods, machinery, food.

LAND
Description Western Africa.
Area 4,361 mi² (11,295 km²).
Highest point 150 ft (50 m).
Lowest point Sea level.

PEOPLE. Gambia's population includes the Mandingo, or Malinke; Fulani; Wolofs; Jola; and Serahuli. Gambians are mainly rural farmers, and literacy is low, with educational opportunities focused in the Banjul area. The population's size varies with the arrival and departure of seasonal Senegalese farm laborers.

ECONOMY AND THE LAND. Gambia's economy relies on peanut production, and crop diversification is a current goal. The Gambia River, which provides a route to the African interior, offers potential for an increased role in trade.

Gambia Map Index

	Lat.	Long.		Lat.	Long.
Bakau	13°29'N	16°41'W	Gambia	13°28'N	16°34'W
Banjul	13°28'N	16°39'W	Georgetown	13°30'N	14°47'W
Basse Santa Su	13°19'N	14°13'W	Gunjur	13°11'N	16°46'W
Brikama	13°15'N	16°39'W	Saint Mary, Cape	13°28'N	16°40'W

Low-lying Gambia is virtually an enclave within Senegal. Bordering the Gambia River are dense mangrove swamps, giving way to flat ground that floods in the rainy season. Behind this lie sand hills and plateaus. The climate of Gambia is subtropical.

HISTORY AND POLITICS. From the thirteenth to the fifteenth centuries the flourishing Mali Empire included the area of Gambia. The Portuguese arrived in the fifteenth century, established slave trading posts, and in 1588 sold trade rights to Britain. During the seventeenth and eighteenth centuries France and Britain competed for control of the river trade. By the late 1800s the Banjul area had become a British colony and the interior a British protectorate. In 1965 Gambia achieved independence as a monarchy, and the country became a republic in 1970. ■

GERMANY, EAST

OFFICIAL NAME German
Democratic Republic

PEOPLE
Population 16,600,000.
Density 397/mi² (153/km²).
Urban 76%.
Capital East Berlin, 1,152,529.
Ethnic groups German.
Languages German.
Religions Protestant 47%, Roman Catholic 7%.
Life expectancy 75 female, 69 male.
Literacy 99%.

POLITICS
Government Socialist republic.
Parties Socialist Unity.
Suffrage Universal, over 18.
Memberships CEMA, UN, Warsaw Pact.
Subdivisions 14 districts, 1 independent city.

ECONOMY
GNP $165,600,000,000.
Per capita $9,903.
Monetary unit Mark.
Trade partners U.S.S.R., Eastern European countries, West Germany.
Exports Machinery, chemical products, textiles.
Imports Raw materials, machinery, fuels.

LAND
Description Eastern Europe.
Area 41,768 mi² (108,179 km²).
Highest point Fichtelberg, 3,983 ft (1,214 m).
Lowest point Sea level.

PEOPLE. The population of East Germany is mainly German and German speaking. A small minority of Slavs exists. East Germans are mostly Protestant, especially Lutheran, although many people remain religiously unaffiliated. The standard of living is relatively high, and citizens benefit from extensive educational and social-insurance systems. The arts also receive much government and public support. The people of East and West Germany are divided by a guarded border but share a cultural heritage of achievements in music, literature, philosophy, and science.

ECONOMY AND THE LAND. Postwar economic expansion emphasized industry, and today East Germany is one of the world's largest industrial producers. The economy is centralized: industry is state owned and most agriculture is collectivized. Mineral resources are limited. The terrain is marked by northern lakes and low hills; central mountains, productive plains, and sandy stretches; and southern uplands. The country's climate is temperate.

HISTORY AND POLITICS. See GERMANY, WEST.

The sandstone cliffs of the Elbsandstein Mountains, shown here, rise along the Czechoslovakian–East German border southeast of Dresden. The region is a popular tourist destination.

GERMANY, WEST

OFFICIAL NAME Federal
Republic of Germany

PEOPLE
Population 61,390,000.
Density 639/mi² (247/km²).
Urban 94%.
Capital Bonn, 293,852.
Ethnic groups German.
Languages German.
Religions Roman Catholic 45%, Protestant 44%.
Life expectancy 76 female, 70 male.
Literacy 99%.

POLITICS
Government Republic.
Parties Christian Democratic Union, Christian Social
Union, Free Democratic, Social Democratic.
Suffrage Universal, over 18.
Memberships EC, NATO, OECD, UN.
Subdivisions 11 states.

ECONOMY
GNP $658,400,000,000.
Per capita $10,682.
Monetary unit Deutsche mark.
Trade partners Western European countries, U.S.
Exports Machinery, motor vehicles, chemicals, iron
and steel products.
Imports Manufactured goods, fuels, raw materials.

LAND
Description Western Europe.
Area 96,019 mi² (248,687 km²).
Highest point Zugspitze, 9,721 ft (2,963 m).
Lowest point Freepsum Lake, 7 ft (2 m) below sea
level.

PEOPLE. West Germany, like East Germany, is
homogeneous, with a Germanic, German-
speaking population. Religious groups include
Roman Catholics and mostly Lutheran Protestants. The populace is generally well educated.
The country is about twice as large as East Germany and has about four times the population.

ECONOMY AND THE LAND. Despite destruction incurred in World War II and Germany's
division into two countries, West Germany has
one of the world's strongest economies. Industry
provides the basis for prosperity, with mining,
manufacturing, construction, and utilities important contributors. The Ruhr district is the nation's most important industrial region, situated
near the Ruhr River in northwest-central Germany and including cities such as Essen and
Dortmund. The Rhine River, the most important
commercial waterway in Europe, is found in the
west. Agriculture remains important in the
south. Germany's terrain varies from northern
plains to western and central uplands and hills
that extend to the southern Bavarian Alps. The
dark green firs of the Black Forest lie in the
southwest. The mild climate is tempered by the
sea in the north, and in the south the winters are
colder because of proximity to the Alps.

HISTORY AND POLITICS. In ancient times Germanic tribes overcame Celtic inhabitants in the
area of Germany and established a northern
stronghold against Roman expansion of Gaul. As
the Roman Empire weakened, the Germanic peoples invaded, deposing the Roman governor of
Gaul in the fifth century A.D. The Franks composed the strongest tribe, and in the ninth century Frankish-controlled territory was expanded
and united under Charlemagne. The 843 Treaty
of Verdun divided Charlemagne's lands into
three kingdoms, with the eastern territory
encompassing modern Germany. Unity did not
follow, however, and Germany remained a dis-
jointed territory of feudal states, duchies, and
independent cities. The Reformation, a movement led by German monk Martin Luther, began
in 1517 and evolved into the Protestant branch of
Christianity. In the eighteenth century the state
of Prussia became the foremost rival of the powerful Austrian state. The rise of Prussian power
and growing nationalism eventually united the
German states into the German Empire in 1871,
and Prussian chancellor Otto von Bismarck installed Prussian king Wilhelm I as emperor. Reconciliation with Austria-Hungary came in 1879,
and Germany allied with Austria in World War I
in 1914. The empire collapsed as a result of the
war, and the Weimar Republic was established in
1919. Instability and disunity arose in the face of
economic problems. Promising prosperity and
encouraging nationalism, Adolf Hitler of the National Socialist, or Nazi, party became chancellor
in 1933. Hitler did away with the freedoms of
speech and assembly and began a genocidal pro-

**Neuschwanstein Castle, shown here, is one of Germany's most spectacular sights. Situated in the West German state of
Bayern, the castle was built by Ludwig II, the king of Bavaria from 1864 to 1866.**

gram to eliminate Jews and other peoples. Hitler's ambitions led to World War II, during which millions of Jews were killed. In April 1945 Hitler committed suicide, and in May Germany unconditionally surrendered to the Allies. The United States, Britain, the Soviet Union, and France divided Germany into four zones of occupation.

East Germany. After World War II, eastern Germany was designated the Soviet-occupied zone. The Communist party combined with the Social Democrats and, following the formation of the western Federal Republic of Germany in 1949, the eastern region proclaimed itself the German Democratic Republic. In 1955 the country became fully independent. Berlin, not included in the occupation zones, was a separate entity under the four Allied nations. When the Soviet Union ceased to participate in Allied negotiations in 1948, the city was divided. The Berlin Wall, constructed in 1961, separates East from West Berlin.

West Germany. The Federal Republic of Germany was established in 1949, composed of the American-, French-, and British-occupied zones. The republic became fully independent in 1955. Military forces of the United States, France, and Britain continue to occupy West Berlin. West German politics have been marked by stability under various chancellors. The Green party, formed in the 1970s by environmentalists, has grown in importance in the 1980s. ■

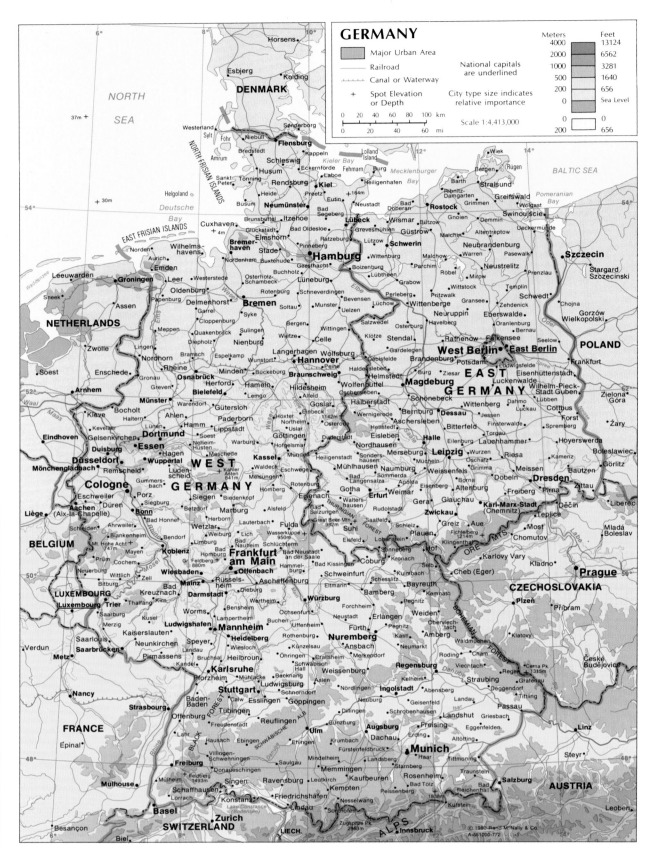

Germany Map Index

	Lat.	Long.
Aachen (Aix-la-Chapelle)	50°47'N	6°05'E
Ahlen	51°46'N	7°53'E
Alps	47°30'N	11°00'E
Altenburg	50°59'N	12°26'E
Amberg	49°27'N	11°52'E
Amrum	54°39'N	8°21'E
Ansbach	49°17'N	10°34'E
Aschaffenburg	49°59'N	9°09'E
Aschersleben	51°45'N	11°27'E
Aue	50°35'N	12°42'E
Augsburg	48°23'N	10°53'E
Baden-Baden	48°46'N	8°14'E
Bad Kreuznach	49°52'N	7°51'E
Bamberg	49°53'N	10°53'E
Bautzen	51°11'N	14°26'E
Bayreuth	49°57'N	11°35'E
Berlin → East Berlin, West Berlin	52°31'N	13°24'E
Bernburg	51°48'N	11°44'E
Bielefeld	52°01'N	8°31'E
Bitterfeld	51°37'N	12°20'E
Black Forest	48°00'N	8°15'E
Bocholt	51°50'N	6°36'E
Bohemian Forest	49°15'N	12°45'E
Bonn	50°44'N	7°05'E
Brandenburg	52°24'N	12°32'E
Braunschweig	52°16'N	10°31'E
Bremen	53°04'N	8°49'E
Bremerhaven	53°33'N	8°34'E
Celle	52°37'N	10°05'E
Chemnitz → Karl-Marx-Stadt	50°50'N	12°55'E
Coburg	50°15'N	10°58'E
Cologne	50°56'N	6°59'E
Constance, Lake	47°35'N	9°25'E
Cottbus	51°45'N	14°19'E
Cuxhaven	53°52'N	8°42'E
Dachau	48°15'N	11°27'E
Danube	48°31'N	13°44'E
Darmstadt	49°53'N	8°40'E
Delmenhorst	53°03'N	8°38'E
Dessau	51°50'N	12°14'E
Deutsche Bay	54°30'N	7°30'E
Döbeln	51°07'N	13°07'E
Dortmund	51°31'N	7°28'E
Dresden	51°03'N	13°44'E
Duisburg	51°25'N	6°46'E
Düren	50°48'N	6°28'E
Düsseldorf	51°12'N	6°47'E
East Berlin	52°30'N	13°25'E
East Frisian Islands	53°44'N	7°25'E
Eberswalde	52°50'N	13°49'E
Eisenach	50°59'N	10°19'E
Eisenhüttenstadt	52°10'N	14°39'E
Eisleben	51°31'N	11°32'E
Elbe	53°50'N	9°00'E
Elmshorn	53°45'N	9°39'E
Emden	53°22'N	7°12'E
Ems	53°20'N	7°00'E
Erfurt	50°58'N	11°01'E
Erlangen	49°36'N	11°01'E

	Lat.	Long.
Eschweiler	50°49'N	6°16'E
Essen	51°28'N	7°01'E
Esslingen	48°45'N	9°16'E
Falkensee	52°33'N	13°04'E
Fehmarn	54°28'N	11°08'E
Feldberg	47°52'N	7°59'E
Fichtelberg	50°26'N	12°57'E
Flensburg	54°47'N	9°26'E
Föhr	54°43'N	8°30'E
Forst	51°44'N	14°39'E
Frankfurt	52°20'N	14°33'E
Frankfurt am Main	50°07'N	8°40'E
Freiberg	50°54'N	13°20'E
Freiburg	47°59'N	7°51'E
Freising	48°23'N	11°44'E
Friedrichshafen	47°39'N	9°28'E
Fulda	50°33'N	9°41'E
Fürth	49°28'N	10°59'E
Gelsenkirchen	51°31'N	7°07'E
Gera	50°52'N	12°04'E
Glauchau	50°49'N	12°32'E
Göppingen	48°42'N	9°40'E
Görlitz	51°09'N	14°59'E
Goslar	51°54'N	10°25'E
Gotha	50°57'N	10°41'E
Göttingen	51°32'N	9°55'E
Greifswald	54°05'N	13°23'E
Greiz	50°39'N	12°12'E
Grosser Feldberg	50°14'N	8°26'E
Güstrow	53°48'N	12°10'E
Gütersloh	51°54'N	8°23'E
Hagen	51°22'N	7°28'E
Halberstadt	51°54'N	11°02'E
Halle	51°29'N	11°58'E
Hamburg	53°33'N	9°59'E
Hameln	52°06'N	9°21'E
Hamm	51°41'N	7°49'E
Hannover	52°24'N	9°44'E
Heidelberg	49°25'N	8°43'E
Heilbronn	49°08'N	9°13'E
Helgoland	54°12'N	7°53'E
Helmstedt	52°13'N	11°00'E
Herford	52°06'N	8°40'E
Hildesheim	52°09'N	9°57'E
Hof	50°18'N	11°55'E
Hohe Acht, Mount	50°23'N	7°00'E
Hoyerswerda	51°26'N	14°14'E
Husum	54°28'N	9°03'E
Ingolstadt	48°46'N	11°27'E
Inn	48°35'N	13°28'E
Isar	48°49'N	12°58'E
Itzehoe	53°55'N	9°31'E
Kaiserslautern	49°26'N	7°46'E
Karl-Marx-Stadt (Chemnitz)	50°50'N	12°55'E
Karlsruhe	49°03'N	8°24'E
Kassel	51°19'N	9°29'E
Kaufbeuren	47°53'N	10°37'E
Kempten	47°43'N	10°19'E
Kiel	54°20'N	10°08'E
Kieler Bay	54°35'N	10°35'E
Kleve	51°48'N	6°09'E
Koblenz	50°21'N	7°35'E

	Lat.	Long.
Konstanz	47°40'N	9°10'E
Landshut	48°33'N	12°09'E
Langerhagen	52°27'N	9°44'E
Lauchhammer	51°30'N	13°47'E
Leer	53°14'N	7°26'E
Leine	52°43'N	9°32'E
Leipzig	51°19'N	12°20'E
Lindau	47°33'N	9°41'E
Lippstadt	51°40'N	8°19'E
Lübeck	53°52'N	10°40'E
Luckenwalde	52°05'N	13°10'E
Lüdenscheid	51°13'N	7°38'E
Ludwigsburg	48°53'N	9°11'E
Ludwigshafen	49°29'N	8°26'E
Lüneburg	53°15'N	10°23'E
Magdeburg	52°07'N	11°38'E
Main	50°00'N	8°18'E
Mainz	50°01'N	8°16'E
Mannheim	49°29'N	8°29'E
Marburg	50°49'N	8°46'E
Mecklenburger Bay	54°20'N	11°40'E
Meissen	51°10'N	13°28'E
Memmingen	47°59'N	10°11'E
Merseburg	51°21'N	11°59'E
Minden	52°17'N	8°55'E
Mönchengladbach	51°12'N	6°28'E
Mosel	50°22'N	7°36'E
Mühlhausen	51°12'N	10°27'E
Munich	48°08'N	11°34'E

	Lat.	Long.
Münster	51°57'N	7°37'E
Naumburg	51°09'N	11°48'E
Neisse	52°04'N	14°46'E
Neubrandenburg	53°33'N	13°15'E
Neumünster	54°04'N	9°59'E
Neunkirchen	49°20'N	7°10'E
Neuruppin	52°55'N	12°48'E
Neustrelitz	53°21'N	13°04'E
Nienburg	52°38'N	9°13'E
Nordhausen	51°30'N	10°47'E
Nordhorn	52°27'N	7°05'E
North Frisian Islands	54°50'N	8°12'E
Nuremberg	49°27'N	11°04'E
Oder	53°32'N	14°38'E
Offenbach	50°08'N	8°47'E
Offenburg	48°28'N	7°57'E
Oldenburg	53°08'N	8°13'E
Ore Mountains	50°30'N	13°10'E
Osnabrück	52°16'N	8°02'E
Paderborn	51°43'N	8°45'E
Passau	48°35'N	13°28'E
Pforzheim	48°54'N	8°42'E
Pirmasens	49°12'N	7°36'E
Pirna	50°58'N	13°56'E
Plauen	50°30'N	12°08'E
Pomeranian Bay	54°00'N	14°15'E
Porz	50°53'N	7°03'E
Potsdam	52°24'N	13°04'E
Rathenow	52°36'N	12°20'E

	Lat.	Long.
Ravensburg	47°47'N	9°37'E
Regensburg	49°01'N	12°06'E
Remscheid	51°11'N	7°11'E
Rendsburg	54°18'N	9°40'E
Reuflingen	48°29'N	9°11'E
Rheine	52°17'N	7°26'E
Rhine	51°52'N	6°03'E
Riesa	51°18'N	13°17'E
Rosenheim	47°51'N	12°07'E
Rostock	54°05'N	12°07'E
Rügen	54°25'N	13°24'E
Ruhr	51°27'N	6°44'E
Rüsselsheim	50°00'N	8°25'E
Saale	51°57'N	11°55'E
Saarbrücken	49°14'N	6°59'E
Saarlouis	49°21'N	6°45'E
Schleswig	54°31'N	9°33'E
Schönebeck	52°01'N	11°44'E
Schwäbische Alb	48°25'N	9°30'E
Schwedt	53°03'N	14°17'E
Schweinfurt	50°03'N	10°14'E
Schwerin	53°38'N	11°25'E
Siegen	50°52'N	8°02'E
Singen	47°46'N	8°50'E
Speyer	49°19'N	8°26'E
Spree	52°32'N	13°13'E
Stade	53°36'N	9°28'E
Stendal	52°36'N	11°51'E
Stralsund	54°19'N	13°05'E
Straubing	48°53'N	12°34'E

	Lat.	Long.
Stuttgart	48°46'N	9°11'E
Suhl	50°37'N	10°41'E
Sylt	54°54'N	8°20'E
Thuringian Forest	50°30'N	11°00'E
Trier	49°45'N	6°38'E
Tübingen	48°31'N	9°02'E
Ulm	48°24'N	10°00'E
Wasserkuppe	50°30'N	9°56'E
Weiden	49°41'N	12°10'E
Weimar	50°59'N	11°19'E
Weissenburg	49°01'N	10°58'E
Weissenfels	51°12'N	11°58'E
Weser	53°32'N	8°34'E
West Berlin	52°31'N	13°24'E
Wetzlar	50°33'N	8°29'E
Wiesbaden	50°05'N	8°14'E
Wilhelm-Pieck-Stadt Guben	51°57'N	14°43'E
Wilhelmshaven	53°31'N	8°08'E
Wismar	53°53'N	11°28'E
Wittenberg	51°52'N	12°39'E
Wittenberge	53°00'N	11°44'E
Wolfenbüttel	52°10'N	10°32'E
Wolfsburg	52°25'N	10°47'E
Worms	49°38'N	8°22'E
Wuppertal	51°16'N	7°11'E
Würzburg	49°48'N	9°56'E
Zittau	50°54'N	14°47'E
Zugspitze Peak	47°25'N	10°59'E
Zwickau	50°44'N	12°29'E

GHANA

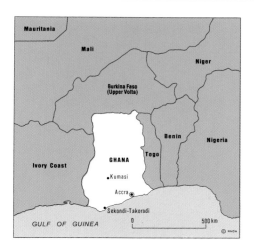

GHANA

	Railroad
+	Spot Elevation or Depth

National capitals are underlined

City type size indicates relative importance

Scale 1:7,238,000

Meters	Feet
1000	3281
500	1640
200	656
0	0
200	656
Below 2000	Below 6562

© 1980 Rand McNally & Co
A-582000-772 1 1-2

OFFICIAL NAME Republic of Ghana

PEOPLE

Population 14,030,000.
Density 152/mi² (59/km²).
Urban 36%.
Capital Accra, 1,045,381.
Ethnic groups Akan, Ewe, Ga.
Languages English, Akan, indigenous.
Religions Christian 42%, indigenous 38%, Muslim 12%.
Life expectancy 56 female, 53 male.
Literacy 30%.

POLITICS

Government Provisional military government.
Parties None.
Suffrage Universal, over 18.
Memberships CW, OAU, UN.
Subdivisions 10 regions.

ECONOMY

GNP $10,500,000,000.
Per capita $895.
Monetary unit Cedi.
Trade partners U.K., U.S., West Germany, Netherlands.
Exports Cocoa, wood, gold.
Imports Manufactured goods, fuels, food, transportation equipment.

LAND

Description Western Africa.
Area 92,100 mi² (238,537 km²).
Highest point Afadjoto, 2,905 ft (885 m).
Lowest point Sea level.

Ghana Map Index

	Lat.	Long.		Lat.	Long.
Accra	5°33'N	0°13'W	Oda	5°55'N	0°59'W
Bawku	11°05'N	0°14'W	*Oti*	8°40'N	0°13'E
Berekum	7°27'N	2°37'W	Prestea	5°27'N	2°08'W
Black Volta	8°41'N	1°33'W	Sekondi-Takoradi	4°59'N	1°43'W
Bolgatanga	10°46'N	0°52'W	Sunyani	7°20'N	2°20'W
Cape Coast	5°05'N	1°15'W	Tamale	9°25'N	0°50'W
Gold Coast	5°20'N	0°45'W	Tarkwa	5°19'N	1°59'W
Ho	6°35'N	0°30'E	Tema	5°38'N	0°01'E
Hohoe	7°09'N	0°28'E	*Three Points,*		
Koforidua	6°03'N	0°17'W	*Cape*	4°45'N	2°06'W
Konongo	6°37'N	1°11'W	*Volta*	5°46'N	0°41'E
Kumasi	6°41'N	1°35'W	*Volta, Lake*	7°30'N	0°15'E
Mampong	7°04'N	1°24'W	Wa	10°04'N	2°29'W
Nsawam	5°50'N	0°20'W	Wenchi	7°42'N	2°07'W
Nyakrom	5°37'N	0°48'W	*White Volta*	9°15'N	1°10'W
Obuasi	6°14'N	1°39'W	Winneba	5°25'N	0°36'W
			Yendi	9°26'N	0°01'W

PEOPLE. Tradition states that Ghanaians are descendants of migrating tribes who traveled down the Volta River valley in the 1200s, and nearly all are black Africans. The Akan, the majority group, are further divided into the Fanti, who live mainly along the coast, and the Ashanti, who inhabit the forests north of the coast. The Ewe and Ga live in the south and southeast. Other groups include the Guan, living on the Volta River plains, and the Moshi-Dagomba in the north. Ghana's more than fifty languages and dialects reflect this ethnic diversity, and English, the official language, is spoken by a minority. Christianity and traditional African religions predominate, but a Muslim minority also exists. Most people live in rural areas, and the literacy rate is low.

ECONOMY AND THE LAND. Agriculture is the economic mainstay, but Ghana's natural resources are diverse. Production of cocoa, the most important export, is concentrated in the Ashanti region, a belt of tropical rain forest extending north from the coastal plain. Resources include forests and mineral deposits, and exploitation of gold, diamonds, manganese ore, and bauxite is currently underway. Ghana's coastal lowlands give way to scrub and plains, the inland Ashanti rain forest, and northern savanna. The climate is tropical.

HISTORY AND POLITICS. The ancestors of today's Ghanaians probably migrated from the northern areas of Mauritania and Mali in the thirteenth century. The Portuguese reached the shore around 1470 and called the area the Gold Coast. The Dutch came soon after, eager to exploit the riches of the region. By the 1640s Portuguese influence on the Gold Coast had given way to the Dutch, and a lucrative slave trade sparked British, German, and Danish interest in the region as well. The 1850s saw the slave trade come to an end, and in subsequent years weakening Dutch and Danish settlements resulted in expanding British control. By 1874 the Gold Coast had become a British colony that extended from the shore of the Gulf of Guinea to the inland Ashanti territory. In 1901, after nearly seventy-five years of British-Ashanti fighting, the African lands also fell to the British. The onetime Ashanti empire became a colony, and the territories to the north were proclaimed a British protectorate. A thriving cacao industry led Britain to invest in transportation systems in the early twentieth century and improve educational and health facilities as well. Following World War I, a League of Nations mandate created British Togoland out of German holdings, and in a 1956 plebiscite, the people voted for Togoland to merge with Ghana when independence was achieved. In 1957 the four united regions became independent Ghana, the first black-ruled Commonwealth nation in Africa. A long history of economic problems plus disunity arising from the merging of the four separate entities led to instability soon after independence. The parliamentary state became a republic in 1960, and civilian rule has alternated with military governments. Ghana follows a foreign policy of nonalignment, and although Ghanaians' loyalties are based on community rather than national allegiance, they are in general agreement on foreign affairs. ■

Palm trees line the shore along the Gulf of Guinea, which borders Ghana in the south. Blue lagoons and white-sand beaches are also found in this coastal region.

GIBRALTAR

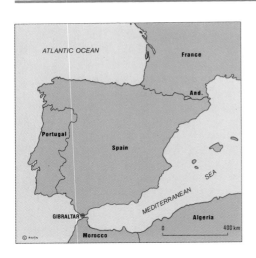

ATLANTIC OCEAN
France
Portugal
Spain
And.
GIBRALTAR
MEDITERRANEAN
SEA
Algeria
Morocco
400 km

OFFICIAL NAME Gibraltar

PEOPLE

Population 30,000.
Density 13,043/mi² (5,000/km²).
Urban 100%.
Capital Gibraltar, 30,000.
Ethnic groups Italian, English, Maltese.
Languages English, Spanish.
Religions Roman Catholic 75%, Anglican 8%, Jewish 2%.
Literacy 100%.

POLITICS

Government Colony (U.K.).
Parties Democratic, Labor/Association for the Advancement of Civil Rights, Socialist Labor.
Suffrage Universal adult Gibraltarians (other U.K. subjects in residence six months or more).
Memberships None.

Subdivisions None.

ECONOMY

Monetary unit Pound.
Trade partners U.K., Morocco, Portugal.
Exports Reexport of tobacco, petroleum, wine.
Imports Manufactured goods, fuels, food.

LAND

Description Southwestern Europe (peninsula on Spain's southern coast).
Area 2.3 mi² (6 km²).
Highest point 1,398 ft (426 m).
Lowest point Sea level.

PEOPLE. Occupying a narrow peninsula on Spain's southern coast, the British colony of Gibraltar has a mixed population of Italian, Maltese, Portuguese, and Spanish descent. A large number of British residents are also present, many of them military personnel. Most are bilingual in English and Spanish.

ECONOMY AND THE LAND. With land unsuited for agriculture and a lack of mineral resources, Gibraltar depends mainly on the British military presence and tourism. More than half of Gibraltar's male population works for British departments or the Gibraltar government. The private sector provides jobs as well, and shipping-related activities, construction, hotels, food services, and retail distributors are employers. The bottling industry provides for earnings in manufacturing. Connected to Spain by an isthmus, Gibraltar consists mainly of the limestone-and-shale ridge known as the Rock of Gibraltar. The climate is mild.

HISTORY AND POLITICS. Drawn by Gibraltar's strategic location at the Atlantic entrance to the Mediterranean, Phoenicians, Carthaginians, Ro-

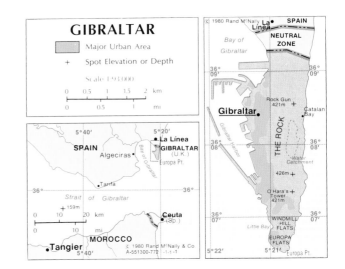

GIBRALTAR
Major Urban Area
+ Spot Elevation or Depth

Gibraltar Map Index

	Lat.	Long.		Lat.	Long.
Europa Point	36°06'N	5°21'W	*Gibraltar, Bay of*	36°09'N	5°22'W
Gibraltar	36°09'N	5°21'W	*The Rock*	36°08'N	5°21'W

mans, Vandals, Visigoths, and Moors all played a role in the land's history. After nearly three hundred years under Spanish control, Gibraltar was captured by Britain in 1704, during the War of the Spanish Succession. It was officially ceded to the British in the 1713 Peace of Utrecht. In a 1967 referendum, residents voted to remain under British control. British-Spanish competition for the colony has continued, however, and the border between Spain and Gibraltar was closed by the Spanish government in 1969 and did not reopen until 1985. ∎

GREECE

The Corinth Canal, shown here, connects the Gulf of Corinth with Saronikós Bay. The canal was constructed between 1882 and 1893.

Shown here is the Erechtheion, a temple on the Acropolis in Athens and a symbol of the mastery of Greek architecture. Construction on the Erechtheion was completed around 410 B.C.

Greek windmills such as this one on Crete pump water to irrigate olive, grape, and grain crops.

GREECE

OFFICIAL NAME Hellenic
Republic

PEOPLE
Population 10,030,000.
Density 197/mi² (76/km²).
Urban 65%.
Capital Athens, 885,737.
Ethnic groups Greek 98%, Turkish 1%.
Languages Greek.
Religions Greek Orthodox 98%, Muslim 1%.
Life expectancy 76 female, 72 male.
Literacy 95%.

POLITICS
Government Republic.
Parties Communist, New Democracy, Panhellenic
Socialist Movement.
Suffrage Universal, over 18.
Memberships EC, NATO, OECD, UN.
Subdivisions 51 departments.

ECONOMY
GNP $38,600,000,000.
Per capita $3,959.
Monetary unit Drachma.
Trade partners West Germany, Italy,
France, U.S.
Exports Textiles, fruits, minerals.
Imports Machinery, transportation equipment,
petroleum, chemicals, consumer goods.

LAND
Description Southeastern Europe.
Area 50,944 mi² (131,944 km²).
Highest point Mt. Olympus, 9,570 ft (2,917 m).
Lowest point Sea level.

PEOPLE. Greece has played a central role in European, African, and Asian cultures for thousands of years, but today its population is almost homogeneous. Native Greek inhabitants are united by a language that dates back three thousand years and a religion that influences many aspects of everyday life. Athens, the capital, was the cultural center of an ancient civilization that produced masterpieces of art and literature and broke ground in philosophy, political thought, and science.

ECONOMY AND THE LAND. The economy of Greece takes its shape from terrain and location. Dominated by the sea and long a maritime trading power, Greece has one of the largest merchant fleets in the world and depends greatly on commerce. The mountainous terrain and poor soil limit agriculture, although Greece is a leading producer of lemons and olives. The service sector, including tourism, provides most of Greece's national income. Inhabitants enjoy a temperate climate, with mild, wet winters, and hot, dry summers.

HISTORY AND POLITICS. Greece's history begins with the early Bronze Age cultures of the Minoans and the Mycenaeans. The city-state, or polis, began to develop around the tenth century B.C., and Athens, a democracy, and Sparta, an oligarchy, gradually emerged as Greece's leaders. The Persian Wars, in which the city-states united to repel a vastly superior army, ushered in the Golden Age of Athens, a cultural explosion in the fifth century B.C. The Parthenon, perhaps Greece's most famous building, was built at this time. Athens was defeated by Sparta in the Peloponnesian War, and by 338 B.C. Philip II of Macedon had conquered all of Greece. His son, Alexander the Great, defeated the Persians and spread Greek civilization and language all over the known world. Greece became a Roman province in 146 B.C. and part of the Byzantine Empire in A.D. 395, but its traditions had a marked influence on these empires. Absorbed into the Ottoman Empire in the 1450s, Greece had gained independence by 1830 and became a constitutional monarchy about fifteen years later. For much of the twentieth century the nation was divided between republicans and monarchists. During World War II Germany occupied Greece, and postwar instability led to a civil war, with Communist rebels eventually losing. Greece was ruled by a repressive military junta from 1967 until 1974, when the regime relinquished power to a civilian government. The Greeks then voted for a republic over a monarchy. ■

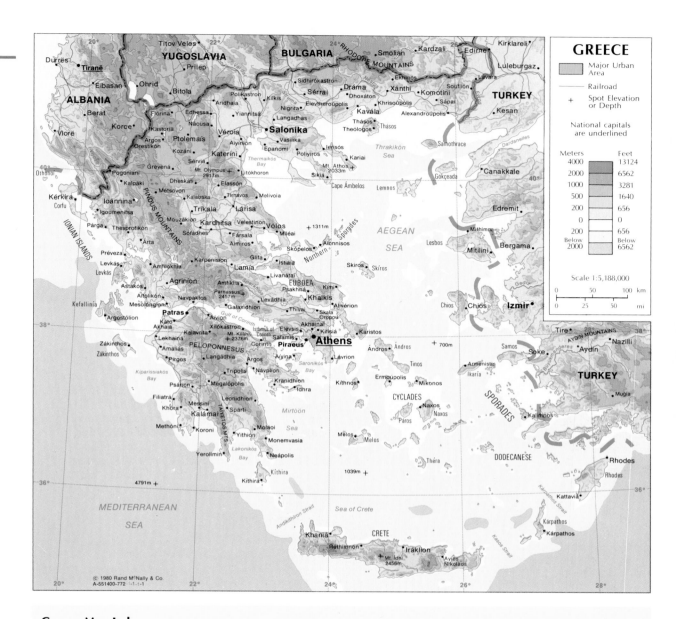

The monasteries of Météora, a valley in Thessaly, were built in the fourteenth century on rocks rising almost vertically from the valley floor. Once accessible only by ladder or rope, the monasteries can now be reached by stairs cut into the rock.

Greece Map Index

	Lat.	Long.		Lat.	Long.		Lat.	Long.		Lat.	Long.
Aegean Sea	38°30′N	25°00′E	Evros	40°52′N	26°12′E	Lamía	38°54′N	22°26′E	Rhodes	36°26′N	28°13′E
Agrínion	38°37′N	21°24′E	Ídhi, Mount	35°18′N	24°43′E	Lárisa	39°38′N	22°25′E	Rhodes	36°10′N	28°00′E
Ámbelos, Cape	39°56′N	23°55′E	Ikaría	37°41′N	26°20′E	Lemnos	39°54′N	25°21′E	Rhodope		
Ándros	37°45′N	24°42′E	Ioánnina	39°40′N	20°50′E	Lesbos	39°10′N	26°20′E	Mountains	41°30′N	24°30′E
Athens	37°58′N	23°43′E	Ionian Islands	38°30′N	20°30′E	Levkás	38°39′N	20°27′E	Salonika	40°38′N	22°56′E
Axios (Vardar)	40°31′N	22°43′E	Iráklion	35°20′N	25°09′E	Mirtóon Sea	36°51′N	23°18′E	Sámos	37°48′N	26°44′E
Chios	38°22′N	26°08′E	Kalámai	37°04′N	22°07′E	Mitilíni	39°06′N	26°32′E	Saronikós Bay	37°54′N	23°12′E
Chios	38°22′N	26°00′E	Kardhítsa	39°21′N	21°55′E	Nestos	40°41′N	24°44′E	Sérrai	41°05′N	23°32′E
Corfu	39°40′N	19°42′E	Kárpathos	35°40′N	27°10′E	Northern			Struma	40°47′N	23°51′E
Corinth, Gulf of	38°19′N	22°04′E	Kárpathos Strait	35°50′N	27°30′E	Sporades	39°17′N	23°23′E	Thásos	40°41′N	24°47′E
Corinth, Isthmus			Kasos Strait	35°30′N	26°30′E	Olympus, Mount	40°05′N	22°21′E	Théra	36°24′N	25°29′E
of	37°55′N	23°00′E	Katerini	40°16′N	22°30′E	Parnassus	38°32′N	22°35′E	Thermaikós Bay	40°23′N	22°47′E
Crete	35°29′N	24°42′E	Kavála	40°56′N	24°25′E	Patras	38°15′N	21°44′E	Thrakikón Sea	40°15′N	24°28′E
Crete, Sea of	35°46′N	23°54′E	Kefallinía	38°15′N	20°35′E	Peloponnesus	37°30′N	22°00′E	Tríkala	39°34′N	21°46′E
Cyclades	37°30′N	25°00′E	Kérkira	39°36′N	19°56′E	Pindus			Véroia	40°31′N	22°12′E
Dodecanese	36°30′N	27°00′E	Khalkis	38°28′N	23°36′E	Mountains	39°49′N	21°14′E	Vólos	39°21′N	22°56′E
Dráma	41°09′N	24°08′E	Khaniá	35°31′N	24°02′E	Piraeus	37°57′N	23°38′E	Xánthi	41°08′N	24°53′E
Euboea	38°34′N	23°50′E	Komotini	41°08′N	25°25′E	Ptolemaís	40°31′N	21°41′E	Zákinthos	37°52′N	20°44′E

GREENLAND

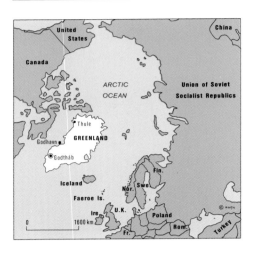

OFFICIAL NAME Greenland

PEOPLE
Population 53,000.
Density 0.06/mi² (0.02/km²).
Urban 75%.
Capital Godthåb, 9,717.
Ethnic groups Greenlander (Inuit and native-born whites) 86%, Danish 14%.
Languages Danish, indigenous.
Religions Lutheran.
Life expectancy 67 female, 60 male.
Literacy 99%.

POLITICS
Government Part of Danish realm.
Parties Atassut, Inuit Atagatigik, Siumut.
Suffrage Universal, over 21.
Memberships None.
Subdivisions 3 counties, 19 communes.

ECONOMY
Monetary unit Danish krone.
Trade partners Denmark, Finland, West Germany, U.S.
Exports Fish and fish products, metallic ores and concentrates.
Imports Petroleum, machinery, transportation equipment, food.

LAND
Description North Atlantic island.
Area 840,004 mi² (2,175,600 km²).
Highest point Gunnbjorn Mtn., 12,139 ft (3,700 m).
Lowest point Sea level.

PEOPLE. Most Greenlanders are of mixed Inuit-Danish ancestry. Descended from an indigenous Arctic people, pure Inuit are a minority and usually follow traditional life-styles.

ECONOMY AND THE LAND. Fishing is the state's economic mainstay, and mining produces zinc and lead. Land regions include an inland plateau, coastal mountains and fjords, and offshore islands. The climate is cold, with warmer temperatures in the southwest.

HISTORY AND POLITICS. Following early immigration of Arctic Inuit, Norwegian Vikings sighted Greenland in the ninth century. Greenland united with Norway in the 1200s and came under Danish rule in the 1300s. In 1953 the island became a province of Denmark and in 1979 gained home rule. ■

Greenland Map Index

	Lat.	Long.		Lat.	Long.
Angmagssalik	65°36'N	37°41'W	Godhavn	69°15'N	53°33'W
Christanshåb	68°50'N	51°12'W	Godthåb	64°11'N	51°44'W
Disko	69°50'N	53°30'W	Julianehåb	60°43'N	46°01'W
Farvel, Cape	59°45'N	44°00'W	Narssag	60°54'N	46°00'W
Frederikshåb	62°00'N	49°43'W	Thule	76°34'N	68°47'W

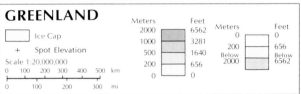

GREENLAND

☐ Ice Cap
+ Spot Elevation
Scale 1:20,000,000

Meters	Feet	Meters	Feet
2000	6562	0	0
1000	3281	200	656
500	1640	Below 2000	Below 6562
200	656		
0	0		

© 1980 Rand McNally & Co.

GRENADA

OFFICIAL NAME Grenada

PEOPLE
Population 114,000.
Density 857/mi² (331/km²).
Urban 75%.
Capital St. George's, 7,500.
Ethnic groups Black.
Languages English.
Religions Roman Catholic, Anglican, other Protestant.
Life expectancy 67 female, 60 male.
Literacy 98%.

POLITICS
Government Parliamentary state.
Parties Democratic Movement, National Democratic.
Suffrage Universal adult.
Memberships CW, OAS, UN.
Subdivisions 6 parishes.

ECONOMY
GNP $119,000,000.
Per capita $870.
Monetary unit East Caribbean dollar.
Trade partners U.K., Benelux countries, U.S., Trinidad and Tobago.
Exports Cocoa, nutmeg, bananas.
Imports Food, machinery, construction materials.

LAND
Description Caribbean island.
Area 133 mi² (344 km²).
Highest point Mt. St. Catherine, 2,756 ft (840 m).
Lowest point Sea level.

PEOPLE. Grenada's culture bears the influences of former British and French rule. The most widely spoken language is English, although a French patois is also spoken, and the majority of the population is Roman Catholic. Most Grenadians are black, but there are small East Indian and European populations.

ECONOMY AND THE LAND. Rich volcanic soils and heavy rainfall have made agriculture the chief economic activity. Also known as the Isle of Spice, Grenada is one of the world's leading producers of nutmeg and mace. Many tropical fruits are also raised, and the small plots of peasant farmers dot the hilly terrain. Another mainstay of the economy is tourism, with visitors drawn by the beaches and tropical climate. There is little industry on Grenada, and high unemployment has plagued the nation in recent years.

HISTORY AND POLITICS. European attempts to colonize Grenada were resisted by the Carib Indians for more than one hundred years after the island's discovery by Christopher Columbus in 1498. The French established the first settlement in 1650 and slaughtered the Caribs, but the British finally gained control in 1783. In 1974 Grenada achieved full independence under Prime Minister Eric Gairy, despite widespread opposition to his policies. In 1979 foes of the regime staged a coup and installed a Marxist government headed by Maurice Bishop. Power struggles resulted, and a military branch of the government seized power in 1983 and executed Bishop and several of his ministers. The United States led a subsequent invasion that deposed the Marxists. ■

GRENADA

+ Spot Elevation or Depth
National capital is underlined
Scale 1:787,000

Grenada Map Index

	Lat.	Long.		Lat.	Long.
Baillies Bacolet	12°02'N	61°41'W	Grenville	12°07'N	61°37'W
Carriacou	12°30'N	61°27'W	Hillsborough	12°28'N	61°28'W
Gouyave	12°10'N	61°44'W	Marquis	12°06'N	61°37'W
Grand Anse Bay	12°02'N	61°46'W	Saint George's	12°03'N	61°45'W
Grand Bay	12°28'N	61°25'W	Salines, Point	12°00'N	61°48'W
Grand Roy	12°08'N	61°45'W	Sauteurs	12°14'N	61°38'W
Grenadine Islands	12°25'N	61°35'W	Tivoli	12°10'N	61°37'W
			Victoria	12°12'N	61°42'W

GUADELOUPE

OFFICIAL NAME Department
of Guadeloupe

PEOPLE
Population 320,000.
Density 466/mi² (180/km²).
Urban 40%.
Capital Basse-Terre,
Basse-Terre I., 13,656.
Ethnic groups Black or mulatto 90%, white 5%,
others 5%.
Languages French, Creole.
Religions Roman Catholic 95%, Hindu 5%.
Life expectancy 72 female, 66 male.
Literacy 70%.

POLITICS
Government Overseas department (France).
Parties Communist, Rally for the Republic, Socialist
Party Federation.
Suffrage Universal, over 18.
Subdivisions 3 arrondissements.

ECONOMY
GNP $998,000,000.
Per capita $3,151.
Monetary unit French franc.
Trade partners France, Martinique, U.S.
Exports Bananas, sugar, rum.
Imports Vehicles, foodstuffs, clothing, building
materials.

LAND
Description Caribbean islands.
Area 687 mi² (1,780 km²).
Highest point Soufrière, Basse-Terre I., 4,813 ft
(1,467 m).
Lowest point Sea level.

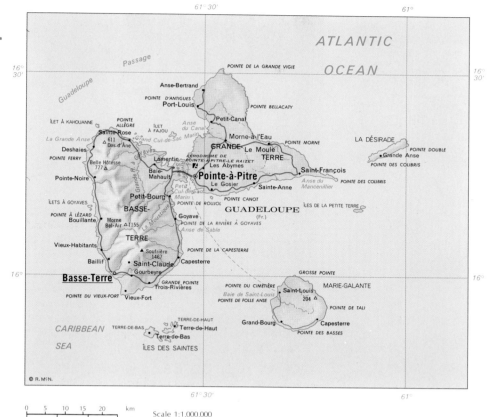

Scale 1:1,000,000

PEOPLE. Most of the people of these French islands in the Caribbean are black or of mixed black and white ancestry. A white community in the Îles des Saintes island group is descended from the original French settlers.

ECONOMY AND THE LAND. Important economic contributors include tourism, agriculture, sugar refining, and rum distilling. A drawbridge crossing a narrow strait connects the volcanic island of Basse-Terre, or Guadeloupe proper, to Grande-Terre, part of a limestone island chain. Together, these two islands are known as Guadeloupe. Other islands include the Îles des

Saintes group, Marie-Galante, La Désirade, St. Barthélemy, the northern section of St. Martin, and Îles de la Petite Terre. The climate is warm with moderating trade winds.

HISTORY AND POLITICS. Around the year 1000 the Carib Indians took the main island from the Arawaks. In 1493 Christopher Columbus arrived, but the first French settlers did not come to the islands until 1635. About ten years later the sugar economy was underway, and slaves were imported from Africa to work the plantations. In 1946 France changed Guadeloupe's status from colony to overseas department. ■

GUAM

OFFICIAL NAME Territory
of Guam

PEOPLE
Population 116,000.
Density 555/mi² (214/km²).
Urban 40%.
Capital Agana, 896.
Ethnic groups Chamorro, white, Filipino.
Languages English, Chamorro.
Religions Roman Catholic.

POLITICS
Government Unicorporated territory (U.S.).
Parties Democratic, Republican.
Suffrage Universal, over 18.
Subdivisions 19 municipalities.

ECONOMY
GNP $690,000,000.
Per capita $6,070.
Monetary unit U.S. dollar.

Trade partners Saudi Arabia, U.S., Japan.
Imports Petroleum, fuels.

LAND
Description North Pacific island.
Area 209 mi² (541 km²).
Highest point Mt. Lamlam, 1,332 ft (406 m).
Lowest point Sea level.

PEOPLE. The main ethnic group in Guam is the Chamorros, who are of mixed Micronesian, Filipino, and Spanish ancestry. Because of the United States military base and its fluctuating personnel, the size and nature of the population vary.

ECONOMY AND THE LAND. The United States military and a growing tourist industry provide employment for the islanders, and there is some light industry as well. Many residents, however, continue to practice subsistence farming. The largest island in the Mariana Islands, Guam has hills and mountains in the south and a flat plateau in the north. The climate is tropical.

HISTORY AND POLITICS. Magellan arrived on Guam in 1521, and in 1565 Spain took formal possession of the island. In 1898, following the Spanish-American War, Spain ceded the island to the United States. It became a major United States military base, and during World War II the Japanese occupied the island. The people of Guam were granted United States citizenship in 1950; however, they do not vote in national elections. ■

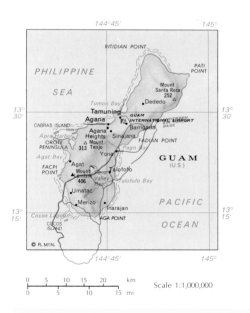

Scale 1:1,000,000

GUATEMALA

OFFICIAL NAME Republic of Guatemala

PEOPLE

Population 8,080,000.
Density 192/mi² (74/km²).
Urban 44%.
Capital Guatemala, 749,784.
Ethnic groups Ladino (mestizo and westernized Indian) 59%, Indian 41%.
Languages Spanish, indigenous.
Religions Roman Catholic, Protestant, indigenous.
Life expectancy 56 female, 54 male.
Literacy 50%.

POLITICS

Government Republic.
Parties Democratic Institutional, National Liberation Movement, National United Front, Revolutionary.
Suffrage Universal, over 18.
Memberships OAS, UN.
Subdivisions 22 departments.

ECONOMY

GDP $8,600,000,000.
Per capita $1,114.
Monetary unit Quetzal.
Trade partners U.S., Central American countries, Japan, West Germany.
Exports Coffee, cotton, sugar.
Imports Manufactured goods, machinery, transportation equipment, chemicals, fuels.

LAND

Description Central America.
Area 42,042 mi² (108,889 km²).
Highest point Tajumulco Volcano; 13,845 ft (4,220 m).
Lowest point Sea level.

PEOPLE. Guatemala's population is made up of majority ladinos and minority Indians. Ladinos include both mestizos, those of Spanish-Indian origin, and westernized Indians of Mayan descent. Classified on the basis of culture rather than race, ladinos follow a Spanish-American life-style and speak Spanish. Nonladino Indians are also of Mayan descent; they generally speak Mayan dialects, and many are poor, uneducated, and isolated from the mainstream of Guatemalan life. Roman Catholicism often combines with traditional Indian religious practice. Population is concentrated in the central highland region.

ECONOMY AND THE LAND. Most Guatemalans practice agriculture in some form. Indians generally operate small, unproductive subsistence farms, and export crops are mainly produced on large plantations on the fertile southern plain that borders the Pacific. Although light industry is growing, it is unable to absorb rural immigrants seeking employment in the cities. Much of the landscape is mountainous, with the Pacific plain and Caribbean lowlands bordering central highlands. Northern rain forests and grasslands are sparsely populated and largely undeveloped. The climate is tropical in low areas and temperate in the highlands.

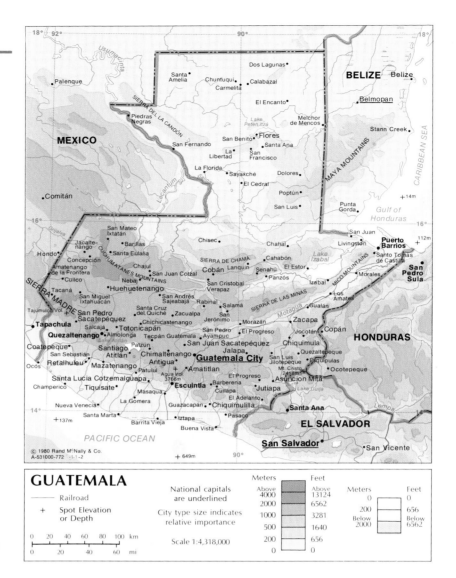

GUATEMALA

— Railroad
+ Spot Elevation or Depth

National capitals are underlined
City type size indicates relative importance

	Meters	Feet
Above	4000	Above 13124
	2000	6562
	1000	3281
	500	1640
	200	656
	0	0

	Meters	Feet
	200	656
	Below 2000	Below 6562

Scale 1:4,318,000

© 1980 Rand McNally & Co.
A-531000-772

HISTORY AND POLITICS. Indians in the region were absorbed into the Mayan civilization that was flourishing in Central America by the fourth century. In 1523 the Spanish defeated the indigenous Indians and went on to establish one of the most influential colonies in Central America. Guatemala joined Costa Rica, El Salvador, Nicaragua, and Honduras in 1821 to declare independence from Spain, and the former Spanish colonies formed the Federation of Central America in 1823. Almost from the start, the federation was marked by dissension, and by 1838 it had, in effect, been dissolved. Following a series of dictatorships, social and economic reform began in 1944 and continued under two successive presidents. The government was ousted in a 1954 revolution, and military rule established. A presidential assassination, accusations of government corruption and human rights violations, guerrilla activities, and violence followed. A 1976 earthquake resulted in thousands of deaths and physical and economic damage. ∎

Shown here are the ruins of Tikal, situated in northern Guatemala in the Petén jungle, an area so impenetrable that the Spanish were not able to conquer the region's inhabitants until 1697. Tikal is one of the largest and most important of the Mayan cities.

The ancient Mayan people founded an advanced civilization, organized into independent, often warring, city-states and suburban agricultural communities. Settlement in the area of Tikal began around 600 B.C., and soon it became a thriving Mayan city-state. Tikal was continuously occupied until A.D. 900, when it was virtually abandoned, as were the other Mayan cities in the Petén region. Excavation of Tikal began in 1956, and the site is one of the most explored of the Mayan ruins.

Guatemala Map Index

	Lat.	Long.
Agua Volcano	14°28'N	90°45'W
Amatitlan	14°29'N	90°37'W
Antigua	14°34'N	90°44'W
Asuncion Mita	14°20'N	89°43'W
Atitlán, Lake	14°42'N	91°12'W
Barrita Vieja	13°55'N	90°54'W
Chajul	15°30'N	91°02'W
Chamá, Sierra de	15°40'N	90°30'W
Chimaltenango	14°40'N	90°49'W
Chiquimula	14°48'N	89°33'W
Chiquimulilla	14°05'N	90°23'W
Chisec	15°49'N	90°17'W
Coatepeque	14°42'N	91°52'W
Dolores	16°31'N	89°25'W
El Cedral	16°26'N	90°03'W
El Encanto	17°17'N	89°34'W
El Estor	15°32'N	89°21'W
Escuintla	14°18'N	90°47'W
Flores	16°56'N	89°53'W
Guatemala City	14°38'N	90°31'W
Honduras, Gulf of	16°10'N	87°50'W
Huehuetenango	15°20'N	91°28'W
Izabal, Lake	15°30'N	89°10'W
Jacaltenango	15°40'N	91°44'W
Jalapa	14°38'N	89°59'W
Jutiapa	14°17'N	89°54'W
Lacantum	16°36'N	90°39'W
La Florida	16°33'N	90°27'W
Los Amates	15°16'N	89°06'W
Madre, Sierra	15°20'N	92°00'W
Mazatenango	14°32'N	91°30'W
Mico Mountains	15°30'N	88°55'W
Minas, Sierra de las	15°10'N	89°40'W
Motagua	15°44'N	88°14'W
Petén Itzá, Lake	16°59'N	89°50'W
Piedras Negras	17°11'N	91°15'W
Puerto Barrios	15°43'N	88°36'W
Quezaltenango	14°50'N	91°31'W
Retalhuleu	14°32'N	91°41'W
Salamá	15°06'N	90°16'W
Salinas	16°28'N	90°33'W
San Benito	16°55'N	89°54'W
San Juan	15°52'N	88°53'W
San Pedro Sacatepéquez	14°58'N	91°46'W
Santa Lucia Cotzemalguapa	14°20'N	91°01'W
Santiago Atitlán	14°38'N	91°14'W
Tajumulco Volcano	15°02'N	91°55'W
Tiquisate	14°17'N	91°22'W
Totonicapán	14°55'N	91°22'W
Zacapa	14°58'N	89°32'W
Zacualpa	15°05'N	90°50'W

GUINEA

OFFICIAL NAME People's Revolutionary Republic of Guinea

PEOPLE
Population 5,655,000.
Density 60/mi² (23/km²).
Urban 19%.
Capital Conakry, 600,000.
Ethnic groups Fulani, Mandingo, Soussou, others.
Languages French, indigenous.
Religions Muslim 75%, indigenous 24%, Christian 1%.
Life expectancy 45 female, 42 male.
Literacy 48% in indigenous languages, 20% in French.

POLITICS
Government Republic.
Parties None.
Suffrage Universal, over 18.
Memberships OAU, UN.
Subdivisions 15 prefectures.

ECONOMY
GNP $1,710,000,000.
Per capita $329.
Monetary unit Syli.
Trade partners Western European countries, U.S., U.S.S.R., China.
Exports Bauxite, alumina, pineapples, coffee.
Imports Petroleum, metals, machinery, transportation equipment, food.

LAND
Description Western Africa.
Area 94,926 mi² (245,857 km²).
Highest point Mont Nimba, 5,748 ft (1,752 m).
Lowest point Sea level.

PEOPLE. Guinea's population is composed of several ethnic groups, with three—the Fulani, Mandingo, and Soussou—forming nearly half the total. Most Guineans are rural farmers, living in hamlets, and the only true urban center is Conakry. Mortality as well as emigration rates are high.

ECONOMY AND THE LAND. Rich soil and a varied terrain suited for diverse crop production have made agriculture an important economic activity. Guinea also has vast mineral reserves, including one of the world's largest bauxite deposits. The terrain is mostly flat along the coast and mountainous in the interior. The climate is tropical on the coast, hot and dry in the north and northeast, and cooler with less humidity in the highlands.

HISTORY AND POLITICS. As part of the Ghana, Mali, and Songhai empires that flourished in West Africa between the fourth and fifteenth centuries, Guinea was a trading center for gold and slaves. The Portuguese arrived on the coast in the 1400s. In the 1890s France declared the area a colony and named it French Guinea. The first of the French colonies in West Africa to attain independence, in 1958, Guinea was also the only colony to reject membership in the French Community. ■

GUINEA
— Railroad

Scale 1:10,667,000

Meters	Feet		Meters	Feet
2000	6562			0
1000	3281		200	656
500	1640		Below	Below
200	656		2000	6562
0	0			

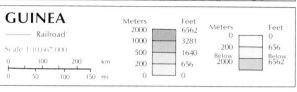

Guinea Map Index

	Lat.	Long.		Lat.	Long.
Conakry	9°31'N	13°43'W	Labé	11°19'N	12°17'W
Dubreka	9°48'N	13°31'W	Niger	11°40'N	8°43'W
Kankan	10°23'N	9°18'W	Nimba Mountains	7°30'N	8°30'W
Kindia	10°04'N	12°51'W	Nzérékoré	7°45'N	8°49'W
Kouroussa	10°39'N	9°53'W	Siguiri	11°25'N	9°10'W

GUINEA-BISSAU

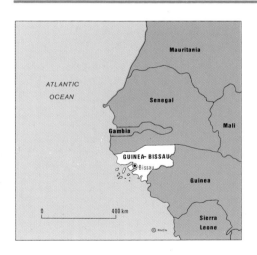

OFFICIAL NAME Republic of Guinea-Bissau

PEOPLE
Population 850,000.
Density 61/mi² (24/km²).
Urban 24%.
Capital Bissau, 109,486.
Ethnic groups Balanta 30%, Fulani 20%, Manjaca 14%, Mandingo 13%.
Languages Portuguese, indigenous.
Religions Indigenous 65%, Muslim 30%, Christian 5%.
Life expectancy 42.
Literacy 9%.

POLITICS
Government Republic.
Parties African Party for the Independence of Guinea-Bissau and Cape Verde.
Suffrage Universal, over 15.

Memberships OAU, UN.
Subdivisions 8 regions, 1 autonomous sector.

ECONOMY
GDP $177,000,000.
Per capita $198.
Monetary unit Peso.
Trade partners Portugal, other Western European countries.
Exports Peanuts, palm kernels, shrimp.
Imports Food, machinery, transportation equipment, fuels.

LAND
Description Western Africa.
Area 13,948 mi² (36,125 km²).
Highest point 1,017 ft (310 m).
Lowest point Sea level.

PEOPLE. Guinea-Bissau's largest ethnic group, the Balanta, mainly inhabit the coastal area. Most practice traditional beliefs, although some are Christian. Predominately Muslim peoples, the Fulani and Mandingo are concentrated in the northwest. The Manjaca inhabit the northern and central coastal regions. The official language is Portuguese, but many speak Crioulo, a creole dialect also spoken in Cape Verde.

ECONOMY AND THE LAND. Guinea-Bissau's economy is dependent upon agriculture, and its soils are relatively productive. Peanuts, cotton, corn, and sorghum are grown in the north, and palm-oil production is concentrated along the coast. Timber is produced primarily in the south. A swamp-covered coastal plain rises to an eastern savanna. The climate is tropical. The country includes the Bijagos Archipelago, lying just off the coast.

HISTORY AND POLITICS. The area of Guinea-Bissau was inhabited by diverse peoples prior to the arrival of the Portuguese in 1446. Ruled as a single colony with Cape Verde, the region soon developed into a base for the Portuguese slave trade. In 1879 it was separated from Cape Verde as Portuguese Guinea, and its status changed to overseas province in 1951. A movement for the independence of Guinea-Bissau and Cape Verde developed in the 1950s, and a coup in Portugal in 1974 resulted in independence the same year. Attempts to unite Guinea-Bissau and Cape Verde have been unsuccessful. ■

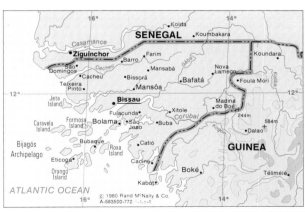

GUINEA-BISSAU
+ Spot Elevation

Scale 1:5,600,000

City type size indicates relative importance

National capitals are underlined

Meters	Feet
1000	3281
500	1640
200	656
0	0
200	656

Guinea-Bissau Map Index

	Lat.	Long.		Lat.	Long.
Bafatá	12°10'N	14°40'W	Bissau	11°51'N	15°35'W
Bijagós Archipelago	11°25'N	16°20'W	Bolama	11°35'N	15°28'W
			Orango Island	11°10'N	16°08'W

GUYANA

OFFICIAL NAME Cooperative
Republic of Guyana

PEOPLE
Population 840,000.
Density 10/mi² (3.9/km²).
Urban 30%.
Capital Georgetown, 72,049.
Ethnic groups East Indian 51%, African and mixed
43%, Amerindian 4%.
Languages English.
Religions Christian 57%, Hindu 33%, Muslim 9%.
Life expectancy 72 female, 67 male.
Literacy 92%.

POLITICS
Government Republic.
Parties People's National Congress, People's
Progressive, United Force.
Suffrage Universal, over 18.
Memberships CW, UN.
Subdivisions 10 regions.

ECONOMY
GNP $430,000,000.
Per capita $539.
Monetary unit Dollar.
Trade partners Caribbean countries, U.K., U.S.
Exports Bauxite, sugar, rice.
Imports Manufactured goods, petroleum, food.

LAND
Description Northeastern South America.
Area 83,000 mi² (214,969 km²).
Highest point Mt. Roraima, 9,094 ft (2,772 m).
Lowest point Sea level.

PEOPLE. Guyana's population is composed of
descendants of black African slaves and East Indian, Chinese, and Portuguese laborers brought
to work sugar plantations. Amerindians, the indigenous peoples of Guyana, are a minority.
Ninety percent of the people live along the fertile
coastal plain, where farming and manufacturing
are concentrated.

ECONOMY AND THE LAND. Agriculture and
mining compose the backbone of the Guyanese
economy. Sugar and rice continue to be important crops and in addition to bauxite, mines
produce manganese, diamonds, and gold. Guyana's inland forests give way to savanna and a
coastal plain. The climate is tropical.

HISTORY AND POLITICS. First gaining European notice in 1498 with the voyages of Christopher Columbus, Guyana was the stage for com-
peting colonial interests—British, French, and
Dutch—until it officially became British Guiana
in 1831. Slavery was abolished several years
later, causing the British to import indentured
laborers, the ancestors of today's majority group.
In 1953 the adoption of a constitution was followed by elections, but British fears of Communist subversion led to the removal of the winner
—Cheddi B. Jagan, leader of the People's Progressive party—and the suspension of the constitution. The People's Progressive party won again

in 1957 and 1961. In the early 1960s racial tensions erupted into riots between East Indians
and blacks, causing the British to postpone independence until another election could be held. In
1964 the People's National Congress won the majority of legislative seats. Independence was
gained in 1966, and the name Guyana adopted.
Guyana became a republic in 1970 and has pursued socialist policies. The two main political
parties continue to reflect Guyana's ethnic divisions: the People's National Congress is supported by blacks, and the People's Progressive party
by East Indians. ■

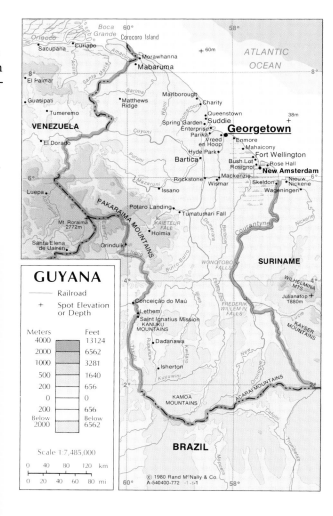

Guyana Map Index

	Lat.	Long.		Lat.	Long.
Acarai Mountains	1°50′N	57°40′W	Marlborough	7°29′N	58°38′W
Bartica	6°24′N	58°37′W	Matthews Ridge	7°30′N	60°10′W
Bush Lot	6°12′N	57°16′W	Morawhanna	8°16′N	59°45′W
Charity	7°24′N	58°36′W	*New*	3°23′N	57°36′W
Corocoro Island	8°30′N	60°10′W	New Amsterdam	6°15′N	57°31′W
Courantyne	5°55′N	57°05′W	Orinduik	4°42′N	60°01′W
Cuyuni	6°23′N	58°41′W	*Pakaraima*		
Dadanawa	2°50′N	59°30′W	*Mountains*	5°30′N	60°00′W
Demerara	6°48′N	58°10′W	Parika	6°52′N	58°25′W
Enmore	6°46′N	57°59′W	Potaro Landing	5°23′N	59°08′W
Enterprise	6°56′N	58°24′W	Queenstown	7°12′N	58°29′W
Essequibo	6°59′N	58°23′W	Rockstone	5°59′N	58°33′W
Fort Wellington	6°24′N	57°36′W	*Roraima, Mount*	5°12′N	60°44′W
Georgetown	6°48′N	58°10′W	Rose Hall	6°16′N	57°21′W
Holmia	4°58′N	59°35′W	Rosignol	6°17′N	57°32′W
Hyde Park	6°30′N	58°16′W	Saint Ignatius		
Ireng	3°33′N	59°51′W	Mission	3°20′N	59°47′W
Isherton	2°19′N	59°22′W	Skeldon	5°53′N	57°08′W
Issano	5°49′N	59°24′W	Spring Garden	6°59′N	58°31′W
Kaieteur Fall	5°10′N	59°28′W	Suddie	7°07′N	58°29′W
Lethem	3°23′N	59°48′W	*Takutu*	3°27′N	60°06′W
Mabaruma	8°12′N	59°47′W	Tumatumari Fall	5°22′N	59°00′W
Mackenzie	6°00′N	58°17′W	Vreed en Hoop	6°48′N	58°11′W
Mahaicony	6°36′N	57°48′W	Wismar	6°00′N	58°18′W

Kaieteur National Park in central Guyana lies in a region of forested highlands and plateaus. Wind and water have molded the park's sandstone and shale into a variety of interesting formations, as the photograph shows.

HAITI

OFFICIAL NAME Republic of
Haiti

PEOPLE
Population 5,305,000.
Density 495/mi² (191/km²).
Urban 26%.
Capital Port-au-Prince, 745,700.
Ethnic groups Black 95%, mulatto and European 5%.
Languages French.
Religions Roman Catholic, Protestant, Voodoo.
Life expectancy 52 female, 49 male.
Literacy 23%.

POLITICS
Government Republic.
Parties Inactive.
Suffrage Universal, over 18.
Memberships OAS, UN.
Subdivisions 9 departments.

ECONOMY
GNP $1,500,000,000.
Per capita $300.
Monetary unit Gourde.
Trade partners U.S., France.
Exports Coffee, light manufactures, bauxite.
Imports Consumer goods, food, industrial
equipment, petroleum products.

LAND
Description Caribbean island (western Hispaniola
Island).

Area 10,714 mi² (27,750 km²).
Highest point La Selle Pk., 8,773 ft (2,674 m).
Lowest point Sea level.

PEOPLE.   The world's oldest black republic, Haiti
has a population composed mainly of descendants of African slaves. Most people are poor
and rural. Although French is the official language, Haitian Creole, a combination of French
and West African languages, is more widely spoken. Religions include Roman Catholicism, Protestantism, and Voodooism, which blends Christian and African beliefs.

ECONOMY AND THE LAND.   Haiti's economy
remains underdeveloped. Most people rely on
subsistence farming, though productivity is hampered by high population density in productive
regions. Coffee is the main commercial crop and
export. Recent growth of light industry is partially attributable to tax exemptions and low labor
costs. Occupying the western third of Hispaniola
Island, Haiti has an overall mountainous terrain
and a tropical climate.

HISTORY AND POLITICS.   Christopher Columbus reached Hispaniola in 1492, and the indigenous Arawak Indians almost completely died out
during subsequent Spanish settlement. Most
Spanish settlers had gone to seek their fortunes
in other colonies by the 1600s, and western Hispaniola came under French control in 1697. Slave
importation increased rapidly, and in less than a
hundred years black Africans far outnumbered
the French. In a 1791 revolution led by Toussaint
L'Ouverture, Jean Jacques Dessalines, and Henri
Christophe, the slaves rose against the French.
By 1804 independence from France had been
achieved, and the area was renamed Haiti. The
eastern region of the island, now the Dominican
Republic, was conquered by Haitians in the
1820s, and it remained part of Haiti until 1844.
Instability increased under various dictatorships
from 1843 to 1915, and United States marines
occupied the country from 1915 to 1934. After a
time of alternating military and civilian rule,
François Duvalier came to office in 1957, declaring himself president-for-life in 1964. His rule
was marked by repression, corruption, and
human rights abuses. His son, Jean-Claude, suc-

ceeded him as president-for-life in 1971, and the
twenty-eight year Duvalier dictatorship ended in
1986 when Jean-Claude Duvalier fled the country
in the midst of great unrest. A new constitution
was approved in 1987, but instability continues. ■

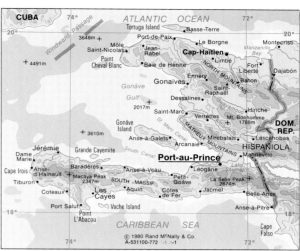

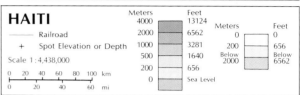

HAITI

	Meters	Feet	Meters	Feet
Railroad	4000	13124	0	0
Spot Elevation or Depth	2000	6562	200	656
Scale 1 : 4,438,000	1000	3281	Below	Below
	500	1640	2000	6562
0 20 40 60 80 100 km	200	656		
0 20 40 60 mi	0	Sea Level		

Haiti Map Index

	Lat.	Long.		Lat.	Long.
Anse-d'Hainault	18°30′N	74°27′W	Les Cayes	18°12′N	73°45′W
Aquin	18°17′N	73°24′W	Macaya Peak	18°25′N	74°00′W
Artibonite	19°15′N	72°47′W	Manzanillo Bay	19°45′N	71°46′W
Bonhomme,			Petit-Goâve	18°26′N	72°52′W
Mount	19°05′N	72°18′W	Port-au-Prince	18°32′N	72°20′W
Cap-Haïtien	19°45′N	72°12′W	Port-de-Paix	19°57′N	72°50′W
Coteaux	18°12′N	74°02′W	Saint-Marc	19°07′N	72°42′W
Gonaïves	19°27′N	72°41′W	*Saint Marc Canal*	18°50′N	72°45′W
Gonâve Gulf	19°00′N	73°30′W	*Saumâtre, Lake*	18°35′N	72°00′W
Gonâve Island	18°51′N	73°03′W	*South Canal*	18°40′N	73°05′W
Hinche	19°09′N	72°01′W	*South Massif*	18°25′N	73°55′W
Jacmel	18°14′N	72°32′W	*Tortuga Island*	20°04′N	72°49′W
Jérémie	18°39′N	74°07′W	Verrettes	19°03′N	72°28′W
La Selle Peak	18°22′N	71°59′W	*Windward*		
Léogâne	18°31′N	72°38′W	*Passage*	20°00′N	73°50′W

**Many Haitians are subsistence farmers, and any surplus crops are often loaded on donkeys and brought
to local markets to trade or sell as in this photo near Cap-Haïtien.**

HONDURAS

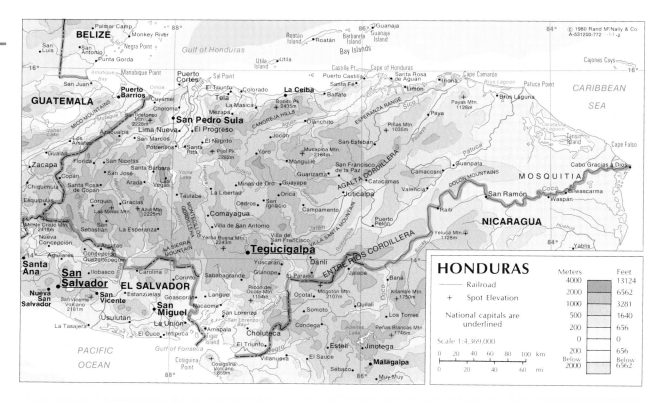

OFFICIAL NAME Republic of Honduras

PEOPLE
Population 4,500,000.
Density 104/mi² (40/km²).
Urban 26%.
Capital Tegucigalpa, 444,749.
Ethnic groups Mestizo 90%, Indian 7%
Languages Spanish.
Religions Roman Catholic 97%.
Life expectancy 59 female, 55 male.
Literacy 60%.

POLITICS
Government Republic.
Parties Liberal, National, National Innovation and Unity.
Suffrage Universal, over 21.
Memberships OAS, UN.
Subdivisions 18 departments.

ECONOMY
GNP $2,620,000,000.
Per capita $675.
Monetary unit Lempira.
Trade partners U.S., Central American countries, West Germany, Japan.
Exports Bananas, coffee, wood, meat.
Imports Manufactured goods, machinery, transportation equipment, chemicals, petroleum.

LAND
Description Central America.
Area 43,277 mi² (112,088 km²).
Highest point Mt. Las Minas, 9,347 ft (2,849 m).
Lowest point Sea level.

Honduras Map Index

	Lat.	Long.		Lat.	Long.
Agalta Cordillera	15°00'N	85°53'W	Corquín	14°34'N	88°52'W
Aguán	15°57'N	85°44'W	Danlí	14°00'N	86°35'W
Amapala	13°17'N	87°40'W	El Progreso	15°21'N	87°49'W
Bay Islands	16°20'N	86°30'W	*Entre Ríos*		
Bonito Peak	15°38'N	86°55'W	*Cordillera*	14°19'N	85°26'W
Brus Lagoon	15°50'N	84°35'W	*Fonseca, Gulf of*	13°10'N	87°40'W
Brus Laguna	15°47'N	84°35'W	Guanaja	16°27'N	85°54'W
Cajones Cays	16°05'N	83°12'W	Guanpata	15°01'N	85°02'W
Camarón, Cabo	16°00'N	85°05'W	*Honduras, Cape*		
Campamento	14°33'N	86°42'W	*of*	16°01'N	86°02'W
Caratasca			*Honduras, Gulf of*	16°10'N	87°50'W
Lagoon	15°23'N	83°55'W	Iriona	15°57'N	85°11'W
Choluteca	13°18'N	87°12'W	*Jalán*	14°39'N	86°12'W
Coco	15°00'N	83°10'W	Juticalpa	14°42'N	86°15'W
Comayagua	14°25'N	87°37'W	La Ceiba	15°47'N	86°50'W
Copán	14°50'N	89°09'W	La Esperanza	14°20'N	88°10'W

	Lat.	Long.		Lat.	Long.
Las Minas			San Francisco de		
Mountain	14°33'N	88°39'W	la Paz	14°55'N	86°14'W
Las Vegas	14°49'N	88°06'W	*San Ildefonso*		
Lempa	13°53'N	88°30'W	*Mountain*	15°31'N	88°17'W
Lima Nueva	15°23'N	87°56'W	San Pedro Sula	15°27'N	88°02'W
Minas de Oro	14°46'N	87°20'W	*Sico*	15°58'N	84°58'W
Mosquitia	15°00'N	84°00'W	Tegucigalpa	14°06'N	87°13'W
Motagua	15°44'N	88°14'W	Tela	15°44'N	87°27'W
Patuca	15°50'N	84°17'W	*Ulúa*	15°53'N	87°44'W
Patuca Point	15°51'N	84°18'W	Utila	16°06'N	86°54'W
Paya	15°37'N	85°17'W	Valencia	14°47'N	85°18'W
Puerto Castilla	16°01'N	86°01'W	*Yerba Buena*		
Puerto Cortés	15°48'N	87°56'W	*Mountain*	14°05'N	87°26'W
Roatán	16°18'N	86°35'W	Yoro	15°09'N	87°07'W
Sabanagrande	13°50'N	87°15'W			

PEOPLE. Most Hondurans are mestizos, of Spanish-Indian descent. Other groups include Indians and descendants of black Africans and Europeans. Most Indians have been assimilated into the majority culture, but a minority continues to practice a traditional Indian life-style. The Spanish language predominates, and English is spoken by a small population of British descent on the northern coast and Bay Islands. Poverty is an ongoing problem for the mainly rural population, and economic and educational improvements mostly affect urban inhabitants.

ECONOMY AND THE LAND. Honduras has an underdeveloped economy based on banana cultivation. Other activities include livestock raising, coffee production, forestry, and some mining. Honduras's terrain is mostly mountainous, with lowlands along some coastal regions. The climate varies from tropical in the lowlands to temperate in the mountains.

HISTORY AND POLITICS. Early in its history Honduras was part of the Mayan Empire. By 1502, when Christopher Columbus arrived to claim the region for Spain, the decline of the Maya had rendered the Indians weakened and unable to stave off Spanish settlement. The Spanish colonial period introduced gold and silver

mines, cattle ranches, and African slaves. In 1821 Honduras, El Salvador, Nicaragua, Costa Rica, and Guatemala declared independence from Spain and, in 1823, formed the Federation of Central America. The unstable union had virtually collapsed by 1838, and the member states became independent as the federation dissolved. Instability, Guatemalan political influence, and the development of a banana economy based on United States–owned plantations marked the

1800s and early 1900s. Frequent revolutions have characterized the twentieth century, and a dictator governed from 1933 to 1948. Since the 1950s civilian governments have alternated with military coups and rule. Controversies focus on issues of poverty, land distribution, and a border dispute with El Salvador. The country has become an important base for United States activities in Central America, evidenced by ongoing United States military maneuvers. ∎

Honduras is bordered by two seas: the Caribbean on the north and a short stretch of the Pacific on the south. The land along the shoreline rises rapidly to the mountains of the interior that cover nearly four-fifths of the nation.

HONG KONG

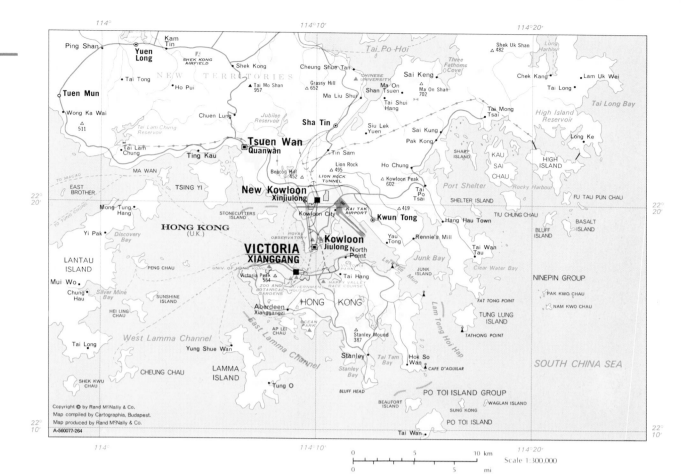

OFFICIAL NAME Hong Kong

PEOPLE
Population 5,435,000.
Density 13,256/mi² (5,123/km²).
Urban 92%.
Capital Hong Kong, 1,183,621.
Ethnic groups Chinese 98%.
Languages Cantonese, English.
Religions Indigenous 90%, Christian 10%.
Life expectancy 76 female, 70 male.
Literacy 75%.

POLITICS
Government Colony (U.K.).
Parties None.
Suffrage Limited to 200,000–300,000 professional or skilled persons.
Memberships None.
Subdivisions 4 census districts.

ECONOMY
GDP $25,900,000,000.
Per capita $4,900.
Monetary unit Dollar.
Trade partners U.S., China, U.K., Japan, West Germany.
Exports Clothing, plastic articles, textiles, electrical equipment.
Imports Raw materials, consumer goods, capital equipment, food.

LAND
Description Eastern Asia.
Area 410 mi² (1,061 km²).
Highest point Tai Mo Shan, 3,140 ft (957 m).
Lowest point Sea level.

PEOPLE. Ethnically, 98 percent of Hong Kong's population is Chinese, but approximately 60 per-

cent of the people were born here and thus are considered British nationals. Cantonese, a Chinese dialect, is spoken by a majority, and both English and Chinese are official languages. The many religions of Hong Kong include Taoism, Confucianism, Buddhism, Islam, and Hinduism as well as indigenous beliefs. There is also a Christian minority and a number of Sikhs and Jews. Hong Kong is one of the world's most densely populated areas.

ECONOMY AND THE LAND. Low taxes, duty-free status, an accessible location, and an excellent natural harbor have helped make Hong Kong an Asian center of trade, finance, manufacturing, and transportation. Situated on the coast of China, Hong Kong borders Guangdong province. The colony consists of the islands of Hong Kong and Lantau, the mainland areas of Kowloon and the New Territories, and many smaller islands. In addition to mountains, the New Territories contain some level areas suitable for agriculture, and the islands are hilly. The climate is tropical, with hot, rainy summers and cool, humid winters.

Hong Kong Map Index

	Lat.	Long.		Lat.	Long.
Aberdeen	22°15′N	114°09′E	New Kowloon	22°20′N	114°10′E
Kowloon	22°18′N	114°10′E	Tsuen Wan	22°22′N	114°07′E
Kwun Tong	22°19′N	114°12′E	Victoria	22°17′N	114°09′E

HISTORY AND POLITICS. Inhabited since ancient times, Hong Kong came under Chinese rule around the third century B.C. The Portuguese made their way to the coast of China in the early sixteenth century, and British attempts at settlement began in the 1600s. In 1839 British opium smuggling led to the Opium War between Britain and China, and a victorious Britain received the island of Hong Kong in an 1842 treaty. In 1860 the British gained control of the Kowloon Peninsula, and in 1898 the New Territories came under British rule through a ninety-nine-year lease with China. British-Chinese discussions are underway concerning the expiration of the New Territories' lease in 1997 and the transfer of the area to China. ■

The original incentive for development of Hong Kong was its excellent location and natural harbor, shown here, but the resourcefulness of Hong Kong's people has made the colony a commercial success. Prior to World War II Hong Kong's major role was that of entrepôt, serving as an intermediate center for trade with China. But the growing population was forced to look elsewhere for earnings when a United Nations trade embargo was placed on China during the Korean War in the 1950s, and the result was Hong Kong's booming manufacturing sector. Today, entrepôt trade is thriving, and Hong Kong is an international center of finance as well.

HUNGARY

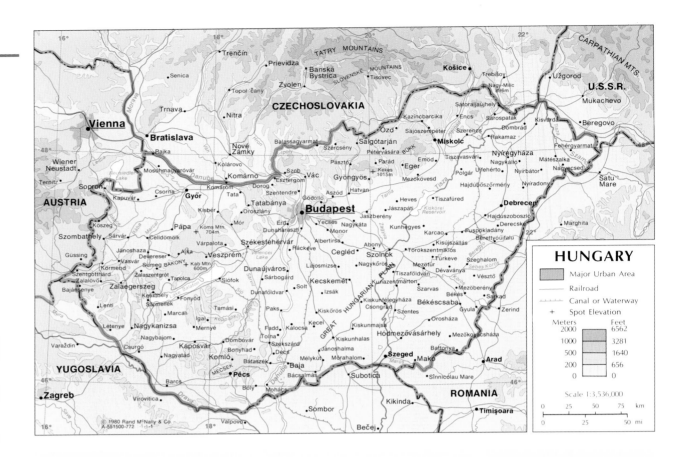

HUNGARY
- Major Urban Area
- Railroad
- Canal or Waterway
- + Spot Elevation

Meters	Feet
2000	6562
1000	3281
500	1640
200	656
0	0

Scale 1:3,536,000

OFFICIAL NAME Hungarian People's Republic

PEOPLE
Population 10,675,000.
Density 297/mi² (115/km²).
Urban 54%.
Capital Budapest, 2,064,000.
Ethnic groups Hungarian 92%, Gypsy 3%, German 3%.
Languages Hungarian.
Religions Roman Catholic 68%, Calvinist 20%, Lutheran 5%.
Life expectancy 73 female, 66 male.
Literacy 98%.

POLITICS
Government Socialist republic.
Parties Socialist Workers'.
Suffrage Universal, over 18.
Memberships CEMA, UN, Warsaw Pact.
Subdivisions 19 counties, 1 city.

ECONOMY
GNP $65,200,000,000.
Per capita $6,901.
Monetary unit Forint.
Trade partners U.S.S.R., West Germany, East Germany.
Exports Machinery, transportation equipment, agricultural products.
Imports Machinery, transportation equipment, fuels, chemicals.

LAND
Description Eastern Europe, landlocked.
Area 35,921 mi² (93,036 km²).
Highest point Kékes, 3,330 ft (1,015 m).
Lowest point Tisza River valley, 259 ft (79 m).

Hungary Map Index

	Lat.	Long.		Lat.	Long.		Lat.	Long.		Lat.	Long.
Baja	46°11′N	18°57′E	Great Hungarian			Marcal	47°41′N	17°32′E	Sopron	47°41′N	16°36′E
Bakony	46°55′N	17°40′E	Plain	46°45′N	19°45′E	Maros	46°15′N	20°13′E	Szamos (Someş)	48°07′N	22°22′E
Balaton, Lake	46°50′N	17°45′E	Gyöngyös	47°47′N	19°56′E	Mecsek	46°15′N	18°05′E	Szeged	46°15′N	20°09′E
Békéscsaba	46°41′N	21°06′E	Győr	47°42′N	17°38′E	Miskolc	48°06′N	20°47′E	Székesfehérvár	47°12′N	18°25′E
Berettyó	46°59′N	21°07′E	Hernad	47°56′N	21°08′E	Nagykanizsa	46°27′N	17°00′E	Szolnok	47°10′N	20°12′E
Bordrog	48°07′N	21°25′E	Hódmezővásárhely	46°25′N	20°20′E	Nagy-Milic	48°35′N	21°28′E	Szombathely	47°14′N	16°38′E
Budapest	47°30′N	19°05′E	Ipoly	47°49′N	18°52′E	Nyíregyháza	47°59′N	21°43′E	Tarna	47°31′N	19°59′E
Bükk	48°05′N	20°30′E	Kapos	46°44′N	18°30′E	Pápa	47°19′N	17°28′E	Tatabánya	47°34′N	18°26′E
Cegléd	47°10′N	19°48′E	Kaposvár	46°22′N	17°47′E	Pécs	46°05′N	18°13′E	Tisza	45°15′N	20°17′E
Danube	45°55′N	18°55′E	Kecskemét	46°54′N	19°42′E	Rába	47°42′N	17°38′E	Vác	47°47′N	19°08′E
Debrecen	47°32′N	21°38′E	Kékes	47°55′N	20°02′E	Répce	47°41′N	17°03′E	Velencei Lake	47°12′N	18°35′E
Drava	45°46′N	18°13′E	Kiskőrei Reservoir	47°35′N	20°40′E	Salgótarján	48°07′N	19°48′E	Veszprém	47°06′N	17°55′E
Dunaújváros	46°58′N	18°57′E	Körös	46°43′N	20°12′E	Sárvíz	46°24′N	18°41′E	Zagyva	47°10′N	20°13′E
Eger	47°54′N	20°23′E	Leitha	47°54′N	17°17′E	Sebes Körös	46°55′N	20°59′E	Zala	46°43′N	17°16′E
			Makó	46°13′N	20°29′E				Zalaegerszeg	46°51′N	16°51′E

The Danube River divides Budapest into eastern Pest and western Buda. Shown here is Pest as viewed from the Buda side.

PEOPLE. Hungary's major ethnic group and language evolved from Magyar tribes who settled the region in the ninth century. Gypsies, Germans, and other peoples compose minorities. Most people are Roman Catholic, and the government supervises religious activities through a state office. The government also controls educational programs, and the literacy rate is high.

ECONOMY AND THE LAND. Following World War II, Hungary pursued a program of industrialization, and the onetime agricultural nation now looks to industry as its main economic contributor. Agriculture is almost completely socialized, and farming remains important, with productivity aided by fertile soils and a mild climate. Economic planning was decentralized in 1968, thus Hungary's economy differs from that of other Soviet-bloc nations. A flat plain dominates the landscape, and the climate is temperate throughout the country.

HISTORY AND POLITICS. In the late 800s Magyar tribes from the east overcame Slavic and Germanic residents and settled the area. In the thirteenth century invading Mongols caused much destruction, and in the early 1500s, after repeated attacks, the Ottoman Turks gained domina-

tion of central Hungary. By the late seventeenth century the entire region had come under the rule of Austria's Hapsburgs. In 1867 Hungary succeeded in obtaining equal status with Austria, and the dual monarchy of Austria-Hungary emerged. Discontent and nationalistic demands increased until 1914, when a Bosnian Serb killed the heir to the Austro-Hungarian throne. Austria-Hungary declared war on Serbia, and World War I began, resulting in a loss of territory and population for Hungary. At the end of the war, in 1918, Hungary became a republic, only to revert to monarchical rule in 1919. Hungary

entered World War II on the side of Germany, and Adolf Hitler set up a pro-Nazi government in Hungary in 1944. The Soviet Union invaded that same year, and a Hungarian-Allied peace treaty was signed in 1947. Coalition rule evolved into a Communist government in 1949. Discontent erupted into rebellion in 1956, a new premier declared Hungary neutral, and Soviet forces entered Budapest to quell the uprising. Since the early sixties, the standard of living has improved and economic and cultural liberties have increased. The country remains allied with the Soviet Union, and Western ties are expanding. ∎

ICELAND

OFFICIAL NAME Republic of
Iceland

PEOPLE
Population 240,000.
Density 6/mi² (2.3/km²).
Urban 89%.
Capital Reykjavík, 84,593.
Ethnic groups Mixed Norwegian and Celtic.
Languages Icelandic.
Religions Lutheran 95%.
Life expectancy 80 female, 74 male.
Literacy 100%.

POLITICS
Government Republic.
Parties Independence, People's Alliance, Progressive,
Social Democratic.
Suffrage Universal, over 20.
Memberships NATO, OECD, UN.
Subdivisions 8 regions.

ECONOMY
GNP $2,200,000,000.
Per capita $9,322.
Monetary unit Króna.
Trade partners U.S., Scandinavian countries, U.K.,
West Germany.

Exports Fish and fish products, animal products,
aluminum.
Imports Machinery, transportation equipment,
petroleum, food, textiles.

LAND
Description North Atlantic island.
Area 39,769 mi² (103,000 km²).
Highest point Hvannadalshnúkur, 6,952 ft (2,119 m).
Lowest point Sea level.

PEOPLE. Most Icelanders are of Norwegian or
Celtic ancestry, live in coastal cities, and belong
to the Lutheran church. Icelandic, the predominant language, has changed little from the Old
Norse of the original settlers and still resembles
the language of twelfth-century Nordic sagas.

ECONOMY AND THE LAND. Fish, found in the
island's rich coastal waters, are the main natural
resource and export. Iceland has a long tradition
based on fishing, but the industry has recently
suffered from decreasing markets and catches.
Glaciers, lakes, hot springs, volcanoes, and a
lava desert limit agricultural land but provide a
scenic terrain. Although the island lies just south
of the Arctic Circle, the climate is moderated by
the Gulf Stream. Summers are damp and cool,
and winters relatively mild but windy. Proximity
to the Arctic Circle puts Iceland in the Land of
the Midnight Sun, resulting in periods of twenty-
four-hour daylight in June.

HISTORY AND POLITICS. Norwegians began
settlement of Iceland around the ninth century.
The world's oldest parliament, the Althing, was
established in Iceland in A.D. 930. Civil wars and
instability during the thirteenth century led to
the end of independence in 1262, when Iceland
came under Norwegian rule. In the fourteenth
century Norway was joined to Denmark's realm,
and rule of Iceland passed to the Danes. The
Althing was abolished in 1800 but reestablished
in 1843. In the 1918 Act of Union, Iceland became a sovereign state but retained its union
with Denmark under a common king. Germany
occupied Denmark in 1940, during World War II;

and British troops, replaced by Americans in
1941, protected Iceland from invasion. Following
a 1944 plebiscite, Iceland left its union with Denmark and became an independent republic. The
country has no military. ■

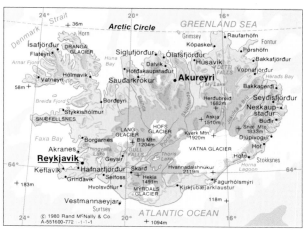

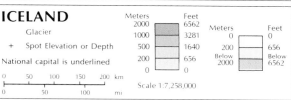

Iceland Map Index

	Lat.	Long.		Lat.	Long.
Akranes	64°18'N	22°02'W	Kverk Mountain	64°43'N	16°38'W
Akureyri	65°44'N	18°08'W	Myrdals Glacier	63°40'N	19°05'W
Breida Fjord	65°15'N	23°15'W	Neskaupstadur	65°10'N	13°43'W
Denmark Strait	67°00'N	24°00'W	Ólafsfjördur	66°06'N	18°38'W
Faxa Bay	64°25'N	23°00'W	Pjórsá	63°47'N	20°48'W
Fontur	66°23'N	14°30'W	Reykjavik	64°09'N	21°51'W
Grimsey	66°34'N	18°00'W	Saudárkrókur	65°46'N	19°41'W
Gull Falls	64°24'N	20°08'W	Seydisfjördur	65°16'N	14°00'W
Hafnarfjördur	64°03'N	21°56'W	Siglufjördur	66°10'N	18°56'W
Horna Lagoon	64°17'N	15°16'W	Snæfellsness	64°50'N	23°00'W
Húna Bay	65°50'N	20°50'W	Surtsey	63°16'N	20°32'W
Húsavík	66°04'N	17°18'W	Thingvalla Lake	64°12'N	21°10'W
Hvannadalshnúkur	64°01'N	16°41'W	Thóris Lake	64°50'N	19°26'W
Ísafjördur	66°08'N	23°13'W	Vatna Glacier	64°25'N	16°50'W
Keflavík	64°02'N	22°36'W	Vestmannaeyjar	63°26'N	20°12'W

**Often called the "Land of Fire and Ice," Iceland is an island of contrasting features, as exemplified by the bubbling geysers shown
here against a backdrop of snow- and glacier-covered mountains. Volcanoes, lakes, a mountainous lava desert, sulfur springs,
canyons, waterfalls, and fast-flowing rivers are also found throughout the island, and areas such as these make up almost 80 percent
of Iceland's total area. Population is concentrated on the 7 percent of the island that borders the sea.**

INDIA

In developing countries such as India, pressure on the land is so great that agriculture must compete with industry. Here, Indian women winnow corn in the traditional way against the backdrop of Calcutta's steelworks. In India as elsewhere, agriculture is losing ground to industry, which seeks "green field" sites to avoid the high cost of reclaiming industrial land.

OFFICIAL NAME Republic of India

PEOPLE
Population 754,600,000.
Density 610/mi² (236/km²).
Urban 23%.
Capital New Delhi, 271,990.
Ethnic groups Indo-Aryan 72%, Dravidian 25%, Mongoloid 3%.
Languages Hindi, English, indigenous.
Religions Hindu 83%, Muslim 11%, Christian 3%, Sikh 2%.
Life expectancy 50 female, 51 male.
Literacy 36%.

POLITICS
Government Republic.
Parties Congress (I), Congress (S), Lok Dal.
Suffrage Universal, over 21.
Memberships CW, UN.
Subdivisions 25 states, 6 union territories.

ECONOMY
GNP $146,000,000,000.
Per capita $209.

Monetary unit Rupee.
Trade partners U.S., U.K., U.S.S.R., Japan.
Exports Engineering goods, textiles, clothing, tea.
Imports Machinery, transportation equipment, petroleum, fertilizer.

LAND
Description Southern Asia.
Area 1,237,061 mi² (3,203,975 km²).
Highest point Kanchenjunga, 28,208 ft (8,598 m).
Lowest point Sea level.
The above information includes part of Jammu and Kashmir.

As the traditional invasion and trade route to India, the Khyber Pass has played an important role in that country's history. The pass lies on the Afghanistan-Pakistan border in the Safed Koh Mountains.

PEOPLE. India's population is composed of two main ethnic groups: the Indo-Aryan and the Dravidian. Found mostly in the north are the Indo-Aryans, a central Asian people who arrived in India around 1500 B.C., pushing the Dravidians to the south, where they remain concentrated today. A Mongoloid minority inhabits the mountains of the far north, and aboriginal groups live in the central forests and mountains. Hindi is the official language, English is spoken by a minority of educated persons, and more than fourteen indigenous languages are in use as well. India is second only to China in population, and although Hindus are the religious majority, the country also has one of the world's largest Muslim populations. Christians, Sikhs, Jains, and Buddhists comprise additional religious minorities.

ECONOMY AND THE LAND. Economic conditions have improved since India became independent from Britain in 1947. Agriculture, upon which most Indians depend, is now more efficient, a result of modernization programs. Industry has expanded as well, and the country ranks high in its number of scientists and skilled laborers. Poverty, unemployment, and underemployment continue to plague the nation, however, partly due to rapid population growth and improved life expectancy. Many natural resources, including coal, iron ore, bauxite, and manganese, remain undeveloped. India is made up of three land regions: the Himalayas along the northern border; the Gangetic plain, a fertile northern region; and the peninsula, made up mostly of the Deccan, a plateau region. The climate ranges from temperate to tropical monsoon.

HISTORY AND POLITICS. India's civilization dates back to 2500 B.C., when the Dravidians flourished in the region. Aryan tribes invaded about one thousand years later, bringing the indigenous beliefs that evolved into Hinduism, and various empires followed. In the sixth or fifth century B.C., Siddhārtha Gautama, who came to be called Buddha, founded Buddhism, a major influence on Indian life until about A.D. 800. Invasions beginning around A.D. 450 brought the Huns, and during the seventh and eighth centuries Arab conquerors introduced Islam. The Mogul Empire, under a series of Muslim rulers, began in the 1500s, and the British East India Company established trading posts in the 1600s. By 1757 the East India Company had become India's major power, and by the 1850s the company controlled nearly all present-day India, Pakistan, and Bangladesh. An Indian rebellion in 1857 caused Britain to take over the East India Company's rule. Demands for independence increased after a controversial massacre of Indians by British troops in 1919, and by 1920 Mohandas Gandhi had emerged as the leader of an independence campaign based on nonviolent disobedience and noncooperation. The nation gained independence in 1947, establishing Pakistan as a separate Muslim state because of Muslim-Hindu hostilities. Recent disputes included a border conflict with China that erupted into fighting in 1959 and 1962 and a disagreement with Pakistan over the mainly Muslim region of Kashmir. In 1984 Sikhs demanding an independent state assassinated Prime Minister Indira Gandhi. India's foreign policy is based on nonalignment. ∎

Each year thousands of Hindu pilgrims come to the holy city of Varanasi to bathe in the Ganges.

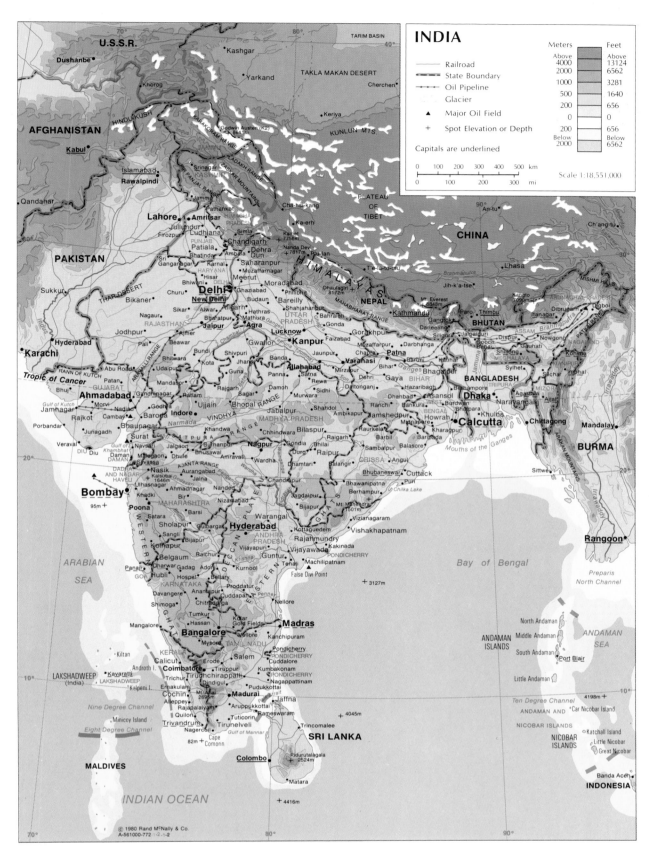

India Map Index

	Lat.	Long.		Lat.	Long.
Agartala	23°49'N	91°16'E	Jamshedpur	22°48'N	86°11'E
Agra	27°11'N	78°01'E	Jodhpur	26°17'N	73°02'E
Ahmadabad	23°02'N	72°37'E	Jullundur	31°19'N	75°34'E
Aijal	23°44'N	92°43'E	Kamet	30°54'N	79°37'E
Ajanta Range	20°30'N	76°00'E	Kanpur	26°28'N	80°21'E
Aligarh	27°53'N	78°05'E	Karakoram Range	35°30'N	77°00'E
Allahabad	25°27'N	81°51'E	Karnataka	14°00'N	76°00'E
Amritsar	31°35'N	74°53'E	Kerala	10°00'N	76°30'E
Anai, Mount	10°10'N	77°04'E	Khambhat, Gulf of	21°00'N	72°30'E
Andaman And Nicobar Islands	10°00'N	93°00'E	Kohima	25°40'N	94°07'E
Andaman Islands	12°00'N	92°45'E	Kolhapur	16°42'N	74°13'E
Andhra Pradesh	16°00'N	79°00'E	Krishna	15°57'N	80°59'E
Aravalli Range	25°00'N	73°30'E	Kutch, Gulf of	22°36'N	69°30'E
Arunachal Pradesh	28°30'N	95°00'E	Ladakh Range	34°00'N	78°00'E
Asansol	23°41'N	86°59'E	Lakshadweep	10°00'N	73°00'E
Assam	26°00'N	92°00'E	Lucknow	26°51'N	80°55'E
Bangalore	12°58'N	77°36'E	Ludhiana	30°54'N	75°51'E
Bareilly	28°21'N	79°25'E	Madhya Pradesh	23°00'N	79°00'E
Baroda	22°18'N	73°12'E	Madras	13°04'N	80°16'E
Belgaum	15°52'N	74°30'E	Madurai	9°56'N	78°07'E
Bengal, Bay of	15°00'N	90°00'E	Maharashtra	19°00'N	76°00'E
Bhagalpur	25°15'N	87°00'E	Manipur	25°00'N	94°00'E
Bhaunagar	21°46'N	72°09'E	Mannar, Gulf of	8°30'N	79°00'E
Bhopal	23°16'N	77°24'E	Meerut	28°59'N	77°42'E
Bhubaneswar	20°14'N	85°50'E	Meghalaya	25°30'N	91°15'E
Bihar	25°00'N	86°00'E	Minicoy Island	8°17'N	73°02'E
Bikaner	28°01'N	73°18'E	Mishmi Hills	29°00'N	96°00'E
Bilaspur	22°05'N	82°09'E	Mizoram	23°30'N	93°00'E
Bombay	18°58'N	72°50'E	Moradabad	28°50'N	78°47'E
Brahmaputra	25°45'N	89°50'E	Nagaland	26°00'N	95°00'E
Calcutta	22°32'N	88°22'E	Nagpur	21°09'N	79°06'E
Calicut	11°15'N	75°46'E	Nanda Devi	30°23'N	79°59'E
Chandigarh	30°44'N	76°55'E	Narmada	21°38'N	72°36'E
Chilka Lake	19°46'N	85°20'E	Nasik	19°59'N	73°48'E
Cochin	9°58'N	76°15'E	New Delhi	28°36'N	77°12'E
Coimbatore	11°00'N	76°58'E	Nicobar Islands	8°00'N	93°30'E
Comorin, Cape	8°04'N	77°34'E	Nine Degree Channel	9°00'N	73°00'E
Cuttack	20°30'N	85°50'E	Orissa	20°00'N	84°00'E
Dadra and Nagar Haveli	20°05'N	73°00'E	Palk Strait	10°00'N	79°45'E
Daman	20°10'N	73°00'E	Panaji	15°29'N	73°50'E
Deccan Plateau	14°00'N	77°00'E	Patiala	30°19'N	76°24'E
Dehra Dun	30°19'N	78°02'E	Patkai Range	27°00'N	96°00'E
Delhi	28°40'N	77°13'E	Patna	25°36'N	85°07'E
Delhi	28°37'N	77°10'E	Pir Panjal Range	33°00'N	75°00'E
Dispur	26°09'N	91°46'E	Pondicherry	11°56'N	79°53'E
Diu	20°42'N	70°59'E	Pondicherry	11°56'N	79°50'E
Eastern Ghats	14°00'N	78°50'E	Poona	18°32'N	73°52'E
Eight Degree Channel	8°00'N	73°00'E	Raipur	21°14'N	81°38'E
Gandhinagar	23°13'N	72°41'E	Rajahmundry	16°59'N	81°47'E
Ganges	24°12'N	88°44'E	Rajasthan	27°00'N	74°00'E
Ganges, Mouths of the	22°00'N	89°00'E	Rajkot	22°18'N	70°47'E
Gangtok	27°20'N	88°37'E	Rann of Kutch	24°00'N	70°00'E
Gaya	24°47'N	85°00'E	Saharanpur	29°58'N	77°33'E
Goa	14°20'N	74°00'E	Salem	11°39'N	78°10'E
Godavari	17°00'N	81°45'E	Satpura Range	22°00'N	78°00'E
Gorakhpur	26°45'N	83°22'E	Shillong	25°34'N	91°53'E
Gujarat	22°00'N	72°00'E	Sholapur	17°41'N	75°55'E
Guntur	16°18'N	80°27'E	Silvassa	20°17'N	73°00'E
Gwalior	26°13'N	78°10'E	Simla	31°06'N	77°10'E
Haryana	29°20'N	76°20'E	Srinagar	34°05'N	74°49'E
Himachal Pradesh	32°00'N	77°00'E	Surat	21°10'N	72°50'E
Himalayas	28°00'N	84°00'E	Tamil Nadu	11°00'N	78°15'E
Howrah	22°35'N	88°20'E	Ten Degree Channel	10°00'N	92°00'E
Hubli	15°21'N	75°10'E	Thar Desert	27°00'N	71°00'E
Hyderabad	17°23'N	78°29'E	Tiruchchirappalli	10°49'N	78°41'E
Imphal	24°49'N	93°57'E	Tirunelveli	8°44'N	77°42'E
Indore	22°43'N	75°50'E	Tripura	24°00'N	92°00'E
Indus	34°40'N	76°15'E	Trivandrum	8°29'N	76°55'E
Itanagar	27°20'N	93°50'E	Ujjain	23°11'N	75°46'E
Jabalpur	23°10'N	79°57'E	Uttar Pradesh	27°00'N	80°00'E
Jaipur	26°55'N	75°49'E	Varanasi	25°20'N	83°00'E
Jammu	32°42'N	74°52'E	Vijayawada	16°31'N	80°37'E
Jammu and Kashmir	34°00'N	76°00'E	Vindhya Range	23°00'N	77°00'E
Jamnagar	22°28'N	70°04'E	Vishakhapatnam	17°42'N	83°18'E
			Warangal	18°00'N	79°35'E
			West Bengal	24°00'N	88°00'E
			Western Ghats	14°00'N	75°00'E
			Zaskar Mountains	33°00'N	78°00'E

Both New Delhi and Delhi are found in the Indian state of Delhi, and while New Delhi serves as modern India's capital and administrative center, the much larger city of Delhi is heir to the legacy of a past capital of the vast Mogul Empire.

In 1526 Delhi was conquered by Babur, the founder of the Mogul Empire in India, and foremost among the architectural structures from the time of the Moguls is Delhi's Red Fort, shown here. Built in the seventeenth century by Shah Jahan, the fort includes a palace, mosque, administrative buildings, and barracks. Within the massive sandstone walls is found the magnificent white marble Diwan-i-Khas, or Hall of Private Audience, in which the famous Peacock throne once stood. Shah Jahan personified the high point in the distinctive art and architecture of the Mogul period, reflected also in the magnificent Taj Mahal.

INDONESIA

OFFICIAL NAME Republic of Indonesia

PEOPLE
Population 166,070,000.
Density 224/mi² (87/km²).
Urban 22%.
Capital Jakarta, Java I., 6,503,449.
Ethnic groups Javanese 45%, Sundanese 14%, Madurese 8%, coastal Malay 8%.
Languages Bahasa Indonesia, Malay-Polynesian languages, English, Dutch.
Religions Muslim 90%, Christian 5%, Hindu 3%.
Life expectancy 55 female, 52 male.
Literacy 64%.

POLITICS
Government Republic.
Parties Democratic, Golkar, Unity Development.
Suffrage Universal, over 17 (no age requirement if married).
Memberships ASEAN, OPEC, UN.
Subdivisions 27 provinces.

ECONOMY
GNP $70,000,000,000.
Per capita $440.
Monetary unit Rupiah.
Trade partners Japan, U.S., Singapore.
Exports Petroleum, natural gas, wood, natural rubber.
Imports Food, machinery, transportation equipment, chemicals, petroleum products.

LAND
Description Southeastern Asian islands.
Area 741,101 mi² (1,919,443 km²).
Highest point Jaya Pk., New Guinea I., 16,503 ft (5,030 m).
Lowest point Sea level.

PEOPLE. Indonesia is the fifth most populous nation in the world. The majority of the people are of Malay stock, which includes several subgroups, such as Javanese, Sundanese, Madurese and coastal Malay. More than two hundred indigenous languages are spoken, but the official, unifying language is Bahasa Indonesia. Most people live in small farm villages and follow ancient customs stressing cooperation. Muslim traders brought Islam to Indonesia, and most of the population is Muslim. Many Indonesians combine spirit worship with Islam or Christianity. Indonesia's rich cultural heritage includes many ancient temples.

ECONOMY AND THE LAND. Indonesia is a leading producer of petroleum in the Far East. The area also has large deposits of minerals and natural gas. Agriculture is still a major economic activity, and rice remains an important crop. Overpopulation threatens the economy and food supply. The nation's more than 13,600 islands form a natural barrier between the Indian and Pacific oceans, making the straits between the islands important for world trade and military strategy. Java, the most industrial and heavily populated island, is characterized by volcanic mountains and narrow fertile plains along the northern coast. Indonesia includes most of Borneo, the third largest island in the world. Other major Indonesian islands are Sulawesi, Sumatra, and Irian Jaga, the western half of New Guinea, which also feature inland mountains and limited coastal plains. The climate is tropical, with seasonal monsoons.

The homeland of the Bugi of Indonesia is in the south of Sulawesi, but they travel throughout Indonesia and Malaysia in their large oceangoing vessels. They often form new settlements on their journeys, and an extended family may well have its members thousands of miles apart. These onetime pirates now carry cargoes of local produce or imported goods.

HISTORY AND POLITICS. Indonesian civilization is more than 2,500 years old and has produced two major empires with influence throughout Southeast Asia. The Portuguese arrived in the sixteenth century but were outnumbered by the Dutch, who eventually gained control of most of the islands and established a plantation colony. An independence movement began early in the twentieth century and slowly gained momentum. Japan encouraged Indonesian nationalism during World War II, and shortly after the Japanese surrender in 1945, Indonesia proclaimed itself an independent republic. Economic and political instability led to an attempted Communist coup in 1965, after which the government outlawed communism, cut its ties with China, and strengthened relations with Western powers. ∎

Hinduism is a minority religion in Indonesia, and here Balinese Hindus perform a cremation rite following the death of a Brahman.

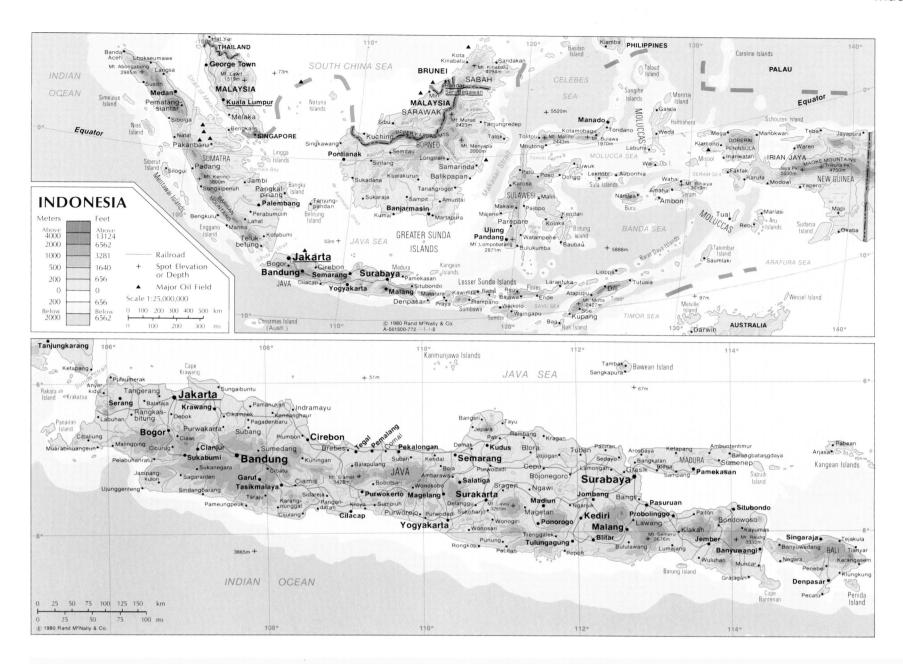

Indonesia Map Index

	Lat.	Long.
Ambon	3°43′S	128°12′E
Arafura Sea	9°00′S	133°00′E
Bali	8°20′S	115°00′E
Balikpapan	1°17′S	116°50′E
Banda Sea	5°00′S	128°00′E
Bandung	6°54′S	107°36′E
Bangil	7°36′S	112°47′E
Bangka Island	1°48′N	125°09′E
Banjarmasin	3°20′S	114°35′E
Bantenan, Cape	8°47′S	114°33′E
Banyuwangi	8°12′S	114°21′E
Barisan Mountains	3°00′S	102°15′E
Belitung Island	2°50′S	107°55′E
Binaiya, Mount	3°11′S	129°26′E
Blitar	8°06′S	112°09′E
Blora	6°57′S	111°25′E
Bogor	6°35′S	106°47′E
Bojonegoro	7°09′S	111°52′E
Bondowoso	7°55′S	113°49′E
Bone Bay	4°00′S	120°40′E
Borneo	0°30′N	114°00′E

	Lat.	Long.
Brebes	6°53′S	109°03′E
Celebes Sea	3°00′N	122°00′E
Cepu	7°09′S	111°35′E
Ciamis	7°20′S	108°21′E
Cianjur	6°49′S	107°08′E
Cilacap	7°44′S	109°00′E
Cirebon	6°44′S	108°34′E
Comal	6°55′S	109°31′E
Denpasar	8°39′S	115°13′E
Dili	8°33′S	125°35′E
Doberai Peninsula	1°30′S	132°30′E
Garut	7°13′S	107°54′E
Greater Sunda Islands	2°00′S	110°00′E
Gresik	7°09′S	112°38′E
Indramayu	6°20′S	108°19′E
Jakarta	6°10′S	106°48′E
Jambi	1°36′S	103°37′E
Java	7°30′S	110°00′E
Java Sea	5°00′S	110°00′E
Jaya Peak	4°05′S	137°11′E

	Lat.	Long.
Jember	8°10′S	113°42′E
Jombang	7°33′S	112°14′E
Kapuas	0°25′S	109°40′E
Karimata Strait	2°05′S	108°40′E
Kediri	7°49′S	112°01′E
Kerinci, Mount	1°42′S	101°16′E
Klakah	7°59′S	113°15′E
Krakatoa	6°07′S	105°24′E
Krawang	6°19′S	107°17′E
Krawang, Cape	5°56′S	107°00′E
Kudus	6°48′S	110°50′E
Kupang	10°10′S	123°35′E
Lawang	7°49′S	112°42′E
Lawu, Mount	7°38′S	111°11′E
Lesser Sunda Islands	9°00′S	120°00′E
Madiun	7°37′S	111°31′E
Madura	7°00′S	113°20′E
Magelang	7°28′S	110°13′E
Magetan	7°39′S	111°20′E
Mahakam	0°35′S	117°17′E
Makassar Strait	2°00′S	117°30′E

	Lat.	Long.
Malacca, Strait of	2°30′N	101°20′E
Malang	7°59′S	112°37′E
Manado	1°29′N	124°51′E
Maoke Mountains	4°00′S	138°00′E
Medan	3°35′N	98°40′E
Mentawai Islands	3°00′S	100°10′E
Moluccas	5°00′S	130°00′E
Musi	2°20′S	104°56′E
New Guinea	5°00′S	137°00′E
Ngawi	7°24′S	111°26′E
Padang	0°57′S	100°21′E
Pakanbaru	0°32′N	101°27′E
Palembang	2°55′S	104°45′E
Pamekasan	7°10′S	113°28′E
Pangkalpinang	2°08′S	106°08′E
Parepare	4°01′S	119°38′E
Pasuruan	7°38′S	112°54′E
Pekalongan	6°53′S	109°40′E
Pemalang	6°54′S	109°22′E
Pematangsiantar	2°57′N	99°03′E
Ponorogo	7°52′S	111°27′E

	Lat.	Long.
Pontianak	0°02′S	109°20′E
Probolinggo	7°45′S	113°13′E
Purwakarta	6°34′S	107°26′E
Purwokerto	7°25′S	109°14′E
Purworejo	7°43′S	110°01′E
Rakata Island	6°10′S	105°26′E
Rangkasbitung	6°21′S	106°15′E
Raung, Mount	8°08′S	114°03′E
Salatiga	7°19′S	110°30′E
Samarinda	0°30′S	117°09′E
Savu Sea	9°40′S	122°00′E
Semarang	6°58′S	110°25′E
Semeru, Mount	8°06′S	112°55′E
Seram Sea	2°30′S	128°00′E
Serang	6°07′S	106°09′E
Singaraja	8°07′S	115°06′E
Situbondo	7°42′S	114°00′E
Slamet, Mount	7°14′S	109°12′E
Sragen	7°26′S	111°02′E
Subang	6°34′S	107°45′E
Sukabumi	6°55′S	106°56′E
Sula Islands	1°52′S	125°22′E

	Lat.	Long.
Sulawesi	2°00′S	121°00′E
Sumatra	1°00′S	103°00′E
Sumedang	6°52′S	107°55′E
Sumenep	7°01′S	113°52′E
Sunda Strait	6°00′S	105°45′E
Surabaya	7°15′S	112°45′E
Surakarta	7°35′S	110°50′E
Tangerang	6°11′S	106°37′E
Tanjungkarang	5°25′S	105°16′E
Tasikmalaya	7°20′S	108°12′E
Tegal	6°52′S	109°08′E
Telukbetung	5°27′S	105°16′E
Timor	9°00′S	125°00′E
Timor Sea	11°00′S	128°00′E
Tomini Bay	0°20′S	121°00′E
Trikora Peak	4°15′S	138°45′E
Tual	5°40′S	132°45′E
Tuban	6°54′S	112°03′E
Tulungagung	8°04′S	111°54′E
Ujung Pandang	5°07′S	119°24′E
Yogyakarta	7°48′S	110°22′E

Elaborately carved houses such as these are found among the Minangkabau people of Sumatra. Much prestige hinges on a building's size, its carvings, and its roof. The adaptation of corrugated iron sheeting to traditional roof design reflects the ingenuity of the Minangkabau.

Terracing of steep slopes in Bali for rice cultivation enables farmers to make maximum use of inherently unsuitable terrain.

IRAN

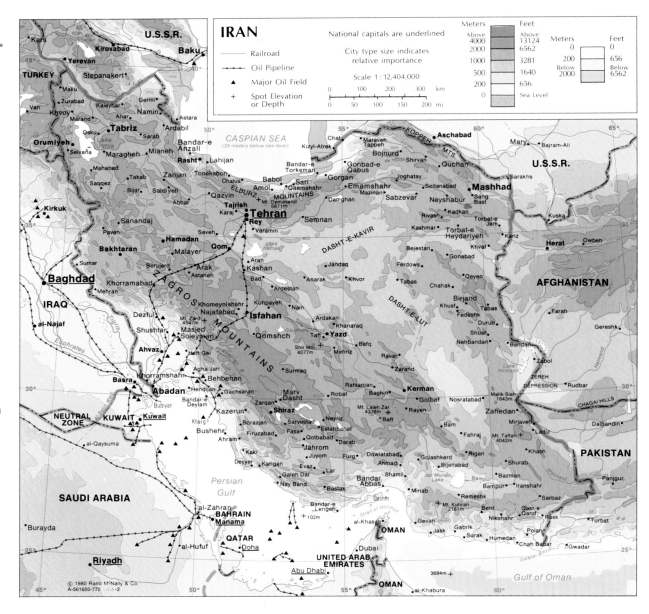

OFFICIAL NAME Islamic
Republic of Iran

PEOPLE
Population 44,500,000.
Density 70/mi² (27/km²).
Urban 49%.
Capital Tehran, 4,496,159.
Ethnic groups Persian 63%, Turkish 18%, other Iranian
13%, Kurdish 3%, Arab 3%.
Languages Farsi, Turkish, Kurdish, Arabic.
Religions Shiite Muslim 93%, Sunni Muslim 5%,
Zoroastrian, Jewish, Christian, Baha'i.
Life expectancy 59 female, 57 male.
Literacy 48%.

POLITICS
Government Republic.
Parties Islamic Republican.
Suffrage Universal, over 15.
Memberships OPEC, UN.
Subdivisions 24 provinces.

ECONOMY
GNP $66,500,000,000.
Per capita $1,621.
Monetary unit Rial.
Trade partners Japan, West Germany, Italy.
Exports Petroleum, carpets, fruits, nuts.
Imports Machinery, military equipment, food.

LAND
Description Southwestern Asia.
Area 636,296 mi² (1,648,000 km²).
Highest point Mt. Demavend, 18,386 ft (5,604 m).
Lowest point Caspian Sea, 92 ft (28 m) below sea
level.

PEOPLE. Most Iranians are of Aryan ancestry,
descended from an Asiatic people who migrated
to the area in ancient times. The Aryan groups
include majority Persians and minority Gilani,
Mazanderani, Kurds, Lur, Bakhtiari, and Baluchi.
Arabs and Turks are among the non-Aryan minorities. Until 1935, when the shah officially
changed its name, Iran was known to the rest of
the world as Persia; Farsi, or Persian, remains the
main language. Nearly all Iranians are Muslim,
mainly of the Shiite sect, and the country is an
Islamic republic, with law based on Islamic
teachings. Minority religious groups, especially
Baha'is, have been victims of persecution.

ECONOMY AND THE LAND. Iran's previously
rapid economic development has slowed as a result of a 1979 revolution and an ongoing war
with Iraq. Small-scale farming, manufacturing,
and trading appear to be current economic
trends. Oil remains the most important export,
although output has decreased due to changes in
economic policy and other factors. Persian carpets also continue as elements of trade. Iran's
terrain consists mainly of a central plateau
marked by desert and surrounded by mountains;
thus agriculture is limited, and the country remains dependent on imported food. The central
region is one of the most arid areas on earth,
and summers throughout most of the country
are long, hot, and dry, with higher humidity

along the Persian Gulf and Caspian coast. Winters are cold in the mountains of the northwest,
but mild on the plain. The Caspian coastal region
is generally subtropical.

HISTORY AND POLITICS. Iran's history is one
of the world's oldest, with a civilization dating
back several thousand years. Around 1500 B.C.
Aryan immigrants began arriving from central
Asia, calling the region Iran, or land of the Ary-
ans, and splitting into two groups: the Medes
and the Persians. In the sixth century B.C. Cyrus
the Great founded the Persian, or Achaemenian,
Empire, which came to encompass Babylonia,
Palestine, Syria, and Asia Minor. Alexander the
Great conquered the region in the fourth century
B.C. Various dynasties followed, and Muslim
Arabs invaded in the A.D. 600s and established
Islam as the major religion. The following centuries saw Iran's boundaries expand and recede
under various rulers, and increasing political
awareness resulted in a 1906 constitution and
parliament. In 1908 oil was discovered in the

region, and modernization programs began during the reign of Reza Shah Pahlavi, who came to
power in 1925. Despite Iran's declared neutrality
in World War II, the Allies invaded, obtaining
rights to use the country as a supply route to the
Soviet Union. The presence of foreign influences
caused nationalism to increase sharply after the
war. Mohammad Reza Pahlavi—who succeeded
his father, Reza Shah Pahlavi, as shah—instituted social and economic reforms during the
sixties, although many Muslims felt the reforms
violated religious law and resented the increasing
Western orientation of the country and the absolute power of the shah. Led by Muslim leader
Ayatollah Ruholla Khomeini, revolutionaries
seized the government in 1979, declaring Iran an
Islamic republic, based upon fundamental Islamic principles. Khomeini remained the religious
leader of Iran, and in 1980 the first president of
the republic was elected. Since 1980 the country
has been involved in a war with Iraq over territorial and other disputes, and internal unrest
continues as well. ■

Iran Map Index

	Lat.	Long.		Lat.	Long.		Lat.	Long.		Lat.	Long.
Abadan	30°20'N	48°16'E	Elburz Mountains	36°00'N	53°00'E	Lut, Dasht-e	33°00'N	57°00'E	Rey	35°35'N	51°25'E
Ahvaz	31°19'N	48°42'E	Emamshahr	36°25'N	55°01'E	Malayer	34°17'N	48°50'E	Sabzevar	36°13'N	57°42'E
Amol	36°23'N	52°20'E	Gonbad-e Qabus	37°17'N	55°17'E	Maragheh	37°23'N	46°13'E	Sanandaj	35°19'N	47°00'E
Arak	34°05'N	49°41'E	Gorgan	36°50'N	54°29'E	Marv Dasht	29°50'N	52°40'E	Sari	36°34'N	53°04'E
Aras	39°40'N	48°00'E	Hamadan	34°48'N	48°30'E	Mashhad	36°18'N	59°36'E	Semnan	35°33'N	53°24'E
Ardabil	38°15'N	48°18'E	Harirud (Tedzhen)	36°35'N	61°40'E	Masjed			Shiraz	29°36'N	52°32'E
Atrak	37°28'N	53°57'E	Hormuz, Strait of	26°34'N	56°15'E	Soleyman	31°58'N	49°18'E	Tabriz	38°05'N	46°18'E
Babol	36°34'N	52°42'E	Isfahan	32°40'N	51°38'E	Mianeh	37°26'N	47°42'E	Tajrish	35°48'N	51°25'E
Bakhtaran	34°19'N	47°04'E	Jaz Murian Lake	27°20'N	58°55'E	Najafabad	32°37'N	51°21'E	Tehran	35°40'N	51°26'E
Bandar Abbas	27°11'N	56°17'E	Kashan	33°59'N	51°29'E	Namin	38°25'N	48°30'E	Torbat-e		
Bandar-e Anzali	37°28'N	49°27'E	Kavir, Dasht-e	34°40'N	54°30'E	Oman, Gulf of	24°30'N	58°30'E	Heydariyeh	35°16'N	59°13'E
Behbehan	30°35'N	50°14'E	Kazerun	29°37'N	51°38'E	Orumiyeh	37°33'N	45°04'E	Urmia, Lake	37°40'N	45°30'E
Birjand	32°53'N	59°13'E	Kerman	30°17'N	57°05'E	Persian Gulf	27°00'N	51°00'E	Yazd	31°53'N	54°25'E
Bojnurd	37°28'N	57°19'E	Khorramabad	33°30'N	48°20'E	Qazvin	36°16'N	50°00'E	Zagros		
Demavend,			Khorramshahr	30°25'N	48°11'E	Qom	34°39'N	50°54'E	Mountains	33°40'N	47°00'E
Mount	35°56'N	52°08'E	Khvoy	38°33'N	44°58'E	Quchan	37°06'N	58°30'E	Zahedan	29°30'N	60°52'E
Dezful	32°23'N	48°24'E	Lahijan	37°12'N	50°01'E	Rasht	37°16'N	49°36'E	Zanjan	36°40'N	48°29'E

IRAQ

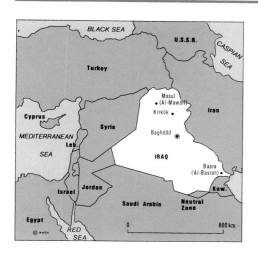

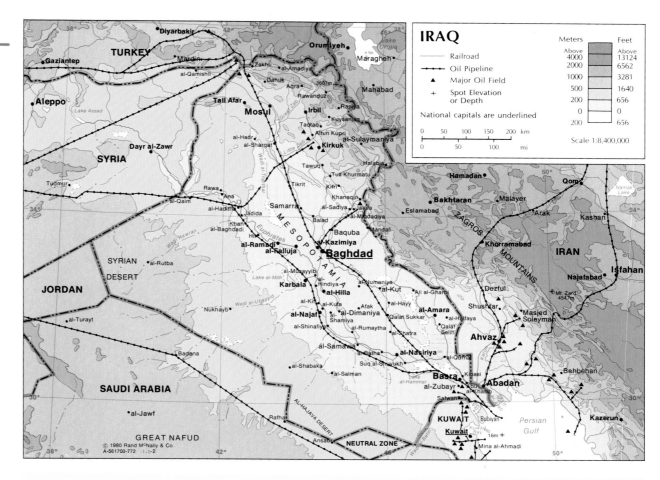

OFFICIAL NAME Republic of
Iraq

PEOPLE
Population 15,255,000.
Density 91/mi² (35/km²).
Urban 68%.
Capital Baghdad, 1,300,000.
Ethnic groups Arab 75%; Kurdish 15%; Turkish,
 Assyrian, and others 10%.
Languages Arabic, Kurdish.
Religions Shiite Muslim 55%, Sunni Muslim 40%,
 Christian 5%.
Life expectancy 58 female, 55 male.
Literacy 70%.

POLITICS
Government Republic.
Parties None (banned).
Suffrage Universal adult.
Memberships AL, OPEC, UN.
Subdivisions 15 provinces, 3 autonomous regions.

ECONOMY
GNP $30,000,000,000.
Per capita $2,150.
Monetary unit Dinar.
Trade partners Japan, West Germany, other Western
 European countries, U.S.
Exports Petroleum, dates.
Imports Construction equipment, machinery, motor
 vehicles.

LAND
Description Southwestern Asia.
Area 167,925 mi² (434,924 km²).
Highest point 11,835 ft (3,607 m).
Lowest point Sea level.

PEOPLE. Descendants of the founders of one of
the world's oldest civilizations inhabit Iraq. Most
Iraqis are Muslim Arabs and Arabic speaking.
The minority Kurds, also mainly Muslim, are
concentrated in the northwest; speak their own
language, Kurdish; and follow a non-Arab life-
style. Kurdish demands for self-rule have led to
occasional rebellion.

ECONOMY AND THE LAND. Oil is the mainstay of Iraq's economy, and nearly all economic
development has focused on the petroleum industry, nationalized in the 1970s. Despite its oil
wealth, the Iraqi economy, like the Iranian, has
been drained by the continuing Iran-Iraq war.
Most farmland lies near the Tigris and Euphrates
rivers; dates are the most important export crop.
The terrain is marked by northeastern mountains, southern and western deserts, and the
plains of upper and lower Iraq, which lie between the Tigris and Euphrates rivers. The climate is generally hot and dry.

HISTORY AND POLITICS. Civilizations such as
the Sumerian, Babylonian, and Parthian flourished in the area of the Tigris and Euphrates in
ancient times. Once known as Mesopotamia, the
region was the setting for many biblical events.
After coming under Persian rule in the sixth cen-

tury B.C., Mesopotamia fell to Alexander the
Great in the fourth century B.C. Invading Arabs
brought the Muslim religion in the seventh century A.D., and for a time Baghdad was the capital and cultural center of the Arab empire.
Thirteenth-century Mongol invaders were followed by Ottoman Turks in the sixteenth century. Ottoman rule continued, and following a
British invasion during World War I, Mesopotamia became a British mandate at the end of the
war. In 1921 the monarchy of Iraq was established, and independence was gained in 1932.

Iraq and other nations formed the Arab League
in 1945 and participated in a war against Israel in
1948. Opposition to monarchical rule increased
during the 1950s; following a 1958 military coup,
the country was declared a republic. Instability,
evidenced by coups, continued into the seventies, and the political climate was further complicated by occasional uprisings by Kurds demanding autonomy. In 1980 a border dispute and
other disagreements with Iran resulted in a continuing war. Foreign policy is often influenced by
the Arab-Israeli conflict. ∎

Iraq Map Index

	Lat.	Long.		Lat.	Long.		Lat.	Long.		Lat.	Long.
al-Amara	31°50′N	47°09′E	al-Nasiriya	31°02′N	46°16′E	Euphrates	31°00′N	47°25′E	Mesopotamia	34°00′N	44°00′E
al-Dimaniya	31°59′N	44°56′E	al-Ramadi	33°25′N	43°17′E	Great Zab	36°00′N	43°21′E	Milh, Lake al-	32°40′N	43°35′E
al-Falluja	33°20′N	43°46′E	al-Samawa	31°18′N	45°17′E	Hammar, Lake			Mosul	36°20′N	43°08′E
Al-Hajava Desert	30°00′N	44°00′E	al-Sulaymaniya	35°33′N	45°26′E	al-	30°50′N	47°10′E	Persian Gulf	29°00′N	49°00′E
al-Hilla	32°29′N	44°25′E	al-Zubayr	30°23′N	47°43′E	Irbil	36°11′N	44°01′E	Samarra	34°12′N	43°52′E
al-Kazimiya	33°22′N	44°20′E	Arab, Shatt al-	29°57′N	48°34′E	Karbala	32°36′N	44°02′E	Syrian Desert	32°00′N	40°00′E
al-Kut	32°25′N	45°49′E	Baghdad	33°21′N	44°25′E	Kirkuk	35°28′N	44°28′E	Tall Afar	36°22′N	42°27′E
al-Najaf	31°59′N	44°20′E	Basra	30°30′N	47°47′E	Little Zab	35°12′N	43°25′E	Tigris	31°00′N	47°25′E

**Bounded by the Tigris and Euphrates rivers, the region of Sumer in Iraq is a landscape of lagoons
dotted with man-made islands and houses, both made of mud and reeds from the swamp.**

IRELAND

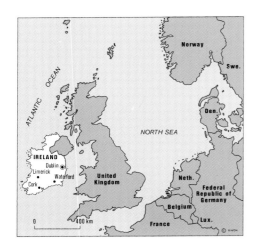

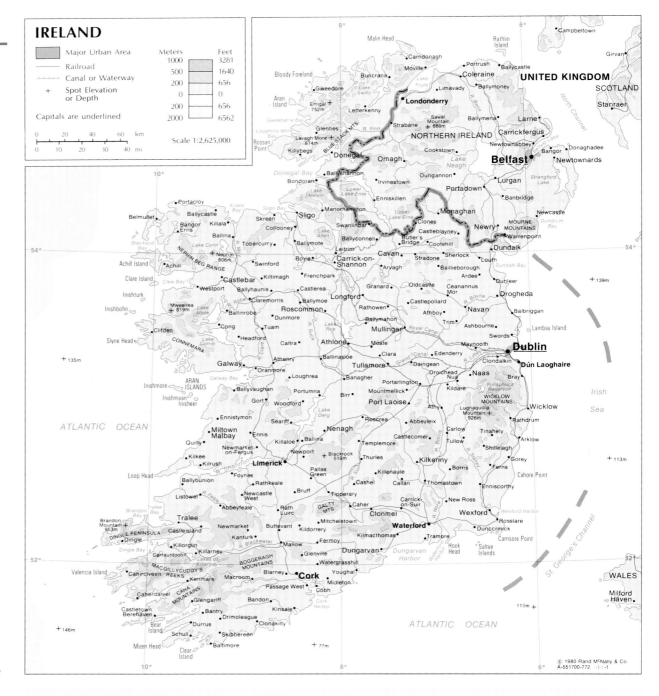

OFFICIAL NAME Ireland

PEOPLE
Population 3,595,000.
Density 132/mi² (51/km²).
Urban 56%.
Capital Dublin, 525,882.
Ethnic groups Celtic, English.
Languages Irish Gaelic, English.
Religions Roman Catholic 94%, Anglican 4%.
Life expectancy 75 female, 71 male.
Literacy 99%.

POLITICS
Government Republic.
Parties Fianna Fail, Fine Gael, Labor.
Suffrage Universal, over 18.
Memberships EC, OECD, UN.
Subdivisions 26 counties.

ECONOMY
GNP $17,000,000,000.
Per capita $5,667.
Monetary unit Pound.
Trade partners U.K., other Western European countries, U.S.
Exports Meat and dairy products, textiles, machinery.
Imports Petroleum, petroleum products, machinery, chemicals, manufactured goods.

LAND
Description Northwestern Europe (five-sixths of island of Ireland).
Area 27,136 mi² (70,283 km²).
Highest point Carrauntoohil, 3,406 ft (1,038 m).
Lowest point Sea level.

PEOPLE. Most of Ireland's population is descended from the Celts, a people who flourished in Europe and Great Britain in ancient times. Irish Gaelic, a form of ancient Celtic, and English are official languages. Most people are Roman Catholic, and Protestants mainly belong to the Church of Ireland, a member of the Anglican Communion. The country has a long literary tradition and has contributed greatly to world literature.

ECONOMY AND THE LAND. Ireland's economy was agricultural until the 1950s, when a program of rapid industrialization began. This expansion has resulted in significant foreign investment, especially by the United States. Most of the Irish labor force is unionized. Agriculture continues to play an important role, however, and food is produced for both domestic consumption and trade. The country of Ireland occupies most of the island of Ireland but excludes Northern Ireland, which is part of the United Kingdom. The fertile central region features green, rolling hills, suitable for farming and pastureland, and is surrounded by coastal highlands. The climate is temperate maritime, with mild summers and winters and plentiful rainfall.

HISTORY AND POLITICS. Around the fourth century B.C. Ireland's indigenous population was conquered by Gaels, a Celtic tribe, from continental Europe and Great Britain. Christianity was introduced by St. Patrick in A.D. 432, and periodic Viking raids began near the end of the eighth century. In the twelfth century the pope made the Norman king of England, Henry II, overlord of the island; the English intervened in a dispute between Irish kings; and centuries of British influence began. As British control grew, so did Irish Catholic hostility, arising from seizure of land by English settlers, the Protestant Reformation, and the elimination of political and religious freedoms. The Protestant majority of present-day Northern Ireland was established in the 1600s, when land taken from the Irish was distributed to English and Scottish Protestants. In 1801 the British Act of Union established the United Kingdom of Great Britain and Ireland. Religious freedom was regained in 1829, but the struggle for independence continued. Most of the Irish depended upon potatoes as a staple food, and hundreds of thousands died or emigrated in the 1840s when the crop failed because of a plant disease. Following an armed rebellion, the Irish Free State, a dominion of Great Britain, was created in 1921, with the predominantly Protestant countries in the north remaining under British rule. The nation became a republic in 1948. Many Irish citizens and Catholics in Northern Ireland continue to demand unification of the country, and the struggle occasionally erupts into violence. Neutrality remains the basis of foreign policy, and the nation is a strong supporter of European unity. ∎

Ireland Map Index

	Lat.	Long.		Lat.	Long.		Lat.	Long.		Lat.	Long.
Achill Island	54°00′N	10°00′W	Cork	51°54′N	8°28′W	Liffey	53°22′N	6°14′W	Rossan Point	54°42′N	8°48′W
Allen, Lake	54°08′N	8°08′W	Corrib, Lake	53°05′N	9°10′W	Limerick	52°40′N	8°38′W	Royal Canal	53°21′N	6°15′W
Aran Islands	53°07′N	9°43′W	Derg, Lake	53°00′N	8°20′W	Longford	53°44′N	7°47′W	Saint George's		
Athlone	53°25′N	7°56′W	Dingle Bay	52°05′N	10°15′W	Loop Head	52°34′N	9°56′W	Channel	52°00′N	6°00′W
Bann	55°10′N	6°45′W	Dingle Peninsula	52°10′N	10°05′W	Mask, Lake	53°35′N	9°20′W	Shannon	52°36′N	9°41′W
Blackwater	51°51′N	7°50′W	Donegal	54°39′N	8°07′W	Milltown Malbay	52°52′N	9°23′W	Sligo	54°17′N	8°28′W
Blue Stack			Donegal Bay	54°30′N	8°30′W	Mizen Head	51°27′N	9°49′W	Slyne Head	53°24′N	10°13′W
Mountains	54°50′N	8°00′W	Drogheda	53°43′N	6°21′W	Monaghan	54°15′N	6°58′W	Strangford Lake	54°30′N	5°36′W
Boyne	53°43′N	6°15′W	Dublin	53°20′N	6°15′W	Mourne			Suir	52°15′N	7°00′W
Carnsore Point	52°10′N	6°22′W	Dundalk	54°01′N	6°25′W	Mountains	54°10′N	6°05′W	Swilly, Lake	55°10′N	7°38′W
Carrauntoohill	52°00′N	9°45′W	Dungarvan	52°05′N	7°37′W	Mullingar	53°32′N	7°20′W	Tralee	52°16′N	9°42′W
Carrick-on-			Dún Laoghaire	53°17′N	6°08′W	Naas	53°13′N	6°39′W	Tullamore	53°16′N	7°30′W
Shannon	53°57′N	8°05′W	Erne, Lower Lake	54°26′N	7°46′W	Navan	53°39′N	6°41′W	Waterford	52°15′N	7°06′W
Castlebar	53°52′N	9°17′W	Erne, Upper Lake	54°14′N	7°32′W	Neagh, Lake	54°37′N	6°25′W	Wexford	52°20′N	6°27′W
Cavan	54°00′N	7°21′W	Finn	54°50′N	7°29′W	Nenagh	52°52′N	8°12′W	Wicklow	52°59′N	6°03′W
Clear Island	51°26′N	9°30′W	Foyle, Lake	55°07′N	7°08′W	Pollaphuca			Wicklow		
Clew Bay	53°50′N	9°50′W	Galway	53°16′N	9°03′W	Reservoir	53°08′N	6°31′W	Mountains	53°02′N	6°24′W
Clonmel	52°21′N	7°42′W	Grand Canal	53°21′N	6°14′W	Port Laoise	53°02′N	7°17′W			
Conn, Lake	54°04′N	9°20′W	Irish Sea	53°00′N	5°20′W	Ree, Lake	53°35′N	8°00′W			
Connemara	53°25′N	9°45′W	Kilkenny	52°39′N	7°15′W	Roscommon	53°38′N	8°11′W			

ISLE OF MAN

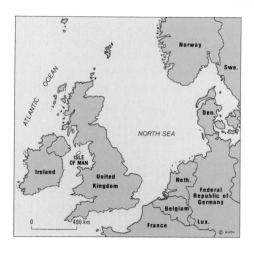

OFFICIAL NAME Isle of Man

PEOPLE
Population 67,000.
Density 303/mi² (117/km²).
Urban 72%.
Capital Douglas, 20,368.
Ethnic groups Manx, British.
Languages English.
Religions Anglican, Methodist.

POLITICS
Government Self-governing territory (U.K.).
Suffrage Universal, over 21.

ECONOMY
GDP $278,000,000.
Per capita $4,150.
Monetary unit British pound sterling.
Trade partners U.K.

Exports Textiles, fish.
Imports Timber, fertilizer.
LAND
Description Northwestern European island.
Area 221 mi² (572 km²).
Highest point Snaefell, 2,036 ft (621 m).
Lowest point Sea level.

PEOPLE. Manx, of Celtic descent, compose the majority population on the Isle of Man. Their language, also called Manx, is virtually extinct, having been replaced by English nearly universally on the island. A dependency of the United Kingdom, the Isle of Man has a minority British population, and the main religion is Anglican.

ECONOMY AND THE LAND. Agricultural activities include livestock raising and dairy farming, and the island's major crops are oats, wheat, barley, and potatoes. Fishing provides for local consumption and export income, and tax incentives have encouraged the development of industry. About 11 percent of the island's income comes from tourism. The Isle of Man is situated midway between Britain and Ireland, and many tourists from the British Isles visit the island annually, attracted by its scenic beauty. In addition, a popular motorcycle race held each year draws international visitors. The rocky coast is marked by cliffs, and moors cover much of the island's interior. Calf of Man, a rocky islet, lies off the southwest shore. The climate is mild.

HISTORY AND POLITICS. Irish missionaries came to the Isle of Man early in its history. The Vikings took the island in the ninth century, and it remained under Norwegian control until 1266. Various rulers and owners followed, including the Scots, Welsh, British, and the earls of Salis-

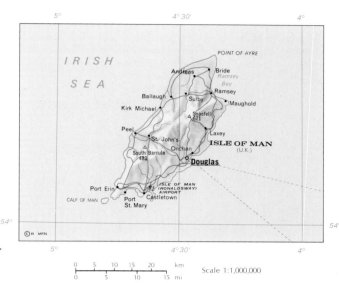

Isle of Man Map Index

	Lat.	Long.		Lat.	Long.
Calf of Man	54°03′N	4°48′W	Peel	54°13′N	4°40′W
Castletown	54°04′N	4°40′W	Port Erin	54°06′N	4°44′W
Douglas	54°09′N	4°28′W	Ramsey	54°20′N	4°21′W

bury and Derby. In 1765 Britain bought the island from the Duke of Atholl. A self-governing territory of the United Kingdom, the Isle of Man has its own legal system; residents are not subject to British laws and acts, although local laws require British approval. The island also has its own legislature, the one-thousand-year-old Tynwald, which is one of the world's oldest legislative bodies. The Crown is represented in the dependency by a lieutenant governor. The Isle of Man is also famous as the birthplace of the Manx cat. ■

ISRAEL

Just as Rome is the focus of Roman Catholicism and Mecca is that of Islam, Jerusalem, shown here, occupies a central position in Judaism. In the Arab-Israeli conflict of 1948, Jordan seized East Jerusalem, comprising the Old City and site of many sacred Jewish shrines. Jerusalem remained divided until the Six-Day War of 1967, when the Israelis took East Jerusalem and destroyed the wall that separated the Israeli and Jordanian sectors. In 1980 the Israeli government proclaimed Jerusalem the permanent capital; many countries, however, do not recognize the capital and maintain their embassies in Tel Aviv–Jaffa.

ISRAEL

OFFICIAL NAME State of Israel

PEOPLE
Population 4,170,000.
Density 505/mi² (195 km²).
Urban 87%.
Capital Jerusalem, 415,000.
Ethnic groups Jewish 85%, Arab 15%.
Languages Hebrew, Arabic, English.
Religions Jewish 85%, Muslim 11%.
Life expectancy 76 female, 73 male.
Literacy 88%.

POLITICS
Government Republic.
Parties Labor Alignment, Likud.
Suffrage Universal, over 18.
Memberships UN.
Subdivisions 6 districts.

ECONOMY
GNP $22,200,000,000.
Per capita $5,612.
Monetary unit Shekel.
Trade partners U.S., U.K., West Germany, other Western European countries.
Exports Polished diamonds, fruits, textiles, clothing, machinery, fertilizer.
Imports Military equipment, rough diamonds, petroleum, machinery, chemicals.

LAND
Description Southwestern Asia.
Area 8,302 mi² (21,501 km²).
Highest point Mt. Meron, 3,963 ft (1,208 m).
Lowest point Dead Sea, 1,312 ft (400 m) below sea level.
The above information excludes the Golan Heights, the West Bank, and Gaza Strip.

PEOPLE. Most Israelis are Jewish immigrants or descendants of Jews who settled in the region in the late 1800s. The two main ethnic groups are the Ashkenazim of central and eastern European origin and the Sephardim of the Mediterranean and Middle East. The non-Jewish population is primarily Arab and Muslim, and many Palestinians inhabit the Israeli-occupied West Bank, which was controlled by Jordan from 1948 to 1967 and whose status is now in dispute. Violence between Arabs and Jews has resulted from Israeli settlement of the West Bank region.

ECONOMY AND THE LAND. Despite drastic levels of inflation and a constant trade deficit, Israel has experienced continuous economic growth. Skilled labor supports the market economy based on services, manufacturing, and commerce. Taxes are a major source of revenue, as are grants and loans from other countries and income from tourism. The country is poor in natural resources, but through improved irrigation and soil conservation, Israel now produces much of its own food. Because of its limited natural resources, Israel must import most of the raw materials it needs for industry. The region's varied terrain includes coastal plains, central mountains, the Jordan Rift Valley, and the desert region of the Negev. Except in the Negev, the climate is temperate.

HISTORY AND POLITICS. Israel comprises much of the historic region of Palestine, known in ancient times as Canaan and the site of most biblical history. The region saw the arrival of the

Israel Map Index

	Lat.	Long.		Lat.	Long.
Acre (Akko)	32°55′N	35°05′E	Kiryath Gath	31°37′N	34°46′E
Aqaba, Gulf of	29°30′N	34°55′E	Kiryath Malachi	31°42′N	34°38′E
Arad	31°15′N	35°13′E	Kiryath Shemona	33°12′N	35°35′E
Ashdod	31°49′N	34°40′E	Kiryath Tivon	32°43′N	35°08′E
Ashqelon			*Kishon*	32°49′N	35°02′E
(Ashkelon)	31°40′N	34°35′E	Lod	31°58′N	34°54′E
Bath Yam	32°00′N	34°45′E	*Meron, Mount*	32°58′N	35°25′E
Beersheba	31°14′N	34°47′E	Nachal Oz	31°28′N	34°29′E
Beth Shean	32°30′N	35°31′E	Nahariyya	33°00′N	35°05′E
Beth Shemesh	31°47′N	34°59′E	Nazareth	32°42′N	35°18′E
Chadera	32°26′N	34°55′E	*Negev*	30°30′N	34°55′E
Chatzor Ha-			Netanya	32°20′N	34°51′E
Geliliith	32°59′N	35°34′E	Ofakim	31°17′N	34°37′E
Dead Sea	31°30′N	35°30′E	Ofula	32°38′N	35°20′E
Dimona	31°04′N	35°02′E	Pardes Chana	32°28′N	34°58′E
Dor	32°37′N	34°55′E	Pethach Tikva	32°05′N	34°53′E
Elat	29°33′N	34°57′E	Ramath Gan	32°05′N	34°49′E
Galilee, Sea of	32°48′N	35°35′E	Ramla	31°55′N	34°52′E
Gaza	31°30′N	34°28′E	*Ramon, Mount*	30°30′N	34°38′E
Gaza Strip	31°25′N	34°20′E	Rehovoth	31°54′N	34°49′E
Gedera	31°49′N	34°46′E	Rishon le Zion	31°58′N	34°48′E
Ha-Arava	31°04′N	35°07′E	Safad	32°58′N	35°30′E
Haifa	32°50′N	35°00′E	Sedroth	31°31′N	34°35′E
Hertzliyya	32°11′N	34°50′E	*Tabor, Mount*	32°41′N	35°23′E
Hula Valley	33°08′N	35°37′E	Tel Aviv-Jaffa	32°04′N	34°46′E
Jerusalem	31°46′N	35°14′E	Tiberias	32°47′N	35°32′E
Jordan	31°46′N	35°33′E	Tirath Karmel	32°46′N	34°58′E
Karmel, Mount	32°44′N	35°02′E	Umm el Fahm	32°31′N	35°09′E
Kefar Sava	32°10′N	34°54′E	Yavne	31°53′N	34°45′E
Khan Yunis	31°21′N	34°19′E			

Hebrews around 1900 B.C. and subsequent immigration and invasion by diverse peoples, including Assyrians, Babylonians, and Persians. In 63 B.C. it became part of the Roman Empire and was renamed Judaea and, finally, Palestine. In the A.D. 600s invading Arabs brought Islam to the area, and by the early 1500s, when Ottoman Turks conquered the region, Muslims made up a majority. During the late 1800s, as a result of oppression in eastern Europe, many Jews immigrated to Palestine, hoping to establish a Jewish state. This movement, called Zionism, and the increasing Jewish population led to Arab-Jewish tensions. Turkey sided with Germany in World War I, and after the war the Ottoman Empire collapsed. Palestine became a mandated territory of Britain in 1920. Jewish immigration, and thus Arab-Jewish hostility, increased during the years of Nazi Germany. Additional unrest arose from conflicting interpretations of British promises and the terms of the mandate. In 1947 Britain turned to the United Nations for help in resolving the problem, and in 1948 the nation of Israel was established. Neighboring Arab countries invaded immediately, and war ensued, during which Israel gained additional land. Despite a 1949 truce, violence continued along the borders, and in response to terrorist attacks, in 1956 Israel invaded the Gaza Strip, an area along the southeast coast of the Mediterranean, and the Sinai Peninsula in northeast Egypt, withdrawing in 1957 when the United Nations Emergency Force arrived. The Six-Day War between Israel and Egypt, Jordan, and Syria broke out in 1967 after Egypt expelled the United Nations force, sent Egyptian troops to the Sinai and Gaza Strip, and closed the Strait of Tiran to Israeli ships. During the war Israel gained control of the Sinai Peninsula; the Gaza Strip; the Golan Heights, a hilly region on the Syria-Israel border; and the West Bank, land west of the Jordan River. On Yom Kippur in 1973, Syrian and Egyptian forces attacked Israeli positions, but Israel drove the Syrians back across the Suez Canal. Following a cease fire, efforts for peace were renewed, resulting in disengagement agreements with Egypt and Syria and, ultimately, a peace treaty with Egypt in 1979. In 1981 Israel annexed the Golan Heights and in 1982 returned the Sinai to Egypt. Both the West Bank and Gaza Strip remain under Israeli administration, and tensions remain between Israel and many of its neighbors. ■

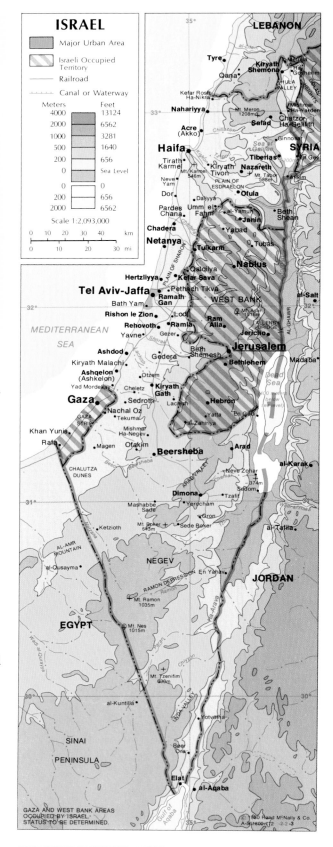

The Wailing Wall in Jerusalem is all that remains of the Jews' holy temple, built in biblical times. Shown here is a bar mitzvah being held at this most sacred place.

ITALY

OFFICIAL NAME Italian
Republic

PEOPLE
Population 56,940,000.
Density 490/mi² (189/km²).
Urban 69%.
Capital Rome, 2,830,569.
Ethnic groups Italian, others.
Languages Italian.
Religions Roman Catholic.
Life expectancy 76 female, 72 male.
Literacy 93%.

POLITICS
Government Republic.
Parties Christian Democratic, Communist, Socialist, Social Movement.
Suffrage Universal, over 18.
Memberships EC, NATO, OECD, UN.
Subdivisions 20 regions.

ECONOMY
GNP $347,000,000,000.
Per capita $5,314.
Monetary unit Lira.
Trade partners West Germany, France, Benelux countries, U.S., U.K.
Exports Machinery, transportation equipment, textiles, food.
Imports Machinery, transportation equipment, food, petroleum.

LAND
Description Southern Europe.
Area 116,319 mi² (301,266 km²).
Highest point Mt. Blanc (Monte Bianco), 15,771 ft (4,807 m).
Lowest point Sea level.

PEOPLE. Italy is populated mainly by Italian Roman Catholics. Most speak Italian; however, dialects differ from region to region. Despite an ethnic homogeneity, the people exhibit diversity in terms of politics and culture. The country has about twelve political parties, and northern inhabitants are relatively prosperous, employed primarily in industry, whereas southerners are generally farmers and often poor.

ECONOMY AND THE LAND. The Italian economy is based on private enterprise, although the government is involved in some industrial and commercial activities. Industry is centered in the north, producing steel, textiles, and chemicals. Much commercial agriculture is also based in the north, taking place on the rich soils of the Po Valley. A hilly terrain makes parts of the south unsuited for crop raising, and livestock grazing is a main activity. Tourism is also important, with visitors drawn by the northern Alps, the sunny south, and the Italian cultural tradition. The island of Sicily produces fruits, olives, and grapes, and Sardinia engages in sheep and wheat raising. Except for the northern Po Valley, narrow coastal areas, and a small section in the south, Italy's terrain is mostly mountainous. But mountains make Italy vulnerable to natural disaster,

and in 1987 catastrophic landslides in the Alps wiped out Sant'Antonio Morignone and isolated the region from the rest of the country. Italy's climate varies from cool in the north to Mediterranean in the south.

HISTORY AND POLITICS. Early influences in Italy included Greeks, Etruscans, and Celts. From the fifth century B.C. to the fifth century A.D., the dominant people were Romans descended from Sabines and neighboring Latins, who inhabited the Latium coast. Following the demise of the Roman Empire, rulers and influences included Byzantines; Lombards, an invading Germanic tribe; and the Frankish king Charlemagne, whom the pope crowned emperor of the Romans in 800. During the eleventh century, Italy became a region of city-states, and their cultural life led to the Renaissance, which started in the 1300s. As the city-states weakened, Italy fell victim to invasion and rule by France, Spain, and Austria, with these countries controlling various regions at different times. In 1861 Victor Emmanuel II, the king of Sardinia, proclaimed Italy a kingdom, and by 1871 the nation included the entire peninsula, with Rome as the capital and Victor Emmanuel as king. In 1922 Benito Mussolini, the leader of Italy's Fascist movement, came to power. By 1925 Mussolini was ruling as dictator, and an almost continuous period of warfare followed. In World War II the country allied with Germany, and a popular resistance movement evolved. The monarchy was ended by plebiscite in 1946, and the country became a republic. There are now many political parties, but the Christian Democratic, Communist, and Socialist parties are dominant. ■

Venice, a seaport in northeast Italy and one of the world's treasure houses of art and architecture, consists of more than 118 islands in a large lagoon. The main water thoroughfare is the Grand Canal, but narrow canals separate most of the islands.

The Dolomites' limestone peaks rise above Cortina d'Ampezzo in northeast Italy.

ITALY

Major Urban Area
Railroad
Glacier
+ Spot Elevation or Depth

National capitals are underlined

City type size indicates relative importance

Meters	Feet
Above 4000	Above 13124
2000	6562
1000	3281
500	1640
200	656
0	0
200	656
Below 2000	Below 6562

Scale 1:6,145,000

0   50   100   150 km
0   50   100 mi

Italy Map Index

	Lat.	Long.		Lat.	Long.
Abruzzi Mountains	42°00′N	14°00′E	Macerata	43°18′N	13°27′E
			Maggiore, Lake	46°00′N	8°40′E
Adrano	37°40′N	14°50′E	Malta Channel	56°44′N	26°53′E
Adriatic Sea	42°30′N	16°00′E	Manfredonia	41°38′N	15°55′E
Agrigento	37°18′N	13°35′E	Manfredonia, Gulf of	41°35′N	16°05′E
Alcamo	37°59′N	12°58′E	Mantova	45°09′N	10°48′E
Alessandria	44°54′N	8°37′E	Maritime Alps	44°15′N	7°10′E
Alghero	40°34′N	8°19′E	Marsala	37°48′N	12°26′E
Alps	46°30′N	8°30′E	Matera	40°40′N	16°37′E
Altamura	40°50′N	16°33′E	Matterhorn	45°59′N	7°43′E
Ancona	43°38′N	13°30′E	Mazara del Vallo	37°39′N	12°36′E
Aosta	45°44′N	7°20′E	Merano	46°40′N	11°09′E
Apennines	43°00′N	13°00′E	Messina	38°11′N	15°33′E
Arezzo	43°25′N	11°53′E	Messina, Strait of	38°15′N	15°35′E
Ascoli Piceno	42°51′N	13°34′E	Milan	45°28′N	9°12′E
Asinara, Gulf of	41°00′N	8°30′E	Modena	44°40′N	10°55′E
Asti	44°54′N	8°12′E	Modica	36°51′N	14°47′E
Augusta	37°13′N	15°13′E	Monfalcone	45°49′N	13°32′E
Avellino	40°54′N	14°47′E	Monferrato	45°08′N	8°27′E
Avezzano	42°02′N	13°25′E	Montecristo Island	42°20′N	10°19′E
Bari	41°07′N	16°52′E	Naples	40°51′N	14°17′E
Barletta	41°19′N	16°17′E	Nebrodi	37°55′N	14°35′E
Bergamo	45°41′N	9°43′E	Novara	45°28′N	8°38′E
Bernina Peak	46°21′N	9°51′E	Novi Ligure	44°46′N	8°47′E
Biella	45°34′N	8°03′E	Nuoro	40°19′N	9°20′E
Blanc, Mount	45°50′N	6°52′E	Padua	45°25′N	11°53′E
Bologna	44°29′N	11°20′E	Palermo	38°07′N	13°21′E
Bolzano	46°31′N	11°22′E	Pantelleria Island	36°47′N	12°00′E
Bonifacio, Strait of	41°01′N	14°00′E	Parma	44°48′N	10°20′E
Brenner Pass	47°00′N	11°30′E	Passero, Cape	36°40′N	15°09′E
Brescia	45°33′N	13°15′E	Pavia	45°10′N	9°10′E
Brindisi	40°38′N	17°56′E	Perugia	43°08′N	12°22′E
Cagliari	39°20′N	9°00′E	Pescara	42°28′N	14°13′E
Caltanissetta	37°29′N	14°04′E	Piacenza	45°01′N	9°40′E
Campobasso	41°34′N	14°39′E	Pinerolo	44°53′N	7°21′E
Capri Island	40°33′N	14°13′E	Piombino	42°55′N	10°32′E
Carbonia	39°11′N	8°32′E	Pisa	43°43′N	10°23′E
Carrara	44°05′N	10°06′E	Po	44°57′N	12°04′E
Caserta	41°04′N	14°20′E	Ponziane Islands	40°55′N	12°57′E
Catania	37°30′N	15°06′E	Pordenone	45°57′N	12°39′E
Catanzaro	38°54′N	16°36′E	Potenza	40°38′N	15°49′E
Cerignola	41°16′N	15°54′E	Prato	43°53′N	11°06′E
Cesena	44°08′N	12°15′E	Ravenna	44°25′N	12°12′E
Chieti	42°21′N	14°10′E	Reggio di Calabria	38°07′N	15°39′E
Chioggia	45°13′N	12°17′E	Rieti	42°24′N	12°51′E
Civitavecchia	42°06′N	11°48′E	Rimini	44°04′N	12°34′E
Comino, Cape	40°31′N	9°50′E	Riviera	45°15′N	9°30′E
Como	45°47′N	9°05′E	Rome	41°54′N	12°29′E
Como, Lake	46°00′N	9°20′E	Rosa, Monte	45°55′N	7°52′E
Cosenza	39°17′N	16°15′E	Rovigo	45°04′N	11°47′E
Cremona	45°07′N	10°02′E	Saint Bernard Pass	45°50′N	7°10′E
Crotone	39°05′N	17°07′E	Salerno	40°41′N	14°47′E
Cuneo	44°23′N	7°32′E	San Benedetto del Tronto	42°57′N	13°53′E
Dolomites	46°25′N	11°50′E	San Remo	43°49′N	7°46′E
Egadi Islands	37°56′N	12°16′E	San Severo	41°41′N	15°23′E
Elba	42°46′N	10°17′E	Santa Maria di Leuca, Cape	39°47′N	18°22′E
Empoli	43°43′N	10°57′E	Sardinia	40°00′N	9°00′E
Enna	37°34′N	14°17′E	Sassari	40°44′N	8°33′E
Eolie Islands	38°30′N	15°00′E	Savona	44°17′N	8°30′E
Etna, Mount	37°46′N	15°00′E	Sciacca	37°30′N	13°06′E
Fabriano	43°20′N	12°54′E	Sicily	37°30′N	14°00′E
Faenza	44°17′N	11°53′E	Sicily, Strait of	37°20′N	11°20′E
Fano	43°50′N	13°01′E	Siena	43°19′N	11°21′E
Ferrara	44°50′N	11°35′E	Spoleto	42°44′N	12°44′E
Florence	43°46′N	11°15′E	Stromboli Island	38°48′N	15°13′E
Foggia	41°27′N	15°34′E	Sulmona	42°03′N	13°55′E
Foligno	42°57′N	12°42′E	Syracuse	37°04′N	15°17′E
Garda, Lake	45°40′N	10°41′E	Taranto	40°28′N	17°15′E
Gela	37°03′N	14°15′E	Taranto, Gulf of	40°10′N	17°20′E
Gennargentu Mountains	39°59′N	9°19′E	Terni	42°34′N	12°37′E
Genoa	44°25′N	8°57′E	Teulada, Cape	38°52′N	8°39′E
Genoa, Gulf of	44°10′N	8°55′E	Tiber	41°44′N	12°14′E
Grande Mountain	42°28′N	13°34′E	Tivoli	41°58′N	12°48′E
Gran Paradiso	45°32′N	7°16′E	Torre Annunziata	40°45′N	14°27′E
Gran Sasso d'Italia Mountains	42°27′N	13°42′E	Trapani	38°01′N	12°31′E
			Trasimeno, Lake	43°08′N	12°06′E
Grosseto	42°46′N	11°08′E	Trento	46°04′N	11°08′E
Iesi	43°31′N	13°14′E	Treviso	45°40′N	12°15′E
Iglesias	39°19′N	8°32′E	Trieste	45°40′N	13°48′E
Imola	44°21′N	11°42′E	Turin	45°03′N	7°40′E
Imperia	43°53′N	8°03′E	Tyrrhenian Sea	40°00′N	12°00′E
Ionian Sea	38°30′N	18°00′E	Udine	46°03′N	13°14′E
Ischia	40°43′N	13°54′E	Ustica Island	38°42′N	13°10′E
Ivrea	45°28′N	7°52′E	Varese	45°48′N	8°48′E
La Marmora Peak	39°59′N	9°19′E	Velino, Mount	42°09′N	13°23′E
L'Aquila	42°22′N	13°22′E	Venice	45°27′N	12°21′E
La Spezia	44°07′N	9°50′E	Venice, Gulf of	45°15′N	13°00′E
Latina	41°28′N	12°52′E	Verbania	45°56′N	8°33′E
Lecce	40°23′N	18°11′E	Verona	45°27′N	11°00′E
Lecco	45°51′N	9°23′E	Vesulius	40°49′N	14°26′E
Legnago	45°11′N	11°18′E	Vicenza	45°33′N	11°33′E
Licata	37°05′N	13°56′E	Viso, Mount	44°40′N	7°07′E
Ligurian Sea	43°30′N	9°00′E	Viterbo	42°25′N	12°06′E
Lipari Island	38°30′N	14°57′E	Zillertaler Alps	47°00′N	11°55′E
Livorno	43°33′N	10°19′E			
Lodi	45°19′N	9°30′E			
Lucca	43°50′N	10°29′E			

Beginning at the French border, Italy's northwest coastal region along the Ligurian Sea is known as the Italian Riviera. The fishing villages that dot the shore have become popular tourist destinations, and chief among these resorts is the town of Portofino, shown here. A beautiful setting, an agreeable climate, and Mediterranean vegetation combine for a quaint atmosphere that draws hundreds of visitors annually.

For hundreds of years Rome has been an international cultural center, and the city today is a blend of the ancient and modern. Here, busy streets wind past Roman ruins and the Colosseum.

IVORY COAST

OFFICIAL NAME Republic of
the Ivory Coast

PEOPLE
Population 9,325,000.
Density 75/mi² (29/km²).
Urban 38%.
Capital Abidjan (de facto), 1,500,000; Yamoussoukro (designated), 35,585.
Ethnic groups Agni, Baule, Krou, Senoufou, Mandingo, others.
Languages French, indigenous.
Religions Indigenous 63%, Muslims 25%, Christian 12%.
Life expectancy 48 female, 46 male.
Literacy 24%.

POLITICS
Government Republic.
Parties Democratic.
Suffrage Universal, over 21.
Memberships OAU, UN.
Subdivisions 34 departments.

ECONOMY
GDP $7,700,000,000.
Per capita $871.
Monetary unit CFA franc.
Trade partners France, other Western European countries, U.S.
Exports Cocoa, coffee, wood.
Imports Machinery, petroleum, motor vehicles, consumer goods.

LAND
Description Western Africa.
Area 123,847 mi² (320,763 km²).
Highest point Mt. Nimba, 5,748 ft (1,752 m).
Lowest point Sea level.

PEOPLE. Ivory Coast is composed almost entirely of black Africans from more than sixty ethnic groups. French is the nation's official language, a result of former French rule, but many indigenous languages are spoken as well. Traditional religions predominate, though a significant number of Ivorians are Muslim or Christian. Most Ivorians live in huts in small villages, but increased numbers have moved to the cities to find work. Overcrowding is a major problem in the cities.

ECONOMY AND THE LAND. Once solely dependent upon the export of cocoa and coffee, Ivory Coast now produces and exports a variety of agricultural goods. Forest land, when cleared, provides rich soil for agriculture—still the country's main activity. Petroleum, textile, and apparel industries also contribute to the strong economy. Ivory Coast pursues a policy of economic liberalism in which foreign investment is encouraged. As a result, foreigners hold high-level positions in most Ivory Coast industries. The hot, humid coastal region gives way to inland tropical forest. Beyond the forest lies savanna, and to the northwest are highlands.

HISTORY AND POLITICS. Ivory Coast once consisted of many African kingdoms. French sailors

Ivory Coast Map Index

	Lat.	Long.		Lat.	Long.
Abengourou	6°44′N	3°29′W	Duékoué	6°45′N	7°21′W
Abidjan	5°19′N	4°02′W	Ferkéssédougou	9°36′N	5°12′W
Aboisso	5°28′N	3°12′W	Gagnoa	6°08′N	5°56′W
Adzopé	6°06′N	3°52′W	Grand-Bassam	5°12′N	3°44′W
Bandama	5°10′N	5°00′W	Katiola	8°08′N	5°06′W
Bandama Blanc	6°54′N	5°31′W	Komoé	5°12′N	3°44′W
Bandama Rouge	6°54′N	5°31′W	Korhogo	9°27′N	5°38′W
Black Volta	8°47′N	2°35′W	Man	7°24′N	7°33′W
Bondoukou	8°02′N	2°48′W	Nimba, Mount	7°35′N	8°25′W
Bonoua	5°16′N	3°36′W	Odienne	9°30′N	7°34′W
Bouaké	7°41′N	5°02′W	Sassandra	4°58′N	6°05′W
Cavally	4°22′N	7°32′W	Sassandra	4°58′N	6°05′W
Daloa	6°53′N	6°27′W	Séguéla	7°57′N	6°40′W
Danané	7°16′N	8°09′W	Tabou	4°25′N	7°21′W
Dimbokro	6°39′N	4°42′W	Toura Mountains	7°40′N	7°25′W
Divo	5°50′N	5°22′W	Yamoussoukro	6°49′N	5°17′W

gave the region its present name when they began trading for ivory and other goods in 1483. Missionaries arrived in 1637, but European settlement was hindered by the rugged coastline and intertribal conflicts. Ivory Coast became a French colony in 1893. Movements toward autonomy began after World War II, and in 1960 Ivory Coast declared itself an independent republic. The nation has enjoyed political stability since independence and has maintained close economic ties with France. Ivory Coast has one political party, which controls the government. Foreign policy stresses favorable relations with the West. ∎

IVORY COAST

	Meters	Feet		
— Railroad	2000	6562	Meters	Feet
+ Spot Elevation	1000	3281	0	0
	500	1640	200	656
	200	656	Below 2000	Below 6562
	0	0		

Scale 1:9,267,000

Villages of thatched huts such as these near Daloa are found in the countryside of the Ivory Coast, where families live in groups called "compounds."

JAMAICA

OFFICIAL NAME Jamaica

PEOPLE
Population 2,170,000.
Density 511/mi² (197/km²).
Urban 50%.
Capital Kingston, 671,000.
Ethnic groups African 76%, Afro-European 15%, East Indian and Afro-East Indian 4%, white 3%.
Languages English.
Religions Anglican, Baptist, other Protestant, Roman Catholic.
Life expectancy 73 female, 69 male.
Literacy 76%.

POLITICS
Government Parliamentary state.
Parties Labor, People's National.
Suffrage Universal, over 18.
Memberships CW, OAS, UN.
Subdivisions 14 parishes.

ECONOMY
GNP $3,000,000,000.
Per capita $1,360.
Monetary unit Dollar.
Trade partners U.S., Venezuela, Caribbean countries.
Exports Alumina, bauxite, sugar, bananas.
Imports Fuels, machinery, transportation equipment, electrical equipment, food.

LAND
Description Caribbean island.
Area 4,244 mi² (10,991 km²).
Highest point Blue Mountain Pk., 7,402 ft (2,256 m).
Lowest point Sea level.

PEOPLE. Most Jamaicans are of African or Afro-European descent, and the majority are Christian. English is the official language, but many Jamaicans also speak a local dialect of English. Population is concentrated on the coastal plains, where the main commercial crops are also grown.

ECONOMY AND THE LAND. Agriculture is the traditional mainstay, and more than a third of the population is engaged in farming. Sugarcane and bananas are principal crops. Mining is also important, and Jamaica is a leading producer of bauxite. The tropical climate, tempered by ocean breezes, makes the island a popular tourist destination. A mountainous inland region is surrounded by coastal plains and beaches.

HISTORY AND POLITICS. Christopher Columbus claimed the island for Spain in 1494. As the enslaved native population died out, blacks were brought from Africa to work plantations. Britain invaded and gained control of Jamaica in the seventeenth century, and for a time the island was one of the most important sugar and slave centers of the New World. In 1838 the British abolished slavery, the plantation economy broke down, and most slaves became independent farmers. Local political control began in the 1930s, and the nation became fully independent in 1962. Since independence the nation has faced unemployment, inflation, and poverty, with periodic social unrest. Jamaica maintains a foreign policy of nonalignment. ■

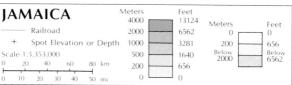

JAMAICA

	Meters	Feet		Meters	Feet
— Railroad	4000	13124		0	0
+ Spot Elevation or Depth	2000	6562		200	656
Scale 1:3,353,000	1000	3281		Below 2000	Below 6562
	500	1640			
	200	656			
	0	0			

Jamaica Map Index

	Lat.	Long.		Lat.	Long.
Alligator Pond	17°52′N	77°34′W	May Pen	17°58′N	77°14′W
Blue Mountain			Montego Bay	18°28′N	77°55′W
Peak	18°03′N	76°35′W	Morant Bay	17°53′N	76°25′W
Blue Mountains	18°06′N	76°40′W	*Morant Point*	17°55′N	76°10′W
Christiana	18°10′N	77°29′W	Ocho Rios	18°25′N	77°07′W
Cockpit Country	18°18′N	77°43′W	Port Antonio	18°11′N	76°28′W
Denham, Mount	18°13′N	77°32′W	*Portland Bight*	17°53′N	77°08′W
Falmouth	18°30′N	77°39′W	*Portland Point*	17°42′N	77°11′W
Frankfield	18°09′N	77°22′W	Port Maria	18°22′N	76°54′W
Kingston	18°00′N	76°48′W	Port Morant	17°54′N	76°19′W
Little London	18°15′N	78°13′W	Saint Ann's Bay	18°26′N	77°08′W
Manchioneal	18°02′N	76°17′W	Savanna-la-Mar	18°13′N	78°08′W
Mandeville	18°02′N	77°30′W	Spanish Town	17°59′N	76°57′W

Jamaica's tourist industry has led to coastal development, such as the hotel complex in Ocho Rios seen here through surrounding vegetation.

JAPAN

OFFICIAL NAME Japan

PEOPLE
Population 120,200,000.
Density 824/mi² (318/km²).
Urban 76%.
Capital Tokyo, Honshu I., 8,351,893.
Ethnic groups Japanese.
Languages Japanese.
Religions Shinto and Buddhist 84%, others 16%.
Life expectancy 79 female, 75 male.
Literacy 99%.

POLITICS
Government Constitutional monarchy.
Parties Clean Government, Communist, Liberal
 Democratic, Socialist.
Suffrage Universal, over 20.
Memberships OECD, UN.
Subdivisions 47 prefectures.

ECONOMY
GNP $1,060,000,000,000.
Per capita $8,947.
Monetary unit Yen.

Trade partners U.S., southeastern Asian countries,
 Western European countries, Saudi Arabia.
Exports Machinery, motor vehicles, textiles,
 manufactured goods.
Imports Petroleum, raw materials, food, machinery.

LAND
Description Eastern Asian islands.
Area 145,834 mi² (377,708 km²).
Highest point Mt. Fuji, Honshu I., 12,388 ft (3,776 m).
Lowest point Hachiro-gata reclamation area, Honshu
 I., 13 ft (4 m) below sea level.

PEOPLE. The Japanese constitute Japan's major ethnic group; minority enclaves include Koreans and Chinese. Shintoism and Buddhism are the principal religions, and most Japanese observe both. Almost all the population lives on the coastal plains. Japan's culture blends East and West, with karate, tea ceremonies, and kimonos balanced by baseball, fast food, and business suits. Although its arts have been greatly influ-

Kyoto, a cultural and religious center of Japan, is the site of temples, shrines, and museums. The Golden Pavilion of the Kinkaku-Ji Temple, shown here, was built in the late 1300s, then rebuilt in the 1950s.

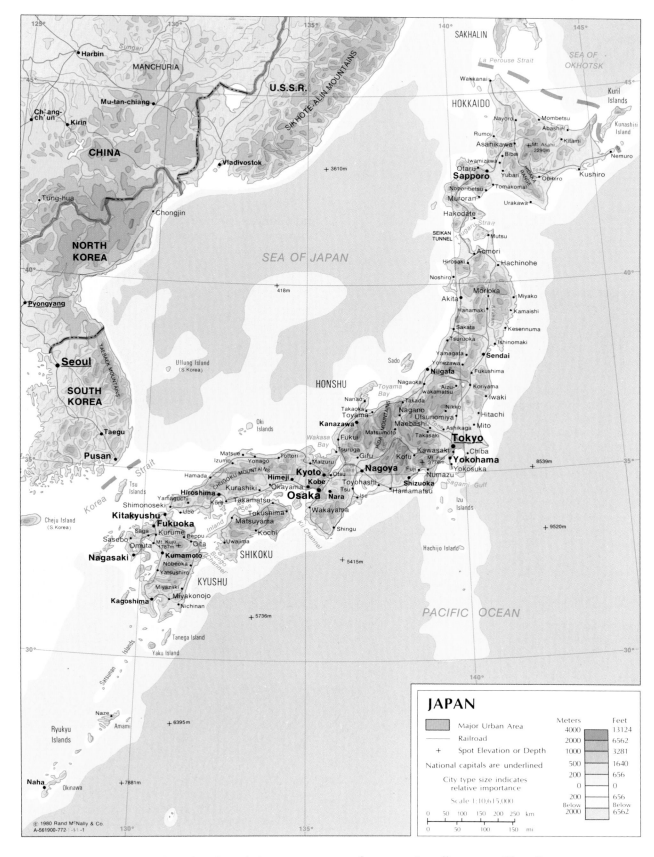

Japan is an international leader in business, industry, and technology. The industrial complex shown here is being built on land reclaimed from the sea at Mizushima, near Kurashiki.

enced by China, Japan has developed distinctive music, literature, and painting.

ECONOMY AND THE LAND. One of the world's leading industrial powers, Japan is remarkable for its economic growth rate since World War II, considering it has few natural resources. It has also become famous for its innovative technology and continues to be a major user of robots in industry. Manufacturing is the basis of the economy, and Japan is a leading shipbuilder and produces machinery, cars, and electronic equipment. Its chemical and iron and steel industries are extremely profitable. Agriculture's part in the economy is small, since little of the rugged island terrain is arable. Fishing still plays a significant role in Japan's economy, though exports in this area have not been as high in recent years. Overseas trade has expanded rapidly since the 1960s, as Japan requires raw materials for its many industries. Trade barriers and the competitiveness of Japanese products overseas have led to trade deficits among Western nations. Japan's mountainous terrain includes both active and dormant volcanoes; earth-

quakes occasionally occur. The climate ranges from subtropical to temperate.

HISTORY AND POLITICS. Legend states that Japan's first emperor was descended from the sun goddess and came to power around 600 B.C. The arrival of Buddhism, Confucianism, and new technologies from China in the fifth and sixth centuries A.D. revolutionized society. Feuding nobles controlled Japan between 1192 and 1867 and ruled as shoguns, or generals, in the name of the emperor. The warrior class, or samurai, developed early in this period. The arrival of Europeans in the sixteenth century caused fear of an invasion among the shoguns, and in the 1630s they dissolved all foreign contacts. Japan's isolation lasted until 1853, when Commodore Matthew Perry of the United States opened the nation to the West with a show of force. The subsequent Meiji Restoration modernized Japan by adopting Western technologies and legal systems and by stressing industrialization and education. Japan embarked on military expansion in the late nineteenth century, annexing Korea in 1910 and adding to its holdings after participat-

ing in World War I as a British ally. It occupied Manchuria in 1931 and invaded China in 1937. As part of the Axis powers in World War II, Japan attacked United States military bases in Pearl Harbor, Hawaii, in 1941. After the United States dropped atomic bombs on Hiroshima and Nagasaki in 1945, Japan surrendered. Allied forces occupied the nation until 1947. At that time the Japanese approved a constitution that shifted political power from the emperor to the people and that abolished the military. To uphold its own security, Japan maintains several branches of a self-defense force. Since the war, Japan has been ruled by conservative governments that seek close relations with the West. ∎

JORDAN

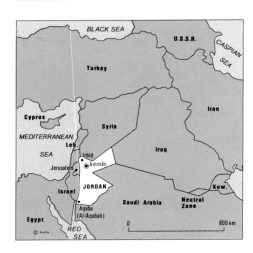

OFFICIAL NAME Hashemite
Kingdom of Jordan

PEOPLE
Population 2,475,000.
Density 70/mi² (27/km²).
Urban 60%.
Capital Ammān, 648,587.
Ethnic groups Arab 98%, Circassian 1%, Armenian
1%.
Languages Arabic, English.
Religions Sunni Muslim 92%, Christian 8%.
Life expectancy 64 female, 60 male.
Literacy 70%.

POLITICS
Government Constitutional monarchy.
Parties None (illegal).
Suffrage Universal, over 20.
Memberships AL, UN.
Subdivisions 5 governorates.

ECONOMY
GNP $4,900,000,000.
Per capita $1,875.
Monetary unit Dinar.
Trade partners Saudi Arabia, U.S., West Germany,
Japan, Iraq, Italy.
Exports Phosphates, fruits, vegetables.
Imports Machinery, transportation equipment,
petroleum, food.

LAND
Description Southwestern Asia.
Area 35,135 mi² (91,000 km²).
Highest point Mt. Ramm, 5,755 ft (1,754 m).
Lowest point Dead Sea, 1,312 ft (400 m) below sea
level.
The above information excludes the West Bank.

PEOPLE. Most Jordanians are Arabs, but there
are Circassian, Armenian, and Kurdish minori-
ties, as well as a small nomadic population, the
Bedouins, in desert areas. A large number of
Jordanians are Palestinian refugees displaced by
Arab-Israeli wars, and these refugees have been

granted citizenship by the Jordanian government.
Many Palestinians also live on the West Bank, a
disputed area that was first part of the Palestine
mandate, then occupied by Jordan from 1948 to
1967, when Israel gained control of the region.

ECONOMY AND THE LAND. A nation with few
natural resources, limited rainfall, and little arable land, Jordan has suffered further economic
damage from an influx of refugees and the
chronic political instability of the Middle East. In
a 1967 war, Jordan lost about half of its farmland
when Israel took the economically active West
Bank, a region that had been under Jordanian
control since 1948. Although cities, desert, and
unproductive land covers more than 80 percent
of Jordan, agriculture remains the most important economic activity and employer. The major
crops are vegetables, fruits, olives, and wheat,
but the nation is not self-sufficient and must rely
on imports to feed its people. Many subsistence
farmers raise goats and sheep. Jordan's main natural resource is phosphate, and the country has
deposits of potash and shale oil as well. Phosphate mining, petroleum refining, cement production, and light industry provide some
income, and tourism has helped to boost a weak
economy that relies heavily on aid and investment from the United States and Arab nations.
The southern section of the Jordan River, which
forms the border between Jordan and the Israeli-
occupied West Bank, runs into the Dead Sea,
and Jordan's terrain is marked by deserts, mountains, and rolling plains. Most of the country has
a Mediterranean climate with hot, dry summers
and cool, wet winters. In the hilly regions, however, both summer and winter temperatures are
lower.

HISTORY AND POLITICS. Jordan is the site of
one of the world's oldest settlements, Jericho,
which dates back to about 8000 B.C., and the
biblical lands of Edom, Moab, Ammon, and Ba-
shan were found here as well. The area's history
includes rule by the Hebrews, Assyrians, Egyptians, Persians, Greeks, and Romans, and around
A.D. 636 Arab Muslims conquered the region.
Rule by the Ottoman Turks began in the sixteenth century, and in World War I Arab armies
helped the British defeat Turkey. At the end of
the war present-day Israel and Jordan became
the British mandate of Palestine, which in 1922
was divided into the mandates of Transjordan,
lying east of the Jordan River, and Palestine,
lying to the west. Transjordan gained full independence in 1946. In 1948 Israel was created
from the Palestine mandate, and Arab-Israeli
fighting ensued. After capturing the West Bank,
Transjordan was renamed Jordan in 1949. During
the Arab-Israeli Six-Day War in 1967, this region
and the Jordanian section of Jerusalem fell to
Israel. As a result of these conflicts, Jordan's
Palestinian-refugee population grew, and a 1970

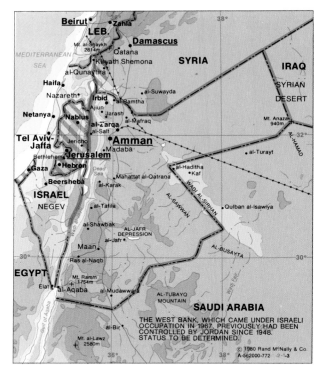

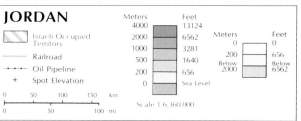

JORDAN

	Meters	Feet
Israeli Occupied Territory	4000	13124
	2000	6562
Railroad	1000	3281
Oil Pipeline	500	1640
Spot Elevation	200	656
	0	Sea Level

Meters	Feet
0	0
200	656
Below 2000	Below 6562

Scale 1:6,360,000

Jordan Map Index

	Lat.	Long.		Lat.	Long.
al-Aqaba	29°31'N	35°00'E	Jayb, Wadi al-	31°04'N	35°07'E
al-Jafr			Jordan	31°46'N	35°33'E
Depression	30°17'N	36°20'E	Maan	30°20'N	36°30'E
al-Zarqa	32°05'N	36°06'E	Madaba	31°43'N	35°48'E
Amman	31°57'N	35°56'E	Ramm, Mount	29°35'N	35°24'E
Aqaba, Gulf of	29°00'N	34°40'E	Ras al-Naqb	30°00'N	35°29'E
Dead Sea	31°30'N	35°30'E	Sawwan, al-	30°45'N	37°15'E
Irbid	32°33'N	35°51'E	Syrian Desert	32°00'N	40°00'E

civil war pitted the government against Palestinian guerrillas, who, like Jordan, desired control of
the West Bank. The guerrillas were expelled following the war, but subsequent Arab-Israeli hostilities led to Jordan's recognition of the Palestine
Liberation Organization and support for the creation of an independent Palestinian state that
would include the West Bank, where controversial Israeli settlements have now been established. However, this stance was again reversed
in favor of an agreement that would unify both
banks of the Jordan River. Jordan is a constitutional monarchy headed by a king. Political parties have been banned since 1957. ■

Jordan has little in the way of
natural resources, but phosphate
mining, depicted here, takes advantage of Jordan's chief mineral
resource, providing jobs and
income. Oil, which was discovered in 1982 at Azraq, and potash, found in the Dead Sea,
offer potential for expanded resource exploitation.

KAMPUCHEA

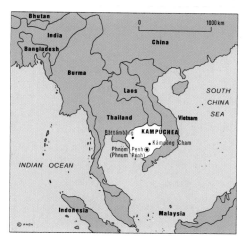

OFFICIAL NAME Democratic
Kampuchea

PEOPLE
Population 6,180,000.
Density 88/mi² (34/km²).
Urban 15%.
Capital Phnom Penh, 400,000.
Ethnic groups Khmer 90%, Chinese 5%.
Languages Khmer.
Religions Theravada Buddhist 95%.
Life expectancy 31 female, 29 male.
Literacy 48%.

POLITICS
Government Socialist republic.
Parties People's Revolutionary, United Front for
National Construction and Defense.
Suffrage Universal, over 18.
Memberships UN.
Subdivisions 20 provinces.

ECONOMY
Monetary unit Riel.
Trade partners Vietnam, U.S.S.R.
Exports Natural rubber.
Imports Food, machinery, petroleum.

LAND
Description Southeastern Asia.
Area 69,898 mi² (181,035 km²).
Highest point Mt. Aoral, 5,948 ft (1,813 m).
Lowest point Sea level.

PEOPLE. The Khmer, one of the oldest peoples
in Southeast Asia, constitute the major ethnic
group in Kampuchea, formerly known as Cambodia. The population has declined significantly
since the mid-1970s due to war, famine, human
rights abuses, and emigration. Because of an
urban-evacuation campaign initiated by the
Khmer Rouge, Kampuchea's previous regime,
most Kampucheans live in rural areas, working
as farmers or laborers. Although the new government does not encourage religious activity, it
was often punished by death during the Khmer
Rouge era, and the practice of Buddhism, the
main religion, is on the rise.

ECONOMY AND THE LAND. Kampuchea's flat
central region and wet climate make it well suited for rice production. Along with rubber, rice
was the mainstay of the economy before the seventies, but the Vietnam and civil wars all but
destroyed agriculture. This sector of the economy
has begun to recover recently. A shortage of
skilled labor, combined with the effects of war,
have held back industry. The terrain is marked
by the central plain, forests, and mountains in
the south, west, and along the Thai border. The
climate is tropical, and there is high rainfall and
humidity.

HISTORY AND POLITICS. Kampuchea traces its
roots to the Hindu kingdoms of Funan and
Chenla, which reigned in the early centuries A.D.
The Angkor Empire dominated until the fifteenth
century, incorporating much of present-day
Laos, Thailand, and Vietnam and constructing

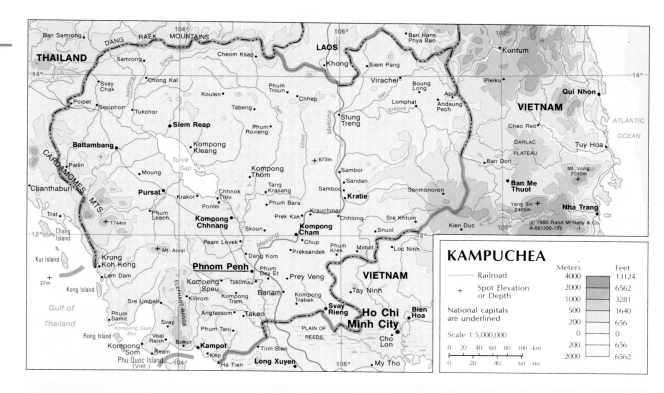

Kampuchea Map Index

	Lat.	Long.		Lat.	Long.		Lat.	Long.		Lat.	Long.
Banam	11°19'N	105°18'E	Kompong Cham	12°00'N	105°27'E	Kong Island	11°20'N	103°00'E	Sen	12°32'N	104°28'E
Battambang	13°06'N	103°12'E	Kompong			Kratie	12°29'N	106°01'E	Siem Reap	13°22'N	103°51'E
Cardamomes			Chhnang	12°15'N	104°40'E	Krung Koh Kong	11°37'N	102°59'E	Sreng	13°21'N	103°27'E
Mountains	12°00'N	103°15'E	Kompong Kleang	13°06'N	104°08'E	*Mekong*	10°55'N	105°12'E	Srepok	13°33'N	106°16'E
Chinit	12°55'N	105°35'E	Kompong Som	10°38'N	103°30'E	Phnom Penh	11°33'N	104°55'E	Stung Treng	13°31'N	105°58'E
Dangraek			Kompong Som			Prey Veng	11°29'N	105°19'E	Svay Rieng	11°05'N	105°48'E
Mountains	14°25'N	103°30'E	*Bay*	10°50'N	103°32'E	Pursat	12°32'N	103°55'E	Takeo	10°59'N	104°47'E
Elephant Range	11°00'N	104°05'E	Kompong Speu	11°27'N	104°32'E	*Pursat*	12°41'N	104°09'E	*Tonle Sap*	13°00'N	104°00'E
Kampot	10°37'N	104°11'E	Kompong Thom	12°42'N	104°54'E	*San*	13°32'N	105°58'E	Virachei	13°59'N	106°49'E

War has taken its toll on Kampuchea, but many colonial structures remain standing, a legacy of French rule.

the stone temples of Angkor Wat, considered one
of Southeast Asia's greatest architectural achievements. By 1431 the Siamese had overrun the
region, and subsequent years saw the rise of the
Siamese, Vietnamese, and Lao. By the mid-1700s
Cambodia's boundaries approximated those of
today, and during the 1800s, as French control in
Indochina expanded, the area became a French
protectorate. Cambodia gained independence in
1953 under King Sihanouk, who, after changing
his title to "prince," became prime minister in
1955 and head of state in 1960. In 1970, after
Sihanouk was ousted, Lon Nol was installed as
prime minister, and the monarchy of Cambodia
changed to the Khmer Republic. During this time
the Vietnam War spilled over the Khmer Republic's borders as United States forces made bomb-

ing raids against what they claimed were North
Vietnamese bases. Resulting anti-American sentiment gave rise to discontent with Lon Nol's pro–
United States regime. The Khmer Communists,
or Khmer Rouge, seized power in 1975 and, led
by Pol Pot, exiled most Kampucheans to the
countryside. An estimated one million died
under the Khmer Rouge, many executed because
they were educated or had links to the former
government. Vietnamese troops supported by
some Kampuchean Communists invaded Kampuchea in late 1978, and by early 1979 they had
overthrown the Khmer Rouge and established
the Democratic Kampuchea. Several insurgent
groups, including the Khmer Rouge, have continued guerrilla warfare against the Vietnamese-
installed government. ■

KENYA

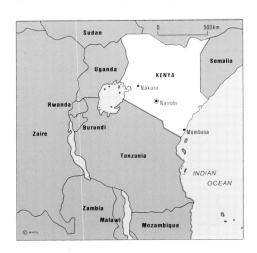

OFFICIAL NAME Republic of
Kenya

PEOPLE
Population 18,970,000.
Density 84/mi² (33/km²).
Urban 13%.
Capital Nairobi, 827,775.
Ethnic groups Kikuyu 21%, Luhya 14%, Luo 13%,
Kalenjin 11%, Kamba 11%, Kisii 6%, Meru 5%.
Languages English, Swahili, indigenous.
Religions Protestant 38%, Catholic 28%, indigenous
26%, Muslim 6%.
Life expectancy 58 female, 54 male.
Literacy 47%.

POLITICS
Government Republic.
Parties Africa National Union.
Suffrage Universal, over 21.
Memberships CW, OAU, UN.
Subdivisions 7 provinces, 1 capital district.

ECONOMY
GDP $6,300,000,000.
Per capita $316.
Monetary unit Shilling.
Trade partners Western European countries, Japan,
Iran, U.S.
Exports Petroleum products, coffee, tea, livestock
products.
Imports Petroleum, machinery, motor vehicles, iron
and steel.

LAND
Description Eastern Africa.
Area 224,961 mi² (582,646 km²).
Highest point Mt. Kenya (Kirinyaga), 17,058 ft (5,199 m)
Lowest point Sea level.

PEOPLE. Nearly all Kenyans are black Africans
belonging to one of more than forty different
groups, each with its own language and culture.
Some groups are nomadic, like the Masai. Arab
and European minorities—found mostly along
the coast—reflect Kenya's history of foreign rule.
Most Kenyans live in the southwestern highlands, raising crops or livestock. Over half of the
citizens practice a form of Christianity, while the
rest pursue indigenous beliefs or Islam. Swahili,
a blend of Bantu and Arabic, is the official language; it serves as a communication link among
Kenya's many ethnic groups. English is also spoken. The national slogan of *harambee,* or "pull
together," illustrates the need for cooperation
among Kenya's diverse groups, and the government promotes national unity. Rapid population
growth has led to unemployment and, combined
with the nation's limited arable land and suscep-
tibility to drought, has affected food supplies and
imports.

ECONOMY AND THE LAND. Scenic terrain,
tropical beaches, and abundant wildlife have
given Kenya a thriving tourist industry, and land
has been set aside for national parks and game
preserves. Agriculture is the primary activity,
even though the northern three-fifths of the

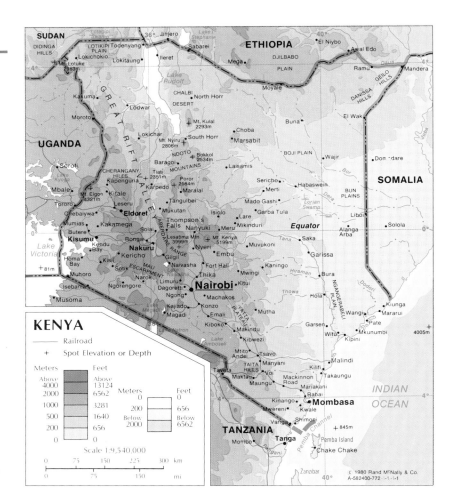

KENYA
— Railroad
+ Spot Elevation or Depth

Scale 1:9,540,000

c 1980 Rand McNally & Co.
A-582400-772 -1-1-1

country is semidesert. The most productive soils
are found in the southwestern highlands, and
coffee is the main export crop. Much of the land
is also used for raising livestock, another leading
economic contributor. Oil from other nations is
refined in Kenya, and food processing and cement production are also significant activities.
Kenya's climate varies from arid in the north to
temperate in the highlands and tropical along the
coast.

HISTORY AND POLITICS.   Remains of early hu-
mans dating back more than two million years
have been found in Kenya. Settlers from other
parts of Africa arrived about 1000 B.C. A thousand years later Arab traders reached the coast;
they controlled the area by the eighth century
A.D. The Portuguese ruled the coast between
1498 and the late 1600s. Kenya came under British control in 1895 and was known as the East
African Protectorate. Opposition to British rule
began to mount in the 1940s as Kenyans demanded a voice in government. The Mau Mau
rebellion of the fifties, an armed revolt, was an
outgrowth of this discontent. Kenya gained independence from Britain in 1963 and became a republic in 1964. Its first president was Jomo Ken-
yatta, a Kikuyu who had been an active leader in
the previous revolt. Recent administrations have
pursued a policy of Africanization, under which
land and other holdings have been transferred
from European to African hands. ■

*Tourism is a mainstay of the Kenyan economy, with people drawn from all over the world to
view the wildlife preserved in game reserves and national parks. Many of these protected
areas were established in the 1900s to protect dying species from hunters and poachers, and in
1977 hunting was made illegal. In this picture, Kilimanjaro in neighboring Tanzania soars above
giraffes in Amboseli National Park.*

KIRIBATI

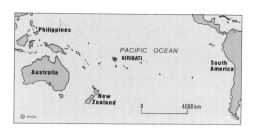

OFFICIAL NAME Republic of
Kiribati

PEOPLE
Population 62,000.
Density 225/mi² (87/km²).
Urban 32%.
Capital Bairiki, Tarawa I., 1,800.
Ethnic groups Micronesian.
Languages English, Gilbertese.
Religions Roman Catholic, Protestant.
Life expectancy 54 female, 50 male.
Literacy 90%.

POLITICS
Government Republic.
Parties Christian Democratic, Gilbertese National. .
Memberships CW.

ECONOMY
GDP $36,000,000.
Per capita $630.
Monetary unit Australian dollar.
Trade partners Australia, New Zealand.
Exports Copra, fish.
Imports Food, fuels, transportation equipment.

LAND
Description Central Pacific islands.

Area 275 mi² (712 km²).
Highest point 265 ft (81 m).
Lowest point Sea level.

PEOPLE. The people of Kiribati, a nation of thirty-three islands in the central Pacific, are mostly Micronesian. Almost all the population lives on the Gilbert Islands in small villages and practices Roman Catholicism or Protestantism. English, the official language, and Gilbertese are spoken.

ECONOMY AND THE LAND. A small, unskilled work force combined with small land area and few natural resources have given Kiribati a subsistence economy. Phosphate deposits have been depleted, and copra is now the main export. Kiribati depends on economic aid from Australia, New Zealand, and Great Britain. One island and three island groups make up Kiribati: Banaba Island, the Kiribati islands, the Phoenix Islands, and part of the Line Islands. Nearly all are coral reefs, composed of hard sand and little soil; many surround a lagoon. The climate is tropical.

HISTORY AND POLITICS. Fijians and Tongans conquered the inhabitants of the islands in the 1300s, and they were followed by invading Samoans in the 1400s. The first European settler arrived in 1837, and in 1892 a British sea captain declared the islands a protectorate. The Gilbert and Ellice islands officially became a British colony in 1916, and soon other islands were merged with the colony. During World War II, Tarawa Island was the scene of battles between United States and Japanese forces. The Ellice Islands became independent in 1978 as the nation of Tuvalu, and the Republic of Kiribati came into existence a year later. ∎

Maps show major islands only.

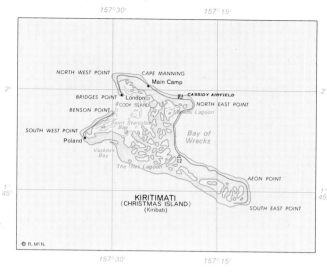

Kiribati Map Index

	Lat.	Long.		Lat.	Long.
Bairiki	1°20'N	173°01'E	Kiritimati	1°52'N	157°20'W
Bonriki	1°23'N	173°09'E	Tarawa	1°25'N	173°00'E
Christmas Island → Kiritimati	1°52'N	157°20'W			

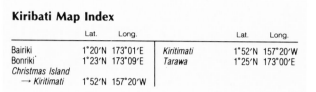

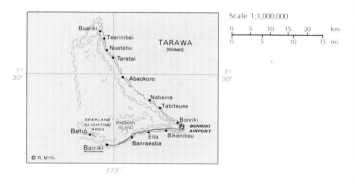

KOREA, NORTH

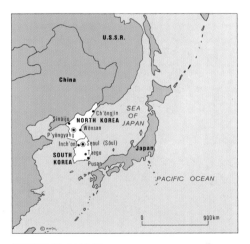

OFFICIAL NAME
Democractic People's
Republic of Korea

PEOPLE
Population 19,855,000.
Density 427/mi² (165/km²).
Urban 33%.
Capital P'yŏngyang, 1,700,000.
Ethnic groups Korean.
Languages Korean.
Religions Buddhist, Confucian.
Life expectancy 65 female, 61 male.
Literacy 95%.

POLITICS
Government Socialist republic.
Parties Workers'.
Suffrage Universal, over 17.
Memberships None.
Subdivisions 9 provinces, 4 special cities.

ECONOMY
GNP $16,200,000,000.
Per capita $786.
Monetary unit Won.
Trade partners U.S.S.R., Japan, West Germany.
Exports Minerals, machinery, textile fibers.
Imports Petroleum, machinery, food, coal.

LAND
Description Eastern Asia.
Area 46,540 mi² (120,538 km²).
Highest point Mt. Paektu, 9,003 ft (2,744 m).
Lowest point Sea level.

PEOPLE. Despite a history of invasions, North Korea has a homogeneous population with virtually no minorities. Korean, the nation's language, is a Uralic tongue; that is, it is related to Japanese, Mongolian, Hungarian, and Finnish. Several dialects are spoken, and unlike South Koreans, North Koreans use the Hankul, or Korean, alphabet exclusively. Prior to the development of the Hankul alphabet in the fifteenth century, Chinese characters were used for writing. Traditionally, Korean religions included Buddhism, Confucianism, and Shamanism. Nineteenth-century missionaries introduced Christianity to Korea, but today Buddhism and Confucianism remain the major faiths, although religious activity has been discouraged by the government. Urban population has grown rapidly since 1953 as the result of an emphasis on manufacturing, but the nation remains more sparsely populated than South Korea because of mass emigration to the south following World War II. In addition, population distribution is uneven, with more people living on the fertile plains near the coast than in the mountainous interior. Educational systems here as in the south have improved since the 1940s. The government pays for all education, and the literacy rate in North Korea is slightly higher than that in South Korea.

ECONOMY AND THE LAND. The division of the Korean peninsula after World War II left North Korea with most of the industry and natural resources but little agricultural land and few skilled workers. The country has succeeded in becoming one of the most industrialized nations in Asia and has overcome its agricultural problems as well. Most industry is government owned, and North Koreans have focused on the development of heavy industry, although light manufacturing has been improving with the aid of automation. Mines produce a variety of minerals and metals, including tungsten, coal, gold, iron ore, and zinc. Farming is collectivized, and output has been aided by irrigation and other modern practices. An economic policy introduced in 1982 aims at increasing farm output through land reclamation, infrastructure development, and other measures. The Soviet Union and China have aided North Korea's development, but the theory of self-reliance is the government's guiding principle. The Korean peninsula juts southward from the land of northwest China. Hills and mountain ranges cover much of North Korea, and about three-fourths of the area is covered with forest, scrub, and brush. Between the ranges lie deep, narrow valleys, oftentimes marked by small cultivated plains. Less than 20 percent of the nation is arable, however. The climate is continental; winters are cold and dry, and summers are hot and humid.

HISTORY AND POLITICS. See KOREA, SOUTH.

KOREA, SOUTH

OFFICIAL NAME Republic of
Korea

PEOPLE
Population 42,315,000.
Density 1,113/mi² (430/km²).
Urban 57%.
Capital Seoul, 8,366,756.
Ethnic groups Korean.
Languages Korean.
Religions Buddhist, Christian, Shamanic, Confucian.
Life expectancy 69 female, 64 male.
Literacy 90%.

POLITICS
Government Republic.
Parties Democratic, Democratic Justice, National.
Suffrage Universal, over 20.
Memberships None.
Subdivisions 9 provinces, 4 independent cities.

ECONOMY
GNP $70,800,000,000.
Per capita $1,800.
Monetary unit Won.
Trade partners U.S., Japan, Middle Eastern countries,
West Germany.
Exports Textiles, transportation equipment,
footwear, electrical machinery.
Imports Petroleum, machinery, transportation
equipment, chemicals.

LAND
Description Eastern Asia.
Area 38,025 mi² (98,484 km²).
Highest point Mt. Halla, 6,398 ft (1,950 m).
Lowest point Sea level.

PEOPLE. The homogeneous quality of South Korea's population is similar to that of North Korea. Population density, however, is much greater in South Korea: about two million Koreans migrated to the south following World War II. The major language, Korean, is written predominantly in the Hankul, or Korean, alphabet, with some Chinese characters. Buddhism is practiced by most South Koreans, although Confucianism has influenced much of life.

ECONOMY AND THE LAND. South Korea was traditionally the peninsula's agricultural zone, and following the 1945 partition of the country, the south was left with little industry and few resources but abundant manpower. The economy has advanced rapidly since 1953, and today agriculture and industry are of almost equal importance. Rice, barley, and beans are principal crops; machinery and textiles are significant manufactured products. Central mountains give way to plains in the south and west, and the climate is temperate.

HISTORY AND POLITICS. Korea's strategic location between the Soviet Union, China, and Japan has made it prey to foreign powers. China conquered the northern part of the peninsula in 108 B.C., influencing culture, religion, and government, and Mongols controlled Korea for most of the thirteenth and fourteenth centuries. The rule of the Yi dynasty began in 1392 and endured until 1910, when Japan annexed Korea. In 1945, following Japan's defeat in World War II, Soviet troops occupied northern Korea while the United States military occupied the south. The Soviet Union, the United States, and Great Britain tried to aid unification of the country but failed, and a subsequent plan for United Nations–supervised elections was opposed by the Soviets. In 1948 two separate governments were formed: the northern Democratic People's Republic of Korea and the southern Republic of Korea. Both governments claimed the peninsula, and relations became strained. After several border clashes, North Korea invaded South Korea in 1950. Chinese Communists fought on the side of North Korea, and United States forces aided the south.

Korea Map Index

	Lat.	Long.		Lat.	Long.
Aoji	42°31'N	130°23'E	Masan	35°11'N	128°32'E
Chechon	37°08'N	128°12'E	Mokpo	34°48'N	126°22'E
Cheju Island	33°20'N	126°30'E	Naktong	35°07'N	128°57'E
Chinju	35°11'N	128°05'E	Namhan	37°31'N	127°18'E
Chongjin	41°47'N	129°50'E	Nampo	38°45'N	125°23'E
Chongju	36°39'N	127°31'E	Paektu, Mount	42°00'N	128°03'E
Chonju	35°49'N	127°08'E	Panmunjom	37°57'N	126°40'E
Chunchon	37°52'N	127°43'E	Pukchong	40°15'N	128°20'E
Chungju	36°58'N	127°58'E	Pukhan	37°31'N	127°18'E
Haeju	38°02'N	125°42'E	Pusan	35°06'N	129°03'E
Halla, Mount	33°22'N	126°32'E	Pyongyang	39°01'N	125°45'E
Hamgyong			Samchok	37°27'N	129°10'E
Mountains	41°50'N	128°30'E	Sariwon	38°31'N	125°44'E
Hamhung	39°54'N	127°32'E	Seoul	37°33'N	126°58'E
Han	37°45'N	126°11'E	Sinuiju	40°05'N	124°24'E
Hungnam	39°50'N	127°38'E	Sobaek		
Hyesan	41°23'N	128°12'E	Mountains	36°00'N	128°00'E
Imjim	37°47'N	126°40'E	Sunchon	34°57'N	127°28'E
Inchon	37°28'N	126°38'E	Suwon	37°17'N	127°01'E
Japan, Sea of	39°00'N	125°00'E	Taebaek		
Kaesong	37°59'N	126°33'E	Mountains	37°40'N	128°50'E
Kanggye	40°58'N	126°34'E	Taedong	38°42'N	125°15'E
Kanghwa Bay	37°20'N	126°35'E	Taegu	35°52'N	128°35'E
Kanghwa Island	37°40'N	126°27'E	Taejon	36°20'N	127°26'E
Kimchaek	40°41'N	129°12'E	Tanchon	40°27'N	128°54'E
Kimchon	36°07'N	128°05'E	Tongjoson Bay	39°30'N	128°00'E
Korea Bay	39°00'N	125°00'E	Tuman	42°18'N	130°41'E
Korea Strait	34°00'N	129°00'E	Uiju	40°12'N	124°32'E
Kum	36°00'N	126°40'E	Unggi	42°20'N	130°24'E
Kunsan	35°58'N	126°41'E	Wonju	37°22'N	127°58'E
Kwangju	35°09'N	126°54'E	Wonsan	39°09'N	127°25'E
Kwanmo, Mount	41°42'N	129°13'E	Yalu	39°55'N	124°22'E
Kyonggi Bay	37°25'N	126°00'E	Yellow Sea	36°00'N	125°00'E

The war ended in 1953 with an armistice, but a permanent peace treaty has never been signed. Both countries continue to claim the entire peninsula. Sporadic fighting has broken out between the north and south in recent years, and tense relations have stalled steps toward reunification.

North Korea. The Democratic People's Republic of Korea was established in 1948, several months after the formation of South Korea. The country incurred about 2.5 million casualties during the war with South Korea. Following the war, the government moved quickly to modernize industry and the military; North Korea maintains one of the world's largest armies. Despite its ties to the Soviet Union and China, North Korea strives for an independent foreign policy based on the country's emphasis on self-reliance.

South Korea. The Republic of Korea came into being on August 15, 1948. Since the war, the country has experienced a presidential overthrow, military rule, and a presidential assassination. Continued claims by students and others of government civil rights abuses erupted in violence in 1979, when civilians and military personnel clashed. The fifth constitution since 1948, initiating the Fifth Republic, was adopted in 1980. ∎

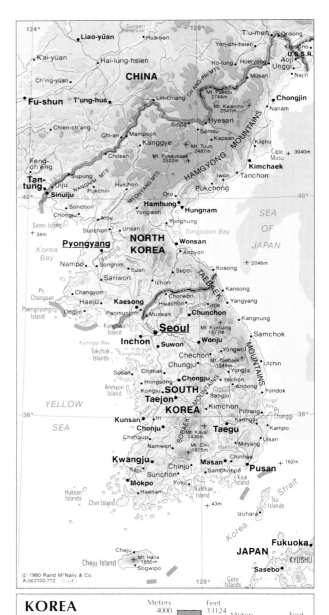

KOREA

— Railroad
+ Spot Elevation or Depth

Meters	Feet
4000	13124
2000	6562
1000	3281
500	1640
200	656

Meters	Feet
0	0
200	656
Below 2000	Below 6562

Scale 1:7,500,000

0 50 100 150 km
0 50 100 mi

Modern Korean artists have much in common with Western artists, and twentieth-century themes are found in most of the country's current artwork. However, the early influences of Chinese art, Buddhism, and Confucianism are still felt and highly respected, and Koreans continue to view ornamental work, such as wall painting, as an art. As shown here, many of the traditional art forms continue to thrive, and South Korean artists working on architectural decorations weave traditional themes and symbols into their work.

KUWAIT

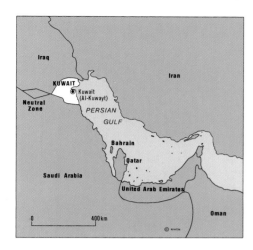

OFFICIAL NAME State of
Kuwait

PEOPLE
Population 1,815,000.
Density 264/mi² (102/km²).
Urban 90%.
Capital Kuwait, 60,365.
Ethnic groups Kuwaiti 39%, other Arab 39%,
Southern Asian 9%, Iranian 4%.
Languages Arabic, English.
Religions Muslim 95%.
Life expectancy 73 female, 68 male.
Literacy 71%.

POLITICS
Government Constitutional monarchy.
Parties None (prohibited).
Suffrage Native-born and naturalized males, over 21
(20-year residency required after naturalization).
Memberships AL, OPEC, UN.
Subdivisions 4 governorates.

ECONOMY
GNP $27,600,000,000.
Per capita $25,850.
Monetary unit Dinar.
Trade partners Japan, Western European countries,
U.S.

Exports Petroleum, petroleum products.
Imports Machinery, transportation equipment,
manufactured goods, food.

LAND
Description Southwestern Asia.
Area 6,880 mi² (17,818 km²).
Highest point 951 ft (290 m).
Lowest point Sea level.

PEOPLE. Kuwait's recent prosperity has drawn
emigrants from the Persian Gulf and beyond,
giving it a diverse population; there are Palestinian, Iranian, and Pakistani minorities. The population has risen dramatically since the thirties,
when the oil industry began. Arabic is the official
language; English is also taught and widely spoken. Almost all residents of Kuwait observe
Islam, the state religion. Most belong to the
Sunni branch, but there is a sizable Shiite community.

ECONOMY AND THE LAND. The economy centers on the largely government-controlled petroleum industry. Kuwait is one of the world's largest oil producers, and its oil reserves are among
the world's most extensive. However, oil production and refining require a limited work force,
and Kuwait has recently tried to diversify to create more jobs. Commercial fishing and shrimp
exporting are gaining importance in Kuwait's
economy. Because of the desert terrain, agriculture is marginal. Kuwait's climate is subtropical.

HISTORY AND POLITICS. Arab nomads settled
Kuwait Bay around A.D. 1700. The Al Sabah dynasty has ruled the nation since the mid-1700s.
Alarmed by the designs of the Turks and Arabs,
Kuwait in 1899 signed an agreement with Britain
in which Britain guaranteed Kuwait's defense.
Drilling for oil began in 1936, and by 1945 Kuwait had become a major exporter. Independence
came in 1961. Iraq immediately made a claim to
the state but was discouraged from attacking by
the arrival of British troops. Official border agreements have never been made between Kuwait
and Iraq. Kuwait briefly cut off oil shipments to

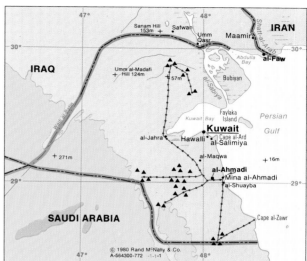

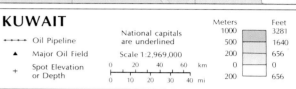

Kuwait Map Index

	Lat.	Long.		Lat.	Long.
Abdulla Bay	29°50′N	48°20′E	Faylaka Island	29°25′N	48°22′E
al-Ahmadi	29°05′N	48°04′E	Hawalli	29°19′N	48°02′E
al-Salimiya	29°18′N	48°03′E	Kuwait	29°20′N	47°59′E
Batin, Wadi al-	29°35′N	47°00′E	Mina al-Ahmadi	29°04′N	48°08′E
Bubiyan	29°47′N	48°10′E	Persian Gulf	29°30′N	48°30′E

Western nations in retaliation for their support of
Israel in the 1967 and 1973 Arab-Israeli wars.
Kuwait's remarkable oil wealth, which transformed it from a poor nation into an affluent
one, has enabled it to offer its citizens a wide
range of benefits and to aid other Arab states.
Poised at the tip of the Persian Gulf, Kuwait
must always be sensitive to the interests of its
many neighbors. The ongoing Iran-Iraq war has
presented a problem, as have tensions among
various religious and ethnic groups. Despite the
conflicts, Kuwait strives to remain neutral. ∎

**Oil has made Kuwait one of the world's richest countries, but activities such as fishing continue
to provide employment. Shown here are fishermen with their nets along Kuwait's coast.**

LAOS

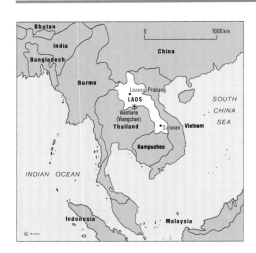

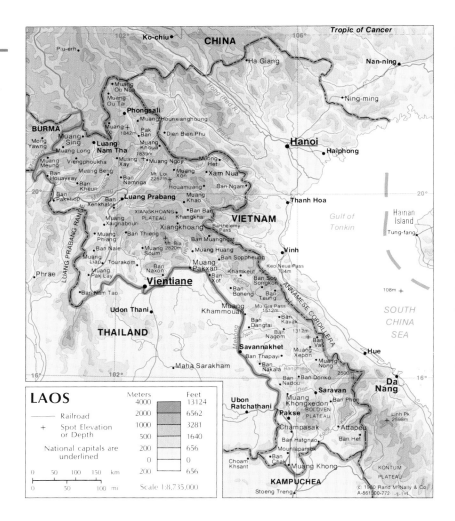

Laos Map Index

	Lat.	Long.
Annamese		
Cordillera	17°00'N	106°00'E
Attapeu	14°48'N	106°50'E
Bia, Mount	18°59'N	103°09'E
Boloven Plateau	15°20'N	106°20'E
Champasak	14°53'N	105°52'E
Chu	19°53'N	105°45'E
Kong	13°32'N	105°58'E
Lik	18°31'N	102°31'E
Luang Nam Tha	20°57'N	101°25'E
Luang Prabang	19°52'N	102°08'E
Luang Prabang		
Range	18°30'N	101°15'E
Mekong	13°55'N	105°58'E
Muang		
Khammouan	17°24'N	104°48'E
Muang Khong	14°07'N	105°51'E
Muang		
Khongxedon	15°34'N	105°49'E
Muang Pakxan	18°22'N	103°39'E
Muang Sing	21°11'N	101°09'E
Mu Gia Pass	17°40'N	105°47'E
Ou	20°04'N	102°13'E
Pakse	15°07'N	105°47'E
Phongsali	21°41'N	102°06'E
Saravan	15°43'N	106°25'E
Savannakhet	16°33'N	104°45'E
Vientiane	17°58'N	102°36'E
Xam Nua	20°25'N	104°02'E
Xiangkhoang	19°20'N	103°22'E

OFFICIAL NAME Lao People's
Democratic Republic

PEOPLE
Population 3,775,000.
Density 41/mi² (16/km²).
Urban 13%.
Capital Vientiane (Viangchan), 174,229.
Ethnic groups Lao 48%; Phoutheung 25%; Tai 14%;
Miao, Yao, and others 13%.
Languages Lao, French.
Religions Buddhist 50%, animist and others 50%.
Life expectancy 45 female, 42 male.
Literacy 28%.

POLITICS
Government Socialist republic.
Parties People's Revolutionary.
Suffrage Universal, over 18.
Memberships UN.
Subdivisions 13 provinces.

ECONOMY
GNP $320,000,000.
Per capita $90.
Monetary unit Kip.
Trade partners Thailand, U.S.S.R., Eastern European
countries, Singapore.
Exports Hydroelectric power, wood, coffee, tin.
Imports Food, petroleum, machinery, transportation
equipment.

LAND
Description Southeastern Asia, landlocked.
Area 91,429 mi² (236,800 km²).
Highest point Mt. Bia, 9,252 ft (2,820 m).
Lowest point 230 ft (70 m).

PEOPLE. Laos is peopled by many ethnic
groups, each with its own customs, religion, and
language. Its history of culturally diverse communities is mirrored in the political divisions of
recent years. The Lao are numerically and politically dominant, and Lao is the official language.
Small Vietnamese and Chinese minorities exist.
Most of Laos's residents are farmers engaged in
rice production.

ECONOMY AND THE LAND. Years of warfare, a
landlocked position, and a poor transportation
system have hindered the development of Laos's
economy. Although agriculture is the basis of the
economy, very little of the fertile land is cultivated. Substantial mineral deposits and large timber
reserves also have not been exploited to their
potential. Manufacturing is limited, partly because of an unskilled work force. Situated in a
mountainous, densely forested region, Laos has
a tropical climate and experiences seasonal monsoons.

HISTORY AND POLITICS. By A.D. 900 the fore-
runners of the Lao had arrived from southern
China. The first united Lao kingdom was founded in 1353 and included much of modern Thailand. It dissolved into three rival states by the
early 1700s, setting the stage for interference by
Burma, Vietnam, and Siam, present-day Thai-

land. In 1899 France made Laos part of French
Indochina. Laos gained some autonomy in 1949,
but this period saw the growth of Communist
and anti-Communist factions whose rivalry
would prevent any unified government until
1975. Although Geneva peace agreements declared Laos's neutrality in 1954 and 1962, the
nation became increasingly embroiled in the Vietnam War as belligerents in that conflict entered
Laos. A protracted civil war began in 1960 between the Pathet Lao, a Communist faction aided

by the North Vietnamese, and government forces
backed by the Thai and South Vietnamese. A
cease-fire was signed in 1973 and a new coalition
government was formed a year later. Following
Communist victories in Vietnam and Kampuchea, the Pathet Lao gained control in 1975
and established the Lao People's Democratic Republic. Opposed to Communist rule, many Lao
abandoned their country to seek refuge in Thailand and the United States. Laos retains close
ties with Vietnam. ∎

**The Mekong, Southeast Asia's largest river, flows through Laos, starting in the country's northern mountains.
Agricultural land on the flood plain along the river's banks is often subject to flooding.**

LEBANON

OFFICIAL NAME Republic of Lebanon

PEOPLE
Population 2,610,000.
Density 650/mi² (251/km²).
Urban 78%.
Capital Beirut, 474,870.
Ethnic groups Arab 93%, Armenian 6%.
Languages Arabic, French, English.
Religions Christian 50%, Muslim and Druze 50%.
Life expectancy 68 female, 65 male.
Literacy 75%.

POLITICS
Government Republic.
Parties Political activity organized along sectarian lines, with numerous groups.
Suffrage Females, over 21 (with elementary education); males, over 21.
Memberships AL, UN.
Subdivisions 6 provinces.

ECONOMY
GDP $4,100,000,000.
Per capita $1,316.
Monetary unit Pound.
Trade partners Middle Eastern countries, Western European countries, U.S.
Exports Fruits, vegetables, textiles.
Imports Metals, machinery, food.

LAND
Description Southwestern Asia.
Area 4,015 mi² (10,400 km²).
Highest point Mt. Sauda, 10,115 ft (3,083 m).
Lowest point Sea level.

PEOPLE. Traditionally home to many diverse groups, Lebanon has recently been shaken by the conflicting demands of its population. Almost all Lebanese are of Arab stock, and Arabic is the official language. Palestinian refugees have settled here since the creation of Israel in 1948, many of them living in refugee camps. Lebanon's religious makeup is notable for its variety, encompassing seventeen recognized sects in a country with an area smaller than that of the U.S. state of Connecticut. There has been no official census since 1932, and although those figures show almost an equal division between Islam and Christianity, recent estimates indicate that Muslims are now a majority. Among Muslims there are members of the majority Shiite, minority Sunni, and Druze sects, while most Christians are Maronites. War and unpredictable violence have created an atmosphere in which most Lebanese are concerned only with day-to-day survival.

ECONOMY AND THE LAND. Situated strategically between the West and the Middle East, Lebanon has long been a center of commerce. Its economy is fueled by the service sector, particularly banking. Prolonged fighting, beginning with the 1975 civil war, has greatly damaged all economic activity. Industry has experienced severe setbacks, and most manufacturing plants have closed or now operate at greatly reduced production rates. Once a popular tourist destination, Lebanon has lost its income from this sector as well, and in addition many Beirut hotels have been destroyed by the fighting. Much of the work force is engaged in agriculture, and a variety of crops is grown. The coastal area consists of a plain, behind which lie mountain ranges sepa-

rated by a fertile valley. The climate of Lebanon is Mediterranean.

HISTORY AND POLITICS. The Phoenicians settled parts of Lebanon about 3000 B.C. and were followed by Egyptian, Assyrian, Persian, Greek, and Roman rulers. Christianity came to the area during the Byzantine Empire, around A.D. 325, and Islam followed in the seventh century, brought by Arab Muslims. In 1516 Lebanon was incorporated into the Ottoman Empire. Between the end of World War I, when the Ottoman Empire collapsed, and 1943, when Lebanon became independent, it was a French mandate. A government in which Muslims and Christians shared power was set up after independence. Opposition to Lebanon's close ties to the West led to a 1958 insurrection, which United States marines put down at the government's request. The Palestine Liberation Organization (PLO), a group working to establish a Palestinian state, began operating from bases in Lebanon and in the late sixties clashed with Israel in southern Lebanon. The presence of the PLO in Lebanon divided Muslims, who generally supported it, from Christians, who opposed it. The increasing Muslim population also demanded a greater voice in the government. Civil war between Muslims and Christians broke out in 1975, and fighting ended the next year with the requested aid of Syrian deterrent forces. Internal instability continued, however, along with Israeli-Palestinian hostilities; in June 1982 Israel invaded Lebanon, driving the

PLO from Beirut and the south. Hundreds of Palestinian refugees were killed by Christian militiamen in September. A multinational peacekeeping force arrived shortly afterward but left after falling victim to terrorist attacks. Israel began a gradual withdrawal from Lebanon in 1985, and Syrian troops yet occupy parts of the country. Internal and international attempts to reconcile warring factions have been unsuccessful, and sporadic violence continues. In 1986, however, the leaders of various factions signed a peace agreement in an attempt to bring an end to the civil war. ∎

Lebanon Map Index

	Lat.	Long.		Lat.	Long.
Alayh	33°48′N	35°36′E	Halba	34°33′N	36°05′E
al-Batrun	34°15′N	35°39′E	Hasbayya	33°24′N	35°41′E
al-Damur	33°44′N	35°27′E	Hermon, Mount	33°26′N	35°51′E
al-Litani	33°20′N	35°14′E	Jazzin	33°32′N	35°34′E
al-Qubayyat	34°34′N	36°17′E	Jubayl	34°07′N	35°39′E
Amyun	34°18′N	35°49′E	Lebanon		
Anti-Lebanon			Mountains	33°50′N	35°40′E
Mountains	33°35′N	36°00′E	Marj Uyun	33°22′N	35°35′E
Baalbek	34°00′N	36°12′E	Orontes	34°27′N	36°32′E
Babda	33°50′N	35°32′E	Ras Balabakk	34°15′N	36°25′E
Beirut	33°53′N	35°30′E	Rashayya	33°30′N	35°51′E
Beirut, Cape	33°54′N	35°28′E	Sidon	33°33′N	35°22′E
Bint Jubayl	33°07′N	35°26′E	Tripoli	34°26′N	35°51′E
Bsharri	34°15′N	36°01′E	Tyre	33°16′N	35°11′E
Burj Hammud	33°53′N	35°32′E	Zhgarta	34°24′N	35°54′E
Ghazir	34°01′N	35°40′E			

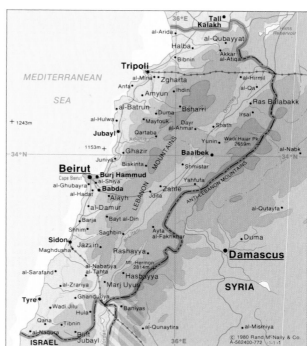

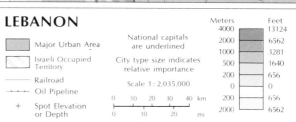

LEBANON

	Meters	Feet
	4000	13124
	2000	6562
	1000	3281
	500	1640
	200	656
	0	0
	200	656
	2000	6562

- Major Urban Area
- Israeli Occupied Territory
- Railroad
- Oil Pipeline
- + Spot Elevation or Depth

National capitals are underlined
City type size indicates relative importance
Scale 1: 2.035.000
0 10 20 30 40 km
0 10 20 mi

A Middle East people of Arab stock, the Bedouins traditionally follow a nomadic life-style in the region's deserts, living in tents and seeking water and pastures to support the raising of camels, sheep, and goats. The nomadic way of life is becoming more difficult to maintain, however, and many Middle East nations have implemented programs to encourage the permanent settlement of the Bedouins.

LESOTHO

OFFICIAL NAME Kingdom of Lesotho

PEOPLE
Population 1,495,000.
Density 128/mi² (49/km²).
Urban 5%.
Capital Maseru, 14,686.
Ethnic groups Sotho.
Languages English, Sesotho.
Religions Christian 80%, indigenous 20%.
Life expectancy 54 female, 51 male.
Literacy 55%.

POLITICS
Government Monarchy.
Parties Basotho National, Basutoland Congress.
Suffrage Universal adult.
Memberships CW, OAU, UN.
Subdivisions 10 districts.

ECONOMY
GNP $569,000,000.
Per capita $424.
Monetary unit Loti.
Trade partners South Africa.
Exports Wool, mohair, food.
Imports Food, construction materials, clothing, vehicles.

LAND
Description Southern Africa, landlocked.
Area 11,720 mi² (30,355 km²).
Highest point Thabana Ntlenyana, 11,425 ft (3,482 m).

PEOPLE. The Sotho, a black African group, constitute Lesotho's majority population. Most Sotho live in the lowlands and raise livestock and crops. The traditional religion is based on ancestor worship, but many Sotho are Christian.

ECONOMY AND THE LAND. Surrounded by South Africa and having few resources, Lesotho is almost entirely dependent on South Africa for economic survival. Much of the male population must seek employment there, usually spending several months a year in South African mines or industries. Livestock raising represents a significant part of Lesotho's economy. Diamond mining, one of the few industries, employs a small portion of the population. Most of the terrain is mountainous; the fairly high elevations give Lesotho a temperate climate.

HISTORY AND POLITICS. Refugees from tribal wars in southern Africa arrived in what is now Lesotho between the sixteenth and nineteenth centuries A.D. Chief Moshoeshoe united the Sotho tribes in 1818 and led them in war against the Boers, settlers of Dutch or Huguenot descent. At Moshoeshoe's request, Basutoland came under British protection in 1868. It resisted

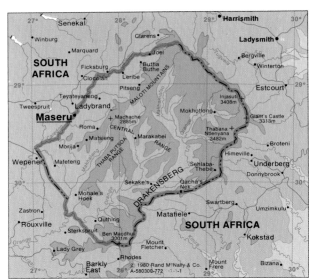

LESOTHO

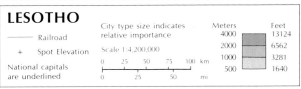

	Railroad
+	Spot Elevation
	National capitals are underlined

City type size indicates relative importance
Scale 1:4,200,000

Lesotho Map Index

	Lat.	Long.		Lat.	Long.
Maseru	29°28'S	27°30'E	Thabana		
Orange	30°20'S	27°22'E	Ntlenyana	29°28'S	29°16'E

attempts at absorption by the Union of South Africa and became the independent Kingdom of Lesotho in 1966. Lesotho, although unforgiving of South Africa's racial policies, is forced by its geographic and economic situation to cooperate with its powerful neighbor. ∎

LIBERIA

OFFICIAL NAME Republic of Liberia

PEOPLE
Population 2,195,000.
Density 51/mi² (20/km²).
Urban 33%.
Capital Monrovia, 243,243.
Ethnic groups African 95%, descendants of freed American slaves 5%.
Languages English, indigenous.
Religions Indigenous 75%, Muslim 15%, Christian 10%.
Life expectancy 55 female, 52 male.
Literacy 24%.

POLITICS
Government Provisional military government.
Parties None (suspended).
Suffrage Property owners, over 18.
Memberships OAU, UN.

Subdivisions 10 counties, 5 territories.

ECONOMY
GDP $800,000,000.
Per capita $385.
Monetary unit U.S. dollar.
Trade partners U.S., West Germany, other Western European countries.
Exports Iron ore, natural rubber, diamonds, wood.
Imports Machinery, petroleum, transportation equipment, food.

LAND
Description Western Africa.
Area 43,000 mi² (111,369 km²).
Highest point Mt. Wuteve, 4,528 ft (1,380 m).
Lowest point Sea level.

PEOPLE. Most Liberians belong to indigenous black groups, which number about twenty. Few are descended from the freed American slaves who founded modern Liberia, but this group —known as Americo-Liberians—has traditionally been politically dominant.

ECONOMY AND THE LAND. Liberia's extensive resources are attractive to foreign nations, and iron-ore mining and rubber production were developed by Western firms. Land regions include a coastal plain, plateaus, and low mountains. The climate is hot and humid.

HISTORY AND POLITICS. Early settlers are thought to have migrated from the north and east between the twelfth and seventeenth centuries A.D. The American Colonization Society, a private United States organization devoted to resettling freed slaves, purchased land in Liberia, and in 1822 the first settlers landed at the site of Monrovia. The settlers declared their independence in 1847, setting up a government based on the United States model. ∎

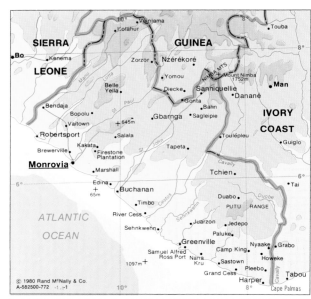

LIBERIA

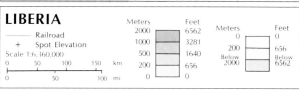

| | Railroad |
| + | Spot Elevation |

Scale 1:6,360,000

Liberia Map Index

	Lat.	Long.		Lat.	Long.
Buchanan	5°57'N	10°02'W	Harper	4°25'N	7°43'W
Gbarnga	7°00'N	9°29'W	Monrovia	6°18'N	10°47'W
Greenville	5°01'N	9°03'W	Robertsport	6°45'N	11°22'W

LIBYA

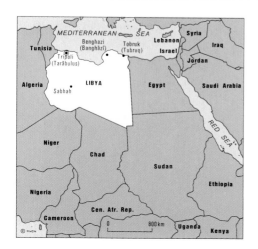

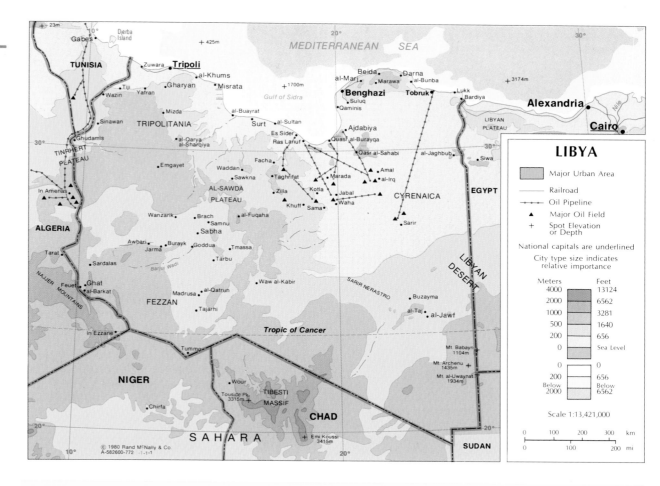

OFFICIAL NAME Socialist
People's Libyan Arab
Jamahiriya

PEOPLE
Population 3,785,000.
Density 5.6/mi² (2.2/km²).
Urban 52%.
Capital Tripoli, 858,500.
Ethnic groups Arab-Berber 97%.
Languages Arabic.
Religions Sunni Muslim 97%.
Life expectancy 59 female, 55 male.
Literacy 50%.

POLITICS
Government Socialist republic.
Parties None.
Suffrage Universal adult.
Memberships AL, OPEC, UN.
Subdivisions 10 provinces.

ECONOMY
GDP $26,500,000,000.
Per capita $7,600.
Monetary unit Pound.
Trade partners Italy, West Germany, Spain, France.
Exports Petroleum.
Imports Machinery, transportation equipment, food,
manufactured goods.

LAND
Description Northern Africa.
Area 679,362 mi² (1,759,540 km²).
Highest point Bette, 7,438 ft (2,267 m).
Lowest point Sabkhat Ghuzzayil, 154 ft (47 m) below
sea level.

Libya Map Index

	Lat.	Long.		Lat.	Long.		Lat.	Long.		Lat.	Long.
Ajdabiya	30°48'N	20°14'E	Beida	32°46'N	21°43'E	Ghat	24°58'N	10°11'E	Tinrhert Plateau	29°00'N	9°00'E
al-Jawf	24°11'N	23°19'E	Benghazi	32°07'N	20°04'E	Libyan Desert	26°00'N	25°00'E	Tobruk	32°05'N	23°59'E
al-Khums	32°39'N	14°16'E	Bette	22°00'N	19°12'E	Misrata	32°23'N	15°06'E	Tripoli	32°54'N	13°11'E
al-Marj	32°30'N	20°54'E	Cyrenaica	31°00'N	22°30'E	Nerastro, Sarir	24°20'N	20°37'E	Tripolitania	31°00'N	15°00'E
Al-Sawda Plateau	28°40'N	15°30'E	Darna	32°46'N	22°39'E	Sabha	27°03'N	14°26'E			
al-Uwaynat,			Fezzan	26°00'N	14°00'E	Sidra, Gulf of	31°30'N	18°00'E			
Mount	21°54'N	24°58'E	Gharyan	32°10'N	13°01'E	Surt	31°12'N	16°35'E			

PEOPLE. The Berbers were the original settlers
of Libya, but today the population is largely
mixed Arab and Berber. Almost all Libyans live
along the coast, although there are some nomadic groups in desert areas. Large migrations from
rural areas to the cities have accompanied Libya's oil-based prosperity. Islam is by far the most
popular religion, and nearly all Libyans speak
Arabic. Traditional social orders still exist, despite
centuries of foreign rule.

ECONOMY AND THE LAND. The discovery of
oil in 1959 propelled Libya from the ranks of the
world's poorest nations to one of its leading oil
producers. It has used its revenues to develop
industry and agriculture in an effort to diversify
the economy. Because most of Libya is covered
by the Sahara Desert, agriculture is limited, and
it has been further hurt by the exodus of Libyan
farmers from the countryside. Libya has a desert
climate except for the coast, which has moderate
temperatures.

HISTORY AND POLITICS. For much of its history Libya was dominated by the empires of the
Mediterranean, from the Phoenician and Carthaginian to the Greek and Roman. In the seventh
century A.D. the area was taken by Muslim
Arabs, whose language and religion transformed
Libyan culture. Although the Ottoman Turks
conquered the region in the sixteenth century,
local rulers remained virtually autonomous. Italy
invaded Libya in 1911, and the country became
an Italian colony. Following World War II, British
and French forces occupied the area until a United Nations resolution made Libya an independent nation in 1951. A monarchy ruled until
1969, when a military coup established a republic
with Colonel Mu'ammar Muhammad al-Qadhafi
in control. Under his leadership, Libya has
backed Arab unity and the Palestinian cause, opposed foreign influences, and created a welfare
system. ■

**Shown here is a desert patrol leaving the Libyan town of
Ghudamis to continue its route through the Sahara.
Ghudamis is situated southwest of Tripoli, where the nations of Algeria and Tunisia meet Libya, and this crossroads
location made Ghudamis a historical Saharan oasis and
stopover for caravans traveling from Tripoli to the Sudan.**

**The Romans captured the town around 20 B.C., and in
the seventh century Arabs took the city. Ghudamis
was occupied by foreign armies when the Italians
arrived in 1924 and when the French came in 1943 during
World War II. Today, Ghudamis remains an important
Saharan oasis and is the site of an airport as well.**

LIECHTENSTEIN

OFFICIAL NAME Principality
of Liechtenstein

PEOPLE
Population 27,000.
Density 435/mi² (169/km²).
Capital Vaduz, 4,980.
Ethnic groups Alemannic 95%, Italian and others 5%.
Languages German.
Religions Roman Catholic 83%, Protestant 7%.
Literacy 100%.

POLITICS
Government Constitutional monarchy.
Parties Fatherland Union, Progressive Citizens'.
Suffrage Universal adult male, limited adult female.
Memberships None.
Subdivisions 11 communes.

ECONOMY
GDP $439,400,000.
Per capita $16,900.
Monetary unit Swiss franc.
Trade partners Switzerland, other Western European
countries.
Exports Metal products, precision instruments,
artificial teeth.

LAND
Description Central Europe, landlocked.
Area 62 mi² (160 km²).
Highest point Vorder-Grauspitz, 8,527 ft (2,599 m).
Lowest point Ruggeller Riet, 1,411 ft (430 m).

PEOPLE. In spite of its location at the crossroads of Europe, Liechtenstein has retained a largely homogeneous ethnicity. Almost all Liechtensteiners are descended from the Alemanni, a Germanic tribe, and many speak the Alemanni dialect. German is the official language.

ECONOMY AND THE LAND. The last few decades have seen the economy shift from agriculture to industry. An economic alliance with Switzerland dating from 1923 has been profoundly beneficial to Liechtenstein: the two nations form a customs union and use the same currency. Other important sources of revenue are tourism, the sale of postage stamps, and taxation of foreign businesses headquartered here. Most of Liechtenstein is covered by the Alps; nonetheless, its climate is mild.

HISTORY AND POLITICS. Early inhabitants of what is now Liechtenstein included the Celts, Romans, and Alemanni, who arrived about A.D. 500. The area became part of the empire of the Frankish king Charlemagne in the late 700s, and following Charlemagne's death, it was divided into the lordships of Vaduz and Schellenberg. By 1719, when the state became part of the Holy Roman Empire, the Austrian House of Liechten-

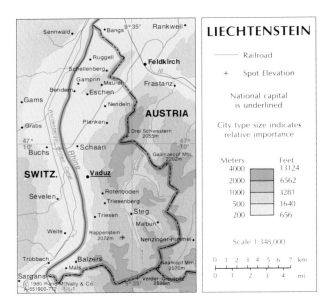

Liechtenstein Map Index

	Lat.	Long.		Lat.	Long.
Balzers	47°04'N	9°30'E	Schaan	47°10'N	9°31'E
Eschen	47°13'N	9°31'E	Vaduz	47°09'N	9°31'E
Rhine	47°16'N	9°32'E	Vorder-Grauspitz	47°03'N	9°36'E

stein had purchased both lordships, uniting them as the Imperial Principality of Liechtenstein. The nation's independence dates from the abolition of the empire by France's Napoleon Bonaparte in 1806. Liechtenstein was neutral in both world wars and has remained unaffected by European conflicts. The government is a hereditary constitutional monarchy; the prince is the chief of state, and the prime minister is the head of government. Women gained limited suffrage in 1984. ∎

LUXEMBOURG

OFFICIAL NAME Grand
Duchy of Luxembourg

PEOPLE
Population 365,000.
Density 366/mi² (141/km²).
Urban 78%.
Capital Luxembourg, 78,924.
Ethnic groups Mixed Celtic, French, and German.
Languages Luxembourgish, French, German.
Religions Roman Catholic 97%.
Life expectancy 76 female, 71 male.
Literacy 100%.

POLITICS
Government Constitutional monarchy.
Parties Christian Socialist, Liberal, Socialist Workers'.
Suffrage Universal, over 18.
Memberships EC, NATO, OECD, UN.
Subdivisions 3 districts.

ECONOMY
GNP $3,400,000,000.
Per capita $9,289.
Monetary unit Franc.
Trade partners West Germany, Belgium, France.
Exports Steel, plastic, and rubber products.
Imports Coal, petroleum, consumer goods.

LAND
Description Western Europe, landlocked.
Area 998 mi² (2,586 km²).
Highest point Buurgplaatz, 1,834 ft (559 m).
Lowest point 427 ft (130 m).

PEOPLE. Luxembourg's population bears the imprint of foreign influences, yet retains an individual character. Most Luxembourgers are a blend of Celtic, French, and German stock. German and French are official languages, as is Luxembourgish, an indigenous German dialect.

ECONOMY AND THE LAND. Luxembourg's steel industry forms the basis of its economy, and the country has compensated for a worldwide drop in the steel market by developing financial services, notably banking. Luxembourg has two distinct regions: the mountainous, wooded north and the open, rolling south, known as Bon Pays. The climate is temperate.

HISTORY AND POLITICS. The present city of Luxembourg developed from a castle built in A.D. 963 by Count Siegfried of Ardennes. Several heavily fortified towns grew up around the castle, and the area became known as the Gibraltar of the North because of those fortifications. The duchy remained semiautonomous until the Burgundians conquered the area in 1443. Various European powers ruled Luxembourg for most of the next four centuries, and in 1815 the duchy was elevated to a grand duchy. It became auton-

omous in 1839 and was recognized in 1867 as an independent state. Luxembourg was occupied by Germany in both world wars. ∎

Luxembourg Map Index

	Lat.	Long.		Lat.	Long.
Dudelange	49°28'N	6°05'E	Moselle	49°43'N	6°30'E
Esch	49°30'N	5°59'E	Our	49°53'N	6°18'E
Luxembourg	49°36'N	6°09'E	Pétange	49°34'N	5°52'E

MACAO

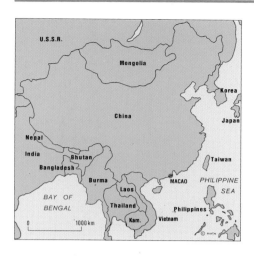

OFFICIAL NAME Macao

PEOPLE
Population 310,000.
Density 51,667/mi² (19,375/km²).
Urban 97%.
Capital Macao, 253,376.
Ethnic groups Chinese 98%, Portuguese 2%.
Languages Portuguese, Chinese dialects.
Religions Buddhist, Roman Catholic.
Literacy Portuguese and Macanese 100%.

POLITICS
Government Overseas province (Portugal).
Parties None. (Civic associations are represented in legislature.)
Suffrage Portuguese, Chinese, and foreign residents, over 18.
Memberships None.
Subdivisions 3 districts.

ECONOMY
GNP $640,000,000.
Per capita $2,246.
Monetary unit Pataca.
Trade partners Hong Kong, China, West Germany, France.
Exports Textiles, clothing.
Imports Food, consumer goods.

LAND
Description Eastern Asia.
Area 6 mi² (16 km²).
Highest point Coloane Alto, 571 ft (174 m).
Lowest point Sea level.

PEOPLE. Situated on the southeastern China coast, 17 miles (27.4 kilometers) west of Hong Kong, Macao is populated almost entirely by Chinese. Because Macao is an overseas province of Portugal, minorities include people of Portuguese and mixed Chinese-Portuguese descent.

ECONOMY AND THE LAND. Tourism, gambling, and light industry help make up Macao's economy; however, its leading industries are clothing and textiles, which employ the majority of the labor force. The province consists of the city of Macao, located on a peninsula, and the nearby islands of Taipa and Coloane. The climate is maritime tropical, with cool winters and warm summers.

HISTORY AND POLITICS. Macao became a Portuguese trading post in 1557. It flourished as the midpoint for trade between China and Japan but declined when Hong Kong became a trading power in the nineteenth century. Although the government is nominally directed by Portugal, any policies relating to Macao are subject to China's approval. Macao is the oldest European settlement in the Far East. ∎

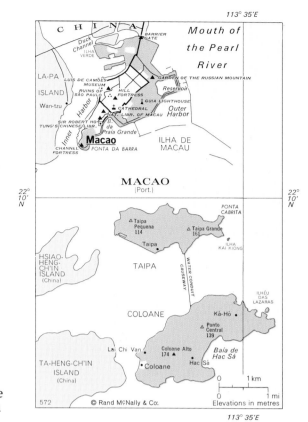

Macao Map Index

	Lat.	Long.		Lat.	Long.
Coloane	22°07′N	113°33′E	Praia Grande,		
Macau	22°12′N	113°33′E	Baia da	22°11′N	113°32′E
			Taipa	22°09′N	113°33′E

MADAGASCAR

OFFICIAL NAME Democratic Republic of Madagascar

PEOPLE
Population 9,775,000.
Density 43/mi² (17/km²).
Urban 18%.
Capital Antananarivo, 484,000.
Ethnic groups 18 Malagasy groups.
Languages Malagasy, French.
Religions Indigenous 52%, Christian 41%, Muslim 7%.
Life expectancy 49 female, 46 male.
Literacy 53%.

POLITICS
Government Socialist republic.
Parties Advance Guard of the Revolution, Congress for Independence.
Suffrage Universal, over 18.
Memberships OAU, UN.
Subdivisions 6 provinces.

Madagascar Map Index

	Lat.	Long.		Lat.	Long.
Ambre, Cape	11°57′S	49°17′E	Manakara	22°08′S	48°01′E
Antananarivo	18°55′S	47°31′E	Mananjary	21°13′S	48°20′E
Antsirabe	19°51′S	47°02′E	Marovoay	16°06′S	46°39′E
Antsiranana	12°16′S	49°17′E	Tananarive →		
Faradofay	25°02′S	47°00′E	Antananarivo	18°55′S	47°31′E
Fianarantsoa	21°26′S	47°05′E	Toamasina	18°10′S	49°23′E
Mahajanga	15°43′S	46°19′E	Toliara	23°21′S	43°40′E

ECONOMY
GDP $3,200,000,000.
Per capita $360.
Monetary unit Franc.
Trade partners France, U.S., West Germany, Japan, Italy.
Exports Coffee, vanilla, sugar, cloves.
Imports Consumer goods, food, machinery, petroleum, fertilizer.

LAND
Description Western Indian Ocean island.
Area 226,658 mi² (587,041 km²).
Highest point Maromokotro, 9,436 ft (2,876 m).
Lowest point Sea level.

PEOPLE. Most of the population is of mixed African and Indonesian descent. The *cotiers*, who live on the coast, are African, while Asians live on the inland plateau.

ECONOMY AND THE LAND. Madagascar's economy is based on agriculture. The climate is tropical on the coastal plains and moderate in the inland highlands.

HISTORY AND POLITICS. Madagascar's first settlers arrived around two thousand years ago. The Portuguese sighted the island in the 1500s, and in 1896 France made the island a colony. Full independence came in 1960. ∎

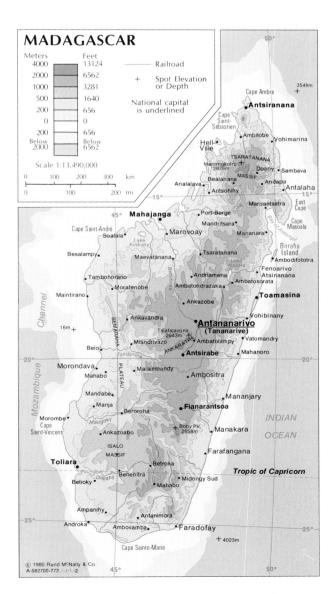

MALAWI

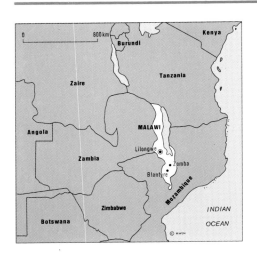

OFFICIAL NAME Republic of Malawi

PEOPLE
Population 6,940,000.
Density 152/mi² (59/km²).
Urban 8%.
Capital Lilongwe, 98,718.
Ethnic groups Chewa, Nyanja, Tumbuka, Yao, Lomwe, others.
Languages Chichewa, English.
Religions Protestant 55%, Roman Catholic 20%, Muslim 20%.
Life expectancy 45 female, 43 male.
Literacy 25%.

POLITICS
Government Republic.
Parties Congress.
Suffrage Universal, over 18.
Memberships CW, OAU, UN.
Subdivisions 3 regions.

ECONOMY
GDP $1,340,000,000.
Per capita $213.
Monetary unit Kwacha.
Trade partners South Africa, U.K., U.S., West Germany.

Exports Tobacco, tea, sugar, peanuts.
Imports Manufactured goods, machinery, fuels, motor vehicles.

LAND
Description Southern Africa, landlocked.
Area 45,747 mi² (118,484 km²).
Highest point Sapitwa, 9,849 ft (3,002 m).
Lowest point 120 ft (37 m).

PEOPLE. Almost all Malawians are black Africans descended from Bantu peoples. The Chewa constitute the majority in the central area, while the Nyanja are dominant in the south and the Tumbuka in the north. Chichewa and English are official languages. The majority of the population is rural, and traditional village customs are prevalent. For the most part, the society is matriarchal. Many Malawians combine Christian or Muslim beliefs with African religious practices.

ECONOMY AND THE LAND. A landlocked nation with limited resources and a largely unskilled work force, Malawi relies almost entirely on agriculture. A recent series of poor harvests, combined with a doubling of population between 1945 and 1966, has contributed to the decline in agricultural output. Among the main exports are tea and tobacco. Many Malawians work part of the year as miners in South Africa, Zambia, and Zimbabwe. Malawi, situated along the Great Rift Valley, has a varied terrain with highlands, plateaus, and lakes. The climate is subtropical, and rainfall varies greatly from north to south.

HISTORY AND POLITICS. Archaeological findings indicate that Malawi has been inhabited for at least fifty thousand years. Bantu-speaking peoples, ancestors of the Malawians, immigrated from the north around A.D. 1400 and soon formed centralized kingdoms. In the 1830s other Bantu groups, involved in the slave trade, invaded the region. The arrival of Scottish missionary David Livingstone in 1859 signaled the start of British influence, and in 1891 the territory became the British protectorate of Nyasaland. For about ten years, beginning in 1953, Nyasaland

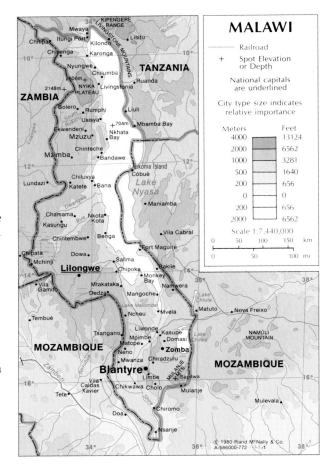

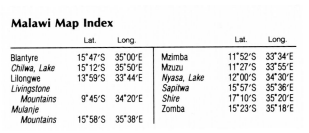

Malawi Map Index

	Lat.	Long.		Lat.	Long.
Blantyre	15°47′S	35°00′E	Mzimba	11°52′S	33°34′E
Chilwa, Lake	15°12′S	35°50′E	Mzuzu	11°27′S	33°55′E
Lilongwe	13°59′S	33°44′E	Nyasa, Lake	12°00′S	34°30′E
Livingstone			Sapitwa	15°57′S	35°36′E
Mountains	9°45′S	34°20′E	Shire	17°10′S	35°20′E
Mulanje			Zomba	15°23′S	35°18′E
Mountains	15°58′S	35°38′E			

was part of the larger Federation of Rhodesia and Nyasaland. Malawi attained independence in 1964 and became a republic in 1966. ∎

MALAYSIA

OFFICIAL NAME Malaysia

PEOPLE
Population 15,500,000.
Density 121/mi² (47/km²).
Urban 30%.
Capital Kuala Lumpur, 937,817.
Ethnic groups Malay 50%, Chinese 36%, Indian 10%.
Languages Malay, Chinese dialects, Tamil.
Religions Muslim, Buddhist, Hindu, Confucian, Christian.

Life expectancy 67 female, 63 male.
Literacy 70%.

POLITICS
Government Constitutional monarchy.
Parties Berjaya, Democratic Action, Islamic, National Front.
Suffrage Universal, over 20.
Memberships ASEAN, CW, UN.
Subdivisions 13 states, 1 federal territory.

ECONOMY
GNP $25,100,000,000.
Per capita $1,750.
Monetary unit Ringgit.
Trade partners Japan, U.S., Singapore, Western European countries.
Exports Petroleum, natural rubber, wood, palm oil, tin.
Imports Machinery, food, transportation equipment, manufactured goods.

LAND
Description Southeastern Asia.
Area 128,430 mi² (332,632 km²).
Highest point Mt. Kinabalu, 13,455 ft (4,101 m).
Lowest point Sea level.

George Town—port city, tourist center, and capital of the Malaysian state of Penang—is situated on a western island also known as Penang. Shown here is a view from the east, looking toward the channel that separates Penang Island from the mainland.

PEOPLE. Malaysia's location at one of Southeast Asia's maritime crossroads has left it with a diverse population, including Malays, Chinese, Indians, and native non-Malay groups. Although mostly rural and often economically disadvan-

taged, the indigenous Malays dominate the nation's political scene. The Chinese population is mainly urban and employed in Malaysia's business, trade, and financial sectors, wielding most of the economic power. There is considerable tension between the Malays and Chinese. Generally Muslim, Hindu, or Buddhist, the Indians are descended from plantation workers who arrived around the turn of the century. Indigenous non-Malay ethnic groups live mainly on northern Borneo, and although each group has its distinctive culture, the various peoples do hold some common customs. Although most inhabitants speak Malay and practice Islam, Malaysia's ethnic groups have resisted assimilation; Chinese, Indian, and Western languages and beliefs are also part of the culture. Most Malaysians live in Peninsular Malaysia.

ECONOMY AND THE LAND. The economy is one of the healthiest in the region, supported by multiple strengths in agriculture, mining, forestry, and fishing. The nation is one of the world's leading producers of rubber, palm oil, and tin, and one of the Far East's largest petroleum exporters. Manufacturing is being developed. The southern portion of the Malay Peninsula in Southeast Asia constitutes Peninsular Malaysia, and East Malaysia consists of the states of Sarawak and Sabah, situated on the northern section of the island of Borneo. The land is characterized by swampy areas, mountains, and rain forests. The climate is tropical and very humid.

HISTORY AND POLITICS. The Malay Peninsula has been inhabited since the late Stone Age. Hindu and Buddhist influences were widespread from the ninth through the fourteenth centuries A.D., after which Islam was introduced. In 1511

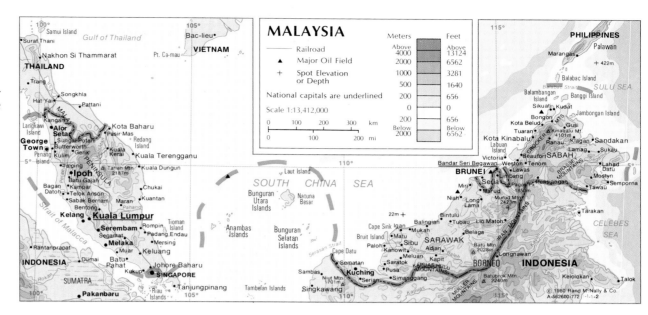

the Portuguese seized Melaka, a trading center, but were soon replaced, first by the Dutch in 1641 and then by the British in 1795. By the early 1900s Britain was in control of present-day Malaysia and Singapore, the areas which were occupied by Japan during World War II. Following the war, the Federation of Malaya was created, a semiautonomous state under British authority. A guerrilla war ensued, waged by Chinese Communists and others who opposed the British. Full independence was gained in 1963 with the unification of Malaysia. Singapore seceded in 1965. In 1969 riots between Malays and Chinese resulted in a suspension of parliamentary democracy lasting almost two years. ■

Malaysia Map Index

	Lat.	Long.		Lat.	Long.
Alor Setar	6°07'N	100°22'E	Kuala Lumpur	3°10'N	101°42'E
Balabac Strait	7°35'N	117°00'E	Kuala		
Borneo	3°00'N	114°00'E	Terengganu	5°20'N	103°08'E
Brassey			Kuching	1°33'N	110°20'E
Mountains	4°54'N	117°30'E	Malacca, Strait		
Crocker			of	2°30'N	101°20'E
Mountains	5°40'N	116°14'E	Malay Peninsula	6°00'N	101°00'E
Datu, Cape	2°06'N	109°39'E	Melaka	2°12'N	102°15'E
George Town	5°25'N	100°20'E	Murud Mountain	3°52'N	115°30'E
Ipoh	4°35'N	101°05'E	Pahang	3°32'N	103°28'E
Iran Mountains	2°05'N	114°55'E	Penang Island	5°23'N	100°15'E
Johor Baharu	1°28'N	103°45'E	Rajang	2°04'N	111°12'E
Kelang	3°02'N	101°27'E	Sabah	5°20'N	117°10'E
Keluang	2°02'N	103°19'E	Sandakan	5°50'N	118°07'E
Kinabalu			Sarawak	2°30'N	113°30'E
Mountain	6°05'N	116°33'E	Seremban	2°43'N	101°56'E
Kota Baharu	6°08'N	102°15'E	Sibu	2°18'N	111°49'E
Kota Kinabalu	5°59'N	116°04'E	Tahan Mountain	4°38'N	102°14'E

MALDIVES

OFFICIAL NAME Republic of Maldives

PEOPLE
Population 175,000.
Density 1,522/mi² (587/km²).
Urban 21%.
Capital Male, Male I., 29,555.
Ethnic groups Mixed Sinhalese, Dravidian, Arab, black.
Languages Divehi.
Religions Sunni Muslim.
Literacy 36%.

POLITICS
Government Republic.
Parties None.
Suffrage Universal, over 21.
Memberships CW, UN.
Subdivisions 19 districts.

ECONOMY
GDP $74,000,000.
Per capita $462.
Monetary unit Rufiyaa.
Trade partners Japan, Sri Lanka, Thailand.
Exports Fish products, clothing.
Imports Food, manufactured goods, machinery, petroleum.

LAND
Description Indian Ocean islands.
Area 115 mi² (298 km²).
Highest point 80 ft (24 m).
Lowest point Sea level.

PEOPLE. Most Maldivians are descended from Sinhalese peoples from Sri Lanka; southern Indians, or Dravidians; and Arabs. Nearly all Maldivians are Sunni Muslims and speak Divehi. Of the Maldives' more than one thousand islands, only about two hundred are inhabited, and the population is concentrated on Male, also the site of the capital. Most unpopulated islands lack drinking-water sources and arable land.

ECONOMY AND THE LAND. The nation draws on its advantages as a union of 1,200 islands to fuel its economy: tourism, shipping, and fishing are the mainstays. Because of limited arable land and infertile soil, agriculture is marginal. The Maldives are flat coral islands, grouped into a chain of nineteen atolls. Seasonal monsoons mark the tropical climate.

HISTORY AND POLITICS. The Maldives are believed to have been originally settled by southern Indian peoples. Arab sailors brought Islam to the islands in the twelfth century A.D. Although a Muslim sultanate remained in power, with two interruptions, from 1153 until 1968, the Portuguese and Dutch controlled the islands intermit-

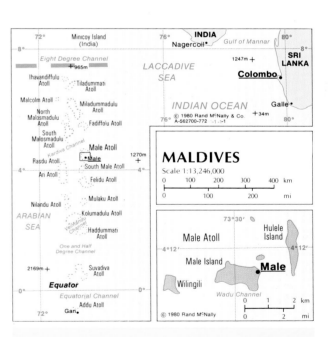

Maldives Map Index

	Lat.	Long.		Lat.	Long.
Addu Atoll	0°38'S	73°10'E	Laccadive Sea	7°00'N	76°00'E
Eight Degree			Male	4°10'N	73°31'E
Channel	8°00'N	73°00'E	Male Atoll	4°25'N	73°30'E
Felidu Atoll	3°30'N	73°30'E	Miladummadulu		
Haddummati			Atoll	6°15'N	73°15'E
Atoll	1°55'N	73°25'E	Suvadiva Atoll	0°30'N	73°15'E
Hulele Island	4°11'N	73°32'E	Tiladummati Atoll	6°50'N	73°05'E
Kardiva Channel	5°00'N	73°20'E	Wadu Channel	4°07'N	73°27'E
Kolumadulu Atoll	2°25'N	73°10'E	Wilingili	4°10'N	73°28'E

tently between the 1500s and the 1700s. The Maldives were a British protectorate from 1887 to 1965, when they achieved independence. A republic was declared three years later. The Republic of Maldives is nonaligned and maintains close ties with other Islamic nations. ■

MALI

OFFICIAL NAME Republic of
Mali

PEOPLE
Population 7,650,000.
Density 16/mi² (6.2/km²).
Urban 17%.
Capital Bamako, 404,022.
Ethnic groups Mande 50%, Fulani 17%, Voltaic 12%,
Songhai 6%.
Languages French, Bambara, indigenous.
Religions Muslim 90%, indigenous 9%, Christian 1%.
Life expectancy 46 female, 43 male.
Literacy 10%.

POLITICS
Government Republic.
Parties Democratic Union.
Suffrage Universal, over 21.
Memberships OAU, UN.
Subdivisions 7 regions, 1 district.

ECONOMY
GDP $1,000,000,000.
Per capita $138.
Monetary unit Franc.
Trade partners France, Ivory Coast, China, Senegal,
U.K., West Germany.
Exports Cotton, livestock, dried fish, peanuts.
Imports Food, machinery, vehicles, petroleum,
chemicals and pharmaceuticals.

LAND
Description Western Africa, landlocked.
Area 478,766 mi² (1,240,000 km²).
Highest point Hombori Tondo, 3,789 ft (1,155 m).
Lowest point 72 ft (22 m).

PEOPLE. The majority of Malians belong to one
of several black groups, although there is a small
nonblack nomadic population. Most Malians are
farmers who live in small villages. The official
language is French, but most people communicate in Bambara, a market language. The population is concentrated in the basins of the Niger
and Senegal rivers, in the south. Heirs of three
ancient empires, Malians have produced a distinct culture.

ECONOMY AND THE LAND. One of the
world's poorest nations, Mali depends primarily
on agriculture but is limited by a climate that
produces drought and a terrain that is almost
half desert. Mineral reserves have not been exploited because of poor transportation and power
facilities. Food processing and textiles account for
most industry. Mali, a landlocked country, faces
a growing national debt due to its dependence
on foreign goods. The climate is hot, with alternating dry and wet seasons.

HISTORY AND POLITICS. Parts of present-day
Mali once belonged to the Ghana, Mali, and
Songhai empires. These wealthy empires, which
ruled from about A.D. 300 to 1600, traded with
the Mediterranean world and were centers of Islamic learning. Fierce native resistance delayed
colonization by the French until 1904, when

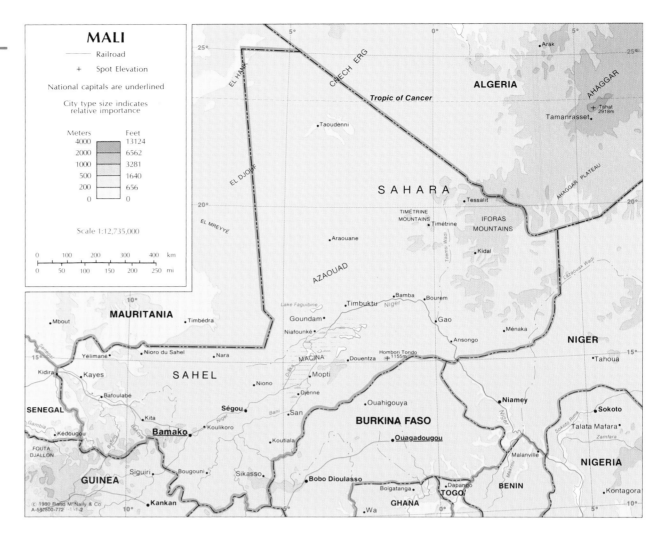

Mali Map Index

	Lat.	Long.		Lat.	Long.		Lat.	Long.		Lat.	Long.
Azaouad	19°00'N	3°00'W	Gao	16°16'N	0°03'W	Niger	14°53'N	0°50'E	Timétrine		
Bafing	13°49'N	10°50'W	Goundam	16°25'N	3°40'W	Sahel	15°00'N	8°00'W	Mountains	19°20'N	0°42'W
Bamako	12°39'N	8°00'W	Hombori Tondo	15°16'N	1°40'W	San	13°18'N	4°54'W			
Bani	14°30'N	4°12'W	Iforas Mountains	20°00'N	2°00'E	Ségou	13°27'N	6°16'W			
Diaka	15°13'N	4°14'W	Kayes	14°27'N	11°26'W	Sikasso	11°19'N	5°40'W			
El Hank	24°30'N	7°00'W	Macina	14°30'N	5°00'W	Tilemsi Wash	16°15'N	0°02'E			
Faguibine, Lake	16°45'N	3°54'W	Mopti	14°30'N	4°12'W	Timbuktu	16°46'N	3°01'W			

French Sudan, as the area was called, was made
part of French West Africa. In 1959 it joined Senegal to form the Federation of Mali. Senegal soon
withdrew from the union, and French Sudan declared itself the Republic of Mali in 1960. Since
independence, Mali has experienced continuing
economic discontent and political instability, including a 1968 military coup. ■

**This agricultural training program in Mali was funded by a loan from the International
Development Association of the World Bank. Developing nations prefer to borrow from such
organizations because there are no political strings attached.**

MALTA

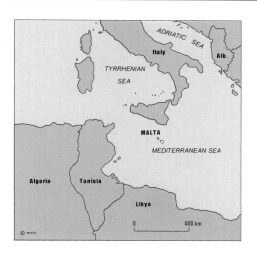

OFFICIAL NAME Republic of
Malta

PEOPLE
Population 360,000.
Density 2,951/mi² (1,139/km²).
Urban 83%.
Capital Valletta, 13,962.
Ethnic groups Mixed Arab, Sicilian, Norman,
Spanish, Italian, English.
Languages Maltese, English.
Religions Roman Catholic 98%.
Life expectancy 74 female, 70 male.
Literacy 83%.

POLITICS
Government Republic.
Parties Labor, Nationalist.
Suffrage Universal, over 18.
Memberships CW, UN.
Subdivisions 13 electoral districts.

ECONOMY
GDP $1,140,000,000.
Per capita $3,499.
Monetary unit Pound.
Trade partners West Germany, Italy, U.K.
Exports Clothing, textiles, petroleum products.
Imports Manufactured goods, machinery, food,
petroleum.

LAND
Description Mediterranean island.
Area 122 mi² (316 km²).
Highest point 829 ft (253 m).
Lowest point Sea level.

PEOPLE. Malta's diverse population reflects centuries of rule by Arabs, Normans, and the British. The official languages are English and Maltese, the latter a blend of Arabic and a Sicilian dialect of Italian.

ECONOMY AND THE LAND. Situated strategically between Europe and Africa, Malta became an important military site for foreign powers with the opening of the Suez Canal in 1869. Its economy was thus shaped by the patterns of war and peace in the Mediterranean but has recently turned toward commercial shipbuilding, construction, manufacturing, and tourism. Its soil is poor and rocky, and most food is imported. Malta, with its hilly terrain, is subtropical in summer and temperate the rest of the year.

HISTORY AND POLITICS. The Phoenicians and Carthaginians first colonized the island of Malta between 1000 and 600 B.C. Malta was made part of the Roman and Byzantine empires and then was ruled successively by Arabs, Normans, and various feudal lords. In the 1500s the Holy Roman Emperor Charles V ceded Malta to the Knights of St. John of Jerusalem, an order of the Roman Catholic church. The Knights' reign,

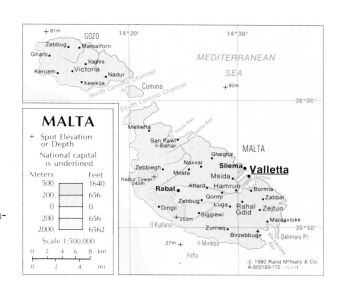

Malta Map Index

	Lat.	Long.		Lat.	Long.
Comino	36°00'N	14°20'E	Rabat	35°52'N	14°25'E
Gozo	36°03'N	14°15'E	Valletta	35°54'N	14°31'E
Malta	35°53'N	14°27'E	Victoria	36°02'N	14°14'E

marked by cultural and architectural achievements, ended with surrender to France's Napoleon Bonaparte in 1798. The Maltese resisted French rule, however, and offered control to Britain, becoming part of the United Kingdom in 1814. Throughout the two world wars Malta was a vital naval base for the Allied forces . It achieved independence from Britain in 1964 and became a republic ten years later. In 1979 the last British and North Atlantic Treaty Organization (NATO) military forces departed, and Malta declared its neutrality and nonalignment. ■

MARSHALL ISLANDS

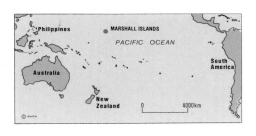

OFFICIAL NAME Republic of
the Marshall Islands

PEOPLE
Population 34,000.
Density 486/mi² (188/km²).
Urban 48%.
Capital Majuro I.
Ethnic groups Micronesian.
Languages English, Malay-Polynesian languages.
Religions Protestant, Roman Catholic.

POLITICS
Government Part of Trust Territory of the Pacific
Islands (U.S.).
Suffrage Universal, over 18.
Subdivisions 33 municipalities.

ECONOMY
GNP $46,300,000.
Per capita $1,301.
Monetary unit U.S. dollar.

LAND
Description North Pacific islands.
Area 70 mi² (181 km²).

PEOPLE. Most Marshall Islanders are Micronesian, although there is a Polynesian minority.

Both English and Malay-Polynesian languages are spoken on the islands.

ECONOMY AND THE LAND. The main industry of the Marshalls is coconut growing, and many islanders continue to practice subsistence farming and fishing. The islands remain dependent upon economic aid from the United States. Part of the area of the Pacific known as Micronesia, the Marshall Islands consist of thirty atolls and five individual islands. The two major island groups are the eastern Ratak Chain and the western Ralik Chain. The coral islands are mostly flat and low-lying, and the climate is hot and rainy.

HISTORY AND POLITICS. The history of the Marshall Islands prior to the arrival of Europeans is largely unknown, but it is likely that the earliest settlers came from Southeast Asia. Spanish ships sailed through the area in the 1500s, but treacherous waters prevented rapid settlement. The islands received their name from Captain John Marshall, a Briton who reached the Marshalls in 1788. In the 1880s, with Britain's approval, the Marshall Islands became a German protectorate, and in 1914, during World War I, Japan seized the islands. Following the war, the Marshall Islands, along with the other islands of the region, were declared a League of Nations mandate under Japanese administration. During World War II the United States captured the islands from Japan, and in 1947 the Marshall Islands were incorporated into the United States Trust Territory of the Pacific Islands established by the United Nations. Between 1946 and 1958 the United States conducted sixty-four nuclear test explosions on the islands of Bikini and Enewetak. Resettlement of these islands began in 1977, and about 50 of the 450 residents displaced

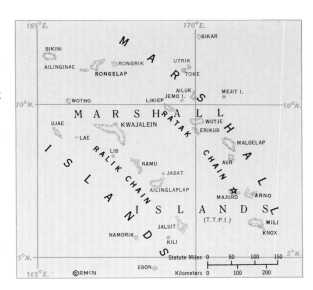

Map shows major islands only.

Marshall Islands Map Index

	Lat.	Long.		Lat.	Long.
Bikini	11°35'N	165°23'E	Ralik Chain	8°00'N	167°00'E
Kwajalein	9°05'N	167°20'E	Ratak Chain	9°00'N	171°00'E
Majuro	7°05'N	171°08'E			

by the tests were allowed to return home. Increasing self-government led to a 1978 constitution that established the Republic of the Marshall Islands. The constitutional government was recognized by a United States order in 1979, in 1982 the Marshall Islands signed a free association compact with the United States, and in 1986 the compact was finalized. Official recognition of the new republic awaits United Nations approval and the dissolution of the trust territory. ■

MARTINIQUE

OFFICIAL NAME Department of Martinique

PEOPLE
Population 320,000.
Density 753/mi² (291/km²).
Urban 46%.
Capital Fort-de-France, 99,844.
Ethnic groups Black and mulatto 90%, white 5%, others 5%.
Languages French, Creole.
Religions Roman Catholic 95%.
Life expectancy 74 female, 67 male.
Literacy 70%.

POLITICS
Government Overseas department (France).
Parties Rally for the Republic, Socialist, Union for French Democracy.
Suffrage Universal, over 18.
Subdivisions 3 arrondissements.

ECONOMY
GDP $1,300,000,000.
Per capita $4,036.
Monetary unit French franc.
Trade partners France, Venezuela, Guadeloupe, Saudi Arabia.
Exports Refined petroleum products, bananas, rum, pineapples.
Imports Petroleum, foodstuffs, building materials.

LAND
Description Caribbean island.
Area 425 mi² (1,100 km²).
Highest point Mt. Pelée, 4,583 ft (1,397 m).
Lowest point Sea level.

PEOPLE. Blacks and people of mixed black-and-French ancestry compose the majority group on Martinique. The culture is a unique blend of French and West Indian life-styles.

ECONOMY AND THE LAND. Martinique's tropical climate and beautiful scenery attract many visitors each year. Agriculture provides additional income, and major products include bananas, sugar, and rum. Forested mountains cover much of the island.

HISTORY AND POLITICS. Carib Indians inhabited the island when Christopher Columbus first sighted it in 1493. Columbus didn't come ashore until his 1502 voyage, and Indian hostility discouraged colonization. French settlement began in 1635, and except for short periods of British rule, the island has remained in French hands. In 1946 Martinique became an overseas department of France. ■

Scale 1:1,000,000

Martinique Map Index

	Lat.	Long.		Lat.	Long.
Fort-de-France	14°36′N	61°05′W	Le Vauclin	14°33′N	60°51′W
La Trinité	14°44′N	60°58′W	Pelée, Montagne	14°48′N	61°10′W
Le Lamentin	14°37′N	61°01′W	Saint-Pierre	14°45′N	61°11′W

MAURITANIA

OFFICIAL NAME Islamic Republic of Mauritania

PEOPLE
Population 1,640,000.
Density 4.1/mi² (1.6/km²).
Urban 23%.
Capital Nouakchott, 150,000.
Ethnic groups Moor-black 40%, Moor 30%, black 30%.
Languages Arabic, French.
Religions Muslim.
Life expectancy 46 female, 43 male.
Literacy 17%.

POLITICS
Government Provisional military government.
Parties None (suspended).
Suffrage Universal adult.
Memberships AL, OAU, UN.
Subdivisions 12 regions, 1 capital district.

ECONOMY
GNP $720,000,000.
Per capita $460.
Monetary unit Ouguiya.
Trade partners France, other Western European countries, Senegal, U.S.
Exports Iron ore, processed fish.
Imports Food, machinery, petroleum, consumer goods.

LAND
Description Western Africa.
Area 397,955 mi² (1,030,700 km²).
Highest point Mt. Jill, 3,002 ft (915 m).
Lowest point Sebkha de Ndrhamcha, 10 ft (3 m) below sea level.

PEOPLE. Most Mauritanians are Moors, descendants of Arabs and Berbers, or of mixed Arab, Berber, and black descent. The Moors, who speak Arabic, are mostly nomadic herdsmen. The remainder of the population is composed of black Africans, who speak several languages and farm in the Senegal River valley. Virtually all Mauritanians are Muslim. Proportionally, the nomadic population has declined recently because of long periods of drought, although overall population is increasing.

ECONOMY AND THE LAND. Mauritania's economy is based on agriculture. Crop production, confined chiefly to the Senegal River valley, has recently fallen because of drought and outmoded cultivation methods. Mining of high-grade iron ore is the primary industrial activity, although fishing and fish processing are also important. Inadequate transportation and communication systems and a war with Western Sahara have virtually crippled the economy. Besides the river valley, land regions include a northern desert and southeastern grasslands. Mauritania has a hot, dry climate.

HISTORY AND POLITICS. Berbers began settling in parts of the area around A.D. 300 and established a network of caravan trading routes. From this time until the late 1500s, sections of the south were dominated by the Ghana, the Mali, and finally the Songhai empires. Contact with Europeans grew between the 1600s and 1800s, and in 1920 France made Mauritania a colony. Mauritania attained independence in 1960, although Morocco claimed the area and did not recognize the state until 1970. During the late seventies Mauritania became embroiled in a war with the Polisario Front, a Western Saharan nationalist group, and Morocco for control of Western Sahara. Mauritania withdrew its troops from the area in 1979. ■

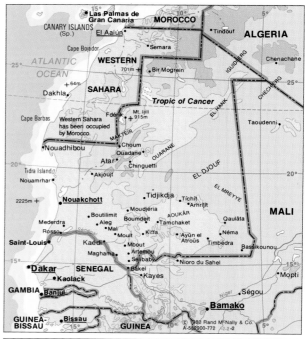

MAURITANIA

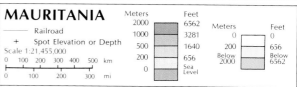

	Meters	Feet		Meters	Feet
	2000	6562		0	0
	1000	3281		200	656
	500	1640		Below 2000	Below 6562
	200	656			
	0	Sea Level			

— Railroad
+ Spot Elevation or Depth
Scale 1:21,455,000

Mauritania Map Index

	Lat.	Long.		Lat.	Long.
Aoukâr	18°00′N	9°30′W	Nouakchott	18°06′N	15°57′W
Atar	20°31′N	13°03′W	Ouarane	21°00′N	10°30′W
Dakhla	23°43′N	15°57′W	Senegal	15°48′N	16°32′W
El Djouf	21°25′N	6°40′W	Tidjikdja	18°33′N	11°25′W
Nouadhibou	20°54′N	17°04′W			

MAURITIUS

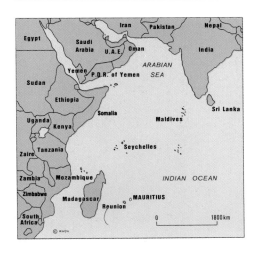

OFFICIAL NAME Mauritius

PEOPLE
Population 1,025,000.
Density 1,297/mi² (501/km²).
Urban 43%.
Capital Port Louis, 147,386.
Ethnic groups Indo-Mauritian 68%, Creole 27%, Sino-Mauritian 3%, Franco-Mauritian 2%.
Languages English, French.
Religions Hindu 51%, Christian 30%, Muslim 17%.
Life expectancy 68 female, 64 male.
Literacy 61%.

POLITICS
Government Parliamentary state.
Parties Labor, Militant Movement, Militant Socialist Movement, Social Democratic.
Suffrage Universal, over 18.
Memberships CW, OAU, UN.
Subdivisions 9 subdivisions.

ECONOMY
GDP $960,000,000.
Per capita $890.
Monetary unit Rupee.

Trade partners U.K., France, South Africa, U.S.
Exports Sugar, clothing, molasses.
Imports Food, petroleum products, capital equipment.

LAND
Description Indian Ocean island.
Area 790 mi² (2,045 km²).
Highest point Petite Rivière Noire Pk., 2,717 ft (828 m).
Lowest point Sea level.

PEOPLE. Mauritius's diverse ethnicity is largely the product of its past as a sugar-producing colony: Creoles are descendants of African slaves and European plantation owners, while the Indian community traces its roots to laborers who replaced the Africans after slavery was abolished. There are also people of Chinese and French descent. Franco-Mauritians now compose most of the nation's elite.

ECONOMY AND THE LAND. Sugar remains fundamental to the economy. Almost all arable land is covered by sugarcane, and sugar and its by-products make up the majority of exports. Attempts have been made at diversification, with tea and tobacco recent introductions. Inflation, unemployment, overpopulation, and low sugar prices cloud the economic outlook. Mauritius is a volcanic island, with a central plateau surrounded by mountains. The nation includes the volcanic island of Mauritius plus Rodrigues Island, the Agalega Islands, and Cargados Carajos Shoals. The climate is tropical.

HISTORY AND POLITICS. Although visited by Arab, Malay, and Portuguese sailors between the tenth and sixteenth centuries A.D., Mauritius was uninhabited until 1598, when the Dutch claimed it. They abandoned the island in 1710 and were followed five years later by the French, who made it a colony. During the 1700s the French used Mauritius, which they called Île de France, as a naval base and established plantations worked by imported slaves. The British ousted the French in 1810 during the Napoleonic Wars, and the 1814 Treaty of Paris recognized British possession. In the nineteenth century indentured workers from India replaced the plantation slaves. In 1965 Britain created the British Indian Ocean Territory from several of Mauritius's dependencies, promising the return of the islands when they were no longer of military value to the United Kingdom. Mauritius gained independence in 1968. ∎

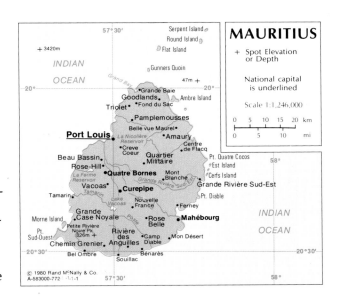

Mauritius Map Index

	Lat.	Long.		Lat.	Long.
Amaury	20°08'S	57°40'E	Port Louis	20°10'S	57°30'E
Beau Bassin	20°13'S	57°27'E	Quartier Militaire	20°15'S	57°35'E
Chemin Grenier	20°29'S	57°27'E	Quatre Bornes	20°15'S	57°28'E
Curepipe	20°19'S	57°31'E	Quatre Cocos,		
Goodlands	20°02'S	57°38'E	Point	20°14'S	57°46'E
Grande Case			Rivière des		
Noyale	20°25'S	57°22'E	Anguilles	20°29'S	57°32'E
Grande Rivière			Rose Belle	20°24'S	57°36'E
Sud-Est	20°17'S	57°46'E	Rose-Hill	20°14'S	57°27'E
Mahébourg	20°24'S	57°42'E	Round Island	19°51'S	57°48'E
Pamplemousses	20°26'S	57°34'E	Sud-Ouest, Point	20°28'S	57°47'E
Petite Rivière			Triolet	20°03'S	57°32'E
Noire Peak	20°24'S	57°24'E	Vacoas	20°18'S	57°29'E

MAYOTTE

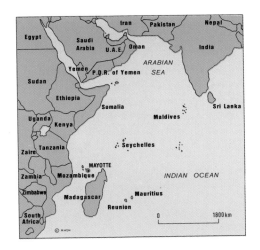

OFFICIAL NAME Territorial Collectivity of Mayotte

PEOPLE
Population 63,000.
Density 438/mi² (169/km²).
Capital Dzaoudzi, 4,147.
Ethnic groups Mahorais.
Languages French, Mahorian.
Religions Sunni Muslim.

POLITICS
Government Territorial collectivity (France).
Parties Mahorian Democratic Rally, Mahorian Popular, Mahorian Rally.

Subdivisions 17 communes.

ECONOMY
Monetary unit French franc.
Trade partners France, Kenya, South Africa, Pakistan, Reunion.
Exports Ylang-ylang, vanilla.
Imports Building materials, transportation equipment, rice, clothing, flour.

LAND
Description Southeastern African islands.
Area 144 mi² (373 km²).

PEOPLE. Of Malagasy descent, Mahorais are the main ethnic group on French-ruled Mayotte, and most of the population is Sunni Muslim. French, the official language, is used for commercial affairs, but most Mahorais speak Mahorian, an Arab dialect of Swahili. Both the French and Malagasy cultures have influenced the people of Mayotte.

ECONOMY AND THE LAND. Mayotte's cash crops include ylang-ylang, vanilla, coffee, copra, cinnamon, and cloves, and the lobster and shrimp industries are expanding. The territorial collectivity comprises the volcanic island of Mayotte; the small island of Pamanzi; and several other islands. The climate is tropical.

HISTORY AND POLITICS. Part of the Comoro archipelago, Mayotte shares much of its early history with the nation of Comoros. The islands served as a link between Madagascar and the African mainland, and Mayotte became a cross-roads for invading Africans, Arabs, Indonesians, and Malagasy. In 1843 France took the island of Mayotte, then eventually expanded its control to the other Comoro Islands. When Comoros became independent in 1975, Mayotte remained under French rule. In 1976 Mayotte's people again voted to retain their ties with France and not join the independent country of Comoros. ∎

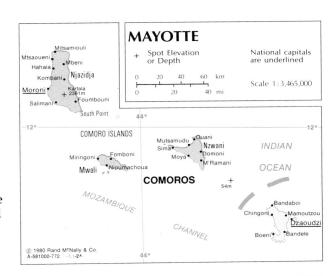

Mayotte Map Index

	Lat.	Long.		Lat.	Long.
Bandaboi	12°43'S	45°09'E	Chingoni	12°48'S	45°08'E
Bandele	12°55'S	45°13'E	Dzaoudzi	12°47'S	45°17'E
Boeni	12°55'S	45°06'E	Mamoutzou	12°47'S	45°14'E

MEXICO

OFFICIAL NAME United
Mexican States

PEOPLE
Population 78,670,000.
Density 103/mi² (40/km²).
Urban 67%.
Capital Mexico City, 9,373,400.
Ethnic groups Mestizo 60%, Amerindian 30%, white
9%.
Languages Spanish.
Religions Roman Catholic 97%, Protestant 3%.
Life expectancy 68 female, 64 male.
Literacy 74%.

POLITICS
Government Republic.
Parties Institutional Revolutionary, National Action,
Unified Socialist.
Suffrage Universal, over 18.
Memberships OAS, UN.
Subdivisions 31 states, 1 federal district.

ECONOMY
GDP $168,000,000,000.
Per capita $2,273.
Monetary unit Peso.
Trade partners U.S., Western European countries,
Japan.
Exports Petroleum, cotton, coffee, minerals.
Imports Machinery, industrial vehicles, intermediate
goods.

LAND
Description Southern North America.

Until about the tenth century A.D., Mexico's Yucatan Peninsula was the site of a flourishing Mayan civilization, and the ruins of Uxmal stand in evidence to that fact. This city was built during the Mayan Late Classic period, which lasted from about A.D. 600 to 900.

The era saw the Maya's greatest achievements in art and science and a blossoming of new architectural styles as well. Uxmal's ancient buildings, such as the one shown here, are examples of the Puuc style of architecture, named after a nearby hilly region.

Area 761,604 mi² (1,972,547 km²).
Highest point Orizaba Pk. (Citlaltépetl Volcano),
18,406 ft (5,610 m).
Lowest point Lake Salada, 26 ft (8 m) below sea level.

PEOPLE. Most Mexicans are mestizos, descended from Indians and the Spaniards who conquered Mexico in the 1500s. Spanish is spoken by most inhabitants, and Roman Catholicism is the most popular religion. Another major ethnic group is composed of indigenous Indians, or Amerindians, some of whom speak only Indian languages and hold traditional religious beliefs. Mexico's rapid population growth has contributed to poverty among rural dwellers, spurring a migration to the cities. A mild climate and fertile soils create a concentration of population on Mexico's central plateau.

ECONOMY AND THE LAND. Mexico is a leading producer of petroleum and silver, a growing manufacturer of iron, steel, and chemicals, and an exporter of coffee and cotton. Foreign visitors —drawn by archaeological sites and warm, sunny weather—make tourism an important activity. Despite vast gains made since the mid-1900s in agriculture and industry, the economy has recently been troubled by inflation, declining oil prices, unemployment arising from the popu-

lation boom, and a trade deficit that has grown with the need for imported materials. In recent years the peso has been significantly devalued, and banks have been nationalized to help reduce a massive international debt. Austerity plans and foreign aid are expected to help revitalize the economy. Terrain and climate are greatly varied, ranging from tropical jungles along the coast to desert plains in the north. A temperate central plateau is bounded by rugged mountains in the south, east, and west.

HISTORY AND POLITICS. Farm settlements grew up in the Valley of Mexico between 6500 and 1500 B.C., and during the subsequent three thousand years the area of present-day Mexico gave birth to the great civilizations of the Olmec, Maya, Toltec, and Aztec Indians. The Aztec Empire was overthrown by the Spanish in 1521, and Mexico became the viceroyalty of New Spain. Although there was much dissatisfaction with Spanish rule, rebellion did not begin until 1810. Formal independence came in 1821. Mexico lost considerable territory, including Texas, to the United States during the Mexican War, from 1846 to 1848. During subsequent years power changed hands frequently as liberals demanding social and economic reforms battled conservatives. A brief span of French imperial rule, from 1864 to 1867, interrupted the struggle. Following a revolution that started in 1910, a new constitution was adopted in 1917, and progress toward reform began, culminating in the separation of church and state and the redistribution of land. Mexico maintains close relations with the United States and is anxious to help mediate a peace in Central America. ■

Many Mexican villages preserve customs and rituals that have been passed down through the ages. These Totonac Indians are taking part in the fiesta of Corpus Christi at Popantla. This festival dates back to pagan times, but today the celebration combines elements of both Roman Catholic and ancient practices.

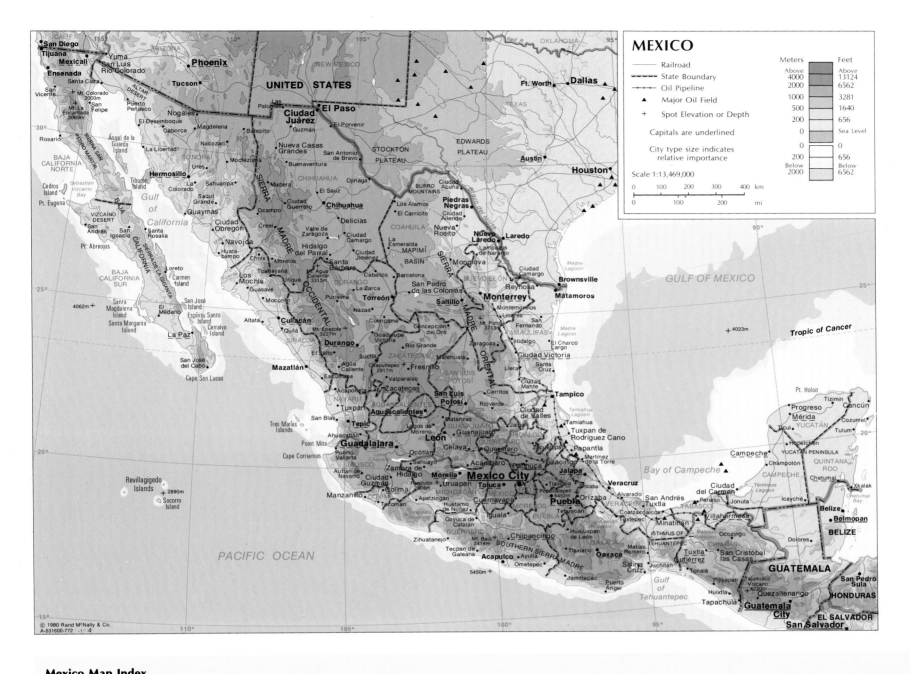

Mexico Map Index

MICRONESIA, FEDERATED STATES OF

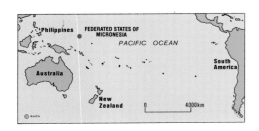

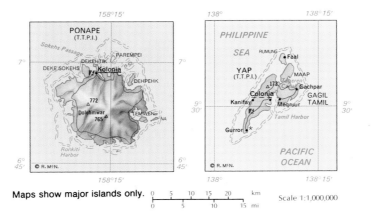

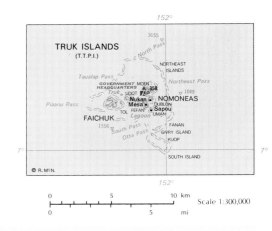

Maps show major islands only.   Scale 1:1,000,000   Scale 1:300,000

OFFICIAL NAME Federated
States of Micronesia

PEOPLE
Population 80,000.
Density 295/mi² (114/km²).
Urban 19%.
Capital Kolonia, Ponape I., 5,549.
Ethnic groups Micronesian.
Languages English, Malay-Polynesian languages.
Religions Protestant, Roman Catholic.

POLITICS
Government Part of Trust Territory of the Pacific
Islands (U.S.).
Suffrage Universal, over 18.
Subdivisions 4 states.

ECONOMY
Monetary unit U.S. dollar.

LAND
Description North Pacific Islands.
Area 271 mi² (702 km²).

PEOPLE. Most inhabitants of Truk, Yap, Kosrae,
and Ponape—the four states of the Federated

States of Micronesia—are Micronesian, a group
of mixed Melanesian, Polynesian, and Malaysian
origin.

ECONOMY AND THE LAND. Subsistence farming and fishing are the primary activities for
most islanders. Coconuts are the main cash crop.
The states continue to depend upon economic
assistance from the United States, however. Each
of the four states comprises a number of islands
and, together with the territory of Palau, forms
the Caroline archipelago, made up of volcanic
and coral islands. The climate is tropical.

HISTORY AND POLITICS. The ancestors of today's population probably arrived in the region
more than 2,500 years ago, although evidence
shows some islands may have been inhabited as
long as 4,000 years ago. Spanish and German
competition for the islands came to an end in
1899 when Germany purchased all the Caroline
and Mariana islands, except Guam, from Spain.
After Japanese occupation during World War I,
the islands became a League of Nations mandate
administered by Japan. In 1947 the islands be-

came part of the Trust Territory of the Pacific
Islands, which was established by the United
Nations and placed under United States administration. In 1978, Truk, Yap, Kosrae, and Ponape,
along with the Marshall Islands and Palau, voted
on a constitution that would unite Micronesia
into a single entity. The Marshall Islands and
Palau rejected the proposal, but Truk, Yap, Kosrae, and Ponape elected to become the Federated
States of Micronesia. The United States recognized the constitution in 1979, and in 1982 a
compact of free association was signed. The compact received final approval in 1986; however, the
change in status from trusteeship to independent
country requires that the United Nations officially rescind the trusteeship. ■

Federated States of Micronesia Map Index

	Lat.	Long.		Lat.	Long.
Colonia	9°31'N	138°08'E	Ponape	6°55'N	158°15'E
Kolonia	6°58'N	158°13'E	Truk Islands	7°25'N	151°47'E
Nukan	7°23'N	151°53'E	Yap	9°31'N	138°06'E

MIDWAY ISLANDS

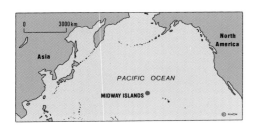

OFFICIAL NAME Midway
Islands

PEOPLE
Population 500.
Density 250/mi² (96/km²).
Ethnic groups American.
Languages English.

POLITICS
Government Unincorporated territory (U.S.).

LAND
Description North Pacific islands.
Area 2 mi² (5.2 km²).
Lowest point Sea level.

PEOPLE. Midway has no native peoples, and
United States military personnel and government
employees constitute the territory's population.
The Midway Islands are within a Naval Defense
Sea Area; therefore, no one can come to the
islands without first receiving permission from
the United States navy.

ECONOMY AND THE LAND. The strategically
situated Midway Islands are used as a United
States naval station and air base. Sand Island is

the site of an airstrip that is used only for military supply flights and as a refueling station for
military aircraft. The meteorological division of
the United States navy operates a weather station on the Midway Islands, conducting research
and providing data for world use. In addition to
the naval property, a portion of the islands has
been designated a national wildlife reserve administered by the United States Department of
the Interior. The bird life protected here includes
albatross, frigate birds, and terns. The islands of
Midway are situated approximately 1,200 miles
(1,931 kilometers) northwest of the U.S. state of
Hawaii. The unincorporated territory is made up
of a coral atoll that encircles two islands, Sand
and Eastern. The climate is tropical.

HISTORY AND POLITICS. In 1859 Captain N. C.
Brooks of the Hawaiian ship *Gambia* discovered
the uninhabited islands, and for a time Midway
was known as Brooks Island. Captain William
Reynolds was the next American to arrive, and
in 1867, sailing on the U.S.S. *Lackawana*, he
claimed Midway as a United States possession.
United States president Theodore Roosevelt declared Midway a naval reservation in 1903, and a
cable relay station was erected that same year.
Development of the island by the United States
continued, and in the 1930s a commercial airport
and facilities for housing airplane travelers over-
night were built. In 1939 construction workers
from the United States began turning Eastern
Island into a submarine and air base. By August
1941 their work had been completed, and in De-
cember of that year the Japanese attacked Midway on their return flight from the bombing of
Pearl Harbor. Throughout World War II, the Japanese were unable to capture the island. From
June 4 to June 6, 1942, United States planes at-

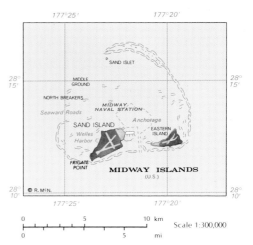

Midway Islands Map Index

	Lat.	Long.		Lat.	Long.
Eastern Island	28°12'N	177°20'W	Sand Islet	28°16'N	177°23'W
Frigate Point	28°11'N	177°24'W	Seaward Roads	28°13'N	177°25'W
Sand Island	28°12'N	177°23'W	Welles Harbor	28°12'N	177°26'W

tacked a Japanese fleet off the shores of Midway.
Four of Japan's aircraft carriers and one cruiser
were destroyed in the battle, virtually crippling
the Japanese navy. Losses on the United
States side included an aircraft carrier and a de-
stroyer. This sea-and-air battle became known as
the Battle of Midway, and many believe the
United States victory at Midway was the turning
point of the war in the Pacific. Today, Midway
continues its role as naval station and air base for
the United States military. The Midway Islands'
political status is that of unincorporated territory
of the United States, and the Department of the
Navy administers the islands. ■

MONACO

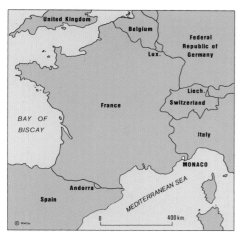

OFFICIAL NAME Principality
of Monaco

PEOPLE
Population 28,000.
Density 46,667/mi² (18,667/km²).
Urban 100%.
Capital Monaco, 25,000.
Ethnic groups French 58%, Monegasque 19%, Italian
17%.
Languages French, Monegasque, Italian, English.
Religions Roman Catholic 95%.
Literacy 99%.

POLITICS
Government Constitutional monarchy.
Parties National and Democratic Union, Socialist.
Suffrage Universal adult.
Memberships None.

ECONOMY
Monetary Unit French franc.

LAND
Description Southern Europe.
Area 0.6 mi² (1.5 km²).
Highest point 459 ft (140 m).
Lowest point Sea level.

PEOPLE. Monaco is inhabited mostly by French
citizens. Monegasques, of indigenous descent,
and Italians form the rest of the population.
Many foreigners have taken up residence, drawn
by the country's tax benefits. French is the official language. Monegasque, a blend of French
and Italian, is also spoken, as are Italian and
English. Most residents are Roman Catholic.

ECONOMY AND THE LAND. Monaco's beautiful seaside location, mild Mediterranean climate,
and famous gambling casino in Monte Carlo
make it a popular tourist haven. Consequently,
tourism forms the backbone of the economy.
Production of chemicals, food products, and perfumes, among other light industries, are additional sources of income. Monaco also profits
from many foreign businesses, attracted by the
favorable tax climate, that are headquartered in
the principality. France and Monaco form a customs union for a mutually beneficial trade system; the French franc is Monaco's official currency. The world's second smallest independent
state in area—after Vatican City—Monaco has
four regions: the old city of Monaco-Ville, site of
the royal palace; Monte Carlo, the resort and
major tourist center; La Condamine, the port
area; and Fontvieille, the rapidly growing industrial section.

HISTORY AND POLITICS. Known to the Phoenicians, Greeks, and Romans, the region became a
Genoese colony in the twelfth century A.D.

Around the turn of the fourteenth century, the
area was granted to the Grimaldi family of
Genoa. France, Spain, and Sardinia had intermittent control of Monaco from 1400 until 1861,
when its autonomy was recognized by the
Franco-Monegasque Treaty. Another treaty, providing for French protection of Monaco, was
signed in 1918. The absolute rule of Monaco's
princes ended with the 1911 constitution. ∎

**The glittering nightlife of Monte Carlo draws thousands
of visitors to Monaco each year, making this Riviera
resort a major contributor to the principality's
tourism-based economy.**

MONGOLIA

OFFICIAL NAME Mongolian
People's Republic

PEOPLE
Population 1,885,000.
Density 3.1/mi² (1.2/km²).
Urban 51%.
Capital Ulan Bator, 435,400.
Ethnic groups Mongol 90%, Kazakh 4%, Chinese 2%,
Russian 2%.
Languages Khalkha Mongol.
Religions Tibetan Buddhist, Muslim.
Life expectancy 65 female, 61 male.
Literacy 80%.

POLITICS
Government Socialist republic.
Parties People's Revolutionary.
Suffrage Universal, over 18.
Memberships CEMA, UN.

Subdivisions 18 provinces, 3 autonomous cities.

ECONOMY
GDP $1,200,000,000.
Per capita $860.
Monetary unit Tugrik.
Trade partners U.S.S.R.
Exports Livestock, animal products, wool, hides,
minerals.
Imports Machinery, petroleum, clothing,
construction materials.

LAND
Description Central Asia, landlocked.
Area 604,250 mi² (1,565,000 km²).
Highest point 14,350 ft (4,374 m).
Lowest point Höh Lake, 1,814 ft (553 m).

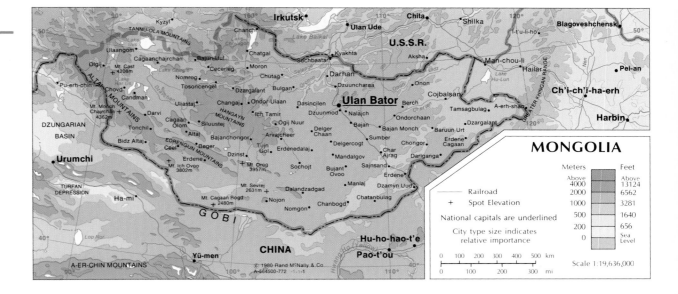

Mongolia Map Index

	Lat.	Long.		Lat.	Long.
Altai Mountains	48°00'N	90°00'E	Monch		
Cherlen	48°48'N	117°00'E	Chajrchan,		
Chovsgol, Lake	51°00'N	100°30'E	Mount	46°45'N	91°30'E
Cojbalsan	48°34'N	114°50'E	Onon	51°42'N	115°50'E
Darhan	49°28'N	105°56'E	Orchon	50°21'N	106°05'E
Gobi	43°00'N	106°00'E	Selenge	52°16'N	106°16'E
Hangayn			Ulan Bator	47°55'N	106°53'E
Mountains	47°30'N	100°00'E	Uvs, Lake	50°20'N	92°45'E

PEOPLE. Mongols, a central Asian people, make
up the vast majority of Mongolia's population.
Several Mongol groups exist, the largest of which
is the Khalkha; Khalkha Mongol is the predominant language. Turkic-speaking Kazakhs as well
as Russians and Chinese constitute minorities.

Tibetan Buddhism was once the most common religion; however, the government now discourages religious practice. The traditional nomadic way of life is becoming less common as recent government policies have led to urbanization and settled agriculture. Animal raising and herding, however, continue as a way of life for the majority of Mongolians.

ECONOMY AND THE LAND. Mongolia's economy, long based on the raising of livestock, has been shaped by the ideal grazing land found in most of the country. But significant economic changes have occurred since 1924, including the collectivization and modernization of farming, the introduction of industry, and the exploitation of mineral resources. Today, herders are organized into collectives, and state farms enable Mongolians to practice large-scale agriculture. Although dependent on Soviet aid, Mongolia has made considerable progress toward diversifying and developing its economy. Mongolia's terrain varies from mountains in the north and west to steppe in the east and desert in the south. Located in the heart of Asia, remote from any moderating body of water, Mongolia has a rigorous continental climate with little precipitation.

HISTORY AND POLITICS. Mongolian tribes were united under the warlord Genghis Khan around A.D. 1200, and he and his successors built one of history's largest land empires. In 1691 the Manchu dynasty of China subdued Outer Mongolia, as the area was then known, but allowed the Mongol rulers autonomy. Until the Mongols ousted the Chinese in 1911, Outer Mongolia remained a Chinese province. In 1912 the state accepted Russian protection but was unable to prevent a subsequent Chinese ad-

For hundreds of years nomadic herders in Mongolia have traveled the plains, seeking grazing land for their livestock and living in circular felt tents called "yurts." This traditional way of life is becoming more rare, however, as government programs aid nomads in settling permanently on farms and in towns. Shown here is a yurt settlement outside the capital city of Ulan Bator.

vance, and in 1919 Outer Mongolia again became a Chinese province. In 1921 a combined Soviet and Mongolian force defeated Chinese and Belorussian, or White Russian, troops, and the Mongolian People's Republic was declared in 1924. A mutual-assistance pact was signed by Mongolia and Russia in 1966. Today Mongolia continues to support Soviet foreign policy. ∎

MONTSERRAT

OFFICIAL NAME Montserrat

PEOPLE
Population 12,000.
Density 300/mi² (117/km²).
Urban 11%.
Capital Plymouth, 1,568.

Ethnic groups Black.
Languages English.
Religions Anglican, Methodist, Roman Catholic.
Literacy 77%.

POLITICS
Government Colony (U.K.).
Parties People's Liberation Movement, Progressive Democratic.
Suffrage Universal, over 18.
Subdivisions 3 parishes.

ECONOMY
GNP $32,400,000.
Per capita $2,760.
Monetary unit Eash Caribbean dollar.
Trade partners U.K., U.S., Trinidad and Tobago.
Exports Plastic bage, electronic parts, textiles, hot peppers.
Imports Machinery and transportation equipment, foodstuffs, manufactured goods.

LAND
Description Caribbean island.
Area 40 mi² (103 km²).
Highest point Chances Pk. 3,000 ft (914 m).
Lowest point Sea level.

PEOPLE. Most of Montserrat's people are black descendants of African slaves, nearly all are English speaking, and the majority belong to the Anglican church. A number of the island's early settlers were Irish, and traces of an Irish brogue can still be heard in the speech of some residents. The culture, however, is distinctly West Indian.

ECONOMY AND THE LAND. The late 1970s and early 1980s saw an influx of light industry to Montserrat, with companies taking advantage of the island's tax benefits. Until recently, agriculture had been on the decline, but emphasis on the production of Sea Island cotton and vegetable crops helped to revive that sector somewhat. Tourism is an important economic contributor, yet the island remains unspoiled by commercialism. The volcanic island of Montserrat is rugged and mountainous, and the climate is tropical.

HISTORY AND POLITICS. Christopher Columbus reached the island in 1493, naming it after the Spanish monastery of Santa Maria de Montserrat. In 1632 British and Irish settlers arrived from St. Christopher, and later in the seventeenth century many more Irish immigrants came to Montserrat via Virginia. Sugar cultivation began in 1650, and Africans were brought as slaves to work on the plantations. In 1664 the French took the island, and the British were not able to regain control until four years later. In 1782 France again overpowered the British for

possession of Montserrat, but it returned to British rule the next year. Slavery was ended in 1834, and the island's sugar, lime, and cotton industries declined soon after. In 1966 Montserrat residents chose to remain a colony rather than become an associate state of the United Kingdom. Although some islanders desire independence, most residents seem to prefer colonial status. ∎

This old, unused sugar mill is a legacy from Montserrat's early colonial period, when sugar and slaves fueled a prosperous economy. Descendants of the slaves now compose Montserrat's major population group.

MOROCCO

OFFICIAL NAME Kingdom of Morocco

PEOPLE
Population 21,750,000.
Density 126/mi² (49/km²).
Urban 42%.
Capital Rabat, 367,620.
Ethnic groups Arab-Berber 99%.
Languages Arabic, Berber dialects, French.
Religions Muslim 99%.
Life expectancy 59 female, 55 male.
Literacy 28%.

POLITICS
Government Constitutional monarchy.
Parties Istiqlal, National Assembly of Independents, Popular Movement, Socialist Union of Popular Forces.
Suffrage Universal, over 20.
Memberships AL, UN.
Subdivisions 39 provinces, 2 prefectures.

ECONOMY
GNP $15,200,000,000.
Per capita $640.
Monetary unit Dirham.
Trade partners France, Spain, Saudi Arabia, West Germany.
Exports Phosphates, food, consumer goods.
Imports Petroleum, food, machinery.

LAND
Description Northern Africa.
Area 172,414 mi² (446,550 km²).
Highest point Mt. Toubkal, 13,665 ft (4,165 m).
Lowest point Sebkha Tah, 180 ft (55 m) below sea level.

PEOPLE. Moroccans are virtually homogeneous in race and culture; most are a mixture of Arab and Berber stocks and speak Arabic. A few Berber dialects are spoken in rural mountain areas, and French and Spanish, the colonial tongues, are common in business and government. The majority of people are Sunni Muslim. The population is concentrated west of the Atlas Mountains, which border the Sahara Desert. Migrations from rural areas to cities, where the standard of living is higher, have been the trend.

ECONOMY AND THE LAND. Although agriculture employs much of the work force and is an important activity, the nation depends on mining for most of its income. Morocco is a leading exporter of phosphates and has other mineral reserves. Fishing and tourism are growing sources of revenue. Such recent developments as severe drought, rising dependency on imported oil, and a costly war in Western Sahara have slowed productivity, while investment by Arab countries has bolstered the economy. Morocco, with its varied terrain of desert, forests, and mountains, has an equally varied climate that is semitropical along the coast, and desert beyond the Atlas Mountains.

HISTORY AND POLITICS. In ancient times Morocco was a province of Carthage and Rome.

Vandals and Byzantine Greeks, the subsequent rulers, were followed in the A.D. 700s by Arabs, who brought Islam. Morocco's strategic position awakened the interest of colonial powers in the 1800s, and by 1912 the area was divided into French and Spanish protectorates. A nationalist movement began in the twenties, occasionally bringing violence, but not until 1956 did Morocco become independent from France. The last of Spain's holdings in Morocco were returned in 1969. War broke out in 1976, when Morocco claimed the northern part of Western Sahara and was challenged by the Saharan nationalist Polisario Front. Although Mauritania, which had been involved in the war and had been fighting for southern Western Sahara, surrendered its claim in 1979, Morocco has continued to battle the Polisario Front. ■

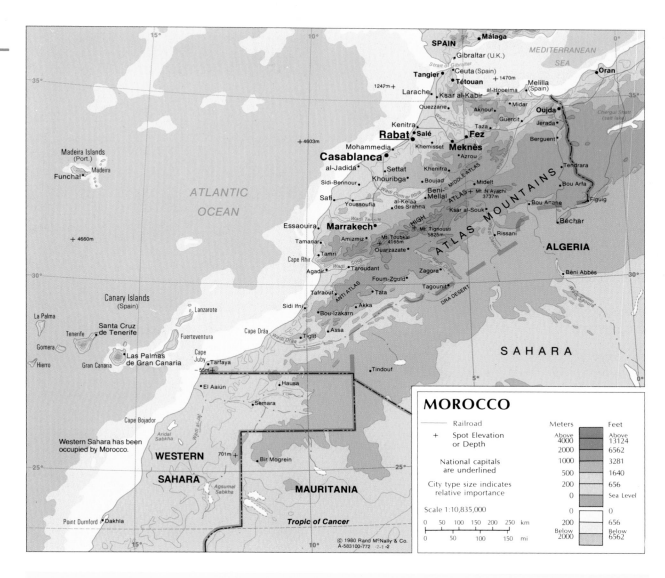

Marrakech, in central Morocco, is a bustling Arab-Berber city with a history dating back to the eleventh century. Colorful gardens, palaces, and mosques add interest to this picturesque town at the foot of the Atlas Mountains, and much of the town's activity takes place in Marrakech's main square, the Djemaa el Fna, shown here. Each day from early morning until sundown, people congregate in the square to watch jugglers, snake charmers, acrobats, and dancers; to listen to storytellers acting out their tales; and to barter for goods with the craftspeople at the bazaars.

Morocco Map Index

	Lat.	Long.		Lat.	Long.		Lat.	Long.		Lat.	Long.
al-Jadida	33°16'N	8°30'W	High Atlas	31°30'N	6°00'W	Moulouya, Wadi	35°05'N	2°25'W	Tangier	35°48'N	5°45'W
Anti Atlas	30°00'N	8°30'W	Juby, Cape	27°58'N	12°55'W	Oujda	34°41'N	1°45'W	Tétouan	35°34'N	5°23'W
Atlas Mountains	32°00'N	4°00'W	Kasar al Kabir	35°01'N	5°54'W	Oum er Rbia,			Tignousti, Mount	31°31'N	6°44'W
Beni-Mellal	32°22'N	6°29'W	Kenitra	34°16'N	6°40'W	Wadi	33°19'N	8°21'W	Toubkal, Mount	31°05'N	7°55'W
Casablanca	33°39'N	7°35'W	Khouribga	32°54'N	6°57'W	Rabat	34°02'N	6°51'W			
Drâa, Wadi	28°43'N	11°09'W	Larache	35°12'N	6°10'W	Rhir, Cape	30°38'N	9°55'W			
Essaouira	31°30'N	9°47'W	Marrakech	31°38'N	8°00'W	Safi	32°20'N	9°17'W			
Fez	34°05'N	4°57'W	Meknès	33°53'N	5°37'W	Salé	34°04'N	6°50'W			
Gibraltar, Strait			Middle Atlas	33°30'N	5°00'W	Sebou, Wadi	34°15'N	6°40'W			
of	35°57'N	5°36'W	Mohammedia	33°44'N	7°24'W	Settat	33°04'N	7°37'W			

MOZAMBIQUE

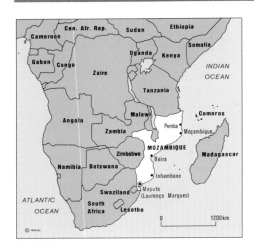

OFFICIAL NAME People's
Republic of Mozambique

PEOPLE
Population 13,700,000.
Density 45/mi² (17/km²).
Urban 15%.
Capital Maputo, 739,077.
Ethnic groups African 99%.
Languages Portuguese, indigenous.
Religions Indigenous 60%, Christian 30%, Muslim 10%.
Life expectancy 48 female, 44 male.
Literacy 14%.

POLITICS
Government Socialist republic.
Parties Liberation Front.
Suffrage Universal adult.
Memberships OAU, UN.
Subdivisions 11 provinces.

ECONOMY
GNP $1,500,000,000.
Per capita $150.
Monetary unit Metical.
Trade partners Portugal, South Africa, U.S., West Germany, U.K.
Exports Cashews, shrimp, sugar, tea, cotton.
Imports Machinery, petroleum, motor vehicles, electrical equipment.

LAND
Description Southern Africa.
Area 302,329 mi² (783,030 km²).
Highest point Mt. Binga, 7,992 ft (2,436 m).
Lowest point Sea level.

PEOPLE. Black Africans belonging to about ten groups compose the vast majority of Mozambique's population. Most black Mozambicans live in rural areas, while small European and Asian minorities live primarily in urban centers. Traditional African religions are followed by a majority, but Islam and Christianity also have adherents. Although Portuguese is the official language, most blacks speak Bantu tongues.

ECONOMY AND THE LAND. Mozambique's underdeveloped economy is largely the product of its colonial past, during which its human and natural resources were neglected. Recent political developments in southern Africa have created more economic woes, as lucrative trade agreements with racially divided neighbors have ceased. The mainstays of the economy are agriculture and transport services. Fishing and mining are being developed, and the Marxist government has allowed some private enterprise. Foreign aid is important. The climate is tropical or subtropical along the coastal plain that covers nearly half of the country, with cooler conditions in the western high plateaus and mountains.

HISTORY AND POLITICS. Bantu-speaking peoples settled in present-day Mozambique around the first century A.D. Subsequent immigrants included Arab traders in the 800s and the Portuguese in the late 1400s. Portuguese trading posts

Mozambique's ocean coastline stretches for 1,534 miles (2,470 kilometers). Busy harbors such as this one handle trade for the nation's landlocked neighbors.

were established, and prospectors and traders made their way inland seeking gold and slaves. In the early 1900s Portugal transferred much of the administration of Mozambique to private companies seeking to profit from the use of Mozambique as a trade route for cheap labor for nearby British colonies. Here as elsewhere in Africa colonial policies benefited European settlers while overlooking the welfare of Mozambique and its native inhabitants. Opposition to foreign rule crystallized with the formation in the early 1960s of the Mozambique Liberation Front, a Marxist nationalist group that initiated an armed campaign against the Portuguese. Mozambique finally attained its independence in 1975, following a 1974 coup in Portugal that installed a government opposed to the country's colonial policies. Since independence Mozambique has had to face many problems, including an ongoing armed struggle against an insurgent group known as the Mozambican National Resistance (MNR, or RENAMO). This antigovernment group was created in the 1970s by the white-minority government that had seized power in Rhodesia, now Zimbabwe, and Mozambique's fight against RENAMO continues to take a heavy toll. In an attempt to ease some of its economic problems, in 1984 Mozambique signed a nonaggression pact with South Africa, whose policies Mozambique opposes. By this agreement South Africa will discontinue its support for RENAMO, and Mozambique will not provide bases for anti-apartheid groups fighting South Africa's current regime. The pact provides for economic benefits as well, but continued guerrilla fighting and food shortages have created a crisis situation in Mozambique. ■

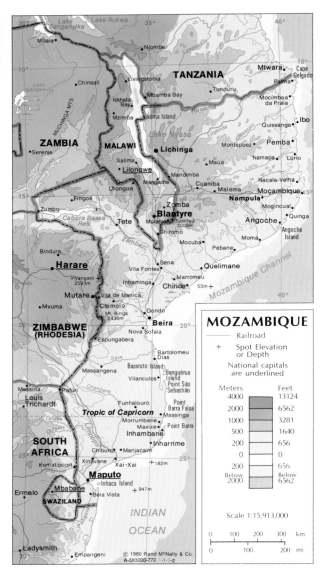

Mozambique Map Index

	Lat.	Long.		Lat.	Long.
Angoche	16°14′S	39°58′E	Maputo	25°58′S	32°35′E
Barra, Point	23°45′S	35°30′E	Moçambique	15°03′S	40°42′E
Beira	19°50′S	34°52′E	Mozambique		
Cabora Bassa			Channel	18°00′S	39°00′E
Reservoir	15°40′S	31°30′E	Nampula	15°07′S	39°15′E
Chilwa, Lake	15°12′S	35°50′E	Nyasa, Lake	12°00′S	34°30′E
Chinde	18°37′S	36°24′E	Pemba	12°57′S	40°30′E
Delgado, Cape	10°40′S	40°35′E	Quelimane	17°53′S	36°51′E
Ibo	12°20′S	40°35′E	Rovuma	10°29′S	40°28′E
Inhaca Island	26°03′S	32°57′E	São Sebastião,		
Inhambane	23°51′S	35°29′E	Point	22°07′S	35°30′E
Inharrime	24°29′S	35°01′E	Save (Sabi)	21°00′S	35°02′E
Limpopo	25°15′S	33°30′E	Tete	16°13′S	33°35′E
Lugenda	11°25′S	38°33′E	Zambezi	18°55′S	36°04′E
Lúrio	13°35′S	40°32′E			

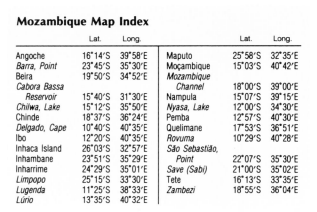

Mozambique's long coastline and natural harbors offer potential for recreational use as well as commercial development.

NAMIBIA

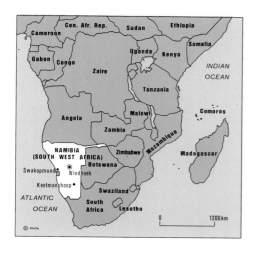

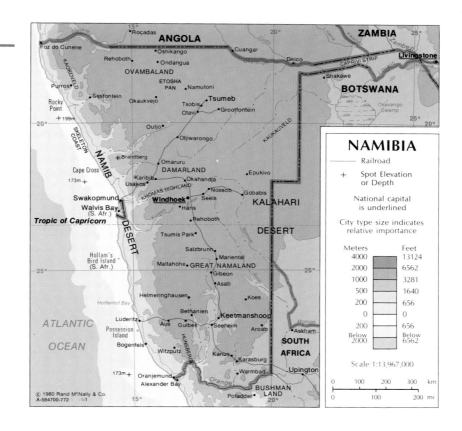

NAMIBIA

— Railroad

+ Spot Elevation
or Depth

National capital
is underlined

City type size indicates
relative importance

Meters		Feet
4000		13124
2000		6562
1000		3281
500		1640
200		656
0		0
200		656
Below 2000		Below 6562

Scale 1:13,967,000

0 100 200 300 km
0 100 200 mi

© 1980 Rand McNally & Co.
A-584700-772 -1-1

Namibia Map Index

	Lat.	Long.
Auob	26°25'S	20°35'E
Brandberg	21°10'S	14°33'E
Caprivi Strip	17°59'S	23°00'E
Cunene	17°20'S	11°50'E
Fish	28°07'S	17°45'E
Kalahari Desert	23°00'S	20°00'E
Kaokoveld	21°00'S	14°20'E
Kaukauveld	20°00'S	20°30'E
Keetmanshoop	26°36'S	18°08'E
Namib Desert	23°00'S	15°00'E
Nossob	26°55'S	20°37'E
Okavango	18°15'S	21°48'E
Orange	28°41'S	16°28'E
Skeleton Coast	21°00'S	13°00'E
Swakopmund	22°41'S	14°34'E
Tsumeb	19°13'S	17°42'E
Windhoek	22°34'S	17°06'E
Zambezi	17°48'S	25°14'E

OFFICIAL NAME Namibia

PEOPLE
Population 1,095,000.
Density 3.4/mi² (1.3/km²).
Urban 45%.
Capital Windhoek, 88,700.
Ethnic groups Black 86%, white 7%, mixed 7%.
Languages Afrikaans, indigenous.
Religions Christian, indigenous.
Life expectancy 53 female, 50 male.
Literacy 100% whites, 28% nonwhites.

POLITICS
Government Under South African administration.
Parties Action Front for the Preservation of the Turnhalle Principles, Democratic Turnhalle Alliance, South West Africa People's Organization.
Suffrage Universal adult.
Memberships None.
Subdivisions 26 districts.

ECONOMY
GNP $2,010,000,000.
Per capita $1,879.
Monetary unit South African rand.
Trade partners South Africa, West Germany, U.K., U.S.
Exports Diamonds, copper, lead, cattle, fish products.
Imports Food, construction materials, manufactured goods.

LAND
Description Southern Africa.
Area 318,261 mi² (824,292 km²).
Highest point Brandberg, 8,461 ft (2,579 m).
Lowest point Sea level.
The above information excludes Walvis Bay.

PEOPLE. The largest ethnic group is black African, composed of many indigenous peoples. South Africans, Britons, and Germans constitute the white minority. Black Namibians speak various native dialects, while the majority of whites speak Afrikaans. Traditional customs and religions are still followed by blacks, but a considerable number have converted to Christianity. Whites control economic and political life in Namibia, which is governed by South Africa.

ECONOMY AND THE LAND. Namibia's economy depends on the mining of diamonds, copper, lead, and other minerals, and Namibia is Africa's fourth-largest exporter of minerals. Recent fluctuations in prices on the world market, however, have cut into profits from the mining sector. Agriculture makes a marginal contribution, but livestock raising is important. Manufacturing remains undeveloped because of an unskilled work force, and Namibia imports most of its finished goods from South Africa, its partner in a customs union. A variety of factors, including continuing drought and political instability, have held back economic growth. Namibia consists of a high plateau that encompasses the Namib Desert and part of the Kalahari Desert. The climate is subtropical.

HISTORY AND POLITICS. Bushmen were probably the area's first inhabitants, followed by other African peoples. European exploration of the coast began in the A.D. 1500s, but the coastal desert prevented foreign penetration. In 1884 Germany annexed all of the territory except for the coastal enclave of Walvis Bay, which had been claimed by Britain in 1878. After South African troops ousted the Germans from the area during World War I, the League of Nations mandated Namibia, then known as South West Africa, to South Africa. Following World War II the United Nations requested that the territory become a trusteeship. South Africa refused to cooperate. In 1966 the United Nations revoked South Africa's mandate, yet South Africa kept control of Namibia. In the 1960s the South West African People's Organization (SWAPO) was formed, a nationalist group made up primarily of dissidents eager to see Namibia gain independence. In 1966 SWAPO began guerrilla raids on South African bases in Namibia, and in 1973 the United Nations recognized SWAPO as the legitimate representative of the Namibian people. A 1978 United Nations plan for the withdrawal of South African troops from Namibia was unsuccessful, and negotiations for independence continued into the late 1980s. ■

These Herero women are wearing the nineteenth-century dress introduced by the wives of missionaries. One of Namibia's many Bantu groups, the Herero were nearly wiped out during German colonial rule.

NAURU

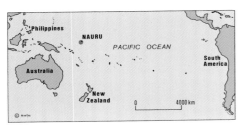

OFFICIAL NAME Republic of
Nauru

PEOPLE
Population 7,800.
Density 951/mi² (371/km²).
Capital Yaren District.
Ethnic groups Nauruan 58%, other Pacific Islander
26%, Chinese 8%, European 8%.
Languages Nauruan, English.
Religions Protestant 67%, Roman Catholic 33%.
Literacy 99%.

POLITICS
Government Republic.
Parties Governing faction (not a formal party), Nauru
(the opposition).
Suffrage Universal adult.
Memberships CW.
Subdivisions 14 districts.

ECONOMY
GNP $155,400,000.
Per capita $21,400.
Monetary unit Australian dollar.
Trade partners Australia, New Zealand.
Exports Phosphates.
Imports Food, fuels, water.

LAND
Description South Pacific island.

Area 8.2 mi² (21 km²).
Highest point 210 ft (64 m).
Lowest point Sea level.

PEOPLE. The original settlers of Nauru were of
Melanesian, Micronesian, and Polynesian stock,
and centuries of intermarriage has resulted in the
homogeneous Nauruan group found on the island today. Their language, Nauruan, is likewise
a mixture of several tongues, combining elements from the languages of the Gilbert, Caroline, Marshall, and Solomon islands. English is
widely spoken as well. Minority groups on
Nauru include immigrants from other Pacific islands, Europeans, and Chinese. All Nauruans
are Christian.

ECONOMY AND THE LAND. Some of the
world's richest phosphate deposits are found on
Nauru, and although tourism provides some
income, phosphate mining is the island's economic mainstay. Unlike most countries dependent upon a single resource, Nauru has planned
for future security by investing profits in long-
term trust funds to support the islanders when
the phosphate deposits are depleted. Agriculture
is limited, and the main crop is coconuts, with
small amounts of vegetables grown mostly by
the Chinese population. Small-scale livestock
raising and fishing provide additional food sources, but aside from this, all food must be imported. However, government subsidies make imports available to citizens at a low cost. The
nation has no taxes, and per capita income is
high. Most of the coral island is a plateau, and
the climate is tropical.

HISTORY AND POLITICS. The island was most
likely settled by castaways from nearby islands
who inadvertently drifted to Nauru's shores.

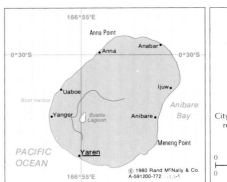
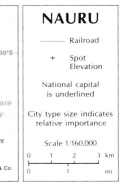

Nauru Map Index

	Lat.	Long.		Lat.	Long.
Anabar	0°30'S	166°57'E	Ijuw	0°30'S	166°57'E
Anibare	0°32'S	166°57'E	*Meneng Point*	0°32'S	166°57'E
Anibare Bay	0°32'S	166°57'E	Uaboe	0°31'S	166°55'E
Anna	0°30'S	166°56'E	Yangor	0°31'S	166°54'E
Anna Point	0°30'S	166°56'E	Yaren	0°32'S	166°55'E
Buada Lagoon	0°31'S	166°55'E			

Noted by a British explorer in 1798, Nauru remained autonomous much longer than most
other Pacific islands. The nineteenth century,
however, saw the arrival of European traders
who furnished the islanders with firearms, exac-
erbating tribal rivalries and leading to much
bloodshed. Germany controlled Nauru from 1881
to 1914, when it surrendered the island to Australia soon after the outbreak of World War I.
Nauru was subsequently mandated to Australia,
Britain, and New Zealand, and World War II
brought Japanese occupation. The island reverted
to Australian rule in 1947 as a trusteeship. It
became independent in 1968 and gained control
of European interests in the phosphate industry
in 1970. ∎

NEPAL

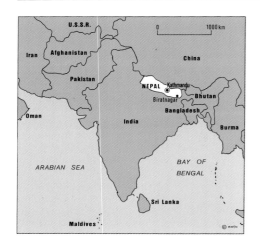

OFFICIAL NAME Kingdom of
Nepal

PEOPLE
Population 16,785,000.
Density 299/mi² (115/km²).
Urban 5%.
Capital Kathmandu, 235,160.
Ethnic groups Brahman, Chetri, Gurung, Magar,
others.
Languages Nepali.
Religions Hindu 88%, Buddhist.
Life expectancy 44 female, 45 male.
Literacy 20%.

POLITICS
Government Constitutional monarchy.
Parties None.
Suffrage Universal, over 21.
Memberships UN.

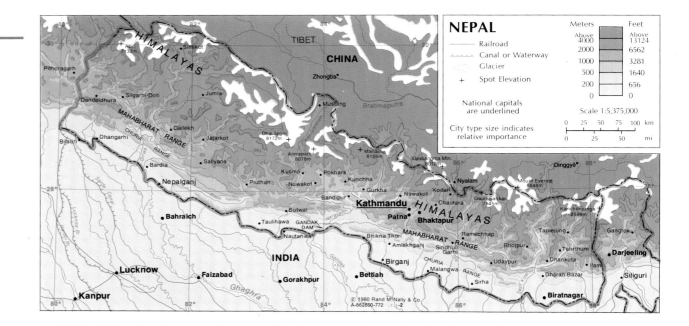

Nepal Map Index

	Lat.	Long.		Lat.	Long.			Lat.	Long.		Lat.	Long.
Bhaktapur	27°42'N	85°27'E	Girwa	28°15'N	81°05'E		Mahabharat			Sun Kosi	26°55'N	87°09'E
Biratnagar	26°29'N	87°17'E	Himalayas	28°00'N	84°00'E		Range	27°40'N	84°30'E	Xixabangma		
Birganj	27°00'N	84°52'E	Kanchenjunga	27°42'N	88°08'E		Manaslu	28°33'N	84°33'E	Mountain	28°22'N	85°50'E
Dhaulagiri	28°42'N	83°30'E	Kathmandu	27°43'N	85°19'E		Nepalganj	28°03'N	81°37'E			
Everest, Mount	27°59'N	86°56'E					Patna	27°41'N	85°20'E			

Subdivisions 14 zones.

ECONOMY
GDP $2,300,000,000.
Per capita $149.
Monetary unit Rupee.
Trade partners India.
Exports Rice, food, jute, wood.

Imports Consumer goods, fuels, machinery,
fertilizer, food.

LAND
Description Southern Asia, landlocked.
Area 56,135 mi² (145,391 km²).
Highest point Mt. Everest, 29,028 ft (8,848 m).
Lowest point 197 ft (60 m).

PEOPLE. Nepal's mixed population results from migrations over the centuries from India, Tibet, and central Asia. Most of Nepal's ruling families have been of Indian descent, and Nepali, the official language, is derived from Sanskrit, an ancient Indian language. Although the majority of the population practices Hinduism, Nepal is the birthplace of Buddha and has been greatly influenced by Buddhism as well. The importance of both religions is reflected in the more than 2,700 shrines in the Kathmandu Valley. Most Nepalese are rural farmers.

ECONOMY AND THE LAND. Because of geographic remoteness and a political policy of isolation lasting until the 1950s, Nepal's economy is one of the least developed in the world. Agriculture, concentrated chiefly in the south, is the most significant activity, even though most of Nepal is covered by the Himalayas, the world's highest mountains. This range—which includes Mount Everest, the world's highest peak—has made tourism increasingly lucrative. Nepal has potential in hydroelectricity and forestry, but inadequate transportation routes, overpopulation, and deforestation present obstacles to development. The country has received financial aid from many nations, partly because of its strategic location between India and China. The climate varies from subtropical in the flat, fertile south to temperate in the central hill country. Himalayan summers are cool and winters severe.

HISTORY AND POLITICS. Several small Hindu-Buddhist kingdoms had emerged in the Kathmandu Valley by about A.D. 300. These states were unified in the late 1700s by the founder of the Shah dynasty. The Rana family wrested control from the Shahs in 1846 and pursued an isola-

The Bhote, an ethnic group related to Tibetans, comprise many different populations whose cultures have developed in isolation from one another. These Bhote come from Yakba, a village in a remote area of western Nepal.

tionist course, which thwarted foreign influence but stunted economic growth. Opposition to the Ranas mounted during the 1930s and 1940s, and in 1951 the Shah monarchy was restored by a revolution. In 1962 the king established a government that gave the crown dominance and abolished political parties. A 1980 referendum narrowly upheld this system. ■

NETHERLANDS

OFFICIAL NAME Kingdom of the Netherlands

PEOPLE
Population 14,465,000.
Density 910/mi² (351/km²).
Urban 88%.
Capital Amsterdam (constitutional), 687,397; The Hague (seat of government), 449,338.
Ethnic groups Dutch 99%, Indonesian and others 1%.
Languages Dutch.
Religions Roman Catholic 40%, Protestant 31%.
Life expectancy 78 female, 74 male.
Literacy 99%.

POLITICS
Government Constitutional monarchy.
Parties Christian Democratic Appeal, Democrats '66, Labor, Liberal.
Suffrage Universal, over 18.

Memberships EC, NATO, OECD, UN.
Subdivisions 16 provinces.

ECONOMY
GNP $137,300,000,000.
Per capita $9,807.
Monetary unit Guilder.
Trade partners West Germany, Belgium, France, U.S., U.K.
Exports Food, machinery, chemicals, petroleum products.

Imports Machinery, petroleum, transportation equipment, food.

LAND
Description Western Europe.
Area 15,892 mi² (41,160 km²).
Highest point Vaalserberg, 1,053 ft (321 m).
Lowest point Prins Alexander polder, 22 ft (6.7 m) below sea level.

About two-fifths of the Netherlands lies below sea level, and early settlers took on the ambitious project of building a nation upon this land covered by seawater, swampland, and lakes. To do this, they created polders by erecting dikes around certain areas and then draining the water. Canals redirected the water's flow, taking it to the North Sea or to farmland for irrigation.

To pump the rerouted water into the fields, the Dutch made wide use of windmills such as those shown here. The windmills also ground grain and powered sawmills. Although the use of windmills dropped off after the invention of the steam engine, they remain a common sight in the Dutch countryside, a reminder of the resourcefulness that made the Netherlands a prosperous nation.

PEOPLE. The country's major ethnic group is the Dutch, for the most part a mixture of Germanic peoples. There are small minorities from the former Dutch possessions of Indonesia and Suriname. Dutch is the official language, but many Netherlanders also speak English or German. Although most Dutch are Christian, the nation has a history of religious tolerance that has drawn countless refugees.

ECONOMY AND THE LAND. A variety of manufacturing strengths—notably the metal, chemical, and food-processing industries—fuels the prosperous economy. Tourism and the production of natural gas are also important. A lack of natural resources obliges the Netherlands to import many goods. The country benefits from its strategic position and has enjoyed success in shipping and trade. Much of the Netherlands, including most farmland, has been reclaimed from the sea through artificial drainage. The land is almost uniformly flat, and proximity to the sea produces a mild, damp climate. The Kingdom of the Netherlands includes the Netherland Antilles, two groups of Caribbean islands, and Aruba.

HISTORY AND POLITICS. The Germanic tribes of the area were conquered in 58 B.C. by the Romans, who were driven out in the A.D. 400s by the Franks. As part of the Low Countries with Belgium and Luxembourg, the Netherlands was dominated successively by Charlemagne, the dukes of Burgundy, the Hapsburgs, and rulers of Spain. Spanish persecution of Dutch Protestants led to a revolt that in 1581 created the Republic of the United Netherlands. In the 1600s the Netherlands became a maritime as well as a colonial power and produced many masterpieces in painting. But a series of wars with England and France ending in 1714 spelled the end of Dutch influence, and the nation fell to France in 1795. With the defeat of Napoleon Bonaparte of France in 1815, the Netherlands was united with Belgium and became an independent kingdom. Belgium seceded in 1830. The Netherlands declared its neutrality in both world wars but was occupied by Germany from 1940 to 1945. The war cost the country many lives and much of its economic strength. Membership in several international economic unions aided recovery. Since the war the Netherlands has abandoned neutrality and now maintains a pro-Western stance in foreign affairs. ■

The Netherlands is an important cheese producer, and cheese markets, such as this one in Gouda, draw local residents as well as tourists.

Netherlands Map Index

	Lat.	Long.		Lat.	Long.		Lat.	Long.		Lat.	Long.
Alkmaar	52°37′N	4°44′E	Gouda	52°01′N	4°43′E	Middelburg	51°30′N	3°37′E	Tilburg	51°34′N	5°05′E
Almelo	52°21′N	6°39′E	Grevelingen	51°45′N	4°00′E	Nijmegen	51°50′N	5°50′E	Utrecht	52°05′N	5°08′E
Ameland	53°25′N	5°45′E	Groningen	53°13′N	6°33′E	Nordhollands			Valkenswaard	51°21′N	5°28′E
Amersfoort	52°09′N	5°24′E	Haarlem	52°23′N	4°38′E	Canal	52°25′N	4°50′E	Veendam	53°06′N	6°58′E
Amsterdam	52°22′N	4°54′E	Harderwijk	52°21′N	5°36′E	Northeast Polder	52°42′N	5°45′E	Veenendaal	52°02′N	5°34′E
Amsterdam-Rhine			Haringvliet	51°47′N	4°10′E	Oldenzaal	52°19′N	6°56′E	Venlo	51°24′N	6°10′E
Canal	51°57′N	5°20′E	Harlingen	53°10′N	5°24′E	Oosterhout	51°38′N	4°51′E	Vlaardingen	51°54′N	4°21′E
Apeldoorn	52°13′N	5°58′E	Heerenveen	52°57′N	5°55′E	Oss	51°46′N	5°31′E	Vlieland	53°15′N	5°00′E
Arnhem	51°59′N	5°55′E	Heerlen	50°54′N	5°59′E	Overflakkee	51°45′N	4°10′E	Vlissingen	51°26′N	3°35′E
Assen	52°59′N	6°34′E	Helmond	51°29′N	5°40′E	Prinses Margriet			Vught	51°40′N	5°17′E
Bergen op Zoom	51°30′N	4°17′E	Hengelo	52°15′N	6°45′E	Canal	53°10′N	5°55′E	Waal	51°55′N	4°30′E
Beverwijk	52°28′N	4°40′E	Hilversum	52°14′N	5°10′E	Rhine	51°52′N	6°02′E	Waalwijk	51°42′N	5°04′E
Breda	51°35′N	4°46′E	Hoogeveen	52°43′N	6°29′E	Rijssen	52°18′N	6°30′E	Waddenzee	53°15′N	5°15′E
Bussum	52°16′N	5°10′E	Hoorn	52°38′N	5°04′E	Roosendaal	51°32′N	4°28′E	Wageningen	51°58′N	5°40′E
Delft	52°00′N	4°21′E	IJmuiden	52°27′N	4°36′E	Rotterdam	51°55′N	4°28′E	Walcheren	51°33′N	3°35′E
Delfzijl	53°19′N	6°46′E	IJssel	52°30′N	6°00′E	Schiedam	51°55′N	4°24′E	Wassenaar	52°07′N	4°24′E
Den Helder	52°54′N	4°45′E	IJsselmeer	52°45′N	5°25′E	Schouwen	51°43′N	3°50′E	Weert	51°15′N	5°43′E
Deventer	52°15′N	6°10′E	Kampen	52°33′N	5°54′E	's Gravenhage			Western Scheldt	51°25′N	3°45′E
Doetinchem	51°58′N	6°17′E	Katwijk aan Zee	52°13′N	4°24′E	→ The Hague	52°06′N	4°18′E	West Frisian		
Dordrecht	51°49′N	4°40′E	Kerkrade	50°52′N	6°04′E	's-Hertogenbosch	51°41′N	5°19′E	Islands	53°26′N	5°30′E
Drachten	53°06′N	6°05′E	Leeuwarden	53°12′N	5°46′E	Sittard	51°00′N	5°53′E	Wilhelmina Canal	51°47′N	4°51′E
Eastern Scheldt	51°30′N	4°00′E	Leiden (Leyden)	52°09′N	4°30′E	Sliedrecht	51°49′N	4°45′E	Winschoten	53°08′N	7°02′E
East Flevoland	52°30′N	5°45′E	Lek	52°00′N	6°00′E	Sneek	53°02′N	5°40′E	Winterswijk	51°58′N	6°44′E
Ede	52°03′N	5°40′E	Leyden →			Soest	52°09′N	5°18′E	Zaandam	52°26′N	4°49′E
Eindhoven	51°26′N	5°28′E	Leiden	52°09′N	4°30′E	South Flevoland	52°22′N	5°20′E	Zandvoort	52°22′N	4°32′E
Emmen	52°47′N	7°00′E	Lower Rhine	51°59′N	6°20′E	Terneuzen	51°20′N	3°50′E	Zeist	52°05′N	5°15′E
Enkhuizen	52°42′N	5°17′E	Maas (Meuse)	51°49′N	5°01′E	Terschelling	53°24′N	5°20′E	Zevenaar	51°56′N	6°05′E
Enschede	52°12′N	6°53′E	Maastricht	50°52′N	5°43′E	Texel	53°05′N	4°45′E	Zutphen	52°08′N	6°12′E
Geleen	50°58′N	5°52′E	Markerwaard	52°33′N	5°15′E	The Hague ('s			Zwolle	52°30′N	6°05′E
Goes	51°30′N	3°54′E	Meppel	52°42′N	6°11′E	Gravenhage)	52°06′N	4°18′E			
Gorinchem	51°50′N	5°00′E	Meuse (Maas)	51°49′N	5°01′E	Tiel	51°54′N	5°25′E			

Places and Possessions of the Netherlands

Entity	Status	Area	Population	Capital / Population
Aruba (Caribbean island)	Self-governing territory	75 mi² (193 km²)	65,000	Oranjestad / 14,700
Curaçao (Caribbean island)	Division of Netherlands Antilles	171 mi² (444 km²)	165,000	Willemstad / 43,547
Netherlands Antilles— Bonaire, Curaçao, Saba, St. Eustatius, St. Maarten (Caribbean islands)	Self-governing territory	309 mi² (800 km²)	185,000	Willemstad / 43,547

NETHERLANDS ANTILLES

OFFICIAL NAME Netherlands Antilles

PEOPLE
Population 185,000.
Density 599/mi² (231/km²).
Urban 32%.
Capital Willemstad, Curaçao I., 43,547.
Ethnic groups Mixed African, Carib Indian, European.
Languages Dutch, Papiamento, English.
Religions Roman Catholic, Protestant, Jewish.

Life Expectancy 66 female, 59 male.
Literacy 95%.

POLITICS
Government Self-governing territory (Netherlands).
Parties Democratic, Democratic Party of Bonaire, Movement for a New Antilles.
Suffrage Universal, over 18.
Subdivisions 3 island territories.

ECONOMY
GDP $1,360,000,000.
Per capita $9,140.
Monetary unit Guilder.
Trade partners Venezuela, U.S., Saudi Arabia, Nigeria.
Exports Petroleum products, phosphate.
Imports Petroleum, food, manufactured goods.

LAND
Description Caribbean islands.
Area 309 mi² (800 km²).
Highest point Saba I., 2,828 ft (862 m).
Lowest point Sea level.

PEOPLE. The people of the Netherlands Antilles are of mixed African, Carib Indian, and European descent. Most people are multilingual, and languages include Dutch, English, and Papiamento, which combines Spanish, Dutch, Portuguese, English, and Indian elements.

ECONOMY AND THE LAND. The economy of the Netherlands Antilles is based on services and tourism, and tax incentives have drawn some industry to the islands. Poor soils and aridity limit agriculture. The mainly volcanic St. Maarten, St. Eustatius, and Saba make up the northern island group; the coral islands of Curaçao and Bonaire constitute the southern islands. The climate is tropical.

HISTORY AND POLITICS. Carib Indians were the original inhabitants of the northern islands,

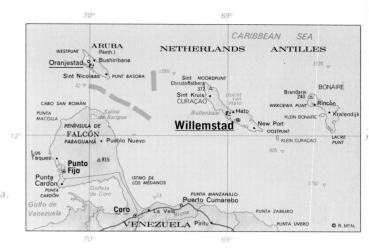

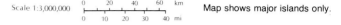

Scale 1:3,000,000

Map shows major islands only.

Netherlands Antilles Map Index

	Lat.	Long.		Lat.	Long.
Bonaire	12°10′N	68°15′W	Kralendijk	12°10′N	68°17′W
Curaçao	12°11′N	69°00′W	New Port	12°03′N	68°49′W
Hato	12°12′N	68°57′W	Willemstad	12°06′N	68°56′W

and Caiquetio Indians resided on the islands to the south. Christopher Columbus reached the northern islands in 1493, and the Spanish arrived at the southern islands in 1499. In the 1630s both groups came under Dutch rule. Some of the islands saw brief periods of French and British rule, but since 1816 all the islands have been under Dutch control. The Netherlands Antilles is a self-governing territory of the Netherlands. Aruba was part of the territory until 1986. ■

NEW CALEDONIA

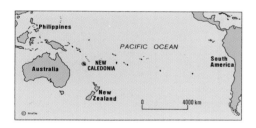

OFFICIAL NAME Territory of New Caledonia and Dependencies

PEOPLE
Population 149,000.
Density 20/mi² (7.8/km²).
Urban 60%.
Capital Nouméa, New Caledonia I., 56,078.
Ethnic groups Melanesian 42%, French 40%, Vietnamese, Indonesian, Chinese, Polynesian.
Languages French, Malay-Polynesian languages.
Religions Roman Catholic 60%, Protestant 30%.

POLITICS
Government Overseas territory (France).
Parties Federation for a New Society, Rally for the Republic, Union Calédonienne.
Suffrage Universal adult.
Memberships None.
Subdivisions 4 divisions.

ECONOMY
GNP $637,000,000.
Per capita $4,000.
Monetary unit CFP franc.
Trade partners France.
Exports Nickel.
Imports Fuels, minerals, machinery, electrical equipment.

LAND
Description South Pacific islands.
Area 7,358 mi² (19,058 km²).
Highest point Mt. Panié, New Caledonia I., 5,341 ft (1,628 m).
Lowest point Sea level.

PEOPLE. New Caledonia's largest ethnic group is Melanesian, or Kanak. The islands are a French overseas territory, and people of French descent form a significant minority.

ECONOMY AND THE LAND. New Caledonia is a leading producer of nickel, and its economy is based on mining. The main island of New Caledonia is mountainous, and smaller islands include the Isle of Pines and the Loyalty and Belep islands. The climate is tropical.

HISTORY AND POLITICS. Melanesians settled the islands around 2000 B.C., and Europeans arrived in 1774. In 1853 France annexed New Caledonia, using the main island as a penal colony until the turn of the century. Officially a French territory since 1946, New Caledonia experienced violence in the 1980s, stemming from the desire of the Kanak population for independence. ■

New Caledonia Map Index

	Lat.	Long.		Lat.	Long.
Koné	21°04′S	164°52′E	Nouméa	22°16′S	166°27′E
Koumac	20°33′S	164°17′E	Thio	21°37′S	166°14′E

Map shows major islands only.

Scale 1:6,000,000

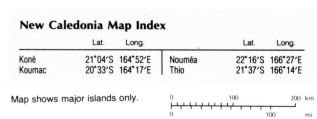

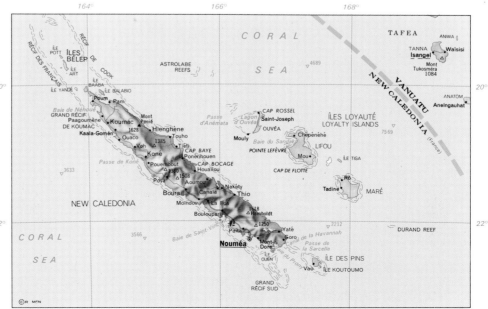

NEW ZEALAND

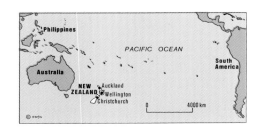

OFFICIAL NAME New Zealand

PEOPLE
Population 3,155,000.
Density 30/mi² (12/km²).
Urban 83%.
Capital Wellington, North I., 134,900.
Ethnic groups European 87%, Maori 9%, Pacific
Islander 2%.
Languages English, Maori.
Religions Anglican 29%, Presbyterian 18%, Roman
Catholic 15%, others 38%.
Life expectancy 76 female, 72 male.
Literacy 98%.

POLITICS
Government Parliamentary state.
Parties Labor, National, New Zealand, Social Credit
Political League.
Suffrage Universal, over 18.
Memberships CW, OECD, UN.
Subdivisions 22 local government regions.

ECONOMY
GNP $25,390,000,000.
Per capita $7,947.
Monetary unit Dollar.
Trade partners Australia, U.S., Japan, U.K.
Exports Wool, meat and dairy products, wood
products.
Imports Machinery, manufactured goods, petroleum,
motor vehicles, chemicals.

LAND
Description South Pacific islands.
Area 103,515 mi² (268,103 km²).
Highest point Mt. Cook, South I., 12,349 ft (3,764 m).
Lowest point Sea level.

PEOPLE. The majority of New Zealanders are
descended from Europeans, mostly Britons, who
arrived in the 1800s. Of Polynesian descent, the
indigenous Maori form the largest minority.
After a period of decline following the arrival of
the Europeans, the Maori population has been
increasing.

ECONOMY AND THE LAND. Industrial and
commercial activities are diversified and profitable. Agriculture, especially livestock raising, remains important for exports, and forestry is expanding. New Zealand consists of two large
islands—North Island and South Island—and
many smaller islands, and the nation administers
several island territories. The scenic terrain is
greatly varied, ranging from fjords and mountains to a volcanic plateau.

HISTORY AND POLITICS. The Maori, the original settlers, are thought to have arrived around
A.D. 1000. Captain James Cook of Britain charted
the islands in the late 1700s. Maori chiefs signed
the 1840 Treaty of Waitangi, establishing British
sovereignty, and British companies began to
send settlers to New Zealand. Subsequent battles
between settlers and Maori ended with the Maori's defeat in 1872, but European diseases and
weapons continued to reduce the Maori population. In 1907 New Zealand became a self-
governing dominion of Britain; formal independence came forty years later. New Zealand
supported Britain in both world wars, but foreign
policy has recently focused on Southeast Asia
and the South Pacific. Advancing Maori rights is
a priority. ■

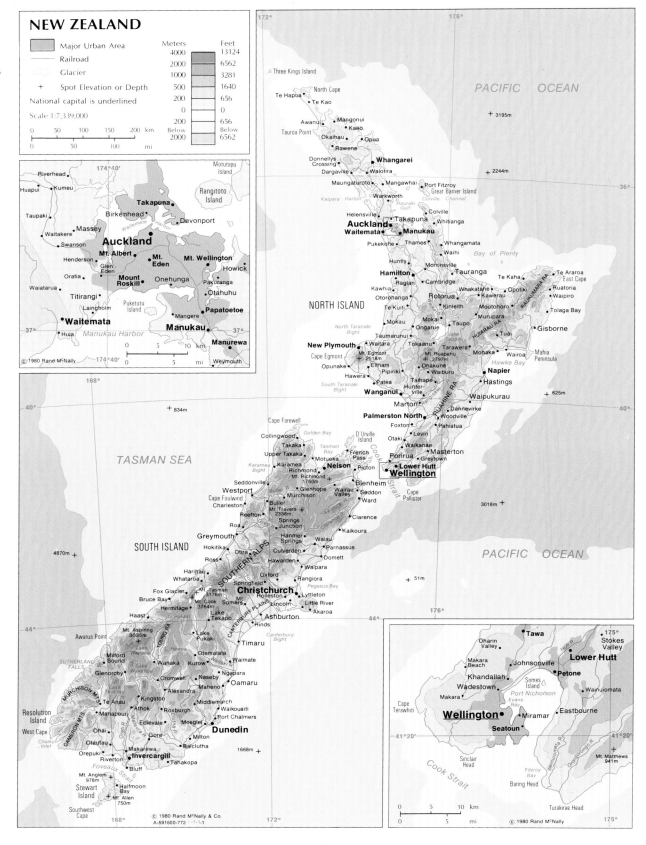

New Zealand Map Index

	Lat.	Long.		Lat.	Long.		Lat.	Long.		Lat.	Long.
Ashburton	43°55'S	171°45'E	Hauraki Gulf	36°20'S	175°05'E	Napier	39°29'S	176°55'E	Sutherland Falls	44°48'S	167°44'E
Auckland	36°52'S	174°46'E	Hawke Bay	39°20'S	177°30'E	Nelson	41°17'S	173°17'E	Takapuna	36°47'S	174°47'E
Blenheim	41°31'S	173°57'E	Howick	36°54'S	174°56'E	New Plymouth	39°04'S	174°05'E	Tasman, Mount	43°34'S	170°09'E
Bruce Bay	43°35'S	169°41'E	Invercargill	46°24'S	168°21'E	Oamaru	45°06'S	170°58'E	Tasman Bay	41°00'S	173°20'E
Canterbury Plains	44°00'S	171°45'E	Johnsonville	41°14'S	174°47'E	Okaihau	35°19'S	173°47'E	Taupo, Lake	38°49'S	175°55'E
Christchurch	43°32'S	172°38'E	Khandallah	41°15'S	174°47'E	Onehunga	36°56'S	174°47'E	Tauranga	37°42'S	176°10'E
Cook, Mount	43°36'S	170°10'E	Lake Pukaki	44°11'S	170°09'E	Ongarue	38°43'S	175°17'E	Tawa	41°10'S	174°51'E
Cook Strait	41°15'S	174°30'E	Lower Hutt	41°13'S	174°55'E	Otahuhu	36°57'S	174°51'E	Te Anau, Lake	45°12'S	167°48'E
Devonport	36°49'S	174°48'E	Manukau	37°02'S	174°54'E	Palmerston North	40°21'S	175°37'E	Te Araroa	37°38'S	178°22'E
Dunedin	45°52'S	170°30'E	Manurewa	37°02'S	174°54'E	Papatoetoe	36°58'S	174°52'E	Te Hapua	34°31'S	172°54'E
Eastbourne	41°18'S	174°54'E	Marton	40°05'S	175°23'E	Petone	41°13'S	174°52'E	Timaru	44°24'S	171°15'E
Egmont, Mount	39°18'S	174°04'E	Massey	36°51'S	174°36'E	Plenty, Bay of	37°40'S	177°00'E	Titirangi	36°56'S	174°40'E
Foveaux Strait	46°35'S	168°00'E	Masterton	40°57'S	175°40'E	Porirua	41°08'S	174°51'E	Wadestown	41°16'S	174°46'E
Gisborne	38°40'S	178°01'E	Maungaturoto	36°06'S	174°22'E	Rotorua	38°09'S	176°15'E	Waipukurau	40°00'S	176°34'E
Glenorchy	44°51'S	168°23'E	Miramar	41°19'S	174°49'E	Ruapehu, Mount	39°17'S	175°34'E	Waitemata	36°56'S	174°42'E
Greymouth	42°28'S	171°12'E	Mount Albert	41°19'S	174°44'E	Seatoun	41°19'S	174°50'E	Wanganui	39°56'S	175°03'E
Hamilton	37°47'S	175°17'E	Mount Eden	36°53'S	174°45'E	Southern Alps	43°30'S	170°30'E	Wellington	41°18'S	174°47'E
Hanmer Springs	42°31'S	172°49'E	Mount Roskill	36°55'S	174°45'E	Stewart Island	47°00'S	167°50'E	Westport	41°45'S	171°36'E
Hastings	39°38'S	176°51'E	Mount Wellington	36°54'S	174°51'E	Stokes Valley	41°11'S	174°58'E	Whangarei	35°43'S	174°19'E

Places and Possessions of New Zealand

Entity	Status	Area	Population	Capital / Population
Cook Islands (South Pacific)	Self-governing territory	91 mi² (236 km²)	16,000	Avarua / 9,525
Niue (South Pacific island)	Self-governing territory	102 mi² (263 km²)	2,900	Alofi / 960
Tokelau (South Pacific islands)	Island territory	4.6 mi² (12 km²)	1,500	None

NICARAGUA

OFFICIAL NAME Republic of
Nicaragua

PEOPLE
Population 2,970,000.
Density 59/mi² (23/km²).
Urban 53%.
Capital Managua, 644,588.
Ethnic groups Mestizo 69%, white 17%, black 9%,
Indian 5%.
Languages Spanish, English.
Religions Roman Catholic 95%.
Life expectancy 59 female, 55 male.
Literacy 66%.

POLITICS
Government Republic.
Parties Sandinista National Liberation Front.
Memberships OAS, UN.
Subdivisions 16 departments.

ECONOMY
GDP $2,500,000,000.
Per capita $846.
Monetary unit Córdoba.
Trade partners Western European countries, Central
American countries.
Exports Cotton, coffee, sugar, meat.
Imports Food, chemicals and pharmaceuticals,
transportation equipment, machinery, petroleum.

LAND
Description Central America.
Area 50,193 mi² (130,000 km²).
Highest point Mt. Mogotón, 6,913 ft (2,107 m).
Lowest point Sea level.

PEOPLE. Nicaraguan society closely reflects the
nation's history as a Spanish colony: most of its
inhabitants are Spanish speaking, Roman Catholic, and mestizo, a mix of Indian and European
stocks. Black communities are found mostly in
the Caribbean region, and many indigenous Indians living along the coast speak English. Population is concentrated in the west, and about half
of the people live in rural areas, supporting
themselves by subsistence farming or, along the
coasts, fishing. Educational reform has resulted
in an improved literacy rate in the past decade.

ECONOMY AND THE LAND. Nicaragua is chiefly an agricultural nation, relying on the production of cotton, coffee, and sugar. Years of instability before a 1979 revolution, a large foreign
debt inherited from the previous regime, and a
continuing civil war have severely hindered economic prosperity. The nation also suffers from a
reliance on imported goods. In 1985 the currency
was sharply devalued, and the United States,
formerly a chief trading partner, announced a
trade embargo. Basic consumer goods are in
short supply. The terrain includes a low-lying
Pacific region, central highlands, and a flat Caribbean area. The climate is tropical.

HISTORY AND POLITICS. Spanish conquistado-
res, who came via Panama in 1522 to what is
now Nicaragua, found a number of independent

Nicaragua Map Index

	Lat.	Long.		Lat.	Long.
Amerique, Sierra			Jinotepe	11°51′N	86°12′W
de	12°12′N	85°19′W	Juigalpa	12°05′N	85°24′W
Bilwaskarma	14°45′N	83°53′W	León	12°26′N	86°53′W
Bluefields	12°00′N	83°45′W	Managua	12°09′N	86°17′W
Boaco	12°30′N	85°30′W	*Managua, Lake*	12°20′N	86°20′W
Bonanza	14°01′N	84°35′W	Masaya	11°58′N	86°06′W
Cabo Gracias a			Matagalpa	12°55′N	85°55′W
Dios	14°59′N	83°10′W	*Mogoton, Mount*	13°45′N	86°23′W
Cárdenas	11°12′N	85°31′W	*Mosquitos, Costa*		
Chinandega	12°37′N	87°09′W	*de*	13°00′N	83°45′W
Cinco Pinos	13°14′N	86°52′W	Nagarote	12°16′N	86°34′W
Coco	15°00′N	83°10′W	*Nicaragua, Lake*	11°30′N	85°30′W
Darién Cordillera	12°55′N	85°30′W	*Ometepe Island*	11°30′N	85°35′W
Diriamba	11°51′N	86°14′W	*Perlas Lagoon*	12°30′N	83°40′W
El Viejo	12°40′N	87°10′W	Puerto Cabezas	14°02′N	83°23′W
Escondido	12°04′N	83°45′W	Punta Gorda	11°31′N	83°47′W
Estelí	13°05′N	86°23′W	Raiti	14°35′N	85°02′W
Fonseca, Gulf of	13°10′N	87°40′W	Rio Grande	12°54′N	83°32′W
Granada	11°56′N	85°57′W	Rivas	11°26′N	85°50′W
Grande de			Rosita	13°53′N	84°24′W
Matagalpa	12°54′N	83°32′W	San Carlos	11°07′N	84°47′W
Isabelia,			*San Juan*	10°56′N	83°42′W
Cordillera	13°45′N	85°15′W	San Juan del		
Jalapa	13°55′N	86°08′W	Norte	10°55′N	83°42′W
Jinotega	13°06′N	86°00′W	Tarica	12°56′N	84°41′W

Indian states. Nicaragua was ruled by Spain as
part of Guatemala until it became independent in
1821. In 1823 the former Spanish colonies of the
region formed the Federation of Central America,
a union which collapsed in 1838, resulting in the
independent Republic of Nicaragua. For the next
century Nicaragua was the stage both for conflict
between the Liberal and Conservative parties
and for United States military and economic involvement. Members of the Somoza family, who
had close ties to the United States, directed a
repressive regime from 1936 to 1979, when the
widely supported Sandinistas overthrew the government. The Sandinistas, who have implemented agrarian reform and improved health care and
education, are opposed by Nicaraguans linked to
the Somoza administration and by others.
Known as contras, these United States–backed
insurgents are fighting the Sandinistas from
within Nicaragua and from Honduras. ■

**Nicaragua, about the size of the U.S. state of Iowa, can be divided into four main geographic
regions. In the country's southwest are Lakes Managua and Nicaragua, north of these a coastal
plain borders the Pacific, and the eastern Caribbean coast is flat and swampy. The nation's
central region, shown in the photograph, is rugged and mountainous, marked by forested
highlands and deep valleys.**

NIGER

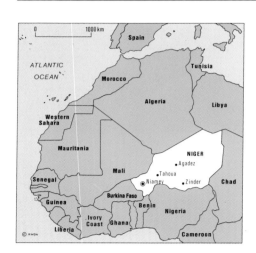

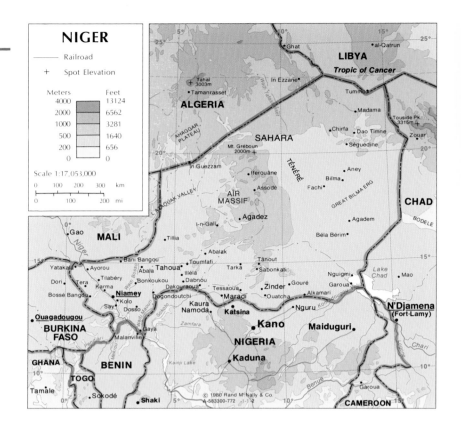

NIGER

- — Railroad
- + Spot Elevation

Meters	Feet
4000	13124
2000	6562
1000	3281
500	1640
200	656
0	0

Scale 1:17,053,000

Niger Map Index

OFFICIAL NAME Republic of Niger

PEOPLE
Population 6,390,000.
Density 13/mi² (5/km²).
Urban 13%.
Capital Niamey, 362,800.
Ethnic groups Hausa 56%, Djerma 22%, Fulani 9%, Tuareg 8%, Beriberi 4%.
Languages French, Hausa, indigenous.
Religions Muslim 80%, indigenous, Christian.
Life expectancy 46 female, 43 male.
Literacy 5%.

POLITICS
Government Provisional military government.
Parties None (banned).
Suffrage Universal adult.
Memberships OAU, UN.
Subdivisions 7 departments.

ECONOMY
GDP $2,000,000,000.
Per capita $425.
Monetary unit CFA franc.
Trade partners France, other Western European countries, Nigeria.
Exports Uranium, livestock, vegetables.
Imports Petroleum, machinery, motor vehicles, food.

LAND
Description Western Africa, landlocked.
Area 489,191 mi² (1,267,000 km²).
Highest point Indoukâl-n-Taghès, 6,634 ft (2,022 m).
Lowest point 650 ft (200 m).

PEOPLE. Nearly all Nigeriens are black Africans belonging to culturally diverse groups. The Hausa and the Djerma constitute the two largest segments of the population, and they live mostly in the south and are farmers. The remainder of Nigeriens are nomadic herdsmen who inhabit the northern desert regions. Although the official language is French, most people speak indigenous tongues. Islam is the most commonly observed religion, but some Nigeriens follow indigenous and Christian beliefs.

ECONOMY AND THE LAND. Niger's economy is chiefly agricultural, but frequent drought makes crop success uncertain. Although farming, including livestock raising, is the major activity for 85 percent of the nation, only 10 percent of the land is cultivated. Subsistence farmers grow mainly millet, sorghum, cassava, and beans. Peanuts are the primary cash crop, but production has suffered greatly because of drought. In 1966 uranium deposits were discovered in northern Niger, and mining of these has provided a sub-stantial income for the nation. A slump in the world uranium market, however, has affected the industry, postponing plans for expansion. Most of northern Niger is covered either by mountains or the Sahara, while savanna is found in the south. The climate is hot and dry.

HISTORY AND POLITICS. Because of its central location in northern Africa, Niger was a crossroads for many peoples during its early history and was dominated by several African empires before European explorers arrived in the 1800s. The area was placed within the French sphere of influence in 1885, but not until 1922 did France make Niger a colony of French West Africa. Gradual moves toward autonomy were made during the forties and fifties, and Niger became fully independent in 1960. Postindependence instability, caused in part by a prolonged drought, led to a 1974 military coup and the banning of political parties. Niger maintains close ties to France. ∎

Despite the ever-present threat of drought, most people in Niger continue to depend on subsistence farming. Residents of the southern savanna grow crops on small plots, while northern herders seek out grazing lands in the mountains and desert. Following a recent drought, the government implemented a program to provide farmers with fertilizers and irrigation. The herders lost an estimated 60 percent of their livestock during the drought, and the government has helped them recoup their losses as well. This nomadic herder has found a grazing area near the town of Iferouâne at the foot of the Aïr Massif.

NIGERIA

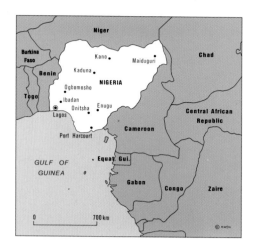

OFFICIAL NAME Federal
Republic of Nigeria

PEOPLE
Population 89,650,000.
Density 251/mi² (97/km²).
Urban 28%.
Capital Lagos, 1,404,000.
Ethnic groups Hausa-Fulani, Yoruba, Ibo, others.
Languages English, Hausa, Yoruba, Ibo, others.
Religions Muslim 47%, Christian 34%, indigenous 18%.
Life expectancy 51 female, 48 male.
Literacy 25–30%.

POLITICS
Government Republic.
Parties None (banned).
Suffrage None.
Memberships CW, OAU, OPEC, UN.
Subdivisions 19 states, 1 federal territory.

ECONOMY
GDP $74,000,000,000.
Per capita $827.
Monetary unit Naira.
Trade partners U.K., other Western European countries, U.S.
Exports Petroleum, cocoa, palm products.
Imports Machinery, transportation equipment, manufactured goods, food.

LAND
Description Western Africa.
Area 356,669 mi² (923,768 km²).
Highest point Mt. Waddi, 7,936 ft (2,419 m).
Lowest point Sea level.

PEOPLE. Nigeria, Africa's most populous nation, contains more than two hundred distinct black African groups, and competition among the many ethnic groups has threatened national unity. The largest groups are the Hausa-Fulani, who dominate the north; the Yoruba, found primarily in the southwest; and the Ibo, who live in the southeast and have historically been active in government and trade. Most Hausa-Fulani are Muslim, and the sizable Christian community is found mainly in the south. Nigerians commonly combine traditional beliefs with Islam or Christianity. Indigenous tongues are more widely spoken than English, the official language.

ECONOMY AND THE LAND. Nigeria's economy is based on mining and agriculture. Petroleum plays an important economic role, but a number of factors—including unskilled labor, poor power facilities, and the worldwide drop in oil prices —have silenced the oil boom of the 1970s and slowed development in other areas. In 1983 and 1985 the government expelled millions of illegal aliens in an effort to revive the economy. The terrain is diverse, encompassing tropical forest, savanna, and semidesert. The climate is predominantly tropical.

HISTORY AND POLITICS. From around 500 B.C. to about A.D. 200 the region was home to the sophisticated Nok civilization. Later cultures that dominated parts of the area included the Hausa, Fulani, and Yoruba. The Portuguese arrived in the 1400s, but the British gained control over the following centuries, uniting the region in 1914 as the Colony and Protectorate of Nigeria. Nigerian calls for self-rule culminated in independence in 1960. Internal tensions began to wrack the new nation, and in 1966 two military coups took place. After subsequent massacres of Ibo, that group declared eastern Nigeria the autonomous state of Biafra. A three-year civil war followed, ending in 1970 with Biafra's surrender. Economic recovery was speeded by the oil boom and government development. Subsequent years have seen coups and elections install short-lived regimes, and political instability continues. ∎

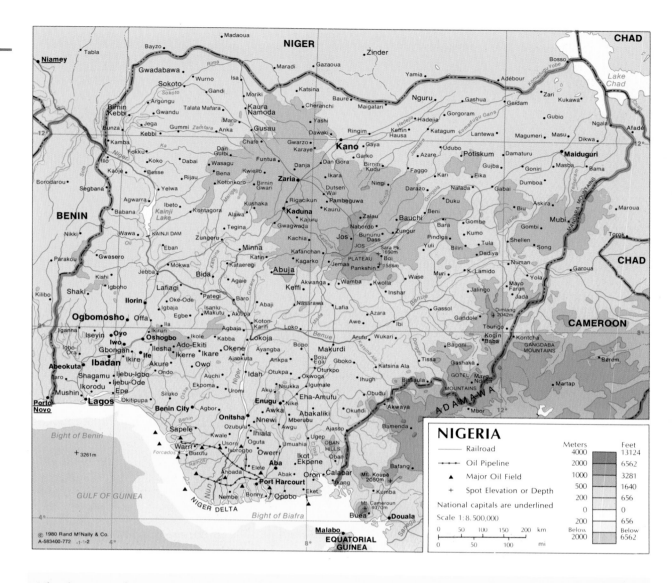

Nigeria Map Index

	Lat.	Long.		Lat.	Long.		Lat.	Long.		Lat.	Long.
Aba	5°06′N	7°21′E	Gongola	9°30′N	12°04′E	Kaduna	8°45′N	5°45′E	Offa	8°09′N	4°44′E
Abakaliki	6°21′N	8°06′E	Gusau	12°12′N	6°40′E	Kainji Lake	10°30′N	4°35′E	Ogbomosho	8°08′N	4°15′E
Abeokuta	7°10′N	3°26′E	Gwadabawa	13°20′N	5°15′E	Kano	12°00′N	8°30′E	Okene	7°33′N	6°15′E
Abuja	9°12′N	7°11′E	Ibadan	7°17′N	3°30′E	Katsina Ala	7°48′N	8°52′E	Onitsha	6°09′N	6°47′E
Ado-Ekiti	7°38′N	5°12′E	Idah	7°07′N	6°43′E	Kaura Namoda	12°35′N	6°35′E	Opobo	4°34′N	7°27′E
Akure	7°15′N	5°12′E	Ife	7°30′N	4°30′E	Keffi	8°51′N	7°52′E	Oron	4°48′N	8°14′E
Awka	6°12′N	7°05′E	Ihiala	5°51′N	6°51′E	Komadugu Gana	13°05′N	12°24′E	Oshogbo	7°47′N	4°34′E
Bauchi	10°19′N	9°50′E	Ijebu-Igbo	6°56′N	4°01′E	Komadugu Yobe	13°43′N	13°20′E	Owerri	5°29′N	7°02′E
Benin City	6°19′N	5°41′E	Ijebu-Ode	6°50′N	3°56′E	Lafiagi	8°52′N	5°25′E	Owo	7°15′N	5°37′E
Benue	7°48′N	6°46′E	Ikare	7°32′N	5°45′E	Lagos	6°27′N	3°24′E	Oyo	7°51′N	3°56′E
Biafra, Bight of	4°00′N	8°00′E	Ikerre	7°31′N	5°14′E	Lokoja	7°47′N	6°45′E	Port Harcourt	4°43′N	7°05′E
Bida	9°05′N	6°01′E	Ikire	7°23′N	4°12′E	Maiduguri	11°51′N	13°10′E	Potiskum	11°43′N	11°05′E
Birnin Kebbi	12°32′N	4°12′E	Ikorodu	6°37′N	3°31′E	Makurdi	7°45′N	8°32′E	Rima	13°04′N	5°10′E
Calabar	4°57′N	8°19′E	Ikot Ekpene	5°12′N	7°40′E	Mandara			Sapele	5°54′N	5°41′E
Chad, Lake	13°20′N	14°00′E	Ilesha	7°38′N	4°45′E	Mountains	10°45′N	13°40′E	Sara Peak	9°41′N	9°17′E
Cross	4°42′N	8°21′E	Ilorin	8°30′N	4°32′E	Minna	9°37′N	6°33′E	Shagamu	6°51′N	3°39′E
Dimlang	8°24′N	11°47′E	Iseyin	7°58′N	3°36′E	Mubi	10°18′N	13°20′E	Shaki	8°39′N	3°25′E
Eha-Amufu	6°40′N	7°46′E	Iwo	7°38′N	4°11′E	Mushin	6°32′N	3°22′E	Sokoto	13°04′N	5°16′E
Enugu	6°27′N	7°27′E	Jamaare	12°06′N	10°14′E	Nguru	12°52′N	10°27′E	Sokoto	11°20′N	4°10′E
Epe	6°37′N	3°59′E	Jos	9°55′N	8°53′E	Niger	5°33′N	6°33′E	Warri	5°31′N	5°45′E
Gbongan	7°29′N	4°21′E	Jos Plateau	9°30′N	9°00′E	Niger Delta	4°50′N	6°00′E	Zamfara	12°05′N	4°02′E
			Kaduna	10°33′N	7°27′E	Nnewi	6°00′N	6°59′E	Zaria	11°07′N	7°44′E

Petroleum plays a major role in the Nigerian economy, but many Nigerians, such as these fishermen along the Niger River, continue to make their living by the traditional methods. Most fishing and farming is carried out on the subsistence level.

NIUE

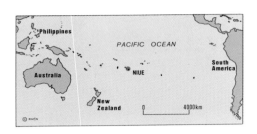

OFFICIAL NAME Niue

PEOPLE
Population 2,900.
Density 28/mi² (11/km²).
Urban 69%.
Capital Alofi, 960.
Ethnic groups Polynesian.
Languages English, Malay-Polynesian languages.
Religions Church of Niue 75%, Mormon 10%.

POLITICS
Government Self-governing territory (New Zealand).
Suffrage Universal adult.

Subdivisions 14 village councils.

ECONOMY
GDP $3,000,000.
Per capita $1,080.
Monetary unit New Zealand dollar.
Trade partners New Zealand, Fiji, Japan.
Exports Coconut products, honey, fruit, handicrafts.
Imports Foodstuffs, manufactured goods, machinery, fuels.

LAND
Description South Pacific island.
Area 102 mi² (263 km²).
Lowest point Sea level.

PEOPLE. Niue has a mainly Polynesian population that speaks indigenous tongues. Because of Niue's association with New Zealand, English is widely spoken.

ECONOMY AND THE LAND. The economy is based on agriculture, and in addition to surplus crops, handicrafts are exported. The coral island's climate is tropical.

HISTORY AND POLITICS. More than one thousand years ago Niue's first inhabitants arrived either from Samoa or another eastern Pacific island. In 1774 Captain James Cook of Britain came to Niue, calling it Savage Island because of the hostility of the inhabitants. The island did not come under British rule until 1900. In 1901 Niue was annexed to New Zealand, and the island became a self-governing territory of New Zealand in 1974. ■

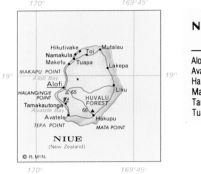

Niue Map Index

	Lat.	Long.
Alofi	19°01'S	169°55'W
Avatele	19°06'S	169°55'W
Hakupu	19°06'S	169°50'W
Makefu	18°59'S	169°55'W
Tamakautonga	19°05'S	169°55'W
Tuapa	18°57'S	169°54'W

Scale 1:1,000,000

NORFOLK ISLAND

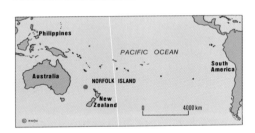

OFFICIAL NAME Territory of Norfolk Island

PEOPLE
Population 1,700.
Density 121/mi² (47/km²).
Capital Kingston.
Ethnic groups Mixed European and Tahitian.

Languages English, Norfolk.
Religions Anglican, Roman Catholic, Uniting Church in Australia.

POLITICS
Government External territory (Australia).

ECONOMY
Monetary unit Australian dollar.
Trade partners Australia, New Zealand.
Exports Norfolk pine seeds, kentia palm seeds, avocados.
Imports Foodstuffs, manufactured goods.

LAND
Description South Pacific island.
Area 14 mi² (36 km²).
Highest point Mt. Bates, 1,047 ft (319 m).
Lowest point Sea level.

The island's population comprises descendants of *Bounty* mutineers, called "islanders," and immigrants from Australia and New Zealand, or "mainlanders." Tourism is the main economic contributor. Of volcanic origin, Norfolk Island has a subtropical climate. Captain James Cook arrived at the uninhabited island in 1774, and for a time Norfolk served as a penal colony. In 1914 Norfolk Island became an external territory of Australia. ■

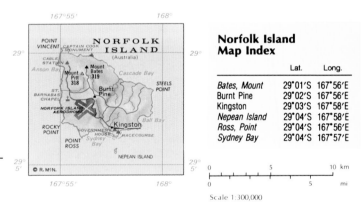

Norfolk Island Map Index

	Lat.	Long.
Bates, Mount	29°01'S	167°56'E
Burnt Pine	29°02'S	167°56'E
Kingston	29°03'S	167°58'E
Nepean Island	29°04'S	167°58'E
Ross, Point	29°04'S	167°56'E
Sydney Bay	29°04'S	167°57'E

Scale 1:300,000

NORTHERN MARIANA ISLANDS

OFFICIAL NAME Northern Mariana Islands

PEOPLE
Population 19,000.
Density 103/mi² (40/km²).
Urban 16%.
Capital Saipan I.
Ethnic groups Chamorro, Micronesian.
Religions Roman Catholic.

POLITICS
Government Part of Trust Territory of the Pacific Islands (U.S.).
Suffrage Universal, over 18.
Subdivisions 4 municipalities.

ECONOMY
Monetary unit U.S. dollar.

LAND
Description North Pacific islands.
Area 184 mi² (477 km²).

The Chamorros, of mixed descent, are a majority. Most income comes from tourism, and the climate is tropical. Inhabited for more than three thousand years, the Northern Marianas were ruled by Spain, Germany, and Japan. In 1947 the United Nations declared the Northern Marianas part of the Trust Territory of the Pacific Islands, under United States administration. Upon the dissolution of the trust territory, the Northern Marianas will officially become a U.S. commonwealth. ■

Map shows major islands only.

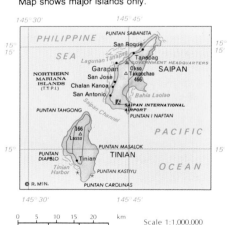

Northern Mariana Islands Map Index

	Lat.	Long.		Lat.	Long.
Garapan	15°12'N	145°43'E	San Roque	15°15'N	145°47'E
Saipan	15°12'N	145°45'E	Tanapag	15°14'N	145°45'E
San Jose	15°09'N	145°43'E	Tinian	15°00'N	145°38'E

NORWAY

OFFICIAL NAME Kingdom of Norway

PEOPLE
Population 4,150,000.
Density 28/mi² (11/km²).
Urban 70%.
Capital Oslo, 448,747.
Ethnic groups Germanic, Lappish.
Languages Norwegian, Lappish.
Religions Lutheran 94%.
Life expectancy 79 female, 74 male.
Literacy 100%.

POLITICS
Government Constitutional monarchy.
Parties Center, Christian People's, Conservative, Labor, Progressive, Socialist Left.
Suffrage Universal, over 18.
Memberships NATO, OECD, UN.
Subdivisions 19 counties.

ECONOMY
GNP $56,200,000,000.
Per capita $13,600.
Monetary unit Krone.
Trade partners U.K., West Germany, Sweden, U.S.
Exports Petroleum, natural gas, metals, paper and wood pulp, chemicals, fish products.
Imports Machinery, transportation equipment, food, iron and steel, textiles, clothing.

LAND
Description Northern Europe.
Area 149,158 mi² (386,317 km²).
Highest point Glittertinden, 8,110 ft (2,472 m).
Lowest point Sea level.

PEOPLE. Because of its relatively remote location in far northern Europe, Norway has seen few population migrations and possesses a virtually homogeneous population, which is predominantly Germanic, Norwegian speaking, and Lutheran. Small communities of Lapps and Finns live in the far north, while most Norwegians live in the south and along the coast. Two mutually intelligible forms of the Norwegian language are taught in schools. The people of Norway enjoy many government-provided social services, including health care, free education through the university level, and a pension plan that guarantees an individual's living standard will be maintained after retirement.

ECONOMY AND THE LAND. Norway's economy, based on shipping, trade, and the mining of offshore oil and natural gas, takes its shape from the nation's proximity to several seas. Shipbuilding, fishing, and forestry are also important activities. Norway is a leading producer of hydroelectricity, which supplies nearly all of Norway's needs and allows for the export of oil and gas. Combined with some government control of the economy, these lucrative activities have given the nation a high standard of living and fairly low unemployment. Only about 3 percent of Norway's land is arable, and agricultural activity is dominated by livestock raising. Mountainous high plateau interspersed with lakes and deep

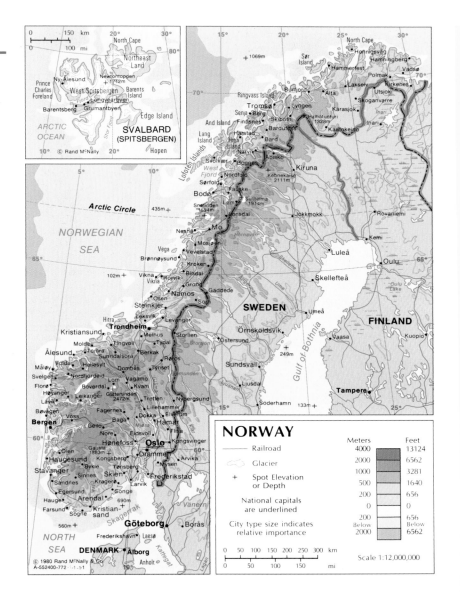

valleys make up Norway's terrain, and the coast is marked by fjords and offshore islands. About one-third of northern Norway lies in the Arctic Circle, but the Gulf Stream gives the nation a much milder climate than other places at the same latitude.

HISTORY AND POLITICS. Parts of present-day Norway were inhabited by about 9000 B.C. Germanic tribes began immigrating to the area about 2000 B.C. Between A.D. 800 and 1100 Viking ships from Norway raided coastal towns throughout Western Europe and also colonized Greenland and Iceland. Unified around 900, Norway was

subsequently shaken by civil war, plague, and the end of its royal line. It entered a union with Denmark in 1380, becoming a Danish province in 1536. Around the end of the Napoleonic Wars, in 1814, Norway became part of Sweden. A long struggle against Swedish rule ended in 1905 as Sweden recognized Norwegian independence, and a Danish prince was made king. Norway was neutral in World War I but endured German occupation during World War II. In 1967 the government initiated a social-welfare system. Norway retains relations with Western nations and the Soviet Union but does not allow foreign military bases or nuclear arms on its soil. ∎

Places and Possessions of Norway

Entity	Status	Area	Population	Capital / Population
Bouvet (South Atlantic islands)	Territory	23 mi² (59 km²)	*None*	None
Jan Mayen (North Atlantic island)	Part of Norway	144 mi² (373 km²)	*No permanent population*	None
Svalbard (North Atlantic islands)	Part of Norway	23,957 mi² (62,049 km²)	*4,200*	Longyearbyen / 3,700

The fishing village of Hammerfest, Norway, is known as the world's northernmost town, yet the Gulf Stream keeps its harbor ice free year-round. Situated on Kvaløya Island southwest of North Cape, Hammerfest lies within the Arctic Circle. This is the Land of the Midnight Sun, and in Hammerfest the sun never sets from May to August and never rises from November to February. This view looking out over the coast shows the sun at midnight during its summer period.

OMAN

OFFICIAL NAME Sultanate of
Oman

PEOPLE
Population 1,025,000.
Density 12/mi² (4.8/km²).
Urban 8%.
Capital Muscat, 6,000.
Ethnic groups Arab, Baluchi, Zanzibari, Indian.
Languages Arabic, Farsi.
Religions Ibadite Muslim 75%, Sunni Muslim, Shiite
Muslim, Hindu.
Life expectancy 50 female, 48 male.
Literacy 20%.

POLITICS
Government Monarchy.
Parties None.
Suffrage None.
Memberships AL, UN.
Subdivisions 1 province, 2 governorates, numerous
districts.

ECONOMY
GNP $6,300,000,000.
Per capita $6,828.
Monetary unit Rial.
Trade partners Japan, United Arab Emirates, U.K.,
other Western European countries.
Exports Petroleum.
Imports Machinery, transportation equipment,
manufactured goods, food.

LAND
Description Southwestern Asia.
Area 82,030 mi² (212,457 km²).
Highest point Mt. Sham, 9,957 ft (3,035 m).
Lowest point Sea level.

PEOPLE. Most of Oman's population is Arab,
Arabic speaking, and belongs to the Ibadite sect
of Islam. Other forms of Islam are also practiced.
There is a significant foreign community that includes Indians, Pakistanis, and East African
blacks. Many of them are guest workers in the
oil industry.

ECONOMY AND THE LAND. Although oil production is the economic mainstay, Oman's reserves are not as vast as those of some other
Arab states, and the government is seeking to
diversify. The mining of natural gas and copper
is being developed, as are agriculture and fishing. A central position in the politically volatile
Persian Gulf and revolutionary internal strife
have led Oman to devote a considerable portion
of its budget to defense. Land regions include a
coastal plain, interior mountains, and desert.
Oman's land borders are undefined and in dispute. A desert climate prevails over most areas
except the coast, which has humid conditions.

HISTORY AND POLITICS. Islam came to Muscat
and Oman, as the nation was known before
1970, in the seventh century A.D. The Portuguese
gained control of parts of the coast in 1508 but
were driven out in 1650 by the Arabs. At about
this time the hereditary sultanate—which absorbed the political power formerly held by the
Ibadite religious leaders, or imams—was founded. Close relations with Britain were cemented in
a 1798 agreement and subsequent treaties, and
British ties have continued to the present. Conflicts between the sultan and Omanis who wanted to be ruled exclusively by their imam erupted

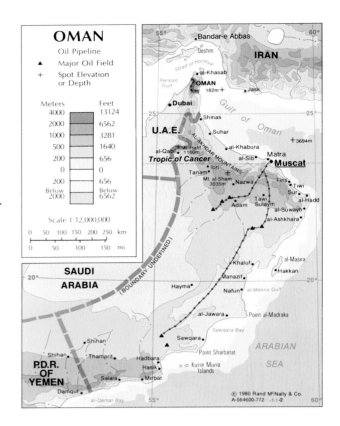

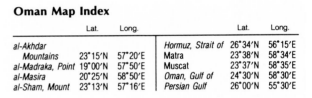

Oman Map Index

	Lat.	Long.		Lat.	Long.
al-Akhdar			Hormuz, Strait of	26°34′N	56°15′E
Mountains	23°15′N	57°20′E	Matra	23°38′N	58°34′E
al-Madraka, Point	19°00′N	57°50′E	Muscat	23°37′N	58°35′E
al-Masira	20°25′N	58°50′E	Oman, Gulf of	24°30′N	58°30′E
al-Sham, Mount	23°13′N	57°16′E	Persian Gulf	26°00′N	55°30′E

intermittently after 1900, and in 1959 the sultan
defeated the rebels with British help and outlawed the office of imam. Marxist insurgency
was put down in 1975. Sultan Qaboos bin Said,
who overthrew his father's regime in 1970, has
liberalized some policies and worked to modernize the nation. Oman is a moderate, pro-Western
Arab state. ∎

PACIFIC ISLANDS, TRUST TERRITORY OF THE

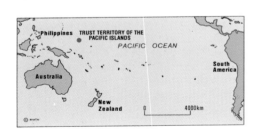

OFFICIAL NAME Trust Territory
of the Pacific Islands

PEOPLE
Population 146,000.
Density 204/mi² (79/km²).
Urban 29%.
Capital Saipan I.
Ethnic groups Micronesian, mixed European.
Languages English, Malay-Polynesian languages.
Religions Protestant, Roman Catholic.

POLITICS
Government United Nations trusteeship (U.S.).
Suffrage Universal, over 18.
Subdivisions 4 constitutional governments.

ECONOMY
GNP 140,000,000.
Per capita $950.
Monetary unit U.S. dollar.

Trust Territory of the Pacific Islands Map Index

	Lat.	Long.		Lat.	Long.
Caroline Islands	8°00′N	147°00′E	Northern Mariana		
Mariana Islands	16°00′N	145°30′E	Islands	16°00′N	149°00′E
Marshall Islands	11°00′N	168°00′E	Palau	7°30′N	134°30′E
Micronesia,					
Federated					
States of	5°00′N	152°00′E			

Exports Coconut products, fish, handicrafts.
Imports Foodstuffs, building materials.

LAND
Description North Pacific islands.
Area 717 mi² (1,857 km²).
Highest point Agrihan I., 3,166 ft (965 m).
Lowest point Sea level.

PEOPLE. Most inhabitants of the more than two
thousand islands that make up the territory are
Micronesian or of mixed descent.

ECONOMY AND THE LAND. Coconuts, fish,
and handicrafts are major products. The territory
consists of the Caroline Islands, the Marshall Islands, and the Northern Marianas. The climate is
tropical.

HISTORY AND POLITICS. The United Nations
established the trust territory under United
States administration in 1947. Upon termination
of the trust territory by the United Nations, the
Marshall Islands, Palau, and the Federated States
of Micronesia will officially become independent
nations, and the Northern Mariana Islands will
be a United States commonwealth. ∎

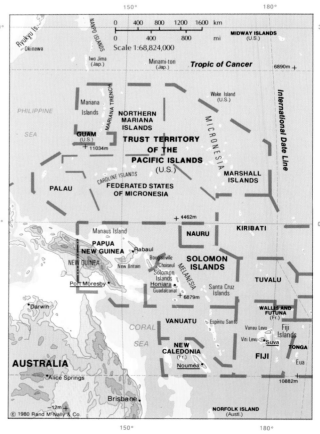

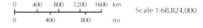

PAKISTAN

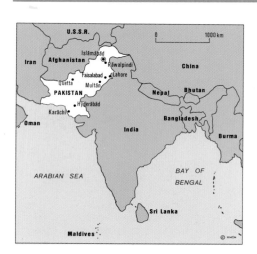

OFFICIAL NAME Islamic Republic of Pakistan

PEOPLE

Population 101,300,000.
Density 298/mi² (115/km²).
Urban 28%.
Capital Islamabad, 201,000.
Ethnic groups Punjabi, Sindhi, Pushtun, Baluchi.
Languages Urdu, English, Punjabi, Sindhi.
Religions Muslim 97%.
Life expectancy 50 female, 51 male.
Literacy 24%.

POLITICS

Government Republic.
Parties None (suspended).
Suffrage Universal, over 18.
Memberships UN.
Subdivisions 5 provinces, 1 capital territory.

ECONOMY

GNP $33,020,000,000.
Per capita $348.
Monetary unit Rupee.
Trade partners Japan, U.S., U.K., West Germany, Kuwait.
Exports Rice, cotton, textiles, light manufactures.
Imports Petroleum, transportation equipment, raw materials, consumer goods.

LAND

Description Southern Asia.
Area 339,732 mi² (879,902 km²).
Highest point K², 28,250 ft (8,611 m).
Lowest point Sea level.
The above information includes part of Jammu and Kashmir.

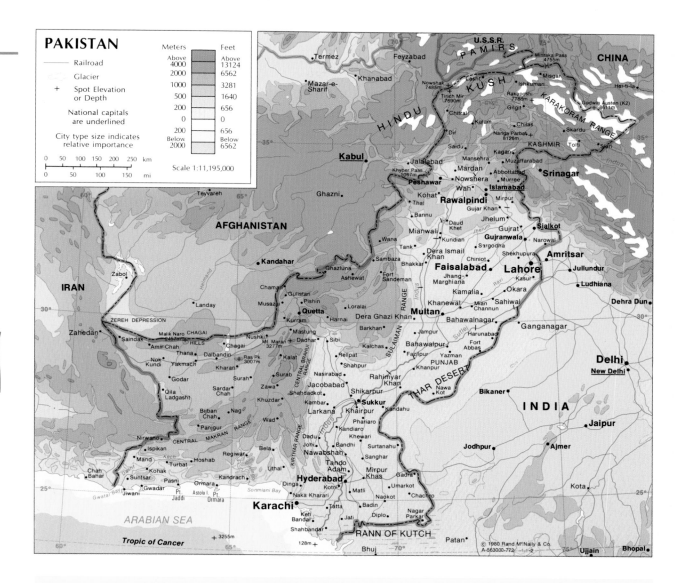

Pakistan Map Index

	Lat.	Long.		Lat.	Long.		Lat.	Long.		Lat.	Long.
Bahawalnagar	29°59'N	73°16'E	Hingol	25°23'N	65°28'E	Kohat	33°35'N	71°26'E	Rann of Kutch	24°00'N	70°00'E
Bahawalpur	29°24'N	71°41'E	Hyderabad	25°22'N	68°22'E	Lahore	31°35'N	74°18'E	Ravi	30°35'N	71°48'E
Central Brahui			Indus	24°20'N	67°47'E	Larkana	27°33'N	68°13'E	Rawalpindi	33°36'N	73°04'E
Range	29°20'N	66°55'E	Islamabad	33°42'N	73°10'E	Mardan	34°21'N	72°02'E	Sahiwal	30°40'N	73°06'E
Central Makran			Jacobabad	28°17'N	68°26'E	Mianwali	32°35'N	71°33'E	Shikarpur	27°57'N	68°38'E
Range	26°40'N	64°30'E	Jhelum	32°56'N	73°44'E	Mintaka Pass	36°58'N	74°54'E	Sialkot	32°30'N	74°31'E
Chenab	29°23'N	71°02'E	Jhelum	31°12'N	72°08'E	Mirpur Khas	25°32'N	69°00'E	Sonmiani Bay	25°15'N	66°30'E
Dasht	25°10'N	61°40'E	Kabul	33°55'N	72°14'E	Multan	30°11'N	71°29'E	Sukkur	27°42'N	68°52'E
Dera Ghazi Khan	30°03'N	70°38'E	Kamalia	30°44'N	72°39'E	Nanga Parbat	35°15'N	74°36'E	Sulaiman Range	30°30'N	70°10'E
Dera Ismail Khan	31°50'N	70°54'E	Karachi	24°52'N	67°03'E	Nawabshah	26°15'N	68°25'E	Sutlej	29°23'N	71°02'E
Faisalabad	31°25'N	73°05'E	Karakoram Range	35°30'N	77°00'E	Nowshera	34°01'N	71°59'E	Tando Adam	25°46'N	68°40'E
Godwin Austen	35°53'N	76°30'E	Kashmir	35°00'N	75°00'E	Okara	30°49'N	73°27'E	Thar Desert	27°00'N	71°00'E
Gujranwala	32°26'N	74°33'E	Khairpur	27°32'N	68°46'E	Peshawar	34°01'N	71°33'E	Tirich Mir	36°15'N	71°50'E
Gujrat	32°34'N	74°05'E	Khanewal	30°18'N	71°56'E	Quetta	30°12'N	67°00'E	Wah	33°48'N	72°42'E
Gwatar Bay	25°04'N	61°36'E	Khyber Pass	34°05'N	71°10'E	Rahimyar Khan	28°25'N	70°18'E	Zhob	32°04'N	69°50'E
Hindu Kush	36°00'N	71°30'E	Kirthar Range	27°00'N	67°10'E	Rakaposhi	36°10'N	74°30'E			

PEOPLE. Pakistan's varied ethnicity is the product of centuries of incursions by different racial types. Today each people is concentrated in a different region and speaks its own language; Urdu, the official language, is not widely spoken. The Punjabis compose the largest ethnic group and have traditionally been influential in government and commerce. Virtually all the people of Pakistan, which was created as a Muslim homeland, follow Islam.

ECONOMY AND THE LAND. Despite recent progress in manufacturing, agriculture remains the economic mainstay. Government planning and foreign assistance have aided all sectors, but Pakistan remains troubled by high population growth, unskilled labor, a trade deficit, and an influx of refugees fleeing the civil war in Afghanistan. Pakistan's terrain includes mountains, fertile plains, and desert. The climate is continental, with extreme variations in temperature and colder winters in the north.

HISTORY AND POLITICS. Around 2500 B.C. the Indus Valley civilization flourished in the area of modern Pakistan. Various empires and immigrants followed, including Aryans, Persians, and Greeks. Invading Arabs introduced Islam to the region in the A.D. 700s. In the 1500s the Mogul Empire of Afghanistan came to include nearly all

of present-day Pakistan, India, and Bangladesh, and as that empire declined, various peoples ruled the area. Through wars and treaties, the British presence in Asia expanded, and by the early twentieth century British India included all of modern Pakistan. Because of hostilities between British India's Muslims and Hindus, the separate Muslim nation of Pakistan was created when British India gained independence in 1947. With its boundaries drawn around the Muslim population centers, Pakistan was formed from

the northeastern and northwestern parts of India, and its eastern region was separated from the west by more than 1,000 miles (1,600 kilometers). East Pakistanis felt that power was unfairly concentrated in the west, and in 1971 a civil war erupted. Aided by India, East Pakistan won the war and became the independent nation of Bangladesh. Subsequent political activity in Pakistan has included martial law and accusations of government corruption. A dispute with India over ownership of the Kashmir region continues. ∎

Although a commercial center and Pakistan's second-largest city, Lahore has a skyline that reflects its Islamic roots and Mogul past. After rule by various peoples, Lahore's golden age came in the sixteenth and seventeenth centuries, after the Moguls had made it a capital of their empire. Many of the city's architectural structures, though not perfectly preserved, reflect that past, especially the palaces, gardens, and mosques.

PALAU

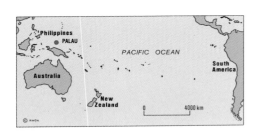

OFFICIAL NAME Republic
of Palau

PEOPLE
Population 13,000.
Density 68/mi² (26/km²).
Urban 51%.
Capital Koror, 6,222.
Ethnic groups Micronesian.
Languages English, Malay-Polynesian languages.
Religions Protestant, Roman Catholic.

POLITICS
Government Part of Trust Territory of the Pacific
Islands (U.S.).
Suffrage Universal, over 18.
Subdivisions 17 municipalities.

ECONOMY
Monetary unit U.S. dollar.

LAND
Description North Pacific islands.
Area 192 mi² (497 km²).

PEOPLE. Palau's majority group is Micronesian,
and languages include English as well as Malay-
Polynesian tongues. The islands are divided into
six states, each with its own governor, but the
village chiefs continue to wield power as well.

ECONOMY AND THE LAND. Government jobs
provide for much employment, but the service
sector is on the rise as tourism expands. Foreign
investment has increased as well. Phosphate deposits on the island of Angaur once fueled a
prosperous export industry, but reserves were
depleted in 1955, and economic plans include
further exploration and exploitation of natural
resources. The United States continues to supply
economic assistance. Palau is made up of a
group of islands in the Caroline Islands. The
northern islands in the group are volcanic, and
the southern islands are coral. The climate is
tropical.

HISTORY AND POLITICS. The Spanish seafarer
Ruy Lopez de Villalobos was the first to sight the
Palau Islands, in 1543. Spaniards controlled the
islands until 1899, when Spain sold Palau to Germany. Following World War I, Palau came under
Japan's jurisdiction as a League of Nations mandate. Japan invested in improvements for certain
islands, constructing a naval base on Peleliu, and
soon an influx of Japanese settlers boosted the
islands' population. Some of World War II's
bloodiest battles between the United States and
Japan took place at Peleliu in 1944. War memori-
als for both Japanese and American soldiers
stand on the island today, and the remains of
warships and planes are found in the offshore
waters. After the war, in 1947, Palau along with
the Northern Marianas, the islands of the Federated States of Micronesia, and the Marshall Islands were declared a United Nations trust territory under United States administration. Palau
adopted a constitution in 1980, declaring itself
the Republic of Palau, and a constitutional government was installed in 1981. After initial problems regarding the status of nuclear weapons in

Palau, a compact of free association with the
United States, which was signed in 1982, was
approved in 1987. Under this agreement, a continuing source of controversy in Palau, the United States has the right to control military and
defense activities, providing economic assistance
in return. However, the fulfillment of the compact is dependent upon United Nations recognition of an independent Palau and termination of
the trust territory agreement. Palau's first consti-
tutionally elected president was assassinated in
1985. ■

Scale 1:3,000,000

Map shows major islands only.

Palau Map Index

	Lat.	Long.		Lat.	Long.
Babelthuap	7°30′N	134°36′E	Melekeok	7°29′N	134°38′E
Kloulklubed	7°02′N	134°15′E	Meyungs	7°20′N	134°27′E
Koror	7°20′N	134°29′E	Ngermechau	7°35′N	134°39′E

PANAMA

OFFICIAL NAME Republic of
Panama

PEOPLE
Population 2,155,000.
Density 72/mi² (28/km²).
Urban 49%.
Capital Panamá, 388,638.
Ethnic groups Mestizo 70%, West Indian 14%, white
10%, Indian 6%.
Languages Spanish, English.
Religions Roman Catholic 93%, Protestant 6%.
Life expectancy 73 female, 69 male.
Literacy 85%.

POLITICS
Government Republic.
Parties Christian Democratic, Democratic
Revolutionary, Liberal, Panameñista.
Suffrage Universal, over 18.

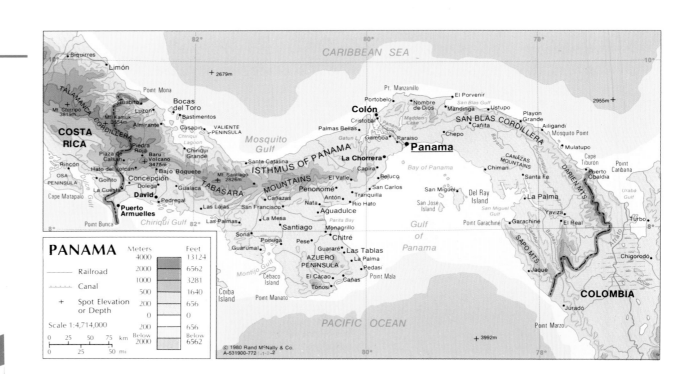

Panama Map Index

	Lat.	Long.		Lat.	Long.		Lat.	Long.		Lat.	Long.
Aguadulce	8°15′N	80°33′W	Chucunaque	8°09′N	77°44′W	Las Lajas	8°15′N	81°52′W	Pedasí	7°32′N	80°02′W
Almirante	9°18′N	82°24′W	Colón	9°22′N	79°54′W	Las Tablas	7°46′N	80°17′W	Penonomé	8°31′N	80°22′W
Azuero Peninsula	7°40′N	80°35′W	Concepción	8°31′N	82°37′W	Mosquitos, Gulf			Puerto Armuelles	8°17′N	82°52′W
Baru Volcano	8°48′N	82°33′W	Darien Mountains	8°20′N	77°22′W	of	9°00′N	81°15′W	San Blas		
Bayano	9°00′N	79°06′W	David	8°26′N	82°26′W	Mulatupo	8°57′N	77°45′W	Cordillera	9°18′N	79°00′W
Bejuco	8°36′N	79°53′W	Del Ray Island	8°22′N	78°55′W	Nombre de Dios	9°35′N	79°28′W	San Miguel	8°27′N	78°56′W
Bocas del Toro	9°20′N	82°15′W	El Real	8°08′N	77°43′W	Palmas Bellas	9°14′N	80°05′W	Santa Catalina	8°47′N	81°20′W
Burica, Point	8°03′N	82°53′W	Garachiné	8°04′N	78°22′W	Panama, Bay of	8°50′N	79°20′W	Santiago	8°06′N	80°59′W
Chepo	9°10′N	79°06′W	Guabito	9°30′N	82°37′W	Panama, Gulf of	8°00′N	79°30′W	Soná	8°01′N	81°19′W
Chiriquí Grande	8°57′N	82°07′W	Guararé	7°49′N	80°17′W	Panama Canal	9°20′N	79°55′W	Tabasara		
Chiriquí Gulf	8°00′N	82°20′W	Jaqué	7°31′N	78°10′W	Panama City	8°58′N	79°31′W	Mountains	8°33′N	81°40′W
Chiriquí Lagoon	9°03′N	82°00′W	La Chorrera	8°53′N	79°47′W	Panama, Isthmus			Ustupo	9°27′N	78°34′W
Chitré	7°58′N	80°26′W	La Palma	7°42′N	80°12′W	of	9°00′N	79°00′W	Yaviza	8°11′N	77°41′W

Memberships OAS, UN.
Subdivisions 9 provinces, 1 territory.
ECONOMY
GNP $3,945,000,000.
Per capita $1,934.
Monetary unit Balboa.
Trade partners U.S., Venezuela, Western European countries, Japan.
Exports Petroleum products, bananas, sugar, shrimp.
Imports Manufactured goods, petroleum, machinery, transportation equipment, food.
LAND
Description Central America.
Area 29,762 mi² (77,082 km²).
Highest point Baru Volcano, 11,401 ft (3,475 m).
Lowest point Sea level.

PEOPLE. Most Panamanians are mestizos, a mixture of Spanish and Indian stocks. Indigenous Indians, blacks from the West Indies, and whites form the rest of the population. Former Spanish rule is reflected by the official language, Spanish, and the predominance of Roman Catholicism. Most people live in the area around the Panama Canal. A wealthy white elite has traditionally directed the government and economy.

ECONOMY AND THE LAND. Because of its strategic location, Panama has long been a center for trade and transportation. The 1914 opening of the Panama Canal, connecting the Atlantic and Pacific oceans, accentuated these strengths and has provided additional revenue and jobs; the

canal area is now Panama's most economically developed region. Agriculture also plays an economic role. The main cash crops include bananas, sugarcane, and coffee, and subsistence farmers raise rice, maize, and beans. The fishing industry is growing in importance, and Panama is a major exporter of shrimp. Oil refining and food processing are expanding industries, and financial services, aided by favorable tax laws and a lack of government controls, contribute to the economy as well. Panama will have to adjust to the economic and technical losses that will accompany the end of United States operation of the canal in 1999. The nation has a mountainous interior and a tropical climate.

HISTORY AND POLITICS. Originally inhabited by Indians, Panama became a Spanish colony in the early 1500s and served as a vital transportation center. In 1821 it overcame Spanish rule and entered the Republic of Greater Colombia. After Colombia vetoed a United States plan to build a canal across the narrow isthmus, Panama, encouraged by the United States, seceded from the republic and became independent in 1903. Eleven years later America completed the canal and established control over it and the Panama Canal Zone. Dissatisfaction with this arrangement resulted in several anti-American riots in the fifties and sixties. A 1968 coup placed the Panamanian National Guard in power, and the movement to end American control of the Canal Zone gained momentum. In 1979 the sovereignty of the Canal Zone was transferred to Panama; it will gain con-

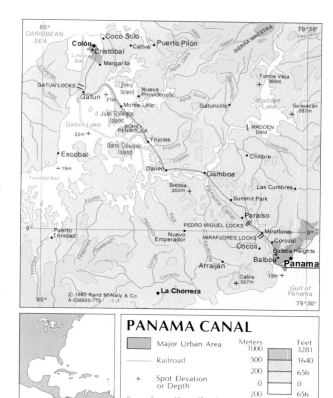

PANAMA CANAL

	Major Urban Area
	Railroad
+	Spot Elevation or Depth

Meters	Feet
1000	3281
500	1640
200	656
0	0
200	656

Scale 1:782,000

trol of the canal in 1999. Some representation has been returned to civilians, but the military continues to exercise considerable control. ∎

PAPUA NEW GUINEA

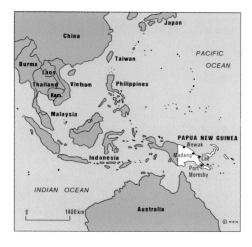

OFFICIAL NAME Papua New Guinea

PEOPLE
Population 3,400,000.
Density 19/mi² (7.3/km²).
Urban 13%.
Capital Port Moresby, New Guinea I., 116,952.
Ethnic groups Melanesian, Papuan, Negrito, Micronesian, Polynesian.
Languages English, Papuan and Negrito languages.
Religions Roman Catholic, Lutheran, indigenous.
Life expectancy 52 female, 50 male.
Literacy 32%.

POLITICS
Government Parliamentary state.
Parties Melanesian Alliance, National, Pangu, Papua Besena, People's Progress, United.
Suffrage Universal adult.
Memberships CW, UN.
Subdivisions 20 provinces.

ECONOMY
GNP $2,000,000,000.
Per capita $650.
Monetary unit Kina.

Trade partners Australia, Japan, Singapore.
Exports Copper, coffee beans, coconut products.
Imports Machinery, manufactured goods, petroleum, food.
LAND
Description South Pacific islands.
Area 178,703 mi² (462,840 km²).
Highest point Mt. Wilhelm, New Guinea I., 14,793 ft (4,509 m).
Lowest point Sea level.

PEOPLE. Almost all inhabitants are Melanesians belonging to several thousand culturally diverse and geographically isolated communities. More than seven hundred languages are spoken, but most people also speak Motu or a dialect of English to communicate with other groups. The most commonly observed religion is Christianity, brought by European missionaries; diverse faiths based on spirit and ancestor worship are also followed.

ECONOMY AND THE LAND. The economic mainstays are agriculture, which employs most of the work force, and the mining of copper and gold. Papua New Guinea has other mineral resources, as well as potential for forestry. The nation consists of the eastern half of New Guinea Island, plus New Britain, New Ireland, Bougainville, and six hundred smaller islands. Terrain includes mountains, volcanoes, broad valleys, and swamps; the climate is tropical.

HISTORY AND POLITICS. Settlers from Southeast Asia are thought to have arrived nearly fifty thousand years ago. Isolated native villages were found by the Spanish and Portuguese in the early 1500s. In 1884 Germany annexed the northeastern part of the island of New Guinea and its offshore islands, and Britain took control of the southeastern section and its islands. Australia assumed administration of the British territory, known as Papua, in 1906 and seized the German regions, or German New Guinea, during World War I. The League of Nations granted Australia a

mandate to New Guinea in 1920. After being occupied by Japan in World War II, Papua and New Guinea were united as an Australian territory from 1945 to 1946. The independent nation of Papua New Guinea came into being in 1975. Bougainville seceded a few months later but rejoined the nation in 1976. ∎

PAPUA NEW GUINEA

+	Spot Elevation or Depth

Scale 1:22,400,000

Papua New Guinea Map Index

	Lat.	Long.		Lat.	Long.
Admiralty Islands	2°10'S	147°00'E	New Hanover	2°30'S	150°15'E
Bismarck			New Ireland	3°20'S	152°00'E
Archipelago	5°00'S	150°00'E	Owen Stanley		
Bismarck Sea	4°00'S	148°00'E	Range	9°20'S	147°55'E
Bougainville	6°00'S	155°00'E	Papua, Gulf of	8°30'S	145°00'E
Fly	8°30'S	143°41'E	Popondetta	8°46'S	148°14'E
Huon Gulf	7°10'S	147°25'E	Port Moresby	9°30'S	147°10'E
Kavieng	2°35'S	150°50'E	Rabaul	4°12'S	152°12'E
Kerema	8°00'S	145°45'E	Sepik	3°51'S	144°34'E
Lae	6°45'S	147°00'E	Solomon Sea	8°00'S	153°00'E
Lorengau	2°00'S	147°15'E	Talasea	5°20'S	150°05'E
Madang	5°15'S	145°50'E	Torres Strait	10°25'S	142°10'E
Mount Hagen	5°50'S	144°15'E	Vanima	2°40'S	141°20'E
New Britain	6°00'S	150°00'E	Wewak	3°35'S	143°40'E
New Guinea	4°00'S	145°00'E	Wilhelm, Mount	5°45'S	145°05'E

PARAGUAY

OFFICIAL NAME Republic of Paraguay

PEOPLE
Population 3,230,000.
Density 21/mi² (7.9/km²).
Urban 39%.
Capital Asunción, 455,517.

Ethnic groups Mestizo 95%.
Languages Spanish, Guarani.
Religions Roman Catholic 97%, Mennonite.
Life expectancy 67 female, 63 male.
Literacy 81%.

POLITICS
Government Republic.
Parties Colorado, Febrerista, Liberal, Radical Liberal.
Suffrage Universal adult.
Memberships OAS, UN.
Subdivisions 20 departments.

ECONOMY
GDP $5,800,000,000.
Per capita $1,411.
Monetary unit Guaraní.
Trade partners Brazil, Argentina, West Germany, Japan, U.S.
Exports Cotton, soybeans, wood products.
Imports Machinery, fuels, motor vehicles, food.

LAND
Description Central South America, landlocked.
Area 157,048 mi² (406,752 km²).
Highest point 2,625 ft (800 m).
Lowest point 151 ft (46 m).

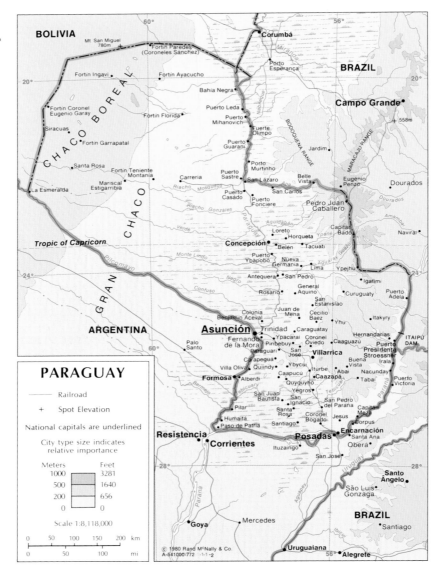

Paraguay Map Index

	Lat.	Long.
Aquidabán	23°11'S	57°32'W
Asunción	25°16'S	57°40'W
Bahía Negra	20°15'S	58°12'W
Bella Vista	22°08'S	56°31'W
Capitán Bado	23°16'S	55°32'W
Carreria	21°59'S	58°35'W
Chaco Boreal	20°30'S	60°30'W
Concepción	23°25'S	57°17'W
Coroneles Sánchez →		
Fortín Paredes	19°20'S	59°58'W
Encarnación	27°20'S	55°54'W
Fernando de la Mora	25°19'S	57°36'W
Fortín Ayacucho	19°58'S	59°47'W
Fortín Coronel Eugenio Garay	20°31'S	62°08'W
Fortín Florida	20°45'S	59°17'W
Fortín Garrapatal	21°27'S	61°30'W
Fortín Ingavi	19°55'S	60°47'W
Fortín Paredes (Coroneles Sánchez)	19°20'S	59°58'W
Fortín Teniente Montania	22°04'S	59°57'W
Fuerte Olimpo	21°02'S	57°54'W
Gran Chaco	23°00'S	60°00'W
La Esmeralda	22°13'S	62°38'W
Mariscal Estigarribia	22°02'S	60°38'W
Monte Lindo	23°56'S	57°12'W
Paraguay	27°18'S	58°38'W
Paraná	27°15'S	58°37'W
Pedro Juan Caballero	22°34'S	55°37'W
Pilcomayo	25°21'S	57°42'W
Puerto Casado	22°20'S	57°55'W
Puerto Fonciere	22°29'S	57°48'W
Puerto Guaraní	21°18'S	57°55'W
Puerto Leda	20°41'S	58°02'W
Puerto Mihanovich	20°52'S	57°59'W
Puerto Sastre	22°06'S	57°59'W
San Carlos	22°16'S	57°18'W
San Lázaro	22°10'S	57°55'W
Santa Rosa	21°46'S	61°43'W
Siracuas	21°03'S	61°46'W
Tebicuary	26°36'S	58°16'W
Trinidad	25°15'S	57°38'W
Verde	23°09'S	57°37'W
Villarrica	25°45'S	56°26'W
Ypejhú	23°54'S	55°20'W

PEOPLE. Paraguay's population displays a homogeneity unusual in South America; most people are a mix of Spanish and Guarani Indian ancestry, are Roman Catholic, and speak both Spanish and Guarani. The small number of unassimilated Guarani live mostly in western Paraguay, known as the Chaco. There are some foreign communities, mostly German, Japanese, and Brazilian. Culture combines Spanish and Indian traditions.

ECONOMY AND THE LAND. Agriculture—based on cotton, soybeans, and cattle—forms the keystone of the economy. Forestry also contributes significantly to Paraguay's exports. The lack of direct access to the sea, an unskilled labor force, and a history of war and instability have resulted in an underdeveloped economy; manufacturing in particular has suffered. There is great potential for hydroelectric power, and it is already under exploitation. The Paraguay River divides the country into the semiarid Chaco plains in the west and the fertile east, where most farming takes place. The climate is tropical.

HISTORY AND POLITICS. The indigenous Guarani formed an agricultural society centered around what is now Asunción. Portuguese and Spanish explorers arrived in the early 1500s, and the region subsequently gained importance as the center of Spanish holdings in southern South America. During the 1700s Jesuit missionaries worked to convert thousands of Indians to Roman Catholicism. After gaining independence in 1811, Paraguay was ruled until 1870 by three successive dictators: José Gaspar Rodriguez de Francia, who held power from 1814 to 1840 and sealed Paraguay off from foreign influence; Carlos Antonio López, who reversed this isolationism during his rule from 1841 to 1862; and his

son, Francisco Solano López, who led Paraguay into a disastrous war against Uruguay, Argentina, and Brazil that cost the nation half its population. A war against Bolivia from 1932 to 1935 increased Paraguay's territory but further weakened its stability. Alternating weak and repressive regimes followed until 1954, when General Alfredo Stroessner came to power. Having restricted almost all opposition, he has since ruled continuously. ■

West of the Paraguay River lies the Chaco, a region of dry plains with a climate harsher than that of eastern

Paraguay. The nation's large cattle ranches are found here, with scenes reminiscent of the American West.

PERU

OFFICIAL NAME Republic of Peru

PEOPLE

Population 19,520,000.
Density 39/mi² (15/km²).
Urban 65%.
Capital Lima, 371,122.
Ethnic groups Indian 45%, mestizo 37%, white 15%.
Languages Spanish, Quechua, Aymara.
Religions Roman Catholic.
Life expectancy 60 female, 56 male.
Literacy 72%.

POLITICS

Government Republic.
Parties American Popular Revolutionary Alliance, Popular Action, Popular Christian, United Left.
Suffrage Universal, over 18.
Memberships OAS, UN.
Subdivisions 24 departments, 1 constitutional province.

ECONOMY

GNP $19,200,000,000.
Per capita $1,018.
Monetary unit Sol.
Trade partners U.S., Japan, Western European countries.
Exports Copper, silver, petroleum, lead, zinc, fish products.
Imports Machinery, transportation equipment, food, manufactured goods.

LAND

Description Western South America.
Area 496,224 mi² (1,285,216 km²).
Highest point Mt. Huascarán, 22,133 ft (6,746 m).
Lowest point Sea level.

PEOPLE. Peru's Indian population constitutes the nation's largest ethnic group and the largest Indian concentration in North or South America. Although whites make up the third largest group after Indians and mestizos, they have historically controlled much of the wealth. The Indians are often geographically and culturally remote from the ruling classes and generally live in poverty.

ECONOMY AND THE LAND. Considerable natural resources have made Peru a leader in the production of minerals—notably copper, lead, and silver—and in fishing. The food-processing, textile, and oil-refining industries also contribute. Productivity has been slowed by a mountainous terrain that impedes transport and communication, earthquakes and other natural disasters, a largely unskilled work force, and years of stringent military rule. Climate varies from arid and mild in the coastal desert to temperate but cool in the Andean highlands and hot and humid in the eastern jungles and plains.

HISTORY AND POLITICS. Several sophisticated Indian cultures arose in the region between 900 B.C. and A.D. 1200, the last of which was the Incan. Builders of an empire stretching from Colombia to Chile, the Inca were conquered by the Spanish by 1533. For almost the next three hundred years Peru was a harshly ruled Spanish colony and center for colonial administration. Independence from Spain, which came in 1821, was achieved largely through the efforts of José de San Martín of Argentina and Simón Bolívar of Venezuela. Spain did not formally recognize Peruvian independence until 1879. Peru was ruled by military officers for the rest of the century. In 1883 it was defeated by Chile and Bolivia in the War of the Pacific and lost its valuable southern nitrate region. Despite a government ban, a reform party gained momentum in the 1930s and 1940s. A moderate reform government was elected in 1963, but instability continued and the government fell in a 1968 military coup. In an attempt to resolve economic inequities, some industries were nationalized and land reform was instituted. A 1975 coup was followed by elections in 1980 and 1985, but the government remained precarious. ∎

Peru Map Index

	Lat.	Long.
Abancay	13°35′S	72°55′W
Acarí	15°26′S	74°37′W
Acomayo	13°55′S	71°41′W
Acuracay	5°35′S	74°10′W
Altiplano	18°00′S	68°00′E
Amazon	4°12′S	69°57′W
Andes	14°00′S	74°00′W
Andoas	2°50′S	76°30′W
Apurímac	11°48′S	74°03′W
Arequipa	16°24′S	71°33′W
Atalaya	10°44′S	73°45′W
Atico	16°14′S	73°39′W
Ausangate Mountain	13°48′S	71°14′W
Ayabaca	4°38′S	79°43′W
Ayacucho	13°07′S	74°13′W
Ayaviri	14°52′S	70°35′W
Barranca	4°50′S	76°42′W
Barranca	4°50′S	76°42′W
Bayovar	5°50′S	81°03′W
Blue Cordillera	9°00′S	75°35′W
Bolognesi	6°35′S	73°10′W
Borja	4°26′S	77°33′W
Caballococha	3°54′S	70°32′W
Cailloma	15°12′S	71°46′W
Cajamarca	7°10′S	78°31′W
Callao	12°04′S	77°09′W
Camaná	16°37′S	72°42′W
Cañete	13°05′S	76°24′W
Caraybamba	14°24′S	73°09′W
Casma	9°28′S	78°19′W
Castilla	5°12′S	80°38′W
Central Cordillera	9°00′S	77°00′W
Cerro de Pasco	10°41′S	76°16′W
Chachapoyas	6°13′S	77°51′W
Chepén	7°13′S	79°27′W
Chiclayo	6°46′S	79°51′W
Chilete	7°14′S	78°51′W
Chimbote	9°05′S	78°36′W
Chincha Alta	13°27′S	76°08′W
Chocope	7°47′S	79°13′W
Chulucanas	5°06′S	80°10′W
Colta	15°10′S	73°18′W
Contamana	7°15′S	74°54′W
Coropuna Mountain	15°31′S	72°42′W
Cotabambas	13°45′S	72°21′W
Cuzco	13°31′S	71°59′W
Eastern Cordillera	11°00′S	74°00′W
Eten	6°54′S	79°52′W
Ferreñafe	6°38′S	79°45′W
Ganso Azul	8°51′S	74°44′W
Guayaquil, Gulf of	3°00′S	80°30′W
Huacho	11°07′S	77°37′W
Huallaga	5°10′S	75°32′W
Huallanca	8°49′S	77°52′W
Huamachuco	7°48′S	78°04′W
Huambo	15°44′S	72°07′W
Huancavelica	12°46′S	75°02′W
Huancayo	12°04′S	75°14′W
Huando	12°29′S	74°58′W
Huánuco	9°55′S	76°14′W
Huaral	11°30′S	77°12′W
Huaraz	9°32′S	77°32′W
Huarmey	10°04′S	78°10′W
Huascarán	9°07′S	77°37′W
Ica	14°04′S	75°42′W
Ilo	17°38′S	71°20′W
Intutu	3°39′S	74°44′W
Iquitos	3°46′S	73°15′W
Jaén	5°42′S	78°47′W
Jauja	11°48′S	75°30′W
Juanjuí	7°11′S	76°45′W
Juliaca	15°30′S	70°08′W
Lagunas	5°14′S	75°38′W
Lamas	6°25′S	76°35′W
Lambayeque	6°42′S	79°55′W
La Merced	11°03′S	75°19′W
La Oroya	11°32′S	75°54′W
Lima	12°03′S	77°03′W

	Lat.	Long.
Machupicchu	13°07′S	72°34′W
Mamara	14°14′S	72°35′W
Manu	12°15′S	70°55′W
Marañón	4°42′S	74°40′W
Masisea	8°36′S	74°19′W
Misti Volcano	16°18′S	71°24′W
Mollendo	17°02′S	72°01′W
Moquegua	17°12′S	70°56′W
Moyobamba	6°03′S	76°58′W
Napo	3°20′S	72°40′W
Nazca	14°50′S	74°57′W
Ocoña	16°26′S	73°07′W
Ollantaitambo	13°16′S	72°16′W
Olmos	5°59′S	79°46′W
Omaguas	4°08′S	73°15′W
Orellana	6°54′S	75°04′W
Pacasmayo	7°24′S	79°34′W
Paita	5°06′S	81°07′W
Palpa	14°32′S	75°11′W
Pampas	12°24′S	74°54′W
Pastaza	4°50′S	76°25′W
Pativilca	10°42′S	77°47′W
Pebas	3°20′S	71°49′W
Pisco	13°42′S	76°13′W
Piura	5°12′S	80°38′W
Pomabamba	8°50′S	77°28′W
Pomata	16°16′S	69°18′W

	Lat.	Long.
Pucallpa	8°23′S	74°32′W
Puerto Bermúdez	10°20′S	74°54′W
Puerto Chicama	7°42′S	79°27′W
Puerto Maldonado	12°36′S	69°11′W
Puerto Padilla	10°15′S	71°39′W
Puerto Portillo	9°46′S	72°45′W
Puerto Victoria	9°54′S	74°58′W
Pullo	15°14′S	73°50′W
Puno	15°50′S	70°02′W
Punta Moreno	7°36′S	78°54′W
Puquio	14°42′S	74°08′W
Putina	14°55′S	69°52′W
Putumayo	2°45′S	70°05′W
Quillabamba	12°49′S	72°43′W
Quincemil	13°16′S	70°38′W
Requena	4°58′S	73°50′W
Reventazón	6°10′S	80°58′W
Rioja	6°05′S	77°09′W
Salaverry	8°14′S	78°58′W
Saña	6°55′S	79°35′W
Sandia	14°17′S	69°26′W
San Nicolás	15°13′S	75°12′W
Santa Clotilde	2°34′S	73°44′W
Santo Tomás	14°29′S	72°06′W
Saquena	4°40′S	73°31′W
Sechura Bay	5°42′S	81°00′W

	Lat.	Long.
Sicuani	14°16′S	71°13′W
Sullana	4°53′S	80°41′W
Suyo	4°30′S	80°00′W
Tacna	18°01′S	70°15′W
Talara	4°34′S	81°17′W
Tamshiyacu	4°05′S	72°58′W
Tarapoto	6°30′S	76°20′W
Tarma	11°25′S	75°42′W
Tarquí	1°35′S	75°15′W
Tingo María	9°09′S	75°56′W
Titicaca, Lake	15°50′S	69°20′W
Trujillo	8°07′S	79°02′W
Tumbes	3°34′S	80°28′W
Ucayali	4°38′S	73°30′W
Uchiza	8°29′S	76°23′W
Urcos	13°42′S	71°38′W
Urubamba	10°44′S	73°45′W
Vilcabamba Cordillera	13°00′S	73°00′W
Vitarte	12°02′S	76°56′W
Western Cordillera	12°30′S	76°00′W
Yavarí	4°21′S	70°02′W
Yurimaguas	5°54′S	76°05′W
Zorritos	3°40′S	80°40′W

PERU

Railroad
Oil Pipeline
▲ Major Oil Field
+ Spot Elevation or Depth

Meters	Feet
Above 4000	Above 13124
2000	6562
1000	3281
500	1640
200	656
0	0
200	656
Below 2000	Below 6562

Scale 1:14,667,000

© 1980 Rand McNally & Co.
A-541100-772

Traces of the ancient civilization of the Incas can be seen throughout Peru. Here, Andean farmers use an Incan rock fortress as a shelter for their llama flock.

PHILIPPINES

OFFICIAL NAME Republic of
the Philippines

PEOPLE
Population 55,140,000.
Density 476/mi² (184/km²).
Urban 37%.
Capital Manila, Luzon I., 1,626,249.
Ethnic groups Christian Malay 92%, Muslim Malay
4%, Chinese 2%.
Languages Pilipino, Spanish, English,
Malay-Polynesian languages.
Religions Roman Catholic 83%, Protestant 9%,
Muslim 5%, Buddhist and others 3%.
Life expectancy 65 female, 61 male.
Literacy 88%.

POLITICS
Government Republic.
Parties Laban, Liberal, Nacionalista, New Society.
Suffrage Universal adult.
Memberships ASEAN, UN.
Subdivisions 73 provinces, 61 chartered cities.

ECONOMY
GNP $39,000,000,000.
Per capita $760.
Monetary unit Peso.
Trade partners U.S., Japan, Western European
countries, Hong Kong.
Exports Coconut products, sugar, wood, textiles,
copper concentrates.
Imports Petroleum, industrial equipment,
transportation equipment, wheat.

LAND
Description Southeastern Asian islands.
Area 115,831 mi² (300,000 km²).
Highest point Mt. Apo, Mindanao I., 9,692 ft
(2,954 m).
Lowest point Sea level.

PEOPLE. Nearly all Filipinos are descended from
Malay peoples. The majority population is
Roman Catholic, a reflection of centuries under
Spanish rule, but a Muslim minority has begun
agitating for autonomy. Other minority groups
include Filipinos of Chinese ancestry and forest
tribes that inhabit the remote areas of Mindanao.
Although nearly ninety native languages and dialects are spoken, Pilipino, English, and Spanish
are the official languages. The wide gap between
rich and poor was inherited from a plantation
economy that concentrated wealth in the hands
of the landowners.

ECONOMY AND THE LAND. The Philippines is
a primarily agricultural nation, relying on rice,
sugar, coconuts, and wood. Fishing is an important activity. Considerable reserves of copper,
nickel, and chromite make mining important,
and manufacturing is developing through government incentives. A dependence on imported
goods, along with inadequate but growing power
and transport systems, has hampered growth.
The archipelago of more than seven thousand
islands is marked by mountains, volcanoes, forests, and inland plains. The climate is tropical
and includes a typhoon season.

Philippines Map Index

	Lat.	Long.		Lat.	Long.
Agusan	9°00'N	125°31'E	Manila	14°35'N	121°00'E
Angeles	15°09'N	120°35'E	Marawi	8°01'N	124°18'E
Apo, Mount	6°59'N	125°16'E	*Masbate Island*	12°15'N	123°30'E
Babuyan Islands	19°10'N	121°40'E	*Mindanao*	8°00'N	125°00'E
Baguio	16°25'N	120°36'E	*Mindanao Sea*	9°10'N	124°25'E
Balabac Island	7°57'N	117°01'E	*Mindoro*	12°50'N	121°05'E
Balabac Strait	7°35'N	117°00'E	*Mindoro Strait*	12°20'N	120°40'E
Basilan Island	6°34'N	122°03'E	*Moro Gulf*	6°51'N	123°00'E
Batan Islands	20°30'N	121°50'E	Naga	10°13'N	123°45'E
Bohol	9°50'N	124°10'E	*Negros*	10°00'N	123°00'E
Bojeador, Cape	18°30'N	120°34'E	Oatbalogan	11°46'N	124°53'E
Cabanatuan	15°29'N	120°58'E	Ormoc	11°00'N	124°37'E
Cagayan	18°22'N	121°37'E	Ozamiz	8°08'N	123°50'E
Cagayan de Oro	8°29'N	124°39'E	*Palawan*	9°30'N	118°30'E
Calamian Group	12°00'N	120°00'E	*Panay*	11°15'N	122°30'E
Catanduanes			*Polillo Islands*	14°50'N	122°05'E
Island	13°45'N	124°15'E	*Pulog, Mount*	16°36'N	120°54'E
Cavite	14°29'N	120°55'E	Quezon City	14°38'N	121°00'E
Cebu	10°18'N	123°54'E	Roxas	12°35'N	121°31'E
Cebu	10°20'N	123°40'E	*Samar*	12°00'N	125°00'E
Celebes Sea	5°00'N	123°00'E	*San Agustin,*		
Datu Piang	7°01'N	124°30'E	*Cape*	6°16'N	126°11'E
Davao	7°04'N	125°36'E	San Fernando	16°37'N	120°19'E
Dumaguete	9°18'N	123°18'E	San Pablo	14°04'N	121°19'E
Escarpada Point	18°31'N	122°13'E	*Sibuyan Sea*	12°50'N	122°40'E
General Santos	6°07'N	125°11'E	*Sulu Archipelago*	6°00'N	121°00'E
Iloilo	10°42'N	122°34'E	*Sulu Sea*	8°00'N	120°00'E
Leyte	10°50'N	124°50'E	Tacloban	11°15'N	125°00'E
Lingayen Gulf	16°15'N	120°14'E	*Tinaca Point*	5°33'N	125°20'E
Luzon	16°00'N	121°00'E	Tuguegarao	17°37'N	121°44'E
Luzon Strait	20°30'N	121°00'E	*Visayan Sea*	11°35'N	123°51'E
Madre, Sierra	16°20'N	122°00'E	Zamboanga	6°54'N	122°04'E

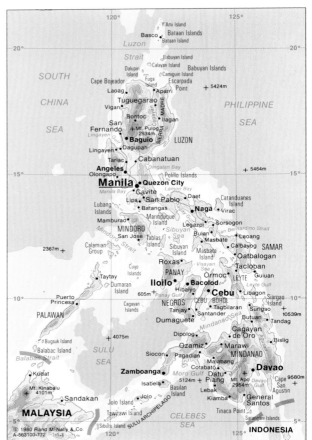

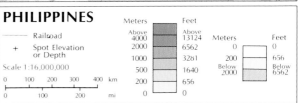

PHILIPPINES

	Meters	Feet				Meters	Feet
Railroad	Above 4000	Above 13124		Meters	Feet		
+ Spot Elevation or Depth	2000	6562		200	0 656		
Scale 1:16,000,000	1000	3281		Below 2000	Below 6562		
	500	1640					
0 100 200 300 400 km	200	656					
0 100 200 mi	0	0					

HISTORY AND POLITICS. It is believed that Ne-
gritos from Borneo and Sumatra made their way
across land bridges to settle the Philippines
about thirty thousand years ago. Around 3000
B.C. the Malay peoples arrived, coming from the
south in a series of migrations, first by land
bridges and then by boat. Chinese merchants
and traders reached the islands in the ninth century. Many who came to trade settled permanently in the Philippines, and these are the ancestors of today's Chinese minority. Islam was
introduced in the fourteenth century by invading
Arabs, but the Malays remained the dominant
group, and Muslim influence was confined mostly to the southern regions. In the 1500s the first
Europeans arrived, and Ferdinand Magellan
claimed the islands for Spain in 1521. By 1565 the
Spanish had secured the Philippines under their
control. The Roman Catholic church became a
dominant influence, and the Malay population
underwent widespread conversion to the colonial
religion. Most Filipinos were not satisfied under
Spanish rule, however, and the more than three
centuries of Spanish rule were marked by rebellions against the colonial power. These generally
small uprisings were easily controlled, but in the
late 1800s Filipino leader Emilio Aguinaldo organized an independence movement that was
put down first by the Spanish and then by the
United States, which gained the islands in 1898
after defeating Spain in the Spanish-American
War. During World War II Japan occupied the
Philippines. Independence came in 1946 and was
followed by a rebellion by Communists demanding land reform; the rebels were defeated in
1954. Ferdinand Marcos was elected president in
1965, instituting a repressive regime marked by
the restriction of civil liberties and consolidation
of presidential power. Charges of vote fraud rid-
dled the 1986 presidential election, in which
Corazon Aquino, wife of assassinated opposition
leader Benigno Aquino, ran against Marcos.
After widespread protests broke out following
Marcos's declaration of victory, he fled the island, and Aquino assumed power. Instability
continued, however, marked by coup attempts,
a growing insurgency group, and unresolved
problems of poverty, social inequity, and
corruption. ∎

**Rice terraces, such as these in Banaue, enable the
Filipinos to produce their major food crop in terrain
otherwise unsuited for agriculture. Despite widespread
cultivation, additional rice must be imported to feed the
nation's large population.**

PITCAIRN

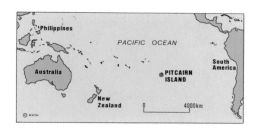

OFFICIAL NAME Pitcairn, Henderson, Dulcie and Oeno Islands

PEOPLE
Population 70.
Density 3.7/mi² (1.4/km²).
Urban 91%.
Capital Adamstown, Pitcairn I., 64.
Ethnic groups Mixed European and Tahitian.
Languages English.
Religions Seventh Day Adventist.

POLITICS
Government Colony (U.K.).
Suffrage Universal, over 18.

ECONOMY
GNP $480,000.
Per capita $6,800.
Monetary unit New Zealand dollar.
Exports Fruits, vegetables, postage stamps.
Imports Fuels, machinery, building materials, foodstuffs.

LAND
Description South Pacific islands.
Area 19 mi² (49 km²).
Lowest point Sea level.

PEOPLE. The population of Pitcairn is of mixed European and Tahitian ancestry, most descendants of the British sailor Fletcher Christian and his fellow mutineers from H.M.S. *Bounty*. Uninhabited for about three years in the late 1850s, Pitcairn has been permanently occupied since 1859. In the past decades emigration to New Zealand has been an ongoing trend.

ECONOMY AND THE LAND. Fertile soil provide for subsistence farming and some export crops as well. Many islanders also engage in fishing and sell handicrafts to the passengers of the ships that dock here. Pitcairn is a rugged, volcanic island, and its shores are nearly inaccessible. The colony includes the uninhabited islands of Henderson, Dulcie, and Oeno. The climate is mild.

HISTORY AND POLITICS. More than six hundred years ago, Polynesians likely lived on Pitcairn off and on, but it was uninhabited when the British admiral Philip Carteret arrived in 1767, naming the island after the midshipman who first sighted it. In 1789 crew members of H.M.S. *Bounty*, led by Fletcher Christian, carried out a mutiny in the South Pacific, and the following year Christian, eight other mutineers, six Tahitian women, and twelve Tahitian men left Tahiti and sailed to Pitcairn. Violence marked the community's early days; by 1800 John Adams was the only surviving adult male. In 1808 a United States ship inadvertently arrived at the island, yet Pitcairn remained largely unheard of until 1814 when the British ships *Briton* and *Tagus* reached its shores. Between 1814 and 1831 the population grew from forty to eighty-six, and concern about drought and dwindling resources caused the Pitcairners to leave for Tahiti. Unable to adjust to the life-style of that island, six

months later they returned to Pitcairn. In 1838 the islanders obtained a constitution and universal adult suffrage, and most Pitcairners trace the island's colonial status back to this time. Pitcairn was again evacuated when the United Kingdom arranged for resettlement on Norfolk Island in 1856, but forty-three Pitcairners returned to the island between 1859 and 1864. Pitcairn was officially made a British colony under the Settlements Act of 1887, and the island continues as a colony of the United Kingdom. ■

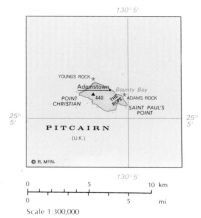

Map shows major island only.

Scale 1:300,000

Pitcairn Map Index

	Lat.	Long.		Lat.	Long.
Adams Rock	25°04'S	130°05'W	Saint Paul's		
Adamstown	25°04'S	130°05'W	Point	25°04'S	130°05'W
Bounty Bay	25°04'S	130°05'W	Youngs Rock	25°03'S	130°07'W
Christian, Point	25°04'S	130°07'W			

POLAND

Palace of King Jan III Sobieski, Warsaw, Poland

POLAND

OFFICIAL NAME Polish
People's Republic

PEOPLE
Population 37,055,000.
Density 307/mi² (119/km²).
Urban 59%.
Capital Warsaw, 1,628,900.
Ethnic groups Polish 99%.
Languages Polish.
Religions Roman Catholic 95%.
Life expectancy 75 female, 70 male.
Literacy 98%.

POLITICS
Government Socialist republic.
Parties United Workers'.
Suffrage Universal, over 18.
Memberships CEMA, UN, Warsaw Pact.
Subdivisions 49 provinces.

ECONOMY
GNP $186,800,000,000.
Per capita $5,160.
Monetary unit Zloty.
Trade partners U.S.S.R., Eastern European countries, West Germany.
Exports Machinery, equipment, fuels, manufactured goods, textiles, food.
Imports Machinery, petroleum, raw materials, food.

LAND
Description Eastern Europe.
Area 120,728 mi² (312,683 km²).
Highest point Rysy, 8,199 ft (2,499 m).
Lowest point Raczki Elbląskie, 5.9 ft (1.8 m) below sea level.

PEOPLE. Prior to World War II, Poland's minority groups included 4.5 million Ukrainians, 3 million Jews, 1 million Byelorussians, and 800,000 Germans, Nazi persecution during the war virtually obliterated the Jewish community and led to the emigration of most other groups as well. The result is today's homogeneous population. Nearly all inhabitants are of Polish descent, and Roman Catholicism, practiced by nearly all Poles, remains a unifying force. The urban population has risen in the postwar period because of government emphasis on industrialization.

ECONOMY AND THE LAND. Government policies since the war have transformed Poland from an agricultural nation into an industrial one. It is a leading producer of coal and has several metal-processing industries. Machinery and textiles are important products. Although most industries are government controlled, the majority of farms are privately owned. Poland's poor soil and short growing season have kept it from achieving agricultural self-sufficiency. Shortages in consumer goods have been chronic since the 1970s, when debts to the West were compounded by the failure of Polish goods in world markets. Poland has a mostly flat terrain—except for mountains in the south—and a temperate climate.

HISTORY AND POLITICS. Slavic tribes inhabited the region of modern Poland several thousand years ago. The Piast dynasty began in the A.D. 900s and established Roman Catholicism as the official religion. In the sixteenth century the Jagiellonian dynasty guided the empire to its height of expansion. A subsequent series of upheavals and wars weakened Poland, and from the 1770s to the 1790s it was partitioned three times, finally disappearing as an independent state. In 1918, following the Allies' World War I victory, Poland regained its independence and, through the 1919 Treaty of Versailles, much of its former territory. World War II began with Germany's invasion of Poland in 1939. A Soviet invasion that same year resulted in a country partitioned between Germany and the Soviet Union. When the Germans attacked the Soviets in 1941, all of Poland fell to the Nazis. Poland came under Communist rule with the end of the war, in 1945, and the British, United States, and Soviet heads of state reached an agreement that shifted Poland's borders to the west. Antigovernment strikes and riots, some spurred by rising food prices, erupted periodically, and following the formation of the trade union Solidarity, the government imposed martial law in 1981. Although martial law was lifted in 1982, many restrictions and tensions remain. ■

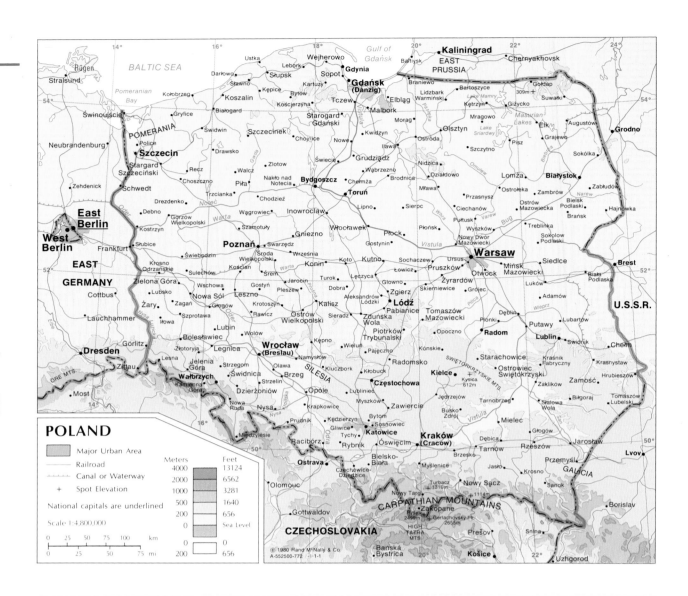

POLAND

Major Urban Area
Railroad
Canal or Waterway
+ Spot Elevation

National capitals are underlined

Scale 1:4,800,000

Meters	Feet
4000	13124
2000	6562
1000	3281
500	1640
200	656
0	Sea Level
200	656

© 1980 Rand McNally & Co
A-552500-772 -1-1-1

Poland Map Index

	Lat.	Long.		Lat.	Long.		Lat.	Long.		Lat.	Long.
Białystok	53°09'N	23°09'E	Koszalin	54°12'N	16°09'E	Otwock	52°07'N	21°16'E	Szczecinek	53°43'N	16°42'E
Biebrza	53°37'N	22°56'E	Kraków (Cracow)	50°03'N	19°58'E	Pabianice	51°40'N	19°22'E	Tarnów	50°01'N	21°00'E
Bielsko-Biała	49°49'N	19°02'E	Kutno	52°15'N	19°23'E	*Pasłęka*	54°26'N	19°45'E	Tczew	54°06'N	18°47'E
Bolesławiec	51°16'N	15°34'E	*Kysica*	50°54'N	20°55'E	Piła	53°10'N	16°44'E	Tomaszów		
Breslau →			Legnica	51°13'N	16°09'E	*Pilica*	51°52'N	21°17'E	Mazowiecki	51°32'N	20°01'E
Wrocław	51°06'N	17°00'E	Leszno	51°51'N	16°35'E	Piotrków			Toruń	53°02'N	18°35'E
Brzeg	50°52'N	17°27'E	Łódź	51°46'N	19°30'E	Trybunalski	51°25'N	19°42'E	*Turbacz*	49°33'N	20°08'E
Bug	52°31'N	21°05'E	Łomża	53°11'N	22°05'E	Płock	52°33'N	19°43'E	*Vistula*	54°22'N	18°55'E
Bydgoszcz	53°08'N	18°00'E	Lubin	51°24'N	16°13'E	*Pomeranian Bay*	54°00'N	14°15'E	Wałbrzych	50°46'N	16°17'E
Carpathian			Lublin	51°15'N	22°35'E	Poznań	52°25'N	16°55'E	Warsaw	52°15'N	21°00'E
Mountains	49°20'N	20°30'E	Malbork	54°02'N	19°01'E	*Prosna*	52°10'N	17°39'E	*Warta*	52°35'N	14°39'E
Chełm	51°10'N	23°28'E	*Mamry, Lake*	54°08'N	21°42'E	Pruszków	52°11'N	20°48'E	Wejherowo	54°37'N	18°15'E
Cracow →			*Masurian Lakes*	53°45'N	21°00'E	Przemyśl	49°47'N	22°47'E	*Wieprz*	51°34'N	21°49'E
Kraków	50°03'N	19°58'E	Mielec	50°18'N	21°25'E	Puławy	51°25'N	21°57'E	*Wkra*	52°27'N	20°44'E
Częstochowa	50°49'N	19°06'E	Mińsk			Racibórz	50°06'N	18°13'E	Włocławek	52°39'N	19°02'E
Danzig →			Mazowiecki	52°11'N	21°34'E	Radom	51°25'N	21°10'E	Wrocław		
Gdańsk	54°23'N	18°40'E	*Narew*	52°26'N	20°42'E	Radomsko	51°05'N	19°25'E	(Breslau)	51°06'N	17°00'E
Dzierżoniów	50°44'N	16°39'E	*Narew*	52°26'N	20°42'E	Rybnik	50°06'N	18°32'E	Zakopane	49°19'N	19°57'E
Elbląg	54°10'N	19°25'E	*Noteć*	52°44'N	15°26'E	*Rysy*	49°12'N	20°04'E	Zamość	50°44'N	23°15'E
Ełk	53°50'N	22°22'E	Nowa Sól	51°48'N	15°44'E	Rzeszów	50°03'N	22°00'E	Żary	51°38'N	15°09'E
Gdańsk (Danzig)	54°23'N	18°40'E	Nowy Sącz	49°38'N	20°42'E	*San*	50°45'N	21°51'E	Zawiercie	50°30'N	19°25'E
Gdańsk, Gulf of	54°40'N	19°15'E	Nysa	50°29'N	17°20'E	Siedlce	52°11'N	22°16'E	Zduńska Wola	51°36'N	18°57'E
Gdynia	54°32'N	18°33'E	*Nysa Kłodzka*	50°49'N	17°50'E	Słupsk	54°28'N	17°01'E	Zgierz	51°52'N	19°25'E
Gniezno	52°31'N	17°37'E	*Nysa Łużicka*	52°04'N	14°46'E	*Sniardwy, Lake*	53°46'N	21°44'E	Zielona Góra	51°56'N	15°31'E
Grudziądz	53°29'N	18°45'E	*Odra (Oder)*	53°32'N	14°38'E	Sopot	54°28'N	18°34'E	Żyrardów	52°04'N	20°25'E
Gwda	53°04'N	16°44'E	Olsztyn	53°48'N	20°29'E	Starachowice	51°03'N	21°04'E			
Inowrocław	52°48'N	18°15'E	*Omulew*	53°05'N	21°32'E	Stargard					
Jarosław	50°02'N	22°42'E	Opole	50°41'N	17°55'E	Szczeciński	53°20'N	15°02'E			
Jelenia Góra	50°55'N	15°46'E	Ostrowiec			Starogard					
Kalisz	51°46'N	18°06'E	Świętokrzyski	50°57'N	21°23'E	Gdański	53°59'N	18°33'E			
Katowice	50°16'N	19°00'E	Ostrów			Świdnica	50°51'N	16°29'E			
Kielce	50°52'N	20°37'E	Wielkopolski	51°39'N	17°49'E	Świnoujście	53°53'N	14°14'E			
Konin	52°13'N	18°16'E	Oświęcim	50°03'N	19°12'E	Szczecin	53°24'N	14°32'E			

PORTUGAL

OFFICIAL NAME Portuguese
Republic

PEOPLE

Population 10,065,000.
Density 283/mi² (109/km²).
Urban 30%.
Capital Lisbon, 807,200.
Ethnic groups Mediterranean, African.
Languages Portuguese.
Religions Roman Catholic 97%.
Life expectancy 75 female, 70 male.
Literacy 80%.

POLITICS

Government Republic.
Parties Communist, Social Democratic, Social
Democratic Center, Socialist.
Suffrage Universal, over 18.
Memberships EC, NATO, OECD, UN.
Subdivisions 18 districts, 2 autonomous regions.

ECONOMY

GNP $23,400,000,000.
Per capita $2,328.
Monetary unit Escudo.
Trade partners U.K., West Germany, other Western
European countries, U.S.
Exports Clothing, textiles, cork and cork products,
wood, food and wine.
Imports Petroleum, industrial machinery,
transportation equipment, cotton, chemicals.

LAND

Description Southern Europe.
Area 35,516 mi² (91,985 km²).
Highest point Pico Pt., 7,713 ft (2,351 m).
Lowest point Sea level.

PEOPLE. Although many invaders have been
drawn by Portugal's long coastline throughout
past centuries, today the population is relatively
homogeneous. One group of invaders, the Romans, laid the basis for the chief language, Portuguese, which developed from Latin. The only
significant minority is composed of black Africans from former colonies. Most Portuguese are
rural and belong to the Roman Catholic church,
which has had a strong influence on society.

ECONOMY AND THE LAND. Despite recent
growth, Portugal's economy remains troubled,
and its reputation as one of Western Europe's
poorest nations continues. Long wars against African independence groups in the Portuguese
colonies had already placed a strain on the economy when a 1974 coup led to the end of Portuguese colonialism and stopped the flow of cheap
raw materials from Africa. A large influx of African refugees followed, an added financial burden
for the state. Agriculture especially has suffered
setbacks, including drought and problem-ridden
reform measures, and the onetime self-sufficient
nation now must import a portion of its food.
Currently the nation is attempting to improve
efficiency in farming, and the government en-
courages the formation of cooperatives. Fishing
continues as an important activity, with island

possessions making a contribution to that sector.
The major manufacturing endeavor is the production of textiles, and other important industries include the manufacture of leather goods,
wood and cork products, and ceramics, mostly
on a small scale. Tourism is of increasing importance, with international visitors drawn by the
nation's history as well as its beaches. Mountains, rolling plains, and flat coastal regions
make up Portugal's terrain, and the climate is
sunny and mild. The Azores, islands in the
North Atlantic, and Madeira, islands off the
northwest coast of Africa, are also part of the
nation of Portugal. The overseas territory of
Macao is situated on the coast of China.

HISTORY AND POLITICS. Inhabited by an Iberi-
an people about five thousand years ago, the
area was later visited by Phoenicians, Celts, and
Greeks before falling to the Romans around the
first century B.C. The Romans were followed by
Germanic Visigoths and in A.D. 711 by North
African Muslims, who greatly influenced Portuguese art and architecture. Spain absorbed Portugal in 1094, and Portugal declared its independence in 1143. About one hundred years later
the last of the Muslims were expelled. Portugal's
golden age—during which its navigators explored the globe and founded colonies in South
America, Africa, and the Far East—lasted from
1385 to the late 1500s. Rival European powers
soon began to seize Portuguese holdings, and in
1580 Spain invaded Portugal, ruling until 1640,
when the Spanish were driven out and independence reestablished. After the 1822 loss of Brazil,
Portugal's most valuable colony, and decades of
opposition, a weakened monarchy was overthrown in 1910. Portugal entered World War I on
the side of the Allies, but the war weakened the
newly established republic, and in 1926 the parliamentary democracy fell to a military coup. Antonio Salazar became prime minister in 1932, ruling as a virtual dictator until 1968. A position of
neutrality during World War II kept Portugal
from suffering the damages of that war, but instability continued nonetheless, with Salazar's fa-

vored treatment of the rich and his refusal to
relinquish Portugal's colonies aggravating the
economic situation further. A 1974 coup toppled
Salazar's successor and set up a military government, events that sparked violence among political parties. Almost all Portuguese colonies gained
independence during the next two years. A democratic government was adopted in 1976, and
since then the nation has been ruled by differing
coalitions. Portugal has close ties to the West and
has sought to improve relations with the Third
World. ■

Portugal Map Index

	Lat.	Long.		Lat.	Long.
Aveiro	40°38′N	8°39′W	Mondego, Cape	40°11′N	8°55′W
Azores	38°30′N	28°00′W	Montijo	38°42′N	8°58′W
Barreiro	38°40′N	9°04′W	Olhão	37°02′N	7°50′W
Beja	38°01′N	7°52′W	Peniche	39°21′N	9°23′W
Braga	41°33′N	8°26′W	Pico Point	38°28′N	28°25′W
Bragança	41°49′N	6°45′W	Ponta Delgada	37°44′N	25°40′W
Cádiz, Gulf of	36°50′N	7°10′W	Portalegre	39°17′N	7°26′W
Caldas da Rainha	39°24′N	9°08′W	Portimão	37°08′N	8°32′W
Carvoeira, Cape	39°21′N	9°24′W	Porto	41°11′N	8°36′W
Castelo Branco	39°49′N	7°30′W	Sado	38°29′N	8°55′W
Chaves	41°44′N	7°28′W	Saint Vincent,		
Coimbra	40°12′N	8°25′W	Cape	37°01′N	9°00′W
Covilha	40°17′N	7°30′W	Santa Maria,		
Douro	41°08′N	8°40′W	Cape	36°58′N	7°54′W
Elvas	38°53′N	7°10′W	Santarem	39°14′N	8°41′W
Espichel, Cape	38°25′N	9°13′W	São João da		
Estrela	40°19′N	7°37′W	Madeira	40°54′N	8°30′W
Estrela			São Miguel	37°47′N	25°30′W
Mountains	40°20′N	7°38′W	Setúbal	38°32′N	8°54′W
Évora	38°34′N	7°54′W	Setúbal, Bay of	38°27′N	8°53′W
Figueira da Foz	40°09′N	8°52′W	Sines, Cape	37°57′N	8°53′W
Funchal	32°38′N	16°54′W	Tagus	38°40′N	9°24′W
Guadiana	37°14′N	7°22′W	Vara Peak	32°45′N	16°56′W
Guarda	40°32′N	7°16′W	Viana do Castelo	41°42′N	8°50′W
Leiria	39°45′N	8°48′W	Vila Nova de		
Lisbon	38°43′N	9°08′W	Gaia	41°08′N	8°37′W
Madeira Islands	32°40′N	16°45′W	Vila Real	41°18′N	7°45′W
Minho	41°52′N	8°51′W	Viseu	40°39′N	7°55′W
Mondego	40°09′N	8°52′W			

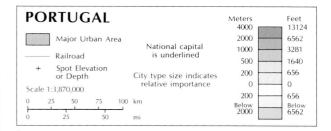

Places and Possessions of Portugal

Entity	Status	Area	Population	Capital / Population
Azores (North Atlantic islands)	Autonomous region	868 mi² (2,247 km²)	255,000	Ponta Delgada / 21,200
Macao (eastern Asia)	Overseas province	6 mi² (16 km²)	310,000	Macao / 253,376
Madeira Islands (northwest of Africa)	Autonomous region	307 mi² (794 km²)	260,000	Funchal / 44,100

PUERTO RICO

Puerto Rico Map Index

	Lat.	Long.		Lat.	Long.		Lat.	Long.		Lat.	Long.
Aguada	18°23′N	67°11′W	Comerío	18°13′N	66°14′W	Guayama	17°59′N	66°07′W	San Germán	18°05′N	67°03′W
Aguadilla	18°26′N	67°09′W	Culebra Island	18°19′N	65°17′W	Guilarte, Mount	18°09′N	66°46′W	San Juan	18°28′N	66°07′W
Arecibo	18°28′N	66°43′W	Dewey	18°18′N	65°18′W	Humacao	18°09′N	65°50′W	San Sebastián	18°20′N	66°59′W
Bayamón	18°24′N	66°09′W	Esperanza	18°06′N	65°28′W	Las Piedras	18°11′N	65°52′W	Santa Isabel	17°58′N	66°24′W
Cabo Rojo	18°05′N	67°09′W	Fajardo	18°20′N	65°39′W	Loíza	18°23′N	65°54′W	Utuado	18°16′N	66°42′W
Caguas	18°14′N	66°02′W	Grande de			Loíza Reservoir	18°17′N	66°00′W	Vieques Island	18°08′N	65°25′W
Cayey	18°07′N	66°10′W	Añasco	18°16′N	67°11′W	Manatí	18°26′N	66°29′W	Vieques Sound	18°15′N	65°23′W
Central Cordillera	18°10′N	66°35′W	Grande de			Mayagüez	18°12′N	67°09′W	Yauco	18°02′N	66°51′W
Coamo	18°05′N	66°22′W	Arecibo	18°29′N	66°42′W	Ponce	18°01′N	66°37′W			
Colonia			Grande de Marati	18°29′N	66°32′W	Punta Mountain	18°10′N	66°36′W			
Providencia	17°59′N	66°00′W	Guánica	17°58′N	66°55′W	Rojo, Cape	17°56′N	67°11′W			

OFFICIAL NAME Commonwealth of Puerto Rico

PEOPLE
Population 3,350,000.
Density 953/mi² (368/km²).
Urban 67%.
Capital San Juan, 422,701.
Languages Spanish, English.
Religions Roman Catholic 85%.
Life expectancy 78 female, 71 male.
Literacy 92%.

POLITICS
Government Commonwealth (U.S.).
Parties Independence, New Progressive, Popular Democratic, Socialist.
Memberships None.
Subdivisions 78 municipalities.

ECONOMY
GNP $12,140,000,000.
Per capita $3,713.
Monetary unit U.S. dollar.
Trade partners U.S., Venezuela, Netherlands Antilles, Virgin Islands.
Exports Clothing, textiles, electrical equipment, sugar, tobacco.
Imports Petroleum, food.

LAND
Description Caribbean island.
Area 3,515 mi² (9,103 km²).
Highest point Punta Mtn., 4,390 ft (1,338 m).
Lowest point Sea level.

PEOPLE. Puerto Rico's chief language, Spanish, and religion, Roman Catholicism, reflect this American Commonwealth's past under Spanish rule. Most of the population is descended from Spaniards and black African slaves. A rising population has caused poverty, housing shortages, and unemployment. Many Puerto Ricans live in the United States, mostly in New York City.

ECONOMY AND THE LAND. Once dependent on such plantation crops as sugar and coffee, Puerto Rico is now a manufacturing nation, specializing in food products and electrical equipment. This transformation was aided by Commonwealth incentives for foreign investors after World War II, also known as Operation Bootstrap. Foreign visitors, attracted by the tropical climate, make tourism another important activity. Economic development has been hurt by a paucity of natural resources and by sensitivity to fluctuations of the United States economy. The island's terrain is marked by mountains, lowlands, and valleys.

HISTORY AND POLITICS. Prior to the arrival of the Europeans, the Arawak Indians inhabited the island of Puerto Rico. Christopher Columbus landed here in 1493, and Spanish settlement began in 1508. In the struggle for control of the island, the Indian population was virtually wiped out, and Indians who survived these early battles soon died of diseases contracted from the settlers. Despite successive attacks by the French, the English, and the Dutch, Puerto Rico remained under Spanish control until 1898, when the United States took possession after the Spanish-American War. A civil government under a United States governor was set up in 1900; seventeen years later Puerto Ricans were made United States citizens. In 1952 the island became a self-governing Commonwealth. Commonwealth status was upheld in a referendum in 1967, but fierce, occasionally violent debate continues over whether Puerto Rico should opt for statehood, continued Commonwealth status, or independence. Puerto Ricans do not vote in United States elections or pay income taxes; however, immigrants to the mainland do have the right to vote and are subject to tax laws. ■

The heart of San Juan is the walled city of Old San Juan, founded in 1521 and situated on an islet connected to the main island by bridges. San Juan Gate, shown here, was once the main entrance to the city.

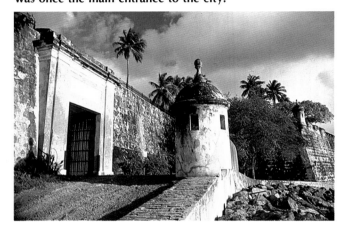

Standing guard over San Juan's harbor is the huge stone structure of El Morro, shown here. Situated in Old San Juan, El Morro was built in 1585 to defend the harbor's entrance from invaders. Because of repeated attacks on the island, the Spanish continued to add to the structure from 1599 to 1609.

QATAR

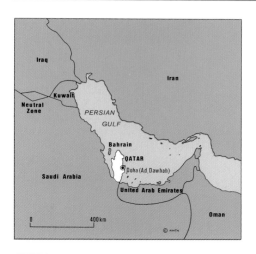

OFFICIAL NAME State of
Qatar

PEOPLE

Population 280,000.
Density 65/mi² (25/km²).
Urban 87%.
Capital Doha, 190,000.
Ethnic groups Arab 40%,
    Pakistani 18%, Indian 18%, Iranian 10%.
Languages Arabic, English.
Religions Muslim 95%.
Life expectancy 60 female, 56 male.
Literacy 40%.

POLITICS

Government Monarchy.
Parties None.
Suffrage None.
Memberships AL, OPEC, UN.
Subdivisions None.

ECONOMY

GDP $7,900,000,000.
Per capita $27,790.
Monetary unit Riyal.
Trade partners U.K., Japan, other Western European
    countries, U.S.
Exports Petroleum.
Imports Machinery, transportation equipment,
    manufactured goods, food.

LAND

Description Southwestern Asia.
Area 4,247 mi² (11,000 km²).
Highest point Aba al-Bawl Hill, 344 ft (105 m).
Lowest point Sea level.

PEOPLE. Qatar's population is distinguished by
a relatively high proportion of Iranians, Pakistanis, and Indians, who began arriving during the
oil boom of the 1950s. Most Qataris are Sunni
Muslims and live in or near Doha, the capital. In
recent years the government has encouraged the
nomadic Bedouins to take up settled life-styles.
Despite a political trend toward a modern welfare state, Qatar retains many elements of a traditional Islamic society.

ECONOMY AND THE LAND. Oil provides the
great majority of Qatar's income. Extensive reserves of natural gas await exploitation. The government has made moves toward economic diversification, investing in agriculture and
industry; fertilizer and cement are important new
products. Most of Qatar is stony desert, and the
climate is hot and arid.

HISTORY AND POLITICS. No strong central
government existed in Qatar before Saudi Muslims gained control in the late eighteenth century. Ottoman Turks occupied the region from 1872
to 1916, when Qatar became a British protector-

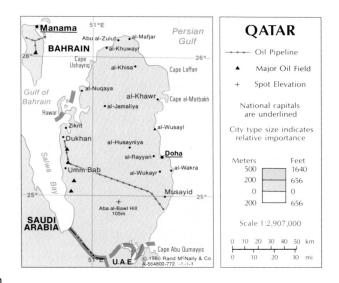

Qatar Map Index

	Lat.	Long.		Lat.	Long.
Aba al-Bawl Hill	24°57'N	51°13'E	Musayid	24°59'N	51°32'E
al-Khawr	25°41'N	51°30'E	*Persian Gulf*	26°10'N	51°40'E
Doha	25°17'N	51°32'E	*Salwa Bay*	25°30'N	50°40'E
Dukhan	25°25'N	50°48'E	Umm Bab	25°12'N	50°48'E

ate. Although oil was discovered in 1940 on the
western side of Qatar's peninsula, the outbreak
of World War II postponed exploitation for another nine years. Qatar became independent in 1971
after failing to agree on the terms of a union
with eight Persian Gulf sheikdoms—today the
United Arab Emirates and Bahrain. Oil revenues
have been used to improve housing, transportation, and public health. Qatar maintains friendly
relations with the West and neighboring Arab
states. ∎

REUNION

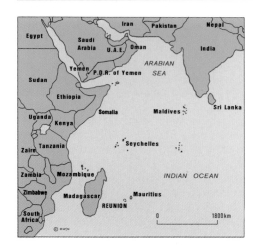

OFFICIAL NAME Department
of Reunion

PEOPLE

Population 545,000.
Density 562/mi² (217/km²).
Urban 41%.
Capital Saint-Denis, 84,400.
Ethnic groups Mixed French, African, Malagasy,
    Chinese, Pakistani, Indian.
Languages French.
Religions Roman Catholic 94%.
Life expectancy 62 female, 56 male.
Literacy 80%.

POLITICS

Government Overseas department (France).
Parties Communist, Popular Movement for
    Liberation, Rally for the Republic, Socialist, Union
    for Democracy.

Suffrage Universal adult.
Memberships None.
Subdivisions 4 districts.

ECONOMY

Monetary unit French franc.
Trade partners France, Mauritius.
Exports Sugar, rum and molasses, perfume essences.
Imports Manufactured goods, food, machinery,
    transportation equipment, petroleum.

LAND

Description Indian Ocean island.
Area 969 mi² (2,510 km²).
Highest point Piton des Neiges, 10,069 ft (3,069 m).
Lowest point Sea level.

PEOPLE. Reunion has a racially mixed population, mainly descended from French settlers, African slaves, and Asian laborers. French is the
official language, but most inhabitants speak a
creole dialect. The mainly Roman Catholic population is densely concentrated in the lowland
areas along the coast. Social stratification is rigid.

ECONOMY AND THE LAND. Reunion's traditional coffee crop was replaced by sugar early on,
and sugar continues as an economic mainstay
today. Industry is based on the production of
sugar by-products, such as rum and molasses.
Unemployment is a problem, and the island remains dependent upon French aid. The mountainous terrain is marked by one active and several
extinct volcanoes. The tropical climate is subject
to occasional cyclones and trade winds, which
bring high rainfall to the south and southeast.

HISTORY AND POLITICS. Although known to
the Arabs and the Portuguese, Reunion was uninhabited when French settlement began in the
1660s. First called Bourbon, the island originally

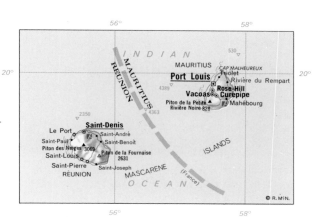

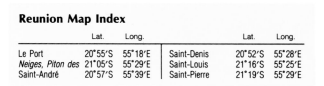

Reunion Map Index

	Lat.	Long.		Lat.	Long.
Le Port	20°55'S	55°18'E	Saint-Denis	20°52'S	55°28'E
Neiges, Piton des	21°05'S	55°29'E	Saint-Louis	21°16'S	55°25'E
Saint-André	20°57'S	55°39'E	Saint-Pierre	21°19'S	55°29'E

served as a stopover on the French shipping
route to India. The French soon developed coffee
and sugar plantations, bringing slaves from Africa to work them. British-French rivalry for control of the area led to brief British rule during the
early 1800s. After several name changes, from
Bourbon to Reunion to Bonaparte and back to
Bourbon again, in 1848 the French settled on the
name Reunion. After the abolition of slavery,
indentured laborers were brought from
Indochina, India, and eastern Africa. Reunion
was a French colony until 1946, when it became
an overseas department. ∎

ROMANIA

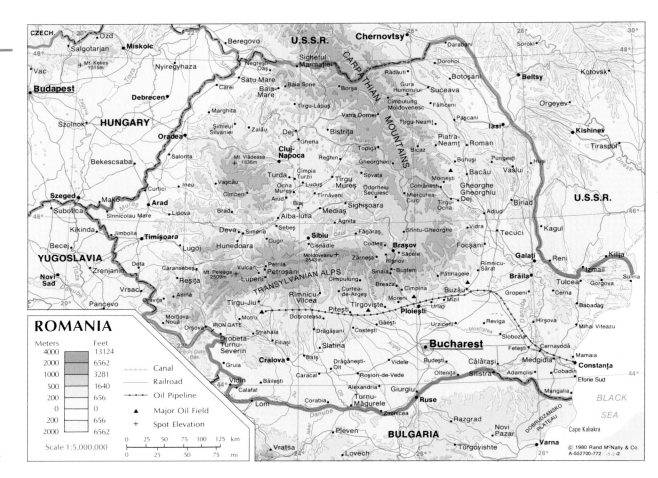

ROMANIA

Meters	Feet
4000	13124
2000	6562
1000	3281
500	1640
200	656
0	0
200	656
2000	6562

······ Canal
───── Railroad
+·+·+ Oil Pipeline
▲ Major Oil Field
+ Spot Elevation

Scale 1:5,000,000

© 1980 Rand McNally & Co.
A-552700-772 -1-2-2

OFFICIAL NAME Socialist
Republic of Romania

PEOPLE
Population 22,860,000.
Density 249/mi² (96/km²).
Urban 50%.
Capital Bucharest, 1,929,360.
Ethnic groups Romanian 88%, Hungarian 8%.
Languages Romanian.
Religions Romanian Orthodox 80%, Roman Catholic 6%.
Life expectancy 74 female, 69 male.
Literacy 98%.

POLITICS
Government Socialist republic.
Parties Communist.
Suffrage Universal, over 18.
Memberships CEMA, UN, Warsaw Pact.
Subdivisions 40 counties, 1 municipality.

ECONOMY
GNP $104,800,000,000.
Per capita $4,238.
Monetary unit Leu.
Trade partners U.S.S.R., West Germany, East Germany.
Exports Machinery, fuels, textiles, wood products, food.
Imports Machinery, fuels, iron ore, motor vehicles.

LAND
Description Eastern Europe.
Area 91,699 mi² (237,500 km²).
Highest point Moldoveanu, 8,343 ft (2,543 m).
Lowest point Sea level.

PEOPLE. The majority population of Romania belongs to the Romanian Orthodox church and traces its roots to Latin-speaking Romans, Thracians, Slavs, and Celts. Minorities concentrated in Transylvania and areas north and west of Bucharest are mainly Roman Catholic Hungarians and Germans. Other minorities include Gypsies, Serbs, Croats, Ukrainians, Greeks, Turks, and Armenians. Almost all inhabitants speak Romanian, although other languages are often spoken by minority groups.

ECONOMY AND THE LAND. Following World War II, Romania's Communist government implemented a program to turn the agricultural nation to industry. The economy is now based on industrial activity, and major products include iron and steel. Farm output suffered during the postwar focus on industrialization, and current plans call for growth in the agricultural as well as the industrial sector. Most agriculture is collectivized, and corn and wheat are major crops. The terrain is marked by a low-lying south-to-northeast plateau that curves around several mountain ranges, including the Carpathians, found in the northern and central regions. The climate is continental, with cold, snowy winters and warm summers.

HISTORY AND POLITICS. First colonized by the Dacians, a Thracian tribe, around the fourth century B.C., the area became the Roman province of Romania in the second century A.D. Invading Bulgars, Goths, Huns, Magyars, Slavs, and Tartars followed the Romans. Between 1250 and 1350 the independent Romanian principalities of Walachia and Moldavia emerged. In the fifteenth and sixteenth centuries Ottoman Turks conquered the principalities, and following a Russian-Turkish war, Russians occupied the states. In 1861 Walachia and Moldavia were united as Romania, in 1878 they gained independence, and in 1881 Romania was proclaimed a kingdom. The nation's government was marked by oppression and a concentration of land and wealth among the aristocracy, and a 1907 rebellion was quelled by the army. In 1919, after a World War I alliance with the Allies, Romania gained Transylvania and other territories. Instability and dissatisfaction, spurred by worldwide economic depression, continued through the 1930s. With the cooperation of Romanian leadership, Germany occupied the country in World War II. In 1944 Soviet troops entered Romania, and the nation subsequently joined the Allies. A Communist government was established in 1945, and in 1947 the king was forced to abdicate and Romania officially became a Communist country. Initially Romania's policies were closely tied to those of the Soviet Union, but renewed nationalism in the sixties led Romanians along an independent course of policy development. However, Romanian relations with the Soviet Union, as well as Western countries, remain friendly. ■

Romania Map Index

	Lat.	Long.
Alba-Iulia	46°04'N	23°35'E
Arad	46°11'N	21°20'E
Argeş	44°04'N	26°37'E
Bacău	46°34'N	26°55'E
Baia-Mare	47°40'N	23°35'E
Bicaz, Lake	47°00'N	26°00'E
Birlad	46°14'N	27°40'E
Bistriţa	47°08'N	24°30'E
Bistriţa	46°30'N	26°57'E
Botoşani	47°45'N	26°40'E
Brăila	45°16'N	27°58'E
Braşov	45°39'N	25°37'E
Bucharest	44°26'N	26°06'E
Buzău	45°09'N	26°49'E
Călăraşi	44°11'N	27°20'E
Carpathian Mountains	47°30'N	25°30'E
Cluj-Napoca	46°47'N	23°36'E
Constanţa	44°11'N	28°39'E

	Lat.	Long.
Craiova	44°19'N	23°48'E
Danube	45°20'N	29°40'E
Dej	47°09'N	23°52'E
Deva	45°53'N	22°55'E
Dîmboviţa	44°14'N	26°27'E
Drobeta-Turnu-Severin	44°38'N	22°39'E
Focşani	45°41'N	27°11'E
Galaţi	45°26'N	28°03'E
Gheorghe Gheorghiu Dej	46°14'N	26°44'E
Giurgiu	43°53'N	25°57'E
Hunedoara	45°45'N	22°54'E
Iasi	47°10'N	27°35'E
Iron Gate Reservoir	44°30'N	22°00'E
Jiu	43°47'N	23°48'E
Lugoj	45°41'N	21°54'E
Lupeni	45°22'N	23°13'E

	Lat.	Long.
Medgidia	44°15'N	28°16'E
Mediaş	46°10'N	24°21'E
Moldoveanu	45°36'N	24°44'E
Mostiştea	44°15'N	27°10'E
Mureş	46°15'N	20°13'E
Olt	43°43'N	24°51'E
Oradea	47°03'N	21°57'E
Peleaga, Mount	45°22'N	22°54'E
Petroşani	45°25'N	23°22'E
Piatra-Neamţ	46°56'N	26°22'E
Piteşti	44°52'N	24°52'E
Ploieşti	44°56'N	26°02'E
Prut	45°28'N	28°12'E
Reşiţa	45°17'N	21°53'E
Rîmnicu-Vîlcea	45°06'N	24°22'E
Roman	46°55'N	26°56'E
Satu Mare	47°48'N	22°53'E
Sibiu	45°48'N	24°09'E

	Lat.	Long.
Sighetul Marmaţiei	47°56'N	23°54'E
Sighişoara	46°13'N	24°48'E
Siret	45°24'N	28°01'E
Slatina	44°26'N	24°22'E
Someş (Szamos)	48°07'N	22°22'E
Suceava	47°39'N	26°19'E
Tecuci	45°50'N	27°26'E
Timişoara	45°45'N	21°13'E
Tîrgovişte	44°56'N	25°27'E
Tîrgu-Jiu	45°02'N	23°17'E
Tîrgu Mureş	46°33'N	24°33'E
Transylvanian Alps	45°30'N	24°15'E
Tulcea	45°11'N	28°48'E
Turda	46°34'N	23°47'E
Turnu-Măgurele	43°45'N	24°53'E
Vaslui	46°38'N	27°44'E

Although Romania's economy is now based on industry, farm villages such as the one shown here remain a common sight throughout much of the Romanian countryside. About 44 percent of Romania's land is arable, and most agriculture is collectivized.

RWANDA

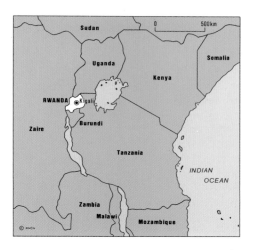

OFFICIAL NAME Republic of
Rwanda

PEOPLE
Population 5,935,000.
Density 584/mi² (225/km²).
Urban 5%.
Capital Kigali, 156,700.
Ethnic groups Hutu 85%, Tutsi 14%, Twa 1%.
Languages Kinyarwanda, French.
Religions Roman Catholic 65%, indigenous 25%,
Protestant 9%, Muslim 1%.
Life expectancy 47 female, 44 male.
Literacy 37%.

POLITICS
Government Republic.
Parties National Revolutionary Movement for
Development.
Suffrage Universal adult.
Memberships OAU, UN.
Subdivisions 10 prefectures.

ECONOMY
GDP $1,388,000,000.
Per capita $270.
Monetary unit Franc.
Trade partners Belgium, Kenya, West Germany,
France, U.S.

Exports Coffee, tea, cassiterite, wolfram.
Imports Food, clothing, machinery, transportation
equipment, petroleum.

LAND
Description Eastern Africa, landlocked.
Area 10,169 mi² (26,338 km²).
Highest point Mt. Karisimbi, 14,787 ft (4,507 m).
Lowest point 3,100 ft (950 m).

PEOPLE. Most Rwandans are Hutu, mainly
farmers of Bantu stock. Minorities include the
Tutsi, a pastoral people that dominated politically
until a Hutu rebellion in 1959, and the Twa,
Pygmies descended from the original population.
Both French and Kinyarwanda are official languages, but most speak Kinyarwanda, a Bantu
tongue. Roman Catholicism is the major religion,
and minority groups practice indigenous beliefs
as well as Protestantism and Islam. Rwanda is
characterized by a high population density and a
high birthrate.

ECONOMY AND THE LAND. Agriculture is the
major activity, although plagued by the erosion
and overpopulation of arable land. Many Rwandans practice subsistence farming, while coffee
and tea are major export crops. The production
and export of minerals such as cassiterite and
wolfram, partly fueled by foreign investment, is
also important. Economic growth has been hindered by Rwanda's landlocked position and underdeveloped transportation system. The terrain
consists mainly of grassy uplands and hills, with
volcanic mountains in the west and northwest.
The climate is mild.

HISTORY AND POLITICS. The Twa, the region's
original inhabitants, were followed by the Hutu.
The Tutsi most likely arrived about the fourteenth century, subjugating the weaker Hutu
and becoming the region's dominant force. The
areas of present-day Rwanda and Burundi became part of German East Africa in the 1890s. In
1919, following World War I, the region was
mandated to Belgium as Ruanda-Urundi, and
following World War II, Ruanda-Urundi was
made a United Nations trust territory under Bel-

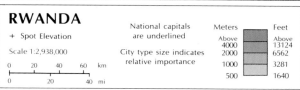

Rwanda Map Index

	Lat.	Long.		Lat.	Long.
Butare	2°36'S	29°44'E	Kibuye	2°03'S	29°21'E
Byumba	1°35'S	30°04'E	Kigali	1°57'S	30°04'E
Cyangugu	2°29'S	28°54'E	Kivu, Lake	2°00'S	29°10'E
Gikongoro	2°29'S	29°34'E	Nyabarongo	2°21'S	30°22'E
Gisenyi	1°42'S	29°15'E	Ruhengeri	1°30'S	29°38'E
Ihema, Lake	1°52'S	30°47'E	Ruzizi	2°45'S	29°00'E
Kagera	1°05'S	30°20'E	Virunga		
Karisimbi, Mount	1°30'S	29°27'E	Mountains	1°30'S	29°30'E
Kibungo	2°10'S	30°32'E			

gian administration. In 1959 a Hutu revolt
against Tutsi domination resulted in the death of
many Tutsi and the flight of many more. Independence was gained in 1962, and the former
territory split into the countries of Rwanda and
Burundi. The military overthrew the nation's
first president in 1973, and a civilian government
was subsequently installed. ■

ST. CHRISTOPHER–NEVIS

OFFICIAL NAME State of
St. Christopher–Nevis

PEOPLE
Population 45,000.
Density 433/mi² (167/km²).
Urban 34%.
Capital Basseterre,
St. Christopher I., 14,725.

Ethnic groups Black.
Languages English.
Religions Anglican, other Protestant, Roman Catholic.
Literacy 80%.

POLITICS
Government Parliamentary state.
Parties Labor, People's Action Movement,
Reformation.
Suffrage Universal adult.
Memberships CW, OAS, UN.
Subdivisions 14 parishes.

ECONOMY
GNP $41,600,000.
Per capita $920.
Monetary unit East Caribbean dollar.
Trade partners U.K., other Western European
countries, U.S.
Exports Sugar, molasses.
Imports Food, manufactured goods, fuels.

LAND
Description Caribbean islands.
Area 104 mi² (269 km²).
Highest point Mt. Misery, St. Christopher I., 3,792 ft
(1,156 m).
Lowest point Sea level.

PEOPLE. Descendants of black Africans constitute the majority population on the islands of St.
Christopher, also known as St. Kitts, and Nevis.
Most inhabitants of St. Christopher live along the
coastal region, and most of Nevis's population is
concentrated near the western town of Charles-
town. English is spoken throughout the islands,
and most people are Protestant, especially Anglican, a legacy of former British rule. Despite this
British influence, the islands are known for their
distinctive West Indian atmosphere.

ECONOMY AND THE LAND. Agriculture and
tourism are the economic mainstays of St. Christopher and Nevis. Sugarcane the major crop, is
cultivated mainly on St. Christopher, while
Nevis produces cotton, fruits, and vegetables.

Agriculture also provides for sugar processing,
the major industrial activity. The attractions of
these vocanic islands include a scenic terrain of
forested mountains, pink- and black-sand beaches, and a tropical climate.

HISTORY AND POLITICS. The more aggressive
Carib Indians conquered the indigenous Arawaks
early in the islands' history. Christopher Columbus sighted St. Christopher and Nevis in 1493,
and although the Spanish, French, and Dutch
knew of the islands, the British were the first to
attempt settlement, on St. Christopher in 1625
and on Nevis three years later. French sailors
arrived on St. Christopher soon afterward, other
French colonists were drawn to the island, and
British-French rivalry for control began. During
the same years, a sugar economy was established, and black Africans were brought to work
the plantations. The competition between Britain
and France came to an end with the signing of
the Treaty of Paris in 1783. which recognized
Britain's right to the islands, and for a time St.
Christopher, Nevis, and Anguilla were ruled as a
single colony. Anguilla was officially made a separate dependency of Britain in 1980, and St.
Christopher and Nevis became independent in
1983. ■

ST. HELENA

OFFICIAL NAME St. Helena

PEOPLE
Population 6,900.
Density 43/mi² (16/km²).
Urban 26%.
Capital Jamestown, 1,516.
Ethnic groups Mixed European, Asian, and African.
Languages English.
Religions Anglican, Baptist, Seventh-Day Adventist.
Literacy 97%.

POLITICS
Government Colony (U.K.).
Parties Labor, Progressive.
Subdivisions 3 administrative areas.

ECONOMY
Monetary unit U.K. pound sterling.
Trade partners U.K., South Africa.
Exports Fish, handicrafts.
Imports Foodstuffs, tobacco, fuels, animal feed, building materials.

LAND
Description South Atlantic islands.
Area 162 mi² (419 km²).
Highest point Queen Mary's Pk., 6,760 ft (2,060 m).
Lowest point Sea level.

PEOPLE. Most of the inhabitants of the island of St. Helena are of mixed European, Asian, and African heritage. St. Helena is a British colony with a distinctly British culture; English is the language spoken on the island, and the major religion is Anglican. Most people work as laborers or farmers, but many islanders have emigrated to Ascension Island, a dependecy of St. Helena, in order to find employment.

ECONOMY AND THE LAND. Subsistence farmers grow crops for local consumption, producing mainly corn, potatoes, and vegetables, and other agricultural activity includes the raising of sheep, cattle, and goats. A crop growers' cooperative assists farmers by providing access to agricultural supplies and local markets. A plentiful supply of fish is found in the offshore waters, fueling a fishing industry that remains important to the colony's economy. In the 1970s a crafts industry was established on the island, and handicrafts, together with fish, constitute the island's exports. However, the colony remains dependent upon economic aid from the United Kingdom. The terrain of the volcanic island is rugged and mountainous. The climate is mild, cooled by South Atlantic trade winds. In addition to the main island of St. Helena, the colony includes the dependencies of Ascension Island and the Tristan da Cunha archipelago, made up of the islands of Tristan da Cunha, Gough, Inaccessible, and Nightingale. These islands are also of volcanic origin, and although the volcano on Tristan da Cunha was thought to be extinct, an unanticipated eruption occurred in 1961.

HISTORY AND POLITICS. The Portuguese navigator João de Nova reached the uninhabited island in 1502, naming it St. Helena after the

mother of the Emperor Constantine the Great. It was not until the late 1500s, however, that St. Helena became widely known, and, in time, it evolved into a stopover for ships traveling the trade routes from Europe to the East Indies. The Dutch were first to officially claim the island, annexing St. Helena to the Netherlands in 1633; they did not, however, attempt settlement. Administration by the British East India Company began in 1659, and the company's administration and British annexation became official in 1661. The British were able to withstand a Dutch attempt to take the island in 1673. From 1815 until his death in 1821 Napoleon Bonaparte was exiled on St. Helena, and it is mainly for this that the island is known today. In 1834 St. Helena became a colony, with administration of the island shifting from the East India Company to the British Crown. Local stories from these early days tell of slavery, mutinies, and harsh governments. In 1922 the British government made Ascension Island a dependency of St. Helena, and in 1938 administration of the Tristan da Cunha island group passed to the St. Helena colony as well. In 1942, during World War II, a weather and radio station was built on the island of Tristan da Cunha by a South African defense unit. The British navy used the station for the rest of the war. St. Helena is administered by a governor assisted by a legislative council. The colony's Progressive party supports continued economic ties to the United Kingdom, while the Labor party wants to decrease St. Helena's dependence on British economic aid. ∎

ST. LUCIA

OFFICIAL NAME St. Lucia

PEOPLE
Population 120,000.
Density 504/mi² (195/km²).
Urban 40%.
Capital Castries, 47,600.
Ethnic groups Black 90%, mixed 6%.
Languages English, French.
Religions Roman Catholic 90%, Anglican 3%, other Protestant 7%.
Life expectancy 72 female, 67 male.
Literacy 78%.

POLITICS
Government Parliamentary state.
Suffrage Universal, over 18.
Memberships CW, OAS, UN.
Subdivisions 10 quarters.

ECONOMY
GDP $121,500,000.
Per capita $980.
Monetary unit East Caribbean dollar.
Trade partners U.K., U.S., Trinidad and Tobago, Barbados.
Exports Bananas, cocoa.
Imports Food, machinery, petroleum, fertilizer.

LAND
Description Caribbean island.
Area 238 mi² (616 km²).
Highest point Mt. Gimie, 3,117 ft (950 m).
Lowest point Sea level.

PEOPLE. St. Lucia's population is composed mainly of descendants of black African slaves, and minority groups include people of African-European descent, whites, and East Indians. During the colonial period the island frequently shifted from British to French control, and its culture reflects both British and French elements. Although English is widely spoken, many St. Lucians speak a dialect of French. Roman Catholicism is the main religion, and the Protestant minority includes Anglicans. The government hopes to slow ongoing movement from the countryside into the cities and thus avoid the problems of housing shortages and unemployment that usually accompany population shifts such as this.

ECONOMY AND THE LAND. Agriculture remains important, and principal crops include bananas, cocoa, and coconuts, which provide the by-products of copra and coconut oil. Economic plans call for a diversification of agricultural output. Tax incentives and relative political stability have caused an increase in industrial development and foreign investment, mainly from the United States. Tourism is becoming increasingly important, with visitors drawn by the tropical climate, mountain scenery, and beaches.

HISTORY AND POLITICS. Arawak Indians arrived between the A.D. 200s and 400s and were conquered by the Caribs between the ninth and eleventh centuries. Dutch, French, and British

rivalry for control began in the seventeenth century, but at first the Europeans were unable to subdue the Caribs. The first successful settlement was established by the French in 1651. After many years of alternating French and British control, St. Lucia came under British rule through the 1814 Treaty of Paris. Internal self-government was gained in 1967, and the island gained full independence in 1979. ∎

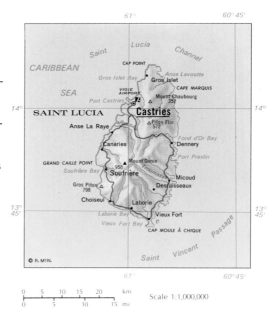

St. Lucia Map Index

	Lat.	Long.		Lat.	Long.
Anse La Raye	13°57′N	61°03′W	Gimie, Mount	13°52′N	61°01′W
Castries	14°01′N	61°00′W	Micoud	13°50′N	60°54′W
Dennery	13°55′N	60°54′W	Soufrière	13°52′N	61°04′W

ST. PIERRE AND MIQUELON

OFFICIAL NAME Department of St. Pierre and Miquelon

PEOPLE
Population 6,200.
Density 67/mi² (26/km²).
Urban 80%.
Capital Saint-Pierre, Saint-Pierre I., 5,371.
Ethnic groups French.
Languages French.
Religions Roman Catholic.
Literacy 99%.

POLITICS
Government Territorial collectivity (France).

ECONOMY
French franc.
Trade partners Canada, France, U.S.
Exports Fish.
Imports Fuels, foodstuffs, transportation equipment.

LAND
Description Description North Atlantic islands.
Area 93 mi² (242 km²).
Highest point Morne de la Grande Montagne, Miquelon I., 787 ft (240 m).
Lowest point Sea level.

PEOPLE. Lying off the coast of Newfoundland in Canada, the territorial collectivity of St. Pierre and Miquelon is the last of France's former North American empire. Most of the colony's 6,200 inhabitants are Roman Catholic decendants of Norman stock. French is spoken throughout the islands, and nearly all residents can read and write.

ECONOMY AND THE LAND. The islands of St. Pierre and Miquelon are barren, rocky, and frequently covered in fog. Agricultural activity is minimal; thin soil and little vegetation cover the islands' granite masses. St. Pierre and Miquelon lie near the fish-rich waters of the Grand Banks. Fishing is the main economic activity and major employer. The primary export is fish, which makes up 88 percent of the total export trade. After fish, shellfish provide for 6 percent and fishmeal 5 percent of exported goods. During the annual fishing season, European as well as local vessels are found in the waters surrounding the islands. Because of the Gulf Stream, St. Pierre's harbor remains ice free throughout the winter, and it is on a shipping route that connects with

Sydney, Australia. St. Pierre and Miquelon is made up of a number of small islands in addition to the two main islands of St. Pierre and Miquelon. The climate is mild and humid, moderated by the Gulf Stream.

HISTORY AND POLITICS. Basque fishermen found their way to the islands in the sixteenth century, and French settlement began in the seventeenth century. In 1713 the British captured the islands, but the 1763 Treaty of Paris returned the islands to French hands. That same treaty ceded the French colony of Acadia to Britain, and when many French inhabitants of Acadia were forced to relocate, some of these established permanent settlements on St. Pierre and Miquelon. British-French rivalry for possession continued, and the British were able to regain control of the islands two more times in the next decades. In 1814 French rule was finally established, with the stipulation that France could not fortify the islands. From 1816 to 1976 the islands were a French overseas territory, and they became self-governing in 1956. A French territorial collectivity, the islands are governed by a privy council and a fourteen-member general council, which the voters of St. Pierre and Miquelon elect by direct vote. The term of each representative is six years. The islands are represented in France by two senators and a councillor, while an appointed commissioner represents France's interests on the islands. ■

ST. VINCENT AND THE GRENADINES

OFFICIAL NAME St. Vincent and the Grenadines

PEOPLE
Population 140,000.
Density 933/mi² (360/km²).
Urban 14%.
Capital Kingstown, St. Vincent I., 23,959.
Ethnic groups Black.
Languages English.
Religions Anglican, Methodist, Roman Catholic.
Life expectancy 60 female, 58 male.
Literacy 82%.

POLITICS
Government Parliamentary state.
Parties Labor, New Democratic.
Suffrage Universal, over 18.
Memberships CW, OAS, UN.
Subdivisions 13 census divisions.

ECONOMY
GNP $69,200,000.
Per capita $539.
Monetary unit East Caribbean dollar.
Trade partners U.K., Trinidad and Tobago, Canada, U.S.

Exports Bananas, arrowroot, copra.
Imports Food, machinery, fertilizer, fuels.

LAND
Description Caribbean islands.
Area 150 mi² (389 km²).
Highest point Soufrière, St. Vincent I., 4,048 ft (1,234 m).
Lowest point Sea level.

PEOPLE. The people of St. Vincent are mainly descended from black African slaves. The colonial influences of Britain and France are evidenced by the languages and religions: English is the official language, a French patois is also spoken, and most people are either Anglican or Roman Catholic.

ECONOMY AND THE LAND. St. Vincent's economy is based on agriculture, especially banana production. Tourism also plays a role, both on the main island of St. Vincent and in the Grenadines. St. Vincent is the largest island, and about one hundred smaller islands make up the Grenadines. The terrain is mountainous, with coastlines marked by sandy beaches, and the climate is tropical.

HISTORY AND POLITICS. The indigenous Arawak Indians were conquered by the Caribs about 1300, and these were the inhabitants that Christopher Columbus found when he reached the area in the late 1400s. The French and British, rivals for the islands of the Caribbean, agreed to let St. Vincent stand as neutral territory, and the Carib Indians remained in control for the next several centuries. In the 1760s, however, British settlement began, and in 1779 the French took St. Vincent. In 1783, by the Treaty of Versailles, St. Vincent and the Grenadines officially passed

into British hands. In the 1790s Caribs that had joined forces with the French began terrorizing the colony, and when the British were finally able to bring the situation under control, the government relocated the Caribs to an island near Honduras. St. Vincent and the Grenadines remained a British dependency until independence was gained in 1979. ■

Map shows major islands only.

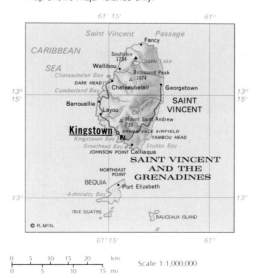

St. Vincent and the Grenadines Map Index

	Lat.	Long.		Lat.	Long.
Bequia	13°01'N	61°13'W	Georgetown	13°16'N	61°08'W
Chateaubelair	13°17'N	61°15'W	Kingstown	13°09'N	61°14'W
Fancy	13°22'N	61°11'W	Layou	13°12'N	61°17'W

SAN MARINO

OFFICIAL NAME Republic of San Marino

PEOPLE
Population 23,000.
Density 958/mi² (377/km²).
Urban 74%.
Capital San Marino, 4,623.
Ethnic groups San Marinese.
Languages Italian.
Religions Roman Catholic.
Literacy 97%.

POLITICS
Government Republic.
Parties Christian Democratic, Communist, Socialist, Unitary Socialist.
Suffrage Universal adult.
Memberships None.
Subdivisions 9 castles.

ECONOMY
Monetary unit Italian lira.
Trade partners Italy.
Exports Construction materials, textiles, wine, postage stamps.
Imports Consumer goods, petroleum, gold.

LAND
Description Southern Europe, landlocked.
Area 24 mi² (61 km²).
Highest point Monte Titano, 2,425 ft (739 m).
Lowest point 174 ft (53 m).

PEOPLE. San Marino is completely surrounded by Italy; thus the San Marinese are ethnically similar to Italians, combining Mediterranean, Alpine, Adriatic, and Nordic roots. Italian is the main language, and Roman Catholicism the major religion. Despite San Marino's similarities to Italy, its long tradition of independence has given its citizens a strong national identity.

ECONOMY AND THE LAND. San Marino and Italy's close economic relationship has resulted in a mutually beneficial customs union; San Marino has no customs restrictions at its borders and receives annual budget subsidiary payments from Italy. Most San Marinese are employed in agriculture; livestock raising is a main activity, and crops include wheat and grapes. Tourism and the sale of postage stamps are major economic contributors, as is industry, which produces construction materials and textiles for export. Located in the Apennine Mountains, San Marino has a rugged terrain and a generally moderate climate.

HISTORY AND POLITICS. San Marino is considered the world's oldest republic. Tradition has it that Marinus, a Christian stonecutter seeking re-

San Marino Map Index

	Lat.	Long.		Lat.	Long.
Borgo Maggiore	43°56′N	12°27′E	Serravalle	43°57′N	12°30′E
Castellaccio	43°54′N	12°27′E	Titano, Mount	43°56′N	12°27′E
San Marino	43°55′N	12°28′E			

ligious freedom in a time of repressive Roman rule, founded the state in the fourth century A.D. Partly because of the protection afforded by its mountainous terrain, San Marino has been able to maintain continuous independence despite attempted invasions. In the 1300s the country became a republic, and the pope recognized its independent status in 1631. San Marino signed its first treaty of friendship with Italy in 1862. In its foreign relations, the country maintains a distinct identity and status. ■

SAO TOME AND PRINCIPE

OFFICIAL NAME Democratic Republic of Sao Tome and Principe

PEOPLE
Population 89,000.
Density 239/mi² (92/km²).
Urban 32%.
Capital São Tomé, São Tomé I., 17,380.
Ethnic groups Mixed African, Portuguese-African.
Languages Portuguese, indigenous.
Religions Roman Catholic, Protestant, Seventh Day Adventist.
Literacy 50%.

POLITICS
Government Republic.
Parties Movement for Liberation.
Suffrage Universal, over 18.
Memberships OAU, UN.
Subdivisions 7 counties.

ECONOMY
GDP $30,000,000.
Per capita $300.
Monetary unit Dobra.
Trade partners Netherlands, Portugal, U.S., West Germany.
Exports Cocoa, copra, palm oil.
Imports Food, machinery, electrical equipment, fuels.

LAND
Description Western African islands.
Area 372 mi² (964 km²).
Highest point São Tomé Pk., São Tomé I., 6,640 ft (2,024 m).
Lowest point Sea level.

PEOPLE. Descendants of African slaves and people of Portuguese-African heritage compose most of Sao Tome and Principe's population. Colonial rule by Portugal is evidenced by the predominance of the Portuguese language and Roman Catholicism..

ECONOMY AND THE LAND. Cocoa dominates Sao Tome and Principe's economy. Copra and palm-oil production is also important, and fishing plays an economic role as well. Through the development of vegetable crops, the government hopes to diversify agricultural output. Part of an extinct volcanic mountain range, Sao Tome and Principe have a mostly mountainous terrain. The climate is tropical.

HISTORY AND POLITICS. When Portuguese explorers arrived in the 1400s, Sao Tome and Principe were uninhabited. Early settlers included Portuguese convicts and exiles. Cultivation of the land and importation of slaves led to a thriving sugar economy by the mid-1500s. In the 1800s, following slave revolts and the decline of sugar

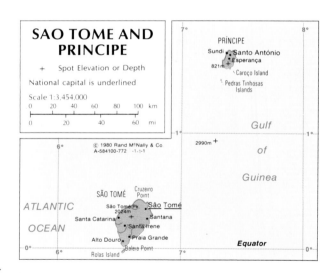

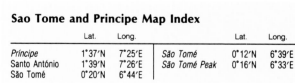

Sao Tome and Principe Map Index

	Lat.	Long.		Lat.	Long.
Príncipe	1°37′N	7°25′E	São Tomé	0°12′N	6°39′E
Santo António	1°39′N	7°26′E	São Tomé Peak	0°16′N	6°33′E
São Tomé	0°20′N	6°44′E			

production, coffee and cocoa became the islands' mainstays, and soon large Portuguese plantations called *rocas* were established. Slavery was abolished by Portugal in 1876, but an international controversy arose in the early 1900s when it was found that Angolan contract workers were being treated as virtual slaves. Decades of unrest led to the 1953 Batepa Massacre, in which Portuguese rulers killed several hundred rioting African workers. A movement for independence began in the late 1950s, and following a 1974 change of government in Portugal, Sao Tome and Principe became independent in 1975. ■

SAUDI ARABIA

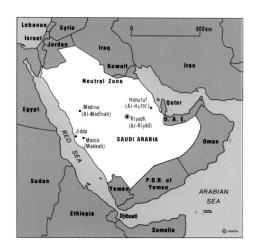

OFFICIAL NAME Kingdom of
Saudi Arabia

PEOPLE
Population 10,970,000.
Density 13/mi² (5.1/km²).
Urban 70%.
Capital Riyadh, 1,000,000.
Ethnic groups Arab
90%, Afro-Asian 10%.
Languages Arabic.
Religions Muslim.
Life expectancy 56 female, 53 male.
Literacy 52%.

POLITICS
Government Monarchy.
Parties None.
Suffrage None.
Memberships AL, OPEC, UN.
Subdivisions 14 districts.

ECONOMY
GDP $120,000,000,000.
Per capita $14,117.
Monetary unit Riyal.
Trade partners Japan, U.S., Western European
countries.
Exports Petroleum, petroleum products.
Imports Manufactured goods, transportation
equipment, construction materials, food.

LAND
Description Southwestern Asia.
Area 830,000 mi² (2,149,690 km²).
Highest point 10,279 ft (3,133 m).
Lowest point Sea level.

PEOPLE. Saudi Arabia is inhabited primarily by
Arab Muslims descended from Semitic peoples
who settled in the region several thousand years
ago. The petroleum industry has attracted a sizable minority of Arabs from other nations, Europeans, and non-Arab Muslims from Africa and
Asia. The country's official language is Arabic,
although English is used among educated Saudis
in business and international affairs. Islam dominates Saudi life, and nearly all the people belong
to the religion's Sunni branch. Various forms of
Christianity and traditional religions are practiced
among foreign workers and indigenous minority
groups. Most live in urban areas, but some Bedouin tribes preserve their nomadic way of life.

ECONOMY AND THE LAND. The economy of
Saudi Arabia has been shaped by its vast deserts
and huge petroleum reserves. The hot, mostly
arid climate has prevented agricultural abun-
dance and stability: the country must import
nearly all its food. Oil was discovered in the
1930s, but the country did not begin rapid economic development until the reserves were aggressively exploited following World War II.
Saudi Arabia is the world's leading exporter of
petroleum, possessing the largest concentration
of known oil reserves in the world. The government is seeking to diversify the economy, improve transportation and communication lines,

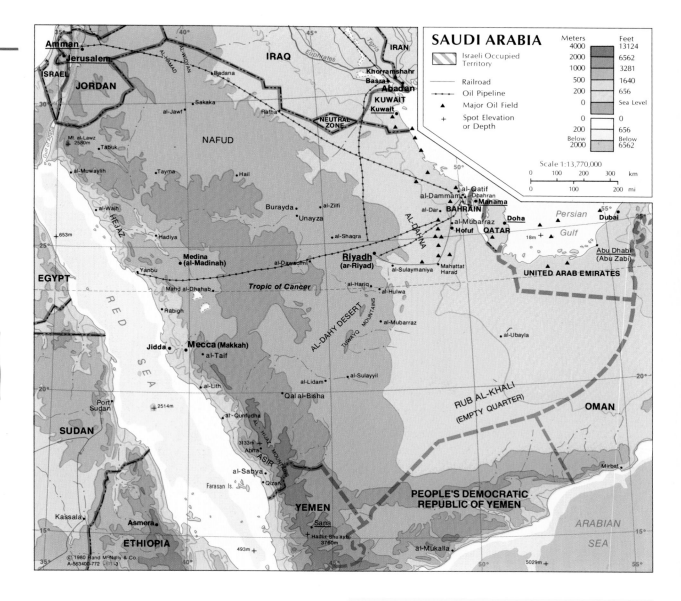

and build agricultural output. Private enterprise
and foreign investment are encouraged. Saudi
Arabia is divided into the western highlands bordering the Red Sea, a central plateau, northern
deserts, the huge Rub al-Khali desert in the
south, and the eastern lowlands. Only the coastal regions receive appreciable rainfall, and some
inland desert areas may go without rain for several years.

HISTORY AND POLITICS. Even though what is
now Saudi Arabia established prosperous trade
routes thousands of years ago, its history begins
with the founding of Islam by Muhammad in the
early 600s A.D. By the end of that century Mecca
and Medina were established as political and religious centers of Islam and remain so today. The
territory split into numerous states that warred
among themselves for over a thousand years.
The Ottoman Turks gained control over the
coastal region of Hejaz in the early 1500s, while
Britain set up protectorates along the southern
and eastern coasts of Arabia during the 1800s.
The Saud family dynasty, founded in the 1400s,
managed to remain a dominant religious and political force. Members of the dynasty fought to
establish the supremacy of Islamic law and unite
the various clans into one nation. In 1932 Ibn
Saud proclaimed the Kingdom of Saudi Arabia
and established a Saud monarchy that has continued despite dissension within the royal family.
Since the 1960s Saudi Arabia has aggressively
sought to upgrade local governments, industry,
education, the status of women, and the standard of living while maintaining Islamic values
and traditions. Saudi Arabia is a dominant member of the Organization of Petroleum Exporting
Countries (OPEC). Despite disagreements with
the West and continuing conflicts with Israel, the
country maintains strong diplomatic and economic ties with the United States and nations of
Western Europe. ■

Saudi Arabia Map Index

	Lat.	Long.		Lat.	Long.
Al-Dahna	24°30′N	48°10′E	Hofuf	25°22′N	49°34′E
Al-Dahy Desert	22°20′N	45°35′E	Jidda	21°30′N	39°12′E
al-Damman	26°26′N	50°07′E	Mecca (Makkah)	21°27′N	39°49′E
Al-Hijaz			Medina (al-		
Mountains	19°45′N	41°55′E	Madinah)	24°28′N	39°36′E
al-Lawz, Mount	28°40′N	35°18′E	Nafud	28°30′N	41°00′E
al-Mubarraz	25°55′N	49°36′E	Persian Gulf	25°00′N	54°00′E
al-Qatif	26°33′N	50°00′E	Qal al-Bisha	20°01′N	42°36′E
al-Sabya	17°09′N	42°37′E	Red Sea	20°00′N	38°00′E
al-Taif	21°16′N	40°24′E	Riyadh (ar-Riyad)	24°38′N	46°43′E
Aqaba, Gulf of	29°00′N	34°40′E	Rub Al-Khali		
Asir	19°00′N	42°00′E	(Empty		
Burayda	26°20′N	43°59′E	Quarter)	20°00′N	51°00′E
Empty Quarter			Tuwayq		
→ Rub Al-			Mountains	23°00′N	46°00′E
Khali	20°00′N	51°00′E	Unayza	26°06′N	43°56′E
Hejaz	24°30′N	38°30′E			

**Saudi Arabia's economy is based on its vast
oil reserves. Here, a drill takes rock samples
from a Saudi Arabian field.**

SENEGAL

SENEGAL

Railroad		
+ Spot Elevation		
National capitals are underlined		

	Meters	Feet
	2000	6562
	1000	3281
	500	1640
	200	656
	0	0
	200	656
	Below 2000	Below 6562

Scale 1:6,529,000

Senegal Map Index

	Lat.	Long.
Casamance	12°33'N	16°46'W
Dakar	14°40'N	17°26'W
Diourbel	14°40'N	16°15'W
Doué	16°38'N	15°02'W
Falémé	14°46'N	12°14'W
Ferlo, Vallée du	15°42'N	15°30'W
Gambia	13°30'N	13°50'W
Guiers, Lake	16°12'N	15°50'W
Kaolack	14°09'N	16°04'W
Kolda	12°53'N	14°57'W
Louga	15°37'N	16°13'W
Mbour	14°24'N	16°58'W
Rufisque	14°43'N	17°17'W
Saint-Louis	16°02'N	16°30'W
Senegal	15°48'N	16°32'W
Thiès	14°48'N	16°56'W
Vert, Cape	14°43'N	17°30'W
Ziguinchor	12°35'N	16°16'W

OFFICIAL NAME Republic of
Senegal

PEOPLE
Population 6,650,000.
Density 88/mi² (34/km²).
Urban 34%.
Capital Dakar, 979,000.
Ethnic groups Wolof 36%, Fulani 17%, Serer 16%,
Toucouleur 9%, Diola 9%, Mandingo 7%.
Languages French, Wolof, indigenous.
Religions Muslim 75%, indigenous 20%, Christian 5%.
Life expectancy 45 female, 43 male.
Literacy 10%.

POLITICS
Government Republic.
Parties Assembly, Democratic, Democratic National,
Socialist.
Suffrage Universal adult.
Memberships OAU, UN.
Subdivisions 10 regions.

ECONOMY
GDP $2,500,000,000.
Per capita $410.
Monetary unit CFA franc.
Trade partners France, other Western European
countries, U.S., Japan.
Exports Peanuts and peanut products, phosphate
rock, canned fish.
Imports Food, consumer goods, machinery,
petroleum, transportation equipment.

LAND
Description Western Africa.
Area 75,955 mi² (196,722 km²).
Highest point 1,906 ft (581 m).
Lowest point Sea level.

PEOPLE. Senegal's diverse population is made
up mostly of black Africans from a number of
ethnic groups, each with its own life-style and
language. The former French colony retains
French as its official language, although many
Senegalese remain unable to speak it. Senegal's
educational system has also been influenced by
its French model, and because of continued ties
with the former colonial power, many Senegalese
live in France temporarily, usually to work and
less frequently to attend school. Most Senegalese
are Muslim; a lesser number of people practice
traditional African faiths, and a small minority
are Roman Catholic. Nearly two-thirds of the
population lives in rural areas, and most people
work as subsistence farmers.

ECONOMY AND THE LAND. Crop growing and
livestock raising are the primary activities that
contribute to Senegal's earnings, and peanuts are
the major export crop. In the early 1980s the
peanuts suffered from drought as well as problems with quality, but government plans to diversify crop output should help the economy to
weather such adverse conditions in the future.
Drought has also affected the production of cotton, Senegal's other major cash crop, and caused
the government to issue a global appeal for food

assistance. Expansion in the fishing industry has
resulted in increased export earnings, and the
government hopes for growth in its tourism industry as well. Senegal's natural resources include deposits of lime phosphate, aluminum
phosphate, and iron ore. Oil has been found
offshore, but a border dispute with Guinea-
Bissau has prevented exploitation of this resource. Industrial activities include oil refining;
textile, chemical, and building-material production; and some light industry. A tax-free zone
has been set up to encourage foreign investment,
but the country lacks the skilled labor needed to
fuel industrial enterprises. Senegal's transportation system ranks among Africa's best, and the
capital city of Dakar is one of Africa's busiest
ports. Still, Senegal remains a poor nation with a
high unemployment rate, and the country continues to rely heavily on foreign aid. The terrain,
which is mainly flat, is highlighted by small plateaus, low massifs, marshy swamps, and a sandy
coast. The climate is marked by dry and rainy
seasons, with differing precipitation patterns in
the south and the more arid north.

HISTORY AND POLITICS. Prehistoric peoples
once inhabited the region of present-day Senegal, and until the late 1500s the Ghana, the Mali,

and, lastly, the Songhai empires dominated parts
of the area. Portuguese traders arriving on the
west coast of Africa in the 1400s found a land of
independent kingdoms, and by negotiating with
the local kings, the Europeans soon had established a prosperous trade. About this time the
modern-day peanut crop was established; the
peanuts provided cheap food for the slaves that
were passed along the trade routes. Other European powers attempting to gain a footing in the
area of Senegal included the British, the French,
and the Dutch. By the early 1800s France had
gained control of the region and in 1895 made
Senegal part of French West Africa. In 1959 Senegal joined with French Sudan, or present-day
Mali, to form the Federation of Mali, which became independent in 1960. However, Senegal
withdrew from the federation later in the year to
found the independent Republic of Senegal. The
new parliamentary government was plagued by
coup attempts and an economy crippled by the
severe droughts of the late 1960s and early 1970s.
In 1982 Senegal formed a union with the Gambia, called the Confederation of Senegambia, to
strengthen economic and military ties between
the two countries. Senegal has maintained close
ties to France and follows a pro-Western foreign
policy. ■

Fertile land is difficult to find in
the regions of Africa that border
the Sahara. A vicious circle is
created as growing populations
force communities to overuse
poor land, thus lowering its productivity even further. These
Senegal villagers, herding goats
on the fringes of the semiarid
Sahel region, are contributing to
the Sahara's southward expansion.

SEYCHELLES

OFFICIAL NAME Republic of
Seychelles

PEOPLE
Population 66,000.
Density 386/mi² (149/km²).
Urban 37%.
Capital Victoria, Mahé I., 15,559.
Ethnic groups Mixed Asian, African, European.
Languages English, French.
Religions Roman Catholic 90%.
Life expectancy 71 female, 65 male.
Literacy 60%.

POLITICS
Government Republic.
Parties People's Progressive Front.
Suffrage Universal adult.
Memberships CW, OAU, UN.

ECONOMY
GDP $128,000,000.
Per capita $1,330.
Monetary unit Rupee.
Trade partners U.K., South Africa, Japan, Singapore.
Exports Copra, cinnamon, vanilla, fish.
Imports Food, manufactured goods, machinery, petroleum, transportation equipment.

LAND
Description Indian Ocean islands.
Area 171 mi² (443 km²).
Highest point Mt. Seychellois, Mahé I., 2,969 ft (905 m).
Lowest point Sea level.

PEOPLE. The majority of Seychellois are of mixed African and European ancestry, while the remainder are Chinese or Indian. Many of the more than one hundred islands are coral atolls, unable to support human life, and the population is concentrated on Mahé, the largest island.

ECONOMY AND THE LAND. A tropical climate, white-sand beaches, and exotic flora and fauna make tourism the mainstay of the economy of Seychelles. In addition, fertile soils produce cinnamon and coconuts. Seychelles is made up of mountainous granite islands and flat coral islands.

HISTORY AND POLITICS. The Portuguese reached the uninhabited islands in the early 1500s, and for more than two hundred years the islands served as little more than pirates' havens. France claimed them in 1756, and by the 1770s white planters and African slaves had begun settlement of Mahé. Following a French-English war, the islands were ceded to Britain in 1814. Seychelles achieved independence in 1976. ∎

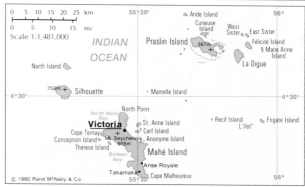

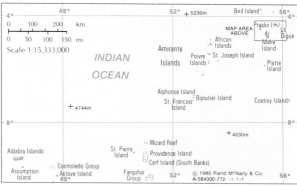

Seychelles Map Index

	Lat.	Long.		Lat.	Long.
Aldabra Islands	9°25'S	46°22'E	Farquhar Group	10°10'S	51°10'E
Amirante Islands	6°00'S	53°10'E	La Digue	4°21'S	55°50'E
Bird Island	3°43'S	55°12'E	Praslin Island	4°19'S	55°44'E
Coetivy Island	7°08'S	56°16'E	Silhouette	4°29'S	55°14'E
Cosmoledo Group	9°43'S	47°35'E	Victoria	4°38'S	55°27'E

SIERRA LEONE

OFFICIAL NAME Republic of
Sierra Leone

PEOPLE
Population 3,855,000.
Density 138/mi² (53/km²).
Urban 25%.
Capital Freetown, 300,000.
Ethnic groups Temne 30%, Mende 30%, Creole 2%, others.
Languages English, Krio, indigenous.
Religions Indigenous 70%, Muslim 25%, Christian 5%.
Life expectancy 49 female, 46 male.
Literacy 15%.

POLITICS
Government Republic.
Parties All People's Congress.
Suffrage Universal, over 21.
Memberships CW, OAU, UN.
Subdivisions 3 provinces, 1 capital district.

ECONOMY
GDP $1,200,000,000.
Per capita $291.
Monetary unit Leone.
Trade partners U.K., other Western European countries, U.S., Japan.
Exports Diamonds, palm kernels, coffee, cocoa, iron ore.
Imports Machinery, food, petroleum, transportation equipment, manufactured goods.

LAND
Description Western Africa.
Area 27,925 mi² (72,325 km²).
Highest point Bintimani, 6,381 ft (1,945 m).
Lowest point Sea level.

PEOPLE. Of Sierra Leone's nearly twenty ethnic groups, the northern Temne and the southern Mende compose majorities. Descendants of American slaves who settled in Freetown on the coast constitute a Creole minority. Krio, an English dialect, is spoken by the Creoles.

ECONOMY AND THE LAND. Mining is Sierra Leone's major economic contributor, producing diamonds, iron ore, and rutile. Although most Sierra Leoneans survive by subsistence farming, agriculture contributes less than one-third of the country's income. Coastal swamps and beaches, forested hills, and mountains characterize the terrain of Sierra Leone. The climate is tropical.

HISTORY AND POLITICS. When the Portuguese began arriving in the 1400s, they found the region inhabited by the Temne. In 1787 the Englishman Granville Sharp settled nearly four hundred freed black American slaves in what is now Freetown. The British declared the area a colony in 1808 and a protectorate in 1896. Sierra Leone became an independent nation in 1961. ∎

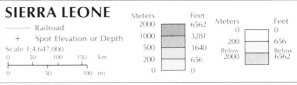

Sierra Leone Map Index

	Lat.	Long.		Lat.	Long.
Bauya	8°11'N	12°34'W	Mano	6°56'N	11°31'W
Bo	7°56'N	11°21'W	Moa	6°59'N	11°36'W
Freetown	8°30'N	13°15'W	Pendembu	8°06'N	10°42'W
Great Scarcies	8°55'N	13°08'W	Pepel	8°35'N	13°03'W
Kenema	7°52'N	11°12'W	Rokel	8°33'N	12°48'W
Little Scarcies	8°51'N	13°09'W	Sewa	7°18'N	12°08'W
Loma Mountains	9°10'N	11°07'W	Sherbro Bay	7°40'N	12°45'W
Lunsar	8°41'N	12°32'W	Sherbro Island	7°45'N	12°55'W
Makeni	8°53'N	12°03'W			

SINGAPORE

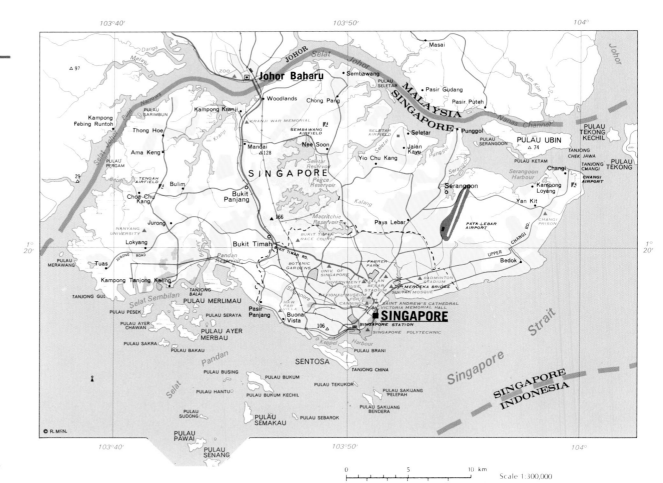

© R. MEN.

Scale 1:300,000

OFFICIAL NAME Republic of Singapore

PEOPLE
Population 2,545,000.
Density 11,361/mi² (4,380/km²).
Urban 100%.
Capital Singapore, 2,502,000.
Ethnic groups Chinese 77%, Malay 15%, Indian 6%.
Languages English, Chinese, Malay, Tamil.
Religions Buddhist, Taoist, Muslim, Hindu, Christian.
Life expectancy 74 female, 70 male.
Literacy 85%.

POLITICS
Government Republic.
Parties People's Action.
Suffrage Universal, over 20.
Memberships ASEAN, CW, UN.

ECONOMY
GDP $14,200,000,000.
Per capita $5,745.
Monetary unit Dollar.
Trade partners Malaysia, U.S., Japan, Saudi Arabia.
Exports Petroleum products, electrical machinery, telecommunications equipment, natural rubber.
Imports Machinery, petroleum, manufactured goods, rice.

LAND
Description Southeastern Asian island.
Area 224 mi² (581 km²).
Highest point Timah Hill, 545 ft (166 m).
Lowest point Sea level.

PEOPLE. Singapore is one of the most densely populated nations in the world. Most of the population is Chinese. A significant minority is Malay, and the remainder is European or Indian. Singapore's languages include Chinese, English, Malay, and Tamil. The main religions —Buddhism, Taoism, Islam, Hinduism, and Christianity—reflect the cultural diversity of the nation. Singapore's society is characterized by a mixture of Western and traditional customs and dress. Nearly all the population lives in the city of Singapore on Singapore Island.

ECONOMY AND THE LAND. Singapore is a leading Asian economic power. The city of Singapore is well known as a financial center and major harbor for trade. The nation's factories produce a variety of goods, such as chemicals, electronic equipment, and machinery, and are among the world leaders in petroleum refining. Singapore has few natural resources, however, and little arable land. Most agricultural output is consumed domestically; Singapore must import much of its raw materials and food. The nation consists of one main island, which is characterized by wet lowlands, and many small offshore islets. Cool sea breezes and a tropical climate make Singapore an attractive spot for tourists.

HISTORY AND POLITICS. Present-day Singapore has been inhabited since prehistoric times. From the 1100s to the 1800s Singapore served

mainly as a trading center and refuge for pirates. The British East India Company, the major colonial force in India, realized Singapore's strategic importance to British trade and gained possession of the harbor in 1819. All Singapore became a Crown colony in 1826. As the port prospered, the island's population grew rapidly. Following World War II, the people of Singapore moved from internal self-government to independence in 1965. The government continues to work in partnership with the business community to fur-

ther Singapore's growth. In foreign policy, the nation remains nonaligned, but as a small country dependent on trade, Singapore is interested in maintaining wide contacts. ■

Singapore Map Index

	Lat.	Long.		Lat.	Long.
Bukit Panjang	1°23'N	103°46'E	Singapore	1°17'N	103°51'E
Paya Lebar	1°22'N	103°53'E	Woodlands	1°27'N	103°46'E
Serangoon	1°22'N	103°54'E			

Singapore's skyscrapers and modern architecture evidence its role as a world leader in trade and finance. A strategic location makes it one of the world's busiest ports.

SOLOMON ISLANDS

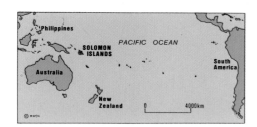

OFFICIAL NAME Solomon
Islands

PEOPLE
Population 270,000.
Density 23/mi² (9.1/km²).
Urban 9%.
Capital Honiara, Guadalcanal I., 16,125.
Ethnic groups Melanesian 93%, Polynesian 4%.
Languages English, Malay-Polynesian languages.
Religions Anglican, Roman Catholic, Methodist, other
Christian.
Literacy 60%.

POLITICS
Government Parliamentary state.
Parties National Democratic, People's Alliance,
United.
Suffrage Universal, over 21.
Memberships CW, UN.
Subdivisions 7 provinces.

ECONOMY
GNP $110,000,000.

Per capita $460.
Monetary unit Dollar.
Trade partners Japan, Australia, U.K., Singapore.
Exports Copra, wood, fish, palm oil.
Imports Machinery, transportation equipment, food,
fuels.

LAND
Description South Pacific islands.
Area 11,506 mi² (29,800 km²).
Highest point Mt. Makarakomburu, Guadalcanal I.,
8,028 ft (2,447 m).
Lowest point Sea level.

PEOPLE. More than 90 percent of the people are
Melanesian, and the remainder are Polynesian,
European, Chinese, and Micronesian. English is
the official language, but some ninety local languages are also spoken. The dominant religion is
Protestantism, and religious minorities include
Roman Catholics and followers of local traditions. The population is primarily rural, and
much of its social structure is patterned on traditional village life.

ECONOMY AND THE LAND. The economy is
based on subsistence farming and exports of fish,
wood, copra, and some spices and palm oil. Terrain ranges from forested mountains to low-lying
coral atolls. The climate is warm and moist, with
heavy annual rainfall.

HISTORY AND POLITICS. Hunter-gatherers
lived on the islands as early as 1000 B.C. Because
of disease and native resistance, early attempts at

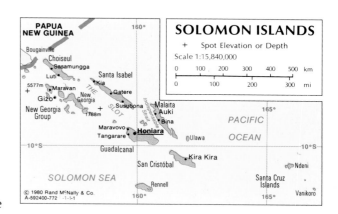

Solomon Islands Map Index

	Lat.	Long.		Lat.	Long.
Auki	8°45′S	160°42′E	Malaita	9°00′S	161°00′E
Choiseul	7°05′S	157°00′E	Rennell	11°40′S	160°10′E
Gizo	8°06′S	156°51′E	San Cristóbal	10°36′S	161°45′E
Guadalcanal	9°32′S	160°12′E	Santa Isabel	8°00′S	159°00′E
Honiara	9°26′S	159°57′E	Tangarare	9°35′S	159°39′E
Kira Kira	10°27′S	161°56′E	The Slot	8°00′S	158°10′E

colonization failed, and Europeans did not firmly
establish themselves until the mid-1800s. Britain
declared the islands a protectorate in 1893. The
area was the site of fierce battles between the
Japanese and Allied forces during World War II,
and following the war, moves were made toward
independence. In 1978 a constitution was adopted, and the Solomon Islands became a sovereign
nation. ■

SOMALIA

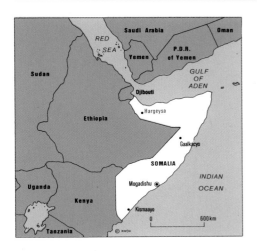

OFFICIAL NAME Somali
Democratic Republic

PEOPLE
Population 6,465,000.
Density 26/mi² (10/km²).
Urban 30%.
Capital Mogadishu, 400,000.
Ethnic groups Somali 99%.
Languages Somali, Arabic, English, Italian.
Religions Sunni Muslim 99%.
Life expectancy 39 female, 38 male.
Literacy 60%.

POLITICS
Government Socialist republic.
Parties Revolutionary Socialist.
Suffrage Universal, over 18.
Memberships AL, OAU, UN.
Subdivisions 16 regions.

ECONOMY
GDP $1,875,000.
Per capita $375.
Monetary unit Shilling.
Trade partners Saudi Arabia, Italy, U.S., U.K.
Exports Livestock, bananas, hides and skins.

Imports Food, petroleum products, transportation
equipment.

LAND
Description Eastern Africa.
Area 246,200 mi² (637,657 km²).
Highest point Surud Ad, 7,897 ft (2,407 m).
Lowest point Sea level.

PEOPLE. Unlike the population in many African
nations, the people of Somalia are remarkably
homogeneous in their language, culture, and
identity. Most are nomadic or seminomadic herders; only a quarter of the people have settled in
permanent communities in southern Somalia.
While Somali is the official language, Arabic, English, and Italian are also spoken. Nearly all the
Somali people are Sunni Muslims. They band
together in large family groups, observing a way
of life that has endured for centuries.

ECONOMY AND THE LAND. Somalia is a developing country that has not yet exploited its rich
deposits of iron ore and gypsum. There is little
manufacturing, and the economy is mainly agricultural, though activity is restricted to the vicini-
ty of the rivers and certain coastal districts. Economic development is hampered by a lack of
railroads and paved highways and by a hot climate with recurring droughts. The terrain ranges
from flatlands in central and southern regions to
northern hills.

HISTORY AND POLITICS. Ancestors of the So-
malis who settled the region were converted by
Arabs to Islam in the A.D. 800s and 900s. They
fought many religious wars with the Christian
kingdom of Ethiopia between the 1300s and
1500s. The British, Italians, and French arrived in
the region in the latter half of the 1800s and
divided the Somali territory among themselves,
with Ethiopia seizing Ogaden in the west. After
World War II Italy was made administrator of its
former colony to prepare it for independence. In
1960 British Somaliland and Italian Somalia
joined to form an independent republic. ■

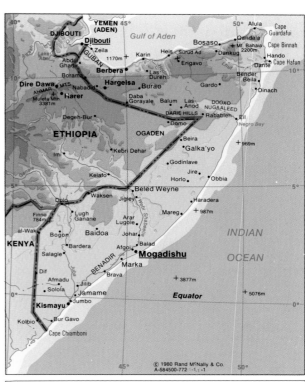

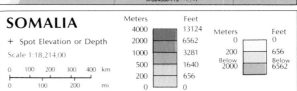

SOMALIA

+ Spot Elevation or Depth
Scale 1:18,214,00

Meters	Feet		Meters	Feet
4000	13124		0	0
2000	6562		200	656
1000	3281		Below 2000	Below 6562
500	1640			
200	656			
0	0			

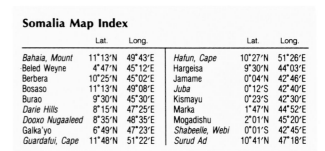

Somalia Map Index

	Lat.	Long.		Lat.	Long.
Bahaia, Mount	11°13′N	49°43′E	Hafun, Cape	10°27′N	51°26′E
Beled Weyne	4°47′N	45°12′E	Hargeisa	9°30′N	44°03′E
Berbera	10°25′N	45°02′E	Jamame	0°04′N	42°46′E
Bosaso	11°13′N	49°08′E	Juba	0°12′S	42°40′E
Burao	9°30′N	45°30′E	Kismayu	0°23′S	42°30′E
Darie Hills	8°15′N	47°25′E	Marka	1°47′N	44°52′E
Dooxo Nugaaleed	8°35′N	48°35′E	Mogadishu	2°01′N	45°20′E
Galka'yo	6°49′N	47°23′E	Shabeelle, Webi	0°01′S	42°45′E
Guardafui, Cape	11°48′N	51°22′E	Surud Ad	10°41′N	47°18′E

SOUTH AFRICA

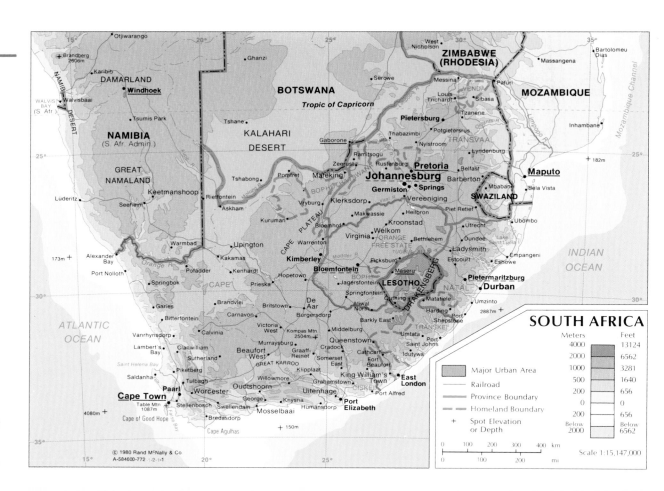

OFFICIAL NAME Republic of
South Africa

PEOPLE
Population 26,855,000.
Density 62/mi² (24/km²).
Urban 53%.
Capital Pretoria (administrative seat), 435,100; Cape Town (seat of legislature), 859,940; Bloemfontein (seat of judiciary), 102,600.
Ethnic groups African 70%, white 18%, Colored 9%, Asian 3%.
Languages Afrikaans, English, indigenous.
Religions Christian.
Life expectancy 56 female, 51 male.
Literacy 70%.

POLITICS
Government Republic.
Parties Conservative, National, Progressive Federal.
Suffrage Whites, over 18 (17 in Natal province).
Memberships UN.
Subdivisions 4 provinces.

ECONOMY
GDP $73,600,000,000.
Per capita $2,500.
Monetary unit Rand.
Trade partners U.S., West Germany, Japan, U.K.
Exports Gold, wool, diamonds.
Imports Motor vehicles, machinery, metals.

LAND
Description Southern Africa.
Area 433,680 mi² (1,123,226 km²).
Highest point eNjesuthi, 11,306 ft (3,446 m).
Lowest point Sea level.
The above information includes Walvis Bay.

South Africa Map Index

	Lat.	Long.		Lat.	Long.		Lat.	Long.		Lat.	Long.
Agulhas, Cape	34°52'S	20°00'E	Germiston	26°15'S	28°05'E	Molopo	28°30'S	20°13'E	*Saint Helena Bay*	32°43'S	18°05'E
Auob	26°25'S	20°35'E	Good Hope, Cape			Mosselbaai	34°11'S	22°08'E	Springs	26°13'S	28°25'E
Barberton	25°48'S	31°03'E	of	34°24'S	18°30'E	Natal	28°40'S	30°40'E	*Table Mountain*	33°57'S	18°25'E
Beaufort West	32°18'S	22°36'E	*Great Karroo*	32°25'S	22°40'E	Olifants	24°10'S	32°40'E	*Transkei*	31°20'S	29°00'E
Bloemfontein	29°12'S	26°07'E	Johannesburg	26°15'S	28°00'E	Orange	28°41'S	16°28'E	*Transvaal*	25°00'S	29°00'E
Bophuthatswana	26°30'S	25°30'E	*Kalahari Desert*	24°00'S	21°30'E	Orange Free			Uitenhage	33°40'S	25°28'E
Cape	31°00'S	23°00'E	Kimberley	28°43'S	24°46'E	State	28°30'S	27°00'E	Upington	28°25'S	21°15'E
Cape Plateau	28°20'S	23°57'E	King William's			Oudtshoorn	33°35'S	22°14'E	*Vaal*	27°40'S	26°09'E
Cape Town	33°55'S	18°22'E	Town	32°51'S	27°22'E	Paarl	33°45'S	18°56'E	*Venda*	23°00'S	31°00'E
De Aar	30°39'S	24°00'E	Klerksdorp	26°58'S	26°39'E	Pietermaritzburg	29°37'S	30°16'E	Vereeniging	26°38'S	27°57'E
Drakensberg	27°00'S	30°00'E	Kroonstad	27°46'S	27°12'E	Pietersburg	23°54'S	29°25'E	Virginia	28°12'S	26°49'E
Durban	29°55'S	30°56'E	Ladysmith	28°34'S	29°45'E	Port Elizabeth	33°58'S	25°40'E	*Walvis Bay*	22°59'S	14°31'E
East London	33°00'S	27°55'E	*Limpopo*	22°25'S	31°20'E	Pretoria	25°45'S	28°10'E	Welkom	27°59'S	26°45'E
False Bay	34°12'S	18°40'E	Mafeking	25°53'S	25°39'E	Queenstown	31°52'S	26°52'E	Worcester	33°39'S	19°27'E

Only about 12 percent of South Africa's land is arable, and the nation's main crops of corn, sugarcane, and wheat are subject to unreliable rainfall and drought. Shown here are wheat fields in southern Cape Province.

PEOPLE. The government of South Africa classifies the country's population into four main groups: black, white, Colored, and Asian. Various black African groups make up the majority population. Whites compose a minority and are either Afrikaners—of Dutch, German, and French descent—or British. Coloreds, people of mixed white, black, and Asian heritage, and Asians, primarily from India, make up the remaining population. Afrikaans and English are the official languages, although the blacks, Coloreds, and Asians speak their own languages as well. The dominant religions are Christian; however, many groups follow traditional practices. The South African government enforces apartheid, a policy of racial segregation widely criticized for violating the rights of blacks, Coloreds, and Asians.

ECONOMY AND THE LAND. The discovery of gold and diamonds in South Africa in the late 1800s shaped the nation's prosperous economy. Revenues from mining promoted industry, and today South Africa is one of the richest and most highly developed countries in Africa. Mining remains a mainstay, as does agriculture; the nation is almost self-sufficient in food production. Many effects of apartheid, including discriminatory systems of education and job reservation, have kept the majority population from the benefits of national prosperity. The varied landscape features coastal beaches, plateaus, mountains, and deep valleys. The climate is temperate. The Republic of South Africa includes the enclave of Walvis Bay, situated on Africa's southwest coast.

HISTORY AND POLITICS.   Southern Africa has been inhabited for many thousands of years. Ancestors of the area's present African population had settled by the time Portuguese explorers reached the Cape of Good Hope in the late 1400s. The first white settlers, ancestors of today's Afrikaners, established colonies in the seventeenth century. Britain gained control of the area in the late eighteenth century, and relations between Afrikaners and the British soon became strained. To escape British rule, many Afrikaners migrated northward to lands occupied by black Africans. The discovery of gold and diamonds in the late 1800s brought an influx of Europeans and further strained relations between Afrikaners and the British, with both groups striving for control of valuable mineral deposits. Two wars broke out, and in 1902 the British defeated the Afrikaners, or Boers, and incorporated the Boer territories into the British Empire. Black Africans were also subdued by the British, and in 1910 the white-controlled Union of South Africa was formed. Afrikaner nationalism grew in the early twentieth century and led to the formation of the National party, which gained control in 1924 and again in 1948. The party began the apartheid system of separation of the races in the late forties, and subsequent decades saw apartheid legislation and increasing racial tension. Apartheid continued in the eighties, despite violence and foreign pressure to abolish the system.   ■

Forests cover about 2 percent of South Africa's land area, and forestry makes a minor contribution to the economy of the nation. Both indigenous trees and imported varieties, including pine, gum, and wattle, are grown, meeting more than 90 percent of South Africa's domestic needs for wood and wood products. The forested land shown here is found in eastern Transvaal.

SPAIN

OFFICIAL NAME Spanish State

PEOPLE
Population 38,515,000.
Density 198/mi² (76/km²).
Urban 91%.
Capital Madrid, 3,188,297.
Ethnic groups Mixed Mediterranean and Nordic.
Languages Spanish.
Religions Roman Catholic 99%.
Life expectancy 76 female, 72 male.
Literacy 97%.

POLITICS
Government Constitutional monarchy.
Parties Popular Alliance, Popular Democratic, Socialist Workers'.
Suffrage Universal, over 18.
Memberships EC, NATO, OECD, UN.
Subdivisions 17 autonomous regions.

ECONOMY
GNP $179,700,000,000.
Per capita $4,746.
Monetary unit Peseta.
Trade partners France, U.S., West Germany, Italy, U.K.
Exports Iron and steel products, machinery, food, automobiles, footwear.
Imports Fuels, machinery, chemicals, iron and steel, food.

LAND
Description Southern Europe.
Area 194,882 mi² (504,741 km²).
Highest point Teide Pk., Tenerife, Canary Is., 12,188 ft (3,715 m).
Lowest point Sea level.

PEOPLE.   The population of Spain is a mixture of ethnic groups from northern Europe and the area surrounding the Mediterranean Sea. Spanish is the official language; however, several regional dialects are commonly spoken. The Basque minority, one of the oldest surviving ethnic groups in Europe, lives mainly in the Pyrenees in northern Spain, preserving its own language and traditions. Since the 1978 constitution, Spain has not had an official religion, yet nearly all its people are Roman Catholic. The country has a rich artistic tradition, blending Moorish and Western cultures.

ECONOMY AND THE LAND.   Following the implementation of an economic-restructuring program in the 1950s, Spain's industrial sector experienced rapid growth, especially in the auto, chemical, machine tool, and shipbuilding industries. Most of these continue as contributors to Spain's economy, although world economic trends have affected Spain as well as other nations. After a boom in the early 1980s, the auto-

mobile industry experienced a decline because of falling demand, and shipbuilding has been influenced by world recession. However, Spain's chemical industry continues to expand. The government hopes that additional economic restructuring will revive these industries, and plans include expansion into high technology and electronics. Formerly the nation's main source of income, agriculture now plays a relatively minor economic role. Tourism is an important contributor; Spain is known for its art and history as well as its beaches and pleasant climate. Spain's terrain is mainly composed of a dry plateau area; mountains cover the northern section, and plains

Spain's scenery, climate, and cultural and historical traditions draw many international visitors to the country. In addition, annual fiestas such as the Seville horse fair, shown here, are colorful attractions.

Spain Map Index

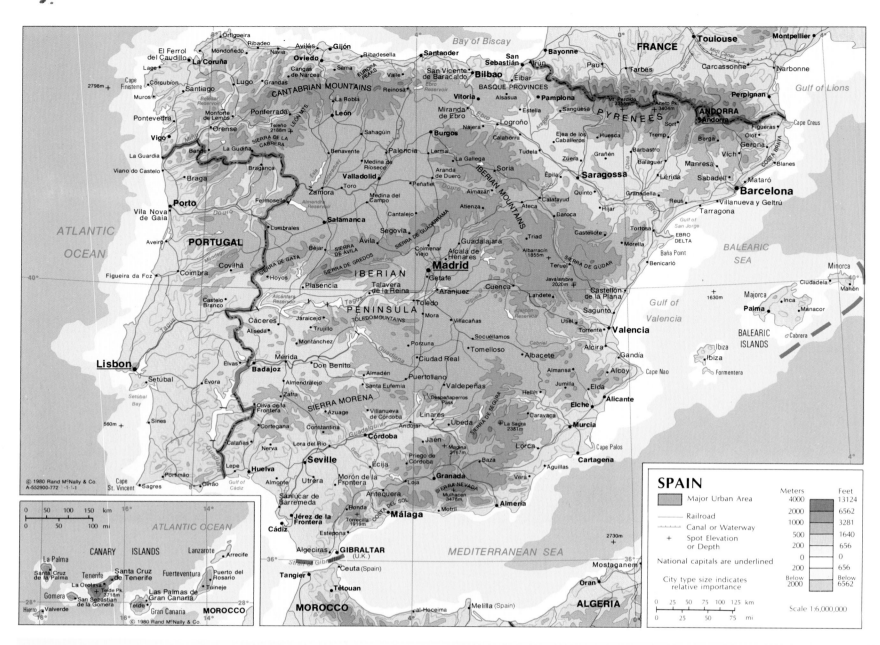

Name	Lat.	Long.
Alarcon Reservoir	39°36'N	2°10'W
Albacete	38°59'N	1°51'W
Alcalá de Henares	40°29'N	3°22'W
Alcántara Reservoir	39°45'N	6°25'W
Alcira	39°09'N	0°26'W
Alcoy	38°42'N	0°28'W
Algeciras	36°08'N	5°30'W
Alicante	38°21'N	0°29'W
Almendra Reservoir	41°15'N	6°10'W
Almería	36°50'N	2°27'W
Aneto Peak	42°38'N	0°40'E
Antequera	37°01'N	4°33'W
Aranjuez	40°02'N	3°36'W
Ávila	40°39'N	4°42'W
Avilés	43°33'N	5°55'W
Badajoz	38°53'N	6°58'W
Balearic Islands	39°30'N	3°00'E
Balearic Sea	40°30'N	2°00'E
Baña Point	40°34'N	0°38'E
Barcelona	41°23'N	2°11'E
Belesar Reservoir	42°45'N	7°40'W
Bilbao	43°15'N	2°58'W
Brava, Costa	41°45'N	3°04'E

Name	Lat.	Long.
Burgos	42°21'N	3°42'W
Cabriel	39°14'N	1°03'W
Cáceres	39°29'N	6°22'W
Cádiz	36°32'N	6°18'W
Cádiz, Gulf of	36°50'N	7°10'W
Canary Islands	28°00'N	15°30'W
Cantabrian Mountains	43°00'N	5°00'W
Cartagena	37°36'N	0°59'W
Castellón de la Plana	39°59'N	0°02'W
Ciudad Real	38°59'N	3°56'W
Córdoba	37°53'N	4°46'W
Creus, Cape	42°19'N	3°19'E
Cuenca	40°04'N	2°08'W
Despeñaperros Pass	38°24'N	3°30'W
Don Benito	38°57'N	5°52'W
Douro	41°08'N	8°40'W
Ebro	42°15'N	1°57'W
Ebro Delta	40°43'N	0°54'E
Ebro Reservoir	43°00'N	3°58'W
Écija	37°32'N	5°05'W
Éibar	43°11'N	2°28'W
Elche	38°15'N	0°42'W
Elda	38°29'N	0°47'W

Name	Lat.	Long.
El Ferrol del Caudillo	43°29'N	8°14'W
Esla	41°29'N	5°43'W
Finisterre, Cape	42°53'N	9°16'W
Fuerteventura	28°20'N	14°00'W
Gandía	38°58'N	0°11'W
Gerona	41°59'N	2°49'E
Getafe	40°18'N	3°43'W
Gibraltar, Strait of	35°57'N	5°36'W
Gijón	43°32'N	5°40'W
Granada	37°13'N	3°41'W
Gran Canaria	28°00'N	15°36'W
Guadalajara	40°38'N	3°10'W
Guadalquivir	36°47'N	6°22'W
Guadiana	37°14'N	7°22'W
Huelva	37°16'N	6°57'W
Iberian Mountains	41°00'N	2°30'W
Iberian Peninsula	40°00'N	5°00'W
Ibiza	38°54'N	1°26'E
Ibiza	39°00'N	1°25'E
Irún	43°21'N	1°47'W
Jaén	37°46'N	3°47'W
Jerez de la Frontera	36°41'N	6°08'W

Name	Lat.	Long.
La Coruña	43°22'N	8°23'W
La Palma	28°40'N	17°52'W
Las Palmas de Gran Canaria	28°06'N	15°24'W
León	42°36'N	5°34'W
Lérida	41°37'N	0°37'E
Linares	38°05'N	3°38'W
Logroño	42°28'N	2°27'W
Lorca	37°40'N	1°42'W
Lugo	43°00'N	7°34'W
Madrid	40°24'N	3°41'W
Majorca	39°30'N	3°00'E
Málaga	36°43'N	4°25'W
Manresa	41°44'N	1°50'E
Mataró	41°32'N	2°27'E
Mérida	38°55'N	6°20'W
Miño	41°52'N	8°51'W
Minorca	40°00'N	4°00'E
Miranda de Ebro	42°41'N	2°57'W
Morena, Sierra	38°00'N	5°00'W
Morón de la Frontera	37°08'N	5°27'W
Mulhacén	37°03'N	3°19'W
Murcia	37°59'N	1°07'W
Nao, Cape	38°44'N	0°14'E
Nevada, Sierra	37°05'N	3°10'W

Name	Lat.	Long.
Orense	42°20'N	7°51'W
Oviedo	43°22'N	5°50'W
Palencia	42°01'N	4°32'W
Palma	39°34'N	2°39'E
Palos, Cape	37°38'N	0°41'W
Pamplona	42°49'N	1°38'W
Perdido, Monte	42°40'N	0°05'E
Plasencia	40°02'N	6°05'W
Ponferrada	42°33'N	6°35'W
Pontevedra	42°26'N	8°38'W
Puertollano	38°41'N	4°07'W
Pyrenees	42°40'N	1°00'E
Sabadell	41°33'N	2°06'E
Sagunto	39°41'N	0°16'W
Salamanca	40°58'N	5°39'W
San Jorge, Gulf of	40°53'N	1°00'E
Sanlúcar de Barremeda	36°47'N	6°21'W
San Sebastián	43°19'N	1°59'W
Santa Cruz de Tenerife	28°27'N	16°14'W
Santander	43°28'N	3°48'W
Santiago	42°53'N	8°33'W
San Vicente de Baracaldo	43°18'N	2°59'W

Name	Lat.	Long.
Saragossa	41°38'N	0°53'W
Segovia	40°57'N	4°07'W
Seville	37°23'N	5°59'W
Sol, Costa del	36°30'N	4°30'W
Soria	41°46'N	2°28'W
Tagus	38°40'N	9°24'W
Talavera de la Reina	39°57'N	4°50'W
Tarragona	41°07'N	1°15'E
Teide Peak	28°16'N	16°38'W
Tenerife	28°19'N	16°34'W
Toledo	39°52'N	4°01'W
Tomelloso	39°10'N	3°01'W
Turia	39°27'N	0°19'W
Úbeda	38°01'N	3°22'W
Utrera	37°11'N	5°47'W
Valdepeñas	38°46'N	3°23'W
Valencia	39°28'N	0°22'W
Valencia, Gulf of	39°50'N	0°30'E
Valladolid	41°39'N	4°43'W
Vich	41°56'N	2°15'E
Vigo	42°14'N	8°43'W
Villanueva y Geltrú	41°14'N	1°44'E
Vitoria	42°51'N	2°40'W
Zamora	41°30'N	5°45'W

extend down the country's eastern coast. Climate in the eastern and southern regions is Mediterranean, while the northwest has more rainfall and less sunshine throughout the year.

HISTORY AND POLITICS. Spain is among the oldest inhabited regions in Europe. For centuries a Roman province, Spain was conquered by the Visigoths in the A.D. 500s, only to change hands again in the 700s when the Arab-Berbers, or Moors, seized control of all but a narrow strip of northern Spain. Christian kings reclaimed the area from the eleventh to the fourteenth centuries. Spain, controlled by the three kingdoms of Navarre, Aragon, and Castile, was united in the late 1400s under King Ferdinand and Queen Isabella. At the height of its empire, Spain claimed territory in North and South America, northern Africa, Italy, and the Canary Islands. However, a

series of wars burdened Spain financially, and in the 1500s, under King Philip II, the area entered a period of decline. Throughout the 1700s and 1800s, the nation lost most of its possessions through treaty or revolution. From 1873 to 1874 Spain's monarchy was replaced by a short-lived republic. The second republic, created in 1931, was brief as well; the election of a leftist coalition in 1936 led to a bitter civil war between an insur-

gent fascist group and supporters of the republic. General Francisco Franco, leader of the successful insurgent army, ruled as dictator of Spain from the end of the war in 1939 until his death in 1975. Spain enjoyed phenomenal economic growth during the 1950s and 1960s; however, that growth declined in the 1970s. Since Franco's death, King Juan Carlos has led the country toward a more democratic form of government. ∎

Places and Possessions of Spain

Entity	Status	Area	Population	Capital / Population
Balearic Islands (Mediterranean Sea)	Province	1,936 mi.² (5,014 km²)	695,000	Palma/304,422
Canary Islands (northwest of Africa)	Part of Spain	2,808 mi² (7,273 km²)	1,475,000	None
Spanish North Africa—Ceuta, Melilla, and small islands (north coast of Africa)	Territory	12 mi² (31 km²)	136,000	None

SRI LANKA

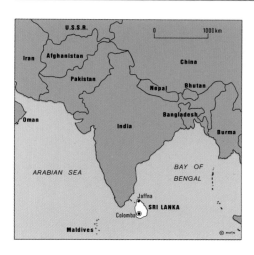

OFFICIAL NAME Democratic
Socialist Republic of
Sri Lanka

PEOPLE
Population 16,070,000.
Density 644/mi² (249/km²).
Urban 22%.
Capital Colombo, 585,776.
Ethnic groups Sinhalese 74%, Tamil 18%, Moor 7%.
Languages Sinhala, Tamil, English.
Religions Buddhist 69%, Hindu 15%, Christian 8%,
Muslim 8%.
Life expectancy 72 female, 67 male.
Literacy 85%.

POLITICS
Government Socialist republic.
Parties All Ceylon Tamil Congress, Freedom, Janatha
Vimukthi Peramuna, United National.
Suffrage Universal, over 18.
Memberships CW, UN.
Subdivisions 24 districts.

ECONOMY
GDP $4,400,000,000.
Per capita $286.
Monetary unit Rupee.
Trade partners U.S., Saudi Arabia, Japan, U.K., West
Germany.
Exports Tea, natural rubber, petroleum products,
textiles.
Imports Petroleum, machinery, transportation
equipment, sugar.

LAND
Description Indian Ocean island.
Area 24,962 mi² (64,652 km²).
Highest point Pidurutalagala, 8,281 ft (2,524 m).
Lowest point Sea level.

PEOPLE. The two principal groups in Sri Lanka
are the majority Sinhalese and the minority Tamils. The Tamils are descended from immigrants
from southern India. Most, known as "Ceylon
Tamils," have lived in Sri Lanka for many centuries. "Indian Tamils" are descendants of Indian
laborers who arrived in the late nineteenth century. Other minorities include the Moors; Burgh-
ers, who are descendants of Dutch, Portuguese,
and British colonists; Malays; and Veddah aborigines. Sinhala is the official language, though
Tamil and English are also widely spoken. Most
Sinhalese are Buddhist, most Tamils are Hindu,
and the majority of the Moors and Malays are
Muslim.

ECONOMY AND THE LAND. Sri Lanka's economy is based on agriculture, which employs nearly half the people in producing tea, rubber, and
coconuts. Sri Lanka also hopes to become self-
sufficient in rice, thus reducing imports of this
staple. Industrial production has increased, and
major exports include graphite and textile products. Sri Lanka is also sponsoring several
internal-development programs. However, continuing high government subsidy and welfare
policies threaten economic growth. Most of Sri

Sri Lanka Map Index

	Lat.	Long.		Lat.	Long.
Adams Bridge	9°04′N	79°37′E	Mahaweli	8°27′N	81°13′E
Adams Peak	6°48′N	80°30′E	Mannar, Gulf of	8°30′N	79°00′E
Anuradhapura	8°21′N	80°23′E	Mannar Island	9°03′N	79°50′E
Badulla	6°59′N	81°03′E	Matale	7°28′N	80°37′E
Batticaloa	7°43′N	81°42′E	Matara	5°56′N	80°33′E
Chilaw	7°34′N	79°47′E	Moratuwa	6°46′N	79°53′E
Colombo	6°56′N	79°51′E	Negombo	7°13′N	79°50′E
Dehiwala-Mount			Palk Strait	10°00′N	79°45′E
Lavinia	6°51′N	79°52′E	Panadura	6°43′N	79°54′E
Dondra Head	5°55′N	80°35′E	Pedro, Point	9°50′N	80°14′E
Galle	6°02′N	80°13′E	Pidurutalagala	7°00′N	80°46′E
Jaffna	9°40′N	80°00′E	Puttalam	8°02′N	79°49′E
Jaffna Lagoon	9°35′N	80°15′E	Ratnapura	6°41′N	80°24′E
Kalutara	6°35′N	79°58′E	Senanayake		
Kandy	7°18′N	80°38′E	Samudra Lake	7°11′N	81°29′E
Kegalla	7°15′N	80°21′E	Sri Lanka	7°00′N	81°00′E
Kelani	6°58′N	79°52′E	Trincomalee	8°34′N	81°14′E
Kurunegala	7°29′N	80°22′E	Weligama	5°58′N	80°25′E

Lanka is composed of a low coastal plain, and
the southern interior is mountainous and forested. The climate is tropical.

HISTORY AND POLITICS. The Sinhalese dynasty was founded by a prince from northern India
in about 500 B.C. Later, the Tamils from southern
India settled in the north of Sri Lanka. European
control began in the 1500s, when the island was
ruled by the Portuguese and Dutch. It became
the British colony of Ceylon in 1802 and the
independent nation of Ceylon in 1948. In 1972
the name was changed to Sri Lanka. Current
concerns of the Sri Lankan government revolve
around the Tamil population. Ceylon Tamils have
full voting rights, whereas most Indian Tamils
lost voting privileges through legislation passed
in 1948. India also refuses to recognize them as
Indian citizens, thus many Indian Tamils remain
stateless. A Sri Lankan–Indian agreement in 1964
provided for repatriation of some Indian Tamils
to India and for Sri Lankan citizenship for others. The agreement has since expired, but Sri
Lanka's government has announced its inten-
tions to grant citizenship to the remaining Indian
Tamils without citizenship status. In addition,
since the 1970s, a group of separatist Ceylon

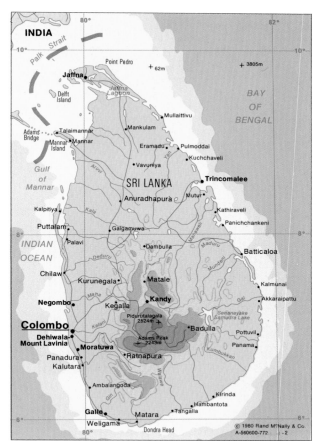

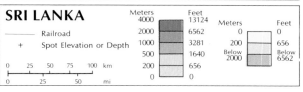

Tamils have been agitating for the right to form
an independent state. Sometimes aided in their
cause by Tamils of southern India, the Ceylon
Tamils have formed an insurgent group, and violence erupts periodically. In foreign affairs, Sri
Lanka pursues a policy of nonalignment. ■

**Sri Lanka's climate and terrain are conducive to tea production, and fields such as this one are
found throughout much of the south and southwest. In 1975 the tea plantations were nationalized, and the government now owns about 60 percent of the land on which tea is cultivated.**

SUDAN

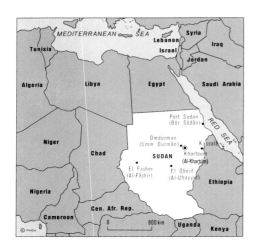

Area 967,500 mi² (2,505,813 km²).
Highest point Kinyeti, 10,456 ft (3,187 m).
Lowest point Sea level.

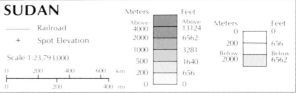

OFFICIAL NAME Democratic
Republic of the Sudan

PEOPLE
Population 21,390,000.
Density 22/mi² (8.5/km²).
Urban 21%.
Capital Khartoum, 333,921.
Ethnic groups Black African 52%, Arab 39%, Beja 6%.
Languages Arabic, indigenous, English.
Religions Sunni Muslim 70%, indigenous 20%,
Christian 5%.
Life expectancy 48 female, 45 male.
Literacy 20%.

POLITICS
Government Republic.
Parties None (outlawed).
Suffrage Universal adult.
Memberships AL, OAU, UN.
Subdivisions 19 provinces.

ECONOMY
GDP $7,100,000,000.
Per capita $345.
Monetary unit Pound.
Trade partners U.K., West Germany, Italy, U.S., Saudi
Arabia, France.
Exports Cotton, gum arabic, peanuts, sesame.
Imports Petroleum products, machinery, textiles,
transportation equipment, food.

LAND
Description Eastern Africa.

PEOPLE. Sudan's population is composed of
two distinct cultures—black African and Arab.
African blacks of diverse ethnicity are a majority
and are concentrated in the south, where they
practice traditional life-styles and beliefs and
speak indigenous languages. Arabic-speaking
Muslims belonging to several ethnic groups live
mainly in northern and central regions. Lack of
cooperation between the two groups continues to
inhibit effective government.

ECONOMY AND THE LAND. The economy is
based on agriculture, and irrigation has made
arid Sudan a leading producer of cotton. However, farm output continues to be vulnerable to
drought, the most recent from 1983 to 1985. Forests provide for production of gum arabic, used
in making candy and perfumes, and other crops
include peanuts and sesame seeds. Economic activity is concentrated near the Nile River and its
branches and near water holes and wells. The
mostly flat terrain is marked by eastern and
western mountains; and southern forests and savanna give way to swampland, scrubland, and
northern desert. The climate varies from desert
in the north to tropical in the south.

HISTORY AND POLITICS. Egypt mounted repeated invasions of what is now northern Sudan
beginning about 300 B.C., but Sudan remained a
collection of small independent states until 1821,
when Egypt conquered and unified the northern
portion. Egypt was unable to establish control
over the south, which was often subject to attacks by slave raiders. In 1881 a Muslim leader
began uniting various groups in a revolt against
Egyptian rule, and success came four years later.
His successor ruled until 1898, when British and
Egyptian forces reconquered the land. Renamed
the Anglo-Egyptian Sudan, the region was ruled
jointly by Egypt and Britain, with British administration dominating. Sudan became independent
in 1956. A series of military coups since that time
has marked the country with political and economic instability. ∎

SUDAN

— Railroad
+ Spot Elevation

Scale 1:23,793,000

	Meters	Feet		Meters	Feet
	Above 4000	Above 13124		0	0
	2000	6562		200	656
	1000	3281		Below 2000	Below 6562
	500	1640			
	200	656			
	0	0			

Sudan Map Index

	Lat.	Long.		Lat.	Long.
al-Arab	9°02′N	29°28′E	Nasser, Lake	21°35′N	31°00′E
al-Fashir	13°38′N	25°21′E	Nile	22°00′N	31°20′E
al-Junayna	13°27′N	22°27′E	Nubian Desert	20°30′N	33°00′E
al-Qadarif	14°20′N	35°24′E	Nyala	12°03′N	24°53′E
al-Ubayyid	13°11′N	30°13′E	Omdurman	15°38′N	32°30′E
Atbara	17°42′N	33°59′E	Port Sudan	19°37′N	37°14′E
Atbara	17°40′N	33°56′E	Red Sea	21°00′N	37°30′E
Blue Nile	15°38′N	32°31′E	Sannar	13°33′N	33°38′E
Fifth Cataract	18°23′N	33°47′E	Shandi	16°42′N	33°26′E
Kassala	15°28′N	36°24′E	Sixth Cataract	16°20′N	32°42′E
Khartoum	15°36′N	32°32′E	Sobat	9°22′N	31°33′E
Kinyeti	3°57′N	32°54′E	Third Cataract	19°49′N	30°19′E
Kurdufan	12°00′N	27°00′E	Uwaynat, Jabal		
Kusti	13°10′N	32°40′E	al-	21°54′N	24°58′E
Malakal	9°31′N	31°39′E	Wad Madani	14°25′N	33°28′E
Marrah, Mount	13°04′N	24°21′E	Waw	7°42′N	28°00′E
Mountain Nile	9°30′N	30°30′E	White Nile	15°38′N	32°31′E

The great civilizations of the Nubia and Kush kingdoms flourished in ancient Sudan. Shown here are the pyramids at Jabal Barkal, legacies of that rich past.

SURINAME

OFFICIAL NAME Republic of Suriname

PEOPLE
Population 375,000.
Density 5.9/mi² (2.3/km²).
Urban 66%.
Capital Paramaribo, 67,718.
Ethnic groups East Indian 37%, Creole 31%, Javanese 15%, Bush Negro 10%, Amerindian 3%.
Languages Dutch, English, Hindi, Sranang Tongo, Javanese.
Religions Hindu, Muslim, Roman Catholic, Moravian, others.
Life expectancy 71 female, 67 male.
Literacy 80%.

POLITICS
Government Republic.
Parties 25 February National Unity Movement.
Suffrage None (suspended).
Memberships OAS, UN.
Subdivisions 9 districts.

ECONOMY
GDP $1,044,000,000.
Per capita $2,916.
Monetary unit Guilder.
Trade partners U.S., Netherlands, other Western European countries, Trinidad and Tobago.
Exports Alumina, bauxite, aluminum, wood and wood products, rice.
Imports Capital equipment, petroleum, iron and steel, food.

LAND
Description Northeastern South America.
Area 63,037 mi² (163,265 km²).
Highest point Juliana Top, 3,749 ft (1,230 m).
Lowest point Sea level.

PEOPLE. Suriname's diverse ethnicity was shaped by the importation of black slaves from Africa and contract laborers from Asia. Descendants of East Indians and Creoles, who are of mixed European–black African stock constitute the two major groups. Minority groups of Javanese, Chinese, and Indian descent live mainly in coastal regions, as does Suriname's European population. Bush Negroes, who compose another minority, are descendants of escaped black slaves, and Amerindians, of Arawak and Carib ancestry, mostly inhabit jungle regions. Dutch is the official language, but most groups have preserved their distinct language, culture, and religion.

ECONOMY AND THE LAND. The economy is based on mining and metal processing, and bauxite and alumina account for the major exports. Agriculture plays an economic role as well and, together with fishing and forestry, offers potential for expansion. The terrain is marked by a narrow coastal swamp, central forests and savanna, and southern jungle-covered hills. The climate is tropical.

HISTORY AND POLITICS. Prior to the arrival of Europeans, present-day Suriname was inhabited

Suriname Map Index

	Lat.	Long.		Lat.	Long.
Albina	5°30'N	54°03'W	Nieuw Nickerie	5°57'N	56°59'W
Berg en Dal	5°09'N	55°04'W	Onverwacht	5°36'N	55°12'W
Brokopondo	5°04'N	54°58'W	Paramaribo	5°50'N	55°10'W
Charlottenburg	5°51'N	54°46'W	Parnam	5°37'N	55°06'W
Coeroeni	3°21'N	57°31'W	Saramacca	5°51'N	55°53'W
Coppename	5°48'N	55°55'W	*Tapanahoni*	4°22'N	54°27'W
Corantijn	5°55'N	57°05'W	Totness	5°53'N	56°19'W
Frederik Willem			Tumuc-Humac		
IV Falls	3°28'N	57°37'W	Mountains	2°00'N	55°00'W
Groningen	5°48'N	55°28'W	Wageningen	5°46'N	56°41'W
Julianatop	3°41'N	56°32'W	Wilhelmina		
Kwakoegron	5°15'N	55°20'W	Range	3°45'N	56°30'W
Litani	3°40'N	54°00'W	W. J. Van		
Marowijne	5°45'N	53°58'W	Blommestein		
Moengo	5°37'N	54°24'W	Lake	4°45'N	55°00'W
Nieuw			*Wonotobo Falls*	4°22'N	57°55'W
Amsterdam	5°53'N	55°05'W			

by indigenous Indians. Christopher Columbus sighted the coast in 1498, but Spanish and Portuguese exploration was slowed by the area's lack of gold. The British established the first settlement in 1651, and in 1665 Jews from Brazil erected the first synagogue in the Western Hemisphere. In 1667 the British traded the area to the Netherlands in exchange for the Dutch colony of New Amsterdam—present-day Manhattan in the U.S. state of New York. Subsequent wars and treaties caused ownership of Suriname to shift among the British, French, and Dutch until 1815, when the Netherlands regained control. In 1954 Suriname became part of the Netherlands, with status equal to that of the Netherlands Antilles. Independence was gained in 1975. In 1980 the military seized power, and a joint military-civilian government was subsequently established. Instability has continued, with occasional coup attempts. The nation pursues a policy of nonalignment but maintains relations with many countries. ■

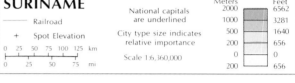

Suriname's bauxite deposits continue to fuel the nation's mining and industrial sectors, despite declining prices and demands for aluminum in the world marketplace. Much of the bauxite is shipped to the United States, but Suriname's factories also process the ore to produce alumina and aluminum for export.

SWAZILAND

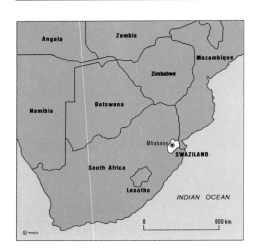

OFFICIAL NAME Kingdom of Swaziland

PEOPLE
Population 660,000.
Density 98/mi² (38/km²).
Urban 15%.
Capital Mbabane, 33,000.
Ethnic groups African 96%, European 3%, mulatto 1%.
Languages English, siSwati.
Religions Christian 57%, indigenous 43%.
Life expectancy 56 female, 51 male.
Literacy 65%.

POLITICS
Government Monarchy.
Parties None.
Suffrage Universal adult.
Memberships CW, OAU, UN.
Subdivisions 4 districts.

ECONOMY
GDP $500,000,000.
Per capita $880.
Monetary unit Lilangeni.
Trade partners South Africa, U.K., U.S.
Exports Sugar, asbestos, wood products, electronics, fruits.
Imports Motor vehicles, petroleum products, machinery, food, chemicals.

LAND
Description Southern Africa, landlocked.
Area 6,704 mi² (17,364 km²).
Highest point Emlembe, 6,109 ft (1,862 m).
Lowest point 70 ft (21 m).

PEOPLE. At least 90 percent of the people of Swaziland are black Africans called Swazi. Very small minorities of white Europeans and people of mixed European and African descent also live in the country. The two official languages are English and siSwati. Government and official business is conducted primarily in English. More than half the Swazi belong to Christian churches, while others practice traditional African religions.

ECONOMY AND THE LAND. Most Swazi are subsistence farmers. Europeans own about one-third of the land in Swaziland and raise most of the cash crops, including fruits, sugar, tobacco, cotton, and wood. About half the nation's income comes from European-owned mining operations. Major exports include asbestos and iron ore. Swaziland also has desposits of coal, pottery clay, gold, and tin. The country's mountain scenery and green forests have brought a growing tourist industry. The climate is temperate.

HISTORY AND POLITICS. According to legend, the Swazi originally came from the area near Maputo. British traders and Dutch farmers from

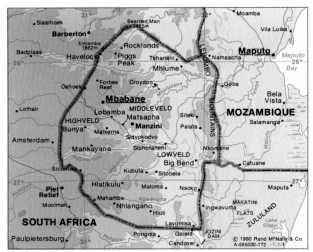

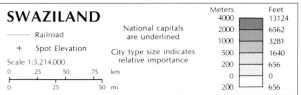

Swaziland Map Index

	Lat.	Long.		Lat.	Long.
Big Bend	26°50′S	31°57′E	Mbabane	26°18′S	31°06′E
Bunya	26°32′S	31°01′E	Mhlume	26°02′S	31°50′E
Emlembe	25°57′S	31°11′E	Nhlangano	27°06′S	31°17′E
Manzini	26°30′S	31°25′E	Piggs Peak	25°38′S	31°15′E
Matsapha	26°29′S	31°23′E	Rocklands	25°55′S	31°20′E

South Africa first reached Swaziland in the 1830s. More whites came in the 1880s when gold was discovered. Swazi leaders unknowingly granted many concessions to the whites at this time. After the Boer War, Britain assumed administration of Swaziland and ruled until 1967. Swaziland became independent in 1968. ■

SWEDEN

Stockholm, Sweden

SWEDEN

OFFICIAL NAME Kingdom of Sweden

PEOPLE

Population 8,335,000.
Density 48/mi² (19/km²).
Urban 83%.
Capital Stockholm, 649,686.
Ethnic groups Swedish, Lappish.
Languages Swedish.
Religions Lutheran 94%.
Life expectancy 79 female, 75 male.
Literacy 99%.

POLITICS

Government Constitutional monarchy.
Parties Center, Communist, Moderate Coalition, People's, Social Democratic.
Suffrage Universal, over 18.
Memberships OECD, UN.
Subdivisions 24 counties.

ECONOMY

GDP $81,000,000,000.
Per capita $10,285.
Monetary unit Krona.
Trade partners West Germany, U.K., Norway, U.S., Denmark, Finland.
Exports Machinery, motor vehicles, wood pulp, paper products, iron and steel products.
Imports Machinery, petroleum, petroleum products, chemicals, food.

LAND

Description Northern Europe.
Area 173,780 mi² (450,089 km²).
Highest point Mt. Kebne, 6,926 ft (2,111 m).
Lowest point Sea level.

PEOPLE. The most significant minorities in the largely urban Swedish population are Swedes of Finnish origin and a small number of Lapps. Sweden is also the home of immigrants from other Nordic countries and Yugoslavia, Greece, and Turkey. Swedish is the main language, although Finns and Lapps often speak other tongues. English is the leading foreign language, especially among students and younger people.

ECONOMY AND THE LAND. Sweden has one of the highest standards of living in the world. Taxes are also high, but the government provides exceptional benefits for most citizens, including free education and medical care, pension payments, four-week vacations, and payments for child care. The nation is industrial and bases its economy on its three most important natural resources—timber, iron ore, and water power. More than a fourth of its exports are lumber or wood products. The iron and steel industry produces high-quality steel used in ball bearings, precision tools, agricultural machinery, aircraft, automobiles, and ships. Swedish farmers rely heavily on dairy products and livestock, and most farms are part of Sweden's agricultural-cooperative movement. Sweden's varied terrain includes mountains, forests, plains, and sandy beaches. The climate is temperate, with cold win-

Sweden Map Index

	Lat.	Long.		Lat.	Long.
Alingsås	57°56'N	12°31'E	Malmberget	67°10'N	20°40'E
Angerman	62°48'N	17°56'E	Malmö	55°36'N	13°00'E
Asnen	56°38'N	14°42'E	Motala	58°33'N	15°03'E
Avesta	60°09'N	16°12'E	Nässjö	57°39'N	14°41'E
Baltic Sea	57°00'N	19°00'E	Norrköping	58°36'N	16°11'E
Boden	65°50'N	21°42'E	Nyköping	58°45'N	17°00'E
Bollnäs	61°21'N	16°25'E	Öland	56°45'N	16°38'E
Bolmen	56°55'N	13°40'E	Örebro	59°17'N	15°13'E
Borås	57°43'N	12°55'E	Örnsköldsvik	63°18'N	18°43'E
Borlänge	60°29'N	15°25'E	Oskarshamn	57°16'N	16°26'E
Bothnia, Gulf of	63°00'N	20°00'E	Östersund	63°11'N	14°39'E
Eskilstuna	59°22'N	16°30'E	Piteå	65°20'N	21°30'E
Fagersta	60°00'N	15°47'E	Piteå	65°14'N	21°32'E
Falun	60°36'N	15°38'E	Sandviken	60°37'N	16°46'E
Gävle	60°40'N	17°10'E	Sarektjåkkå	67°25'N	17°46'E
Göteborg	57°43'N	11°58'E	Siljan	60°50'N	14°45'E
Gotland	57°30'N	18°33'E	Skalka	66°50'N	18°46'E
Halmstad	56°39'N	12°50'E	Skellefteå	64°46'N	20°57'E
Härnösand	62°38'N	17°56'E	Skellefteå	64°42'N	21°06'E
Hässleholm	56°09'N	13°46'E	Skövde	58°24'N	13°50'E
Helsingborg	56°03'N	12°42'E	Söderhamn	61°18'N	17°03'E
Huddinge	59°14'N	17°59'E	Södertälje	59°12'N	17°37'E
Hudiksvall	61°44'N	17°07'E	Sommen	58°01'N	15°15'E
Jönköping	57°47'N	14°11'E	Stockholm	59°20'N	18°03'E
Kalmar	56°40'N	16°22'E	Storavan	65°40'N	18°15'E
Kalmar	56°40'N	16°25'E	Storsjön	63°12'N	14°18'E
Karlskoga	59°20'N	14°31'E	Sundsvall	62°23'N	17°18'E
Karlskrona	56°10'N	15°35'E	Torneå	65°48'N	24°08'E
Karlstad	59°22'N	13°30'E	Trelleborg	55°22'N	13°10'E
Katrineholm	59°00'N	16°12'E	Uddevalla	58°21'N	11°55'E
Kebne, Mount	67°53'N	18°33'E	Uddjaur	65°55'N	17°49'E
Kiruna	67°51'N	20°16'E	Umeå	63°50'N	20°15'E
Klara	59°23'N	13°32'E	Umeå	63°47'N	20°16'E
Köping	59°31'N	16°00'E	Uppsala	59°52'N	17°38'E
Kristianstad	56°02'N	14°08'E	Vänern, Lake	58°55'N	13°30'E
Lidköping	58°30'N	13°10'E	Varberg	57°06'N	12°15'E
Linköping	58°25'N	15°37'E	Västerås	59°37'N	16°33'E
Ljungan	62°19'N	17°23'E	Västervik	57°45'N	16°38'E
Ljusnan	61°12'N	17°08'E	Vättern, Lake	58°24'N	14°36'E
Ludvika	60°09'N	15°11'E	Växjö	56°52'N	14°49'E
Luleå	65°34'N	22°10'E	Visby	57°38'N	18°18'E
Luleå	65°35'N	22°03'E	Yänersborg	58°22'N	12°19'E
Mälaren	59°30'N	17°12'E			

ters in the north. Northern Sweden lies in the Land of the Midnight Sun and experiences periods of twenty-four hours of daylight in summer and darkness in winter.

HISTORY AND POLITICS. Inhabitants of what is now Sweden began to trade with the Roman Empire about 50 B.C. Successful sailing expeditions by Swedish Vikings began about A.D. 800. In the fourteenth century the kingdom came under Danish rule but left the union in 1523 and declared its independence. The Swedish king offered protection to the followers of Martin Luther, and Lutheranism was soon declared the state religion. By the late 1660s Sweden had become one of the great powers of Europe; it suffered a military defeat by Russia in 1709, however, and gradually lost most of its European possessions. An 1809 constitution gave most of the executive power of the government to the king. Despite this, the power of the Parliament gradually increased, and parliamentary rule was adopted in 1917. A 1975 constitution reduced the king's role to a ceremonial one. Sweden remained neutral during both world wars. ■

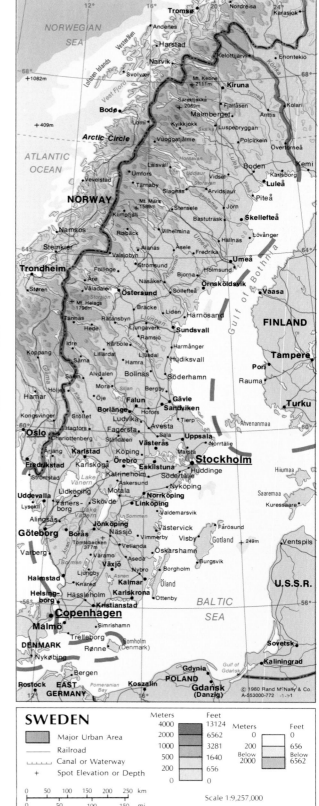

SWEDEN

	Meters	Feet		Meters	Feet
Major Urban Area	4000	13124		0	0
Railroad	2000	6562		200	656
Canal or Waterway	1000	3281		Below 2000	Below 6562
Spot Elevation or Depth	500	1640			
	200	656			
	0	0			

Scale 1:9,257,000

0 50 100 150 200 250 km
0 50 100 150 mi

The Scandinavian nations are known for their mountains, lakes, and forests, and in parts of Sweden, trees cover the countryside as far as the eye can see. In these remote areas, log cabins are scattered across the landscape, and many different types of wood products are manufactured, all with the clear-cut lines that are the trademark of Scandinavian design. The log cabins in this picture are situated near a lake in Hjarpesto, Sweden.

SWITZERLAND

OFFICIAL NAME Swiss
Confederation

PEOPLE
Population 6,485,000.
Density 408/mi² (157/km²).
Urban 58%.
Capital Bern, 145,300.
Ethnic groups German 65%, French 18%, Italian 10%,
   Romansch 1%.
Languages German, French, Italian.
Religions Roman Catholic 49%, Protestant 48%.
Life expectancy 78 female, 74 male.
Literacy 99%.

POLITICS
Government Republic.
Parties Christian Democratic People's, People's,
   Radical Democratic, Social Democratic.
Suffrage Universal, over 20.
Memberships OECD.
Subdivisions 26 cantons.

ECONOMY
GNP $95,600,000,000.
Per capita $14,270.
Monetary unit Franc.
Trade partners West Germany, France, Italy, U.S.,
   U.K.
Exports Machinery, electric appliances, chemicals,
   precision instruments, watches, textiles.
Imports Machinery, metals and metal products,
   petroleum, motor vehicles, iron and steel, food,
   chemicals.

LAND
Description Central Europe, landlocked.
Area 15,943 mi² (41,293 km²).
Highest point Monte Rosa (Dufourspitze), 15,203 ft
   (4,634 m).
Lowest point Lago Maggiore, 633 ft (193 m).

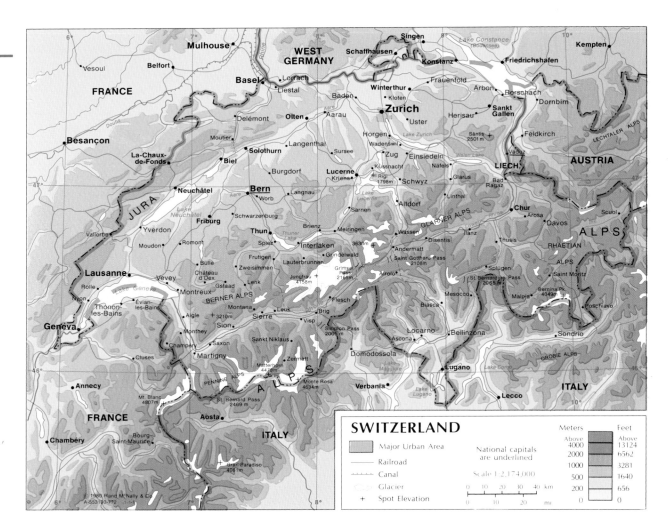

Switzerland Map Index

	Lat.	Long.		Lat.	Long.		Lat.	Long.		Lat.	Long.
Aarau	47°23'N	8°03'E	Friburg	46°48'N	7°09'E	Lugano, Lake	46°00'N	9°00'E	Sankt Gallen	47°25'N	9°23'E
Aare	47°37'N	8°13'E	Geneva	46°12'N	6°09'E	Maggiore, Lake	46°00'N	8°40'E	Schaffhausen	47°42'N	8°38'E
Alps	46°25'N	10°00'E	Geneva, Lake	46°25'N	6°30'E	Martigny	46°06'N	7°04'E	Schwyz	47°02'N	8°40'E
Altdorf	46°53'N	8°39'E	Glarner Alps	46°55'N	9°00'E	Matterhorn	45°59'N	7°43'E	Sierre	46°18'N	7°32'E
Arbon	47°31'N	9°26'E	Grimsel Pass	46°34'N	8°21'E	Montreux	46°26'N	6°55'E	Simplon Pass	46°15'N	8°02'E
Baden	47°29'N	8°18'E	Herisau	47°23'N	9°17'E	Neuchâtel	46°59'N	6°56'E	Sion	46°14'N	7°21'E
Basel	47°33'N	7°35'E	Horgen	47°15'N	8°36'E	Neuchâtel, Lake	46°52'N	6°50'E	Solothurn	47°13'N	7°32'E
Bellinzona	46°11'N	9°02'E	Inn	46°56'N	10°29'E	Olten	47°21'N	7°54'E	Thun	46°45'N	7°37'E
Bern	46°57'N	7°26'E	Interlaken	46°41'N	7°51'E	Pennine Alps	46°05'N	7°50'E	Thuner Lake	46°40'N	7°45'E
Berner Alps	46°30'N	7°30'E	Jungfrau	46°32'N	7°58'E	Rhaetian Alps	46°30'N	10°00'E	Uster	47°21'N	8°43'E
Bernina Peak	46°21'N	9°51'E	Jura	46°45'N	6°30'E	Rhine	47°35'N	7°35'E	Vevey	46°28'N	6°51'E
Biel	47°10'N	7°12'E	La-Chaux-de-			Rhône	46°08'N	5°57'E	Walen Lake	47°07'N	9°12'E
Burgdorf	47°04'N	7°37'E	Fonds	47°06'N	6°50'E	Rigi	47°05'N	8°30'E	Winterthur	47°30'N	8°43'E
Chur	46°51'N	9°32'E	Langenthal	47°13'N	7°47'E	Rorschach	47°29'N	9°30'E	Yverdon	46°47'N	6°39'E
Constance			Lausanne	46°31'N	6°38'E	Rosa, Monte	45°55'N	7°52'E	Zug	47°10'N	8°31'E
(Bodensee),			Liestal	47°29'N	7°44'E	Saint Bernardino			Zurich	47°23'N	8°32'E
Lake	47°35'N	9°25'E	Locarno	46°10'N	8°48'E	Pass	46°20'N	9°00'E	Zurich, Lake	47°13'N	8°45'E
Davos	46°48'N	9°50'E	Lower Rhine	46°49'N	9°25'E	Saint Bernard					
Delémont	47°22'N	7°21'E	Lucerne	47°03'N	8°18'E	Pass	45°50'N	7°10'E			
Einsiedeln	47°08'N	8°45'E	Lucerne, Lake	47°00'N	8°28'E	Saint Gotthard					
Frauenfeld	47°34'N	8°54'E	Lugano	46°01'N	8°58'E	Pass	46°33'N	8°34'E			

PEOPLE. About seven hundred years ago, the
inhabitants of the area of present-day Switzerland began joining together for mutual defense
against invading peoples. Despite this union,
and partly because of the isolation imposed by a
mountainous terrain, the Swiss were able to preserve their regional languages and customs.
German, French, and Italian are all official languages, and Romansch, which is based on Latin,
is spoken by inhabitants of the canton, or state,
of Graubunden. Dialects often differ from community to community, and Swiss German differs
markedly from standard spoken German. Because of the nation's multicultural, multilingual
nature, most of the people of Switzerland are
fluent in two or more languages. The population
is concentrated on a central plain located between mountain ranges.

ECONOMY AND THE LAND. The Alps and Jura
Mountains cover nearly 70 percent of Switzerland, making much of the land unsuited for agriculture but providing the basis for a thriving
tourist industry. The central plain contains rich
cropland and holds Switzerland's major cities
and manufacturing facilities, many specializing in

high-quality, precision products. Switzerland is
also an international banking and finance center.
Straddling the ranges of the central Alps, Switzerland has a terrain of mountains, hills, and plateaus. The climate is temperate but varies with
altitude.

HISTORY AND POLITICS. Helvetic Celts inhabited the area of present-day Switzerland when
Julius Caesar conquered the region, annexing it
to the Roman Empire. As the Roman Empire
declined, northern and western Germanic tribes
began a series of invasions, and in the 800s the
region became part of the empire of the Frankish
king Charlemagne. In 1291 leaders of the three
Swiss cantons signed an agreement declaring
their freedom and promising mutual aid against
any foreign ruler. The confederation was the beginning of modern Switzerland. Over the next
few centuries Switzerland became a military
power, expanding its territories until 1515, when
it was defeated by France. Soon after, Switzerland adopted a policy of permanent neutrality.
The country was again conquered by France during the French Revolution; however, after Napoleon's final defeat in 1815, the Congress of Vienna guaranteed Switzerland's neutrality, a
guarantee that has never been broken. ■

**Matterhorn is known internationally as one of the
earth's most magnificent mountain peaks. Situated just
southwest of the Swiss town of Zermatt, near the Swiss-
Italian border in the Pennine Alps, the peak was first
scaled in 1865 by the British climber Edward Whymper.
The mountain's pyramid shape, with its sheer sides, was
formed by ice and enlarging cirques.**

SYRIA

OFFICIAL NAME Syrian Arab Republic

PEOPLE
Population 10,485,000.
Density 147/mi² (57/km²).
Urban 48%.
Capital Damascus, 1,201,000.
Ethnic groups Arab 90%, Kurdish, Armenian, Circassian, Turkish.
Languages Arabic.
Religions Sunni Muslim 74%, other Muslim 16%, Christian 10%.
Life expectancy 67 female, 64 male.
Literacy 50%.

POLITICS
Government Socialist republic.
Parties Arab Socialist, Arab Socialist Resurrectionist, Arab Socialist Union, Communist, Socialist Unionist Movement.
Suffrage Universal, over 18.
Memberships AL, UN.
Subdivisions 13 provinces, 1 capital district.

ECONOMY
GDP $18,400,000,000.
Per capita $1,957.
Monetary unit Pound.
Trade partners Italy, France, Iraq, Saudi Arabia, Romania, West Germany.
Exports Petroleum, textiles, cotton, fruits, vegetables.
Imports Machinery, fuels, metal products, textiles, food.

LAND
Description Southwestern Asia.
Area 71,498 mi² (185,180 km²).
Highest point Mt. Hermon, 9,232 ft (2,814 m).
Lowest point 655 ft (200 m) below sea level.

PEOPLE. Most Syrians are Arabic-speaking descendants of Semites, a people who settled the region in ancient times. The majority is Sunni Muslim, and Islam is a powerful cultural force. Only a small percentage is Christian. Non-Arab Syrians include Kurds and Armenians, who speak their own languages and maintain their own customs. French is widely understood, and English is spoken in larger cities. The population is evenly divided between urban and rural settlements.

ECONOMY AND THE LAND. Syria is a developing country with great potential for economic growth. Textile manufacturing is a major industry, and oil, the main natural resource, provides for expanding activity in oil refining. The plains and river valleys are fertile, but rainfall is irregular and irrigation is necessary to sustain agriculture. Most farms are small, with cotton and wheat the major products. The terrain is marked by mountains, the Euphrates River valley, and a semiarid plateau. The climate is hot and dry, with relatively cold winters.

HISTORY AND POLITICS. Syria was the site of

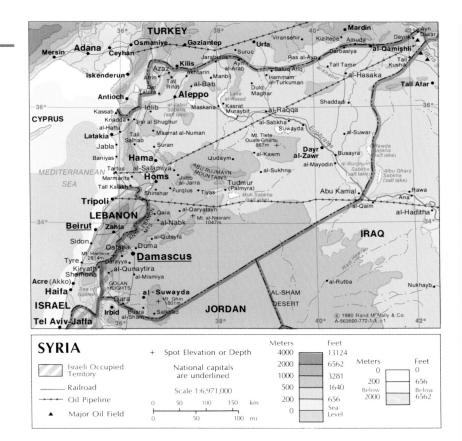

SYRIA

	+ Spot Elevation or Depth
Israeli Occupied Territory	National capitals are underlined
Railroad	
Oil Pipeline	Scale 1:6,971,000
▲ Major Oil Field	

Meters / Feet
4000 / 13124
2000 / 6562
1000 / 3281
500 / 1640
200 / 656
0 / Sea Level

Meters / Feet
0 / 0
200 / 656
Below 2000 / Below 6562

© 1980 Rand McNally & Co.
A-563600-772-1-3-1-1

Syria Map Index

	Lat.	Long.
Abu Kamal	34°27′N	40°55′E
al-Assad, Lake	36°05′N	38°10′E
al-Bab	36°22′N	37°31′E
Aleppo	36°12′N	37°10′E
al-Hasaka	36°29′N	40°45′E
al-Jabul Sabkha	36°03′N	37°39′E
al-Khabur	35°08′N	40°26′E
al-Nabk	34°01′N	36°44′E
al-Qamishli	37°02′N	41°14′E
al-Qunaytira	33°07′N	35°49′E
al-Raqqa	35°56′N	39°01′E
al-Salamiya	35°01′N	37°03′E
al-Suwayda	32°42′N	36°34′E
Anti-Lebanon Mountains	33°35′N	36°00′E
Azaz	36°35′N	37°03′E
Damascus	33°30′N	36°18′E
Dara	32°37′N	36°06′E
Dayr al-Zawr	35°20′N	40°09′E
Duma	33°35′N	36°24′E
Euphrates	34°30′N	41°00′E
Galilee, Sea of	32°48′N	35°35′E
Ghin, Mount	32°39′N	36°43′E
Golan Heights	32°55′N	35°42′E
Hama	35°08′N	36°45′E
Hermon, Mount	33°26′N	35°51′E
Homs	34°44′N	36°43′E
Idlib	35°55′N	36°38′E
Jabla	35°21′N	35°55′E
Latakia	35°31′N	35°47′E
Muh Sabkha	34°30′N	38°20′E
Orontes	36°02′N	35°58′E
Palmyra → Tudmur	34°33′N	38°17′E
Qatana	33°26′N	36°05′E
Tigris	37°05′N	42°20′E
Tudmur (Palmyra)	34°33′N	38°17′E

one of the world's most ancient civilizations, and Damascus and other Syrian cities were centers of world trade as early as 2500 B.C. Greater Syria, as the area was called until the end of World War I, originally included much of modern Israel, Jordan, Lebanon, and parts of Turkey. The region was occupied and ruled by several empires, including the Phoenician, Assyrian, Babylonian, Persian, and Greek, before coming under Roman rule in 64 B.C. During subsequent years Christianity arose in the part of Greater Syria called Palestine. In 636 the region fell to Arab Muslims, who governed until 1260, when Egypt gained control. In 1516 Syria became part of the Turkish Ottoman Empire, and during World War I Syria

aided Britain in defeating the Turks and Germans in return for independence. After the war Greater Syria was divided into the League of Nations mandates of Syria, Lebanon, and Palestine, which in 1922 was further divided into Transjordan and Palestine. The mandate of Syria was placed under French administration. When Syria gained independence in 1946, many nationals wanted to reunite Greater Syria, But Lebanon and Transjordan had also become independent nations, and in 1948 Israel was created from the remaining Palestine mandate. Syria joined with its Arab allies in opposing the state of Israel, participating in the 1967 and 1973 Arab-Israeli wars. ■

About half of Syria's population lives in rural areas, and livestock raising on the subsistence level remains a major activity for many inhabitants of the countryside and small villages.

TAIWAN

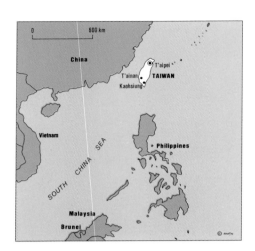

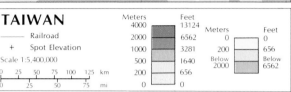

TAIWAN
- ──── Railroad
- ＋ Spot Elevation
- Scale 1:5,400,000

Taiwan Map Index

	Lat.	Long.		Lat.	Long.
Chia-i	23°29'N	120°27'E	Ma-tsu Island	26°09'N	119°56'E
Chi-lung	25°08'N	121°44'E	Pan-ch'iao	25°02'N	121°26'E
Chung-hua	24°03'N	120°33'E	Pei-kang	23°35'N	120°19'E
Chungyang			Pescadores	23°30'N	119°30'E
Range	23°30'N	121°00'E	P'ing-tung	22°40'N	120°29'E
Hsin-chu	24°48'N	120°58'E	Quemoy	24°27'N	118°23'E
Hsüeh Peak	24°24'N	121°12'E	T'ai-nan	23°00'N	120°11'E
Hua-lien	23°58'N	121°36'E	Taipei	25°03'N	121°30'E
I-lan	24°45'N	121°44'E	Taiwan Strait	24°00'N	19°00'E
Kaohsiung	22°38'N	120°17'E	Yu Mountain	23°28'N	120°57'E

OFFICIAL NAME Taiwan

PEOPLE
Population 19,090,000.
Density 1,373/mi² (530/km²).
Urban 66%.
Capital Taipei, 2,270,983.
Ethnic groups Taiwanese 84%, Chinese 14%, aborigine 2%.
Languages Chinese dialects.
Religions Buddhist, Confucian, and Taoist 93%; Christian 5%.
Life expectancy 75 female, 70 male.
Literacy 90%.

POLITICS
Government Republic.
Parties Kuomintang.
Suffrage Universal, over 20.
Memberships None.
Subdivisions 16 counties, 5 cities, 2 special municipalities.

ECONOMY
GNP $49,800,000,000.
Per capita $2,673.
Monetary unit New Taiwan dollar.
Trade partners U.S., Japan, Hong Kong.
Exports Textiles, electrical machinery, plastics, metal products, plywood, canned food.
Imports Petroleum, machinery, chemicals, food, base metals.

LAND
Description Eastern Asian island.
Area 13,900 mi² (36,002 km²).
Highest point Yu Mtn. 13,114 ft (3,997 m).
Lowest point Sea level.

PEOPLE. The majority of Taiwan's inhabitants are descendants of Chinese who migrated from the coast of China in the eighteenth and nineteenth centuries. In 1949, when the Communists came to power on the mainland following a civil war, many business, bureaucratic, and military people arrived on Taiwan, coming from all parts of the mainland. A small group of aborigines lives in the mountains in central Taiwan and are most likely of Malay-Polynesian origin. Taiwan's languages are mainly various dialects of Chinese. Mandarin, the official Chinese dialect, is spoken almost universally and is the language used in Taiwan's classrooms. The native Taiwanese population generally speak a variant of the southern Fujian dialect, and a dialect known as "Hakka" is spoken in certain areas of the northwest, south, and east. A period of Japanese rule from the late 1800s to the 1940s has resulted in fluency in Japanese among the older population. Most religious practices combine Buddhist and Taoist beliefs with the Confucian ethical code.

ECONOMY AND THE LAND. Since World War II, Taiwan's economy has shifted its emphasis from agriculture to industry. During the 1960s the industrial sector implemented labor-intensive methods to create a successful light industry, aided by foreign investment from the United

States, Japan, and Western Europe as well as Chinese emigrants living overseas. To keep pace with current world trends, Taiwan is now turning to modern technology and expanding economic activity to include heavy industry. Although only one-quarter of the island is arable, farmland is intensely cultivated, with some areas producing two and three crops a year. Fishing is also important; however, much food must be imported. The island's terrain is marked by steep eastern mountains sloping to a fertile western region. The capital of Taipei administers the Penghu Islands and about twenty offshore islands as well as the island of Taiwan. The climate is maritime subtropical.

HISTORY AND POLITICS. Chinese migration to Taiwan began as early as A.D. 500. Dutch traders claimed the island in 1624 and used it as a base for trade with China and Japan. It was ruled by China's Manchu dynasty from 1683 until 1895, when China ceded Taiwan to Japan after the first Sino-Japanese war. Following fifty years of Japanese rule, China regained possession of Taiwan after World War II. A civil war in mainland China between Nationalist and Communist forces ended with the victory of the Communists in 1949, and Nationalist leader Chiang Kai-shek fled to Taiwan, proclaiming Taipei the provisional capital of Nationalist China. Although the Peo-

ple's Republic of China replaced Taiwan in the United Nations in 1971, the supporters of Nationalist China continue to claim they are the legitimate rulers of China and refuse to recognize the People's Republic. Since 1971 international recognition of Nationalist China has virtually ceased, and nearly all nations now view Taiwan as part of the People's Republic. Despite this, Taiwan retains informal relations with many countries. ∎

Forest-covered mountains, rushing streams, and serene lakes, such as Sun Moon Lake, shown here, make Taiwan an island of scenic beauty.

TANZANIA

OFFICIAL NAME United
Republic of Tanzania

PEOPLE
Population 21,525,000.
Density 59/mi² (23/km²).
Urban 13%.
Capital DaresSalaam, 757,346.
Ethnic groups African 99%.
Languages Swahili, English, indigenous.
Religions Christian 35%, Muslim 35%, indigenous 30%.
Life expectancy 53 female, 50 male.
Literacy 66%.

POLITICS
Government Republic.
Parties Chama Cha Mapinduzi.
Suffrage Universal, over 18.
Memberships CW, OAU, UN.
Subdivisions 25 regions.

ECONOMY
GDP $5,200,000,000.
Per capita $281.
Monetary unit Shilling.
Trade partners West Germany, U.K., U.S., other Western European countries.
Exports Coffee, cotton, sisal, cashews, diamonds, cloves.
Imports Manufactured goods, machinery, transportation equipment, textiles, petroleum.

LAND
Description Eastern Africa.
Area 364,900 mi² (945,087 km²).
Highest point Kilimanjaro, 19,340 ft (5,895 m).
Lowest point Sea level.

PEOPLE. The largely rural African population of Tanzania consists of more than 130 ethnic groups, most speaking a distinct language. Religious beliefs are nearly evenly divided among Christian, Muslim, and traditional religions.

ECONOMY AND THE LAND. Agriculture accounts for the greatest portion of export earnings and employs 80 percent of the work force. Two-thirds of the land cannot be cultivated, however, because of lack of water and tsetse fly infestation. The mainland farmers grow cassava, corn, and beans, and Zanzibar and Pemba islands are well known sources of cloves. Mainland Tanzania, or Tanganyika, is characterized by hot and humid coastal plains, an arid central plateau, and temperate lake and highland areas. The climate is equatorial and characterized by monsoons.

HISTORY AND POLITICS. The northern mainland has fossil remains of some of humanity's earliest ancestors. Subsequent early inhabitants were gradually displaced by Bantu farmers and Nilotes. Arabs were trading with coastal groups as early as the eighth century, and by the early 1500s the Portuguese had claimed the coastal region. They were displaced in the 1700s by Arabs, who subsequently established a lucrative slave trade. Germans began colonizing the coast in 1884 and six years later signed an agreement

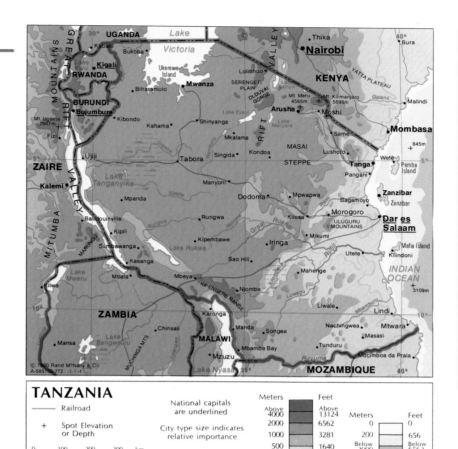

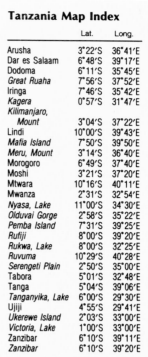

TANZANIA

— Railroad

+ Spot Elevation or Depth

National capitals are underlined

City type size indicates relative importance

Scale 1:13,116,000

Meters	Feet
Above 4000	Above 13124
2000	6562
1000	3281
500	1640
200	656
0	0

Meters	Feet
0	0
200	656
Below 2000	Below 6562

Tanzania Map Index

	Lat.	Long.
Arusha	3°22'S	36°41'E
Dar es Salaam	6°48'S	39°17'E
Dodoma	6°11'S	35°45'E
Great Ruaha	7°56'S	37°52'E
Iringa	7°46'S	35°42'E
Kagera	0°57'S	31°47'E
Kilimanjaro, Mount	3°04'S	37°22'E
Lindi	10°00'S	39°43'E
Mafia Island	7°50'S	39°50'E
Meru, Mount	3°14'S	36°40'E
Morogoro	6°49'S	37°40'E
Moshi	3°21'S	37°20'E
Mtwara	10°16'S	40°11'E
Mwanza	2°31'S	32°54'E
Nyasa, Lake	11°00'S	34°30'E
Olduvai Gorge	2°58'S	35°22'E
Pemba Island	7°31'S	39°25'E
Rufiji	8°00'S	39°20'E
Rukwa, Lake	8°00'S	32°25'E
Ruvuma	10°29'S	40°28'E
Serengeti Plain	2°50'S	35°00'E
Tabora	5°01'S	32°48'E
Tanga	5°04'S	39°06'E
Tanganyika, Lake	6°00'S	29°30'E
Ujiji	4°55'S	29°41'E
Ukerewe Island	2°03'S	33°00'E
Victoria, Lake	1°00'S	33°00'E
Zanzibar	6°10'S	39°11'E
Zanzibar	6°10'S	39°20'E

with Great Britain that secured German dominance along the coast and made Zanzibar a British protectorate. After World War I Britain received part of German East Africa from the League of Nations as a mandate and renamed it Tanganyika. The area became a trust territory under the United Nations following World War II. Nationalist movements soon emerged throughout East Africa, and the first Tanganyikan political party was organized in 1954. The country achieved independence in 1961, and two years later Zanzibar received its independence as a constitutional monarchy under the sultan. A 1964 revolt by the African majority overthrew the sultan, and Zanzibar and Tanganyika subsequently united as Tanzania. ∎

One of Africa's most memorable landscapes is the Ngorongoro Crater in Tanzania. The crater is situated within the Ngorongoro Conservation Area.

THAILAND

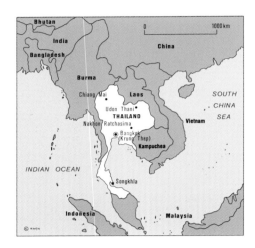

OFFICIAL NAME Kingdom of Thailand

PEOPLE
Population 52,220,000.
Density 264/mi² (102/km²).
Urban 17%.
Capital Bangkok, 5,153,902.
Ethnic groups Thai 75%, Chinese 14%.
Languages Thai.
Religions Buddhist 95%, Muslim 4%.
Life expectancy 65 female, 61 male.
Literacy 84%.

POLITICS
Government Constitutional monarchy.
Suffrage Universal, over 20.
Memberships ASEAN, UN.
Subdivisions 73 provinces.

ECONOMY
GNP $38,400,000,000.
Per capita $800.
Monetary unit Baht.
Trade partners Japan, Western European countries, U.S.
Exports Rice, natural rubber, sugar, tapioca, corn, tin.
Imports Machinery, transportation equipment, petroleum, chemicals, base metals.

LAND
Description Southeastern Asia.
Area 198,115 mi² (513,115 km²).
Highest point Inthanon, 8,530 ft (2,600 m).
Lowest point Sea level.

PEOPLE. Thailand's society is relatively homogeneous. More than 85 percent of its people speak varying dialects of Thai and share a common culture and common religion, Buddhism. Malay-speaking Muslims and Chinese immigrants compose small minorities. Thai society is rural, with most people living in the rice-growing regions. The government has sponsored a successful family-planning program, which has greatly reduced the annual population growth rate.

ECONOMY AND THE LAND. Thailand's economy is based on agriculture, and it is the only developing country able to export large quantities of rice its main food crop, each year. The nation's famed temples and other architectural structures make tourism the largest source of foreign income. Forests produce teak and rattan, and tin is another valuable natural resource. Future industrialization may hinge on deposits of coal and natural gas. The cost of feeding, clothing, and sheltering hundreds of thousands of refugees from Vietnam, Laos, and Kampuchea has been a major drain on the Thai economy. A mountainous and heavily forested nation, Thailand has a tropical climate, dominated by monsoons, high temperatures, and humidity.

HISTORY AND POLITICS. Thai communities were established as early as 4000 B.C., although a Thai kingdom founded in the thirteenth century

A.D. began the history of modern Thailand. In the late 1700s Burmese armies overwhelmed the kingdom. Rama I, founder of the present dynasty, helped to drive the invaders from the country in 1782. He subsequently renamed the nation Siam and established a capital at Bangkok. Siam allowed Europeans to live within its borders during the period of colonial expansion, but the nation never succumbed to foreign rule. As a result, Siam was the only South and Southeast Asian country never colonized by a European power. In 1932 a revolt changed the government from an absolute monarchy to a constitutional monarchy. Military officers assumed control in 1938, and the nation reverted to its former name, Thailand, in 1939. The country was invaded by Japan in World War II. Since the war, Thailand has experienced military coups, martial law, and other problems that arise from political instability. The king remains the formal head of state, but the prime minister wields the nation's political power. ■

Thailand Map Index

	Lat.	Long.		Lat.	Long.
Bangkok	13°45′N	100°31′E	Nan	15°42′N	100°09′E
Bilauktaung			Nong Khai	17°52′N	102°44′E
Range	13°00′N	99°00′E	Pa Sak	14°21′N	100°35′E
Chao Phraya	13°32′N	100°36′E	Phetchabun		
Chi	15°11′N	104°43′E	Range	16°20′N	100°55′E
Chiang Mai	18°47′N	98°59′E	Phitsanulok	16°50′N	100°15′E
Chon Buri	13°22′N	100°59′E	Phra Nakhon Si		
Dangraek			Ayutthaya	14°21′N	100°33′E
Mountains	14°25′N	103°30′E	Phuket	7°53′N	98°24′E
Hat Yai	7°01′N	100°28′E	Phuket Island	8°00′N	98°22′E
Inthanon			Ping	15°42′N	100°09′E
Mountain	18°35′N	98°29′E	Ranong	9°58′N	98°38′E
Khon Kaen	16°26′N	102°50′E	Salween	17°50′N	97°45′E
Kra, Isthmus of	10°20′N	99°00′E	Songkhla	7°12′N	100°36′E
Malay Peninsula	6°00′N	101°00′E	Surat Thani	9°08′N	99°19′E
Mekong	15°20′N	105°34′E	Thailand, Gulf of	10°00′N	101°00′E
Mun	15°19′N	105°30′E	Trang	7°33′N	99°36′E
Nakhon Pathom	13°49′N	100°03′E	Ubon		
Nakhon			Ratchathani	15°14′N	104°54′E
Ratchasima	14°58′N	102°07′E	Udon Thani	17°26′N	102°46′E
Nakhon Sawan	15°41′N	100°07′E	Yom	15°52′N	100°16′E
Nakhon Si					
Thammarat	8°26′N	99°58′E			

THAILAND

Railroad

+ Spot Elevation or Depth

National capitals are underlined

City type size indicates relative importance

Meters	Feet
4000	13124
2000	6562
1000	3281
500	1640
200	656
0	0
200	656
2000	6562

Scale 1:11,280,000

© 1980 Rand McNally & Co.
A-563800-772 -1-1-1

Asia is the home of the world's great religions, and the influence of Buddhism and other faiths can be seen throughout the countries of Southeast Asia. In Thailand about 95 percent of the people are Buddhist, and the culture and life-style reflect this majority belief. Most men serve as monks at some point in their lives, and in the villages the monks also act as schoolteachers.

Well known for the beauty of its temples, or *wats*, Thailand claims to be the site of more than 25,000 of these structures. Because Buddhist practices here are sometimes influenced by other Eastern faiths, temple decorations may incorporate symbols from Hinduism or Islam. The Marble Temple, shown here, is in Bangkok, Thailand.

TOGO

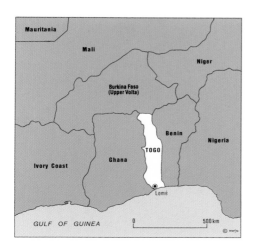

OFFICIAL NAME Republic of Togo

PEOPLE
Population 2,965,000.
Density 135/mi² (52/km²).
Urban 17%.
Capital Lomé, 235,000.
Ethnic groups Ewe, Mina, Kabyè, others.
Languages French, indigenous.
Religions Indigenous 70%, Christian 20%, Muslim 10%.
Life expectancy 50 female, 46 male.
Literacy 18%.

POLITICS
Government Republic.
Parties Rally of the People.
Suffrage Universal adult.
Memberships OAU, UN.
Subdivisions 21 circumscriptions.

ECONOMY
GNP $950,000,000.
Per capita $340.
Monetary unit CFA franc.
Trade partners France, other Western European countries.
Exports Phosphates, cocoa, coffee, palm kernels.

Imports Consumer goods, fuels, machinery, food.
LAND
Description Western Africa.
Area 21,925 mi² (56,785 km²).
Highest point Baumann Pk., 3,235 ft (986 m).
Lowest point Sea level.

PEOPLE. Almost all the people of Togo are black Africans, coming primarily from the Ewe, Mina, and Kabyè ethnic groups. Most of the population lives in the south and practices traditional religions. There are, however, significant Christian and Muslim minorities.

ECONOMY AND THE LAND. Togo is an agricultural country, although productive land is scarce. Fishing is a major industry in the coastal areas. Togo has one of the world's largest phosphate reserves. Much of Togo is mountainous, with a sandy coastal plain. The climate is hot and humid.

HISTORY AND POLITICS. Togo's original inhabitants were probably the ancestors of the present-day central mountain people. Ewes entered the south in the 1300s, and refugees from war-torn northern countries settled in the north between the 1500s and 1800s. For two hundred years European ships raided the coastal region in search of slaves. In 1884 Germany claimed the territory. After World War I Togoland became a League of Nations mandate administered by Britain and France. The mandate was made a United Nations trust territory following World War II and remained under British and French auspices. British Togoland voted to join the Gold Coast and nearby British-administered territories in 1957 and became the independent nation of Ghana. French Togoland voted to become a republic in 1956 with internal self-government within the French Union, although the United Nations did not accept this method of ending the trusteeship. Togo peacefully severed its ties with France in 1960 and became independent the same year. Internal political strife and military dominance of the government have characterized Togo's years of independence. ■

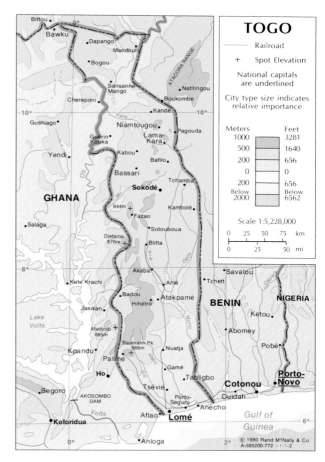

Togo Map Index

	Lat.	Long.		Lat.	Long.
Anécho	6°14′N	1°36′E	Niamtougou	9°46′N	1°06′E
Atakpamé	7°32′N	1°08′E	*Oti*	9°30′N	0°15′E
Bassari	9°15′N	0°47′E	Palimé	6°54′N	0°38′E
Baumann Peak	6°52′N	0°46′E	Sokodé	8°59′N	1°08′E
Lama-Kara	9°33′N	1°12′E	Tabligbo	6°35′N	1°30′E
Lomé	6°08′N	1°13′E	Tsévié	6°25′N	1°13′E
Mono	6°17′N	1°51′E			

TOKELAU

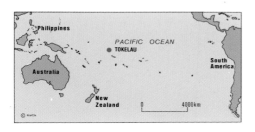

OFFICIAL NAME Tokelau

PEOPLE
Population 1,500.
Density 326/mi² (125/km²).
Ethnic groups Polynesian.
Languages English, Tokelauan.
Religions Congregational 70%, Roman Catholic 30%.

POLITICS
Government Island territory (New Zealand).
Suffrage Universal adult.

ECONOMY
GDP $1,000,000.
Per capita $670.
Monetary unit New Zealand dollar.
Trade partners New Zealand.
Exports Postage stamps, handicrafts.
Imports Foodstuffs, machinery, fuels.

LAND
Description South Pacific islands.
Area 4.6 mi² (12 km²).
Lowest point Sea level.

PEOPLE. Most of Tokelau's people are Polynesian, but widespread intermarriage in the nineteenth-century between Polynesians and beachcombers of American, Portuguese, Scottish, French, and German stock gave many a mixed ancestry. Tokelauan, a language with similarities to Samoan and Tuvaluan, is spoken throughout the islands. The Tokelauans share some cultural characteristics with Samoans, but the life-style of the atolls is more closely related to that of Tuvalu. All Tokelauans are Christian, either Congregational or Roman Catholic. A resettlement program beginning in the 1960s and lasting until the mid-1970s resulted in the emigration of many Tokelauans to New Zealand.

ECONOMY AND THE LAND. Tokelau has few natural resources, and many inhabitants are dependent upon money sent from relatives who have emigrated to New Zealand. Agriculture provides for the production of copra, but all other farming is done at the subsistence level. Coconuts, breadfruit, papaw, and other fruits are grown for food. In an attempt to diversify crop production, the government has tested various types of seeds, but poor-quality soil continues to limit the potential of agriculture. Fish and shellfish are found throughout the waters around the islands, and the islanders hope to improve the size of the catch through the use of various mechanical aids. Industrial activities include the production of copra, woodwork, and woven craft items, such as mats and bags. Tokelau consists of three coral atolls: Atafu, Nukunonu, and Fakaofo. The climate is tropical.

HISTORY AND POLITICS. According to tradition, the ancestors of today's population came from Samoa, Rarotonga, and Nanumanga. In 1765 a British commodore sighted the uninhabited island of Atafu, and another Briton came upon Atafu and Nukunonu in 1791. The Europeans did not know of the island of Fakaofo until 1835, when an American whaling ship sailed past. Following nearly twenty years under unofficial British administration, the islands of Tokelau formally became a British protectorate in 1889. Britain placed the islands with Western Samoa, then Tonga, and then Gilbert and Ellice Islands Colony. Administrative problems arose, however, because of distance, and New Zealand began administering the islands from Western Samoa in 1925. In 1948 the Tokelau Islands Act placed the islands within the international boundaries of New Zealand. The islands continue as a territory of New Zealand. ■

TONGA

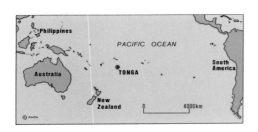

OFFICIAL NAME Kingdom of Tonga

PEOPLE
Population 107,000.
Density 396/mi² (153/km²).
Urban 28%.
Capital Nukualofa, Tongatapu I., 18,312.
Ethnic groups Tongan 98%.
Languages Tongan, English.
Religions Christian.
Life expectancy 58 female, 58 male.
Literacy 93%.

POLITICS
Government Constitutional monarchy.
Parties None.
Suffrage Literate adults, over 21 (males must be taxpayers).
Memberships CW.

ECONOMY
GNP $50,000,000.
Per capita $520.
Monetary unit Pa'anga.
Trade partners Australia, New Zealand, U.S.
Exports Copra, bananas, coconut products.
Imports Food, machinery, petroleum.

LAND
Description South Pacific islands.
Area 270 mi² (699 km²).
Highest point 3,432 ft (1,046 m).
Lowest point Sea level.

PEOPLE. Almost all Tongans are Polynesian and follow the Wesleyan Methodist religion. About two-thirds of the population lives on the main island of Tongatapu.

ECONOMY AND THE LAND. Tonga's economy is dominated by both subsistence and plantation agriculture. Manufacturing is almost nonexistent. Most of the islands are coral reefs; many have fertile soil. The climate is subtropical.

HISTORY AND POLITICS. Tonga has been settled since at least 500 B.C. In the late 1700s a civil war broke out among three lines of kings who sought to establish rulership. In 1822 Wesleyan Methodist missionaries converted one of the warring kings to Christianity. His faction prevailed, and he ruled as George Tupou I, founder of the present dynasty. Tonga came under British protection in 1900 but retained its autonomy in internal matters. The nation became fully independent in 1970 and maintains close relations with Great Britain as well as its Pacific neighbors. ■

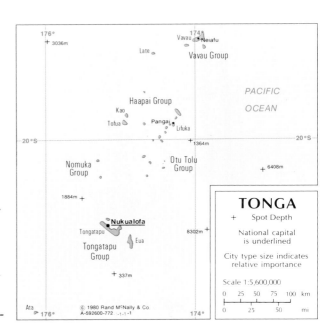

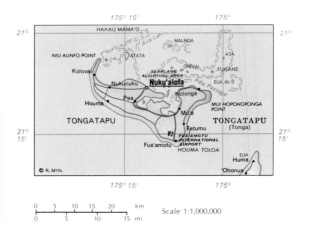

Tonga Map Index

	Lat.	Long.		Lat.	Long.
Eua	21°22'S	174°56'W	Nukualofa	21°08'S	175°12'W
Haapai Group	19°42'S	174°29'W	Pangai	19°48'S	174°21'W
Late	18°48'S	174°39'W	Tofua	19°45'S	175°04'W
Lifuka	19°48'S	174°21'W	Tongatapu	21°10'S	175°10'W
Neiafu	18°39'S	173°59'W	Tongatapu Group	21°10'S	175°10'W
Nomuka Group	20°13'S	174°42'W	Vavau Group	18°40'S	174°00'W

TRINIDAD AND TOBAGO

OFFICIAL NAME Republic of Trinidad and Tobago

PEOPLE
Population 1,240,000.
Density 626/mi² (242/km²).
Urban 49%.
Capital Port of Spain, Trinidad I., 65,906.
Ethnic groups Black 43%, East Indian 40%, mixed 14%, white 1%, Chinese 1%.
Languages English.
Religions Roman Catholic 36%, Hindu 23%, Protestant 13%, Muslim 6%.
Life expectancy 74 female, 70 male.
Literacy 89%.

POLITICS
Government Republic.
Parties Democratic Action Congress, People's National Movement, United Labor Front.
Suffrage Universal, over 18.
Memberships CW, OAS, UN.
Subdivisions 9 counties.

ECONOMY
GNP $7,316,000,000.
Per capita $6,651.
Monetary unit Dollar.
Trade partners U.S., Saudi Arabia, U.K., Indonesia.
Exports Petroleum, petroleum products, amonia, fertilizer, food.
Imports Petroleum, machinery, transportation equipment, food, manufactured goods.

LAND
Description Caribbean islands.
Area 1,980 mi² (5,128 km²).
Highest point El Cerro Del Aripo, Trinidad I., 3,085 ft (940 m).
Lowest point Sea level.

PEOPLE. The two islands of Trinidad and Tobago form a single country, but Trinidad has nearly all the total land mass and population. About a third of all Trinidadians are black African, a third are East Indian, and a third are European, Chinese, and of mixed descent. Most Tobagonians are black African.

ECONOMY AND THE LAND. Agriculture and tourism are important, but the economy is based on oil, which accounts for about 80 percent of the nation's exports. Trinidad is also one of the world's chief sources of natural asphalt and possesses supplies of natural gas. The islands are characterized by tropical rain forests, scenic beaches, and fertile farmland.

HISTORY AND POLITICS. Trinidad was occupied by Arawak Indians when Christopher Columbus arrived and claimed the island for Spain in 1498. The island remained under Spanish rule until 1797, when the British captured it and ruled for more than 150 years. Tobago changed hands among the Dutch, French, and British until 1814, when Britain took control. In 1888 Trinidad and Tobago became a single British colony, and they achieved independence in 1962. A separatist movement on Tobago has caused the government to give that island more control over its internal affairs. ■

Trinidad and Tobago Map Index

	Lat.	Long.		Lat.	Long.
Arenal Point	10°03'N	61°56'W	Pierreville	10°18'N	61°01'W
Arima	10°38'N	61°17'W	Point Fortin	10°11'N	61°41'W
Aripo, El Cerro del	10°43'N	61°15'W	Port of Spain	10°39'N	61°31'W
Basse Terre	10°08'N	61°18'W	Princes Town	10°16'N	61°23'W
Blanchisseuse	10°47'N	61°18'W	Rio Claro	10°18'N	61°11'W
Bonasse	10°05'N	61°52'W	Roxborough	11°15'N	60°35'W
Chaguanas	10°31'N	61°25'W	San Fernando	10°17'N	61°28'W
Débé	10°12'N	61°27'W	Sangre Grande	10°35'N	61°07'W
Dragons Mouth	10°45'N	61°46'W	Scarborough	11°11'N	60°44'W
Galera Point	10°49'N	60°55'W	Serpents Mouth	10°00'N	62°00'W
Guayaguayare	10°08'N	61°02'W	Siparia	10°08'N	61°30'W
La Brea	10°15'N	61°37'W	Tobago	11°15'N	60°40'W
Moriah	11°15'N	60°43'W	Toco	10°50'N	60°57'W
Paria, Gulf of	10°30'N	61°50'W	Trinidad	10°30'N	61°15'W
			Tunapuna	10°38'N	61°23'W

TUNISIA

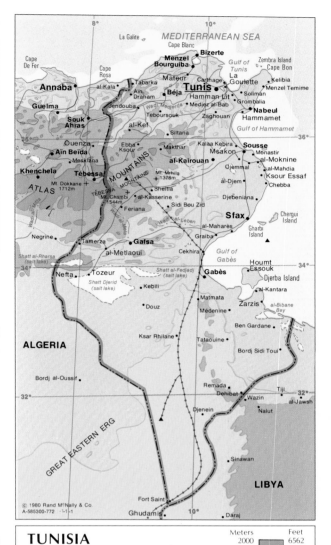

OFFICIAL NAME Republic of
Tunisia

PEOPLE
Population 7,295,000.
Density 115/mi² (45/km²).
Urban 52%.
Capital Tunis, 550,404.
Ethnic groups Arab 98%, European 1%.
Languages Arabic, French.
Religions Muslim 98%, Christian 1%.
Life expectancy 63 female, 59 male.
Literacy 62%.

POLITICS
Government Republic.
Parties Communist, Destourian Socialist, Movement
of Popular Unity, Social Democrats.
Suffrage Universal, over 21.
Memberships AL, OAU, UN.
Subdivisions 23 governorates.

ECONOMY
GNP $8,700,000,000.
Per capita $1,183.
Monetary unit Dinar.
Trade partners France, Italy, West Germany, Greece,
U.S.
Exports Petroleum, textiles, phosphates, olive oil.
Imports Machinery, petroleum, transportation
equipment, food, consumer goods.

LAND
Description Northern Africa.
Area 63,170 mi² (163,610 km²).
Highest point Mt. Chambi, 5,066 ft (1,544 m).
Lowest point Chott el Gharsa, 56 ft (17 m) below sea
level.

PEOPLE. Tunisians are descended from indigenous African peoples and from Arab groups.
Nearly all Tunisians are Muslim. Arabic is the
official language, and French is widely spoken.
Tunisia is a leader in the Arab world in promoting rights for women, and its society is marked
by a large middle class and equitable land distribution.

ECONOMY AND THE LAND. Tunisia is an agricultural country; wheat, barley, citrus fruits, and
olives are important crops. Oil from deposits discovered in the 1960s supplies domestic needs
and serves as a major export, along with phosphates. Tourism is a growing industry, and despite an unemployment problem, Tunisia has a
more balanced economy than many of its neighbors. Tunisia's terrain ranges from a well-watered
and fertile northern area to more arid central and
southern regions.

HISTORY AND POLITICS. Phoenicians began
the Carthaginian Empire in Tunisia about 1100
B.C. In 146 B.C. Romans conquered Carthage and
ruled Tunisia for six hundred years. Arab Muslims from the Middle East gained control of most
of North Africa in the seventh century, influencing the religion and overall culture of the region.
Tunisia became part of the Turkish Ottoman Empire in the late 1500s, and in 1881 France succeeded in establishing a protectorate in the area.
Nationalistic calls for Tunisian independence
began before World War I and gained momentum
by the 1930s. When Tunisia gained independence
in 1956, more than half of the European population emigrated, severely damaging the economy.
A year later Tunisia abolished its monarchy and
became a republic. The nation maintains a nonaligned stance and has established friendly relations with East and West. ■

TUNISIA

Meters	Feet
2000	6562
1000	3281
500	1640
200	656
0	Sea Level
0	0
200	656
2000	6562

Railroad — National capitals are underlined
Oil Pipeline
▲ Major Oil Field — City type size indicates relative importance
+ Spot Elevation

Scale 1:6,000,000

**Tunisia's population is concentrated along the coast, but
village scenes such as this one are common in the nation's semiarid mountain and steppe regions. Most of
the inhabitants of these central and southern regions are
of Berber stock and live in houses made of stone or
mud. In some rural regions, however, people continue
to live in tents.**

TURKEY

OFFICIAL NAME Republic of
Turkey

PEOPLE
Population 50,730,000.
Density 169/mi² (65/km²).
Urban 45%.
Capital Ankara, 1,877,755.
Ethnic groups Turkish 85%, Kurdish 12%.
Languages Turkish, Kurdish.
Religions Muslim 98%.
Life expectancy 64 female, 60 male.
Literacy 70%.

POLITICS
Government Republic.
Parties Motherland, Nationalist Democracy, Populist.
Suffrage Universal, over 21.
Memberships NATO, OECD, UN.
Subdivisions 67 provinces.

ECONOMY
GNP $53,800,000,000.
Per capita $1,096.
Monetary unit Lira.
Trade partners Iraq, West Germany, U.S., Libya, other
Western European countries.
Exports Cotton, tobacco, fruits, nuts, food, textiles.
Imports Petroleum, machinery, transportation
equipment, metals, fertilizer.

LAND
Description Southeastern Europe and southwestern
Asia.
Area 300,948 mi² (779,452 km²).
Highest point Mt. Ararat, 16,804 ft (5,122 m).
Lowest point Sea level.

PEOPLE. Turkey's majority group is Turkish, descended from an Asian people who migrated from Russia and Mongolia around A.D. 900. About half the Turkish population lives in cities and half in rural areas. Kurds, the largest minority group, live in the country's mountainous regions. Arabs and whites compose smaller minorities. Nearly all the population is Sunni Muslim. The changing status of women and the extent of Islamic influence on daily life are key issues in Turkish society.

ECONOMY AND THE LAND. Post–World War II economic development in Turkey was rapid. Although industrialization has greatly increased since 1950, agriculture remains the major employer and an important contributor. The most productive lands lie along the mild coast, but wheat and barley are grown on an interior plateau. The climate is Mediterranean along the coast, while the inland plateau region has hot summers and cold, snowy winters.

HISTORY AND POLITICS. Hittites began migrating to the area from Europe or central Asia around 2000 B.C. Successive dominant groups included Phrygians, Greeks, Persians, and Romans. Muslims and Christians battled for control during the Crusades of the eleventh and twelfth centuries. In the 1300s Ottoman Turks began to build what would become a vast empire. The Republic of Turkey was founded by Mustafa Kemal in 1923, after the collapse of the six-hundred-year-old Ottoman Empire. In 1960 the Turkish government was overthrown by Turkish military forces, who subsequently set up a provisional government, adopted a new constitution, and held free elections. In the sixties and seventies disputes with Greece over Cyprus, populated by majority Greeks and minority Turks, flared into violence, and radical groups committed terrorist acts against the government, which changed hands several times. Turkey's generals assumed power in 1980 and restored order to the country. The government returned to civilian rule in 1983. ■

Turkey Map Index

	Lat.	Long.		Lat.	Long.		Lat.	Long.		Lat.	Long.
Adana	37°01'N	35°18'E	Corum	40°33'N	34°58'E	Kayseri	38°43'N	35°30'E	Samsun	41°17'N	36°20'E
Adapazari	40°46'N	30°24'E	*Dardanelles*	40°15'N	26°25'E	*Keban, Lake*	38°50'N	39°15'E	Sivas	39°45'N	37°02'E
Aegean Sea	39°00'N	25°00'E	Denizli	37°46'N	29°06'E	*Kelkit*	40°46'N	36°32'E	Soke	37°45'N	27°24'E
Afyon	38°45'N	30°33'E	Diyarbakir	37°55'N	40°14'E	Kirikkale	39°50'N	33°31'E	Tarsus	36°55'N	34°53'E
Aksaray	38°23'N	34°03'E	Edirne	41°40'N	26°34'E	Kirsehir	39°09'N	34°10'E	*Taurus*		
Aksehir	38°21'N	31°25'E	*Egridir, Lake*	38°02'N	30°53'E	*Kizil*	41°44'N	35°58'E	*Mountains*	37°00'N	33°00'E
Alexandretta, Gulf			Elazig	38°41'N	39°14'E	Konya	37°52'N	32°31'E	*Tigris*	37°20'N	42°12'E
of	36°30'N	35°40'E	Eregli	37°31'N	34°04'E	Kozan	37°27'N	35°49'E	Tokat	40°19'N	36°34'E
Ankara	39°56'N	32°52'E	Erzincan	39°44'N	39°29'E	Kutahya	39°25'N	29°59'E	Trabzon	41°00'N	39°43'E
Antakya (Antioch)	36°14'N	36°07'E	Erzurum	39°55'N	41°17'E	Malatya	38°21'N	38°19'E	Turhal	40°24'N	36°06'E
Antalya	36°53'N	30°42'E	Eskisehir	39°46'N	30°32'E	Manisa	38°36'N	27°26'E	*Tuz, Lake*	38°45'N	33°25'E
Antalya, Gulf of	36°30'N	31°00'E	*Euphrates*	36°50'N	38°00'E	Maras	37°36'N	36°55'E	Urfa	37°08'N	38°46'E
Ararat, Mount	39°42'N	44°18'E	Gaziantep	37°05'N	37°22'E	*Marmara, Sea of*	40°40'N	28°15'E	Usak	38°41'N	29°25'E
Bafra	41°34'N	35°56'E	*Gelidonya, Cape*	36°13'N	30°25'E	Mersin	36°48'N	34°38'E	Uskudar	41°01'N	29°01'E
Balikesir	39°39'N	27°53'E	Iskenderun	36°37'N	36°07'E	Merzifon	40°53'N	35°29'E	Van	38°28'N	43°20'E
Beysehir, Lake	37°40'N	31°30'E	Isparta	37°46'N	30°33'E	*Murat*	38°39'N	39°50'E	*Van, Lake*	38°33'N	42°46'E
Boldavin	38°42'N	31°04'E	Istanbul	41°01'N	28°58'E	Nevsehir	38°38'N	34°43'E	Yozgat	39°50'N	34°48'E
Bolu	40°44'N	31°37'E	Izmir	38°25'N	27°09'E	Nigde	37°59'N	34°42'E	Zile	40°18'N	35°54'E
Bosporus	41°06'N	29°04'E	Izmit	40°46'N	29°55'E	Nizip	37°01'N	37°46'E	Zonguldak	41°27'N	31°49'E
Bursa	40°11'N	29°04'E	Karabuk	41°12'N	32°37'E	Osmaniya	37°05'N	36°14'E			
Carsamba	41°12'N	36°44'E	Karaman	37°11'N	33°14'E	Polatli	39°36'N	32°09'E			
Ceyhan	37°04'N	35°47'E	Kars	40°36'N	43°05'E	*Sakarya*	39°40'N	30°55'E			

The Troglodyte dwellings shown here are found in Turkey's Cappadocia region. The Troglodytes were a primitive people who inhabited the caves and tunnels of rocky hillsides. They were given their name by the ancient Greeks.

TURKS AND CAICOS ISLANDS

OFFICIAL NAME Turks and
  Caicos Islands

PEOPLE
Population 8,100.
Density 49/mi² (19/km²).
Urban 43%.
Capital Grand Turk, Grand Turk I., 3,146.
Ethnic groups Black.
Languages English.
Religions Baptist, Methodist, Anglican.
Literacy 99%.

POLITICS
Government Colony (U.K.).
Parties People's Democratic Movement, Progressive
  National.
Suffrage Universal, over 18.
Subdivisions 3 districts.

ECONOMY
GDP $15,000,000.
Per capita $2,020.
Monetary unit U.S. dollar.
Trade partners U.S., U.K.
Exports Crawfish, conch.
Imports Foodstuffs, tobacco, clothing.

LAND
Description Carribbean islands.
Area 166 mi² (430 km²).
Highest point Grand Turk I., 157 ft (48 m).
Lowest point Sea level.

PEOPLE. The population of Turks and Caicos is mostly black. English is the main language, although Haitian Creole is spoken by a group of immigrants. A trend of emigration is reversing as the islands' economy develops and employment opportunities expand.

ECONOMY AND THE LAND. Since the completion of a major resort in 1984, Turks and Caicos tourism industry has expanded, with visitors drawn by the beautiful beaches and offshore coral reefs. Financial services are on the rise as well; tax benefits, coupled with minimal government control, continue to attract foreign investors. More than thirty islands and cays compose Turks and Caicos. Six of the main islands are inhabited, along with several of the cays. The terrain is flat with some low hills. The climate is tropical, tempered by trade winds.

HISTORY AND POLITICS. The islands' first inhabitants were the Lucayan Indians. It is likely that present-day Turks and Caicos, rather than San Salvador in the Bahamas, was Christopher Columbus's first New World landfall in 1492. The Spaniard Ponce de Léon arrived in 1515, and soon the islands became a center for pirate activity. In 1678 settlers from Bermuda made their way to the islands, establishing a sea salt operation that endured as a successful enterprise until 1964. Until the 1760s, when the British secured the islands, Turks and Caicos saw invasions by both the Spanish and the French. Following the American Revolution, British Loyalists fled the United States for Turks and Caicos, establishing a plantation economy fueled by slaves. At various times the islands were joined with the Bahamas and Jamaica, and when Jamaica gained independence in 1962, Turks and Caicos became a separate colony. ∎

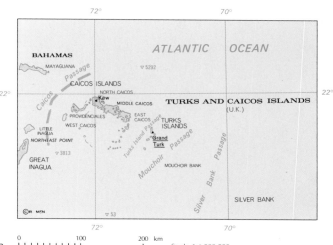

Turks and Caicos Islands Map Index

	Lat.	Long.		Lat.	Long.
Caicos Islands	21°56'N	71°58'W	North Caicos	21°56'N	71°59'W
Grand Turk	21°28'N	71°08'W	Providenciales	21°47'N	72°17'W
Kew	21°54'N	72°02'W	Turks Islands	21°24'N	71°07'W

TUVALU

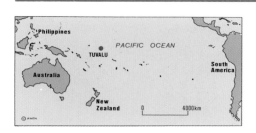

OFFICIAL NAME Tuvalu

PEOPLE
Population 8,200.
Density 820/mi² (315/km²).
Capital Funafuti, Funafuti I., 2,191.
Ethnic groups Polynesian 96%.
Languages Tuvaluan, English.
Religions Christian.
Life expectancy 60 female, 57 male.
Literacy 50%.

POLITICS
Government Parliamentary state.
Parties None.
Memberships CW.
Subdivisions 8 island councils.

ECONOMY
GNP $4,000,000.
Per capita $570.
Monetary unit Australian dollar.
Trade partners U.K., Australia.
Exports Copra.
Imports Food, fuels.

LAND
Description South Pacific islands.
Area 10 mi² (26 km²).
Highest point 15 ft (5 m).
Lowest point Sea level.

PEOPLE. The small island nation of Tuvalu has a largely Polynesian population centered in rural villages. Many Polynesians also have European blood, a result of intermarriage wtih mutineers and traders who settled here in the nineteenth century. Tuvaluans speak the Tuvaluan language, derived from Polynesian and related to Samoan. On the island of Nui a dialect of Gilbertese, the language of early invaders, is also spoken. Because of historical ties to Great Britain, many Tuvaluans also speak English. The majority of Tuvaluans live on the island of Funafuti, which is also the site of the nation's capital. Vaitupu is the next most heavily populated, followed by Niutao, and Nanumea. Most Tuvaluans are Christian, belonging to the Church of Tuvalu, an offshoot of the Congregationalist faith brought by missionaries. Minority faiths include Seventh-Day Adventist and Bahái, among others. Of the nine coral islands, only eight are permanently inhabited.

ECONOMY AND THE LAND. The soil of the Tuvaluan coral-reef islands is poor, and there are few natural resources other than coconut palms. Copra is the primary export, and many Tuvaluans weave mats and baskets for export. Tuvalu has minimal manufacturing and no mining. The nation consists of nine islands, most of them atolls surrounding lagoons. Although there are nine islands, the name Tuvalu means "light standing together." The climate is tropical.

HISTORY AND POLITICS. The first inhabitants of the islands of Tuvalu most likely came from Samoa, although traditon holds that emigrants form Tonga and the Gilbert Islands were also early settlers. In 1568 a Spanish sea captain sighted the islands of Nui, and the same Spaniard sailed past Niulakita in 1595. This was an era of widespread European exploration and expansion, however, and these islands were virtually forgotten during the next centuries. In 1781 another Spaniard reached Nanumanga and Nanumea, and in 1819 the captain of a British ship made his way to Nukufetau and Funafuti, naming the latter Ellice after the ship's owner. Throughout the early decades of the 1800s, Western sailing expeditions continued to arrive in the region, reaching Nukulaelae, Niutao, Vaitupu, and, more than two centuries after their first discovery, Nui and Niulakita. The entire island group soon came to be known as the Ellice Islands. During the mid-1800s many European whalers settled permanently on the islands, in time establishing a coconut export business, the predecessor of today's economic contributor. The 1860s saw a decline in the islands' indigenous population. As slavery became outlawed in European colonies, many natives were shipped to other islands or to South America to work as plantation laborers. In addition, European diseases took their toll on the original inhabitants. Also during the 1860s British missionaries who had been active elsewhere in the Pacific came to the Ellice Islands and established Christianity as the primary belief. In 1916 the Ellice Islands were officially joined with the Gilbert Islands to the northwest as the Gilbert and Ellice Islands Colony under the British Crown. When the British began planning for the colony's eventual independence, Ellice Islanders requested a state separate from the Gilbertese, a result of rivalries between the inhabitants of the two island groups. In 1975 the Ellice Islands were separated from the Gilberts and renamed Tuvalu. In 1978 Tuvalu officially became an independent nation. The Gilbert Islands became independent Kiribati one year later. ∎

UGANDA

OFFICIAL NAME Republic of
Uganda

PEOPLE
Population 14,505,000.
Density 159/mi² (61/km²).
Urban 7%.
Capital Kampala, 458,423.
Ethnic groups African 99%.
Languages English, Swahili, Luganda, indigenous.
Religions Roman Catholic 33%, Protestant 33%,
Muslim 16%, indigenous.
Life expectancy 49 female, 46 male.
Literacy 52%.

POLITICS
Government Republic.
Parties Democratic, Uganda Patriotic Movement,
Uganda People's Congress.
Suffrage Universal adult.
Memberships CW, OAU, UN.
Subdivisions 10 provinces.

ECONOMY
GDP $4,800,000,000.
Per capita $357.
Monetary unit Shilling.
Trade partners Kenya, U.S., U.K.
Exports Coffee, cotton, tea.
Imports Petroleum products, machinery, textiles,
metals, transportation equipment.

LAND
Description Eastern Africa, landlocked.
Area 91,134 mi² (236,036 km²).
Highest point Margherita Pk., 16,763 ft (5,109 m).
Lowest point 2,000 ft (650 m).

PEOPLE. Uganda is a predominantly rural nation with a largely African population composed of various ethnic groups. Numerous differences divide Uganda's varied groups and have traditionally inspired conflict. Though English is the official language of Uganda, Luganda and Swahili are widely used, as well as indigenous Bantu and Nilotic languages. Most Ugandans are Christian; Muslims and followers of traditional beliefs compose significant minorities.

ECONOMY AND THE LAND. Despite attempts to diversify the economy, the country remains largely agricultural. Uganda is able to meet most of its own food needs, and coffee, cotton, and tea are grown commercially. Copper deposits account for most mining activity. Though Uganda straddles the equator, temperatures are modified by altitude. Most of the country is plateau, and Uganda benefits from proximity to several major lakes.

HISTORY AND POLITICS. Arab traders who traveled to the interior of Uganda in the 1830s found sophisticated kingdoms that had developed over several centuries. British explorers tracking the source of the Nile River arrived in the 1860s and were followed by European missionaries. Britain quickly became a dominant force in eastern Africa, and part of modern Uganda became a British protectorate in 1894. Subsequent border adjustments brought Uganda to its present boundaries in 1926. After increasing demands for independence, moves toward autonomy began in the mid-1950s. Independence came in 1962 and was followed by internal conflicts and power struggles. In 1971 Major General Idi Amin Dada led a successful coup against President Obote and declared himself president. His dictatorship was rife with corruption, economic decline, and disregard for human rights. Amin was driven from Uganda by a force of Tanzanian troops and Ugandan exiles in 1979.

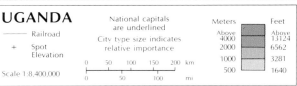

Uganda Map Index

	Lat.	Long.		Lat.	Long.
Albert, Lake	1°40'N	31°00'E	Kampala	0°19'N	32°25'E
Albert Nile	3°36'N	32°02'E	Kyoga, Lake	1°30'N	33°00'E
Arua	3°01'N	30°55'E	Langia		
Edward, Lake	0°25'S	29°30'E	Mountains	3°35'N	33°40'E
Elgon, Mount	1°08'N	34°33'E	Margherita Peak	0°22'N	29°51'E
Entebbe	0°04'N	32°28'E	Masaka	0°20'S	31°44'E
Fort Portal	0°40'N	30°17'E	Mbale	1°05'N	34°10'E
George, Lake	0°02'N	30°12'E	Moroto	2°32'N	34°46'E
Gulu	2°47'N	32°18'E	Ruwenzori	0°23'N	29°54'E
Jinja	0°26'N	33°12'E	Sese Islands	0°20'S	32°20'E
Kabale	1°15'S	29°59'E	Soroti	1°43'N	33°37'E
Kabalega Falls	2°17'N	31°41'E	Victoria, Lake	1°00'S	33°00'E
Kafu	1°08'N	31°05'E	Victoria Nile	2°14'N	31°26'E
Kagera	0°57'S	31°47'E			

President Obote returned to power in 1980 but was forced from office in a 1985 military coup. Uganda follows a nonaligned foreign policy. ■

Kampala, shown here, is the capital and economic center of Uganda. Situated on the equator, it lies on the plateau north of Lake Victoria.

UNION OF SOVIET SOCIALIST REPUBLICS

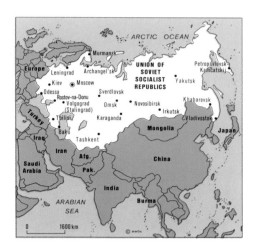

OFFICIAL NAME Union of
Soviet Socialist Republics

PEOPLE
Population 275,590,000.
Density 32/mi² (12/km²).
Urban 64%.
Capital Moscow, 8,202,000.
Ethnic groups Russian 52%, Ukrainian 16%, others
32%.
Languages Russian; other Slavic, Altaic, and
Indo-European languages.
Religions Russian Orthodox 18%, Muslim 9%.
Life expectancy 75 female, 70 male.
Literacy 100%.

POLITICS
Government Socialist republic.
Parties Communist.
Suffrage Universal, over 18.
Memberships CEMA, UN, Warsaw Pact.
Subdivisions 15 Soviet Socialist Republics.

ECONOMY
GNP $1,715,000,000,000.
Per capita $6,352.
Monetary unit Ruble.
Trade partners Eastern European countries, Finland,
West Germany, France.
Exports Petroleum, petroleum products, natural gas,
machinery, manufactured goods, metals.
Imports Food, machinery, steel products, consumer
goods.

LAND
Description Eastern Europe and northern Asia.
Area 8,600,383 mi² (22,274,900 km²).
Highest point Communism Pk., 24,590 ft (7,495 m).
Lowest point Vpadina Karagiye, 433 ft (132 m) below
sea level.

PEOPLE. The varied population of the U.S.S.R.
is composed of more than one hundred distinct
groups. Nearly three-quarters of the people are
Eastern Slavs, and more than 70 percent of this
group are Russians. The remaining Slavs are
Ukrainians and Belorussians. The rest of the
population belongs to Turkic, Finno-Ugric, Cau-
casian, other Indo-European groups, and a mixture of peoples including Inuit. Each ethnic
group speaks its own language, which is sometimes further divided into dialects, and in all
more than one hundred distinct languages, using
five different alphabets, are recognized in the
U.S.S.R. Russian is the most widely spoken.
About 70 percent of the Soviet people proclaim
themselves atheists. Although religious practice

is discouraged by the state, and churches have
no legal status, Russian Orthodox, Islam, Roman
Catholicism, and Protestantism are actively practiced. There is also a significant Jewish minority,
whose problems with emigration have become
the focus of international attention.

ECONOMY AND THE LAND. As an industrial
power, the U.S.S.R. ranks second only to the
United States. Mining, steel production, and
other heavy industries predominate. The economy is controlled by the state, and economic policies are administered through a series of five-
year plans, which emphasize industrial and
technological growth. The Soviet economy is suffering from low productivity, energy shortages,
and a lack of skilled labor, problems the government hopes can be alleviated by increased use of
technology and science. The U.S.S.R. trades primarily with members of the Council for Mutual
Economic Assistance (CEMA), although trade
with the West has risen sharply in the past few
years. Though the country contains some of the
world's most fertile land, long winters and hot,
dry summers keep many crop yields low. Geographically, the Soviet Union is the largest nation
in the world. Its land is richly endowed with
minerals, and the terrain is widely varied, consisting of low mountain ranges, desert and a vast
plain marked by tundra, steppe, and forests.
Several climatic zones are found here as well,
ranging from polar in the far north to subtropical
and semiarid in the south.

HISTORY AND POLITICS. Inhabited as early as
the Stone Age, what is now the U.S.S.R. was
much later invaded successively by Scythians,
Sarmatians, Goths, Huns, Bulgars, Slavs, and
others. By A.D. 989 Byzantine cultural influence
had become predominant. Various groups and
regions were slowly incorporated into a single
state. In 1547 Ivan IV was crowned czar of all
Russia, beginning a tradition of czarist rule that
lasted until the 1917 Russian Revolution, when
the Bolsheviks came to power and named Vladimir Ilyich Lenin as head of the first Soviet government. The Bolsheviks established a Communist state and weathered a bitter civil war. Joseph

**Shown here is an eleventh-century church in the city of
Novgorod. One of the oldest cities in the U.S.S.R., this
northwestern city has preserved much of its ancient
heritage.**

Stalin succeeded Lenin as head of state in 1924
and initiated a series of political purges that lasted through the 1930s. The Soviet Union became
embroiled in World War II, siding with the Allies,
losing over twenty million people, and suffering
widespread destruction of its cities and countryside. It emerged from the war with extended
influence, however, having annexed part of Finland and several Eastern European nations. Following Stalin's death in 1953, the Soviet Union
experienced a liberalization of policies under Ni-
kita Krushchev. In 1964 Leonid Brezhnev worked
to consolidate and strengthen the power of the
Secretariat and Politburo of the Communist
party. Mikhail S. Gorbachev, the youngest Soviet
leader in decades, took office in 1985. ∎

**Depicted here is the Spassity Tower, one of eighteen
towers in the wall that encircles the Kremlin. Now the
seat of government in the center of Moscow, the original Kremlin was built as a walled city in 1147 and
housed the government, religious institutions, and resi-
dences.**

In this picture a basket of caviar is being carried for weighing at a fish factory in Kamchatka. The livelihood of the people in this far eastern region of the U.S.S.R. depends on the world's demand for this delicacy.

Reindeer, shown here with their herders in the Yakut Autonomous Republic, are important to the agricultural development of this cold Siberian northland. Fishing, trapping, and cattle raising are also carried out in the region.

The Summer Palace in Leningrad, shown here, reflects the splendor of the life-style of the czars. Russia was ruled by the czars for nearly four hundred years, from the sixteenth to the early twentieth century.

Cotton, shown here being piled high before processing, is a valuable crop in this dry Turkmen region, lying just north of Iran and Afghanistan in the Soviet Union.

UNION OF SOVIET SOCIALIST REPUBLICS

— Railroad
++++ Canal or Waterway
— Republic Boundary
— Oil Pipeline
▲ Major Oil Field
+ Spot Elevation or Depth

Capitals are underlined

City type size indicates relative importance

Scale 1:25,929,000

Meters Above	Feet Above
4000	13124
2000	6562
1000	3281
500	1640
200	656
0	Sea Level

Meters 200 Below 2000 — Feet 656 Below 6562

0 200 400 600 km
0 200 400 mi

© 1980 Rand McNally & Co.
A-570000-772

This picture shows the changing of the guard at Lenin's Tomb at the Kremlin in Red Square, Moscow. Vladimir Ilyich Lenin was one of the leaders of the 1917 Russian Revolution, and he was the first head of the Soviet government.

The beautiful golden domes of the Kremlin create a unique scene and recollect a past that was richly influenced by the eastern arm of the Christian church. The Byzantine culture and architecture of this early period of the Soviet Union's development continues to stand, colorful and flamboyant, in sharp contrast to the state-influenced culture of the twentieth century.

Union of Soviet Socialist Republics Map Index

UNITED ARAB EMIRATES

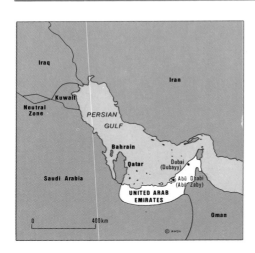

OFFICIAL NAME United Arab
Emirates

PEOPLE
Population 1,600,000.
Density 50/mi² (19/km²).
Urban 81%.
Capital Abu Dhabi, 100,000.
Ethnic groups Emirian 19%, other Arab 23%, South
Asian 50%.
Languages Arabic, Farsi, English.
Religions Muslim 96%.
Life expectancy 65 female, 61 male.
Literacy 56%.

POLITICS
Government Federation of monarchs.
Parties None.
Suffrage None.
Memberships AL, OPEC, UN.

Subdivisions 7 emirates.

ECONOMY
GDP $30,000,000,000.
Per capita $30,000.
Monetary unit Dirham.
Trade partners Japan, Western European countries,
U.S.
Exports Petroleum.
Imports Machinery, consumer goods, food.

LAND
Description Southwestern Asia.
Area 32,278 mi² (83,600 km²).

PEOPLE. The United Arab Emirates is a predominantly urban federation of seven independent states, each with its own ruling emir. The indigenous population is mostly Arab and Muslim, but only a small percentage of residents are U.A.E. citizens. Other groups include foreigners attracted by jobs in industry, especially Asians and Western Europeans.

ECONOMY AND THE LAND. Most of the United Arab Emirates is desert, which explains agriculture's small economic role. However, the federation is rich in oil, and major deposits, primarily in Abu Dhabi, account for nearly all of the Emirian national budget.

HISTORY AND POLITICS. Centuries ago Arab rulers gained control of the region, formerly called the Trucial Coast, and Islam spread to the area in the A.D. 600s. In 1820 Arabian emirs signed the first of a number of treaties with the United Kingdom. Mutual self-interest led to an 1892 treaty that granted Britain exclusive rights to Trucial territory and government activity in return for military protection. Britain formally withdrew from Trucial affairs in 1971, and six of

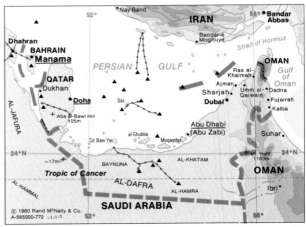

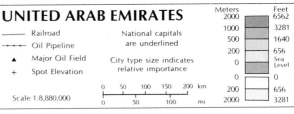

United Arab Emirates Map Index

	Lat.	Long.		Lat.	Long.
Abu Dhabi (Abu Zabi)	24°28′N	54°22′E	Hormuz, Strait of	26°34′N	56°15′E
Al-Dafra	23°25′N	53°25′E	Muqayshit	24°12′N	53°42′E
Das	25°09′N	52°53′E	Persian Gulf	25°00′N	53°00′E
Dubai	25°18′N	55°18′E	Sharjah	25°22′N	55°23′E

the Trucial emirates entered into a loose federation called the United Arab Emirates, which included Abu Dhabi, Dubai, Ash Shariqah, Ajman, Umm al Qaywayn, and Al Fujayrah. The seventh, Ras al Khaymah, joined in early 1972. ∎

UNITED KINGDOM

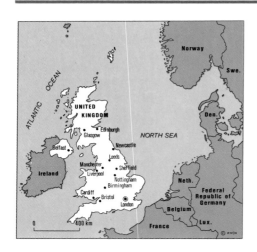

OFFICIAL NAME United
Kingdom of Great Britain
and Northern Ireland

PEOPLE
Population 56,040,000.
Density 596/mi² (230/km²).
Urban 76%.
Capital London, England, 6,851,400.
Ethnic groups English 81%, Scottish 10%, Irish 2%,
Welsh 2%, Ulster 2%.
Languages English.
Religions Anglican, Roman Catholic, Presbyterian.
Life expectancy 76 female, 72 male.
Literacy 99%.

POLITICS
Government Constitutional monarchy.
Parties Conservative, Labor, Liberal, Social
Democratic.

Suffrage Universal, over 18.
Memberships CW, NATO, OECD, UN.
Subdivisions 54 counties in England and Wales,
12 regions in Scotland and island areas,
26 districts in Northern Ireland.

ECONOMY
GNP $482,700,000,000.
Per capita $8,620.
Monetary unit Pound sterling.
Trade partners U.S., West Germany, other Western
European countries.
Exports Machinery, transportation equipment,
petroleum, manufactured goods.
Imports Machinery, food, crude materials,
manufactured goods.

LAND
Description Northwestern European islands.
Area 94,092 mi² (243,694 km²).
Highest point Ben Nevis, Scotland, 4,406 ft (1,343 m).
Lowest point Holme Fen, England, 9 ft (3 m) below
sea level.

PEOPLE. The ancestry of modern Britons reflects many centuries of invasions and migrations from Scandinavia and the European continent. Today Britons are a mixture of Celtic, Roman, Anglo-Saxon, Norse, and Norman influences. English is the official language, although Celtic languages such as Welsh and Scottish Gaelic are also spoken. Anglican is the dominant religion in England, while many Scots practice Presbyterianism. A sizable minority is Roman Catholic. The population is primarily urban and suburban, with a significant percentage living in the southeastern corner of England.

ECONOMY AND THE LAND. A land of limited natural resources, the United Kingdom has relied on trading and, more recently, manufacturing to achieve its stature as a world power. Access to

the sea is a traditional economic and political asset: the country maintains a large merchant fleet, which at one time dominated world trade. The industrial revolution developed quickly in Great Britain, and the country continues to be a leading producer of transportation equipment, metal products, and other manufactured goods. Agriculture is hindered by climate and limited suitable land, but intensive, mechanized farming methods have allowed the nation to produce half of its food supply. Livestock raising is especially important. Extensive deposits of coal and iron ore make mining important and have contributed to industry. London maintains its position as an international financial center. The United Kingdom includes Scotland, England, Wales, Northern Ireland, and several offshore islands. The varied terrain is marked by several mountain ranges, moors, rolling hills, and plains. The climate is tempered by proximity to the sea but is subject to frequent changes. Great Britain administers many overseas possessions.

HISTORY AND POLITICS. Little is known of the earliest inhabitants of Britain, but evidence such as Stonehenge indicates the existence of a developed culture before the Roman invasion in the 50s B.C. Britain began to interact with the rest of Europe while under Roman rule, and the Norman period after A.D. 1066 fostered the establishment of many cultural and political traditions that continue to be reflected in British life. Scotland came under the British Crown in 1603, and in 1707 England and Scotland agreed to unite as Great Britain. Ireland had been conquered by the early seventeenth century, and the 1801 British Act of Union established the United Kingdom of Great Britain and Ireland. Colonial and economic expansion had taken Great Britain to the Far

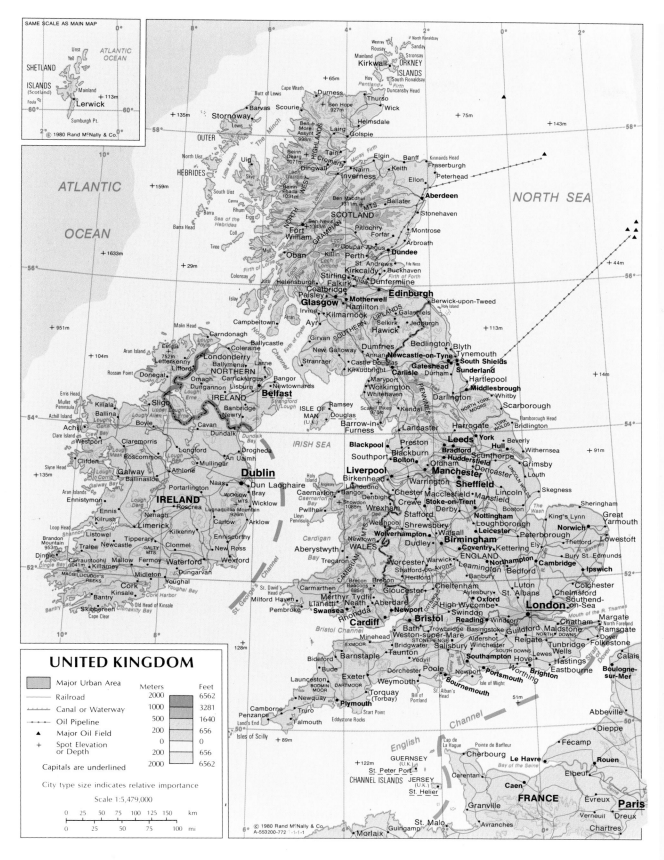

UNITED KINGDOM

	Meters	Feet
	2000	6562
	1000	3281
	500	1640
	200	656
	0	0
	200	656
	2000	6562

Major Urban Area
Railroad
Canal or Waterway
Oil Pipeline
▲ Major Oil Field
+ Spot Elevation or Depth
Capitals are underlined

City type size indicates relative importance

Scale 1:5,479,000

0 25 50 75 100 125 150 km
0 25 50 75 100 mi

© 1980 Rand McNally & Co.
A-553200-772

United Kingdom Map Index

	Lat.	Long.		Lat.	Long.
Aberdare	51°43'N	3°27'W	Lowestoft	52°29'N	1°45'E
Aberdeen	57°10'N	2°04'W	Luton	51°53'N	0°25'W
Aberystwyth	52°25'N	4°05'W	Macclesfield	53°16'N	2°07'W
Anglesey	53°15'N	4°20'W	Macdhui, Ben	57°04'N	3°40'W
Arran	55°35'N	5°15'W	Maidstone	51°17'N	0°32'E
Avon	52°25'N	1°31'W	Mainland	59°00'N	3°10'W
Ayr	55°28'N	4°38'W	Mainland	60°20'N	1°22'W
Barnstaple	51°05'N	4°04'W	Manchester	53°30'N	2°15'W
Barrow-in-Furness	54°07'N	3°14'W	Mansfield	53°09'N	1°11'W
Bath	51°23'N	2°22'W	Margate	51°24'N	1°24'E
Bedford	52°08'N	0°29'W	Merthyr Tydfil	51°46'N	3°23'W
Bedlington	55°08'N	1°35'W	Middlesbrough	54°35'N	1°14'W
Belfast	54°35'N	5°55'W	Moray Firth	57°50'N	3°30'W
Birkenhead	53°24'N	3°02'W	Motherwell	55°48'N	4°00'W
Birmingham	52°30'N	1°50'W	Mull	56°27'N	6°00'W
Blackburn	53°45'N	2°29'W	Neath	51°40'N	3°48'W
Blackpool	53°50'N	3°03'W	Ness, Loch	57°15'N	4°30'W
Blyth	55°07'N	1°30'W	Nevis, Ben	56°48'N	5°01'W
Bolton	53°35'N	2°26'W	Newcastle-on-Tyne	54°59'N	1°35'W
Bournemouth	50°43'N	1°54'W	Newport	52°01'N	4°51'W
Bradford	53°48'N	1°45'W	Northampton	52°14'N	0°54'W
Brighton	50°50'N	0°08'W	North Channel	55°10'N	5°40'W
Bristol	51°27'N	2°35'W	Northern Ireland	54°40'N	6°45'W
Bristol Channel	51°20'N	4°00'W	North Foreland	51°23'N	1°27'E
Caernarfon	53°08'N	4°16'W	North Uist	57°37'N	7°22'W
Cambrian Mountains	52°35'N	3°35'W	North West Highlands	57°30'N	5°00'W
Cambridge	52°13'N	0°08'E	Norwich	52°38'N	1°18'E
Cardiff	51°29'N	3°13'W	Nottingham	52°58'N	1°10'W
Cardigan Bay	52°30'N	4°20'W	Oban	56°25'N	5°29'W
Carlisle	54°54'N	2°25'W	Oldham	53°33'N	2°07'W
Channel Islands	49°20'N	2°20'W	Orkney Islands	59°00'N	3°00'W
Chatham	51°23'N	0°32'E	Outer Hebrides	57°50'N	7°32'W
Chelmsford	51°44'N	0°28'E	Oxford	51°46'N	1°15'W
Cheltenham	51°54'N	2°04'W	Paisley	55°50'N	4°26'W
Chester	53°12'N	2°54'W	Pennines	54°10'N	2°05'W
Clyde, Firth of	55°42'N	5°00'W	Pentland Firth	58°44'N	3°13'W
Coatbridge	55°52'N	4°01'W	Perth	56°24'N	3°28'W
Colchester	51°54'N	0°54'E	Peterborough	52°35'N	0°15'W
Cotswold Hills	51°45'N	2°10'W	Plymouth	50°23'N	4°10'W
Coventry	52°25'N	1°30'W	Poole	50°43'N	1°59'W
Crewe	53°05'N	2°27'W	Portland, Bill of	50°31'N	2°27'W
Darlington	54°31'N	1°34'W	Portsmouth	50°48'N	1°05'W
Derby	52°55'N	1°29'W	Preston	53°46'N	2°42'W
Doncaster	53°32'N	1°07'W	Ramsgate	51°20'N	1°25'E
Dover, Strait of	51°00'N	1°30'E	Reading	51°28'N	0°59'W
Dudley	52°30'N	2°05'W	Reigate	51°14'N	0°13'W
Dumfries	55°04'N	3°37'W	Rhondda	51°40'N	3°27'W
Duncansby Head	58°39'N	3°01'W	Saint Albans	51°46'N	0°21'W
Dundee	56°28'N	3°00'W	Saint Alban's Head	50°34'N	2°04'W
Dunfermline	56°04'N	3°29'W	Saint David's Head	51°55'N	5°19'W
Eastbourne	50°46'N	0°17'E	Saint George's Channel	52°00'N	6°00'W
Edinburgh	55°57'N	3°13'W	Salisbury	51°05'N	1°48'W
England	52°30'N	1°30'W	Scafell Pikes	54°27'N	3°12'W
English Channel	50°20'N	1°00'W	Scarborough	54°17'N	0°24'W
Exeter	50°43'N	3°31'W	Scilly, Isles of	49°55'N	6°20'W
Falkirk	56°00'N	3°48'W	Scotland	57°00'N	4°00'W
Folkestone	51°05'N	1°11'E	Scunthorpe	53°36'N	0°38'W
Forth, Firth of	56°05'N	2°55'W	Sheffield	53°23'N	1°30'W
Fort William	56°49'N	5°07'W	Shetland Islands	60°30'N	1°30'W
Foyle, Lake	55°07'N	7°08'W	Shrewsbury	52°43'N	2°45'W
Gateshead	54°58'N	1°37'W	Skye	57°15'N	6°10'W
Glasgow	55°53'N	4°15'W	Snowdon	53°04'N	4°05'W
Gloucester	51°53'N	2°14'W	Southampton	50°55'N	1°25'W
Grampian Mountains	56°45'N	4°00'W	Southend-on-Sea	51°33'N	0°43'E
Great Yarmouth	52°37'N	1°44'E	Southern Uplands	55°30'N	3°30'W
Grimsby	53°35'N	0°05'W	Southport	53°39'N	3°01'W
Guildford	51°14'N	0°35'W	South Shields	55°00'N	1°25'W
Hamilton	55°47'N	4°03'W	South Uist	57°15'N	7°24'W
Harrogate	54°00'N	1°33'W	Stafford	52°48'N	2°07'W
Hartlepool	54°42'N	1°11'W	Stirling	56°07'N	3°57'W
Hastings	50°51'N	0°36'E	Stoke-on-Trent	53°00'N	2°10'W
Hawick	55°25'N	2°47'W	Stornoway	58°12'N	6°23'W
High Wycombe	51°38'N	0°46'W	Sunderland	54°55'N	1°23'W
Hove	50°49'N	0°10'W	Swansea	51°38'N	3°57'W
Huddersfield	53°39'N	1°47'W	Swindon	51°34'N	1°47'W
Hull	53°45'N	0°20'W	Taunton	51°01'N	3°06'W
Humber	53°40'N	0°10'W	Thames	51°28'N	0°43'E
Inverness	57°27'N	4°15'W	The Minch	58°05'N	5°55'W
Ipswich	52°04'N	1°10'E	The Wash	52°55'N	0°15'E
Irish Sea	53°30'N	5°20'W	Torbay →		
Islay	55°46'N	6°10'W	Torquay	50°28'N	3°30'W
Jura	56°00'N	5°50'W	Torquay (Torbay)	50°28'N	3°30'W
Kettering	52°24'N	0°44'W	Trent	53°42'N	0°41'W
Kilmarnock	55°36'N	4°30'W	Tunbridge Wells	51°08'N	0°16'E
Kinnairds Head	57°42'N	2°00'W	Tynemouth	55°01'N	1°24'W
Kirkcaldy	56°07'N	3°10'W	Wales	52°30'N	3°30'W
Kirkwall	58°59'N	2°58'W	Walsall	52°35'N	1°58'W
Lancaster	54°03'N	2°48'W	Warrington	53°24'N	2°37'W
Land's End	50°03'N	5°44'W	Weston-super-Mare	51°21'N	2°59'W
Leamington	52°18'N	1°31'W	Weymouth	50°36'N	2°28'W
Leeds	53°50'N	1°35'W	Wight, Isle of	50°40'N	1°20'W
Leicester	52°38'N	1°05'W	Wolverhampton	52°36'N	2°08'W
Lerwick	60°09'N	1°09'W	Worcester	52°11'N	2°13'W
Lewis	58°10'N	6°40'W	Workington	54°39'N	3°35'W
Lincoln	53°14'N	0°33'W	Worthing	50°48'N	0°23'W
Liverpool	53°25'N	2°55'W	Wrath, Cape	58°37'N	5°01'W
Llanetti	51°42'N	4°10'W	Wrexham	53°03'N	3°00'W
Lleyn Peninsula	52°54'N	4°30'W	York	53°58'N	1°05'W
Lomond, Loch	56°08'N	4°38'W			
London	51°30'N	0°10'W			
Londonderry	55°00'N	7°19'W			
Lorne, Firth of	56°20'N	5°40'W			
Loughborough	52°47'N	1°11'W			

East, America, Africa, and India, but the nation's influence began to diminish at the end of the nineteenth century as the industrial revolution strengthened other nations. World War I significantly weakened the United Kingdom, and after the war the British Empire lost several components, including southern Ireland in 1921. The period following World War II saw the demise of the empire, with many former colonies gaining independence. ■

The Tower of London is a well-known landmark on the north bank of the River Thames. Construction on the White Tower, shown in the picture, began in the ninth century, and the tower served as a royal fortress to control the port area. Over time, the structure expanded as walls and buildings were built to surround the White Tower.

For centuries the Tower of London was used as a prison, gaining much notoriety during this period, and until the seventeenth century it was a royal residence.

Places and Possessions of the United Kingdom

Entity	Status	Area	Population	Capital/Population
Anguilla (Caribbean island)	Associated state	35 mi² (91 km²)	7,000	The Valley/760
Ascension (South Atlantic island)	Dependency of St. Helena	34 mi² (88 km²)	1,400	Georgetown
Bermuda (North Atlantic islands)	Colony	21 mi² (53 km²)	70,000	Hamilton/1,600
British Indian Ocean Territory Indian Ocean islands)	Colony	23 mi² (60 km²)	None	None
Cayman Islands (Caribbean sea)	Colony	100 mi² (259 km²)	22,000	Georgetown/7,617
Channel Islands (northwest Europe)	Dependency	75 mi² (195 km²)	132,000	None
Falkland Islands (South Atlantic)	Colony	4,700 mi² (12,173 km²)	2,000	Stanley/1,050
Gibraltar (southwestern Europe)	Colony	2.3 mi² (6 km²)	30,000	Gibraltar/30,000
Guernsey and dependencies (northwest Europe islands)	Bailiwick of Channel Islands	30 mi² (77 km²)	78,000	St. Peter Port/16,982
Hong Kong (eastern Asia)	Colony	410 mi² (1,061 km²)	5,435,000	Hong Kong/1,183,621
Isle of Man (northwest Europe)	Self-governing territory	221 mi² (572 km²)	67,000	Douglas/20,368
Jersey (northwest Europe island)	Bailiwick of Channel Islands	45 mi² (117 km²)	54,000	St. Helier/24,941
Montserrat (Caribbean island)	Colony	40 mi² (103 km²)	12,000	Plymouth/1,568
Orkney Islands (northwest Europe)	Part of Scotland	376 mi² (974 km²)	19,000	Kirkwall/5,713
Pitcairn and dependencies (South Pacific islands)	Colony	19 mi² (49 km²)	50	Adamstown/64
St. Helena and dependencies (South Atlantic islands)	Colony	162 mi² (419 km²)	6,900	Jamestown/1,516
Shetland Islands (northwest Europe)	Part of Scotland	551 mi² (1,427 km²)	29,000	Lerwick/6,333
South Georgia and dependencies (South Atlantic islands)	Administered from the Falkland Islands	1,580 mi² (4,092 km²)	22	None
Tristan da Cunha (South Atlantic island)	Dependency of St. Helena	40 mi² (104 km²)	300	Edinburgh
Turks and Caicos Islands (Caribbean Sea)	Colony	166 mi² (430 km²)	8,100	Grand Turk/3,146
Virgin Islands, British (Caribbean islands)	Colony	59 mi² (153 km²)	13,000	Road Town/2,479

The photograph above shows Caerphilly Castle in Mid Glamorgan County, Wales. Built in the thirteenth century, the castle is typical of the many old fortresses dotting the countryside of the United Kingdom.

The usually bustling docks of the River Clyde in industrial Glasgow, Scotland, are shown here in an idle evening hour.

Shown below are the ruins of Melrose Abbey, near Galashiels, Scotland. Melrose Abbey, which exemplifies the late medieval churches built in Scotland, was constructed in the tenth century. Frequently ruined and rebuilt, the structure was ultimately left unfinished.

The Derwent Reservoir and the hills near Newcastle show the variety of the English landscape.

UNITED STATES

OFFICIAL NAME United
States of America

PEOPLE
Population 237,640,000.
Density 65/mi² (25/km²).
Urban 74%.
Capital Washington D.C., 618,400.
Ethnic groups White 80%, black 11%, Spanish 6%.
Languages English.
Religions Protestant, Roman Catholic, Jewish, others.
Life expectancy 78 female, 73 male.
Literacy 100%.

POLITICS
Government Republic.
Parties Democratic, Republican.
Suffrage Universal, over 18.
Memberships NATO, OECD, OAS, UN.
Subdivisions 50 states, 1 federal district.

ECONOMY
GNP $3,363,300,000,000.
Per capita $12,530.
Monetary unit Dollar.
Trade partners Canada, Japan, Western European
countries, Mexico.
Exports Machinery, chemicals, transportation
equipment, food.
Imports Petroleum, machinery, transportation
equipment.

LAND
Description Central North America.
Area 3,679,245 mi² (9,529,200 km²).
Highest point Mt. McKinley, 20,320 ft (6,194 m).
Lowest point Death Valley, 282 ft (86 m) below sea
level.

PEOPLE. The diverse population of the United
States is mostly composed of whites, many descended from eighteenth- and nineteenth-
century immigrants; blacks, mainly descended
from African slaves; peoples of Spanish and
Asian origin; and indigenous Indians, Inuit, and
Hawaiians. Religions encompass the world's
major faiths; predominating are Protestantism,
Roman Catholicism, and Judaism. English is the
official language, though Spanish is spoken by
many, and other languages are often found in
ethnic enclaves.

ECONOMY AND THE LAND. The United States
is an international economic power, and all sectors of the economy are highly developed. Soils
are fertile, and farm output is high, with much
land under cultivation. Mineral output includes
petroleum and natural gas, coal, copper, lead,
and zinc, but high consumption makes the United States dependent on foreign oil. The country
is also a leading manufacturer, and the service
sector is developed as well. The terrain is marked
by mountains, prairies, woodlands, and deserts.
The climate varies regionally, from mild year-
round along the Pacific coast and in the South to
temperate in the Northeast and Midwest. In addition to forty-eight contiguous states, the coun-

try includes the subarctic state of Alaska, northwest of Canada, and the tropical state of Hawaii,
an island group in the Pacific.

HISTORY AND POLITICS. Thousands of years
ago Asiatic peoples, ancestors of American Indians, crossed the Bering Strait land bridge and
spread across North and South America. Vikings
reached North America around A.D. 1000, and
Christopher Columbus arrived in 1492. Early explorations by Portugal and Spain were followed
in 1607 by England's establishment of a colony at
Jamestown, Virginia. Thirteen British colonies
waged a successful war of independence against
England from 1775 to 1783, although America
had declared its independence in 1776. United
States expansion continued westward throughout
the nineteenth century. The issues of black slavery and states' rights led to the American Civil
War from 1861 to 1865, a struggle that pitted the
North against the South and resulted in the end
of slavery. Opportunities for prosperity accompanied the industrial revolution in the late nineteenth century and led to a large influx of immigrants. From 1917 to 1918 the country joined
with the Allies in World War I. A severe economic depression began in 1929, and the United
States did not really recover until military spending during World War II stimulated industry and
the economy in general. Allied victory came in
1945. Postwar conflicts included the Korean War,
taking place in the early fifties, and the Vietnam
War, which involved the United States from the
late 1950s to 1973. ■

**Washington, D.C., was one of the first modern cities to be developed along a prescribed plan.
The French architect L'Enfant created an innovative radial design for the new nation's seat of
government. The capitol building shown above serves as the hub in the plan, and major streets
radiate from it, much as spokes in a wheel, forming the basic street pattern upon which the
city grew. Throughout Washington, monuments and parks serve as secondary hubs for other
radiating streets.**

United States Map Index

	Lat.	Long.		Lat.	Long.
Alabama	32°50'N	87°00'W	Miami	25°46'N	80°11'W
Alaska	65°00'N	153°00'W	Michigan	44°00'N	85°00'W
Albany	42°39'N	73°45'W	Michigan, Lake	44°00'N	87°00'W
Albuquerque	35°05'N	106°39'W	Milwaukee	43°02'N	87°54'W
Aleutian Islands	52°00'N	176°00'W	Minneapolis	44°58'N	93°15'W
Anchorage	61°13'N	149°54'W	Minnesota	46°00'N	94°15'W
Annapolis	38°58'N	76°29'W	Mississippi	32°50'N	89°30'W
Appalachian Mountains	41°00'N	77°00'W	Mississippi	29°00'N	89°15'W
Arizona	34°00'N	112°00'W	Missouri	38°30'N	93°30'W
Arkansas	34°50'N	92°30'W	Missouri	38°50'N	90°08'W
Arkansas	33°48'N	91°04'W	Mitchell, Mount	35°46'N	82°16'W
Atlanta	33°44'N	84°23'W	Mobile	30°41'N	88°02'W
Augusta	44°18'N	69°46'W	Montana	47°00'N	110°00'W
Austin	30°16'N	97°44'W	Montgomery	32°23'N	86°18'W
Baltimore	39°17'N	76°36'W	Montpelier	44°15'N	72°34'W
Baton Rouge	30°27'N	91°09'W	Nashville	36°09'N	86°47'W
Beaumont	30°05'N	94°06'W	Nebraska	41°30'N	100°00'W
Bering Strait	65°30'N	169°00'W	Nevada	39°00'N	117°00'W
Birmingham	33°31'N	86°48'W	Nevada, Sierra	38°00'N	119°15'W
Bismarck	46°48'N	100°47'W	Newark	40°44'N	74°10'W
Blue Ridge	37°00'N	82°00'W	New Hampshire	43°35'N	71°40'W
Boise	43°36'N	116°12'W	New Haven	41°18'N	72°56'W
Boston	42°21'N	71°03'W	New Jersey	40°15'N	74°30'W
Buffalo	42°53'N	78°52'W	New Mexico	34°30'N	106°00'W
California	37°30'N	119°30'W	New Orleans	29°57'N	90°04'W
Canaveral, Cape	28°27'N	80°32'W	New York	40°43'N	74°01'W
Carson City	39°10'N	119°46'W	New York	43°00'N	106°00'W
Cascade Range	45°00'N	121°30'W	Norfolk	36°50'N	76°17'W
Charleston	32°46'N	79°55'W	North Carolina	35°30'N	80°00'W
Charleston	38°20'N	81°37'W	North Dakota	47°30'N	100°15'W
Charlotte	35°13'N	80°50'W	Oakland	37°48'N	122°16'W
Chattanooga	35°02'N	85°18'W	Ohio	40°15'N	82°45'W
Chesapeake Bay	38°40'N	76°25'W	Ohio	36°59'N	89°08'W
Cheyenne	41°08'N	104°49'W	Okeechobee, Lake	26°55'N	80°45'W
Chicago	41°51'N	87°39'W	Oklahoma	35°30'N	98°00'W
Cincinnati	39°09'N	84°27'W	Oklahoma City	35°28'N	97°30'W
Cleveland	41°29'N	81°41'W	Olympia	47°02'N	122°53'W
Coast Ranges	41°00'N	123°30'W	Omaha	41°15'N	95°56'W
Colorado	41°00'N	107°00'W	Ontario, Lake	43°45'N	78°00'W
Colorado	32°27'N	114°50'W	Oregon	44°00'N	121°00'W
Columbia	34°00'N	81°02'W	Orlando	28°32'N	81°22'W
Columbia	46°15'N	124°05'W	Ozark Plateau	37°00'N	93°00'W
Columbus	39°57'N	82°59'W	Pecos	29°42'N	101°22'W
Concord	43°12'N	71°32'W	Pennsylvania	40°45'N	77°30'W
Connecticut	41°45'N	72°45'W	Philadelphia	39°57'N	75°09'W
Connecticut	41°17'N	72°21'W	Phoenix	33°26'N	112°04'W
Dallas	32°46'N	96°47'W	Pierre	44°22'N	100°21'W
Death Valley	36°30'N	117°00'W	Pittsburgh	40°26'N	79°59'W
Delaware	39°10'N	75°30'W	Portland	45°31'N	122°40'W
Denver	39°44'N	104°59'W	Providence	41°49'N	71°24'W
Des Moines	41°36'N	93°36'W	Rainier, Mount	46°52'N	121°46'W
Detroit	42°20'N	83°03'W	Raleigh	35°46'N	78°38'W
Dover	39°09'N	75°31'W	Red	31°00'N	91°40'W
El Paso	31°45'N	106°29'W	Rhode Island	41°40'N	71°30'W
Erie, Lake	42°15'N	81°00'W	Richmond	37°33'N	77°27'W
Florida	29°00'N	82°00'W	Riverside	33°57'N	117°23'W
Florida, Straits of	25°00'N	79°45'W	Rochester	43°09'N	77°36'W
Fort Wayne	41°07'N	85°07'W	Rocky Mountains	48°00'N	116°00'W
Fort Worth	32°43'N	97°19'W	Sacramento	38°34'N	121°29'W
Frankfort	38°12'N	84°52'W	Saginaw	43°25'N	83°56'W
Georgia	32°50'N	83°15'W	Saint Lawrence	45°00'N	74°40'W
Gila	32°43'N	114°33'W	Saint Louis	38°37'N	90°11'W
Grande, Rio (Bravo del Norte)	25°55'N	97°09'W	Saint Paul	44°57'N	93°05'W
Grand Rapids	42°58'N	85°40'W	Saint Petersburg	27°46'N	82°40'W
Great Basin	40°00'N	117°00'W	Salem	44°56'N	123°02'W
Great Plains	40°00'N	100°00'W	Salt Lake City	40°45'N	111°53'W
Great Salt Lake	41°10'N	112°30'W	San Antonio	29°25'N	98°29'W
Greenville	34°51'N	82°23'W	San Diego	32°42'N	117°09'W
Harrisburg	40°16'N	76°53'W	San Francisco	37°46'N	122°25'W
Hartford	41°46'N	72°41'W	San Jose	37°20'N	121°53'W
Hatteras, Cape	35°13'N	75°32'W	Santa Fe	35°41'N	105°56'W
Hawaii	20°00'N	157°45'W	Scranton	41°24'N	75°39'W
Helena	46°35'N	112°02'W	Seattle	47°36'N	122°19'W
Honolulu	21°18'N	157°51'W	Shreveport	32°30'N	93°44'W
Houston	29°45'N	95°21'W	Snake	46°12'N	119°02'W
Hudson	40°42'N	74°02'W	South Carolina	34°00'N	81°00'W
Huron, Lake	44°30'N	82°15'W	South Dakota	44°15'N	100°00'W
Idaho	45°00'N	115°00'W	Spokane	47°39'N	117°25'W
Illinois	40°00'N	89°00'W	Springfield	39°48'N	89°38'W
Indiana	40°00'N	86°15'W	Superior, Lake	48°00'N	88°00'W
Indianapolis	39°46'N	86°09'W	Syracuse	43°02'N	76°08'W
Iowa	42°15'N	93°15'W	Tallahassee	30°26'N	84°16'W
Jackson	32°17'N	90°11'W	Tampa	27°56'N	82°27'W
Jacksonville	30°19'N	81°39'W	Tennessee	35°50'N	85°30'W
Jefferson City	38°34'N	92°10'W	Tennessee	37°04'N	88°33'W
Juan de Fuca, Strait of	48°18'N	124°00'W	Texas	31°30'N	99°00'W
Juneau	58°20'N	134°27'W	The Everglades	26°00'N	80°40'W
Kansas	38°30'N	98°15'W	Toledo	41°39'N	83°33'W
Kansas City	39°05'N	94°34'W	Topeka	39°02'N	95°40'W
Kentucky	37°30'N	85°15'W	Trenton	40°13'N	74°44'W
Knoxville	35°57'N	83°55'W	Tucson	32°13'N	110°55'W
Lansing	42°43'N	84°33'W	Tulsa	36°09'N	95°59'W
Las Vegas	36°10'N	115°08'W	Utah	39°30'N	111°30'W
Lincoln	40°48'N	96°40'W	Vermont	43°50'N	72°45'W
Little Rock	34°44'N	92°17'W	Virginia	37°30'N	78°45'W
Long Beach	33°46'N	118°11'W	Washington	38°53'N	77°02'W
Long Island	40°50'N	73°00'W	Washington	47°30'N	120°30'W
Los Angeles	34°03'N	118°14'W	Washington, Mount	44°15'N	71°15'W
Louisiana	31°15'N	92°15'W	West Palm Beach	26°42'N	80°03'W
Louisville	38°15'N	85°45'W	West Virginia	38°45'N	80°30'W
McKinley, Mount	63°30'N	151°00'W	Whitney, Mount	36°35'N	118°18'W
Madison	43°04'N	89°24'W	Wichita	37°41'N	97°20'W
Maine	45°15'N	69°15'W	Wisconsin	44°45'N	89°30'W
Maryland	39°00'N	76°45'W	Woods, Lake of the	49°15'N	94°45'W
Massachusetts	42°20'N	71°50'W	Worcester	42°15'N	71°48'W
Memphis	35°08'N	90°02'W	Wyoming	43°00'N	107°30'W
Mexico, Gulf of	25°00'N	90°00'W	Youngstown	41°05'N	80°38'W
			Yukon	62°33'N	163°59'W

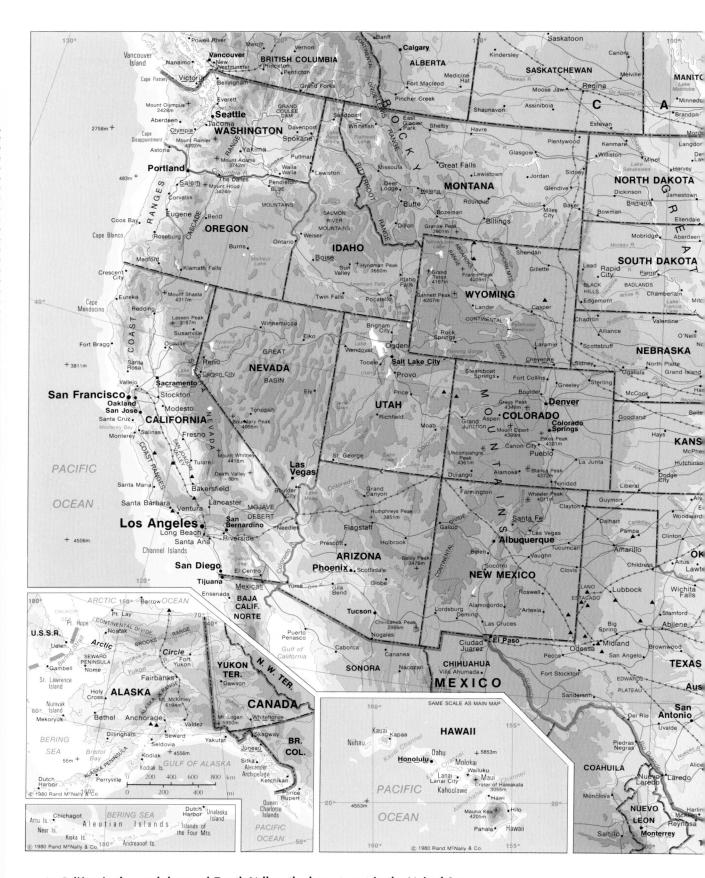

In California the sand dunes of Death Valley, the lowest spot in the United States, lie in the shadow of the Sierra Mountains, illustrating the extremes of the United States landscape.

Sunshine Peak, shown above, stands over 14,000 (4,267 meters) feet high. It is one of the highest peaks in the San Juan Mountains of southwest Colorado, which are a part of the Rocky Mountains.

Orange, Vermont, a typical New England community, reflects the traditional image of the region's scenic beauty and quiet atmosphere.

The cypress trees of Winter Haven, shown below, flourish in the subtropics of Florida, attesting to the range of climates found in a land that encompasses Arctic wastes and fertile plains.

Places and Possessions of the United States

Entity	Status	Area	Population	Capital/Population
American Samoa South Pacific islands)	Unincorporated territory	77 mi² (199 km²)	35,000	Pago Pago/3,075
Guam (North Pacific island)	Unincorporated territory	209 mi² (541 km²)	116,000	Agana/896
Johnston Atoll (North Pacific)	Unincorporated territory	1.2 mi² (3.0 km²)	300	None
Marshall Islands (North Pacific)	Part of Trust Territory of the Pacific Islands	70 mi² (181 km²)	34,000	Majuro (island)
Micronesia, Federated States of (North Pacific Islands)	Part of Trust Territory of the Pacific Islands	271 mi² (702 km²)	80,000	Kolonia/5,549
Midway Islands (North Pacific)	Unincorporated territory	2 mi² (5.2 km²)	500	None
Northern Mariana Islands (North Pacific)	Part of Trust Territory of the Pacific Islands	184 mi² (477 km²)	19,000	Saipan (island)
Pacific Islands, Trust Territory of the (North Pacific)	UN trusteeship under United States administration	717 mi² (1,857 km²)	146,000	Saipan
Palau (North Pacific islands)	Part of Trust Territory of the Pacific islands	192 mi² (497 km²)	13,000	Koror/6,222
Puerto Rico (Caribbean island)	Commonwealth	3,515 mi² (9,103 km²)	3,350,000	San Juan/422,701
Virgin Islands, United States (Caribbean Sea)	Unincorporated territory	133 mi² (344 km²)	105,000	Charlotte Amalie/11,842
Wake Island (North Pacific)	Unincorporated territory	3 mi² (7.8 km²)	300	None

**The Grand Canyon, Arizona, shown above, is the world's most stunning exhibition of the erosive power of running water.
This spectacular formation was carved over a period of ten million years. In its present form, it is 277 miles (446 kilometers)
long, 600 feet (183 meters) to 18 miles (29 kilometers) wide, with a maximum depth of 6,000 feet (1,829 meters).**

URUGUAY

OFFICIAL NAME Oriental Republic of Uruguay

PEOPLE

Population 2,930,000.
Density 43/mi² (17/km²).
Urban 84%.
Capital Montevideo, 1,229,748.
Ethnic groups White 85–90%, mestizo 5–10%, black 3–5%.
Languages Spanish.
Religions Roman Catholic 66%, Protestant 2%, Jewish 2%, others 30%.
Life expectancy 74 female, 69 male.
Literacy 94%.

POLITICS

Government Republic.
Parties Colorado, National.
Suffrage Universal, over 18.
Memberships OAS, UN.
Subdivisions 19 departments.

ECONOMY

GDP $9,400,000,000.
Per capita $3,201.
Monetary unit Nuevo peso.
Trade partners Brazil, Argentina, U.S., West Germany, other Western European countries.
Exports Wool, hides, meat, textiles, leather products.
Imports Petroleum, machinery, transportation equipment, chemicals, metals.

LAND

Description Southern South America.
Area 68,037 mi² (176,215 km²).
Highest point Mt. Catedral, 1,686 ft. (514 m).
Lowest point Sea level.

PEOPLE. Most Uruguayans are white descendants of nineteenth- and twentieth-century immigrants from Spain, Italy, and other European countries. Mestizos, of Spanish-Indian ancestry, and blacks round out the population. Spanish is the official language, and Roman Catholicism is the major religion, with small Protestant and Jewish minorities. Many Uruguayans claim to follow no religion.

ECONOMY AND THE LAND. Uruguay's fertile soil, grassy plains, and temperate climate provide the basis for agriculture and are especially conducive to livestock raising. The country has virtually no mineral resources, and petroleum exploration has been unrewarding. However, refinement of imported fuel is a major industry, and Uruguay has significant hydroelectric potential.

HISTORY AND POLITICS. Uruguay's original inhabitants were Indians. The first European settlement was established by the Portuguese in the 1680s, followed by a Spanish settlement in the 1720s. By the 1770s Spain had gained control of the area, but in the 1820s Portugal once again came to power, annexing present-day Uruguay to Brazil. Nationalistic feelings in the early nineteenth century led to an 1828 war by Uruguayan patriots and Argentina against Brazil, and independence was achieved. Political instability continued until progressive programs were established in the early twentieth century, leading to increased immigration from Mediterranean Europe. Political unrest, caused in part by economic depression, resurfaced in the 1970s, leading to military intervention in the government. ∎

Uruguay Map Index

	Lat.	Long.		Lat.	Long.
Aceguá	31°52′S	54°12′W	Merinos	32°24′S	56°54′W
Aiguá	34°12′S	54°45′W	Minas	34°23′S	55°14′W
Animas Mountain	34°46′S	55°19′W	Mirim Lagoon	32°45′S	52°50′W
Ansina	31°54′S	55°28′W	Montevideo	34°53′S	56°11′W
Arapey	30°58′S	57°32′W	Negro	33°24′S	58°22′W
Artigas	30°24′S	56°28′W	Nueva Palmira	33°53′S	58°25′W
Atlantida	34°46′S	55°45′W	Palermo	33°48′S	55°59′W
Baltasar Brum	30°44′S	57°19′W	Palmitas	33°31′S	57°49′W
Belén	30°47′S	57°47′W	Pando	34°43′S	55°57′W
Cardozo	32°38′S	56°21′W	Paso del Cerro	31°29′S	55°50′W
Carlos Reyles	33°03′S	56°29′W	Paso de los		
Carmelo	34°00′S	58°17′W	Toros	32°49′S	56°31′W
Cebollati	33°16′S	53°47′W	Paysandú	32°19′S	58°05′W
Cerro Chato	33°06′S	55°08′W	Piedra Sola	32°04′S	56°21′W
Cerro Colorado	33°52′S	55°33′W	Plata, Rio de la	35°00′S	57°00′W
Chapicuy	31°39′S	57°54′W	Puntas del Sauce	33°51′S	57°01′W
Chuy	33°41′S	53°27′W	Quebracho	31°57′S	57°53′W
Colón	33°53′S	54°43′W	Retamosa	33°35′S	54°44′W
Colonia del			Rio Branco	32°34′S	53°25′W
Sacramento	34°28′S	57°51′W	Río Negro		
Colonia Lavallesa	31°06′S	57°01′W	Reservoir	32°45′S	56°00′W
Curtina	32°09′S	56°07′W	Rivera	30°54′S	55°31′W
Dolores	33°33′S	58°13′W	Rocha	34°29′S	54°20′W
Durazno	33°22′S	56°31′W	Salto	31°23′S	57°58′W
Florencio			San Gregorio	32°37′S	55°40′W
Sanchez	33°53′S	57°24′W	San José de		
Florida	34°06′S	56°13′W	Mayo	34°30′S	56°42′W
Fraile Muerto	32°31′S	54°32′W	Santa Ana Hills	31°15′S	55°15′W
Francia	32°33′S	56°37′W	Santa Clara de		
Fray Bentos	33°08′S	58°18′W	Olimar	32°55′S	54°58′W
Fray Marcos	34°11′S	55°15′W	Santa Lucia	34°27′S	56°24′W
Goñi	33°31′S	56°24′W	Sarandí del Yi	33°21′S	55°38′W
Grand Hills	33°15′S	55°07′W	Tacuarembó	31°44′S	55°59′W
Guareim	30°12′S	57°36′W	Tranqueras	31°12′S	55°45′W
Guichón	32°21′S	57°12′W	Treinta y Tres	33°14′S	54°23′W
José Battle y			Trinidad	33°32′S	56°54′W
Ordóñez	33°28′S	55°07′W	Uruguay	34°12′S	58°18′W
Juan L. Lacaze	34°26′S	57°27′W	Valle Edén	31°50′S	56°09′W
La Cruz	33°58′S	56°15′W	Velázquez	34°02′S	54°17′W
La Paz	34°46′S	56°15′W	Vergara	32°56′S	53°57′W
Lascano	33°40′S	54°12′W	Yaguarí	31°31′S	54°58′W
Las Piedras	34°44′S	56°13′W	Yaguarón	32°39′S	53°12′W
Maldonado	34°54′S	54°57′W	Yi	33°07′S	57°08′W
Melo	32°22′S	54°11′W	Young	32°41′S	57°38′W
Mercedes	33°16′S	58°01′W			

Montevideo, set in a bay on the shore of the Rio de la Plata, is the capital, major port and the industrial center of Uruguay.

VANUATU

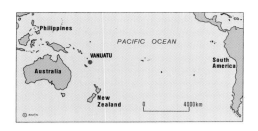

OFFICIAL NAME Republic of
Vanuatu

PEOPLE
Population 130,000.
Density 23/mi² (8.8/km²).
Urban 18%.
Capital Port Vila, Efate I., 10,158.
Ethnic groups Melanesian 90%, French 8%.
Languages Bislama, English, French.
Religions Christian.
Literacy 10–20%.

POLITICS
Government Republic.
Parties National.
Memberships CW, UN.
Subdivisions 4 districts.

ECONOMY
Monetary unit Vatu.
Trade partners Australia, France, Japan.
Exports Copra, frozen fish, meat.
Imports Food, manufactured goods, fuels.

LAND
Description South Pacific islands.
Area 5,714 mi² (14,800 km²).

Highest point Mt. Tabwemasana, Espiritu Santo I.,
6,165 ft (1,879 m).
Lowest point Sea level.

PEOPLE. The majority of Vanuatuans are Melanesian, with Asian, European, and Polynesian
minorities. Languages include English and
French, the languages of former rulers; and
Bislama, a mixture of English and Melanesian.

ECONOMY AND THE LAND. The economy is
based on agriculture, and copra is the primary
export crop. The more than eighty islands of
Vanuatu are characterized by narrow coastal
plains, mountainous interiors, and a mostly hot,
rainy climate.

HISTORY AND POLITICS. In 1606 Portuguese
explorers encountered indigenous Melanesians
on islands that now compose Vanuatu. In 1774
British captain James Cook named the islands the
New Hebrides. To resolve conflicting interests,
Great Britain and France formed a joint naval
commission to oversee the area in 1887 and a
condominium government in 1906. The New
Hebrides became the independent Republic of
Vanuatu in 1980. ∎

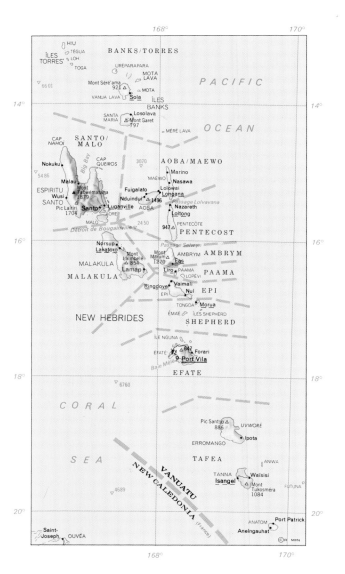

Vanuatu Map Index

	Lat.	Long.		Lat.	Long.
Espiritu Santo	15°15′S	166°50′E	Norsup	16°05′S	167°23′E
Isangel	19°32′S	169°16′E	Port Vila	17°44′S	168°19′E
Lamap	16°26′S	167°43′E	Santo	15°32′S	167°08′E

VATICAN CITY

OFFICIAL NAME State of the
Vatican City

PEOPLE
Population 700.
Density 3,500/mi² (1,750/km²).
Urban 100%.
Capital Vatican City, 700.
Ethnic groups Italian.
Languages Italian, Latin.
Religions Roman Catholic.
Literacy 100%.

POLITICS
Government Ecclesiastical state.
Parties None.
Suffrage Roman Catholic cardinals less than 80 years
old.
Memberships None.
Subdivisions None.

ECONOMY
Monetary unit Italian lira.

LAND
Description Southern Europe, landlocked (within the
city of Rome, Italy).
Area 0.2 mi² (0.4 km²).
Highest point 245 ft (75 m).
Lowest point 62 ft (19 m).

PEOPLE. The Vatican City, the smallest independent state in the world, is the administrative and
spiritual center of the Roman Catholic church,
and the state is the home of the pope, the
church's head. The population of Vatican City is
made up of about five hundred Vatican nationals
plus administrative and diplomatic workers of
more than a dozen nationalities. Italians predominate, but there is a large Swiss population as
well. A number of the Swiss residents are members of the Swiss Guard, a military corps made
up of Roman Catholic citizens of Switzerland.
Roman Catholicism is the state's official religion,
and the official language is Italian, although official acts of the Holy See are drawn up in Latin.

ECONOMY AND THE LAND. The Vatican City
does not engage in commerce per se, but it does
issue its own coins and postage stamps. The
state's income comes from three main sources:
the Istituto per le Opere di Religione; contributions from church members; and interest earned
on the church's investments. Economic problems
include an increasing deficit, caused in part by
salary increases for Vatican employees. Lying on
a hill west of the Tiber River, the Vatican City is
an urban enclave in northwestern Rome, Italy.
The Vatican City enjoys a mild climate moderated
by the Mediterranean Sea.

HISTORY AND POLITICS. For centuries the
popes of the Roman Catholic church ruled the
Papal States, an area across central Italy, which
included Rome. The popes' temporal authority
gradually was reduced to the city of Rome,
which itself was eventually annexed by the Kingdom of Italy in 1870. Denying these rulings, the
pope declared himself a prisoner in the Vatican,
a status that lasted fifty-nine years. The Vatican
City has been an independent sovereign state
since 1929, when Italy signed the Treaty of the
Lateran in return for papal dissolution of the
Papal States. The pope heads all branches of government, though day-to-day responsibilities are
delegated to staff members. ∎

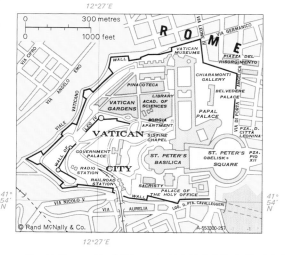

Vatican City Map Index

	Lat.	Long.		Lat.	Long.
Belvedere Palace	41°54′N	12°27′E	Saint Peter's		
Saint Peter's			Square	41°54′N	12°27′E
Basilica	41°54′N	12°27′E	Sistine Chapel	41°54′N	12°27′E

VENEZUELA

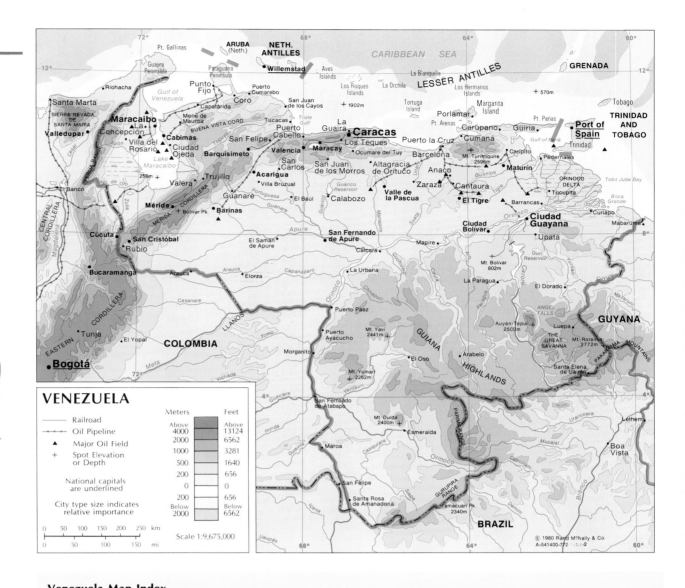

VENEZUELA

	Meters	Feet
Railroad	Above 4000	Above 13124
Oil Pipeline	2000	6562
▲ Major Oil Field	1000	3281
+ Spot Elevation or Depth	500	1640
	200	656
National capitals are underlined	0	0
	200 Below 2000	656 Below 6562
City type size indicates relative importance		

Scale 1:9,675,000

© 1980 Rand McNally & Co.
A-541400-772 -L1-2

OFFICIAL NAME Republic of
Venezuela

PEOPLE
Population 16,040,000.
Density 46/mi² (18/km²).
Urban 76%.
Capital Caracas, 3,041,000.
Ethnic groups Mestizo 67%, white 21%, black 10%,
Indian 2%.
Languages Spanish.
Religions Roman Catholic 96%, Protestant 2%.
Life expectancy 70 female, 66 male.
Literacy 86%.

POLITICS
Government Republic.
Parties Democratic Action, Movement Toward
Socialism, Social Christian.
Suffrage Universal, over 18.
Memberships OAS, OPEC, UN.
Subdivisions 20 states, 2 federal territories, 2 federal
areas.

ECONOMY
GDP $69,300,000,000.
Per capita $4,716.
Monetary unit Bolívar.
Trade partners U.S., Canada, West Germany, Japan,
Italy.
Exports Petroleum, iron ore.
Imports Machinery, transportation equipment,
manufactured goods, chemicals, food.

LAND
Description Northern South America.
Area 352,144 mi² (912,050 km²).
Highest point Bolívar Pk., 16,427 ft (5,007 m).
Lowest point Sea level.

PEOPLE. Spanish colonial rule of Venezuela is
reflected in its predominantly mestizo population, of Spanish-Indian blood, and its official language of Spanish. Minorities include Europeans,
blacks, and Indians, who generally speak local
languages. Nearly all Venezuelans are Roman
Catholic, further evidence of former Spanish
domination. Protestants and lesser numbers of
Jews and Muslims compose small minorities, and
traditional religious practices continue among
some Indians.

ECONOMY AND THE LAND. Since the expansion of the petroleum industry in the 1920s, Venezuela has experienced rapid economic growth,
but the economy has been hampered by uneven-
ly distributed wealth, a high birthrate, and fluctuations in the price of oil. Partly because of the
emphasis on oil production, agriculture has declined; its contribution to the gross national
product is minimal, and Venezuela must import
much of its food. Manufacturing and hydroelectric power are being developed. The varied
Venezuelan landscape is dominated by the
Andes Mountains, a coastal zone, high plateaus,
and plains, or llanos. The climate is tropical, but
temperatures vary with altitude. Most of the
country experiences rainy and dry seasons.

Venezuela Map Index

	Lat.	Long.		Lat.	Long.		Lat.	Long.		Lat.	Long.
Acarigua	9°33′N	69°12′W	Cumaná	10°28′N	64°10′W	Maroa	2°43′N	67°33′W	San Carlos	9°40′N	68°36′W
Altagracia de			Curiapo	8°33′N	61°00′W	Maturín	9°45′N	63°11′W	San Cristóbal	7°46′N	72°14′W
Orituco	9°52′N	66°23′W	Cuyuni	6°57′N	60°20′W	Mene de Mauroa	10°43′N	71°01′W	San Felipe	10°20′N	68°44′W
Anaco	9°27′N	64°28′W	El Baúl	8°57′N	68°17′W	Mérida	8°36′N	71°08′W	San Fernando de		
Angel Falls	5°57′N	62°30′W	El Dorado	6°44′N	61°38′W	Mérida Cordillera	8°40′N	71°00′W	Apure	7°54′N	67°28′W
Apure	7°37′N	66°25′W	Elorza	7°03′N	69°31′W	Meta	6°12′N	67°28′W	San Fernando de		
Arabelo	4°55′N	64°13′W	El Oso	4°59′N	65°25′W	Morganito	5°04′N	67°44′W	Atabapo	4°03′N	67°42′W
Arauca	7°24′N	66°35′W	El Samán de			Ocumare del Tuy	10°07′N	66°46′W	San Juan de los		
Auyán-Tepuí	5°55′N	62°32′W	Apure	7°55′N	68°44′W	Orinoco	8°37′N	62°15′W	Cayos	11°10′N	68°25′W
Barcelona	10°08′N	64°42′W	El Tigre	8°55′N	64°15′W	Orinoco Delta	9°15′N	61°30′W	San Juan de los		
Barinas	8°38′N	70°12′W	Esmeralda	3°10′N	65°33′W	Pakaraima			Morros	9°55′N	67°21′W
Barquisimeto	10°04′N	69°19′W	Guanare	9°03′N	69°45′W	Mountains	5°30′N	60°40′W	Santa Elena de		
Barrancas	8°42′N	62°11′W	Guárico Reservoir	9°05′N	67°25′W	Paraguaná			Uairén	4°37′N	61°08′W
Bolívar Peak	8°30′N	71°02′W	Guiana Highlands	5°00′N	64°00′W	Peninsula	11°55′N	70°00′W	Santa Rosa de		
Cabimas	10°23′N	71°28′W	Guiria	10°34′N	62°18′W	Paria, Gulf of	10°20′N	62°00′W	Amanadona	1°29′N	66°55′W
Caicara	7°37′N	66°10′W	Guri Reservoir	7°30′N	62°50′W	Parima Range	2°30′N	64°00′W	Trujillo	9°22′N	70°26′W
Calabozo	8°56′N	67°26′W	La Concepción	10°38′N	71°50′W	Pedernales	9°58′N	62°16′W	Tucacas	10°48′N	68°19′W
Cantaura	9°19′N	64°21′W	La Guaira	10°36′N	66°56′W	Peñas, Point	10°40′N	61°40′W	Tucupita	9°04′N	62°03′W
Capatárida	11°11′N	70°37′W	La Paragua	6°50′N	63°20′W	Perija Range	10°00′N	73°00′W	Upata	8°01′N	62°24′W
Caracas	10°30′N	66°56′W	La Urbana	7°08′N	66°56′W	Porlamar	10°57′N	63°51′W	Valencia	10°11′N	68°00′W
Caripito	10°08′N	63°06′W	Llanos	5°00′N	70°00′W	Portuguesa	7°57′N	67°32′W	Valera	9°19′N	70°37′W
Caroní	8°21′N	62°43′W	Los Teques	10°21′N	67°02′W	Puerto Ayacucho	5°40′N	67°35′W	Valle de la		
Carúpano	10°40′N	63°14′W	Luepa	5°43′N	61°31′W	Puerto Cabello	10°28′N	68°01′W	Pascua	9°13′N	66°00′W
Casiquiare	2°01′N	67°07′W	Mapire	7°45′N	64°42′W	Puerto Cumarebo	11°29′N	69°21′W	Venezuela, Gulf of		
Ciudad Bolívar	8°08′N	63°33′W	Maracaibo	10°40′N	71°37′W	Puerto la Cruz	10°13′N	64°38′W		11°30′N	71°00′W
Ciudad Guayana	8°22′N	62°40′W	Maracaibo, Lake	9°50′N	71°30′W	Puerto Páez	6°13′N	67°28′W	Villa Bruzual	9°20′N	69°06′W
Ciudad Ojeda	10°12′N	71°19′W	Maracay	10°15′N	67°36′W	Punto Fijo	11°42′N	70°13′W	Villa del Rosario	10°19′N	72°19′W
Coro	11°25′N	69°41′W	Margarita Island	11°00′N	64°00′W	Rubio	7°43′N	72°22′W	Zaraza	9°21′N	65°19′W

HISTORY AND POLITICS. The original inhabitants of modern Venezuela included Arawak and
Carib Indians. In 1498 Christopher Columbus
was the first European to visit Venezuela. The
area became a colony of Spain and was briefly
under German rule. Independence was achieved
in 1821 under the guidance of Simón Bolívar,
Venezuela's national hero. Venezuela became a
sovereign state in 1830. The nineteenth century
saw political instability and revolutionary fervor,
followed by a succession of dictators in the twentieth century. Since 1958 Venezuela has tried to
achieve a representative form of government
and has held a number of democratic elections.
Venezuela supported Argentina during that
country's 1982 conflict with Britain over the Falkland Islands, and the current Venezuelan administration aims at closer relations with the countries of the Caribbean. ■

**The Laguna Canaima, with its spectacular waterfalls and
pristine jungle, is the focal point of Canaima National
Park, about 250 miles (402 kilometers) southeast of
Caracas.**

VIETNAM

OFFICIAL NAME Socialist
Republic of Vietnam

PEOPLE
Population 58,930,000.
Density 463/mi² (179/km²).
Urban 19%.
Capital Hanoi, 819,913.
Ethnic groups Vietnamese 85–90%, Chinese 3%.
Languages Vietnamese.
Religions Buddhist, Confucian, Taoist, Roman
  Catholic, animist, Muslim.
Life expectancy 54 female, 51 male.
Literacy 78%.

POLITICS
Government Socialist republic.
Parties Communist.
Suffrage Universal, over 18.
Memberships CEMA. UN.
Subdivisions 39 provinces, 3 municipalities, 1 special
  zone.

ECONOMY
GNP $10,700,000,000.
Per capita $189.
Monetary unit Dông.
Trade partners U.S.S.R., Eastern European countries,
  Japan.
Exports Agricultural products, handicrafts, coal,
  minerals.
Imports Petroleum, steel products, railroad
  equipment, chemicals, medicines.

LAND
Description Southeastern Asia.
Area 127,242 mi² (329,556 km²).
Highest point Fan Si Pan, 10,312 ft (3,143 m).
Lowest point Sea level.

PEOPLE. Despite centuries of foreign invasion
and domination, the people of Vietnam remain
remarkably homogeneous. Ethnic Vietnamese,
basically a Mongoloid group, compose the majority population. Chinese make up a minority, re-
siding mainly in urban areas, but in 1979, following the eruption of violence along the Vietnam-
China border, many of the Chinese residents fled
the country. Other minorities include tribal
groups that inhabit the nation's highland regions, among them the northern Nung, Meo,
Tahi, Muong, and Man and the southern Monta-
gnards. Although the government does not encourage religious activity, many Vietnamese continue to practice their faiths. Chinese influence
can still be seen in the majority religions of Taoism, Confucianism, and Buddhism, and Islam
and Roman Catholicism are practiced as well,
often influenced by traditions of animism and
ancestor worship. The official language of the
country is Vietnamese, but a history of foreign
intervention is reflected in the wide use of
French, English, Chinese, and Russian.

ECONOMY AND THE LAND. Since the unification of the nation in 1975, the economy has
made great progress toward recovery from the
devastation of war, although the economy of the

Vietnam Map Index

	Lat.	Long.		Lat.	Long.
Annamese			Hon Gay	20°57′N	107°05′E
Cordillera	17°00′N	106°00′E	Hue	16°28′N	107°36′E
Bac Lieu	9°17′N	105°44′E	*Kontum Plateau*	13°55′N	108°05′E
Bac Ninh	21°11′N	106°03′E	Lac Giao	12°40′N	108°03′E
Ca	18°46′N	105°47′E	*Linh Peak*	15°04′N	107°59′E
Ca Mau, Point	8°38′N	104°44′E	Long Xuyen	10°23′N	105°25′E
Cam Pha	21°01′N	107°19′E	*Ma*	19°47′N	105°56′E
Cam Ranh	11°54′N	109°09′E	*Mekong*	10°33′N	105°24′E
Can Tho	10°02′N	105°47′E	My Tho	10°21′N	106°21′E
Chau Phu	10°42′N	105°07′E	Nam Dinh	20°25′N	106°10′E
Con Son	8°43′N	106°36′E	Nha Thang	12°15′N	109°11′E
Da	21°15′N	105°20′E	Ninh Binh	20°15′N	105°59′E
Dac Lac Plateau	12°50′N	108°05′E	Phan Rang	11°34′N	108°59′E
Da Lat	11°56′N	108°25′E	Phan Thiet	10°56′N	108°06′E
Da Nang	16°04′N	108°13′E	*Phu Quoc*	10°12′N	104°00′E
Fan Si Pan	22°15′N	103°46′E	Phu Vinh	9°56′N	106°20′E
Gia Dinh	10°48′N	106°42′E	Qui Nhon	13°46′N	109°14′E
Ha Giang	22°50′N	104°59′E	Rach Gia	10°01′N	105°05′E
Hai Duong	20°56′N	106°19′E	Son Tay	21°08′N	105°30′E
Haiphong	20°52′N	106°41′E	Thai Nguyen	21°36′N	105°50′E
Hanoi	21°02′N	105°51′E	Thanh Hoa	19°48′N	105°46′E
Hoa Binh	20°50′N	105°20′E	Viet Tri	21°18′N	105°26′E
Ho Chi Minh City	10°45′N	106°40′E	Vinh	18°40′N	105°40′E
			Vinh Long	10°15′N	105°58′E

north, with its established state-controlled economic system, remains distinct from that of the
south, with its history of private enterprise. Agriculture is centered in the fertile southern
plains, and the farm industry continues to employ nearly 70 percent of the people. Following
unification, a program of collectivization was implemented in the south, cultivated land was expanded, and urban residents were relocated to
rural areas to provide a labor force for the new
farmlands and cooperatives. The government has
since returned small plots to the peasant farmers
in an attempt to relieve some of the problems
caused by collectivization. Rice is the staple food
crop, and in 1983 the country was self-sufficient
in food production for the first time in its history. Northern Vietnam is rich in mineral resources, but expansion of the war-damaged mining industry has been slowed by lack of skilled
personnel and a poor transportation network.
The north is also the site of most of the nation's
industrial development, and although United
States bombing raids during the war destroyed
nearly 70 percent of Vietnam's industrial resources, the country has recovered much of its
losses. Despite its potential, Vietnam's economic
picture is not likely to improve until the country
can resolve its political and social problems. In
addition, the nation is vulnerable to natural disaster and afflicted by rapid population growth.
Forested mountains and high plateaus mark the
landscape of Vietnam, and the climate is tropical.

HISTORY AND POLITICS. The first Vietnamese
were Mongoloid immigrants from China and Indonesia. Centuries of rule by the Chinese came
to an end in the 1400s when Vietnam gained
independence, but civil strife continued for nearly two centuries. French missionary activity
began in the early seventeenth century, and by
1883 all of present-day Vietnam, Kampuchea,
and Laos were under French rule. During World
War II, until its defeat in 1945, Japan occupied
French Indochina. In the confusion following the
war, Communist leader Ho Chi Minh, founder of
a Vietnamese independence movement, entered
Hanoi and declared Vietnam an independent republic. The republic came to an end in 1946 with
the arrival of the French military, but the struggle for independence continued, with Ho Chi
Minh's supporters opposed by French and Vietnamese forces armed by the United States. In
1954 Ho Chi Minh gained control of the north,
and a subsequent agreement reached in Geneva
divided the country into North and South Vietnam, pending national elections. Fearful of a
Communist victory in the upcoming elections, in
1955 Ngo Dinh Diem declared the south an independent republic with himself as president, effec-
tively suppressing all opposition. He was, however, unable to eliminate the influence of the
northern Communists; United States support of

This street scene in Nha Trang, a city on the mountainous southeast coast reflects two problems common to
many regions in Vietnam. There is overcrowding because of the influx of refugees from agricultural areas to
the south, and there is a lack of adequate transportation
with which to efficiently move goods between the widely separated interdependent parts of the country.

the south increased, and uprisings and rebellions
escalated into a war. Communist victory and
unification of the country as the Socialist Republic of Vietnam was achieved in 1975. Vietnamese
military policy has resulted in armed conflict
with China and the occupation of Kampuchea,
and the country remains dependent on aid from
both Communist and non-Communist states. ■

VIRGIN ISLANDS, BRITISH

OFFICIAL NAME British Virgin Islands

PEOPLE
Population 13,000.
Density 220/mi² (85/km²).
Urban 12%.
Capital Road Town, Tortola I., 2,479.
Ethnic groups Black.
Languages English.
Religions Methodist, Anglican, Church of God.
Literacy 98%.

POLITICS
Government Colony (U.K.).
Parties Independent, United, Virgin Islands.
Suffrage Universal, over 18.

ECONOMY
GNP $77,100,000.
Per capita $5,900.
Monetary unit U.S. dollar.
Trade partners Virgin Islands (U.S.), U.S.
Exports Fish, sand and gravel, fruits and vegetables.
Imports Automobiles, foodstuffs, building materials, machinery.

LAND
Description Caribbean islands.
Area 59 mi² (153 km²).
Highest point Mt. Sage, Tortola I., 1,730 ft (527 m).
Lowest point Sea level.

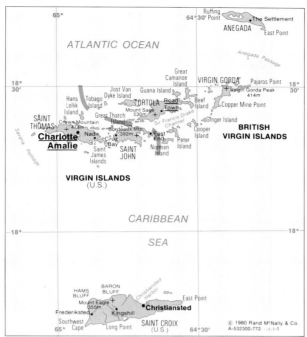

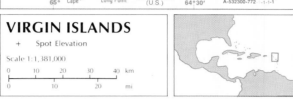

VIRGIN ISLANDS
+ Spot Elevation
Scale 1:1,381,000

© 1980 Rand McNally & Co.
A-532300-772 -1-1-1

Virgin Islands Map Index

	Lat.	Long.		Lat.	Long.
Anegada	18°45'N	64°20'W	Road Town	18°27'N	64°37'W
Anegada Passage	18°30'N	63°40'W	Sage, Mount	18°25'N	64°39'W
Charlotte Amalie	18°21'N	64°56'W	Saint Croix	17°45'N	64°45'W
Christiansted	17°45'N	64°42'W	Saint John	18°20'N	64°45'W
Crown Mountain	18°21'N	64°58'W	Saint Thomas	18°21'N	64°55'W
Cruz Bay	18°20'N	64°48'W	Sir Francis Drake		
East End	18°21'N	64°40'W	Channel	18°25'N	64°30'W
Frederiksted	17°43'N	64°53'W	The Settlement	18°44'N	64°19'W
Kingshill	17°44'N	64°48'W	Tortola	18°27'N	64°36'W
Nadir	18°19'N	64°53'W	Virgin Gorda	18°30'N	64°24'W

VIRGIN ISLANDS, UNITED STATES

OFFICIAL NAME Virgin Islands of the United States

PEOPLE
Population 105,000.
Density 789/mi² (305/km²).
Urban 39%.
Capital Charlotte Amalie, St. Thomas I., 11,842.
Ethnic groups Black, Hispanic, White.
Languages English, Spanish.
Religions Protestant, Roman Catholic.

POLITICS
Government Unincorporated territory (U.S.).
Suffrage Universal, over 18.
Subdivisions 3 islands.

ECONOMY
GNP $890,000,000.
Per capita $8,470.
Monetary unit U.S. dollar.
Trade partners U.S., Soviet Union, Nigeria.
Exports Manufactured goods, chemicals.
Imports Fuels, foodstuffs, manufactured goods.

LAND
Description Caribbean islands.
Area 133 mi² (344 km²).
Highest point Crown Mtn., St. Thomas I., 1,556 (474 m).
Lowest point Sea level.

WAKE ISLAND

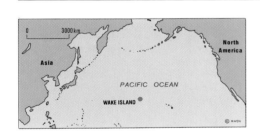

OFFICIAL NAME Wake Island

PEOPLE
Population 300.
Density 100/mi² (38/km²).
Ethnic groups American.
Languages English

POLITICS
Government Unincorporated territory (U.S.).

LAND
Description North Pacific island.
Area 3.0 mi² (7.8 km²).
Highest point 21 ft (6 m).
Lowest point Sea level.

PEOPLE.   A possession of the United States, Wake Island has a population of about three hundred employees of the United States government and military. The three islets have no indigenous population, and there are no ethnic groups other than the Americans. For a period of several months during 1975, however, a large group of Vietnamese refugees en route to the United States were held here until transportation could be arranged. The United States government has considered using Wake Island as the

relocation site for former inhabitants of the Bikini Atoll, which will remain uninhabitable well into the twenty-first century because of radiation resulting from United States nuclear weapons tests.

ECONOMY AND THE LAND.   Wake Island is a United States military base and the site of an American weather station. The work force consists of air force personnel, civilians employed by the air force, and employees of the National Oceanographic and Atmospheric Association. Commercial as well as military flights use Wake Island as a stopover, generally only in emergency situations during flights from Honolulu to Tokyo or Guam. The atoll, situated midway between Hawaii and Guam, is made up of three islets: Wake, Peale, and Wilkes. The climate is tropical, with occasional typhoons.

HISTORY AND POLITICS.   Pacific tradition holds that early Marshall Islanders used the three islets as a collection ground for birds and turtles. The first European to arrive was the Spanish explorer Mendana, who came in 1568 and found the atoll uninhabited. More than two centuries later, in 1796, the British sea captain William Wake reached the island and gave it his name. During the eighteenth century, seafarers knew the atoll as Halcyon and Helsion as well as Wake Island, and a United States expedition led by Commodore Wilkes officially charted Wake Island in 1840. The Americans built a cable relay station on Wake Island in 1899, annexing the island to the United States. The island's significance was its location; a commercial air station, constructed in 1935, provided a stopover for flights to the East, and in 1939, the United States military established a naval and air base. Following the bombing of Pearl Harbor and the capture of

Guam in 1941, the Japanese moved on to seize Wake Island. American bombing raids continued from 1942 until 1945, but the Japanese were able to hold the island, and United States personnel did not return until after the Japanese surrendered to the Allies in 1945. After a period of administration by the United States Federal Aviation Administration, jurisdiction of the island passed to the United States Air Force. Wake Island is currently administered by the air force in conjunction with the United States Department of the Interior. ∎

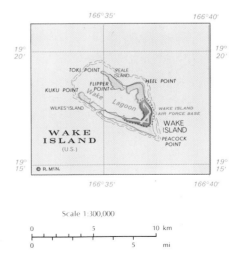

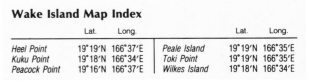

Wake Island Map Index

	Lat.	Long.		Lat.	Long.
Heel Point	19°19'N	166°37'E	Peale Island	19°19'N	166°35'E
Kuku Point	19°18'N	166°34'E	Toki Point	19°19'N	166°35'E
Peacock Point	19°16'N	166°37'E	Wilkes Island	19°18'N	166°34'E

WALLIS AND FUTUNA

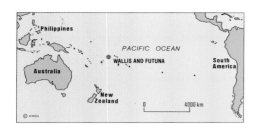

OFFICIAL NAME Territory of the Wallis and Futuna Islands

PEOPLE
Population 12,000.
Density 122/mi² (47/km²).
Capital Mata-Utu, Île Uvéa, 558.
Ethnic groups Polynesian.
Languages French, Wallisian, Futunan.
Religions Roman Catholic.
Life expectancy 63 female, 62 male.

POLITICS
Government Overseas territory (France).
Parties Rally for the Republic, Republican.
Suffrage Universal adult.
Subdivisions 3 districts.

ECONOMY
GNP $7,900,000.
Per capita $650.
Monetary unit CFP franc.

LAND
Description South Pacific islands.
Area 98 mi² (255 km²).
Highest point Mt. Singavi, Île Futuna, 2,500 ft (762 m).
Lowest point Sea level.

PEOPLE. The French overseas territory of Wallis and Futuna consists of two main island groups, and the population is made up of Roman Catholic Polynesians. Despite this seeming homogeneity, each island has its own language. Inhabitants of Wallis Island, known locally as Uvea, speak Wallisian, or East Uvean, a tongue related to Tongan. Futunan, often called East Futunan, is spoken on Futuna Island, and this language is related to Samoan. Although the majority of the people over age forty-five cannot speak French, it remains the official language. The current birthrate in the islands is high, and more than half the population is under twenty years old.

ECONOMY AND THE LAND. Most islanders engage in subsistence activities, and family income comes mainly from government employment or money sent home by emigrants working in New Caledonia. Small-scale crop production can, for the most part, meet the needs of the islanders, but a lack of fertile land, inefficient farming methods, soil depletion, and traditional division of the land into tiny plots leave little hope for the development of a successful farm industry. One-time coconut plantations on Wallis ceased operation following a beetle infestation, and production of copra on Futuna is minimal. Most of the coconut crop is now used to feed pigs and other livestock. Fishing, a traditional food source, remains important throughout the islands and provides the staple of the islanders' diet. Since 1960 the government has attempted programs to improve both agriculture and fishing, but by 1985 the territorial assembly president had declared all such programs a failure. There is potential for a tourism industry; however, local chiefs holding traditional views generally oppose development of the islands for tourism, and hotel facilities and

restaurants remain minimal. Two island groups make up Wallis and Futuna. Wallis consists of a main volcanic island and about nineteen uninhabited islets. Futuna and nearby Alofi were formerly known as the Hoorn Islands. Futuna, not to be confused with the island of Futuna in Vanuatu, is mountainous, and because Alofi has no fresh-water supply, the small island remains without a permanent population. The climate is tropical, with a cyclone season between October and March.

HISTORY AND POLITICS. Wallis was probably settled in the mid-1400s or 1500s by immigrants from Tonga, and rivalry between chiefs marked its early years. The first settlers on Futuna likely came from Samoa, and tradition holds that some inhabitants are descendants of crew members of a Marshall Islands ship that docked on Futuna early in the island's history. In 1616 Dutch mariners reached Futuna and Alofi, naming them the Hoorn Islands for a town in the Netherlands. Captain Samuel Wallis of Britain came to Wallis in 1767, and he was followed by other Europeans in 1781 and 1791. Ongoing contact with Europeans began in the 1820s when many area whalers who came ashore for food and water remained as settlers. French missionaries began their work in the 1830s, and after initial hostilities and the murder of a priest on Futuna, Roman Catholicism was universally accepted on the islands. In 1842 local chiefs requested protection from the French government, and Wallis and Futuna became a French protectorate in 1887. Following a 1959 referendum to change the islands' status, Wallis and Futuna became an overseas territory of France in 1961. ∎

WESTERN SAHARA

OFFICIAL NAME Western Sahara

PEOPLE
Population 170,000.
Density 1.7/mi² (0.6/km²).
Capital El Aaiún, 20,000.
Ethnic groups Arab, Berber.
Languages Arabic.
Religions Muslim.
Literacy Saharans, 5%; Moroccans, 20%.

POLITICS
Government Occupied by Morocco.
Parties Polisario Front.
Memberships OAU.

ECONOMY
Monetary unit Moroccan dirham, Mauritanian ouguiya.
Trade partners Controlled by Morocco.

Exports Phosphates.
Imports Fuels, food.

LAND
Description Northwestern Africa.
Area 102,703 mi² (266,000 km²).
Highest point 2,640 ft (805 m).
Lowest point Sea level.

PEOPLE. Most Western Saharans are nomadic Arabs or Berbers. Because these nomads often cross national borders in their wanderings, the population of Western Sahara is in a constant state of flux. Islam is the principal religion, and Arabic is the dominant language.

ECONOMY AND THE LAND. Most of Western Sahara is barren, rocky desert, with a sandy soil that severely limits agriculture. Mining of major phosphate deposits began in 1972; phosphates are now the primary export. Western Sahara is almost completely arid; rainfall is negligible except along the coast.

HISTORY AND POLITICS. By the fourth century B.C. Phoenicians and Romans had visited the area. Spain explored the region in the sixteenth century and gained control of the region in 1860. Spanish Sahara was designated a province of Spain in 1958. Spanish control ceased in 1976, and the area became known as Western Sahara. Mauritania and Morocco subsequently divided the territory, and Morocco gained control of valuable phosphate deposits. Fighting soon broke out between an independence movement, the Polisario Front, and troops from Morocco and Mauritania. In 1979 Mauritania gave up its claim to the area and withdrew. Morocco claimed the territory that Mauritania had given up; fighting between Morocco and the Polisario Front continued into the 1980s. ∎

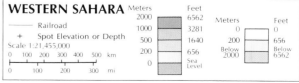

WESTERN SAHARA

	Meters	Feet
Railroad	2000	6562
+ Spot Elevation or Depth	1000	3281
Scale 1:21,455,000	500	1640
	200	656
	0	Sea Level

Meters	Feet
200	0
Below 2000	656
	Below 6562

0 100 200 300 400 500 km
0 100 200 300 mi

Western Sahara Map Index

	Lat.	Long.		Lat.	Long.
Barbas, Cape	22°18'N	16°41'W	El Aaiún	27°09'N	13°12'W
Bojador, Cape	26°08'N	14°30'W	Semara	26°44'N	11°41'W
Dakhla	23°43'N	15°57'W			

WESTERN SAMOA

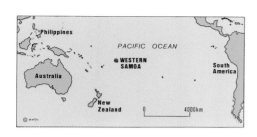

OFFICIAL NAME Independent State of Western Samoa

PEOPLE
Population 160,000.
Density 146/mi² (56/km²).
Urban 21%.
Capital Apia, Upolu I., 33,784.
Ethnic groups Samoan, Euronesian.
Languages Samoan, English.
Religions Christian.
Life expectancy 64 female, 61 male.
Literacy 90%.

POLITICS
Government Constitutional monarchy.
Parties None.
Suffrage 45 members of Legislative Assembly elected by matais, 2 elected by adults without traditional family ties.
Memberships CW, UN.
Subdivisions 21 districts.

ECONOMY
GNP $130,000,000.
Per capita $770.
Monetary unit Talà.
Trade partners New Zealand, U.S., Australia, West Germany.

Exports Copra, cocoa, wood, bananas.
Imports Food, manufactured goods, petroleum, machinery.

LAND
Description South Pacific islands.
Area 1,097 mi² (2,842 km²).
Highest point Mauga Silisili, Savai'i I., 6,096 ft (1,858 m).
Lowest point Sea level.

PEOPLE. Most Western Samoans are of Polynesian descent, and a significant minority are of mixed Samoan and European heritage. The majority of Western Samoans are Christian and practice a variety of faiths introduced by European missionaries and traders. Samoan, a Polynesian tongue, is the principal language, but English is spoken by the islands' urban residents and younger inhabitants. The population is concentrated on the main islands of Upolu and Savai'i.

ECONOMY AND THE LAND. The tropical climate of Western Samoa is suited for agriculture, which is the country's chief economic reliance. Bananas, coconuts, and tropical fruits are the most important crops. Western Samoa is made up of the large islands of Upolu and Savai'i, the smaller islands of Manono and Apolima, and several uninhabited islets. The islands are volcanic, and much of Savai'i is wasteland created by lava flows.

HISTORY AND POLITICS. Polynesians settled the Samoan islands more than two thousand years ago. Dutch explorers visited the islands in the early 1700s, and English missionaries arrived in 1830. Rivalry between the islands' royal families increased, along with competition for influ-

ence among the United Kingdom, the United States, and Germany. In 1900 the United States annexed Eastern Samoa, and Germany obtained Western Samoa. By the end of World War I, New Zealand had gained control of Western Samoa. Growing demand for independence led to United Nations intervention, and gradual steps toward self-government were taken. The islands became fully independent in 1962. The nation maintains friendly relations with New Zealand and neighboring Pacific islands. ∎

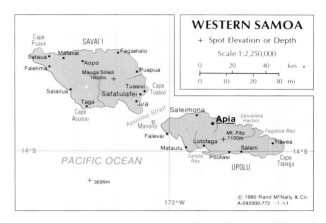

Western Samoa Map Index

	Lat.	Long.		Lat.	Long.
Aopo	13°29'S	172°30'W	Puava, Cape	13°26'S	172°43'W
Apia	13°50'S	171°44'W	Safata Bay	14°00'S	171°50'W
Apolima Strait	14°50'S	172°10'W	Safatulafei	13°40'S	172°07'W
Fagamalo	13°25'S	172°21'W	Salailua	13°41'S	172°34'W
Falelima	13°32'S	172°41'W	Salani	14°00'S	171°33'W
Falevai	13°55'S	171°59'W	Saleimona	13°49'S	171°51'W
Fito, Mount	13°55'S	171°44'W	Saluafata Harbor	13°50'S	171°34'W
Iva	13°41'S	172°10'W	Sataua	13°28'S	172°40'W
Lotofaga	13°59'S	171°50'W	Savai'i	13°35'S	172°25'W
Matautu	13°57'S	171°56'W	Taga	13°46'S	172°28'W
Matavai	13°28'S	172°35'W	Tapaga, Cape	14°01'S	171°23'W
Mauga Silisili	13°35'S	172°27'W	Tiavea	13°57'S	171°24'W
Poutasi	14°01'S	171°41'W	Tuasivi	13°40'S	172°07'W
Puapua	13°34'S	172°09'W	Upolu	13°55'S	171°45'W

YEMEN

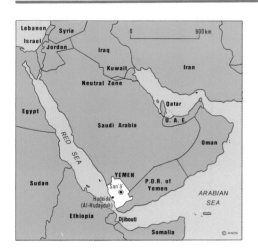

OFFICIAL NAME Yemen Arab Republic

PEOPLE
Population 5,985,000.
Density 79/mi² (31/km²).
Urban 12%.
Capital San'ā, 277,800.
Ethnic groups Arab 90%, Afro-Arab 10%.
Languages Arabic.
Religions Muslim.
Life expectancy 44 female, 42 male.
Literacy 15%.

POLITICS
Government Republic.
Parties General People's Congress.
Memberships AL, UN.
Subdivisions 11 provinces.

ECONOMY
GNP $3,800,000,000.

Per capita $740.
Monetary unit Riyal.
Trade partners P.D.R. Yemen, China, U.S.S.R., Saudi Arabia, Japan.
Exports Khat, cotton, coffee, hides.
Imports Manufactured goods, petroleum products, textiles, food.

LAND
Description Southwestern Asia.
Area 75,290 mi² (195,000 km²).
Highest point Mt. Nabi Shuayb, 12,336 ft (3,760 m).
Lowest point Sea level.

PEOPLE. Nearly all the inhabitants of the Yemen Arab Republic, or North Yemen, are Arab and Arabic speaking. The predominant religion is Islam, and the population is nearly equally divided into Shiite and Sunni Muslims.

ECONOMY AND THE LAND. Yemen has a terrain suited for agriculture, which is the mainstay of the nation's economy. The landscape of the Yemen Arab Republic varies from arid lowlands to the fertile, well-cultivated highlands that dominate the country's center. The climate is temperate inland and hot and dry along the coast.

HISTORY AND POLITICS. From earliest times Yemen has been occupied by trade empires, and it was part of the Kingdom of Sheba in the 900s B.C. The Ottoman Empire ruled Yemen from the sixteenth century until 1918, when the Turkish military withdrew and gave control to the highland Zaidis. In 1962 the Yemeni army deposed the Imam Badr and established the Yemen Arab Republic. A civil war resulted, ending in 1968 with the reconciliation of royalist and republican forces. Political instability and civil unrest have continued, however. ∎

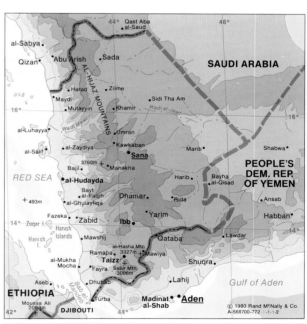

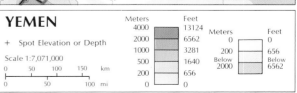

Yemen Map Index

	Lat.	Long.		Lat.	Long.
al-Hudayda	14°48'N	42°57'E	Sada	16°52'N	43°37'E
Ibb	14°01'N	44°10'E	Sana	15°23'N	44°12'E
Mandeb, Bab el-	12°40'N	43°20'E	Taizz	13°38'N	44°04'E

YEMEN, PEOPLE'S DEMOCRATIC REPUBLIC OF

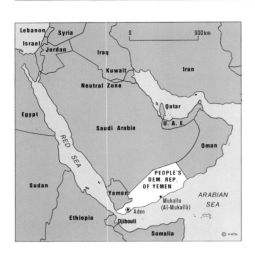

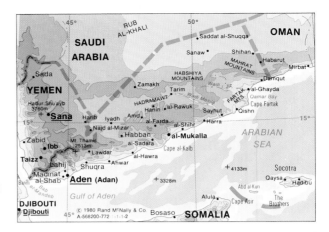

OFFICIAL NAME People's Democratic Republic of Yemen

PEOPLE
Population 2,180,000.
Density 17/mi² (6.5/km²).
Urban 38%.
Capital Aden, 271,600.
Ethnic groups Arab.
Languages Arabic.
Religions Sunni Muslim.
Life expectancy 47 female, 44 male.
Literacy 25%.

POLITICS
Government Socialist republic.

Parties Socialist.
Suffrage Universal, over 18.
Memberships AL, UN.
Subdivisions 6 governorates.

ECONOMY
GNP $792,000,000.
Per capita $430.
Monetary unit Dinar.
Trade partners Yemen, U.K., Japan, Persian Gulf countries, U.S.S.R.
Exports Petroleum products, fish products, hides and skins.
Imports Petroleum, food, machinery, transportation equipment.

LAND
Description Southwestern Asia.
Area 128,560 mi² (332,968 km²).
Highest point 8,255 ft (2,516 m).
Lowest point Sea level.

PEOPLE. Most inhabitants of the People's Democratic Republic of Yemen, or South Yemen, are Arab, with small minorities of Indians, Pakistanis, and East Africans. Islam is the dominant religion, and nearly all South Yemenis belong to the Sunni sect. Small numbers of Christians, Hindus, and Jews also exist.

ECONOMY AND THE LAND. Arable land is limited by South Yemen's arid climate, although most Yemenis are subsistence farmers and nomadic herders. Petroleum products are South Yemen's major industrial export. However, both crude oil and food must be imported for the population, and the diminished oil market is a continuing problem. The terrain is marked by a mountainous interior and a flat, sandy coast. The climate is hot and dry.

HISTORY AND POLITICS. Between 1200 B.C. and A.D. 525 the area of present-day Yemen was at the center of the Minaean, Sabaean, and Himyarite cultures. Christian Ethiopians and Persians also proliferated before the introduction of Islam in the seventh century. Yemen's coastal area came under the control of the British in 1839, and Aden became an important center of trade. Regional instability caused Britain to expand eastward and establish the protectorate of Aden in the 1930s. By the mid-1960s Aden had become the focus of Arab nationalists, and in 1967 Britain granted independence to the People's Republic of South Yemen. After a Marxist coup in 1970, the country was renamed the People's Democratic Republic of Yemen. During the 1970s border clashes erupted with the Yemen Arab Republic, but North and South Yemen continue to express a wish to unify Yemen. ∎

People's Democratic Republic of Yemen Map Index

	Lat.	Long.		Lat.	Long.
Aden (Adan)	12°45′N	45°12′E	Madinat al-Shab	12°50′N	44°56′E
al-Kalb, Cape	14°02′N	48°40′E	Mandeb, Bab el-	12°40′N	43°20′E
al-Mukalla	14°32′N	49°08′E	Masila, Wadi	15°10′N	51°05′E
Bana, Wadi	13°03′N	45°24′E	Shuqra	13°21′N	45°42′E
Habban	14°21′N	47°05′E	Socotra	12°30′N	54°00′E
Lahij	13°02′N	44°54′E	Thamir, Mount	13°53′N	45°30′E

YUGOSLAVIA

Montenegro province in southern Yugoslavia

YUGOSLAVIA

OFFICIAL NAME Socialist Federal Republic of Yugoslavia

PEOPLE
Population 23,075,000.
Density 234/mi² (90/km²).
Urban 39%.
Capital Belgrade, 936,200.
Ethnic groups Serb 36%, Croatian 20%, Bosnian 9%, Slovene 8%, Albanian 8%, Macedonian 6%, Montenegrin 3%, Hungarian 2%.
Languages Serbo-Croatian, Slovene, Macedonian.
Religions Serbian Orthodox 41%, Roman Catholic 32%, Muslim 12%.
Life expectancy 73 female, 69 male.
Literacy 85%.

POLITICS
Government Socialist republic.
Parties League of Communists.
Suffrage Universal, over 18.
Memberships OECD, UN.
Subdivisions 6 republics, 2 autonomous provinces.

ECONOMY
GNP $53,900,000,000.
Per capita $2,370.
Monetary unit Dinar.
Trade partners U.S.S.R., West Germany, Italy, U.S., Czechoslovakia.
Exports Food, leather goods and shoes, machinery, textiles, wood products.
Imports Machinery, petroleum, iron and steel, chemicals.

LAND
Description Eastern Europe.
Area 98,766 mi² (255,804 km²).
Highest point Triglav, 9,396 ft (2,864 m).
Lowest point Sea level.

PEOPLE. The population of Yugoslavia is one of the most diverse in Eastern Europe, composed of nearly twenty distinct ethnic groups in addition to the main Serbian and Croatian groups. Serbo-Croatian, Slovene, and Macedonian are major languages, and religions are diverse as well, often dividing along ethnic lines. Most Yugoslavs work in industry, resulting in a steady urban shift since World War II and a corresponding rise in the standard of living.

ECONOMY AND THE LAND. Since 1945 Yugoslavia's economy has made a successful transition from agriculture to industry. Once modeled on that of the Soviet Union, the economy today is somewhat decentralized, based on the theory of workers' self-management. Decisions on production, prices, and income are made to benefit society as a whole, though wealth has tended to concentrate in the highly industrialized north, resulting in increasing social tension. Agriculture also plays a part in the economic picture, and farming is helped by the moderate climate along the coast of the Adriatic Sea, with stronger seasonal variations in the mountainous inland regions.

YUGOSLAVIA

	Major Urban Area
	Railroad
	Canal or Waterway
	Republic Boundary
	Autonomous Region Boundary
+	Spot Elevation

Meters	Feet
4000	13124
2000	6562
1000	3281
500	1640
200	656
0	0
200	656
2000	6562

Scale 1:4,752,000

City type size indicates relative importance

© 1980 Rand McNally & Co.
A-553400-772 -1-1-1

Yugoslavia Map Index

	Lat.	Long.		Lat.	Long.		Lat.	Long.		Lat.	Long.
Ada	45°48′N	20°08′E	Kočani	41°55′N	22°25′E	Pančevo	44°52′N	20°39′E	Svetozarevo	43°58′N	21°16′E
Banja Luka	44°46′N	17°11′E	Koper	45°33′N	13°44′E	Peć	42°40′N	20°19′E	Tetovo	42°01′N	20°58′E
Bečej	45°37′N	20°03′E	Korčula	42°57′N	16°50′E	Pirot	43°09′N	22°35′E	Tisa	45°15′N	20°17′E
Belgrade	44°50′N	20°30′E	Kosovo and			Požarevac	44°37′N	21°11′E	Titograd	42°26′N	19°14′E
Bitola	41°01′N	21°20′E	Metohija	42°30′N	21°00′E	Prilep	41°20′N	21°33′E	Titovo Užice	43°51′N	19°51′E
Bor	44°05′N	22°07′E	Kosovska			Priština	42°39′N	21°10′E	Titov Veles	41°41′N	21°48′E
Bosnia and			Mitrovica	42°53′N	20°52′E	Prizren	42°12′N	20°44′E	Triglav	46°23′N	13°50′E
Hercegovina	44°15′N	17°30′E	Kragujevac	44°01′N	20°55′E	Pula	44°51′N	13°50′E	Tuzla	44°32′N	18°41′E
Brač	43°20′N	16°40′E	Kraljevo	43°43′N	20°41′E	Rijeka	45°20′N	14°27′E	Valjevo	44°16′N	19°53′E
Brčko	44°53′N	18°48′E	Kranj	46°15′N	14°21′E	Šabac	44°45′N	19°42′E	Varaždin	46°19′N	16°20′E
Čačak	43°53′N	20°21′E	Krk	45°05′N	14°35′E	Sarajevo	43°52′N	18°25′E	Vardar (Axios)	41°07′N	22°30′E
Celje	46°14′N	15°16′E	Kruševac	43°35′N	21°20′E	Sava	44°50′N	20°26′E	Velebit	44°38′N	15°03′E
Cres	44°50′N	14°25′E	Kumanovo	42°08′N	21°43′E	Scutari, Lake	42°12′N	19°18′E	Velika Morava	44°43′N	21°03′E
Croatia	45°10′N	15°30′E	Leskovac	42°59′N	21°57′E	Serbia	44°00′N	21°00′E	Velika Plana	44°20′N	21°04′E
Danube	44°12′N	22°40′E	Ljubljana	46°03′N	14°31′E	Šibenik	43°44′N	15°54′E	Vinkovci	45°17′N	18°49′E
Dinara	43°50′N	16°35′E	Macedonia	41°50′N	22°00′E	Sisak	45°29′N	16°23′E	Vis	43°03′N	16°12′E
Drava	45°33′N	18°55′E	Maribor	46°33′N	15°39′E	Skopje	41°59′N	21°26′E	Vojvodina	45°30′N	20°00′E
Dubrovnik	42°38′N	18°07′E	Montenegro	42°30′N	19°18′E	Slavonski Brod	45°10′N	18°01′E	Vranje	42°33′N	21°54′E
Hvar	43°09′N	16°45′E	Mostar	43°20′N	17°49′E	Slovenia	46°15′N	15°10′E	Vrbas	45°35′N	19°39′E
Iron Gate			Mura (Mur)	46°18′N	16°53′E	Smederevo	44°40′N	20°56′E	Vršac	45°07′N	21°18′E
Reservoir	44°30′N	22°00′E	Nikšić	42°46′N	18°56′E	Sombor	45°46′N	19°07′E	Zadar	44°07′N	15°14′E
Istria	45°15′N	14°00′E	Niš	43°19′N	21°54′E	Split	43°31′N	16°27′E	Zagreb	45°48′N	15°58′E
Julian Alps	46°00′N	14°00′E	Novi Pazar	43°08′N	20°31′E	Sremska			Zaječar	43°54′N	22°17′E
Južna Morava	43°42′N	21°23′E	Novi Sad	45°15′N	19°50′E	Mitrovica	44°58′N	19°37′E	Zapadna Morava	43°42′N	21°23′E
Karawanken	46°30′N	14°25′E	Ohrid	41°07′N	20°47′E	Štip	41°44′N	22°12′E	Zenica	44°12′N	17°55′E
Karlovac	45°29′N	15°34′E	Ohrid, Lake	41°02′N	20°43′E	Subotica	46°06′N	19°39′E	Zrenjanin	45°23′N	20°24′E
Kikinda	45°50′N	20°28′E	Osijek	45°33′N	18°41′E						

HISTORY AND POLITICS. Yugoslavia has been inhabited for at least 100,000 years, its peoples including Illyrians, Thracians, Greeks, Celts, and Romans. In A.D. 395 the Roman Empire was divided into the West Roman Empire and the Byzantine Empire, with the dividing line through present-day Yugoslavia. People in the western region became Roman Catholic and used the Roman alphabet, while Byzantines adopted the Eastern Orthodox faith and the Cyrillic alphabet. Slavic migrations led to the establishment of independent Slavic states such as Serbia and Croatia, and calls for Slavic unity began in the early 1800s. In 1914 a Slavic patriot assassinated Archduke Ferdinand of Austria-Hungary and triggered World War I. The Kingdom of Serbs, Croats, and Slovenes was formed in 1918, but infighting encouraged King Alexander I to declare himself dictator in 1929 and change the new country's name to Yugoslavia, which was retained after Alexander's assassination in 1934. Germany and the other Axis powers invaded Yugoslavia during World War II and were opposed by a partisan army organized by Josip Broz Tito, who assumed leadership when Yugoslavia became a Communist republic in 1945. Tito's policy of nonalignment, the cornerstone of Yugoslavia's foreign policy, caused the Soviet Union to break off diplomatic relations from 1948 to 1955. United States aid from the 1940s to the 1960s encouraged a shift toward Western trade and broadened political and cultural exchanges as well. Tito's course of independence and interaction with non-aligned nations continued after his death in 1980. ■

ZAIRE

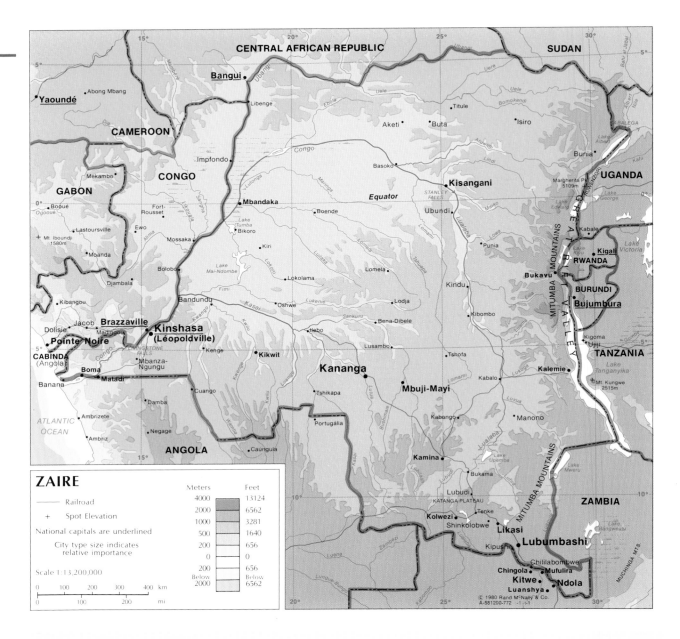

ZAIRE

	Meters	Feet
—— Railroad	4000	13124
+ Spot Elevation	2000	6562
	1000	3281
National capitals are underlined	500	1640
City type size indicates relative importance	200	656
	0	0
Scale 1:13,200,000	200	656
	Below 2000	Below 6562

Scale 0 100 200 300 400 km
0 100 200 mi

© 1980 Rand McNally & Co.
A-581200-772

OFFICIAL NAME Republic of
Zaire

PEOPLE
Population 32,625,000.
Density 36/mi² (14/km²).
Urban 34%.
Capital Kinshasa, 2,700,000.
Ethnic groups Mongo, Luba, Kongo,
Mangbetu-Azande, others.
Languages French, Lingala, Swahili, Kikongo,
Tshiluba.
Religions Roman Catholic 50%, Protestant 20%,
Kimbanguist 10%, Muslim 10%, indigenous 10%.
Life expectancy 52 female, 48 male.
Literacy 15% female, 40% male.

POLITICS
Government Republic.
Parties Popular Movement of the Revolution.
Suffrage Universal, over 18.
Memberships OAU, UN.
Subdivisions 8 regions, 1 federal district.

ECONOMY
GDP $3,400,000,000.
Per capita $570.
Monetary unit Zaire.
Trade partners Belgium, U.S., West Germany.
Exports Copper, cobalt, diamonds, petroleum,
coffee.
Imports Petroleum products, food, machinery,
consumer goods, transportation equipment.

LAND
Description Central Africa.
Area 905,567 mi² (2,345,409 km²).
Highest point Margherita Pk., 16,763 ft (5,109 m).
Lowest point Sea level.

Zaire Map Index

	Lat.	Long.		Lat.	Long.		Lat.	Long.		Lat.	Long.
Aketi	2°44'N	23°46'E	Kamina	8°44'S	25°00'E	Likasi	10°59'S	26°44'E	Matadi	5°49'S	13°27'E
Albert, Lake	1°40'N	31°00'E	Kananga	5°54'S	22°25'E	Livingstone Falls	4°50'S	14°30'E	Mbandaka	0°04'N	18°16'E
Banana	6°01'S	12°24'E	Kasai (Cassai)	3°06'S	16°57'E	Loange	4°17'S	20°02'E	Mbanza-Ngungu	5°15'S	14°52'E
Bandundu	3°18'S	17°20'E	Katanga Plateau	10°00'S	26°00'E	Lokoro	1°43'S	18°23'E	Mbuji-Mayi	6°09'S	23°38'E
Boma	5°51'S	13°03'E	Kikwit	5°02'S	18°49'E	Lualaba	0°26'N	25°20'E	Mitumba		
Bukavu	2°30'S	28°52'E	Kindu	2°57'S	25°56'E	Luapula	9°26'S	28°33'E	Mountains	6°00'S	29°00'E
Bunia	1°34'N	30°15'E	Kinshasa			Lubudi	9°57'S	25°58'E	Mweru, Lake	8°45'S	29°40'E
Bushimaie	6°02'S	23°45'E	(Léopoldville)	4°18'S	15°18'E	Lubumbashi	11°40'S	27°28'E	Ruwenzori	0°23'N	29°54'E
Buta	2°48'N	24°44'E	Kipushi	11°46'N	27°14'E	Lulua	5°02'S	21°07'E	Shinkolobwe	11°02'S	26°35'E
Congo	6°04'S	12°24'E	Kisangani	0°30'S	25°12'E	Maiko	0°14'N	25°33'E	Stanley Falls	0°30'N	25°12'E
Ebola	3°20'N	20°57'E	Kivu, Lake	2°00'S	29°10'E	Mai-Ndombe,			Tanganyika, Lake	6°00'S	29°30'E
Edward, Lake	0°25'S	29°30'E	Kolwezi	10°43'S	25°28'E	Lake	2°00'S	18°20'E	Ubangi	0°30'S	17°42'E
Isiro	2°47'N	27°37'E	Kwango	3°14'S	17°23'E	Manono	7°18'S	27°25'E	Ubundi	0°21'S	25°29'E
Kalemie	5°56'S	29°12'E	Kwilu	3°22'S	17°22'E	Margherita Peak	0°22'N	29°51'E	Upemba, Lake	8°36'S	26°26'E

PEOPLE. The diverse population of Zaire is composed of more than two hundred African ethnic groups, with Bantu peoples accounting for the majority. Belgian settlers introduced French, but hundreds of indigenous languages are more widely spoken. Much of the population is Christian, another result of former European rule. Many non-Christians practice traditional or syncretic faiths such as Kimbanguism. The majority of Zairians are rural farmers.

ECONOMY AND THE LAND. Zaire is rich in mineral resources, particularly copper, cobalt, diamonds, and petroleum; mining has supplanted agriculture in economic importance and now dominates the economy. Agriculture continues to employ most Zairians, however, and subsistence farming is practiced in nearly every region. Industrial activity—especially petroleum refining and hydroelectric production—is growing. Zaire's terrain is composed of mountains and plateaus. The climate is equatorial, with hot and humid weather in the north and west, and cooler and drier conditions in the south and east.

HISTORY AND POLITICS. The earliest inhabitants of modern Zaire were probably Pygmies who settled in the area thousands of years ago.

By the A.D. 700s sophisticated civilizations had developed in what is now southeastern Zaire. Portuguese explorers visited a coastal kingdom in the 1480s. In the early 1500s the Portuguese began the forced emigration of black Africans for slavery. Other Europeans came to the area as the slave trade grew, but the interior remained relatively unexplored until the 1870s. Belgian king Leopold II realized the potential value of the region and declared the area his private state, with himself as ruler. In 1885 the other European powers recognized his claim, and the Congo Free State became King Leopold's private possession. In 1908 the king ceded control of the Congo Free State to the Belgian government, and the colony was renamed the Belgian Congo. Nationalist sentiment grew until rioting broke out in 1959. Independence was granted in 1960, and a weak government assumed control of what was by then called the Congo. Violent civil disorder, provincial secession, and political assassination characterized the next five years. The country stabilized under the rule of President Mobutu Sese Seko, a former army general. Zaire took its present name in 1971. ■

The dugout canoes are assembled on the Zaire River, which provides over 9,000 miles (14,481 kilometers) of navigable waterways for Zaire.

ZAMBIA

ZAMBIA

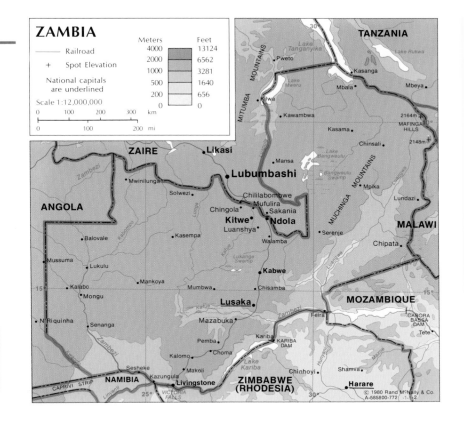

Railroad

+ Spot Elevation

National capitals
are underlined

Scale 1:12,000,000

Meters	Feet
4000	13124
2000	6562
1000	3281
500	1640
200	656
0	0

Zambia Map Index

	Lat.	Long.
Bangweulu, Lake	11°05'S	29°45'E
Chililabombwe	12°18'S	27°43'E
Chingola	12°32'S	27°52'E
Chipata	13°39'S	32°40'E
Kabwe	14°27'S	28°27'E
Kafue	15°56'S	28°55'E
Kariba, Lake	17°00'S	28°00'E
Kitwe	12°49'S	28°13'E
Kwando	18°27'S	23°32'E
Livingstone	17°50'S	25°53'E
Luanshya	13°08'S	28°24'E
Luapula	9°26'S	28°33'E
Lukanga Swamp	14°25'S	27°45'E
Lusaka	15°25'S	28°17'E
Mafinga Hills	10°00'S	33°30'E
Mazabuka	15°51'S	27°46'E
Muchinga Mountains	12°00'S	31°45'E
Mweru, Lake	8°45'S	29°40'E
Ndola	12°58'S	28°38'E
Victoria Falls	17°55'S	25°51'E
Zambezi	15°38'S	30°27'E

OFFICIAL NAME Republic of Zambia

PEOPLE
Population 6,660,000.
Density 23/mi² (8.8/km²).
Urban 43%.
Capital Lusaka, 538,469.
Ethnic groups African 99%.
Languages English, indigenous.
Religions Christian 50–75%, Muslim and Hindu 1%, indigenous.
Life expectancy 52 female, 49 male.
Literacy 54%.

POLITICS
Government Republic.
Parties United National Independence.
Suffrage Universal, over 18.
Memberships CW, OAU, UN.
Subdivisions 9 provinces.

ECONOMY
GDP $2,900,000,000.
Per capita $476.
Monetary unit Kwacha.
Trade partners U.K., South Africa, Japan, West Germany, Saudi Arabia.
Exports Copper, cobalt, zinc, lead, tobacco.
Imports Machinery, transportation equipment, fuels, manufactured goods, food.

LAND
Description Southern Africa, landlocked.
Area 290,586 mi² (752,614 km²).
Highest point 7,100 ft (2,164 m).
Lowest point 1,081 ft (329 m).

PEOPLE. Virtually all Zambians are black Africans belonging to one of more than seventy Bantu-speaking ethnic groups. Besides the indigenous Bantu languages, many speak English, a reflection of decades of British influence. Although most Zambians are Christian, small minorities are Hindu, Muslim, or hold indigenous beliefs. Most Zambians are subsistence farmers in small villages; however, the mining industry has caused many people to move to urban areas, where wages are rising.

ECONOMY AND THE LAND. Mining and processing of copper form the cornerstone of Zambia's economy, and Zambia Consolidated Copper Mines is one of the world's largest copper-mining operations. Zambia also has deposits of lead, zinc, and cobalt, and cobalt is now the nation's second most important export, after copper. Despite the importance of mining, about two-thirds of Zambia's labor force is employed in agriculture. Most of these workers are subsistence farmers, and the lack of large-scale farming necessitates the import of food. The government hopes to attain self-sufficiency through investment in agriculture; however, drought continues to threaten output. The landlocked nation of Zambia is marked by high plateaus and great rivers. The climate is subtropical.

HISTORY AND POLITICS. European explorers arriving in the nineteenth century found an established society of Bantu-speaking inhabitants. In 1888 Cecil Rhodes and the British South Africa Company obtained a mineral-rights concession from local chiefs, and Northern and Southern Rhodesia—now Zambia and Zimbabwe, respectively—came within the British sphere of influence. Northern Rhodesia became a British protectorate in 1924. In 1953 Northern Rhodesia was combined with Southern Rhodesia and Nyasaland, now Malawi, to form a federation, despite African-nationalist opposition to the European minority-controlled government in Southern Rhodesia. The federation was dissolved in 1963, and Northern Rhodesia became the independent Republic of Zambia in 1964. Zambia follows a foreign policy of nonalignment. ■

The picture below shows Bemba women making flour from millet. The Bemba people are a populous ethnic group who gain their livelihood by practicing shifting cultivation of finger millet on the relatively poor soils of northern Zambia.

Only a small portion of the arid savanna vegetation and climatic region which covers most of Zambia is shown in the picture above. Not only is much of this region subject to drought it is also infested by the tsetse fly. These are the major factors limiting the main economic activities to subsistence farming and copper mining.

ZIMBABWE

OFFICIAL NAME Republic of Zimbabwe

PEOPLE
Population 8,190,000.
Density 54/mi² (21/km²).
Urban 23%.
Capital Harare, 656,011.
Ethnic groups Shona 77%, Ndebele 19%, European 3%.
Languages English, ChiShona, Si Ndebele.
Religions Christian, indigenous.
Life expectancy 57 female, 53 male.
Literacy 45–55%.

POLITICS
Government Republic.
Parties African National Union, African People's Union, Republican Front, United African National Council.
Suffrage Universal, over 18 (whites, mixed, and Asians vote separately for 20 seats in House of Assembly).
Memberships CW, OAU, UN.
Subdivisions 8 provinces.

ECONOMY
GDP $7,100,000,000.
Per capita $880.
Monetary unit Dollar.
Trade partners South Africa, U.K., U.S., West Germany.
Exports Tobacco, asbestos, copper, tin, chrome, gold, nickel.
Imports Machinery, petroleum products, transportation equipment.

LAND
Description Southern Africa, landlocked.
Area 150,804 mi² (390,580 km²).
Highest point Inyangani, 8,504 ft (2,592 m).
Lowest point 530 ft (162 m).

PEOPLE. The great majority of Zimbabweans are black Africans of Bantu descent, with a small but economically significant minority of white Europeans. Most Zimbabweans are subsistence farmers who live in small villages. The influence of British colonization can be seen in the official language, English, and in the influence of Christianity.

ECONOMY AND THE LAND. Zimbabwe's natural mineral resources have played a key role in the country's sustained economic growth. The subtropical climate supports a successful farm industry, including crop growing and large-scale cattle ranching, and more than 50 percent of Zimbabwe's population is employed in agriculture. However, three years of drought in the early 1980s took their toll on agricultural profits and affected the cattle industry in particular. The mining industry provides for export income, and deposits of asbestos, copper, tin, chromium ore, gold, and nickel are found within the nation's borders. Although Zimbabwe is a landlocked nation marked by high plateaus, transportation of

ZIMBABWE (RHODESIA)

——— Railroad

+ Spot Elevation

National capitals are underlined

City type size indicates relative importance

Scale 1:7,512,000

Meters	Feet
4000	13124
2000	6562
1000	3281
500	1640
200	656
0	0

goods is facilitated by an excellent system of paved roads and railways.

HISTORY AND POLITICS. Zimbabwe was populated by Bantu groups until European exploration in the nineteenth century. British influence began in 1888, when Cecil Rhodes and the British South Africa Company obtained mineral rights to the area from local chiefs, and eventually the region was divided under British rule as Southern Rhodesia, or present-day Zimbabwe, and Northern Rhodesia, or modern Zambia. In 1953 Southern Rhodesia, Northern Rhodesia, and Nyasaland, now Malawi, formed a federation that ended in discord after ten years; Zambia and Malawi gained their independence, and Southern Rhodesia, which remained under British control, became Rhodesia. In response to British pressure to accept black-majority rule, Rhodesian whites declared independence from the United Kingdom in 1965, which led to economic sanctions imposed by the United Nations. These sanctions and years of antigovernment violence finally forced agreement to the principle of black-majority rule. In 1980 the Zimbabwe African National Union–Patriotic Front won a majority of seats in the House of Representatives, and Rhodesia became independent Zimbabwe. Despite Zimbabwe's move toward stability since independence, some internal unrest continues. ∎

Victoria Falls, in a mile-long chasm, is formed as the Zambezi River drops over 300 feet (483 meters).

INDEX

INTRODUCTION TO THE INDEX

This universal index includes in a single alphabetical list the names of major features that appear on the reference maps. Each place name is followed by the name of the country or continent in which it is located, the page number of the map on which it appears, and its approximate geographic coordinates.

Names The names of cities appear in the index in regular type. The names of all other features, such as rivers, mountains, or countries appear in *italics*.

All names are written with an initial capital letter except for a few Arabic names such as al-Uqsur. Capitalization of non-initial words in a name generally follows local practice.

Abbreviations of names on the maps have been standardized as much as possible. Names that are abbreviated on the maps are generally spelled out in full in the index.

Country names and names of features that extend beyond the boundaries of one country are followed by the name of the continent in which each is located. Country

designations follow the names of all other places in the index. The locations of places in the United States, Canada, and the United Kingdom are further defined by abbreviations that indicate the state, province, or political division in which each is located.

All abbreviations used in the index are defined in the List of Abbreviations below.

Alphabetization Names are alphabetized in the order of the letters of the English alphabet. Spanish *ll* and *ch,* for example, are not treated as distinct letters. Furthermore, diacritical marks are disregarded in alphabetization—German or Scandinavian *ä* or *ö* are treated as *a* or *o.*

The names of physical features may appear inverted, since they are always alphabetized under the proper, not the generic, part of the name, thus: "Gilbraltar, Strait of." Otherwise every entry, whether consisting of one word or more, is alphabetized as a single continuous entity. "Ladysmith," for example, appears after "La Dorada" and before "la Esmeralda." Names beginning with articles (Le

Havre, Den Helder, al-Mansurah) are not inverted. Names beginning "Mc" are alphabetized as though spelled "Mac," and names beginning "St.," "Ste." and "Sainte" as though spelled "Saint."

In the case of identical names, towns are listed first, then political divisions, then physical features. Entries that are completely identical are listed alphabetically by country name.

Page References and Geographic Coordinates The page references and geographic coordinates are found in the last three columns of each entry.

Page references to two-page maps always refer to the left-hand page.

Geographic coordinates for point features, such as cities and mountain peaks, indicate the locations of the symbols. For extensive areal features, such as countries or mountain ranges, locations are given for the approximate centers of the features. Those for linear features, such as canals and rivers, are given for the locations of the terminating points or mouths.

LIST OF ABBREVIATIONS

Ab., Can.	Alberta, Can.	Dom. Rep.	Dominican Republic	La., U.S.	Louisiana, U.S.	Nmb.	Namibia	St. Hel.	St. Helena	
Afg.	Afghanistan			Leb.	Lebanon	Nor.	Norway	St. Luc.	St. Lucia	
Afr.	Africa	Ec.	Ecuador	Leso.	Lesotho	Norf. I.	Norfolk Island	S. Tom./P.	Sao Tome and Principe	
Ak., U.S.	Alaska, U.S.	El Sal.	El Salvador	Lib.	Liberia	N.S., Can.	Nova Scotia, Can.			
Al., U.S.	Alabama, U.S.	Eng., U.K.	England, U.K.	Liech.	Liechtenstein	N.T., Can.	Northwest Territories, Can.	St. P./M.	St. Pierre and Miquelon	
Alb.	Albania	Eq. Gui.	Equatorial Guinea	Lux.	Luxembourg					
Alg.	Algeria	Eth.	Ethiopia	Ma., U.S.	Massachusetts, U.S.	Nv., U.S.	Nevada, U.S.	St. Vin.	St. Vincent and the Grenadines	
Am. Sam.	American Samoa	Eur.	Europe			N.Y., U.S.	New York, U.S.			
And.	Andorra	Faer. Is.	Faeroe Islands	Madag.	Madagascar	N.Z.	New Zealand	Sur.	Suriname	
Ang.	Angola	Falk. Is.	Falkland Islands	Malay.	Malaysia	Oc.	Oceania	Swaz.	Swaziland	
Ant.	Antarctica	Fin.	Finland	Mald.	Maldives	Oh., U.S.	Ohio, U.S.	Swe.	Sweden	
Antig.	Antigua and Barbuda	Fl., U.S.	Florida, U.S.	Marsh. Is.	Marshall Islands	Ok., U.S.	Oklahoma, U.S.	Switz.	Switzerland	
		Fr.	France	Mart.	Martinique	On., Can.	Ontario, Can.	Tai.	Taiwan	
Ar., U.S.	Arkansas, U.S.	F.R.Ger.	Federal Republic of Germany (West Ger.)	Maur.	Mauritania	Or., U.S.	Oregon, U.S.	Tan.	Tanzania	
Arg.	Argentina			May.	Mayotte	Pa., U.S.	Pennsylvania, U.S.	T./C. Is.	Turks and Caicos Islands	
Aus.	Austria			Mb., Can.	Manitoba, Can.	Pak.	Pakistan			
Austl.	Australia			Md., U.S.	Maryland, U.S.	Pan.	Panama	Thai.	Thailand	
Az., U.S.	Arizona, U.S.	Fr. Gu.	French Guiana	Me., U.S.	Maine, U.S.	Pap. N. Gui.	Papua New Guinea	Tn., U.S.	Tennessee, U.S.	
Bah.	Bahamas	Fr. Poly.	French Polynesia	Mex.	Mexico			Tok.	Tokelau	
Bahr.	Bahrain	F.S.A.T.	French Southern and Antarctic Territory	Mi., U.S.	Michigan, U.S.	Para.	Paraguay	Trin.	Trinidad and Tobago	
Barb.	Barbados			Micron.	Federated States of Micronesia	P.D.R.Yem.	People's Democratic Republic of Yemen			
B.A.T.	British Antarctic Territory	Ga., U.S.	Georgia, U.S.					T.T.P.I.	Trust Territory of the Pacific Islands	
		Gam.	Gambia	Mid. Is.	Midway Islands					
B.C., Can.	British Columbia, Can.	Ger.D.R.	German Democratic Republic (East Ger.)	Mn., U.S.	Minnesota, U.S.					
				Mo., U.S.	Missouri, U.S.	P.E., Can.	Prince Edward Island, Can.	Tun.	Tunisia	
Bdi.	Burundi			Mon.	Monaco			Tur.	Turkey	
Bel.	Belgium			Mong.	Mongolia	Phil.	Philippines	Tx., U.S.	Texas, U.S.	
Ber.	Bermuda	Gib.	Gibraltar	Monts.	Montserrat	Pit.	Pitcairn	U.A.E.	United Arab Emirates	
Bhu.	Bhutan	Grc.	Greece	Mor.	Morocco	Pol.	Poland			
B.I.O.T.	British Indian Ocean Territory	Gren.	Grenada	Moz.	Mozambique	Port.	Portugal	Ug.	Uganda	
		Grnld.	Greenland	Mrts.	Mauritius	P.Q., Can.	Quebec, Can.	U.K.	United Kingdom	
Bngl.	Bangladesh	Guad.	Guadeloupe	Ms., U.S.	Mississippi, U.S.	P.R.	Puerto Rico	Ur.	Uruguay	
Bol.	Bolivia	Guat.	Guatemala	Mt., U.S.	Montana, U.S.	Reu.	Reunion	U.S.	United States	
Boph.	Bophuthatswana	Gui.	Guinea	Mwi.	Malawi	R.I., U.S.	Rhode Island, U.S.	U.S.S.R.	Union of Soviet Socialist Republics	
Bots.	Botswana	Gui.-B.	Guinea-Bissau	N.A.	North America	Rom.	Romania			
Braz.	Brazil	Guy.	Guyana	N.B., Can.	New Brunswick, Can.	Rw.	Rwanda			
Bru.	Brunei	Hi., U.S.	Hawaii, U.S.			S.A.	South America	Ut., U.S.	Utah, U.S.	
Bul.	Bulgaria	H.K.	Hong Kong	N.C., U.S.	North Carolina, U.S.	S. Afr.	South Africa	Va., U.S.	Virginia, U.S.	
Ca., U.S.	California, U.S.	Hond.	Honduras			Sau. Ar.	Saudi Arabia	Vat.	Vatican City	
Cam.	Cameroon	Hung.	Hungary	N. Cal.	New Caledonia	S.C., U.S.	South Carolina, U.S.	Ven.	Venezuela	
Can.	Canada	Ia., U.S.	Iowa, U.S.	N.D., U.S.	North Dakota, U.S.			V.I., Br.	Virgin Islands, British	
Cay. Is.	Cayman Islands	I.C.	Ivory Coast			Scot., U.K.	Scotland, U.K.			
Cen. Afr. Rep.	Central African Republic	Ice.	Iceland	Ne., U.S.	Nebraska, U.S.	S.D., U.S.	South Dakota, U.S.	Viet.	Vietnam	
		Id., U.S.	Idaho, U.S.	Neth.	Netherlands			V.I.U.S.	Virgin Islands (U.S.)	
Chile	Chile	Il., U.S.	Illinois, U.S.	Neth. Ant.	Netherlands Antilles	Sen.	Senegal			
Christ. I.	Christmas Island	In., U.S.	Indiana, U.S.			Sey.	Seychelles	Vt., U.S.	Vermont, U.S.	
Co., U.S.	Colorado, U.S.	Indon.	Indonesia	Nf., Can.	Newfoundland, Can.	Sing.	Singapore	Wa., U.S.	Washington, U.S.	
Col.	Colombia	I. of Man	Isle of Man			Sk., Can.	Saskatchewan, Can.	Wales, U.K.	Wales, U.K.	
Com.	Comoros	Ire.	Ireland	N.H., U.S.	New Hampshire, U.S.			Wal./F.	Wallis and Futuna	
C.R.	Costa Rica	Isr.	Israel			S. Kor.	South Korea	Wi., U.S.	Wisconsin, U.S.	
Ct., U.S.	Connecticut, U.S.	Isr. Occ.	Israeli Occupied Territories	Nic.	Nicaragua	S.L.	Sierra Leone	W. Sah.	Western Sahara	
C.V.	Cape Verde			Nig.	Nigeria	S. Mar.	San Marino	W. Sam.	Western Samoa	
Cyp.	Cyprus	Jam.	Jamaica	N. Ire., U.K.	Northern Ireland, U.K.	Sol. Is.	Solomon Islands	W.V., U.S.	West Virginia, U.S.	
Czech.	Czechoslovakia	Jord.	Jordan			Som.	Somalia	Wy., U.S.	Wyoming, U.S.	
D.C., U.S.	District of Columbia, U.S.	Kam.	Kampuchea	N.J., U.S.	New Jersey, U.S.	Sp. N. Afr.	Spanish North Africa	Yk.,Can.	Yukon Territory, Can.	
		Kir.	Kiribati	N. Kor.	North Korea					
De., U.S.	Delaware, U.S.	Ks., U.S.	Kansas, U.S.	N.M., U.S.	New Mexico, U.S.	Sri L.	Sri Lanka	Yugo.	Yugoslavia	
Den.	Denmark	Kuw.	Kuwait	N. Mar. Is.	Northern Mariana Islands	St. C.-N.	St. Christopher-Nevis	Zam.	Zambia	
Dji.	Djibouti	Ky., U.S.	Kentucky, U.S.					Zimb.	Zimbabwe	
Dom.	Dominica									

A

Name	Page	Lat.	Long.
Aachen (Aix-la-Chapelle), Ger., W.	**64**	50°47′N	6°05′E
Aalst, Bel.	**19**	50°56′N	4°02′E
Aarau, Switz.	**160**	47°23′N	8°03′E
Aare, Switz.	**160**	47°37′N	8°13′E
Aba, Nig.	**127**	5°06′N	7°21′E
Aba al-Bawl Hill, Qatar	**141**	24°57′N	51°13′E
Abadan, Iran	**82**	30°20′N	48°16′E
Abakaliki, Nig.	**127**	6°21′N	8°06′E
Abakan, U.S.S.R.	**172**	53°43′N	91°26′E
Abancay, Peru	**135**	13°35′S	72°55′W
Abaya, Lake, Eth.	**54**	6°20′N	37°55′E
Abbé, Lake, Dji.	**49**	11°09′N	41°47′E
Abdulla Bay, Asia	**99**	29°50′N	48°20′E
Abéché, Chad	**36**	13°49′N	20°49′E
Abengourou, I.C.	**90**	6°44′N	3°29′W
Åbenrå, Den.	**48**	55°02′N	9°26′E
Abeokuta, Nig.	**127**	7°10′N	3°26′E
Aberdare, Wales, U.K.	**175**	51°43′N	3°27′W
Aberdare Range, Kenya	**96**	0°25′S	36°38′E
Aberdeen, H.K.	**75**	22°15′N	114°09′E
Aberdeen, Scot., U.K.	**175**	57°10′N	2°04′W
Aberystwyth, Wales, U.K.	**175**	52°25′N	4°05′W
Abidjan, I.C.	**90**	5°19′N	4°02′W
Abnub, Egypt	**52**	27°16′N	31°09′E
Aboisso, I.C.	**90**	5°28′N	3°12′W
Abomey, Benin	**20**	7°11′N	1°59′E
Abrahams Bay, Bah.	**16**	22°21′N	72°55′W
Abruzzi Mountains, Italy	**88**	42°00′N	14°00′E
Abu Dhabi (Abu Zabi), U.A.E.	**174**	24°28′N	54°22′E
Abuja, Nig.	**127**	9°12′N	7°11′E
Abu Kamal, Syria	**161**	34°27′N	40°55′E
Abunã, Braz.	**24**	9°42′S	65°23′W
Abu Tij, Egypt	**52**	27°02′N	31°19′E
Abu Zabi, *see* Abu Dhabi, U.A.E.	**174**	24°28′N	54°22′E
Acajutla, El Sal.	**53**	13°36′N	89°50′W
Acámbaro, Mex.	**113**	20°02′N	100°44′W
Acaponeta, Mex.	**113**	22°30′N	105°22′W
Acapulco, Mex.	**113**	16°51′N	99°55′W
Acarai Mountains, S.A.	**72**	1°50′N	57°40′W
Acari, Peru	**135**	15°26′S	74°37′W
Acarigua, Ven.	**183**	9°33′N	69°12′W
Accra, Ghana	**65**	5°33′N	0°13′W
Aceguá, Ur.	**181**	31°52′S	54°12′W
Acevedo, Arg.	**11**	33°45′S	60°27′W
Achill Island, Ire.	**84**	54°00′N	10°00′W
Achinsk, U.S.S.R.	**172**	56°17′N	90°30′E
Acomayo, Peru	**135**	13°55′S	71°41′W
Aconcagua, Arg.	**11**	32°39′S	70°01′W
Acre (Akko), Isr.	**86**	32°55′N	35°05′E
Acre, Braz.	**24**	9°00′S	70°00′W
Acuracay, Peru	**135**	5°35′S	74°10′W
Ada, Yugo.	**189**	45°48′N	20°08′E
Adamaoua, Afr.	**31**	7°00′N	12°00′E
Adams Bridge, Asia	**155**	9°04′N	79°37′E
Adams Peak, Sri L.	**155**	6°48′N	80°30′E
Adams Rock, Pit.	**137**	25°04′S	130°05′W
Adamstown, Pit.	**137**	25°04′S	130°05′W
Adana, Tur.	**168**	37°01′N	35°18′E
Adapazari, Tur.	**168**	40°46′N	30°24′E
Adare, Cape, Ant.	**8**	71°17′S	170°14′E
Addis Ababa (Adis Abeba), Eth.	**54**	9°00′N	38°50′E
Addu Atoll, Mald.	**107**	0°38′S	73°10′E
Adelaide, Austl.	**14**	34°55′S	138°35′E
Adelaide, Bah.	**16**	25°00′N	77°31′W
Aden (Adan), Yem., P.D.R.	**188**	12°45′N	45°12′E
Aden, Gulf of	**188**	12°30′N	48°00′E
Admiralty Islands, Pap. N. Gui.	**133**	2°10′S	147°00′E
Admiralty Mountains, Ant.	**8**	71°45′S	168°30′E
Ado-Ekiti, Nig.	**127**	7°38′N	5°12′E
Adrano, Italy	**88**	37°40′N	14°50′E
Adriatic Sea, Eur.	**88**	42°30′N	16°00′E
Adwa, Eth.	**54**	14°10′N	38°55′E
Adzopé, I.C.	**90**	6°06′N	3°52′W
Aegean Sea	**67**	38°30′N	25°00′E
Ærø, Den.	**48**	54°53′N	10°20′E
Afadjoto, Ghana	**65**	7°05′N	0°35′E
Afghanistan, Asia	**2**	33°00′N	65°00′E
Afyon, Tur.	**168**	38°45′N	30°33′E
Agadez, Niger	**126**	16°58′N	7°59′E
Agalta Cordillera, Hond.	**74**	15°00′N	85°53′W
Agana, Guam	**69**	13°28′N	144°45′E
Agartala, India	**79**	23°49′N	91°16′E
Agat, Guam	**69**	13°24′N	144°39′E
Agen, Fr.	**58**	44°12′N	0°37′E
Agra, India	**79**	27°11′N	78°01′E
Agrigento, Italy	**88**	37°18′N	13°35′E
Agrinion, Grc.	**67**	38°37′N	21°24′E
Agua Caliente, Mex.	**113**	23°20′N	105°20′W
Agua Caliente, Mount, Mex.	**113**	26°27′N	106°12′W
Aguada, P.R.	**140**	18°23′N	67°11′W
Aguada de Guerra, Arg.	**11**	41°04′S	68°25′W
Aguada de Pasajeros, Cuba	**45**	22°23′N	80°51′W
Aguadilla, P.R.	**140**	18°26′N	67°09′W
Aguadulce, Pan.	**132**	8°15′N	80°33′W
Aguán, Hond.	**74**	15°57′N	85°44′W
Aguascalientes, Mex.	**113**	21°53′N	102°18′W
Agua Volcano, Guat.	**70**	14°28′N	90°45′W
Agulhas, Cape, S. Afr.	**152**	34°52′S	20°00′E
Agusan, Phil.	**136**	9°00′N	125°31′E
Ahaggar, Alg.	**4**	23°00′N	6°30′E
Ahaggar Plateau, Alg.	**4**	21°00′N	6°00′E
Ahlen, Ger., W.	**64**	51°46′N	7°53′E
Ahmadabad, India	**79**	23°02′N	72°37′E
Ahmar Mountains, Eth.	**54**	9°15′N	41°00′E
Ahuacatlán, Mex.	**113**	21°03′N	104°29′W
Ahuachapán, El Sal.	**53**	13°55′N	89°51′W
Ahvaz, Iran	**82**	31°19′N	48°42′E
Ahvenanmaa, Fin.	**57**	60°15′N	20°00′E
Aiguá, Ur.	**181**	34°12′S	54°45′W
Aijal, India	**79**	23°44′N	92°43′E
Air Massif, Niger	**126**	18°00′N	8°30′E
Aisne, Fr.	**58**	49°26′N	2°50′E
Aissa, Mount, Alg.	**4**	32°51′N	0°30′W
Ajaccio, Fr.	**58**	41°55′N	8°44′E
Ajanta Range, India	**79**	20°30′N	76°00′E
Ajdabiya, Libya	**103**	30°48′N	20°14′E
Aketi, Zaire	**190**	2°44′N	23°46′E
Akhmim, Egypt	**52**	26°34′N	31°44′E
Akita, Japan	**93**	39°43′N	140°07′E
Akko, *see* Acre, Isr.	**86**	32°55′N	35°05′E
Akobo, Afr.	**54**	7°48′N	33°03′E
Akranes, Ice.	**77**	64°18′N	22°02′W
Akron, Oh., U.S.	**178**	41°04′N	81°31′W
Aksaray, Tur.	**168**	38°23′N	34°03′E
Aksehir, Tur.	**168**	38°21′N	31°25′E
Akure, Nig.	**127**	7°15′N	5°12′E
Akureyri, Ice.	**77**	65°44′N	18°08′W
Alabama, U.S.	**178**	32°50′N	87°00′W
Alagoas, Braz.	**24**	9°00′S	36°00′W
Alagoinhas, Braz.	**24**	12°07′S	38°26′W
al-Ahmadi, Kuw.	**99**	29°05′N	48°04′E
Alajuela, C.R.	**44**	10°01′N	84°13′W
al-Akhdar Mountains, Oman	**130**	23°15′N	57°20′E
al-Amara, Iraq	**83**	31°50′N	47°09′E
Alamor, Ec.	**51**	4°02′S	80°02′W
Alaotra, Lake, Madag.	**105**	17°30′S	48°30′E
al-Aqaba, Jord.	**94**	29°31′N	35°00′E
al-Arab, Sudan	**156**	9°02′N	29°28′E
Alarcon Reservoir, Spain	**154**	39°36′N	2°10′W
al-Ard, Cape, Kuw.	**99**	29°21′N	48°05′E
Alaska, U.S.	**178**	65°00′N	153°00′W
al-Assad, Lake, Syria	**161**	36°05′N	38°10′E
Alausí, Ec.	**51**	2°12′S	78°50′W
Alayh, Leb.	**101**	33°48′N	35°36′E
al-Bab, Syria	**161**	36°22′N	37°31′E
Albacete, Spain	**154**	38°59′N	1°51′W
al-Badari, Egypt	**52**	26°59′N	31°25′E
Alba-Iulia, Rom.	**142**	46°04′N	23°35′E
Albania, Eur.	**3**	41°00′N	20°00′E
Albany, N.Y., U.S.	**178**	42°39′N	73°45′W
al-Batrun, Leb.	**101**	34°15′N	35°39′E
Albert, Lake, Afr.	**170**	1°40′N	31°00′E
Alberta, Can.	**32**	54°00′N	113°00′W
Albert Canal, Bel.	**19**	50°39′N	5°37′E
Albert Nile, Ug.	**170**	3°36′N	32°02′E
Albina, Sur.	**157**	5°30′N	54°03′W
Ålborg, Den.	**48**	57°03′N	9°56′E
Ålborg Bay, Den.	**48**	56°45′N	10°30′E
Albuquerque, N.M., U.S.	**178**	35°05′N	106°39′W
Albury, Austl.	**14**	36°05′S	146°55′E
Alcalá de Henares, Spain	**154**	40°29′N	3°22′W
Alcamo, Italy	**88**	37°59′N	12°58′E
Alcántara Reservoir, Spain	**154**	39°45′N	6°25′W
Alcira, Spain	**154**	39°09′N	0°26′W
Alcoy, Spain	**154**	38°42′N	0°28′W
Aldabra Islands, Sey.	**149**	9°25′S	46°22′E
Al-Dafra, U.A.E.	**174**	23°25′N	53°25′E
Al-Dahna, Sau. Ar.	**147**	24°30′N	48°10′E
Al-Dahy Desert, Sau. Ar.	**147**	22°20′N	45°35′E
al-Damman, Sau. Ar.	**147**	26°26′N	50°07′E
al-Damur, Leb.	**101**	33°44′N	35°27′E
Aldan, U.S.S.R.	**172**	63°28′N	129°35′E
Alderney, Guernsey	**36**	49°43′N	2°12′W
al-Dimaniya, Iraq	**83**	31°59′N	44°56′E
Aleksinac, Yugo.	**189**	43°32′N	21°43′E
Alemania, Arg.	**11**	25°36′S	65°38′W
Alençon, Fr.	**58**	48°26′N	0°05′E
Aleppo, Syria	**161**	36°12′N	37°10′E
Alessandria, Italy	**88**	44°54′N	8°37′E
Ålesund, Nor.	**129**	62°28′N	6°09′E
Aleutian Islands, Ak., U.S.	**178**	52°00′N	176°00′W
Alexander Island, Ant.	**8**	71°00′S	70°00′W
Alexandretta, Gulf of, Tur.	**168**	36°30′N	35°40′E
Alexandria, Egypt	**52**	31°12′N	29°54′E
al-Faiyum, Egypt	**52**	29°19′N	30°50′E
al-Falluja, Iraq	**83**	33°20′N	43°46′E
Alfaro, Ec.	**51**	2°12′S	79°50′W
al-Fashir, Sudan	**156**	13°38′N	25°21′E
al-Fashn, Egypt	**52**	28°49′N	30°54′E
Algeciras, Spain	**154**	36°08′N	5°30′W
Algeria, Afr.	**4**	28°00′N	3°00′E
Alghero, Italy	**88**	40°34′N	8°19′E
Algiers, Alg.	**4**	36°47′N	3°03′E
al-Hadd, Bahr.	**16**	26°15′N	50°39′E
Al-Hajava Desert, Asia	**83**	30°00′N	44°00′E
al-Hasaka, Syria	**161**	36°29′N	40°45′E
al-Hasha Mountain, Yemen	**187**	13°43′N	44°31′E
Al-Hijaz Mountains, Sau. Ar.	**147**	19°45′N	41°55′E
al-Hilla, Iraq	**83**	32°29′N	44°25′E
al-Hudayda, Yemen	**187**	14°48′N	42°57′E
Alicante, Spain	**154**	38°21′N	0°29′W
Alice Springs, Austl.	**14**	23°42′S	133°53′E
Alice Town, Bah.	**16**	25°44′N	79°17′W
Aligarh, India	**79**	27°53′N	78°05′E
Alima, Congo	**43**	1°36′S	16°36′E
Alingsås, Swe.	**159**	57°56′N	12°31′E
al-Jabul Sabkha, Syria	**161**	36°03′N	37°39′E
al-Jadida, Mor.	**117**	33°16′N	8°30′W
al-Jafr Depression, Jord.	**94**	30°17′N	36°20′E
al-Jawf, Libya	**103**	24°11′N	23°19′E
al-Junayna, Sudan	**156**	13°27′N	22°27′E
al-Kairouan, Tun.	**167**	35°41′N	10°07′E
al-Kalb, Cape, Yem., P.D.R.	**188**	14°02′N	48°40′E
al-Kasserine, Tun.	**167**	35°11′N	8°48′E
al-Kazimiya, Iraq	**83**	33°22′N	44°20′E
al-Kef, Tun.	**167**	36°11′N	8°43′E
al-Khabur, Asia	**161**	35°08′N	40°26′E
al-Khawr, Qatar	**141**	25°41′N	51°30′E
al-Khums, Libya	**103**	32°39′N	14°16′E
Alkmaar, Neth.	**122**	52°37′N	4°44′E
al-Kut, Iraq	**83**	32°25′N	45°49′E
Allahabad, India	**79**	25°27′N	81°51′E
Allanmyo, Burma	**29**	19°22′N	95°13′E
al-Lawz, Mount, Sau. Ar.	**147**	28°40′N	35°18′E
Allen, Lake, Ire.	**84**	54°08′N	8°08′W
Allentown, Pa., U.S.	**178**	40°36′N	75°28′W
Allier, Fr.	**58**	45°05′N	3°35′E
Alligator Pond, Jam.	**91**	17°52′N	77°34′W
al-Litani, Leb.	**101**	33°20′N	35°14′E
All Saints, Antig.	**9**	17°03′N	61°48′W
Alma-Ata, U.S.S.R.	**172**	43°15′N	76°57′E
al-Madraka, Point, Oman	**130**	19°00′N	57°50′E
al-Mahalla al-Kubra, Egypt	**52**	30°58′N	31°10′E
al-Mansha, Egypt	**52**	26°28′N	31°48′E
al-Mansurah, Egypt	**52**	31°03′N	31°23′E
al-Marj, Libya	**103**	32°30′N	20°54′E
al-Masira, Oman	**130**	20°25′N	58°50′E
al-Masira Gulf, Oman	**130**	20°10′N	58°10′E
Almeirim, Braz.	**24**	1°32′S	52°34′W
Almelo, Neth.	**122**	52°21′N	6°39′E
Almendra Reservoir, Spain	**154**	41°15′N	6°10′W
Almeria, Spain	**154**	36°50′N	2°27′W
al-Metlaoui, Tun.	**167**	34°20′N	8°24′E
al-Minya, Egypt	**52**	28°06′N	30°45′E
Almirante, Pan.	**132**	9°18′N	82°24′W
al-Moknine, Tun.	**167**	35°38′N	10°54′E
al-Mubarraz, Sau. Ar.	**147**	25°55′N	49°36′E
al-Muharraq, Bahr.	**16**	26°16′N	50°37′E
al-Mukalla, Yem., P.D.R.	**188**	14°32′N	49°08′E
al-Nabk, Syria	**161**	34°01′N	36°44′E
al-Najaf, Iraq	**83**	31°59′N	44°20′E
al-Nasiriya, Iraq	**83**	31°02′N	46°16′E
Alofi, Niue	**128**	19°01′S	169°55′W
Alor Setar, Malay.	**107**	6°07′N	100°22′E
Alps, Eur.	**160**	46°25′N	10°00′E
al-Qadarif, Sudan	**156**	14°20′N	35°24′E
al-Qamishli, Syria	**161**	37°02′N	41°14′E
al-Qatif, Sau. Ar.	**147**	26°33′N	50°00′E
al-Qubayyat, Leb.	**101**	34°34′N	36°17′E
al-Qunaytira, Syria	**161**	33°07′N	35°49′E
al-Ramadi, Iraq	**83**	33°25′N	43°17′E
al-Raqqa, Syria	**161**	35°56′N	39°01′E
al-Rifa al-Gharbi, Bahr.	**16**	26°07′N	50°33′E
Als, Den.	**48**	54°59′N	9°55′E
al-Sabiya, Kuw.	**99**	29°35′N	48°10′E
al-Sabya, Sau. Ar.	**147**	17°09′N	42°37′E
al-Salamiya, Syria	**161**	35°01′N	37°03′E
al-Salimiya, Kuw.	**99**	29°18′N	48°03′E
al-Samawa, Iraq	**83**	31°18′N	45°17′E
Al-Sawda Plateau, Libya	**103**	28°40′N	15°30′E
al-Sham, Mount, Oman	**130**	23°13′N	57°16′E
al-Sulaymaniya, Iraq	**83**	35°33′N	45°26′E
al-Suwayda, Syria	**161**	32°42′N	36°34′E
Alta Gracia, Arg.	**11**	31°40′S	64°26′W
Altagracia de Orituco, Ven.	**183**	9°52′N	66°23′W
al-Taif, Sau. Ar.	**147**	21°16′N	40°24′E
Altai Mountains, Asia	**115**	48°00′N	90°00′E
Altamura, Italy	**88**	40°50′N	16°33′E
Altar Desert, Mex.	**113**	31°50′N	114°15′W
Altata, Mex.	**113**	24°38′N	107°55′W
Altdorf, Switz.	**160**	46°53′N	8°39′E
Altenburg, Ger., E.	**64**	50°59′N	12°26′E
Altiplano, S.A.	**22**	18°00′S	68°00′W
Alto Araguaia, Braz.	**24**	17°19′S	53°12′W
al-Ubayyid, Sudan	**156**	13°11′N	30°13′E
al-Uqsur, Egypt	**52**	25°41′N	32°39′E
al-Uwaynat, Mount, Afr.	**103**	21°54′N	24°58′E
Alvarado, Mex.	**113**	18°46′N	95°46′W
al-Zarqa, Jord.	**94**	32°05′N	36°06′E
Alzette, Eur.	**104**	49°22′N	6°09′E
al-Zubayr, Iraq	**83**	30°23′N	47°43′E
Amager, Den.	**48**	55°37′N	12°37′E
Amami, Japan	**93**	28°15′N	129°20′E
Amapá, Braz.	**24**	2°03′N	50°48′W
Amapá, Braz.	**24**	1°00′N	52°00′W
Amapala, Hond.	**74**	13°17′N	87°40′W
Amatitlan, Guat.	**70**	14°29′N	90°37′W
Amaury, Mrts.	**111**	20°08′S	57°40′E
Amazon, S.A.	**24**	0°05′S	50°00′W
Amazonas, Braz.	**24**	4°00′S	58°00′W
Ambato, Ec.	**51**	1°15′S	78°37′W
Ambelos, Cape, Grc.	**67**	39°56′N	23°55′E
Amberg, Ger., W.	**64**	49°27′N	11°52′E
Ambon, Indon.	**81**	3°43′S	128°12′E
Ambositra, Madag.	**105**	20°31′S	47°15′E
Ambre, Cape, Madag.	**105**	11°57′S	49°17′E
Ameland, Neth.	**122**	53°25′N	5°45′E
American Highland, Ant.	**8**	72°30′S	78°00′E
American Samoa, Oc.	**5**	14°20′S	170°00′W
Amerique, Sierra de, Nic.	**125**	12°12′N	85°19′W
Amersfoort, Neth.	**122**	52°09′N	5°24′E
Amery Ice Shelf, Ant.	**8**	69°30′S	72°00′E
Amiens, Fr.	**58**	49°54′N	2°18′E
Amirante Islands, Sey.	**149**	6°00′S	53°10′E
Amman, Jord.	**94**	31°57′N	35°56′E
Amol, Iran	**82**	36°23′N	52°20′E
Amritsar, India	**79**	31°35′N	74°53′E
Amrum, Ger., W.	**64**	54°39′N	8°21′E
Amsterdam, Neth.	**122**	52°22′N	4°54′E
Amsterdam-Rhine Canal, Neth.	**122**	51°57′N	5°20′E
Amstetten, Aus.	**15**	48°07′N	14°53′E
Amubri, C.R.	**44**	9°31′N	82°56′W
Amu Darya, Asia	**172**	43°40′N	59°01′E
Amundsen Sea, Ant.	**8**	72°30′S	112°00′W
Amur, Asia	**172**	52°56′N	141°10′E
Amyun, Leb.	**101**	34°18′N	35°49′E
Anabar, Nauru	**120**	0°30′S	166°57′E
Anaco, Ven.	**183**	9°27′N	64°28′W
Anai, Mount, India	**79**	10°10′N	77°04′E
Ana Maria, Gulf of, Cuba	**45**	21°25′N	78°40′W
Anápolis, Braz.	**24**	16°20′S	48°58′W
Anchorage, Ak., U.S.	**178**	61°13′N	149°54′W
Ancona, Italy	**88**	43°38′N	13°30′E
Ancón de Sardinas Bay, S.A.	**51**	1°30′N	79°00′W
Ancud, Chile	**37**	41°52′S	73°50′W
Andalgalá, Arg.	**11**	27°36′S	66°19′W
Andaman And Nicobar Islands, India	**79**	10°00′N	93°00′E
Andaman Islands, India	**79**	12°00′N	92°45′E
Andaman Sea, Asia	**29**	10°00′N	95°00′E
Andamarca, Bol.	**22**	18°49′S	67°31′W
Anderlecht, Bel.	**19**	50°50′N	4°18′E
Andes, S.A.	**135**	14°00′S	74°00′W
Andhra Pradesh, India	**79**	16°00′N	79°00′E
And Island, Nor.	**129**	69°08′N	15°54′E
Andizhan, U.S.S.R.	**172**	40°45′N	72°22′E
Andkhvoy, Afg.	**2**	36°56′N	65°08′E
Andoas, Peru	**135**	2°50′S	76°30′W
Andorra, And.	**5**	42°30′N	1°31′E
Andorra, Eur.	**5**	42°30′N	1°30′E
Andorra Valley, And.	**5**	42°30′N	1°30′E
Andropov, U.S.S.R.	**172**	58°03′N	38°52′E
Ándros, Grc.	**67**	37°45′N	24°42′E
Andros Island, Bah.	**16**	24°26′N	77°57′W
Andros Town, Bah.	**16**	24°43′N	77°47′W
Anécho, Togo	**165**	6°14′N	1°36′E
Anegada, V.I., Br.	**185**	18°45′N	64°20′W
Anegada Passage, V.I., Br.	**185**	18°30′N	63°40′W
Aneto Peak, Spain	**154**	42°38′N	0°40′E
Angara, U.S.S.R.	**172**	58°06′N	93°00′E
Ángel de la Guarda Island, Mex.	**113**	29°20′N	113°25′W
Angeles, Phil.	**136**	15°09′N	120°35′E
Angel Falls, Ven.	**183**	5°57′N	62°30′W
Angerman, Swe.	**159**	62°48′N	17°56′E
Angers, Fr.	**58**	47°28′N	0°33′W
Anglesey, Wales, U.K.	**175**	53°15′N	4°20′W
Angmagssalik, Grnld.	**68**	65°36′N	37°41′W
Angoche, Moz.	**118**	16°14′S	39°58′E
Angol, Chile	**37**	37°48′S	72°43′W
Angola, Afr.	**6**	12°30′S	18°30′E
Angoulême, Fr.	**58**	45°39′N	0°09′E
Anibare, Nauru	**120**	0°32′S	166°57′E
Anibare Bay, Nauru	**120**	0°32′S	166°57′E
Anie Peak, Eur.	**58**	42°57′N	0°43′W
Animas Mountain, Ur.	**181**	34°46′S	55°19′W
Ankara, Tur.	**168**	39°56′N	32°52′E
Ankaratra, Madag.	**105**	19°25′S	47°12′E
Anna, Nauru	**120**	0°30′S	166°56′E
Annaba, Alg.	**4**	36°54′N	7°46′E
Annamese Cordillera, Asia	**100**	17°00′N	106°00′E
Anna Point, Nauru	**120**	0°30′S	166°56′E
Annapolis, Md., U.S.	**178**	38°58′N	76°29′W
Annecy, Fr.	**58**	45°54′N	6°07′E
Annobón Island, Eq. Gui.	**53**	1°25′S	5°36′E
Ans, Bel.	**19**	50°39′N	5°32′E
Ansbach, Ger., W.	**64**	49°17′N	10°34′E
Anse-d'Hainault, Haiti	**73**	18°30′N	74°27′W
Anse La Raye, St. Luc.	**144**	13°57′N	61°03′W
Anshan, China	**38**	41°08′N	122°59′E
Ansina, Ur.	**181**	31°54′S	55°28′W
Antakya (Antioch), Tur.	**168**	36°14′N	36°07′E
Antalaha, Madag.	**105**	14°53′S	50°16′E
Antalya, Tur.	**168**	36°53′N	30°42′E
Antalya, Gulf of, Tur.	**168**	36°30′N	31°00′E
Antananarivo, Madag.	**105**	18°55′S	47°31′E
Antarctica	**8**	87°00′S	60°00′E
Antarctic Peninsula, Ant.	**8**	69°30′S	65°00′W
Antequera, Spain	**154**	37°01′N	4°33′W
Anti Atlas, Mor.	**117**	30°00′N	8°30′W
Antigua, Guat.	**70**	14°34′N	90°44′W
Antigua and Barbuda, N.A.	**9**	17°03′N	61°48′W
Anti-Lebanon Mountains, Asia	**101**	33°35′N	36°00′E
Antofagasta, Chile	**37**	23°39′S	70°24′W
Antofalla Volcano, Arg.	**11**	25°34′S	67°55′W
Antongil, Bay of, Madag.	**105**	15°45′S	49°50′E
Antsirabe, Madag.	**105**	19°51′S	47°02′E
Antsiranana, Madag.	**105**	12°16′S	49°17′E
Antwerp, Bel.	**19**	51°13′N	4°25′E
Anuradhapura, Sri L.	**155**	8°21′N	80°23′E
Aoji, Kor., N.	**98**	42°31′N	130°23′E
Aomori, Japan	**93**	40°39′N	140°45′E
Aopo, W. Sam.	**187**	13°29′S	172°30′W
Aosta, Italy	**88**	45°44′N	7°20′E
Aoukalé, Afr.	**35**	9°17′N	22°42′E
Aoukâr, Maur.	**110**	18°00′N	9°30′W
Apaporis, S.A.	**42**	1°23′S	69°25′W
Apatzingán [de la Constitución], Mex.	**113**	19°05′N	102°21′W
Apeldoorn, Neth.	**122**	52°13′N	5°58′E
Apennines, Italy	**88**	43°00′N	13°00′E
Apia, W. Sam.	**187**	13°50′S	171°44′W
Aplahoue, Benin	**20**	6°56′N	1°41′E
Apo, Mount, Phil.	**136**	6°59′N	125°16′E
Apolima Strait, W. Sam.	**187**	14°50′S	172°10′W
Apolo, Bol.	**22**	14°43′S	68°31′W
Apostolos Andreas, Cape, Cyp.	**46**	35°42′N	34°35′E
Appalachian Mountains, N.A.	**178**	41°00′N	77°00′W
Approuague, Fr. Gu.	**60**	4°38′N	51°58′W
Apure, Ven.	**183**	7°37′N	66°25′W
Apurímac, Peru	**135**	11°48′S	74°03′W
Aqaba, Gulf of	**52**	29°00′N	34°40′E
Aquidabán, Para.	**134**	23°11′S	57°32′W
Aquidauana, Braz.	**24**	20°28′S	55°48′W
Aquin, Haiti	**73**	18°17′N	73°24′W
Arab, Shatt al-, Asia	**83**	29°57′N	48°34′E
Arabelo, Ven.	**183**	4°55′N	64°13′W
Arabian Desert, Egypt	**52**	28°00′N	32°00′E
Aracaju, Braz.	**24**	10°55′S	37°04′W
Arad, Isr.	**86**	31°15′N	35°13′E
Arad, Rom.	**142**	46°11′N	21°20′E
Arafura Sea	**81**	9°00′S	133°00′E
Araguaia, Braz.	**24**	5°21′S	48°41′W
Arak, Iran	**82**	34°05′N	49°41′E
Aral Sea, U.S.S.R.	**172**	45°00′N	60°00′E
Aran Islands, Ire.	**84**	53°07′N	9°43′W
Aranjuez, Spain	**154**	40°02′N	3°36′W
Arapey, Ur.	**181**	30°58′S	57°32′W
Araraquara, Braz.	**24**	21°47′S	48°10′W
Ararat, Mount, Tur.	**168**	39°42′N	44°18′E
Aras, Asia	**82**	39°40′N	48°00′E
Arauca, Col.	**42**	7°05′N	70°45′W
Arauca, S.A.	**183**	7°24′N	66°35′W
Aravalli Range, India	**79**	25°00′N	73°30′E
Arbon, Switz.	**160**	47°31′N	9°26′E
Arcachon, Fr.	**58**	44°37′N	1°12′W
Arcatao, El Sal.	**53**	14°05′N	88°45′W
Ardabil, Iran	**82**	38°15′N	48°18′E
Ardenne Plateau, Eur.	**19**	50°10′N	5°45′E
Arecibo, P.R.	**140**	18°28′N	66°43′W
Arenal Point, Trin.	**166**	10°03′N	61°56′W
Arendal, Nor.	**129**	58°27′N	8°48′E
Arenillas, Ec.	**51**	3°33′S	80°04′W
Arequipa, Peru	**135**	16°24′S	71°33′W
Arequito, Arg.	**11**	33°09′S	61°28′W
Arezzo, Italy	**88**	43°25′N	11°53′E
Argentina, S.A.	**11**	34°00′S	64°00′W
Argentino, Lake, Arg.	**11**	50°13′S	72°25′W
Argeş, Rom.	**142**	44°04′N	26°37′E
Arghandab, Asia	**2**	31°27′N	64°23′E
Argyle, Lake, Austl.	**14**	16°15′S	128°45′E
Århus, Den.	**48**	56°09′N	10°13′E
Arica, Chile	**37**	18°29′S	70°20′W
Arica, Col.	**42**	2°08′S	71°47′W
Arima, Trin.	**166**	10°38′N	61°17′W
Aripo, El Cerro del, Trin.	**166**	10°43′N	61°15′W
Aripuanã, Braz.	**24**	9°10′S	60°38′W
Aripuanã, Braz.	**24**	5°07′S	60°24′W
Arizona, U.S.	**178**	34°00′N	112°00′W
Arkansas, U.S.	**178**	34°50′N	92°30′W
Arkansas, U.S.	**178**	33°48′N	91°04′W
Arkhangelsk, U.S.S.R.	**172**	64°34′N	40°32′E
Armant, Egypt	**52**	25°37′N	32°32′E
Armenia, Col.	**42**	4°31′N	75°41′W
Arnauti, Cape, Cyp.	**46**	35°06′N	32°17′E
Arnhem, Neth.	**122**	51°59′N	5°55′E
Arnhem Land, Austl.	**14**	13°10′S	134°30′E
Arran, Scot., U.K.	**175**	55°35′N	5°15′W
Arras, Fr.	**58**	50°17′N	2°47′E
Artemisa, Cuba	**45**	22°49′N	82°46′W
Artibonite, Haiti	**73**	19°15′N	72°47′W
Artigas, Ur.	**181**	30°24′S	56°28′W
Arua, Ug.	**170**	3°01′N	30°55′E
Aruba, N.A.	**123**	12°30′N	69°58′W
Arue, Fr. Poly.	**60**	17°32′S	149°32′W
Arunachal Pradesh, India	**79**	28°30′N	95°00′E
Arusha, Tan.	**163**	3°22′S	36°41′E
Asadabad, Afg.	**2**	34°52′N	71°09′E
Asahi, Mount, Japan	**93**	43°40′N	142°51′E
Asahikawa, Japan	**93**	43°46′N	142°22′E
Asansol, India	**79**	23°41′N	86°59′E
Aschaffenburg, Ger., W.	**64**	49°59′N	9°09′E
Aschersleben, Ger., E.	**64**	51°45′N	11°27′E
Ascoli Piceno, Italy	**88**	42°51′N	13°34′E
Asenovgrad, Bul.	**27**	42°01′N	24°52′E
Ashburton, N.Z.	**124**	43°55′S	171°45′E
Ashburton, Austl.	**14**	21°40′S	114°56′E
Ashdod, Isr.	**86**	31°49′N	34°40′E
Ashkelon, *see* Ashqelon, Isr.	**86**	31°40′N	34°35′E
Ashkhabad, U.S.S.R.	**172**	37°57′N	58°23′E
Ashmore Reef, Austl.	**14**	12°14′S	123°05′E
Ashqelon (Ashkelon), Isr.	**86**	31°40′N	34°35′E
Asinara, Gulf of, Italy	**88**	41°00′N	8°30′E
Asir, Sau. Ar.	**147**	19°00′N	42°00′E
Asmera, Eth.	**54**	15°20′N	38°53′E
Asnen, Swe.	**159**	56°38′N	14°42′E
Aspiring, Mount, N.Z.	**124**	44°23′S	168°44′E
Assal, Lake, Dji.	**49**	11°41′N	42°25′E
Assam, India	**79**	26°00′N	92°00′E
Assen, Neth.	**122**	52°59′N	6°34′E
Asti, Italy	**88**	44°54′N	8°12′E
Astra, Arg.	**11**	45°45′S	67°30′W
Astrakhan, U.S.S.R.	**172**	46°21′N	48°03′E
Asunción, Para.	**134**	25°16′S	57°40′W
Asuncion Mita, Guat.	**70**	14°20′N	89°43′W
Aswan, Egypt	**52**	24°05′N	32°53′E
Asyut, Egypt	**52**	27°11′N	31°11′E
Atacama Desert, Chile	**37**	24°30′S	69°15′W
Atakora Range, Benin	**20**	10°30′N	1°20′E
Atakpamé, Togo	**165**	7°32′N	1°08′E
Atalaya, Peru	**135**	10°44′S	73°45′W
Atar, Maur.	**110**	20°31′N	13°03′W
Atbara, Sudan	**156**	17°42′N	33°59′E
Atbara, Afr.	**156**	17°40′N	33°56′E
Athens, Grc.	**67**	37°58′N	23°43′E
Athlone, Ire.	**84**	53°25′N	7°56′W
Atico, Peru	**135**	16°14′S	73°39′W
Atitlán, Lake, Guat.	**70**	14°42′N	91°12′W
Atlanta, Ga., U.S.	**178**	33°44′N	84°23′W
Atlantida, Ur.	**181**	34°46′S	55°45′W
Atlas Mountains, Afr.	**4**	33°00′N	2°00′W
Atrak, Asia	**82**	37°28′N	53°57′E
Atrato, Col.	**42**	8°17′N	76°58′W
Attapeu, Laos	**100**	14°48′N	106°50′E
Auckland, N.Z.	**124**	36°52′S	174°46′E
Auderghem, Bel.	**19**	50°49′N	4°26′E
Aue, Ger., E.	**64**	50°35′N	12°42′E
Augsburg, Ger., W.	**64**	48°23′N	10°53′E
Augusta, Italy	**88**	37°13′N	15°13′E
Augusta, Me., U.S.	**178**	44°19′N	69°46′W
Auki, Sol. Is.	**151**	8°45′S	160°42′E
Auob, Afr.	**119**	26°25′S	20°35′E
Aurillac, Fr.	**58**	44°56′N	2°26′E
Ausangate Mountain, Peru	**135**	13°48′S	71°14′W
Austin, Tx., U.S.	**178**	30°16′N	97°44′W
Australia, Oc.	**14**	25°00′S	135°00′E
Australian Capital Territory, Austl.	**14**	35°30′S	149°00′E
Austria, Eur.	**15**	47°20′N	13°20′E
Autlán de Navarro, Mex.	**113**	19°46′N	104°22′W
Auxerre, Fr.	**58**	47°48′N	3°34′E
Auyán-Tepuí, Ven.	**183**	5°55′N	62°32′W
Avarua, Cook Is.	**44**	21°12′S	159°46′W
Avatele, Niue	**128**	19°06′S	169°55′W
Avatiu, Cook Is.	**44**	21°12′S	159°47′W
Aveiro, Port.	**139**	40°38′N	8°39′W
Avellaneda, Arg.	**11**	34°39′S	58°23′W
Avellino, Italy	**88**	40°54′N	14°47′E
Avesta, Swe.	**159**	60°09′N	16°12′E
Avezzano, Italy	**88**	42°02′N	13°25′E
Avignon, Fr.	**58**	43°57′N	4°49′E
Ávila, Spain	**154**	40°39′N	4°42′W
Avilés, Spain	**154**	43°33′N	5°55′W
Avon, Eng., U.K.	**175**	52°25′N	1°31′W
Awali, Bahr.	**16**	26°05′N	50°33′E
Awash, Eth.	**54**	11°45′N	41°05′E
Awka, Nig.	**127**	6°12′N	7°05′E
Axios (Vardar), Eur.	**67**	40°31′N	22°43′E
Ayabaca, Peru	**135**	4°38′S	79°43′W
Ayacucho, Arg.	**11**	37°09′S	58°29′W
Ayacucho, Peru	**135**	13°07′S	74°13′W
Ayapel, Col.	**42**	8°19′N	75°09′W
Ayaviri, Peru	**135**	14°52′S	70°35′W
Ayo Ayo, Bol.	**22**	17°05′S	68°00′W
Ayr, Scot., U.K.	**175**	55°28′N	4°38′W
Ayutla [de los Libres], Mex.	**113**	16°54′N	99°13′W
Azaouad, Mali	**108**	19°00′N	3°00′W

K

Name	Page	Lat.	Long.
Kabale, Ug.	170	1°15'S	29°59'E
Kabalega Falls, Ug.	170	2°17'N	31°41'E
Kabul, Afg.	2	34°31'N	69°12'E
Kabul, Asia	131	33°55'N	72°14'E
Kabwe, Zam.	191	14°27'S	28°27'E
Kadoma, Zimb.	192	18°21'S	29°55'E
Kaduna, Nig.	127	10°33'N	7°27'E
Kaduna, Nig.	127	8°45'N	5°45'E
Kaesong, Kor., N.	98	37°59'N	126°33'E
Kafu, Ug.	170	1°08'N	31°05'E
Kafue, Zam.	191	15°56'S	28°55'E
Kagera, Afr.	163	0°57'S	31°47'E
Kagoshima, Japan	93	31°36'N	130°33'E
Kaieteur Fall, Guy.	72	5°10'N	59°28'W
Kaifeng, China	38	34°51'N	114°21'E
Kainji Lake, Nig.	127	10°30'N	4°35'E
Kaiserslautern, Ger., W.	64	49°26'N	7°46'E
Kajaani, Fin.	57	64°14'N	27°41'E
Kajaki, Lake, Afg.	2	32°22'N	65°16'E
Kalahari Desert, Afr.	23	23°00'S	22°00'E
Kalámai, Grc.	67	37°04'N	22°07'E
Kalemie, Zaire	190	5°56'S	29°12'E
Kalgoorlie, Austl.	14	30°45'S	121°28'E
Kalinin, U.S.S.R.	172	56°52'N	35°55'E
Kalisz, Pol.	138	51°46'N	18°06'E
Kalmar, Swe.	159	56°40'N	16°22'E
Kalmar, Swe.	159	56°40'N	16°25'E
Kalundborg, Den.	48	55°41'N	11°06'E
Kalutara, Sri L.	155	6°35'N	79°58'E
Kamalia, Pak.	131	30°44'N	72°39'E
Kama Reservoir, U.S.S.R.	172	58°52'N	56°15'E
Kamchatka Peninsula, U.S.S.R.	172	56°00'N	160°00'E
Kamchiya, Bul.	27	43°02'N	27°53'E
Kamenjak, Cape, Yugo.	189	44°46'N	13°55'E
Kamet, Asia	79	30°54'N	79°37'E
Kamina, Zaire	190	8°44'S	25°00'E
Kamloops, B.C., Can.	32	50°40'N	120°20'W
Kampala, Ug.	170	0°19'N	32°25'E
Kampen, Neth.	122	52°33'N	5°54'E
Kampot, Kam.	95	10°37'N	104°11'E
Kampuchea, Asia	95	13°00'N	105°00'E
Kâmuk, Mount, C.R.	44	9°17'N	83°04'W
Kananga, Zaire	190	5°54'S	22°25'E
Kanazawa, Japan	93	36°34'N	136°39'E
Kanchenjunga, Asia	120	27°42'N	88°08'E
Kandahar, Afg.	2	31°32'N	65°30'E
Kandavu Passage, Fiji	56	18°45'S	178°00'E
Kandy, Sri L.	155	7°18'N	80°38'E
Kangaroo Island, Austl.	14	35°50'S	137°06'E
Kanggye, Kor., N.	98	40°58'N	126°36'E
Kanghwa Bay, Kor., S.	98	37°20'N	126°35'E
Kanghwa Island, Kor., S.	98	37°40'N	126°27'E
Kankan, Gui.	71	10°23'N	9°18'W
Kano, Nig.	127	12°00'N	8°30'E
Kanpur, India	79	26°28'N	80°21'E
Kansas, U.S.	178	38°30'N	98°15'W
Kansas City, Mo., U.S.	178	39°05'N	94°34'W
Kanye, Bots.	23	24°59'S	25°19'E
Kaohsiung, Tai.	162	22°38'N	120°17'E
Kaokoveld, Nmb.	119	21°00'S	14°20'E
Kaolack, Sen.	148	14°09'N	16°04'W
Kapfenberg, Aus.	15	47°26'N	15°18'E
Kapos, Hung.	76	46°44'N	18°30'E
Kaposvár, Hung.	76	46°22'N	17°47'E
Kaptai, Bngl.	17	22°21'N	92°17'E
Kapuas, Indon.	81	0°25'S	109°40'E
Kapuskasing, On., Can.	32	49°25'N	82°26'W
Kara-Bogaz Gulf, U.S.S.R.	172	41°00'N	53°15'E
Karabuk, Tur.	168	41°12'N	32°37'E
Karachi, Pak.	131	24°52'N	67°03'E
Karaganda, U.S.S.R.	172	49°50'N	73°10'E
Karakoram Range, Asia	131	35°30'N	77°00'E
Kara Kum, U.S.S.R.	172	39°00'N	60°00'E
Karaman, Tur.	168	37°11'N	33°14'E
Kara Sea, U.S.S.R.	172	76°00'N	80°00'E
Karawanken, Eur.	15	46°30'N	14°25'E
Karbala, Iraq	83	32°36'N	44°02'E
Kardhitsa, Grc.	67	39°21'N	21°55'E
Kardiva Channel, Mald.	107	5°00'N	73°20'E
Karhula, Fin.	57	60°31'N	26°57'E
Kariba, Zimb.	192	16°30'S	28°45'E
Kariba, Lake, Afr.	192	17°00'S	28°00'E
Karimata Strait, Indon.	81	2°05'S	108°40'E
Karimganj, Bngl.	17	24°52'N	92°22'E
Karisimbi, Mount, Afr.	143	1°30'S	29°27'E
Karl-Marx-Stadt (Chemnitz), Ger., E.	64	50°50'N	12°55'E
Karlovac, Yugo.	189	45°29'N	15°34'E
Karlovy Vary, Czech.	47	50°11'N	12°52'E
Karlskoga, Swe.	159	59°20'N	14°31'E
Karlskrona, Swe.	159	56°10'N	15°35'E
Karlsruhe, Ger., W.	64	49°03'N	8°24'E
Karlstad, Swe.	159	59°22'N	13°30'E
Karmel, Mount, Isr.	86	32°44'N	35°02'E
Karnaphuli Reservoir, Bngl.	17	22°42'N	92°12'E
Karnataka, India	79	14°00'N	76°00'E
Kárpathos, Grc.	67	35°40'N	27°10'E
Kárpathos Strait, Grc.	67	35°50'N	27°30'E
Karre Mountains, C.A.R.	35	6°33'N	15°40'E
Kars, Tur.	168	40°36'N	43°05'E
Kartala, Com.	43	11°45'S	43°22'E
Kasai (Cassai), Afr.	190	3°06'S	16°57'E
Kasar al Kabir, Mor.	117	35°01'N	5°54'W
Kashan, Iran	82	33°59'N	51°29'E
Kashi, China	38	39°29'N	75°59'E
Kashmir, Pak.	131	35°00'N	75°00'E
Kasos Strait, Grc.	67	35°30'N	26°30'E
Kassala, Sudan	156	15°28'N	36°24'E
Kassel, Ger., W.	64	51°19'N	9°29'E
Katanga Plateau, Zaire	190	10°00'S	26°00'E
Katerina, Mount, Egypt	52	28°31'N	33°57'E
Katerini, Grc.	67	40°16'N	22°30'E
Kathmandu, Nepal	120	27°43'N	85°19'E
Katiola, I.C.	90	8°08'N	5°06'W
Katowice, Pol.	138	50°16'N	19°00'E
Katrineholm, Swe.	159	59°00'N	16°12'E
Katsina Ala, Afr.	127	7°48'N	8°52'E
Kattegat, Eur.	48	57°00'N	11°00'E
Katwijk aan Zee, Neth.	122	52°13'N	4°24'E
Kaufbeuren, Ger., W.	64	47°53'N	10°37'E
Kaukauveld, Afr.	119	20°00'S	20°30'E
Kaura Namoda, Nig.	127	12°35'N	6°35'E
Kavajë, Alb.	3	41°11'N	19°33'E
Kavála, Grc.	67	40°56'N	24°25'E
Kavieng, Pap. N. Gui.	133	2°35'S	150°50'E
Kavir, Dasht-e, Iran	82	34°40'N	54°30'E
Kaw, Fr. Gu.	60	4°29'N	52°02'W
Kawasaki, Japan	93	35°32'N	139°43'E
Kawn Umbu, Egypt	52	24°28'N	32°57'E
Kayes, Mali	108	14°27'N	11°26'W
Kayseri, Tur.	168	38°43'N	35°30'E
Kazakh Steppe, U.S.S.R.	172	49°00'N	72°00'E
Kazan, U.S.S.R.	172	55°49'N	49°08'E
Kazanluk, Bul.	27	42°37'N	25°24'E
Kazerun, Iran	82	29°37'N	51°38'E
Keban, Lake, Tur.	168	38°50'N	39°15'E
Kebne, Mount, Swe.	159	67°53'N	18°33'E
Kecskemét, Hung.	76	46°54'N	19°42'E
Kediri, Indon.	81	7°49'S	112°01'E
Keetmanshoop, Nmb.	119	26°36'S	18°08'E
Kefallinía, Grc.	67	38°15'N	20°35'E
Kefar Sava, Isr.	86	32°10'N	34°54'E
Keffi, Nig.	127	8°51'N	7°52'E
Keflavík, Ice.	77	64°02'N	22°36'W
Kegalla, Sri L.	155	7°15'N	80°21'E
Keiyasi, Fiji	56	17°54'S	177°45'E
Kékes, Hung.	76	47°55'N	20°02'E
Kelang, Malay.	107	3°02'N	101°27'E
Kelani, Sri L.	155	6°58'N	79°52'E
Kelkit, Tur.	168	40°46'N	36°32'E
Keluang, Malay.	107	2°02'N	103°19'E
Kemerovo, U.S.S.R.	172	55°20'N	86°05'E
Kemi, Fin.	57	65°49'N	24°32'E
Kemi, Fin.	57	65°47'N	24°30'E
Kemijärvi, Fin.	57	66°40'N	27°25'E
Kemijarvi, Fin.	57	66°36'N	27°24'E
Kemps Bay, Bah.	16	24°02'N	77°33'W
Kempten, Ger., W.	64	47°43'N	10°19'E
Kenema, S.L.	149	7°52'N	11°12'W
Kenitra, Mor.	117	34°16'N	6°40'W
Kentucky, U.S.	178	37°30'N	85°15'W
Kenya, Afr.	96	1°00'N	38°00'E
Kenya, Mount, Kenya	96	0°10'S	37°20'E
Kerala, India	79	10°00'N	76°30'E
Kerch, U.S.S.R.	172	45°22'N	36°27'E
Kerema, Pap. N. Gui.	133	8°00'S	145°45'E
Kerinci, Mount, Indon.	81	1°42'S	101°16'E
Kerkira, Grc.	67	39°36'N	19°56'E
Kerkrade, Neth.	122	50°52'N	6°04'E
Kerman, Iran	82	30°17'N	57°05'E
Kerulen, Asia	38	48°48'N	117°00'E
Ketou, Benin	20	7°22'N	2°36'E
Kettering, Eng., U.K.	175	52°24'N	0°44'W
Kew, T./C. Is.	169	21°54'N	72°02'W
Khabarovsk, U.S.S.R.	172	48°27'N	135°06'E
Khairpur, Pak.	131	27°32'N	68°46'E
Khalkis, Grc.	67	38°28'N	23°36'E
Khambhat, Gulf of, India	79	21°00'N	72°30'E
Khanabad, Afg.	2	36°41'N	69°07'E
Khandallah, N.Z.	124	41°15'S	174°47'E
Khanewal, Pak.	131	30°18'N	71°56'E
Khaniá, Grc.	67	35°31'N	24°02'E
Khanka, Lake, Asia	38	45°00'N	132°24'E
Khan Yunis, Isr. Occ.	86	31°21'N	34°19'E
Kharkov, U.S.S.R.	172	50°00'N	36°15'E
Khartoum, Sudan	156	15°36'N	32°32'E
Khaskovo, Bul.	27	41°56'N	25°33'E
Kholm, Afg.	2	36°42'N	67°41'E
Khon Kaen, Thai.	164	16°26'N	102°50'E
Khorramabad, Iran	82	33°30'N	48°20'E
Khorramshahr, Iran	82	30°25'N	48°11'E
Khouribga, Mor.	117	32°54'N	6°57'W
Khowst, Afg.	2	33°22'N	69°57'E
Khrysokhou Bay, Cyp.	46	35°06'N	32°25'E
Khulna, Bngl.	17	22°48'N	89°33'E
Khvoy, Iran	82	38°33'N	44°58'E
Khyber Pass, Asia	131	34°05'N	71°10'E
Kia, Sol. Is.	151	7°33'S	158°26'E
Kiberi, Pap. N. Gui.	133	7°25'S	143°48'E
Kibumbu, Bdi.	30	3°32'S	29°45'E
Kibungo, Rw.	143	2°10'S	30°32'E
Kibuye, Rw.	143	2°03'S	29°21'E
Kičevo, Yugo.	189	41°31'N	20°57'E
Kiel, Ger., W.	64	54°20'N	10°08'E
Kielce, Pol.	138	50°52'N	20°37'E
Kieler Bay, Ger., W.	64	54°35'N	10°35'E
Kiev, U.S.S.R.	172	50°26'N	30°31'E
Kigali, Rw.	143	1°57'S	30°04'E
Kii Channel, Japan	93	33°55'N	134°55'E
Kikinda, Yugo.	189	45°50'N	20°28'E
Kikwit, Zaire	190	5°02'S	18°49'E
Kilimanjaro, Mount, Tan.	163	3°04'S	37°22'E
Kilkenny, Ire.	84	52°39'N	7°15'W
Killarney, Lake, Bah.	16	25°03'N	77°27'W
Kilmarnock, Scot., U.K.	175	55°36'N	4°30'W
Kimberley, S. Afr.	152	28°43'S	24°46'E
Kimberley Plateau, Austl.	14	17°00'S	127°00'E
Kimchaek, Kor., N.	98	40°41'N	129°12'E
Kimchon, Kor., S.	98	36°07'N	128°05'E
Kinabalu Mountain, Malay.	107	6°05'N	116°33'E
Kindia, Gui.	71	10°04'N	12°51'W
Kindu, Zaire	190	2°57'S	25°56'E
King Island, Austl.	14	39°50'S	144°00'E
Kingshill, V.I.U.S.	185	17°44'N	64°48'W
Kingston, On., Can.	32	44°18'N	76°34'W
Kingston, Jam.	91	18°00'N	76°48'W
Kingston, Norf. I.	128	29°03'S	167°58'E
Kingstown, St. Vin.	145	13°09'N	61°14'W
King William's Town, S. Afr.	152	32°51'S	27°22'E
Kinkony, Lake, Madag.	105	16°08'S	45°50'E
Kinnairds Head, Scot., U.K.	175	57°42'N	2°00'W
Kinshasa (Léopoldville), Zaire	190	4°18'S	15°18'E
Kinyeti, Sudan	156	3°57'N	32°54'E
Kipushi, Zaire	190	11°46'N	27°14'E
Kira Kira, Sol. Is.	151	10°27'S	161°56'E
Kirghiz Steppe, U.S.S.R.	172	49°00'N	81°00'E
Kiribati, Oc.	97	1°25'N	173°00'E
Kirikkale, Tur.	168	39°50'N	33°31'E
Kiritimati, Kir.	97	1°52'N	157°20'W
Kirkcaldy, Scot., U.K.	175	56°07'N	3°10'W
Kirkland Lake, On., Can.	32	48°09'N	80°02'W
Kirkuk, Iraq	83	35°28'N	44°28'E
Kirkwall, Scot., U.K.	175	58°59'N	2°58'W
Kirov, U.S.S.R.	172	58°38'N	49°42'E
Kirsehir, Tur.	168	39°09'N	34°10'E
Kirthar Range, Pak.	131	27°00'N	67°10'E
Kiruna, Swe.	159	67°51'N	20°16'E
Kiryath Gath, Isr.	86	31°37'N	34°46'E
Kiryath Malachi, Isr.	86	31°42'N	34°38'E
Kiryath Shemona, Isr.	86	33°12'N	35°35'E
Kiryath Tivon, Isr.	86	32°43'N	35°08'E
Kisangani, Zaire	190	0°30'S	25°12'E
Kishinev, U.S.S.R.	172	47°00'N	28°50'E
Kishon, Isr.	86	32°49'N	35°02'E
Kishorganj, Bngl.	17	24°26'N	90°46'E
Kiskörei Reservoir, Hung.	76	47°35'N	20°40'E
Kismayu, Som.	151	0°23'S	42°30'E
Kisumu, Kenya	96	0°06'S	34°45'E
Kitakami, Japan	93	38°25'N	141°19'E
Kitakyushu, Japan	93	33°53'N	130°50'E
Kitimat, B.C., Can.	32	54°03'N	128°33'W
Kitridge Point, Barb.	18	13°10'N	59°25'W
Kitwe, Zam.	191	12°49'S	28°13'E
Kivu, Lake, Afr.	143	2°00'S	29°10'E
Kizil, Tur.	168	41°44'N	35°58'E
Kladno, Czech.	47	50°08'N	14°05'E
Klagenfurt, Aus.	15	46°38'N	14°18'E
Klakah, Indon.	81	7°59'S	113°15'E
Klaksvík, Faer. Is.	55	62°14'N	6°36'W
Klara, Eur.	159	59°23'N	13°32'E
Klerksdorp, S. Afr.	152	26°58'S	26°39'E
Klet', Czech.	47	48°52'N	14°17'E
Kleve, Ger., W.	64	51°48'N	6°09'E
Klosterneuburg, Aus.	15	48°18'N	16°20'E
Kloulklubed, Palau	132	7°02'N	134°15'E
Klyuchevskaya Sopka Volcano, U.S.S.R.	172	56°04'N	160°38'E
Knittelfeld, Aus.	15	47°14'N	14°50'E
Knjaževac, Yugo.	189	43°34'N	22°16'E
Knoxville, Tn., U.S.	178	35°57'N	83°55'W
Kobar Sink, Eth.	54	14°00'N	40°30'E
Kobe, Japan	93	34°41'N	135°10'E
Koblenz, Ger., W.	64	50°21'N	7°35'E
Kočani, Yugo.	189	41°55'N	22°25'E
Kochi, Japan	93	33°33'N	133°33'E
Koforidua, Ghana	65	6°03'N	0°17'W
Kofu, Japan	93	35°39'N	138°35'E
Køge, Den.	48	55°27'N	12°11'E
Køge Bay, Den.	48	55°30'N	12°20'E
Kogon, Gui.	71	11°09'N	14°42'W
Kohat, Pak.	131	33°35'N	71°26'E
Kohima, India	79	25°40'N	94°07'E
Kokkola, Fin.	57	63°50'N	23°07'E
Koko Nor, China	38	36°50'N	100°20'E
Kokopo, Pap. N. Gui.	133	4°20'S	152°15'E
Kola Peninsula, U.S.S.R.	172	67°30'N	37°00'E
Kolda, Sen.	148	12°53'N	14°57'W
Kolding, Den.	48	55°31'N	9°29'E
Kolhapur, India	79	16°42'N	74°13'E
Kolonia, Micron.	114	6°58'N	158°13'E
Kolumadulu Atoll, Mald.	107	2°25'N	73°10'E
Kolwezi, Zaire	190	10°43'S	25°28'E
Kolyma, U.S.S.R.	172	69°30'N	161°00'E
Komadugu Gana, Nig.	127	13°05'N	12°24'E
Komadugu Yobe, Afr.	127	13°43'N	13°20'E
Komandorskiye Islands, U.S.S.R.	172	55°00'N	167°00'E
Komárno, Czech.	47	47°45'N	18°09'E
Komoé, Afr.	90	5°12'N	3°44'W
Komotini, Grc.	67	41°08'N	25°25'E
Kompong Cham, Kam.	95	12°00'N	105°27'E
Kompong Chhnang, Kam.	95	12°15'N	104°40'E
Kompong Kleang, Kam.	95	13°06'N	104°08'E
Kompong Som, Kam.	95	10°38'N	103°30'E
Kompong Som Bay, Kam.	95	10°50'N	103°32'E
Kompong Speu, Kam.	95	11°27'N	104°32'E
Kompong Thom, Kam.	95	12°42'N	104°54'E
Komsomolsk, U.S.S.R.	172	50°35'N	137°02'E
Koné, N. Cal.	123	21°04'S	164°52'E
Kong, Asia	100	13°32'N	105°58'E
Kong Island, Kam.	95	11°20'N	103°00'E
Konin, Pol.	138	52°13'N	18°16'E
Konkama, Eur.	57	68°29'N	22°17'E
Konkouré, Gui.	71	9°58'N	13°42'W
Konongo, Ghana	65	6°37'N	1°11'W
Konstanz, Ger., W.	64	47°40'N	9°10'E
Kontum Plateau, Viet.	184	13°55'N	108°05'E
Konya, Tur.	168	37°52'N	32°31'E
Koper, Yugo.	189	45°33'N	13°44'E
Köping, Swe.	159	59°31'N	16°00'E
Koppeh Mountains, Asia	82	37°50'N	58°00'E
Koprivnica, Yugo.	189	46°10'N	16°50'E
Korab Mountains, Eur.	3	41°47'N	20°34'E
Koralpe, Aus.	15	46°50'N	14°58'E
Korçë, Alb.	3	40°37'N	20°46'E
Korčula, Yugo.	189	42°57'N	16°50'E
Korea, Asia	98	38°00'N	127°00'E
Korea Bay, Asia	38	39°00'N	124°00'E
Korea Strait, Asia	93	34°00'N	129°00'E
Korhogo, I.C.	90	9°27'N	5°38'W
Korinthos, Grc.	67	37°56'N	22°56'E
Kormakiti, Cape, Cyp.	46	35°24'N	32°56'E
Korolevu, Fiji	56	18°13'S	177°44'E
Koror, Palau	132	7°20'N	134°29'E
Koros, Eur.	76	46°43'N	20°12'E
Koro Sea, Fiji	56	18°00'S	179°50'E
Korovou, Fiji	56	17°57'S	178°21'E
Korsør, Den.	48	55°20'N	11°09'E
Kortrijk, Bel.	19	50°50'N	3°16'E
Kosciusko, Mount, Austl.	14	36°27'S	148°16'E
Košice, Czech.	47	48°43'N	21°15'E
Kosovo and Metohija, Yugo.	189	42°30'N	21°00'E
Kosovska Mitrovica, Yugo.	189	42°53'N	20°52'E
Koszalin, Pol.	138	54°12'N	16°09'E
Kota Baharu, Malay.	107	6°08'N	102°15'E
Kota Kinabalu, Malay.	107	5°59'N	116°04'E
Kotka, Fin.	57	60°28'N	26°55'E
Kotor Bay, Yugo.	189	42°25'N	18°35'E
Kotto, C.A.R.	35	4°14'N	22°02'E
Koula-Moutou, Gabon	61	1°08'S	12°29'E
Koumac, N. Cal.	123	20°33'S	164°17'E
Koundougou, Burkina	28	11°44'N	4°31'W
Kourou, Fr. Gu.	60	5°09'N	52°39'W
Kouroussa, Gui.	71	10°39'N	9°53'W
Kowloon, H.K.	75	22°18'N	114°10'E
Kowt-e Ashrow, Afg.	2	34°27'N	68°48'E
Kozan, Tur.	168	37°27'N	35°49'E
Kra, Isthmus of, Asia	164	10°20'N	99°00'E
Kragujevac, Yugo.	189	44°01'N	20°55'E
Krakatoa, Indon.	81	6°07'S	105°24'E
Kraków (Cracow), Pol.	138	50°03'N	19°58'E
Kralendijk, Neth. Ant.	123	12°10'N	68°17'W
Kraljevica, Yugo.	189	45°16'N	14°34'E
Kraljevo, Yugo.	189	43°43'N	20°41'E
Kranj, Yugo.	189	46°15'N	14°21'E
Krasnodar, U.S.S.R.	172	45°02'N	39°00'E
Krasnoyarsk, U.S.S.R.	172	56°01'N	92°50'E
Kratie, Kam.	95	12°29'N	106°01'E
Krawang, Indon.	81	6°19'S	107°17'E
Krawang, Cape, Indon.	81	5°56'S	107°00'E
Krems, Aus.	15	48°25'N	15°36'E
Krishna, India	79	15°57'N	80°59'E
Kristiansand, Nor.	129	58°10'N	8°00'E
Kristianstad, Swe.	159	56°02'N	14°08'E
Kristiansund, Nor.	129	63°07'N	7°45'E
Krivoj Rog, U.S.S.R.	172	47°55'N	33°21'E
Krk, Yugo.	189	45°05'N	14°35'E
Kroonstad, S. Afr.	152	27°46'S	27°12'E
Krujë, Alb.	3	41°30'N	19°48'E
Krung Koh Kong, Kam.	95	11°37'N	102°59'E
Kruševac, Yugo.	189	43°35'N	21°20'E
Ksour Essaf, Tun.	167	35°25'N	11°00'E
Kuala Lumpur, Malay.	107	3°10'N	101°42'E
Kuala Terengganu, Malay.	107	5°20'N	103°08'E
Kuching, Malay.	107	1°33'N	110°20'E
Kudus, Indon.	81	6°48'S	110°50'E
Kufstein, Aus.	15	47°35'N	12°10'E
Kuibyshev, U.S.S.R.	172	53°12'N	50°09'E
Kuito, Ang.	6	12°22'S	16°56'E
Kuju, Mount, Japan	93	33°05'N	131°15'E
Kuku Point, Wake I.	185	19°18'N	166°34'E
Kula, Yugo.	189	45°36'N	19°32'E
Kula Kangri, Bhu.	21	28°03'N	90°27'E
Kum, Kor., N.	98	36°00'N	126°40'E
Kumamoto, Japan	93	32°48'N	130°43'E
Kumanovo, Yugo.	189	42°08'N	21°43'E
Kumasi, Ghana	65	6°41'N	1°35'W
Kumon Range, Burma	29	26°30'N	97°15'E
Kunlun Mountains, China	38	36°30'N	88°00'E
Kunming, China	38	25°05'N	102°40'E
Kunsan, Kor., S.	98	35°58'N	126°41'E
Kuopio, Fin.	57	62°54'N	27°41'E
Kupang, Indon.	81	10°10'S	123°35'E
Kurashiki, Japan	93	34°35'N	133°46'E
Kurdufan, Sudan	156	12°00'N	27°00'E
Kurdzhali, Bul.	27	41°39'N	25°22'E
Kurgan, U.S.S.R.	172	55°26'N	65°18'E
Kuril Islands, U.S.S.R.	172	46°10'N	152°00'E
Kursk, U.S.S.R.	172	51°42'N	36°12'E
Kurume, Japan	93	33°19'N	130°31'E
Kurunegala, Sri L.	155	7°29'N	80°22'E
Kusti, Sudan	156	13°10'N	32°40'E
Kutahya, Tur.	168	39°25'N	29°59'E
Kutch, Gulf of, India	79	22°36'N	69°30'E
Kutno, Pol.	138	52°15'N	19°23'E
Kuujjuak, P.Q., Can.	32	58°06'N	68°25'W
Kuwait, Kuw.	99	29°20'N	47°59'E
Kuwait, Asia	99	29°30'N	47°45'E
Kuwait Bay, Kuw.	99	29°30'N	48°00'E
Kvarner, Yugo.	189	44°45'N	14°15'E
Kverk Mountain, Ice.	77	64°43'N	16°38'W
Kwahu Plateau, Ghana	65	6°30'N	0°30'W
Kwajalein, Marsh. Is.	109	9°05'N	167°20'E
Kwakoegron, Sur.	157	5°15'N	55°20'W
Kwando, Afr.	191	18°27'S	23°32'E
Kwangju, Kor., S.	98	35°09'N	126°54'E
Kwango, Afr.	190	3°14'S	17°23'E
Kwanmo, Mount, Kor., N.	98	41°42'N	129°13'E
Kweichow Plateau, China	38	27°00'N	107°00'E
Kwekwe, Zimb.	192	18°55'S	29°49'E
Kwilu, Afr.	190	3°22'S	17°22'E
Kwun Tong, H.K.	75	22°19'N	114°12'E
Kyaikto, Burma	29	17°18'N	97°01'E
Kyoga, Lake, Ug.	170	1°30'N	33°00'E
Kyonggi Bay, Asia	98	37°25'N	126°00'E
Kyoto, Japan	93	35°00'N	135°45'E
Kyrenia, Cyp.	46	35°20'N	33°19'E
Kysica, Pol.	138	50°54'N	20°55'E
Kyushu, Japan	93	33°00'N	131°00'E
Kyustendil, Bul.	27	42°17'N	22°41'E
Kyzyl Kum, U.S.S.R.	172	42°00'N	64°00'E

L

Name	Page	Lat.	Long.
La Banda, Arg.	11	27°44'S	64°15'W
Labé, Gui.	71	11°19'N	12°17'W
Labe (Elbe), Eur.	47	50°53'N	14°14'E
Labrador, Nf., Can.	32	54°00'N	62°00'W
Labrador Sea, N.A.	32	57°00'N	53°00'W
La Brea, Trin.	166	10°15'N	61°37'W
La Broa Bay, Cuba	45	22°35'N	82°00'W
Labutta, Burma	29	16°09'N	94°46'E
La Calera, Chile	37	32°47'S	71°12'W
Lacantum, N.A.	70	16°36'N	90°39'W
Laccadive Sea, Asia	107	7°00'N	76°00'E
La Ceiba, Hond.	74	15°47'N	86°50'W
Lac Giao, Viet.	184	12°40'N	108°03'E
La-Chaux-de-Fonds, Switz.	160	47°06'N	6°50'E
Lachlan, Austl.	14	34°21'S	143°57'E
La Chorrera, Col.	42	0°44'S	73°01'W
La Chorrera, Pan.	132	8°53'N	79°47'W
La Colorado, Mex.	113	28°41'N	110°25'W
La Concepción, Ven.	183	10°38'N	71°50'W
La Coruña, Spain	154	43°22'N	8°23'W
La Cruz, C.R.	44	11°04'N	85°39'W
La Cruz, Ur.	181	33°58'S	56°15'W
Ladakh Range, Asia	79	34°00'N	78°00'E
La Digue, Sey.	149	4°21'S	55°50'E
Ladoga, Lake, U.S.S.R.	172	61°00'N	31°30'E
La Dorada, Col.	42	5°27'N	74°40'W
Ladysmith, S. Afr.	152	28°34'S	29°45'E
Lae, Pap. N. Gui.	133	6°45'S	147°00'E
La Encantada, Mount, Mex.	113	31°00'N	115°24'W
La Esmeralda, Mex.	113	27°17'N	103°39'W
La Esmeralda, Para.	134	22°13'S	62°38'W
Læsø, Den.	48	57°16'N	11°01'E
La Esperanza, Hond.	74	14°20'N	88°10'W
La Estrella, Bol.	22	16°30'S	63°45'W
Lafiagi, Nig.	127	8°52'N	5°25'E
La Florida, Guat.	70	16°33'N	90°27'W
La Galite, Tun.	167	37°32'N	8°56'E
Lågen, Nor.	129	61°08'N	10°25'E
Laghouat, Alg.	4	33°50'N	2°59'E
Lagos, Nig.	127	6°27'N	3°24'E
Lagos de Moreno, Mex.	113	21°21'N	101°55'W
La Goulette, Tun.	167	36°49'N	10°18'E
La Guaira, Ven.	183	10°36'N	66°56'W
La Guardia, Bol.	22	17°54'S	63°20'W
Lagunas, Peru	135	5°14'S	75°38'W
Lagunillas, Bol.	22	19°38'S	63°43'W
La Hague, Cape, Fr.	58	49°43'N	1°57'W
Lahij, Yem., P.D.R.	188	13°02'N	44°54'E
Lahijan, Iran	82	37°12'N	50°01'E
Lahore, Pak.	131	31°35'N	74°18'E
Lahti, Fin.	57	60°58'N	25°40'E
La Isabela, Cuba	45	22°57'N	80°01'W
Lake Pukaki, N.Z.	124	44°11'S	170°09'E
Lakshadweep, India	79	10°00'N	73°00'E
Laleh Zar, Mount, Iran	82	29°24'N	56°46'E
La Libertad, El Sal.	53	13°29'N	89°19'W
La Louvière, Bel.	19	50°28'N	4°11'E
Lama-Kara, Togo	165	9°33'N	1°12'E
Lamap, Vanuatu	182	16°26'S	167°43'E
La Marmora Peak, Italy	88	39°59'N	9°19'E
Lamas, Peru	135	6°25'S	76°35'W
La Massana, And.	5	42°32'N	1°31'E
Lambaréné, Gabon	61	0°42'S	10°13'E
Lambasa, Fiji	56	16°26'S	179°24'E
Lambayeque, Peru	135	6°42'S	79°55'W
Lambert Glacier, Ant.	8	71°00'S	70°00'E
La Merced, Peru	135	11°03'S	75°19'W
Lamia, Grc.	67	38°54'N	22°26'E
Lampazos de Naranjo, Mex.	113	27°01'N	100°31'W
Lancaster, Eng., U.K.	175	54°03'N	2°48'W
Land's End, Eng., U.K.	175	50°03'N	5°44'W
Landshut, Ger., W.	64	48°33'N	12°09'E
Langeland, Den.	48	54°50'N	10°50'E
Langenthal, Switz.	160	47°13'N	7°47'E
Langerhagen, Ger., W.	64	52°27'N	9°44'E
Langia Mountains, Ug.	170	3°35'N	33°40'E
Lang Island, Nor.	129	68°44'N	14°50'E
Lansing, Mi., U.S.	178	42°43'N	84°33'W
Lanzhou, China	38	36°03'N	103°41'E
Laon, Fr.	58	49°34'N	3°40'E
La Oroya, Peru	135	11°32'S	75°54'W
Laos, Asia	100	18°00'N	105°00'E
La Palma, El Sal.	53	14°19'N	89°11'W
La Palma, Pan.	132	7°42'N	80°12'W
La Palma, Spain	154	28°40'N	17°52'W
La Pampa, Arg.	11	38°30'S	65°00'W
La Paragua, Ven.	183	6°50'N	63°20'W
La Paz, Arg.	11	30°45'S	59°39'W
La Paz, Bol.	22	16°30'S	68°09'W
La Paz, Mex.	113	24°10'N	110°18'W
La Paz, Ur.	181	34°46'S	56°15'W
La Perouse Strait, Asia	93	45°45'N	142°00'E
La Plata, Arg.	11	34°55'S	57°57'W
Lappeenranta, Fin.	57	61°04'N	28°11'E
Laptev Sea, U.S.S.R.	172	76°00'N	126°00'E
L'Aquila, Italy	88	42°22'N	13°22'E
Larache, Mor.	117	35°12'N	6°10'W
Laredo, Tx., U.S.	178	27°30'N	99°30'W
La Rioja, Arg.	11	29°26'S	66°51'W
La Rioja, Arg.	11	30°00'S	67°30'W
Lárisa, Grc.	67	39°38'N	22°25'E
Larkana, Pak.	131	27°33'N	68°13'E
Larnaca, Cyp.	46	34°55'N	33°38'E
La Rochelle, Fr.	58	46°10'N	1°10'W
La Romana, Dom. Rep.	50	18°25'N	68°58'W
Larsen Ice Shelf, Ant.	8	68°30'S	62°30'W
Lascano, Ur.	181	33°40'S	54°12'W
La Selle Peak, Haiti	73	18°22'N	71°59'W
La Serena, Chile	37	29°54'S	71°16'W
Las Flores, Arg.	11	36°03'S	59°07'W
Lashio, Burma	29	22°56'N	97°45'E
Las Lajas, Arg.	11	38°31'S	70°22'W
Las Lajas, Pan.	132	8°15'N	81°52'W
Las Lomitas, Arg.	11	24°42'S	60°36'W
Las Minas Mountain, Hond.	74	14°33'N	88°39'W
Las Ovejas, Arg.	11	37°01'S	70°45'W
Las Palmas de Gran Canaria, Spain	154	28°06'N	15°24'W
La Spezia, Italy	88	44°07'N	9°50'E
Las Piedras, Bol.	22	11°06'S	66°10'W
Las Piedras, P.R.	140	18°11'N	65°52'W
Las Piedras, Ur.	181	34°44'S	56°13'W
Las Plumas, Arg.	11	43°43'S	67°15'W
Las Ramas, Ec.	51	1°50'S	79°48'W
Las Rosas, Arg.	11	32°28'S	61°34'W
Las Tablas, Pan.	132	7°46'N	80°17'W
Las Vegas, Hond.	74	14°49'N	88°06'W
Las Vegas, Nv., U.S.	178	36°10'N	115°08'W
Latacunga, Ec.	51	0°56'S	78°37'W
Latakia, Syria	161	35°31'N	35°47'E
La Tasajera, El Sal.	53	13°16'N	88°52'W
Late, Tonga	166	18°48'S	174°39'W
Latina, Italy	88	41°28'N	12°52'E
La Trinité, Mart.	110	14°44'N	60°58'W
La Tuque, P.Q., Can.	32	47°26'N	72°47'W
Lauchhammer, Ger., E.	64	51°30'N	13°47'E
Lau Group, Fiji	56	18°20'S	178°30'E
Launceston, Austl.	14	41°26'S	147°08'E
La Unión, El Sal.	53	13°20'N	87°51'W
La Urbana, Ven.	183	7°08'N	66°56'W
Lausanne, Switz.	160	46°31'N	6°38'E
Lautaro, Chile	37	38°31'S	72°27'W
Lautoka, Fiji	56	17°37'S	177°27'E

Name	Page	Lat.	Long.
Laval, Fr.	**58**	48°04′N	0°46′W
La Vega, Dom. Rep.	**50**	19°13′N	70°31′W
Lawang, Indon.	**81**	7°49′S	112°42′E
Lawu, Mount, Indon.	**81**	7°38′S	111°11′E
Layou, St. Vin.	**145**	13°12′N	61°17′W
La Zarca, Mex.	**113**	25°50′N	104°44′W
Leamington, Eng., U.K.	**175**	52°18′N	1°31′W
Lebanon, Asia	**101**	33°50′N	35°50′E
Lebanon Mountains, Leb.	**101**	33°50′N	35°40′E
Lebombo Mountains, Afr.	**158**	26°30′S	32°00′E
Lebu, Chile	**37**	37°37′S	73°39′W
Lecce, Italy	**88**	40°23′N	18°11′E
Lecco, Italy	**88**	45°51′N	9°23′E
Lechtaler Alps, Aus.	**15**	47°15′N	10°30′E
Leeds, Eng., U.K.	**175**	53°50′N	1°35′W
Leer, Ger., W.	**64**	53°14′N	7°26′E
Leeuwin, Cape, Austl.	**14**	34°22′S	115°08′E
Leewarden, Neth.	**122**	53°12′N	5°46′E
Legnago, Italy	**88**	45°11′N	11°18′E
Legnica, Pol.	**138**	51°13′N	16°09′E
Le Havre, Fr.	**58**	49°30′N	0°08′E
Leicester, Eng., U.K.	**175**	52°38′N	1°05′W
Leiden (Leyden), Neth.	**122**	52°09′N	4°30′E
Leine, Ger., W.	**64**	52°43′N	9°32′E
Leipzig, Ger., E.	**64**	51°19′N	12°20′E
Leiria, Port.	**139**	39°45′N	8°48′W
Leitha, Eur.	**76**	47°54′N	17°17′E
Lek, Neth.	**122**	52°00′N	6°00′E
Le Lamentin, Mart.	**110**	14°37′N	61°01′W
Le Mans, Fr.	**58**	48°00′N	0°12′E
Lemnos, Grc.	**67**	39°54′N	25°21′E
Lempa, N.A.	**53**	13°14′N	88°49′W
Lena, U.S.S.R.	**172**	72°25′N	126°40′E
Leningrad, U.S.S.R.	**172**	59°55′N	30°15′E
Lens, Fr.	**58**	50°26′N	2°50′E
Leoben, Aus.	**15**	47°23′N	15°06′E
Léogâne, Haiti	**73**	18°31′N	72°38′W
León, Mex.	**113**	21°07′N	101°40′W
León, Nic.	**125**	12°26′N	86°53′W
León, Spain	**154**	42°36′N	5°34′W
Leonora, Austl.	**14**	28°53′S	121°20′E
Léopoldville, *see* Kinshasa, Zaire	**190**	4°18′S	15°18′E
Le Port, Reu.	**141**	20°55′S	55°18′E
Le Puy, Fr.	**58**	45°02′N	3°53′E
Lérida, Spain	**154**	41°37′N	0°37′E
Lerwick, Scot., U.K.	**175**	60°09′N	1°09′W
Lesatima Mountain, Kenya	**96**	0°19′S	36°37′E
Lesbos, Grc.	**67**	39°10′N	26°20′E
Les Cayes, Haiti	**73**	18°12′N	73°45′W
Leskovac, Yugo.	**189**	42°59′N	21°57′E
Lesotho, Afr.	**102**	29°30′S	28°30′E
Lesser Khingan Range, China	**38**	50°00′N	126°25′E
Lesser Sunda Islands, Indon.	**81**	9°00′S	120°00′E
Leszno, Pol.	**138**	51°51′N	16°35′E
Lethbridge, Ab., Can.	**32**	49°42′N	112°50′W
Lethem, Guy.	**72**	3°23′N	59°48′W
Leuven, Bel.	**19**	50°53′N	4°42′E
Le Vauclin, Mart.	**110**	14°33′N	60°51′W
Levkás, Grc.	**67**	38°39′N	20°27′E
Levuka, Fiji	**56**	17°41′S	178°50′E
Lewis, Scot., U.K.	**175**	58°10′N	6°40′W
Leyden, *see* Leiden, Neth.	**122**	52°09′N	4°30′E
Leyte, Phil.	**136**	10°50′N	124°50′E
Lhasa, China	**38**	29°40′N	91°09′E
Liaoyuan, China	**38**	42°54′N	125°07′E
Liberec, Czech.	**47**	50°46′N	15°03′E
Liberia, C.R.	**44**	10°38′N	85°27′W
Liberia, Afr.	**102**	6°30′N	9°30′W
Libreville, Gabon	**61**	0°23′N	9°27′E
Libya, Afr.	**103**	27°00′N	17°00′E
Libyan Desert, Afr.	**52**	24°00′N	25°00′E
Licata, Italy	**88**	37°05′N	13°56′E
Lidköping, Swe.	**159**	58°30′N	13°10′E
Liechtenstein, Eur.	**104**	47°09′N	9°35′E
Liège, Bel.	**19**	50°38′N	5°34′E
Lienz, Aus.	**15**	46°50′N	12°47′E
Liestal, Switz.	**160**	47°29′N	7°44′E
Liffey, Ire.	**84**	53°22′N	6°14′W
Lifuka, Tonga	**166**	19°48′S	174°21′W
Ligurian Sea, Eur.	**88**	43°30′N	9°00′E
Lik, Laos	**100**	18°31′N	102°31′E
Likasi, Zaire	**190**	10°59′S	26°44′E
Likouala, Congo	**43**	1°13′S	16°48′E
Lille, Fr.	**58**	50°38′N	3°04′E
Lilongwe, Mwi.	**106**	13°59′S	33°44′E
Lima, Peru	**135**	12°03′S	77°03′W
Lima Nueva, Hond.	**74**	15°23′N	87°56′W
Limassol, Cyp.	**46**	34°40′N	33°02′E
Lim Bay, Den.	**48**	56°55′N	9°10′E
Limerick, Ire.	**84**	52°40′N	8°38′W
Limoges, Fr.	**58**	45°50′N	1°16′E
Limón, C.R.	**44**	10°00′N	83°02′W
Limpopo, Afr.	**118**	25°15′S	33°30′E
Linares, Chile	**37**	35°51′S	71°36′W
Linares, Mex.	**113**	24°52′N	99°34′W
Linares, Spain	**154**	38°05′N	3°38′W
Lincoln, Arg.	**11**	34°52′S	61°32′W
Lincoln, Eng., U.K.	**175**	53°14′N	0°33′W
Lincoln, Ne., U.S.	**178**	40°48′N	96°40′W
Lindau, Ger., W.	**64**	47°33′N	9°41′E
Lindenows Fjord, Grnld.	**68**	60°45′N	43°30′W
Lindi, Tan.	**163**	10°00′S	39°43′E
Lingayen Gulf, Phil.	**136**	16°15′N	120°14′E
Linh Peak, Viet.	**184**	15°04′N	107°59′E
Linköping, Swe.	**159**	58°25′N	15°37′E
Linz, Aus.	**15**	48°18′N	14°18′E
Lionel Town, Jam.	**91**	17°48′N	77°14′W
Lions, Gulf of, Fr.	**58**	43°00′N	4°00′E
Lipari Island, Italy	**88**	38°30′N	14°57′E
Lippstadt, Ger., W.	**64**	51°40′N	8°19′E
Lisbon, Port.	**139**	38°43′N	9°08′W
Lismore, Austl.	**14**	28°48′S	153°17′E
Litani, S.A.	**157**	3°40′N	54°00′W
Little Belt, The, Den.	**48**	55°20′N	9°45′E
Little London, Jam.	**91**	18°15′N	78°13′W
Little Rock, Ar., U.S.	**178**	34°44′N	92°17′W
Little Scarcies, Afr.	**149**	8°51′N	13°09′W
Little Zab, Asia	**83**	35°12′N	43°25′E
Liuzhou, China	**38**	24°22′N	109°32′E
Liverpool, Eng., U.K.	**175**	53°25′N	2°55′W
Livingstone, Zam.	**191**	17°50′S	25°53′E
Livingstone Falls, Afr.	**190**	4°50′S	14°30′E
Livingstone Mountains, Tan.	**106**	9°45′S	34°20′E
Livo, Fin.	**57**	65°24′N	26°48′E
Livorno, Italy	**88**	43°33′N	10°19′E
Ljubljana, Yugo.	**189**	46°03′N	14°31′E
Ljungan, Swe.	**159**	62°19′N	17°23′E
Ljusnan, Swe.	**159**	61°12′N	17°08′E
Llanetti, Wales, U.K.	**175**	51°42′N	4°10′W
Llanos, S.A.	**183**	5°00′N	70°00′W
Llera, Mex.	**113**	23°19′N	99°01′W
Lleyn Peninsula, Wales, U.K.	**175**	52°54′N	4°30′W
Loa, Chile	**37**	21°26′S	70°04′W
Loange, Afr.	**190**	4°17′S	20°02′E
Lobamba, Swaz.	**158**	26°27′S	31°12′E
Lobería, Arg.	**11**	38°09′S	58°47′W
Lobito, Ang.	**6**	12°20′S	13°34′E
Locarno, Switz.	**160**	46°10′N	8°48′E
Lod, Isr.	**86**	31°58′N	34°54′E
Lodi, Italy	**88**	45°19′N	9°30′E
Łódź, Pol.	**138**	51°46′N	19°30′E
Loess Plateau, China	**38**	37°00′N	106°00′E
Lofoten Islands, Nor.	**129**	68°30′N	15°00′E
Logan, Mount, Yk., Can.	**32**	60°34′N	140°24′W
Logone, Afr.	**36**	12°06′N	15°02′E
Logroño, Spain	**154**	42°28′N	2°27′W
Loire, Fr.	**58**	47°16′N	2°11′W
Loíza, P.R.	**140**	18°23′N	65°54′W
Loiza Reservoir, P.R.	**140**	18°17′N	66°00′W
Loja, Ec.	**51**	4°00′S	79°13′W
Loken tekojärvi, Fin.	**57**	67°55′N	27°40′E
Lokeren, Bel.	**19**	51°06′N	4°00′E
Lokoja, Nig.	**127**	7°47′N	6°45′E
Lokoro, Zaire	**190**	1°43′S	18°23′E
Lolland, Den.	**48**	54°46′N	11°30′E
Lolotique, El Sal.	**53**	13°33′N	88°21′W
Loma Mountains, S.L.	**149**	9°10′N	11°07′W
Lomé, Togo	**165**	6°08′N	1°13′E
Lommel, Bel.	**19**	51°14′N	5°18′E
Lomond, Loch, Scot., U.K.	**175**	56°08′N	4°38′W
Łomża, Pol.	**138**	53°11′N	22°05′E
London, On., Can.	**32**	42°59′N	81°14′W
London, Eng., U.K.	**175**	51°30′N	0°10′W
Londonderry, N. Ire., U.K.	**175**	55°00′N	7°19′W
Longa, Ang.	**6**	10°15′S	13°30′E
Long Beach, Ca., U.S.	**178**	33°46′N	118°11′W
Longford, Ire.	**84**	53°44′N	7°47′W
Long Island, N.Y., U.S.	**178**	40°50′N	73°00′W
Longitudinal Valley, Chile	**37**	36°00′S	72°00′W
Longreach, Austl.	**14**	23°26′S	144°15′E
Long Xuyen, Viet.	**184**	10°23′N	105°25′E
Loop Head, Ire.	**84**	52°34′N	9°56′W
Lopatka, Cape, U.S.S.R.	**172**	50°52′N	156°40′E
Lop Nor, China	**38**	40°20′N	90°15′E
Lora, Lake, Asia	**2**	29°20′N	64°50′E
Lorca, Spain	**154**	37°40′N	1°42′W
Lord Howe Island, Austl.	**14**	31°33′S	159°05′E
Lorengau, Pap. N. Gui.	**133**	2°00′S	147°15′E
Loreto, Bol.	**22**	15°13′S	64°40′W
Loreto, Mex.	**113**	26°01′N	111°21′W
Lorian Swamp, Kenya	**96**	0°40′N	39°35′E
Lorne, Firth of, Scot., U.K.	**175**	56°20′N	5°40′W
Los Alamos, Mex.	**113**	28°40′N	103°30′W
Los Amates, Guat.	**70**	15°16′N	89°06′W
Los Angeles, Chile	**37**	37°28′S	72°21′W
Los Angeles, Ca., U.S.	**178**	34°03′N	118°14′W
Los Antiguos, Arg.	**11**	46°33′S	71°37′W
Los Blancos, Arg.	**11**	23°36′S	62°36′W
Los Chacos, Bol.	**22**	14°33′S	62°11′W
Los Chiles, C.R.	**44**	11°02′N	84°43′W
Los Chonos Archipelago, Chile	**37**	45°00′S	74°00′W
Los Frentones, Arg.	**11**	26°25′S	61°25′W
Los Mochis, Mex.	**113**	25°45′N	108°57′W
Los Palacios, Cuba	**45**	22°35′N	83°15′W
Los Teques, Ven.	**183**	10°21′N	67°02′W
Lot, Fr.	**58**	44°18′N	0°20′E
Lota, Chile	**37**	37°05′S	73°10′W
Lotikipi Plain, Afr.	**96**	4°36′N	34°55′E
Lotofaga, W. Sam.	**187**	13°59′S	171°50′W
Loubomo, Congo	**43**	4°12′S	12°41′E
Louga, Sen.	**148**	15°37′N	16°13′W
Loughborough, Eng., U.K.	**175**	52°47′N	1°11′W
Louisiade Archipelago, Pap. N. Gui.	**133**	11°00′S	153°00′E
Louisiana, U.S.	**178**	31°15′N	92°15′W
Louisville, Ky., U.S.	**178**	38°15′N	85°45′W
Lovech, Bul.	**27**	43°08′N	24°43′E
Lower Hutt, N.Z.	**124**	41°13′S	174°55′E
Lower Rhine, Neth.	**122**	51°59′N	6°20′E
Lower Rhine, Switz.	**160**	46°49′N	9°25′E
Lowestoft, Eng., U.K.	**175**	52°29′N	1°45′E
Loyauté, Îles (Loyalty Islands), N. Cal.	**123**	21°00′S	167°00′E
Loznica, Yugo.	**189**	44°32′N	19°13′E
Lualaba, Zaire	**190**	0°26′N	25°20′E
Luanda, Ang.	**6**	8°48′S	13°14′E
Luang Nam Tha, Laos	**100**	20°57′N	101°25′E
Luang Prabang, Laos	**100**	19°52′N	102°08′E
Luang Prabang Range, Asia	**100**	18°30′N	101°15′E
Luangue, Afr.	**6**	7°00′S	19°33′E
Luanshya, Zam.	**191**	13°08′S	28°24′E
Luapula, Afr.	**190**	9°26′S	28°33′E
Lubango, Ang.	**6**	14°55′S	13°30′E
Lübeck, Ger., W.	**64**	53°52′N	10°40′E
Lubin, Pol.	**138**	51°24′N	16°13′E
Lublin, Pol.	**138**	51°15′N	22°35′E
Lubudi, Zaire	**190**	9°57′S	25°58′E
Lubumbashi, Zaire	**190**	11°40′S	27°28′E
Lucca, Italy	**88**	43°50′N	10°29′E
Lucerne, Switz.	**160**	47°03′N	8°18′E
Lucerne, Lake, Switz.	**160**	47°00′N	8°28′E
Luckenwalde, Ger., E.	**64**	52°05′N	13°10′E
Lucknow, India	**79**	26°51′N	80°55′E
Lüda (Dairen), China	**38**	38°53′N	121°35′E
Lüdenscheid, Ger., W.	**64**	51°13′N	7°38′E
Ludhiana, India	**79**	30°54′N	75°51′E
Ludvika, Swe.	**159**	60°09′N	15°11′E
Ludwigsburg, Ger., W.	**64**	48°53′N	9°11′E
Ludwigshafen, Ger., W.	**64**	49°29′N	8°26′E
Luena, Ang.	**6**	11°47′S	19°52′E
Luepa, Ven.	**183**	5°43′N	61°31′W
Lugano, Switz.	**160**	46°01′N	8°58′E
Lugano, Lake, Eur.	**160**	46°00′N	9°00′E
Lugenda, Afr.	**118**	11°25′S	38°33′E
Lugo, Spain	**154**	43°00′N	7°34′W
Lugoj, Rom.	**142**	45°41′N	21°54′E
Lukanga Swamp, Zam.	**191**	14°25′S	27°45′E
Luleå, Swe.	**159**	65°34′N	22°10′E
Luleå, Swe.	**159**	65°35′N	22°03′E
Lulua, Zaire	**190**	5°02′S	21°07′E
Lundi, Zimb.	**192**	21°43′S	32°34′E
Lüneburg, Ger., W.	**64**	53°15′N	10°23′E
Lungué-Bungo, Afr.	**6**	13°27′S	22°00′E
Lunsar, S.L.	**149**	8°41′N	12°32′W
Lupeni, Rom.	**142**	45°22′N	23°13′E
Lúrio, Moz.	**118**	13°35′S	40°32′E
Lusaka, Zam.	**191**	15°25′S	28°17′E
Lushnje, Alb.	**3**	40°56′N	19°42′E
Lüshun, China	**38**	38°48′N	121°16′E
Lut, Dasht-e, Iran	**82**	33°00′N	57°00′E
Luti, Sol. Is.	**151**	7°14′S	156°59′E
Luton, Eng., U.K.	**175**	51°53′N	0°25′W
Luxembourg, Lux.	**104**	49°36′N	6°09′E
Luxembourg, Eur.	**104**	49°54′N	6°05′E
Luzhou, China	**38**	28°58′N	105°25′E
Luzon, Phil.	**136**	16°00′N	121°00′E
Luzon Strait, Asia	**136**	20°30′N	121°00′E
Lvov, U.S.S.R.	**172**	49°50′N	24°00′E
Lyon, Fr.	**58**	45°45′N	4°51′E

M

Name	Page	Lat.	Long.
Ma, Asia	**184**	19°47′N	105°56′E
Maan, Jord.	**94**	30°20′N	36°30′E
Maas (Meuse), Eur.	**122**	51°49′N	5°01′E
Maastricht, Neth.	**122**	50°52′N	5°43′E
Mababe Depression, Bots.	**23**	18°50′S	24°15′E
Mabaduan, Pap. N. Gui.	**133**	9°16′S	142°44′E
Mabaruma, Guy.	**72**	8°12′N	59°47′W
Macao, Asia	**105**	22°14′N	113°35′E
Macao, Macao	**105**	22°12′N	113°33′E
Macapá, Braz.	**24**	0°02′N	51°03′W
Macará, Ec.	**51**	4°23′S	79°57′W
Macas, Ec.	**51**	2°19′S	78°07′W
Macau, Braz.	**24**	5°07′S	36°38′W
Macaya Peak, Haiti	**73**	18°25′N	74°00′W
Macclesfield, Eng., U.K.	**175**	53°16′N	2°07′W
Macdhui, Ben, Scot., U.K.	**175**	57°04′N	3°40′W
Macdonnell Ranges, Austl.	**14**	23°45′S	133°20′E
Macedonia, Yugo.	**189**	41°50′N	22°00′E
Maceió, Braz.	**24**	9°40′S	35°43′W
Macerata, Italy	**88**	43°18′N	13°27′E
Machachi, Ec.	**51**	0°30′S	78°34′W
Machala, Ec.	**51**	3°16′S	79°58′W
Machupicchu, Peru	**135**	13°07′S	72°34′W
Macina, Mali	**108**	14°30′N	5°00′W
Mackay, Austl.	**14**	21°09′S	149°11′E
Mackenzie, Guy.	**72**	6°00′N	58°17′W
Mackenzie, N.T., Can.	**32**	69°15′N	134°08′W
McKinley, Mount, Ak., U.S.	**178**	63°30′N	151°00′W
Macleod, Lake, Austl.	**14**	24°00′S	113°35′E
McMurdo Sound, Ant.	**8**	77°30′S	165°00′E
Macquarie, Austl.	**14**	30°07′S	147°24′E
Madaba, Jord.	**94**	31°43′N	35°48′E
Madagascar, Afr.	**105**	19°00′S	46°00′E
Madang, Pap. N. Gui.	**133**	5°15′S	145°50′E
Madaripur, Bngl.	**17**	23°10′N	90°12′E
Madeira, S.A.	**24**	3°22′S	58°45′W
Madeira Islands, Port.	**139**	32°40′N	16°45′W
Madelegabel, Eur.	**15**	47°18′N	10°18′E
Madera, Mex.	**113**	29°12′N	108°07′W
Madhya Pradesh, India	**79**	23°00′N	79°00′E
Madinat al-Shab, Yem., P.D.R.	**188**	12°50′N	44°56′E
Madinat Isa, Bahr.	**16**	26°10′N	50°33′E
Madison, Wi., U.S.	**178**	43°04′N	89°24′W
Madiun, Indon.	**81**	7°37′S	111°31′E
Madras, India	**79**	13°04′N	80°16′E
Madre, Sierra, N.A.	**70**	15°20′N	92°00′W
Madre, Sierra, Phil.	**136**	16°20′N	122°00′E
Madre de Dios, S.A.	**22**	10°59′S	66°08′W
Madre Lagoon, Mex.	**113**	25°00′N	97°40′W
Madre Occidental, Sierra, Mex.	**113**	25°00′N	105°00′W
Madre Oriental, Sierra, Mex.	**113**	22°00′N	99°30′W
Madrid, Spain	**154**	40°24′N	3°41′W
Madura, Indon.	**81**	7°00′S	113°20′E
Madurai, India	**79**	9°56′N	78°07′E
Maebashi, Japan	**93**	36°23′N	139°04′E
Maestra, Sierra, Cuba	**45**	20°00′N	76°45′W
Mafeking, S. Afr.	**152**	25°53′S	25°39′E
Mafia Island, Tan.	**163**	7°50′S	39°50′E
Mafinga Hills, Afr.	**191**	10°00′S	33°30′E
Magadan, U.S.S.R.	**172**	59°34′N	150°48′E
Magadi, Lake, Kenya	**96**	1°52′S	36°17′E
Magangue, Col.	**42**	9°14′N	74°45′W
Magdalena, Bol.	**22**	13°20′S	64°08′W
Magdalena, Col.	**42**	11°06′N	74°51′W
Magdeburg, Ger., E.	**64**	52°07′N	11°38′E
Magdelena, Mex.	**113**	20°55′N	103°57′W
Magelang, Indon.	**81**	7°28′S	110°13′E
Magellan, Strait of, S.A.	**37**	54°00′S	71°00′W
Magetan, Indon.	**81**	7°39′S	111°20′E
Maggiore, Lake, Eur.	**160**	46°00′N	8°40′E
Maghagha, Egypt	**52**	28°39′N	30°50′E
Magnitogorsk, U.S.S.R.	**172**	53°27′N	59°04′E
Magwe, Burma	**29**	20°09′N	94°55′E
Mahabharat Range, Nepal	**120**	27°40′N	84°30′E
Mahaicony, Guy.	**72**	6°36′N	57°48′W
Mahajanga, Madag.	**105**	15°43′S	46°19′E
Mahakam, Indon.	**81**	0°35′S	117°17′E
Maharashtra, India	**79**	19°00′N	76°00′E
Mahaut, Dom.	**49**	15°21′N	61°25′W
Mahaweli, Sri L.	**155**	8°27′N	81°13′E
Mahébourg, Mrts.	**111**	20°24′S	57°42′E
Mahmud-e Eragi, Afg.	**2**	35°01′N	69°20′E
Maidstone, Eng., U.K.	**175**	51°17′N	0°32′E
Maiduguri, Nig.	**127**	11°51′N	13°10′E
Maiko, Zaire	**190**	0°14′N	25°33′E
Main, Ger., W.	**64**	50°00′N	8°18′E
Mai-Ndombe, Lake, Zaire	**190**	2°00′S	18°20′E
Maine, U.S.	**178**	45°15′N	69°15′W
Mainland, Scot., U.K.	**175**	59°00′N	3°10′W
Mainland, Scot., U.K.	**175**	60°20′N	1°22′W
Mainz, Ger., W.	**64**	50°01′N	8°16′E
Maio, C.V.	**34**	15°15′N	23°10′W
Maipú, Arg.	**11**	36°52′S	57°52′W
Maipú, Chile	**37**	33°31′S	70°46′W
Maisí, Cape, Cuba	**45**	20°15′N	74°09′W
Maitland, Austl.	**14**	32°44′S	151°33′E
Majorca, Spain	**154**	39°30′N	3°00′E
Majuro, Marsh. Is.	**109**	7°05′N	171°08′E
Makassar Strait, Indon.	**81**	2°00′S	117°30′E
Makefu, Niue	**128**	18°59′S	169°55′W
Makeni, S.L.	**149**	8°53′N	12°03′W
Makgadikgadi Salt Pans, Bots.	**23**	20°45′S	25°30′E
Makhachkala, U.S.S.R.	**172**	42°58′N	47°30′E
Makó, Hung.	**76**	46°13′N	20°29′E
Makokou, Gabon	**61**	0°34′N	12°52′E
Makurdi, Nig.	**127**	7°45′N	8°32′E
Malabo, Eq. Gui.	**53**	3°45′N	8°47′E
Malacca, Strait of, Asia	**107**	2°30′N	101°20′E
Málaga, Col.	**42**	6°42′N	72°44′W
Málaga, Spain	**154**	36°43′N	4°25′W
Malaita, Sol. Is.	**151**	9°00′S	161°00′E
Malakal, Sudan	**156**	9°31′N	31°39′E
Malang, Indon.	**81**	7°59′S	112°37′E
Malanje, Ang.	**6**	9°32′S	16°20′E
Mälaren, Swe.	**159**	59°30′N	17°12′E
Malargüe, Arg.	**11**	35°28′S	69°35′W
Malatya, Tur.	**168**	38°21′N	38°19′E
Malawi, Afr.	**106**	13°30′S	34°00′E
Malayer, Iran	**82**	34°17′N	48°50′E
Malay Peninsula, Asia	**107**	6°00′N	101°00′E
Malaysia, Asia	**107**	2°30′N	112°30′E
Malbork, Pol.	**138**	54°02′N	19°01′E
Maldives, Asia	**107**	3°15′N	73°00′E
Maldonado, Ur.	**181**	34°54′S	54°57′W
Male, Mald.	**107**	4°10′N	73°31′E
Male Atoll, Mald.	**107**	4°25′N	73°30′E
Malheureux, Cape, Sey.	**149**	4°48′S	55°32′E
Mali, Afr.	**108**	17°00′N	4°00′W
Mallawi, Egypt	**52**	27°44′N	30°50′E
Malmberget, Swe.	**159**	67°10′N	20°40′E
Malmö, Swe.	**159**	55°36′N	13°00′E
Maloti Mountains, Leso.	**102**	29°05′S	28°20′E
Malpaso Reservoir, Mex.	**113**	17°10′N	93°40′W
Malta, Eur.	**109**	35°50′N	14°35′E
Malta, Malta	**109**	35°53′N	14°27′E
Malta Channel, Eur.	**88**	56°44′N	26°53′E
Mamara, Peru	**135**	14°14′S	72°35′W
Mamoré, S.A.	**22**	10°23′S	65°23′W
Mamoutzou, May.	**111**	12°47′S	45°14′E
Mampong, Ghana	**65**	7°04′N	1°24′W
Mamry, Lake, Pol.	**138**	54°08′N	21°42′E
Man, I.C.	**90**	7°24′N	7°33′W
Mana, Fr. Gu.	**60**	5°44′N	53°54′W
Manado, Indon.	**81**	1°29′N	124°51′E
Managua, Nic.	**125**	12°09′N	86°17′W
Managua, Lake, Nic.	**125**	12°20′N	86°20′W
Manakara, Madag.	**105**	22°08′S	48°01′E
Manama, Bahr.	**16**	26°13′N	50°35′E
Mananjary, Madag.	**105**	21°13′S	48°20′E
Manaslu, Nepal	**120**	28°33′N	84°33′E
Manatí, P.R.	**140**	18°26′N	66°29′W
Manaus, Braz.	**24**	3°08′S	60°01′W
Manchester, Eng., U.K.	**175**	53°30′N	2°15′W
Manchioneal, Jam.	**91**	18°02′N	76°17′W
Mand, Iran	**82**	28°11′N	51°17′E
Mandalay, Burma	**29**	22°00′N	96°05′E
Mandara Mountains, Afr.	**127**	10°45′N	13°40′E
Mandeb, Bab el-	**54**	12°40′N	43°20′E
Mandeville, Jam.	**91**	18°02′N	77°30′W
Manfredonia, Italy	**88**	41°38′N	15°55′E
Manfredonia, Gulf of, Italy	**88**	41°35′N	16°05′E
Mango Creek, Belize	**20**	16°32′N	88°29′W
Manicoré, Braz.	**24**	5°49′S	61°17′W
Manila, Phil.	**136**	14°35′N	121°00′E
Manipur, India	**79**	25°00′N	94°00′E
Manisa, Tur.	**168**	38°36′N	27°26′E
Manitoba, Can.	**32**	54°00′N	97°00′W
Manizales, Col.	**42**	5°05′N	75°32′W
Mankayana, Swaz.	**158**	26°42′S	31°00′E
Mannar, Gulf of, Asia	**79**	8°30′N	79°00′E
Mannar Island, Sri L.	**155**	9°03′N	79°50′E
Mannheim, Ger., W.	**64**	49°29′N	8°29′E
Mano, Afr.	**149**	6°56′N	11°31′W
Manono, Zaire	**190**	7°18′S	27°25′E
Manresa, Spain	**154**	41°44′N	1°50′E
Mansfield, Eng., U.K.	**175**	53°09′N	1°11′W
Manta, Ec.	**51**	0°57′S	80°44′W
Mantova, Italy	**88**	45°09′N	10°48′E
Mantua, Cuba	**45**	22°17′N	84°17′W
Manu, Peru	**135**	12°15′S	70°50′W
Manua Islands, Am. Sam.	**5**	14°13′S	169°35′W
Manukau, N.Z.	**124**	37°02′S	174°54′E
Manukau Harbor, N.Z.	**124**	37°01′S	174°44′E
Manurewa, N.Z.	**124**	37°02′S	174°54′E
Manzanillo, Cuba	**45**	20°21′N	77°07′W
Manzanillo, Mex.	**113**	19°03′N	104°20′W
Manzanillo Bay, N.A.	**73**	19°45′N	71°46′W
Manzini, Swaz.	**158**	26°30′S	31°25′E
Maoke Mountains, Indon.	**81**	4°00′S	138°00′E
Mapire, Ven.	**183**	7°45′N	64°42′W
Maputo, Moz.	**118**	25°58′S	32°35′E
Maraã, Braz.	**24**	1°50′S	65°22′W
Marabá, Braz.	**24**	5°21′S	49°07′W
Maracaibo, Ven.	**183**	10°40′N	71°37′W
Maracaibo, Lake, Ven.	**183**	9°50′N	71°30′W
Maracay, Ven.	**183**	10°15′N	67°36′W
Maradi, Niger	**126**	13°29′N	7°06′E
Maragheh, Iran	**82**	37°23′N	46°13′E
Marajo Island, Braz.	**24**	1°00′S	49°30′W
Maranhão, Braz.	**24**	5°00′S	45°00′W
Marañón, Peru	**135**	4°42′S	74°40′W
Maras, Tur.	**168**	37°36′N	36°55′E
Marathon, On., Can.	**32**	48°40′N	86°25′W
Maravan, Sol. Is.	**151**	7°51′S	156°42′E
Maravovo, Sol. Is.	**151**	9°17′S	159°38′E
Marawi, Phil.	**136**	8°01′N	124°18′E
Marburg, Ger., W.	**64**	50°49′N	8°46′E
Marcal, Hung.	**76**	47°41′N	17°32′E
Marca Point, Ang.	**6**	16°31′S	11°42′E
March, Eur.	**15**	48°10′N	16°59′E
Mar Chiquita, Lake, Arg.	**11**	30°42′S	62°36′W
Marcos Juárez, Arg.	**11**	32°42′S	62°06′W
Marcos Paz, Arg.	**11**	34°46′S	58°50′W
Mardan, Pak.	**131**	34°21′N	72°02′E
Mar del Plata, Arg.	**11**	38°00′S	57°33′W
Margarita Island, Ven.	**183**	11°00′N	64°00′W
Margate, Eng., U.K.	**175**	51°24′N	1°24′E
Margherita Peak, Afr.	**190**	0°22′N	29°51′E
Margow Desert, Afg.	**2**	30°45′N	63°10′E
María Grande, Arg.	**11**	31°39′S	59°54′W
Mariana Islands, Pac. I.	**130**	16°00′N	145°30′E
Marianao, Cuba	**45**	23°05′N	82°26′W
Maribor, Yugo.	**189**	46°33′N	15°39′E
Marie Byrd Land, Ant.	**8**	80°00′S	120°00′W
Marigot, Dom.	**49**	15°32′N	61°18′W
Marília, Braz.	**24**	22°13′S	49°56′W
Maringá, Braz.	**24**	23°25′S	51°55′W
Mariscal Estigarribia, Para.	**134**	22°02′S	60°38′W
Maritime Alps, Eur.	**88**	44°15′N	7°10′E
Maritsa, Eur.	**27**	41°42′N	26°19′E
Marj Uyun, Leb.	**101**	33°22′N	35°35′E
Marka, Som.	**151**	1°47′N	44°52′E
Markerwaard, Neth.	**122**	52°33′N	5°15′E
Markham, Mount, Ant.	**8**	82°51′S	161°21′E
Marlborough, Guy.	**72**	7°29′N	58°38′W
Marmara, Sea of	**168**	40°40′N	28°15′E
Marne, Fr.	**58**	48°49′N	2°24′E
Maroa, Ven.	**183**	2°43′N	67°33′W
Maromokotro, Madag.	**105**	14°01′S	48°59′E
Marondera, Zimb.	**192**	18°10′S	31°36′E
Maroni, S.A.	**60**	5°45′N	53°58′W
Maros, Eur.	**76**	46°15′N	20°13′E
Marovoay, Madag.	**105**	16°06′S	46°39′E
Marowijne, S.A.	**157**	5°45′N	53°58′W
Marquis, Gren.	**68**	12°06′N	61°37′W
Marrah, Mount, Sudan	**156**	13°04′N	24°21′E
Marrakech, Mor.	**117**	31°38′N	8°00′W
Marsala, Italy	**88**	37°48′N	12°26′E
Marsa Matruh, Egypt	**52**	31°21′N	27°14′E
Marsaxlokk Bay, Malta	**109**	35°49′N	14°33′E
Marseille, Fr.	**58**	43°18′N	5°24′E
Marshall Islands, Oc.	**109**	9°00′N	168°00′E
Marsh Harbour, Bah.	**16**	26°33′N	77°03′W
Martaban, Gulf of, Burma	**29**	16°30′N	97°00′E
Martigny, Switz.	**160**	46°06′N	7°04′E
Martínez de la Torre, Mex.	**113**	20°04′N	97°03′W
Martinique, N.A.	**110**	14°40′N	61°00′W
Marton, N.Z.	**124**	40°05′S	175°23′E
Marv Dasht, Iran	**82**	29°50′N	52°40′E
Maryland, U.S.	**178**	39°00′N	76°45′W
Masaka, Ug.	**170**	0°20′S	31°44′E
Masan, Kor., S.	**98**	35°11′N	128°32′E
Masaya, Nic.	**125**	11°58′N	86°06′W
Masbate Island, Phil.	**136**	12°15′N	123°30′E
Maseru, Leso.	**102**	29°28′S	27°30′E
Mashaba Mountains, Zimb.	**192**	18°45′S	30°32′E
Mashhad, Iran	**82**	36°18′N	59°36′E
Masila, Wadi, Yem., P.D.R.	**188**	15°10′N	51°05′E
Masisea, Peru	**135**	8°36′S	74°19′W
Masjed Soleyman, Iran	**82**	31°58′N	49°18′E
Mask, Lake, Ire.	**84**	53°35′N	9°20′W
Massachusetts, U.S.	**178**	42°20′N	71°50′W
Massey, N.Z.	**124**	36°51′S	174°36′E
Masterton, N.Z.	**124**	40°57′S	175°40′E
Masurian Lakes, Pol.	**138**	53°45′N	21°00′E
Mat, Alb.	**3**	41°39′N	19°34′E
Matadi, Zaire	**190**	5°49′S	13°27′E
Matagalpa, Nic.	**143**	12°55′N	85°55′W
Matale, Sri L.	**155**	7°28′N	80°37′E
Matamoros, Mex.	**113**	25°53′N	97°30′W
Matane, P.Q., Can.	**32**	48°51′N	67°32′W
Matanzas, Cuba	**45**	23°03′N	81°35′W
Matanzas, Mex.	**113**	21°37′N	101°38′W
Matara, Sri L.	**155**	5°56′N	80°33′E
Mataró, Spain	**154**	41°32′N	2°27′E
Matautu, W. Sam.	**187**	13°57′S	171°56′W
Matavai, W. Sam.	**187**	13°28′S	172°35′W
Matavera, Cook Is.	**44**	21°13′S	159°44′W
Matehuala, Mex.	**113**	23°39′N	100°39′W
Matera, Italy	**88**	40°40′N	16°37′E
Mateur, Tun.	**167**	37°03′N	9°40′E
Matías Romero, Mex.	**113**	16°53′N	95°02′W
Mato Grosso, Braz.	**24**	15°00′S	59°57′W
Mato Grosso, Braz.	**24**	11°00′S	55°00′W
Mato Grosso do Sul, Braz.	**24**	20°30′S	53°30′W
Mato Grosso Plateau, Braz.	**24**	15°30′S	56°00′W
Matra, Oman	**130**	23°38′N	58°34′E
Matsapha, Swaz.	**158**	26°29′S	31°23′E
Ma-tsu Island, Tai.	**162**	26°09′N	119°56′E
Matsuyama, Japan	**93**	33°50′N	132°45′E
Matterhorn, Eur.	**160**	45°59′N	7°43′E
Matthews Ridge, Guy.	**72**	7°30′N	60°10′W
Matthew Town, Bah.	**16**	20°57′N	73°40′W
Maturín, Ven.	**183**	9°45′N	63°11′W
Maués, Braz.	**24**	3°24′S	57°42′W
Mau Escarpment, Kenya	**96**	0°40′S	36°02′E
Mauga Silisili, W. Sam.	**187**	13°35′S	172°27′W
Maungaturoto, N.Z.	**124**	36°06′S	174°22′E
Mauritania, Afr.	**110**	20°00′N	12°00′W
Mauritius, Afr.	**111**	20°17′S	57°33′E

Name	Page	Lat.	Long.
Mawlaik, Burma	29	23°38′N	94°24′E
Mayagüez, P.R.	140	18°12′N	67°09′W
Maya Mountains, N.A.	20	16°40′N	88°50′W
Mayotte, Afr.	111	12°50′S	45°10′E
May Pen, Jam.	91	17°58′N	77°14′W
Mayumba, Gabon	61	3°25′S	10°39′E
Mazabuka, Zam.	191	15°51′S	27°46′E
Mazara del Vallo, Italy	88	37°39′N	12°36′E
Mazar-e Sharif, Afg.	2	36°42′N	67°06′E
Mazatenango, Guat.	70	14°32′N	91°30′W
Mazatlán, Mex.	113	23°13′N	106°25′W
Mbabane, Swaz.	158	26°18′S	31°06′E
Mbabo, Mount, Cam.	31	7°16′N	12°09′E
Mbaiki, C.A.R.	35	3°53′N	18°00′E
Mbale, Ug.	170	1°05′N	34°10′E
Mbandaka, Zaire	190	0°04′N	18°16′E
M'banza Congo, Ang.	6	6°16′S	14°15′E
Mbanza-Ngungu, Zaire	190	5°15′S	14°52′E
Mbini, Eq. Gui.	53	1°35′N	9°37′E
Mbini, Afr.	53	1°35′N	9°37′E
Mbomou, Afr.	35	4°08′N	22°26′E
Mbour, Sen.	148	14°24′N	16°58′W
M'Bridge, Ang.	6	7°14′S	12°52′E
Mbua, Fiji	56	16°48′S	178°37′E
Mbuji-Mayi, Zaire	190	6°09′S	23°38′E
Mbutha, Fiji	56	16°39′S	179°50′E
Mecca (Makkah), Sau. Ar.	147	21°27′N	39°49′E
Mechelen, Bel.	19	51°02′N	4°28′E
Mecklenburger Bay, Eur.	64	54°20′N	11°40′E
Mecsek, Hung.	76	46°15′N	18°05′E
Medan, Indon.	81	3°35′N	98°40′E
Médanos, Arg.	11	38°50′S	62°41′W
Medellín, Col.	42	6°15′N	75°35′W
Medgidia, Rom.	142	44°15′N	28°16′E
Mediaş, Rom.	142	46°10′N	24°21′E
Medicine Hat, Ab., Can.	32	50°03′N	110°40′W
Medina (al-Madinah), Sau. Ar.	147	24°28′N	39°36′E
Medjerda, Wadi, Afr.	167	37°07′N	10°13′E
Meekatharra, Austl.	14	26°36′S	118°29′E
Meerut, India	79	28°59′N	77°42′E
Meghalaya, India	79	25°30′N	91°15′E
Mehtar Lam, Afg.	2	34°39′N	70°10′E
Meiktila, Burma	29	20°52′N	95°52′E
Meissen, Ger., E.	64	51°10′N	13°28′E
Mekerrhane Sabkha, Alg.	4	26°19′N	1°20′E
Meknès, Mor.	117	33°53′N	5°37′W
Mekong, Asia	184	10°33′N	105°24′E
Mékrou, Afr.	20	12°24′N	2°49′E
Melaka, Malay.	107	2°12′N	102°15′E
Melbourne, Austl.	14	37°49′S	144°58′E
Melekeok, Palau	132	7°29′N	134°38′E
Melilla, Sp. N. Afr.	117	35°19′N	2°58′W
Melincue, Arg.	11	33°39′S	61°27′W
Melipillo, Chile	37	33°42′S	71°13′W
Melo, Ur.	181	32°22′S	54°11′W
Melrhir Shatt, Alg.	4	34°20′N	6°20′E
Melun, Fr.	58	48°32′N	2°40′E
Melville Bay, Grnld.	68	75°30′N	63°00′W
Melville Island, Austl.	14	11°40′S	131°00′E
Melville Island, N.T., Can.	32	75°15′N	110°00′W
Memmingen, Ger., W.	64	47°59′N	10°11′E
Memphis, Tn., U.S.	178	35°08′N	90°02′W
Méndez, Ec.	51	2°43′S	78°19′W
Mendoza, Arg.	11	32°53′S	68°49′W
Mendoza, Arg.	11	34°30′S	68°30′W
Mene de Mauroa, Ven.	183	10°43′N	71°01′W
Meneng Point, Nauru	120	0°32′S	166°57′E
Menongue, Ang.	6	14°36′S	17°48′E
Mentawai Islands, Indon.	81	3°00′S	100°10′E
Menzel Bourguiba, Tun.	167	37°10′N	9°48′E
Meppel, Neth.	122	52°42′N	6°11′E
Merano, Italy	88	46°40′N	11°09′E
Mercedes, Arg.	11	34°39′S	59°27′W
Mercedes, Arg.	11	29°12′S	58°05′W
Mercedes, Ur.	181	33°16′S	58°01′W
Mergui, Burma	29	12°26′N	98°36′E
Mergui Archipelago, Burma	29	12°00′N	98°00′E
Mérida, Mex.	113	20°58′N	89°37′W
Mérida, Spain	154	38°55′N	6°20′W
Mérida, Ven.	183	8°36′N	71°08′W
Mérida Cordillera, Ven.	183	8°40′N	71°00′W
Merinos, Ur.	181	32°24′S	56°54′W
Meron, Mount, Isr.	86	32°58′N	35°25′E
Merredin, Austl.	14	31°29′S	118°16′E
Merseburg, Ger., E.	64	51°21′N	11°59′E
Mersin, Tur.	168	36°48′N	34°38′E
Merthyr Tydfil, Wales, U.K.	175	51°46′N	3°23′W
Meru, Mount, Tan.	163	3°14′S	36°40′E
Merzifon, Tur.	168	40°53′N	35°29′E
Mesayitonia, Cyp.	46	34°42′N	33°03′E
Mesopotamia, Iraq	83	34°00′N	44°00′E
Messina, Italy	88	38°11′N	15°33′E
Messina, Strait of, Italy	88	38°15′N	15°35′E
Meta, S.A.	42	6°12′N	67°28′W
Metán, Arg.	11	25°29′S	64°57′W
Metapan, El Sal.	53	14°20′N	89°27′W
Metz, Fr.	58	49°08′N	6°10′E
Meulebeke, Bel.	19	50°57′N	3°17′E
Meuse (Maas), Eur.	122	51°49′N	5°01′E
Mexicali, Mex.	113	32°40′N	115°29′W
Mexico, N.A.	113	23°00′N	102°00′W
Mexico, Gulf of, N.A.	178	25°00′N	90°00′W
Mexico City, Mex.	113	19°24′N	99°09′W
Meymaneh, Afg.	2	35°55′N	64°47′E
Meyungs, Palau	132	7°20′N	134°27′E
Mhlume, Swaz.	158	26°02′S	31°50′E
Miami, Fl., U.S.	178	25°46′N	80°11′W
Mianeh, Iran	82	37°26′N	47°42′E
Mianwali, Pak.	131	32°35′N	71°33′E
Miches, Dom. Rep.	50	18°59′N	69°03′W
Michigan, U.S.	178	44°00′N	85°00′W
Michigan, Lake, U.S.	178	44°00′N	87°00′W
Mico Mountains, Guat.	70	15°30′N	88°55′W
Micoud, St. Luc.	144	13°50′N	60°54′W
Micronesia, Federated States of, Oc.	114	6°55′N	158°15′E
Middelburg, Neth.	122	51°30′N	3°37′E
Middelfart, Den.	48	55°30′N	9°45′E
Middle Atlas, Mor.	117	33°30′N	5°00′W

Name	Page	Lat.	Long.
Middlesbrough, Eng., U.K.	175	54°35′N	1°14′W
Middlesex, Belize	20	17°02′N	88°31′W
Midway Islands, Oc.	114	28°13′N	177°22′W
Mielec, Pol.	138	50°18′N	21°25′E
Miguel Alemán Reservoir, Mex.	113	18°13′N	96°32′W
Mikhaylovgrad, Bul.	27	43°25′N	23°13′E
Mikkeli, Fin.	57	61°41′N	27°15′E
Mikongo Mountains, Gabon	61	0°15′N	10°55′E
Miladummadulu Atoll, Mald.	107	6°15′N	73°15′E
Milagro, Ec.	51	2°07′S	79°36′W
Milan, Italy	88	45°28′N	9°12′E
Milh, Lake al-, Iraq	83	32°40′N	43°35′E
Milltown Malbay, Ire.	84	52°52′N	9°23′W
Milo, Gui.	71	11°04′N	9°14′W
Milwaukee, Wi., U.S.	178	43°02′N	87°54′W
Mina al-Ahmadi, Kuw.	99	29°04′N	48°08′E
Minas, Ur.	181	34°23′S	55°14′W
Minas, Sierra de las, Guat.	70	15°10′N	89°40′W
Minas de Oro, Hond.	74	14°46′N	87°20′W
Minas Gerais, Braz.	24	18°00′S	44°00′W
Minatitlán, Mex.	113	17°59′N	94°31′W
Mindanao, Phil.	136	8°00′N	125°00′E
Mindanao Sea, Phil.	136	9°10′N	124°25′E
Minden, Ger., W.	64	52°17′N	8°55′E
Mindoro, Phil.	136	12°50′N	121°05′E
Mindoro Strait, Phil.	136	12°20′N	120°40′E
Minho, Eur.	139	41°52′N	8°51′W
Minicoy Island, India	79	8°17′N	73°02′E
Minna, Nig.	127	9°37′N	6°33′E
Minneapolis, Mn., U.S.	178	44°58′N	93°15′W
Minnesota, U.S.	178	46°00′N	94°15′W
Miño, Eur.	154	41°52′N	8°51′W
Minorca, Spain	154	40°00′N	4°00′E
Minsk, U.S.S.R.	172	53°54′N	27°34′E
Mińsk Mazowiecki, Pol.	138	52°11′N	21°34′E
Mintaka Pass, Pak.	131	36°58′N	74°54′E
Minuf, Egypt	52	30°28′N	30°56′E
Miramar, Arg.	11	38°16′S	57°51′W
Miramar, N.Z.	124	41°19′S	174°49′E
Miranda de Ebro, Spain	154	42°41′N	2°57′W
Miravalles Volcano, C.R.	44	10°45′N	85°10′W
Mirim Lagoon, S.A.	181	32°45′S	52°50′W
Mirpur Khas, Pak.	131	25°32′N	69°00′E
Mirtóon Sea, Grc.	67	36°51′N	23°18′E
Misiones, Arg.	11	27°00′S	55°00′W
Miskolc, Hung.	76	48°06′N	20°47′E
Misrata, Libya	103	32°23′N	15°06′E
Mississippi, U.S.	178	32°50′N	89°30′W
Mississippi, U.S.	178	29°00′N	89°15′W
Missouri, U.S.	178	38°30′N	93°30′W
Missouri, U.S.	178	38°50′N	90°08′W
Mistassini, P.Q., Can.	32	50°25′N	73°52′W
Misti Volcano, Peru	135	16°18′S	71°24′W
Mita, Point, Mex.	113	20°47′N	105°33′W
Mitchell, Mount, N.C., U.S.	178	35°46′N	82°16′W
Mitilini, Grc.	67	39°06′N	26°32′E
Mito, Japan	93	36°22′N	140°28′E
Mitsiwa, Eth.	54	15°38′N	39°28′E
Mitú, Col.	42	1°08′N	70°03′W
Mitumba Mountains, Zaire	190	6°00′S	29°00′E
Miyakonojo, Japan	93	31°44′N	131°04′E
Mizen Head, Ire.	84	51°27′N	9°49′W
Mizoram, India	79	23°30′N	93°00′E
Mizque, Bol.	22	17°56′S	65°19′W
Mjøsa, Nor.	129	60°40′N	11°00′E
Mladá Boleslav, Czech.	47	50°23′N	14°59′E
Mladenovac, Yugo.	189	44°26′N	20°42′E
Mljet, Yugo.	189	42°45′N	17°30′E
Mo, Nor.	129	66°15′N	14°08′E
Moa, Afr.	149	6°59′N	11°36′W
Mobaye, C.A.R.	35	4°19′N	21°11′E
Mobile, Al., U.S.	178	30°41′N	88°02′W
Moçambique, Moz.	118	15°03′S	40°42′E
Mochudi, Bots.	23	24°28′S	26°05′E
Móco, Mount, Ang.	6	12°28′S	15°10′E
Mocorito, Mex.	113	25°29′N	107°55′W
Moctezuma, Mex.	113	29°48′N	109°42′W
Modena, Italy	88	44°40′N	10°55′E
Modica, Italy	88	36°51′N	14°47′E
Mödling, Aus.	15	48°05′N	16°17′E
Moe, Austl.	14	38°10′S	146°15′E
Moengo, Sur.	157	5°37′N	54°24′W
Mogadishu, Som.	151	2°01′N	45°20′E
Mogaung, Burma	29	25°18′N	96°56′E
Mogoton, Mount, Nic.	125	13°45′N	86°23′W
Mohammedia, Mor.	117	33°44′N	7°24′W
Mokpo, Kor., S.	98	34°48′N	126°22′E
Mol, Bel.	19	51°11′N	5°06′E
Molepolole, Bots.	23	24°25′S	25°30′E
Mollendo, Peru	135	17°02′S	72°01′W
Molopo, Afr.	152	28°30′S	20°13′E
Moluccas, Indon.	81	5°00′S	130°00′E
Mombasa, Kenya	96	4°03′S	39°40′E
Momi, Fiji	56	17°55′S	177°17′E
Møn, Den.	48	55°00′N	12°20′E
Monaghan, Ire.	84	54°15′N	6°58′W
Monch Chajrchan, Mount, Mong.	115	46°45′N	91°30′E
Monchengladbach, Ger., W.	64	51°12′N	6°28′E
Monclova, Mex.	113	26°54′N	101°25′W
Mondego, Port.	139	40°09′N	8°52′W
Mondego, Cape, Port.	139	40°11′N	8°55′W
Monfalcone, Italy	88	45°49′N	13°32′E
Monferrato, Italy	88	45°08′N	8°27′E
Mongolia, Asia	115	46°00′N	105°00′E
Mongos Range, C.A.R.	35	8°45′N	23°00′E
Mono, Afr.	165	6°17′N	1°51′E
Monrovia, Lib.	102	6°18′N	10°47′W
Mons, Bel.	19	50°27′N	3°56′E
Montana, U.S.	178	47°00′N	110°00′W
Montauban, Fr.	58	44°01′N	1°21′E
Monteagudo, Bol.	22	19°49′S	63°59′W
Monte Alegre, Braz.	24	2°01′S	54°04′W
Monte Caseros, Arg.	11	30°15′S	57°39′W
Monte Cristi, Dom. Rep.	50	19°52′N	71°39′W
Montecristi, Ec.	51	1°03′S	80°40′W

Name	Page	Lat.	Long.
Monte Cristo, Bol.	22	14°43′S	61°14′W
Montecristo Island, Italy	88	42°20′N	10°19′E
Monte Cristo Mountain, N.A.	53	14°25′N	89°21′W
Montego Bay, Jam.	91	18°28′N	77°55′W
Monte Lindo, Para.	134	23°56′S	57°12′W
Montemorelos, Mex.	113	25°12′N	99°49′W
Montenegro, Yugo.	189	42°30′N	19°18′E
Monteria, Col.	42	8°46′N	75°53′W
Monterrey, Mex.	113	25°40′N	100°19′W
Montes Claros, Braz.	24	16°43′S	43°52′W
Montevideo, Ur.	181	34°53′S	56°11′W
Montgomery, Al., U.S.	178	32°23′N	86°18′W
Montijo, Port.	139	38°42′N	8°58′W
Montpelier, Vt., U.S.	178	44°15′N	72°34′W
Montpellier, Fr.	58	43°36′N	3°53′E
Montreal, P.Q., Can.	32	45°31′N	73°34′W
Montreux, Switz.	160	46°26′N	6°55′E
Montsinéry, Fr. Gu.	60	4°54′N	52°30′W
Monywa, Burma	29	22°05′N	95°08′E
Moorea, Fr. Poly.	60	17°32′S	149°50′W
Moose Jaw, Sk., Can.	32	50°23′N	105°32′W
Moosonee, On., Can.	32	51°17′N	80°39′W
Mopti, Mali	108	14°30′N	4°12′W
Moquegua, Peru	135	17°12′S	70°56′W
Moradabad, India	79	28°50′N	78°47′E
Morant Bay, Jam.	91	17°53′N	76°25′W
Morant Point, Jam.	91	17°55′N	76°10′W
Moratuwa, Sri L.	155	6°46′N	79°53′E
Morava, Eur.	47	48°10′N	16°59′E
Morawhanna, Guy.	72	8°16′N	59°45′W
Moray Firth, Scot., U.K.	175	57°50′N	3°30′W
Morelia, Mex.	113	19°42′N	101°07′W
Morelos, Mex.	113	26°42′N	107°40′W
Morena, Sierra, Spain	154	38°00′N	5°00′W
Morganito, Ven.	183	5°04′N	67°44′W
Morghab (Murgab), Asia	2	35°50′N	63°05′E
Moriah, Trin.	166	11°15′N	60°43′W
Morioka, Japan	93	39°42′N	141°09′E
Morne-à-l'Eau, Guad.	69	16°21′N	61°31′W
Morobe, Pap. N. Gui.	133	7°45′S	147°35′E
Morocco, Afr.	117	30°00′N	9°00′W
Morogoro, Tan.	163	6°49′S	37°40′E
Moro Gulf, Phil.	136	6°51′N	123°00′E
Morón, Arg.	11	34°39′S	58°37′W
Morón, Cuba	45	22°06′N	78°38′W
Morondava, Madag.	105	20°17′S	44°17′E
Morón de la Frontera, Spain	154	37°08′N	5°27′W
Moroni, Com.	43	11°41′S	43°16′E
Moroto, Ug.	170	2°32′N	34°46′E
Morphou, Cyp.	46	35°12′N	32°59′E
Morphou Bay, Cyp.	46	35°10′N	32°50′E
Morro, Ec.	51	2°39′S	80°19′W
Mors, Den.	48	56°50′N	8°45′E
Moscow (Moskva), U.S.S.R.	172	55°45′N	41°49′E
Mosel, Eur.	64	50°22′N	7°36′E
Moshi, Tan.	163	3°21′S	37°20′E
Mosquera, Col.	42	2°30′N	78°29′W
Mosquitia, Hond.	74	15°00′N	84°00′W
Mosquitos, Costa de, Nic.	125	13°00′N	83°45′W
Mosquitos, Gulf of, Pan.	132	9°00′N	81°15′W
Mosselbaai, S. Afr.	152	34°11′S	22°08′E
Mossendjo, Congo	43	2°57′S	12°44′E
Mossoró, Braz.	24	5°11′S	37°20′W
Most, Czech.	47	50°32′N	13°39′E
Mostar, Yugo.	189	43°20′N	17°49′E
Mostiștea, Rom.	142	44°15′N	27°10′E
Mosul, Iraq	83	36°20′N	43°08′E
Motagua, N.A.	70	15°44′N	88°14′W
Motala, Swe.	159	58°33′N	15°03′E
Motherwell, Scot., U.K.	175	55°48′N	4°00′W
Mouila, Gabon	61	1°52′S	11°01′E
Moulins, Fr.	58	46°34′N	3°20′E
Moulmein, Burma	29	16°30′N	97°38′E
Moulmeingyun, Burma	29	16°23′N	95°16′E
Moulouya, Wadi, Mor.	117	35°05′N	2°25′W
Moundou, Chad	36	8°34′N	16°05′E
Mountain Nile, Sudan	156	9°30′N	30°30′E
Mount Albert, N.Z.	124	36°53′S	174°44′E
Mount Eden, N.Z.	124	36°53′S	174°45′E
Mount Gambier, Austl.	14	37°50′S	140°46′E
Mount Hagen, Pap. N. Gui.	133	5°50′S	144°15′E
Mount Isa, Austl.	14	20°44′S	139°30′E
Mount Roskill, N.Z.	124	36°55′S	174°45′E
Mount Wellington, N.Z.	124	36°54′S	174°51′E
Moura, Braz.	24	1°27′S	61°38′W
Mourne Mountains, N. Ire., U.K.	84	54°10′N	6°05′W
Moussa Ali, Afr.	49	12°28′N	42°24′E
Moxos Plain, Bol.	22	15°00′S	65°00′W
Moyobamba, Peru	135	6°03′S	76°58′W
Mozambique, Afr.	118	18°15′S	35°00′E
Msaken, Tun.	167	35°44′N	10°35′E
Msida, Malta	109	35°54′N	14°29′E
Mtwara, Tan.	163	10°16′S	40°11′E
Muang Khammouan, Laos	100	17°24′N	104°48′E
Muang Khong, Laos	100	14°07′N	105°51′E
Muang Khongxedon, Laos	100	15°34′N	105°49′E
Muang Pakxan, Laos	100	18°22′N	103°39′E
Muang Sing, Laos	100	21°11′N	101°09′E
Muara Island, Bru.	26	5°00′N	115°06′E
Mubi, Nig.	127	10°18′N	13°20′E
Muchinga Mountains, Zam.	191	12°00′S	31°45′E
Mudanjiang, China	38	44°35′N	129°36′E
Mu Gia Pass, Asia	100	17°40′N	105°47′E
Muhammad, Cape, Egypt	52	27°44′N	34°15′E
Muharraq Island, Bahr.	16	26°16′N	50°37′E
Mühlhausen, Ger., E.	64	51°12′N	10°27′E
Muh Sabkha, Syria	161	34°30′N	38°20′E
Muisne, Ec.	51	0°36′N	80°02′W
Mulanje Mountains, Afr.	106	15°58′S	35°38′E
Mulatupo, Pan.	132	8°57′N	77°45′W
Mulchén, Chile	37	37°43′S	72°14′W
Mulhacén, Spain	154	37°03′N	3°19′W
Mulhouse, Fr.	58	47°45′N	7°20′E
Mull, Scot., U.K.	175	56°27′N	6°00′W

Name	Page	Lat.	Long.
Mullingar, Ire.	84	53°32′N	7°20′W
Multan, Pak.	131	30°11′N	71°28′E
Mun, Thai.	164	15°19′N	105°30′E
Munich, Ger., W.	64	48°08′N	11°34′E
Munku-Sardyk, Mount, Asia	172	51°45′N	100°32′E
Münster, Ger., W.	64	51°57′N	7°37′E
Muqayshit, U.A.E.	174	24°12′N	53°42′E
Mura (Mur), Eur.	189	46°18′N	16°53′E
Muramuya, Bdi.	30	3°16′S	29°37′E
Murat, Tur.	168	38°39′N	39°50′E
Murchison, Austl.	14	27°42′S	114°09′E
Murchison Mountains, N.Z.	124	20°11′S	134°26′E
Murcia, Spain	154	37°59′N	1°07′W
Mureș, Eur.	142	46°15′N	20°13′E
Murgab (Morghab), Asia	2	38°18′N	61°12′E
Muri, Cook Is.	44	21°14′S	159°43′W
Muroran, Japan	93	42°18′N	140°59′E
Murray, Austl.	14	35°22′S	139°22′E
Murrumbidgee, Austl.	14	34°43′S	143°12′E
Murud Mountain, Malay.	107	3°52′N	115°30′E
Mürzzuschlag, Aus.	15	47°36′N	15°41′E
Musala, Bul.	27	42°11′N	23°34′E
Musayid, Qatar	141	24°59′N	51°32′E
Muscat, Oman	130	23°37′N	58°35′E
Mushin, Nig.	127	6°32′N	3°22′E
Musi, Indon.	81	2°20′S	104°56′E
Mutare, Zimb.	192	18°58′S	32°40′E
Muyinga, Bdi.	30	2°51′S	30°20′E
Mvoung, Gabon	61	0°04′N	12°18′E
Mwali, Com.	43	12°15′S	43°45′E
Mwanza, Tan.	163	2°31′S	32°54′E
Mweru, Lake, Afr.	191	8°45′S	29°40′E
Myingyan, Burma	29	21°28′N	95°23′E
Myitkyina, Burma	29	25°23′N	97°24′E
Mymensingh, Bngl.	17	24°45′N	90°24′E
Myrdals Glacier, Ice.	77	63°40′N	19°05′W
My Tho, Viet.	184	10°21′N	106°21′E
Mzimba, Mwi.	106	11°52′S	33°34′E
Mzuzu, Mwi.	106	11°27′S	33°55′E

N

Name	Page	Lat.	Long.
Naas, Ire.	84	53°13′N	6°39′W
Nabeul, Tun.	167	36°27′N	10°44′E
Nablus, Jord.	94	32°13′N	35°16′E
Nachal Oz, Isr.	86	31°28′N	34°29′E
Nacozari [de Garcia], Mex.	113	30°24′N	109°39′W
Nadir, V.I.U.S.	185	18°19′N	64°53′W
Næstved, Den.	48	55°14′N	11°46′E
Nafud, Sau. Ar.	147	28°30′N	41°00′E
Naga, Phil.	136	10°13′N	123°45′E
Naga Hills, Asia	29	26°00′N	95°00′E
Nagaland, India	79	26°00′N	95°00′E
Nagano, Japan	93	36°39′N	138°11′E
Nagarote, Nic.	125	12°16′N	86°34′W
Nagasaki, Japan	93	32°48′N	129°55′E
Nagoya, Japan	93	35°10′N	136°55′E
Nagpur, India	79	21°09′N	79°06′E
Nagua, Dom. Rep.	50	19°23′N	69°50′W
Nagykanizsa, Hung.	76	46°27′N	17°00′E
Nagy-Milic, Eur.	76	48°35′N	21°28′E
Naha, Japan	93	26°13′N	127°40′E
Nahariyya, Isr.	86	33°00′N	35°05′E
Nairobi, Kenya	96	1°17′S	36°49′E
Naivasha, Lake, Kenya	96	0°46′S	36°21′E
Najafabad, Iran	82	32°37′N	51°21′E
Najjer Plateau, Alg.	4	25°10′N	8°00′E
Nakhodka, U.S.S.R.	172	42°48′N	132°52′E
Nakhon Pathom, Thai.	164	13°49′N	100°03′E
Nakhon Ratchasima, Thai.	164	14°58′N	102°07′E
Nakhon Sawan, Thai.	164	15°41′N	100°07′E
Nakhon Si Thammarat, Thai.	164	8°26′N	99°58′E
Nakskov, Den.	48	54°50′N	11°09′E
Naktong, Kor., S.	98	35°07′N	128°57′E
Nakuru, Kenya	96	0°17′S	36°04′E
Namak, Lake, Iran	82	34°45′N	51°36′E
Nambouwalu, Fiji	56	16°59′S	178°42′E
Nam Dinh, Viet.	184	20°25′N	106°10′E
Namhan, Kor., S.	98	37°31′N	127°18′E
Namib Desert, Nmb.	119	23°00′S	15°00′E
Namibia, Afr.	119	22°00′S	17°00′E
Namin, Iran	82	38°25′N	48°30′E
Namoi, Austl.	14	30°00′S	148°07′E
Namos, Nor.	129	64°29′N	11°30′E
Nampo, Kor., N.	98	38°45′N	125°23′E
Nampula, Moz.	118	15°07′S	39°15′E
Namur, Bel.	19	50°28′N	4°52′E
Nan, Thai.	164	15°42′N	100°09′E
Nanaimo, B.C., Can.	32	49°10′N	123°56′W
Nanchang, China	38	28°34′N	115°56′E
Nancy, Fr.	58	48°41′N	6°12′E
Nanda Devi, India	79	30°23′N	79°59′E
Nandi, Fiji	56	17°48′S	177°25′E
Nanduri, Fiji	56	16°27′S	179°09′E
Nanga Parbat, Pak.	131	35°15′N	74°36′E
Nanjing, China	38	32°03′N	118°47′E
Nan Mountains, China	38	25°00′N	112°00′E
Nanning, China	38	22°48′N	108°20′E
Nan Shan, China	38	39°06′N	98°40′E
Nantes, Fr.	58	47°13′N	1°33′W
Nanuque, Braz.	24	17°50′S	40°21′W
Nanyang, China	38	33°00′N	112°32′E
Nao, Cape, Spain	154	38°44′N	0°14′E
Naogaon, Bngl.	17	24°47′N	88°56′E
Napier, N.Z.	124	39°29′S	176°55′E
Naples, Italy	88	40°51′N	14°17′E
Napo, S.A.	135	3°20′S	72°40′W
Nara, Japan	93	34°41′N	135°50′E
Naranjal, Ec.	51	2°42′S	79°37′W
Narayanganj, Bngl.	17	23°37′N	90°30′E
Narbonne, Fr.	58	43°11′N	3°00′E
Narew, Eur.	138	52°26′N	20°42′E
Narmada, India	79	21°38′N	72°36′E
Narodnaya, Mount, U.S.S.R.	172	65°01′N	60°01′E
Narssag, Grnld.	68	60°54′N	46°00′W
Nashville, Tn., U.S.	178	36°09′N	86°47′W

Name	Page	Lat.	Long.
Nasik, India	79	19°59′N	73°48′E
Näsi Lake, Fin.	57	61°37′N	23°42′E
Nassau, Bah.	16	25°05′N	77°21′W
Nasser, Lake, Afr.	52	22°40′N	32°00′E
Nassjö, Swe.	159	57°39′N	14°41′E
Natal, Braz.	24	5°47′S	35°13′W
Natal, S. Afr.	152	28°40′S	30°40′E
Natashquan, P.Q., Can.	32	50°12′N	61°49′W
Natewa Bay, Fiji	56	16°35′S	179°40′E
Nattas Mountain, Fin.	57	68°12′N	27°20′E
Naumburg, Ger., E.	64	51°09′N	11°48′E
Nauru, Oc.	120	0°32′S	166°55′E
Nausori, Fiji	56	18°02′S	175°32′E
Navan, Ire.	84	53°39′N	6°41′W
Navia, Arg.	11	34°47′S	66°35′W
Navojoa, Mex.	113	27°06′N	109°26′W
Navua, Fiji	56	18°14′S	178°10′E
Nawabshah, Pak.	131	26°15′N	68°25′E
Nazaré, Braz.	24	13°02′S	39°00′W
Nazareth, Isr.	86	32°42′N	35°18′E
Nazas, Mex.	113	25°14′N	104°08′W
Nazca, Peru	135	14°50′S	74°57′W
N'dalatando, Ang.	6	9°18′S	14°54′E
N'djamena (Fort-Lamy), Chad	36	12°07′N	15°03′E
Ndola, Zam.	191	12°58′S	28°38′E
Ndoto Mountains, Kenya	96	1°45′N	37°07′E
Neagh, Lake, N. Ire., U.K.	84	54°37′N	6°25′W
Neath, Wales, U.K.	175	51°40′N	3°48′W
Neblina Peak, S.A.	24	0°48′N	66°02′W
Nebraska, U.S.	178	41°30′N	100°00′W
Nebrodi, Italy	88	37°55′N	14°35′E
Necochea, Arg.	11	38°33′S	58°45′W
Nefta, Tun.	167	33°52′N	7°33′E
Negev, Isr.	86	30°30′N	34°55′E
Negombo, Sri L.	155	7°13′N	79°50′E
Negro, Arg.	11	41°02′S	62°47′W
Negro, S.A.	24	3°08′S	59°55′W
Negro, S.A.	181	33°24′S	58°22′W
Negros, Phil.	136	10°00′N	123°00′E
Neiafu, Tonga	166	18°39′S	173°59′W
Neiges, Piton des, Reu.	141	21°05′S	55°29′E
Neisse, Eur.	64	52°04′N	14°46′E
Neiva, Col.	42	2°56′N	75°18′W
Nelson, N.Z.	124	41°17′S	173°17′E
Nelson, Mb., Can.	32	57°04′N	92°30′W
Nenagh, Ire.	84	52°52′N	8°12′W
Nepal, Asia	120	28°00′N	84°00′E
Nepalganj, Nepal	120	28°03′N	81°37′E
Nepean Island, Norf. I.	128	29°04′S	167°58′E
Nerastro, Sarir, Libya	103	24°20′N	20°37′E
Neskaupstadur, Ice.	77	65°10′N	13°43′W
Ness, Loch, Scot., U.K.	175	57°15′N	4°30′W
Nestos, Eur.	67	40°41′N	24°44′E
Netanya, Isr.	86	32°20′N	34°51′E
Netherlands, Eur.	122	52°15′N	5°30′E
Netherlands Antilles, N.A.	123	12°15′N	68°45′W
Netrakona, Bngl.	17	24°53′N	90°43′E
Neubrandenburg, Ger., E.	64	53°33′N	13°15′E
Neuchâtel, Switz.	160	46°59′N	6°56′E
Neuchatel, Lake, Switz.	160	46°52′N	6°50′E
Neumünster, Ger., W.	64	54°04′N	9°59′E
Neunkirchen, Aus.	15	47°43′N	16°05′E
Neunkirchen, Ger., W.	64	49°20′N	7°10′E
Neuquén, Arg.	11	38°57′S	68°04′W
Neuquén, Arg.	11	39°00′S	70°00′W
Neuruppin, Ger., E.	64	52°55′N	12°48′E
Neusiedler Lake, Eur.	15	47°50′N	16°46′E
Neustrelitz, Ger., E.	64	53°21′N	13°04′E
Neuvo Mundo, Mount, Bol.	22	21°55′S	66°53′W
Nevada, U.S.	178	39°00′N	117°00′W
Nevada, Sierra, Spain	154	37°05′N	3°10′W
Nevada, Sierra, Ca., U.S.	178	38°00′N	119°15′W
Neve Mountains, Ang.	6	13°52′S	13°26′E
Nevers, Fr.	58	47°00′N	3°09′E
Nevis, Ben, Scot., U.K.	175	56°48′N	5°01′W
Nevsehir, Tur.	168	38°38′N	34°43′E
New, Belize	20	18°22′N	88°24′W
New, Guy.	72	3°23′N	57°36′W
New Amsterdam, Guy.	72	6°15′N	57°31′W
Newark, N.J., U.S.	178	40°44′N	74°10′W
New Britain, Pap. N. Gui.	133	6°00′S	150°00′E
New Brunswick, Can.	32	46°30′N	66°15′W
New Caledonia, Oc.	123	21°30′S	165°30′E
Newcastle, Austl.	14	32°56′S	151°46′E
Newcastle-on-Tyne, Eng., U.K.	175	54°59′N	1°35′W
New Delhi, India	79	28°36′N	77°12′E
Newfoundland, Can.	32	52°00′N	56°00′W
New Georgia Group, Sol. Is.	151	8°15′S	157°00′E
New Guinea	130	5°00′S	140°00′E
New Hampshire, U.S.	178	43°35′N	71°40′W
New Hanover, Pap. N. Gui.	133	2°30′S	150°15′E
New Haven, Ct., U.S.	178	41°18′N	72°56′W
New Ireland, Pap. N. Gui.	133	3°20′S	152°00′E
New Jersey, U.S.	178	40°15′N	74°30′W
New Kowloon, H.K.	75	22°20′N	114°10′E
New Mexico, U.S.	178	34°30′N	106°00′W
New Orleans, La., U.S.	178	29°57′N	90°04′W
New Plymouth, N.Z.	124	39°04′S	174°05′E
New Port, Neth. Ant.	123	12°03′N	68°49′W
Newport, Wales, U.K.	175	52°01′N	4°51′W
New Providence, Bah.	16	25°02′N	77°24′W
New South Wales, Austl.	14	33°00′S	146°00′E
Newtontoppen, Sval.	129	79°02′N	17°30′E
New York, N.Y., U.S.	178	40°43′N	74°01′W
New York, U.S.	178	43°00′N	106°00′W
New Zealand, Oc.	124	41°00′S	174°00′E
Neyshabur, Iran	82	36°12′N	58°50′E
Ngami, Lake, Bots.	23	20°37′S	22°40′E
Ngangerabeli Plain, Kenya	96	1°30′S	40°15′E
Ngau, Fiji	56	18°02′S	179°18′E
Ngawi, Indon.	81	7°24′S	111°26′E
Ngermechau, Palau	132	7°35′N	134°39′E

Name	Page	Lat.	Long.
Petit-Goâve, Haiti	**73**	18°26'N	72°52'W
Petone, N.Z.	**124**	41°13'S	174°52'E
Petropavlovsk, U.S.S.R.	**172**	54°54'N	69°06'E
Petropavlovsk-Kamchatsk, U.S.S.R.	**172**	53°01'N	158°39'E
Petroşani, Rom.	**142**	45°25'N	23°22'E
Petrozavodsk, U.S.S.R.	**172**	61°47'N	34°20'E
Pforzheim, Ger., W.	**64**	48°54'N	8°42'E
Phan Rang, Viet.	**184**	11°34'N	108°59'E
Phan Thiet, Viet.	**184**	10°56'N	108°06'E
Phetchabun Range, Thai.	**164**	16°20'N	100°55'E
Philadelphia, Pa., U.S.	**178**	39°57'N	75°09'W
Philippines, Asia	**136**	13°00'N	122°00'E
Phitsanulok, Thai.	**164**	16°50'N	100°15'E
Phnom Penh, Kam.	**95**	11°33'N	104°55'E
Phoenix, Az., U.S.	**178**	33°26'N	112°04'W
Phongsali, Laos	**100**	21°41'N	102°06'E
Phra Nakhon Si Ayutthaya, Thai.	**164**	14°21'N	100°33'E
Phuket, Thai.	**164**	7°53'N	98°24'E
Phuket Island, Thai.	**164**	8°00'N	98°22'E
Phu Quoc, Viet.	**184**	10°12'N	104°00'E
Phu Vinh, Viet.	**184**	9°56'N	106°20'E
Piacenza, Italy	**88**	45°01'N	9°40'E
Piatra-Neamţ, Rom.	**142**	46°56'N	26°22'E
Piauí, Braz.	**24**	7°00'S	43°00'W
Pico, C.V.	**34**	14°56'N	24°21'W
Pico Point, Port.	**139**	38°28'N	28°25'W
Pidurutalagala, Sri L.	**155**	7°00'N	80°46'E
Piedras Negras, Guat.	**70**	17°11'N	91°15'W
Piedras Negras, Mex.	**113**	28°42'N	100°31'W
Piedra Sola, Ur.	**181**	32°04'S	56°21'W
Pieksämäki, Fin.	**57**	62°18'N	27°08'E
Pielinen, Fin.	**57**	63°15'N	29°40'E
Pierre, S.D., U.S.	**178**	44°22'N	100°21'W
Pierreville, Trin.	**166**	10°18'N	61°01'W
Pietermaritzburg, S. Afr.	**152**	29°37'S	30°16'E
Pietersburg, S. Afr.	**152**	23°54'S	29°25'E
Piggs Peak, Swaz.	**158**	25°38'S	31°15'E
Pigs, Bay of, Cuba	**45**	22°07'N	81°10'W
Pihlaja Lake, Fin.	**57**	61°45'N	28°50'E
Pijijiapan, Mex.	**113**	15°42'N	93°14'W
Pila, Arg.	**11**	36°01'S	58°08'W
Piła, Pol.	**138**	53°10'N	16°44'E
Pilcomayo, S.A.	**11**	25°21'S	57°42'W
Pilica, Pol.	**138**	51°52'N	21°17'E
Pillaro, Ec.	**51**	1°10'S	78°32'W
Pinar del Rio, Cuba	**45**	22°25'N	83°42'W
Piñas, Ec.	**51**	3°42'S	79°42'W
Pindus Mountains, Grc.	**67**	39°49'N	21°14'E
Pinerolo, Italy	**88**	44°53'N	7°21'E
Ping, Thai.	**164**	15°42'N	100°09'E
P'ing-tung, Tai.	**162**	22°40'N	120°29'E
Piombino, Italy	**88**	42°55'N	10°32'E
Piotrków Trybunalski, Pol.	**138**	51°25'N	19°42'E
Piracicaba, Braz.	**24**	22°43'S	47°38'W
Pirae, Fr. Poly.	**60**	17°32'S	149°33'W
Piraeus, Grc.	**67**	37°57'N	23°38'E
Pirmassens, Ger., W.	**64**	49°12'N	7°36'E
Pirna, Ger., E.	**64**	50°58'N	13°56'E
Pirot, Yugo.	**189**	43°09'N	22°35'E
Pirovano, Arg.	**11**	36°30'S	61°34'W
Pir Panjal Range, Asia	**79**	33°00'N	75°00'E
Pisa, Italy	**88**	43°43'N	10°23'E
Pisagua, Chile	**37**	19°36'S	70°13'W
Pisco, Peru	**135**	13°42'S	76°13'W
Pitalito, Col.	**42**	1°51'N	76°02'W
Pitcairn, Oc.	**137**	25°04'S	130°06'W
Piteå, Swe.	**159**	65°20'N	21°30'E
Piteå, Swe.	**159**	65°14'N	21°32'E
Piteşti, Rom.	**142**	44°52'N	24°52'E
Pittsburgh, Pa., U.S.	**178**	40°26'N	79°59'W
Piura, Peru	**135**	5°12'S	80°38'W
Pjórsá, Ice.	**77**	63°47'N	20°48'W
Placetas, Cuba	**45**	22°19'N	79°40'W
Plana des Lles Peak, Eur.	**5**	42°28'N	1°40'E
Planeta Rica, Col.	**42**	8°25'N	75°36'W
Plasencia, Spain	**154**	40°02'N	6°05'W
Plata, Rio de la, S.A.	**11**	35°00'S	57°00'W
Plato, Col.	**42**	9°47'N	74°47'W
Plauen, Ger., E.	**64**	50°30'N	12°08'E
Playa Bonita, C.R.	**44**	9°39'N	84°27'W
Plenty, Bay of, N.Z.	**124**	37°40'S	177°00'E
Pleven, Bul.	**27**	43°25'N	24°37'E
Pljevlja, Yugo.	**189**	43°21'N	19°21'E
Płock, Pol.	**138**	52°33'N	19°43'E
Ploieşti, Rom.	**142**	44°56'N	26°02'E
Plovdiv, Bul.	**27**	42°09'N	24°45'E
Plymouth, Eng., U.K.	**175**	50°23'N	4°10'W
Plzeň, Czech.	**47**	49°45'N	13°23'E
Po, Italy	**88**	44°57'N	12°04'E
Pobé, Benin	**20**	6°58'N	2°41'E
Pobedy, Mount, U.S.S.R.	**172**	65°12'N	146°12'E
Pobedy Peak, Asia	**172**	42°02'N	80°05'E
Pogradec, Alb.	**3**	40°54'N	20°39'E
Pointe-à-Pitre, Guad.	**69**	16°14'N	61°32'W
Pointe-Noire, Congo	**40**	4°48'S	11°51'E
Point Fortin, Trin.	**166**	10°11'N	61°41'W
Poitiers, Fr.	**58**	46°35'N	0°20'E
Poland, Eur.	**138**	52°00'N	19°00'E
Polatli, Tur.	**168**	39°36'N	32°09'E
Pol-e Khomri, Afg.	**2**	35°56'N	68°43'E
Polillo Islands, Phil.	**136**	14°50'N	122°05'E
Pollaphuca Reservoir, Ire.	**84**	53°08'N	6°31'W
Pomabamba, Peru	**135**	8°50'S	77°28'W
Pomata, Peru	**135**	16°16'S	69°18'W
Pomeranian Bay, Eur.	**64**	54°00'N	14°15'E
Ponape, Micron.	**114**	6°55'N	158°15'E
Ponce, P.R.	**140**	18°01'N	66°37'W
Pondicherry, India	**79**	11°56'N	79°53'E
Pondicherry, India	**79**	11°56'N	79°50'E
Ponferrada, Spain	**154**	42°33'N	6°35'W
Ponorogo, Indon.	**81**	7°52'S	111°27'E
Ponta Delgada, Port.	**139**	37°44'N	25°40'W
Ponta Grossa, Braz.	**24**	25°05'S	50°09'W
Ponta Porã, Braz.	**24**	22°32'S	55°43'W
Ponte Nova, Braz.	**24**	20°24'S	42°54'W
Pontevedra, Spain	**154**	42°26'N	8°38'W
Pontianak, Indon.	**81**	0°02'S	109°20'E
Ponziane Islands, Italy	**88**	40°55'N	12°57'E
Poole, Eng., U.K.	**175**	50°43'N	1°59'W

Name	Page	Lat.	Long.
Poona, India	**79**	18°32'N	73°52'E
Poopó, Lake, Bol.	**22**	18°45'S	67°07'W
Popayán, Col.	**42**	2°27'N	76°36'W
Popocatépetl, Mex.	**113**	19°02'N	98°38'W
Popondetta, Pap. N. Gui.	**133**	8°46'S	148°14'E
Porco, Bol.	**22**	19°50'S	65°59'W
Pordenone, Italy	**88**	45°57'N	12°39'E
Pori, Fin.	**57**	61°29'N	21°47'E
Porirua, N.Z.	**124**	41°08'S	174°51'E
Porlamar, Ven.	**183**	10°57'N	63°51'W
Portage la Prairie, Mb., Can.	**32**	49°59'N	98°18'W
Portalegre, Port.	**139**	39°17'N	7°26'W
Port Antonio, Jam.	**91**	18°11'N	76°28'W
Port-au-Prince, Haiti	**73**	18°32'N	72°20'W
Port-de-Paix, Haiti	**73**	19°57'N	72°50'W
Port Elizabeth, S. Afr.	**152**	33°58'S	25°40'E
Port Erin, I. of Man	**85**	54°06'N	4°44'W
Port-Gentil, Gabon	**61**	0°43'S	8°47'E
Port Harcourt, Nig.	**127**	4°43'N	7°05'E
Port Hedland, Austl.	**14**	20°19'S	118°34'E
Portillo, Cuba	**45**	19°55'N	77°11'W
Portimão, Port.	**139**	37°08'N	8°32'W
Portland, Or., U.S.	**178**	45°31'N	122°40'W
Portland, Bill of, Eng., U.K.	**175**	50°31'N	2°27'W
Portland Bight, Jam.	**91**	17°53'N	77°08'W
Portland Point, Jam.	**91**	17°42'N	77°11'W
Port Laoise, Ire.	**84**	53°02'N	7°17'W
Port Lincoln, Austl.	**14**	34°44'S	135°52'E
Port-Louis, Guad.	**69**	16°25'N	61°32'W
Port Louis, Mrts.	**111**	20°10'S	57°30'E
Port Maria, Jam.	**91**	18°22'N	76°54'W
Port Morant, Jam.	**91**	17°54'N	76°19'W
Port Moresby, Pap. N. Gui.	**133**	9°30'S	147°10'E
Porto, Port.	**139**	41°11'N	8°36'W
Porto Alegre, Braz.	**24**	30°04'S	51°11'W
Porto Esperança, Braz.	**24**	19°37'S	57°27'W
Port of Spain, Trin.	**166**	10°39'N	61°31'W
Porto Nacional, Braz.	**24**	10°42'S	48°25'W
Porto-Novo, Benin	**20**	6°29'N	2°37'E
Porto Velho, Braz.	**24**	8°46'S	63°54'W
Portoviejo, Ec.	**51**	1°03'S	80°27'W
Port Said, Egypt	**52**	31°16'N	32°18'E
Portsmouth, Dom.	**49**	15°35'N	61°28'W
Portsmouth, Eng., U.K.	**175**	50°48'N	1°05'W
Port Sudan, Sudan	**156**	19°37'N	37°14'E
Porttipahdan tekojärvi, Fin.	**57**	68°08'N	26°40'E
Portugal, Eur.	**139**	39°30'N	8°00'W
Portuguesa, Ven.	**183**	7°57'N	67°32'W
Port Vila, Vanuatu	**182**	17°44'S	168°19'E
Porz, Ger., W.	**64**	50°53'N	7°03'E
Posadas, Arg.	**11**	27°23'S	55°53'W
Potaro Landing, Guy.	**72**	5°23'N	59°08'W
Potenza, Italy	**88**	40°38'N	15°49'E
Potiskum, Nig.	**127**	11°43'N	11°05'E
Potosí, Bol.	**22**	20°40'S	67°00'W
Potosí, Mount, Mex.	**113**	24°52'N	100°13'W
Potsdam, Ger., E.	**64**	52°24'N	13°04'E
Poutasi, W. Sam.	**187**	14°01'S	171°41'W
Povungnituk, P.Q., Can.	**32**	60°02'N	77°10'W
Powell River, B.C., Can.	**32**	49°52'N	124°33'W
Požarevac, Yugo.	**189**	44°37'N	21°11'E
Poznań, Pol.	**138**	52°25'N	16°55'E
Prague, Czech.	**47**	50°05'N	14°26'E
Praia, C.V.	**34**	14°55'N	23°31'W
Praia Grande, Baia da, Macau	**105**	22°11'N	113°32'E
Prainha, Braz.	**24**	1°48'S	53°29'W
Praslin Island, Sey.	**149**	4°19'S	55°44'E
Prato, Italy	**88**	43°53'N	11°06'E
Přerov, Czech.	**47**	49°27'N	17°27'E
Prešov, Czech.	**47**	49°00'N	21°15'E
Prespa, Lake, Eur.	**3**	40°55'N	21°00'E
Prestea, Ghana	**65**	5°27'N	2°08'W
Preston, Eng., U.K.	**175**	53°46'N	2°42'W
Pretoria, S. Afr.	**152**	25°45'S	28°10'E
Prey Veng, Kam.	**95**	11°29'N	105°19'E
Priboj, Yugo.	**189**	43°35'N	19°31'E
Příbram, Czech.	**47**	49°42'N	14°01'E
Prievidza, Czech.	**47**	48°47'N	18°37'E
Prijedor, Yugo.	**189**	44°59'N	16°43'E
Prijepolje, Yugo.	**189**	43°23'N	19°39'E
Prilep, Yugo.	**189**	41°20'N	21°33'E
Prince Albert, Sk., Can.	**32**	53°12'N	105°46'W
Prince Edward Island, Can.	**32**	46°20'N	63°20'W
Prince George, B.C., Can.	**32**	53°55'N	122°45'W
Prince Rupert, B.C., Can.	**32**	54°19'N	130°19'W
Princes Town, Trin.	**166**	10°16'N	61°23'W
Príncipe, S. Tom./P.	**146**	1°37'N	7°25'E
Prinses Margriet Canal, Neth.	**122**	53°10'N	5°55'E
Priština, Yugo.	**189**	42°39'N	21°10'E
Prizren, Yugo.	**189**	42°12'N	20°44'E
Probolinggo, Indon.	**81**	7°45'S	113°13'E
Progreso, Mex.	**113**	21°17'N	89°40'W
Prokuplje, Yugo.	**189**	43°14'N	21°36'E
Prome, Burma	**29**	18°49'N	95°13'E
Propriá, Braz.	**24**	10°13'S	36°51'W
Prosna, Pol.	**138**	52°10'N	17°39'E
Prostějov, Czech.	**47**	49°29'N	17°07'E
Providence, R.I., U.S.	**178**	41°49'N	71°24'W
Providenciales, T./C. Is.	**169**	21°47'N	72°17'W
Pruszków, Pol.	**138**	52°11'N	20°48'E
Prut, Eur.	**142**	45°28'N	28°12'E
Przemyśl, Pol.	**138**	49°47'N	22°47'E
Ptolemaís, Grc.	**67**	40°31'N	21°41'E
Puapua, W. Sam.	**187**	13°34'S	172°09'W
Puava, Cape, W. Sam.	**187**	13°26'S	172°43'W
Pucallpa, Peru	**135**	8°23'S	74°32'W
Pucará, Bol.	**22**	18°43'S	64°11'W
Puebla, Mex.	**113**	19°03'N	98°12'W
Puebloviejo, Ec.	**51**	1°34'S	79°30'W
Puerto Acosta, Bol.	**22**	15°32'S	69°15'W
Puerto Aisen, Chile	**37**	45°24'S	72°42'W
Puerto Alegre, Bol.	**22**	13°53'S	61°36'W
Puerto Ángel, Mex.	**113**	15°40'N	96°29'W
Puerto Armuelles, Pan.	**132**	8°17'N	82°52'W
Puerto Asís, Col.	**42**	0°30'N	76°31'W
Puerto Ayacucho, Ven.	**183**	5°40'N	67°35'W

Name	Page	Lat.	Long.
Puerto Ayora, Ec.	**51**	0°44'S	90°19'W
Puerto Baquerizo Moreno, Ec.	**51**	0°54'S	89°36'W
Puerto Barrios, Guat.	**70**	15°43'N	88°36'W
Puerto Bermúdez, Peru	**135**	10°20'S	74°54'W
Puerto Berrío, Col.	**42**	6°29'N	74°24'W
Puerto Cabello, Ven.	**183**	10°28'N	68°01'W
Puerto Cabezas, Nic.	**125**	14°02'N	83°23'W
Puerto Carreño, Col.	**42**	6°12'N	67°22'W
Puerto Casado, Para.	**134**	22°20'S	57°55'W
Puerto Castilla, Hond.	**74**	16°01'N	86°01'W
Puerto Chicama, Peru	**135**	7°42'S	79°27'W
Puerto Cortés, Hond.	**74**	15°48'N	87°56'W
Puerto Cumarebo, Ven.	**183**	11°29'N	69°21'W
Puerto Deseado, Arg.	**11**	47°45'S	65°54'W
Puerto El Triuto, El Sal.	**53**	13°17'N	88°33'W
Puerto Fonciere, Para.	**134**	22°29'S	57°48'W
Puerto Guaraní, Para.	**134**	21°18'S	57°55'W
Puerto Jiménez, C.R.	**44**	8°33'N	83°19'W
Puerto la Cruz, Ven.	**183**	10°13'N	64°38'W
Puerto Leda, Para.	**134**	20°41'S	58°02'W
Puerto Leguízamo, Col.	**42**	0°12'S	74°46'W
Puerto Libertad, Arg.	**11**	25°55'S	54°36'W
Puertollano, Spain	**154**	38°41'N	4°07'W
Puerto Madryn, Arg.	**11**	42°46'S	65°03'W
Puerto Maldonado, Peru	**135**	12°36'S	69°11'W
Puerto Mihanovich, Para.	**134**	20°52'S	57°59'W
Puerto Montt, Chile	**37**	41°28'S	72°57'W
Puerto Natales, Chile	**37**	51°44'S	72°31'W
Puerto Padilla, Peru	**135**	10°15'S	71°39'W
Puerto Padre, Cuba	**45**	21°12'N	76°36'W
Puerto Páez, Ven.	**183**	6°13'N	67°28'W
Puerto Peñasco, Mex.	**113**	31°20'N	113°33'W
Puerto Plata, Dom. Rep.	**50**	19°48'N	70°41'W
Puerto Portillo, Peru	**135**	9°46'S	72°45'W
Puerto Rico, Bol.	**22**	11°05'S	67°38'W
Puerto Rico, N.A.	**140**	18°15'N	66°30'W
Puerto Sastre, Para.	**134**	22°06'S	57°59'W
Puerto Siles, Bol.	**22**	12°48'S	65°05'W
Puerto Suárez, Bol.	**22**	18°57'S	57°51'W
Puerto Sucre, Bol.	**22**	10°48'S	65°23'W
Puerto Vallarta, Mex.	**113**	20°37'N	105°15'W
Puerto Victoria, Peru	**135**	9°54'S	74°58'W
Puerto Viejo, C.R.	**44**	9°39'N	82°45'W
Pujili, Ec.	**51**	0°57'S	78°41'W
Pukchong, Kor., N.	**98**	40°15'N	128°20'E
Pukë, Alb.	**3**	42°03'N	19°54'E
Pukhan, Asia	**98**	37°31'N	127°18'E
Pula, Yugo.	**189**	44°52'N	13°50'E
Pulacayo, Bol.	**22**	20°25'S	66°41'W
Pullo, Peru	**135**	15°14'S	73°50'W
Pulog, Mount, Phil.	**136**	16°36'N	120°54'E
Puná Island, Ec.	**51**	2°50'S	80°08'W
Punata, Bol.	**22**	17°32'S	65°50'W
Puno, Peru	**135**	15°50'S	70°02'W
Punta Alta, Arg.	**11**	38°53'S	62°05'W
Punta Arenas, Chile	**37**	53°09'S	70°55'W
Punta Delgada, Arg.	**11**	42°46'S	63°38'W
Punta Gorda, Belize	**20**	16°07'N	88°48'W
Punta Gorda, Nic.	**125**	11°31'N	83°47'W
Punta Moreno, Peru	**135**	7°36'S	78°54'W
Punta Mountain, P.R.	**140**	18°10'N	66°36'W
Puntarenas, C.R.	**44**	9°58'N	84°50'W
Puntas del Sauce, Ur.	**181**	33°51'S	57°01'W
Punto Fijo, Ven.	**183**	11°42'N	70°13'W
Puquio, Peru	**135**	14°42'S	74°08'W
Purísima, Mex.	**113**	25°25'N	105°26'W
Pursat, Kam.	**95**	12°32'N	103°55'E
Pursat, Kam.	**95**	12°41'N	104°09'E
Purus, S.A.	**24**	3°42'S	61°28'W
Purwakarta, Indon.	**81**	6°34'S	107°26'E
Purwokerto, Indon.	**81**	7°25'S	109°14'E
Purworejo, Indon.	**81**	7°43'S	110°01'E
Pusan, Kor., S.	**98**	35°06'N	129°03'E
Puławy, Pol.	**138**	51°25'N	21°57'E
Putina, Peru	**135**	14°55'S	69°52'W
Puttalam, Sri L.	**155**	8°02'N	79°49'E
Putumayo (Içá), S.A.	**42**	2°55'S	69°40'W
Puula Lake, Fin.	**57**	61°50'N	26°42'E
Puyo, Ec.	**51**	1°28'S	77°59'W
Pyhä, Fin.	**57**	64°28'N	24°13'E
Pyinmana, Burma	**29**	19°44'N	96°13'E
Pyongyang, Kor., N.	**98**	39°01'N	125°45'E
Pyrenees, Eur.	**154**	42°40'N	1°00'E
Pyu, Burma	**29**	18°29'N	96°26'E

Q

Name	Page	Lat.	Long.
Qal al-Bisha, Sau. Ar.	**147**	20°01'N	42°36'E
Qal'eh-ye Now, Afg.	**2**	34°59'N	63°08'E
Qataba, Yemen	**187**	13°51'N	44°42'E
Qatana, Syria	**161**	33°26'N	36°05'E
Qatar, Asia	**141**	25°00'N	51°10'E
Qattara Depression, Egypt	**52**	30°00'N	27°30'E
Qazvin, Iran	**82**	36°16'N	50°00'E
Qeshm, Iran	**82**	26°45'N	55°45'E
Qingdao, China	**38**	36°06'N	120°19'E
Qinhuangdao, China	**38**	39°56'N	119°36'E
Qin Mountains, China	**38**	34°00'N	108°00'E
Qiqihar, China	**38**	47°19'N	123°55'E
Qom, Iran	**82**	34°39'N	50°54'E
Qomsheh, Iran	**82**	32°01'N	51°52'E
Quaregnon, Bel.	**19**	50°26'N	3°51'E
Quartier Militaire, Mrts.	**111**	20°15'S	57°35'E
Quatre Bornes, Mrts.	**111**	20°15'S	57°28'E
Quatre Cocos, Point, Mrts.	**111**	20°14'S	57°46'E
Quchan, Iran	**82**	37°06'N	58°30'E
Quebec, P.Q., Can.	**32**	46°49'N	71°14'W
Quebec, Can.	**32**	52°00'N	72°00'W
Quebracho, Ur.	**181**	31°57'S	57°53'W
Queen Charlotte Islands, B.C., Can.	**32**	53°00'N	132°00'W
Queen Elizabeth Islands, N.T., Can.	**32**	78°00'N	95°00'W
Queen Maud Land, Ant.	**8**	72°30'S	12°00'E
Queen Maud Mountains, Ant.	**8**	86°00'S	160°00'W
Queensland, Austl.	**14**	22°00'S	145°00'E
Queenstown, Guy.	**72**	7°12'N	58°29'W
Queenstown, S. Afr.	**152**	31°52'S	26°52'E
Quelimane, Moz.	**118**	17°53'S	36°51'E
Quemoy, Tai.	**162**	24°27'N	118°23'E
Quepos, C.R.	**44**	9°27'N	84°09'W
Querétaro, Mex.	**113**	20°36'N	100°23'W
Quetta, Pak.	**131**	30°12'N	67°00'E
Quevedo, Ec.	**51**	1°02'S	79°29'W
Quezaltenango, Guat.	**70**	14°50'N	91°31'W
Quezon City, Phil.	**136**	14°38'N	121°00'E
Quibdó, Col.	**42**	5°42'N	76°40'W
Quilá, Mex.	**113**	24°23'N	107°13'W
Quillabamba, Peru	**135**	12°49'S	72°43'W
Quillacas, Bol.	**22**	19°14'S	66°58'W
Quillacollo, Bol.	**22**	17°26'S	66°17'W
Quillota, Chile	**37**	32°53'S	71°16'W
Quilpué, Chile	**37**	33°03'S	71°27'W
Quimper, Fr.	**58**	48°00'N	4°06'W
Quincemil, Peru	**135**	13°16'S	70°38'W
Qui Nhon, Viet.	**184**	13°46'N	109°14'E
Quito, Ec.	**51**	0°13'S	78°30'W
Qus, Egypt	**52**	25°55'N	32°45'E

R

Name	Page	Lat.	Long.
Rába, Eur.	**76**	47°42'N	17°38'E
Rabat, Malta	**109**	35°52'N	14°25'E
Rabat, Mor.	**117**	34°02'N	6°51'W
Rabaul, Pap. N. Gui.	**133**	4°12'S	152°12'E
Rach Gia, Viet.	**184**	10°01'N	105°05'E
Racibórz, Pol.	**138**	50°06'N	18°13'E
Radom, Pol.	**138**	51°25'N	21°10'E
Radomsko, Pol.	**138**	51°05'N	19°25'E
Rafaela, Arg.	**11**	31°16'S	61°29'W
Rahal Gdid, Malta	**109**	35°52'N	14°30'E
Rahimyar Khan, Pak.	**131**	28°25'N	70°18'E
Rainier, Mount, Wa., U.S.	**178**	46°52'N	121°46'W
Raipur, India	**79**	21°14'N	81°38'E
Raiti, Nic.	**125**	14°35'N	85°02'W
Rajahmundry, India	**79**	16°59'N	81°47'E
Rajang, Malay.	**107**	2°04'N	111°12'E
Rajasthan, India	**79**	27°00'N	74°00'E
Rajkot, India	**79**	22°18'N	70°47'E
Rajshahi, Bngl.	**17**	24°22'N	88°36'E
Rakaposhi, Pak.	**131**	36°10'N	74°30'E
Rakata Island, Indon.	**81**	6°10'S	105°26'E
Raleigh, N.C., U.S.	**178**	35°46'N	78°38'W
Ralik Chain, Marsh. Is.	**109**	8°00'N	167°00'E
Ramath Gan, Isr.	**86**	32°05'N	34°49'E
Ramla, Isr.	**86**	31°55'N	34°52'E
Ramm, Mount, Jord.	**94**	29°35'N	35°24'E
Ramon, Mount, Isr.	**86**	30°30'N	34°38'E
Ramsey, I. of Man	**85**	54°20'N	4°21'W
Ramsgate, Eng., U.K.	**175**	51°20'N	1°25'E
Ramu, Bngl.	**17**	21°25'N	92°07'E
Rancagua, Chile	**37**	34°10'S	70°45'W
Randers, Den.	**48**	56°28'N	10°03'E
Rangitikei, N.Z.	**124**	40°18'S	175°14'E
Rangkasbitung, Indon.	**81**	6°21'S	106°15'E
Rangoon, Burma	**29**	16°47'N	96°10'E
Rangpur, Bngl.	**17**	25°45'N	89°15'E
Rann of Kutch, Asia	**79**	24°00'N	70°00'E
Ranong, Thai.	**164**	9°58'N	98°38'E
Rarotonga, Cook Is.	**44**	21°14'S	159°46'W
Ras al-Naqb, Jord.	**94**	30°00'N	35°29'E
Ras Balabakk, Leb.	**101**	34°15'N	36°25'E
Ras Dashen, Mount, Eth.	**54**	13°10'N	38°26'E
Rashayya, Leb.	**101**	33°30'N	35°51'E
Rashid, Egypt	**52**	31°24'N	30°25'E
Rasht, Iran	**82**	37°16'N	49°36'E
Ratak Chain, Marsh. Is.	**109**	9°00'N	171°00'E
Rathenow, Ger., E.	**64**	52°36'N	12°20'E
Ratnapura, Sri L.	**155**	6°41'N	80°24'E
Raukumara Range, N.Z.	**124**	37°47'S	178°02'E
Rauma, Fin.	**57**	61°08'N	21°30'E
Raung, Mount, Indon.	**81**	8°08'S	114°03'E
Ravelo, Bol.	**22**	18°48'S	65°32'W
Ravenna, Italy	**88**	44°25'N	12°12'E
Ravensburg, Ger., W.	**64**	47°47'N	9°37'E
Ravensthorpe, Austl.	**14**	33°35'S	120°02'E
Ravi, Asia	**131**	30°35'N	71°48'E
Rawalpindi, Pak.	**131**	33°36'N	73°04'E
Rawson, Arg.	**11**	34°36'S	60°04'W
Razgrad, Bul.	**27**	43°32'N	26°31'E
Reading, Eng., U.K.	**175**	51°28'N	0°59'W
Real Cordillera, Bol.	**22**	17°00'S	67°10'W
Recife, Braz.	**24**	8°03'S	34°54'W
Red, see Yuan, Asia	**38**	20°17'N	106°34'E
Red, U.S.	**178**	31°00'N	91°40'W
Red Deer, Ab., Can.	**32**	52°16'N	113°48'W
Red Sea	**147**	20°00'N	38°00'E
Red Volta, Afr.	**28**	10°55'N	0°35'W
Ree, Lake, Ire.	**84**	53°35'N	8°00'W
Regensburg, Ger., W.	**64**	49°01'N	12°06'E
Reggio di Calabria, Italy	**88**	38°07'N	15°39'E
Regina, Sk., Can.	**32**	50°25'N	104°39'W
Régina, Fr. Gu.	**60**	4°19'N	52°08'W
Rehovoth, Isr.	**86**	31°54'N	34°49'E
Reigate, Eng., U.K.	**175**	51°14'N	0°13'W
Reims, Fr.	**58**	49°15'N	4°02'E
Ré Island, Fr.	**58**	46°12'N	1°25'W
Remanso, Braz.	**24**	9°41'S	42°04'W
Rémire, Fr. Gu.	**60**	4°53'N	52°17'W
Remscheid, Ger., W.	**64**	51°11'N	7°11'E
Rendsburg, Ger., W.	**64**	54°18'N	9°40'E
Reng Mountain, Bngl.	**17**	21°59'N	92°36'E
Rengo, Chile	**37**	34°25'S	70°52'W
Rennell, Sol. Is.	**151**	11°40'S	160°10'E
Rennes, Fr.	**58**	48°05'N	1°41'W
Répce, Eur.	**76**	47°41'N	17°03'E
Requena, Peru	**135**	4°58'S	73°50'W
Resistencia, Arg.	**11**	27°27'S	58°59'W
Reşiţa, Rom.	**142**	45°17'N	21°53'E
Resolution Island, N.Z.	**124**	45°40'S	166°40'E
Retalhuleu, Guat.	**70**	14°32'N	91°41'W
Retamosa, Ur.	**181**	33°35'S	54°44'W
Reutlingen, Ger., W.	**64**	48°29'N	9°11'E
Reunion, Afr.	**141**	21°06'S	55°36'E
Reventazón, Peru	**135**	6°10'S	80°58'W
Revillagigedo Islands, Mex.	**113**	19°00'N	111°30'W
Rey, Iran	**82**	35°35'N	51°25'E
Reyes, Bol.	**22**	14°19'S	67°23'W

Name	Page	Lat.	Long.
Reykjavík, Ice.	**77**	64°09'N	21°51'W
Reynosa, Mex.	**113**	26°07'N	98°18'W
Rhaetian Alps, Eur.	**160**	46°30'N	10°00'E
Rheine, Ger., W.	**64**	52°17'N	7°26'E
Rhine, Eur.	**64**	51°52'N	6°03'E
Rhir, Cape, Mor.	**117**	30°38'N	9°55'W
Rhode Island, U.S.	**178**	41°40'N	71°30'W
Rhodes, Grc.	**67**	36°26'N	28°13'E
Rhodes, Grc.	**67**	36°10'N	28°00'E
Rhodope Mountains, Eur.	**27**	41°30'N	24°30'E
Rhondda, Wales, U.K.	**175**	51°40'N	3°27'W
Rhône, Eur.	**58**	43°20'N	4°50'E
Ribeirão Prêto, Braz.	**24**	21°10'S	47°48'W
Riberalta, Bol.	**22**	10°59'S	66°06'W
Richmond, Va., U.S.	**178**	37°33'N	77°27'W
Riesa, Ger., E.	**64**	51°18'N	13°17'E
Rieti, Italy	**88**	42°24'N	12°51'E
Riga, U.S.S.R.	**172**	56°57'N	24°06'E
Rigestan Desert, Afg.	**2**	31°00'N	65°00'E
Rigi, Switz.	**160**	47°05'N	8°30'E
Rijeka, Yugo.	**189**	45°20'N	14°27'E
Rijssen, Neth.	**122**	52°18'N	6°30'E
Rima, Nig.	**127**	13°04'N	5°10'E
Rimini, Italy	**88**	44°04'N	12°34'E
Rimnicu-Vîlcea, Rom.	**142**	45°06'N	24°22'E
Rinconada, Arg.	**11**	22°26'S	66°10'W
Ringkøbing Bay, Den.	**48**	56°00'N	8°15'E
Ringsted, Den.	**48**	55°27'N	11°49'E
Ringvass Island, Nor.	**129**	69°55'N	19°15'E
Riobamba, Ec.	**51**	1°40'S	78°38'W
Rio Branco, Braz.	**24**	9°58'S	67°48'W
Rio Branco, Ur.	**181**	32°34'S	53°25'W
Rio Claro, Trin.	**166**	10°18'N	61°11'W
Rio Colorado, Arg.	**11**	39°01'S	64°05'W
Rio Cuarto, Arg.	**11**	33°08'S	64°20'W
Rio de Janeiro, Braz.	**24**	22°54'S	43°14'W
Rio de Janeiro, Braz.	**24**	22°00'S	42°30'W
Rio Gallegos, Arg.	**11**	51°38'S	69°13'W
Rio Grande, Arg.	**11**	53°47'S	67°42'W
Rio Grande, Braz.	**24**	32°02'S	52°05'W
Rio Grande, Mex.	**113**	23°50'N	103°02'W
Rio Grande, Nic.	**125**	12°54'N	83°32'W
Rio Grande do Norte, Braz.	**24**	5°45'S	36°00'W
Rio Grande do Sul, Braz.	**24**	30°00'S	54°00'W
Rioja, Peru	**135**	6°05'S	77°09'W
Rio Mulato, Bol.	**22**	19°42'S	66°47'W
Rio Negro, Arg.	**11**	40°00'S	67°00'W
Rio Negro Reservoir, Ur.	**181**	32°45'S	56°00'W
Rioverde, Mex.	**113**	21°56'N	99°59'W
Rishon le Zion, Isr.	**86**	31°58'N	34°48'E
Rivas, Nic.	**125**	11°26'N	85°50'W
Rivera, Ur.	**181**	30°54'S	55°31'W
Riverside, Ca., U.S.	**178**	33°57'N	117°23'W
Riviera, Italy	**88**	45°15'N	9°30'E
Rivière des Anguilles, Mrts.	**111**	20°29'S	57°32'E
Rivière-du-Loup, P.Q., Can.	**32**	47°50'N	69°32'W
Riyadh (ar-Riyad), Sau. Ar.	**147**	24°38'N	46°43'E
Road Town, V.I., Br.	**185**	18°27'N	64°37'W
Roatán, Hond.	**74**	16°18'N	86°35'W
Robertsport, Lib.	**102**	6°45'N	11°22'W
Roboré, Bol.	**22**	18°20'S	59°45'W
Rocafuerte, Ec.	**51**	0°55'S	80°28'W
Rocha, Ur.	**181**	34°29'S	54°20'W
Rochester, N.Y., U.S.	**178**	43°09'N	77°36'W
Rockefeller Plateau, Ant.	**8**	80°00'S	135°00'W
Rockhampton, Austl.	**14**	23°23'S	150°31'E
Rocklands, Swaz.	**158**	25°55'S	31°20'E
Rockstone, Guy.	**72**	5°59'N	58°33'W
Rocky Mountains, N.A.	**178**	48°00'N	116°00'W
Rodonit, Cape, Alb.	**3**	41°35'N	19°27'E
Roeselare, Bel.	**19**	50°57'N	3°08'E
Rogagua, Lake, Bol.	**22**	13°43'S	66°54'W
Rojas, Arg.	**11**	34°12'S	60°44'W
Rojo, Cape, P.R.	**140**	17°56'N	67°11'W
Rokel, S.L.	**149**	8°33'N	12°48'W
Roman, Rom.	**142**	46°55'N	26°56'E
Romania, Eur.	**142**	46°00'N	25°30'E
Rome, Italy	**88**	41°54'N	12°29'E
Ronde Island, Gren.	**68**	12°18'N	61°35'W
Rondônia, Braz.	**24**	10°52'S	61°57'W
Rondônia, Braz.	**24**	11°00'S	63°00'W
Rønne, Den.	**48**	55°06'N	14°42'E
Ronne Ice Shelf, Ant.	**8**	78°30'S	61°00'W
Ronse, Bel.	**19**	50°45'N	3°36'E
Roosendaal, Neth.	**122**	51°32'N	4°28'E
Roosevelt Island, Ant.	**8**	79°30'S	162°00'W
Roque Perez, Arg.	**11**	35°25'S	59°20'W
Roraima, Braz.	**24**	1°00'N	61°00'W
Roraima, Mount, S.A.	**72**	5°12'N	60°44'W
Rorschach, Switz.	**160**	47°29'N	9°30'E
Rosa, Monte, Eur.	**160**	45°55'N	7°52'E
Rosario, Arg.	**11**	32°57'S	60°40'W
Rosario, Mex.	**113**	30°01'N	115°40'W
Rosario del Tala, Arg.	**11**	32°18'S	59°09'W
Roscommon, Ire.	**84**	53°38'N	8°11'W
Roseau, Dom.	**49**	15°18'N	61°24'W
Rose Belle, Mrts.	**111**	20°24'S	57°36'E
Rose Hall, Guy.	**72**	6°16'N	57°21'W
Rose-Hill, Mrts.	**111**	20°14'S	57°27'E
Rosenheim, Ger., W.	**64**	47°51'N	12°07'E
Rosignol, Guy.	**72**	6°17'N	57°32'W
Rosita, Nic.	**125**	13°53'N	84°24'W
Roskilde, Den.	**48**	55°39'N	12°05'E
Ross, Point, Norf. I.	**128**	29°04'S	167°56'E
Rossan Point, Ire.	**84**	54°42'N	8°48'W
Ross Ice Shelf, Ant.	**8**	81°30'S	175°00'W
Ross Sea, Ant.	**8**	76°00'S	175°00'W
Rostock, Ger., E.	**64**	54°05'N	12°07'E
Rostov-on-Don, U.S.S.R.	**172**	47°14'N	39°42'E
Rotondo, Mount, Fr.	**58**	42°13'N	9°03'E
Rotorua, N.Z.	**124**	38°09'S	176°15'E
Rotterdam, Neth.	**122**	51°55'N	4°28'E
Roubaix, Fr.	**58**	50°42'N	3°10'E
Rouen, Barb.	**18**	13°05'N	59°34'W
Rouen, Fr.	**58**	49°26'N	1°05'E
Round Island, Mrts.	**111**	19°51'S	57°48'E
Roura, Fr. Gu.	**60**	4°44'N	52°20'W
Rouyn, P.Q., Can.	**32**	48°15'N	79°01'W
Rovaniemi, Fin.	**57**	66°34'N	25°48'E

Name	Page	Lat.	Long.
Rovigo, Italy	88	45°04'N	11°47'E
Rovuma, Afr.	118	10°29'S	40°28'E
Roxa Island, Gui.-B.	71	11°15'N	15°40'W
Roxas, Phil.	136	12°35'N	121°31'E
Roxborough, Trin.	166	11°15'N	60°35'W
Royal Canal, Ire.	84	53°21'N	6°15'W
Ruahine Range, N.Z.	124	40°00'S	176°06'E
Ruapehu, Mount, N.Z.	124	39°17'S	175°34'E
Rub Al-Khali (Empty Quarter), Sau. Ar.	147	20°00'N	51°00'E
Rubio, Ven.	183	7°43'N	72°22'W
Rudolf, Lake, Afr.	96	3°30'N	36°05'E
Rufiji, Tan.	163	8°00'S	39°20'E
Rufino, Arg.	11	34°16'S	62°42'W
Rufisque, Sen.	148	14°43'N	17°17'W
Rügen, Ger., E.	64	54°25'N	13°24'E
Rugwero, Lake, Afr.	30	2°25'S	30°15'E
Ruhengeri, Rw.	143	1°30'S	29°38'E
Ruhr, Ger., W.	64	51°27'N	6°44'E
Rukwa, Lake, Tan.	163	8°00'S	32°25'E
Rum Cay, Bah.	16	23°40'N	74°53'W
Rurrenabaque, Bol.	22	14°28'S	67°34'W
Ruse, Bul.	27	43°50'N	25°57'E
Rüsselsheim, Ger., W.	64	50°00'N	8°25'E
Rutana, Bdi.	30	3°55'S	30°00'E
Ruvubu, Afr.	30	2°23'S	30°47'E
Ruvuma, Afr.	163	10°29'S	40°28'E
Ruwenzori, Afr.	170	0°23'N	29°54'E
Ruyigi, Bdi.	30	3°29'S	30°15'E
Ruzizi, Afr.	30	3°16'S	29°14'E
Rwanda, Afr.	143	2°30'S	30°00'E
Rybnik, Pol.	138	50°06'N	18°32'E
Rysy, Eur.	138	49°12'N	20°04'E
Ryukyu Islands, Japan	93	26°30'N	128°00'E
Rzeszów, Pol.	138	50°03'N	22°00'E

S

Name	Page	Lat.	Long.
Saale, Eur.	64	51°57'N	11°55'E
Saarbrücken, Ger., W.	64	49°14'N	6°59'E
Saarlouis, Ger., W.	64	49°21'N	6°45'E
Saavedra, Arg.	11	37°45'S	62°22'W
Šabac, Yugo.	189	44°45'N	19°42'E
Sabadell, Spain	154	41°33'N	2°06'E
Sabah, Malay.	107	5°20'N	117°10'E
Sabana de la Mar, Dom. Rep.	50	19°04'N	69°23'W
Sabanagrande, Hond.	74	13°50'N	87°15'W
Sabha, Libya	103	27°03'N	14°26'E
Sabzevar, Iran	82	36°13'N	57°42'E
Sacramento, Ca., U.S.	178	38°34'N	121°29'W
Sada, Yemen	187	16°52'N	43°37'E
Sado, Japan	93	38°00'N	138°25'E
Sado, Port.	139	38°29'N	8°55'W
Safad, Isr.	86	32°58'N	35°30'E
Safata Bay, W. Sam.	187	14°00'S	171°50'W
Safatulafei, W. Sam.	187	13°40'S	172°07'W
Safi, Mor.	117	32°20'N	9°17'W
Safid Mountains, Afg.	2	34°30'N	63°30'E
Sagami Gulf, Japan	93	35°00'N	139°30'E
Sage, Mount, V.I., Br.	185	18°25'N	64°39'W
Saginaw, Mi., U.S.	178	43°25'N	83°56'W
Sagua de Tánamo, Cuba	45	20°35'N	75°14'W
Sagua la Grande, Cuba	45	22°49'N	80°05'W
Sagunto, Spain	154	39°41'N	0°16'W
Saharanpur, India	79	29°58'N	77°33'E
Sahel, Mali	108	15°00'N	8°00'W
Sahiwal, Pak.	131	30°40'N	73°06'E
Sahuaripa, Mex.	113	29°03'N	109°14'W
Sahuayo, Mex.	113	20°04'N	102°43'W
Saidpur, Bngl.	17	25°47'N	88°54'E
Saint Albans, Eng., U.K.	175	51°46'N	0°21'W
Saint Alban's Head, Eng., U.K.	175	50°34'N	2°04'W
Saint-André, Reu.	141	20°57'S	55°39'E
Saint-André, Cape, Madag.	105	16°11'S	44°27'E
Saint Ann's Bay, Jam.	91	18°26'N	77°08'W
Saint Anthony, Nf., Can.	32	51°22'N	55°35'W
Saint Bernardino Pass, Switz.	160	46°20'N	9°00'E
Saint Bernard Pass, Eur.	160	45°50'N	7°10'E
Saint-Brieuc, Fr.	58	48°31'N	2°47'W
Saint Croix, V.I.U.S.	185	17°45'N	64°45'W
Saint David's Head, Wales, U.K.	175	51°55'N	5°19'W
Saint David's Island, Ber.	21	32°22'N	64°39'W
Saint-Denis, Reu.	141	20°52'S	55°28'E
Saint-Élie, Fr. Gu.	60	4°50'N	53°17'W
Saintes, Fr.	58	45°45'N	0°52'W
Saint-Étienne, Fr.	58	45°26'N	4°24'E
Saint-François, Guad.	69	16°15'N	61°17'W
Saint George, Ber.	21	32°22'N	64°40'W
Saint-Georges, Fr. Gu.	60	3°54'N	51°48'W
Saint George's, Gren.	68	12°03'N	61°45'W
Saint George's Channel, Eur.	175	52°00'N	6°00'W
Saint George's Island, Ber.	21	32°22'N	64°40'W
Saint-Germain, Fr.	58	48°54'N	2°05'E
Saint Gotthard Pass, Switz.	160	46°33'N	8°34'E
Saint Helena Bay, S. Afr.	152	32°43'S	18°05'E
Saint Helier, Jersey	36	49°12'N	2°37'W
Saint Ignatius Mission, Guy.	72	3°20'N	59°47'W
Saint John, N.B., Can.	32	45°16'N	66°03'W
Saint John, Jersey	36	49°15'N	2°08'W
Saint John, V.I.U.S.	185	18°20'N	64°45'W
Saint John, Lib.	102	6°40'N	9°10'W
Saint Johns, Antig.	9	17°06'N	61°51'W
Saint John's, Nf., Can.	32	47°34'N	52°43'W
Saint-Laurent-du-Maroni, Fr. Gu.	60	5°30'N	54°02'W
Saint Lawrence, N.A.	32	49°30'N	67°00'W
Saint Lawrence, Gulf of, Can.	32	48°00'N	62°00'W
Saint-Louis, Guad.	69	15°57'N	61°19'W
Saint-Louis, Reu.	141	21°16'S	55°25'E
Saint-Louis, Sen.	148	16°02'N	16°30'W
Saint Louis, Mo., U.S.	178	38°37'N	90°11'W

Name	Page	Lat.	Long.
Saint Lucia, N.A.	144	13°53'N	60°58'W
Saint-Malo, Fr.	58	48°39'N	2°01'W
Saint-Malo, Gulf of, Eur.	58	48°45'N	2°00'W
Saint-Marc, Haiti	73	19°07'N	72°42'W
Saint Marc Canal, Haiti	73	18°50'N	72°45'W
Sainte-Marie, Cape, Madag.	105	25°36'S	45°08'E
Saint Mary, Cape, Gam.	62	13°28'N	16°40'W
Saint-Mathieu Point, Fr.	58	48°20'N	4°46'W
Saint-Nazaire, Fr.	58	47°17'N	2°12'W
Saint Paul, Mn., U.S.	178	44°57'N	93°05'W
Saint Paul, Lib.	102	7°10'N	10°00'W
Saint Paul, Cape, Ghana	65	5°49'N	0°57'E
Saint Paul's Point, Pit.	137	25°04'S	130°05'W
Saint Peter Port, Guernsey	36	49°27'N	2°32'W
Saint Peter's Basilica, Vat.	182	41°54'N	12°27'E
Saint Petersburg, Fl., U.S.	178	27°46'N	82°40'W
Saint Peter's Square, Vat.	182	41°54'N	12°27'E
Saint-Pierre, Mart.	110	14°45'N	61°11'W
Saint-Pierre, Reu.	141	21°19'S	55°29'E
Saint Thomas, V.I.U.S.	185	18°21'N	64°55'W
Saint-Vincent, Cape, Madag.	105	21°57'S	43°16'E
Saint Vincent, Cape, Port.	139	37°01'N	9°00'W
Saint Vincent and the Grenadines, N.A.	145	13°15'N	61°12'W
Saipan, N. Mar. Is.	128	15°12'N	145°45'E
Sajama, Mount, Bol.	22	18°06'S	68°54'W
Sakarya, Tur.	168	39°40'N	30°55'E
Sakété, Benin	20	6°43'N	2°40'E
Sakhalin, U.S.S.R.	172	51°00'N	143°00'E
Sal, C.V.	34	16°45'N	22°55'W
Saladillo, Arg.	11	35°38'S	59°46'W
Salado, Arg.	11	31°42'S	60°44'W
Salado, Arg.	11	35°44'S	57°21'W
Salailua, W. Sam.	187	13°41'S	172°34'W
Salamá, Guat.	70	15°06'N	90°16'W
Salamanca, Spain	154	40°58'N	5°39'W
Salamat, Chad	36	9°27'N	18°06'E
Salani, W. Sam.	187	14°00'S	171°33'W
Salatiga, Indon.	81	7°19'S	110°30'E
Salaverry, Peru	135	8°14'S	78°58'W
Saldungaray, Arg.	11	38°12'S	61°47'W
Salé, Mor.	117	34°04'N	6°50'W
Saleimoa, W. Sam.	187	13°49'S	171°51'W
Salekini, Gam.	62	13°29'N	15°58'W
Salem, India	79	11°39'N	78°10'E
Salem, Or., U.S.	178	44°56'N	123°02'W
Salerno, Italy	88	40°41'N	14°47'E
Salgótarján, Hung.	76	48°07'N	19°48'E
Salina Cruz, Mex.	113	16°10'N	95°12'W
Salinas, Ec.	51	2°13'S	80°58'W
Salinas, N.A.	70	16°28'N	90°33'W
Salines, Point, Gren.	68	12°00'N	61°48'W
Salisbury, Eng., U.K.	175	51°05'N	1°48'W
Salonika, Grc.	67	40°38'N	22°56'E
Salta, Arg.	11	24°47'S	65°25'W
Salta, Arg.	11	25°00'S	64°30'W
Saltillo, Mex.	113	25°25'N	101°00'W
Salt Lake City, Ut., U.S.	178	40°45'N	111°53'W
Salto, Arg.	11	34°17'S	60°15'W
Salto, Ur.	181	31°23'S	57°58'W
Saluafata Harbor, W. Sam.	187	13°50'S	171°34'W
Salvador, Braz.	24	12°59'S	38°31'W
Salwa Bay, Asia	141	25°30'N	50°40'E
Salween, Asia	29	16°31'N	97°37'E
Salzburg, Aus.	15	47°48'N	13°02'E
Samalut, Egypt	52	28°18'N	30°42'E
Samaná, Dom. Rep.	50	19°13'N	69°19'W
Samaná Bay, Dom. Rep.	50	19°10'N	69°25'W
Samar, Phil.	136	12°00'N	125°00'E
Samarinda, Indon.	81	0°30'S	117°09'E
Samarkand, U.S.S.R.	172	39°40'N	66°48'E
Samarra, Iraq	83	34°12'N	43°52'E
Samborombón Bay, Arg.	11	36°00'S	57°12'W
Samborondón, Ec.	51	1°57'S	79°44'W
Sambre, Eur.	19	50°28'N	4°52'E
Samchok, Kor., S.	98	37°27'N	129°10'E
Samo, Pap. N. Gui.	133	3°58'S	152°51'E
Sámos, Grc.	67	37°48'N	26°44'E
Samsø, Den.	48	55°52'N	10°37'E
Samsun, Tur.	168	41°17'N	36°20'E
San, Mali	108	13°18'N	4°54'W
San, Asia	95	13°32'N	105°58'E
San, Eur.	138	50°45'N	21°51'E
Saña, Peru	135	6°55'S	79°35'W
Sana, Yemen	187	15°23'N	44°12'E
Sanaga, Cam.	31	3°35'N	9°38'E
San Agustín, Cape, Phil.	136	6°16'N	126°11'E
San Alejo, El Sal.	53	13°26'N	87°58'W
Sanandaj, Iran	82	35°19'N	47°00'E
Sanandita, Bol.	22	21°40'S	63°35'W
San Andrés, Mex.	113	27°14'N	114°14'W
San Andrés Tuxtla, Mex.	113	18°27'N	95°13'W
San Antonio, Belize	20	16°15'N	89°02'W
San Antonio, Chile	37	33°35'S	71°38'W
San Antonio, Tx., U.S.	178	29°25'N	98°29'W
San Antonio, Cape, Arg.	11	36°40'S	56°42'W
San Antonio, Cape, Cuba	45	21°52'N	84°57'W
San Antonio de Bravo, Mex.	113	30°10'N	104°42'W
San Antonio de los Baños, Cuba	45	22°53'N	82°30'W
San Antonio Oeste, Arg.	11	40°44'S	64°56'W
San Benedetto del Tronto, Italy	88	42°57'N	13°53'E
San Benito, Guat.	70	16°55'N	89°54'W
San Bernardo, Chile	37	33°36'S	70°43'W
San Blas, Mex.	113	21°31'N	105°16'W
San Blas Cordillera, Pan.	132	9°18'N	79°00'W
San Borja, Bol.	22	14°49'S	66°51'W
San Carlos, Arg.	11	27°45'S	55°54'W
San Carlos, Chile	37	36°25'S	71°58'W
San Carlos, Eq. Gui.	53	3°27'N	8°33'E
San Carlos, Nic.	125	11°07'N	84°47'W
San Carlos, Para.	134	22°16'S	57°18'W
San Carlos, Ven.	183	9°40'N	68°36'W

Name	Page	Lat.	Long.
San Carlos de Bariloche, Arg.	11	41°09'S	71°18'W
Sánchez, Dom. Rep.	50	19°14'N	69°36'W
San Cristóbal, Dom. Rep.	50	18°25'N	70°06'W
San Cristóbal, Ven.	183	7°46'N	72°14'W
San Cristóbal, Sol. Is.	151	10°36'S	161°45'E
San Cristobal Island, Ec.	51	0°50'S	89°26'W
San Cristóbal las Casas, Mex.	113	16°45'N	92°38'W
Sancti-Spiritus, Cuba	45	21°56'N	79°27'W
Sancy Hill, Fr.	58	45°32'N	2°49'E
Sandakan, Malay.	107	5°50'N	118°07'E
Sand Hill, Belize	20	17°36'N	88°22'W
Sandia, Peru	135	14°17'S	69°26'W
San Diego, Ca., U.S.	178	32°42'N	117°09'W
Sand Island, Mid. Is.	114	28°12'N	177°23'W
Sand Islet, Mid. Is.	114	28°16'N	177°23'W
Sandlands Village, Bah.	16	25°02'N	77°18'W
Sandviken, Swe.	159	60°37'N	16°46'E
San Enrique, Arg.	11	35°47'S	60°22'W
San Felipe, Chile	37	32°45'S	70°44'W
San Felipe, Col.	42	1°55'N	67°06'W
San Felipe, Mex.	113	31°00'N	114°52'W
San Felipe, Ven.	183	10°20'N	68°44'W
San Fernando, Chile	37	34°35'S	71°00'W
San Fernando, Mex.	113	24°50'N	98°10'W
San Fernando, Phil.	136	16°37'N	120°19'E
San Fernando, Trin.	166	10°17'N	61°28'W
San Fernando de Apure, Ven.	183	7°54'N	67°28'W
San Fernando de Atabapo, Ven.	183	4°03'N	67°42'W
San Francisco, Arg.	11	31°26'S	62°05'W
San Francisco, Ca., U.S.	178	37°46'N	122°25'W
San Francisco, Cape, Ec.	51	0°40'N	80°05'W
San Francisco de la Paz, Hond.	74	14°55'N	86°14'W
San Francisco de Macoris, Dom. Rep.	50	19°18'N	70°15'W
San Gabriel, Ec.	51	0°36'N	77°49'W
Sangay Volcano, Ec.	51	2°00'S	78°20'W
San German, P.R.	140	18°05'N	67°03'W
Sangha, Congo	43	2°00'N	15°00'E
Sangolqui, Ec.	51	0°19'S	78°28'W
San Gregorio, Ur.	181	32°37'S	55°40'W
Sangre Grande, Trin.	166	10°35'N	61°07'W
San Ignacio, Bol.	22	14°53'S	65°36'W
San Ignacio, Bol.	22	16°23'S	60°59'W
San Ignacio, Mex.	113	27°27'N	112°51'W
San Ildefonso Mountain, Hond.	74	15°31'N	88°17'W
San Isidro, Arg.	11	34°27'S	58°30'W
San Javier, Bol.	22	14°34'S	64°42'W
San Javier, Bol.	22	16°20'S	62°38'W
San Joaquín, Bol.	22	13°04'S	64°49'W
San Jorge, Arg.	11	31°54'S	61°52'W
San Jorge, Gulf of, Spain	154	40°53'N	1°00'E
San Jorge Gulf, Arg.	11	46°00'S	67°00'W
San José, C.R.	44	9°56'N	84°05'W
San Jose, N. Mar. Is.	128	15°09'N	145°43'E
San Jose, Ca., U.S.	178	37°20'N	121°53'W
San José de Chiquitos, Bol.	22	17°51'S	60°47'W
San José del Cabo, Mex.	113	23°03'N	109°41'W
San José del Guaviare, Col.	42	2°35'N	72°38'W
San José de Mayo, Ur.	181	34°30'S	56°42'W
San José de Ocoa, Dom. Rep.	50	18°33'N	70°30'W
San Juan, Arg.	11	31°32'S	68°31'W
San Juan, Dom. Rep.	50	18°40'N	71°05'W
San Juan, Guat.	70	15°52'N	88°53'W
San Juan, P.R.	140	18°28'N	66°07'W
San Juan, Arg.	11	31°00'S	69°00'W
San Juan, N.A.	125	10°56'N	83°42'W
San Juan del Norte, Nic.	125	10°55'N	83°42'W
San Juan de los Cayos, Ven.	183	11°10'N	68°25'W
San Juan de los Morros, Ven.	183	9°55'N	67°21'W
San Juanillo, C.R.	44	10°02'N	85°44'W
San Juan Sacatepéquez, Guat.	70	14°43'N	90°39'W
San Julián, Arg.	11	49°18'S	67°43'W
Sankt Gallen, Switz.	160	47°25'N	9°23'E
Sankt Pölten, Aus.	15	48°12'N	15°37'E
Sankt Veit, Aus.	15	47°20'N	13°09'E
San Lázaro, Para.	134	22°10'S	57°55'W
San Lorenzo, Arg.	11	32°45'S	60°44'W
San Lorenzo, Ec.	51	1°17'N	78°50'W
Sanlúcar de Barremeda, Spain	154	36°47'N	6°21'W
San Lucas, Bol.	22	20°06'S	65°07'W
San Lucas, Ec.	51	3°45'S	79°15'W
San Luis, Arg.	11	33°18'S	66°21'W
San Luis, Cuba	45	20°12'N	75°51'W
San Luis, Arg.	11	34°00'S	66°00'W
San Luis, Cape, Mex.	113	22°52'N	109°53'W
San Luis, Lake, Bol.	22	13°45'S	64°00'W
San Luis Potosí, Mex.	113	22°09'N	100°59'W
San Luis Rio Colorado, Mex.	113	32°29'N	114°48'W
San Marcelino, El Sal.	53	13°22'N	89°03'W
San Marino, S. Mar.	146	43°55'N	12°28'E
San Marino, Eur.	146	43°56'N	12°25'E
San Martín, Bol.	22	13°08'S	63°43'W
San Martín, Lake, S.A.	37	49°00'S	72°40'W
San Matías Bay, Arg.	11	41°30'S	64°15'W
San Miguel, Bol.	22	16°42'S	61°01'W
San Miguel, Ec.	51	1°44'S	79°01'W
San Miguel, El Sal.	53	13°29'N	88°11'W
San Miguel, Pan.	132	8°27'N	78°56'W
San Miguel, Bol.	22	13°52'S	63°56'W
Sannar, Sudan	156	13°33'N	33°38'E
San Nicolás, Peru	135	15°13'S	75°12'W
San Nicolas de los Arroyos, Arg.	11	33°20'S	60°13'W
Sanniquellie, Lib.	102	7°22'N	8°43'W
San Pablo, Phil.	136	14°04'N	121°19'E
San Pedro, Arg.	11	33°40'S	59°40'W

Name	Page	Lat.	Long.
San Pedro, Bol.	22	14°20'S	64°50'W
San Pedro de las Colonias, Mex.	113	25°45'N	102°59'W
San Pedro de Macoris, Dom. Rep.	50	18°27'N	69°18'W
San Pedro Sacatepéquez, Guat.	70	14°58'N	91°46'W
San Pedro Sula, Hond.	74	15°27'N	88°02'W
San Rafael, Arg.	11	34°36'S	68°20'W
San Rafael Oriente, El Sal.	53	13°23'N	88°21'W
San Ramón, Bol.	22	13°17'S	64°43'W
San Ramón de la Nueva Orán, Arg.	11	23°08'S	64°20'W
San Remo, Italy	88	43°49'N	7°46'E
San Roque, N. Mar. Is.	128	15°15'N	145°47'E
San Salvador, Arg.	11	31°37'S	58°30'W
San Salvador, El Sal.	53	13°42'N	89°12'W
San Salvador (Watling I.), Bah.	16	24°02'N	74°28'W
San Salvador de Jujuy, Arg.	11	24°11'S	65°18'W
San Salvador Island, Ec.	51	0°14'S	90°45'W
San Sebastián, P.R.	140	18°20'N	66°59'W
San Sebastián, Spain	154	43°19'N	1°59'W
San Severo, Italy	88	41°41'N	15°23'E
Santa Ana, Bol.	22	13°45'S	65°35'W
Santa Ana, Bol.	22	15°31'S	67°30'W
Santa Ana, Ec.	51	1°13'S	80°23'W
Santa Ana, El Sal.	53	13°59'N	89°34'W
Santa Ana Hills, S.A.	181	31°15'S	55°15'W
Santa Ana Volcano, El Sal.	53	13°50'N	89°38'W
Santa Bárbara, Mex.	113	26°48'N	105°49'W
Santa Catalina, Pan.	132	8°47'N	81°20'W
Santa Catarina, Braz.	24	27°00'S	50°00'W
Santa Clara, Cuba	45	22°24'N	79°58'W
Santa Clara, Mex.	113	29°17'N	107°01'W
Santa Clara de Olimar, Ur.	181	32°55'S	54°58'W
Santa Clotilde, Peru	135	2°34'S	73°44'W
Santa Cruz, Arg.	11	50°01'S	68°31'W
Santa Cruz, Bol.	22	17°48'S	63°10'W
Santa Cruz, C.R.	44	10°16'N	85°36'W
Santa Cruz, Mex.	113	23°05'N	97°50'W
Santa Cruz, Arg.	11	49°00'S	70°00'W
Santa Cruz Cabrália, Braz.	24	16°17'S	39°02'W
Santa Cruz de Tenerife, Spain	154	28°28'N	16°14'W
Santa Cruz Island, Ec.	51	0°38'S	90°23'W
Santa Cruz Islands, Sol. Is.	151	11°00'S	166°15'E
Santa Elena, Ec.	51	2°14'S	80°51'W
Santa Elena, Cape, C.R.	44	10°54'N	85°57'W
Santa Elena de Uairén, Ven.	183	4°37'N	61°08'W
Santa Fe, Arg.	11	31°38'S	60°42'W
Santa Fé, Cuba	45	21°45'N	82°45'W
Santa Fe, N.M., U.S.	178	35°41'N	105°56'W
Santa Fe, Arg.	11	31°00'S	61°00'W
Santa Inés Island, Chile	37	53°45'S	72°45'W
Santa Isabel, Arg.	11	36°15'S	66°56'W
Santa Isabel, P.R.	140	17°58'N	66°24'W
Santa Isabel, Sol. Is.	151	8°00'S	159°00'E
Santa Isabel Peak, Eq. Gui.	53	3°35'N	8°46'E
Santa Lucia, Ur.	181	34°27'S	56°24'W
Santa Lucia Cotzemalguapa, Guat.	70	14°20'N	91°01'W
Santa María, Arg.	11	26°41'S	66°02'W
Santa Maria, Cape, Ang.	6	13°25'S	12°32'E
Santa Maria, Cape, Port.	139	36°58'N	7°54'W
Santa Maria di Leuca, Cape, Italy	88	39°47'N	18°22'E
Santa Marta, Col.	42	11°15'N	74°13'W
Santana do Livramento, Braz.	24	30°53'S	55°31'W
Santander, Spain	154	43°28'N	3°48'W
Santarém, Braz.	24	2°26'S	54°42'W
Santarem, Port.	139	39°14'N	8°41'W
Santa Rosa, Arg.	11	36°37'S	64°17'W
Santa Rosa, Para.	134	21°46'S	61°43'W
Santa Rosa de Amanadona, Ven.	183	1°29'N	66°55'W
Santa Rosa de Sucumbios, Ec.	51	0°22'N	77°10'W
Santa Rosalía, Mex.	113	27°19'N	112°17'W
Santiago, Bol.	22	18°19'S	59°34'W
Santiago, Chile	37	33°27'S	70°40'W
Santiago, Pan.	132	8°06'N	80°59'W
Santiago, Spain	154	42°53'N	8°33'W
Santiago, Mex.	113	21°36'N	105°26'W
Santiago Atitlán, Guat.	70	14°38'N	91°14'W
Santiago de Cuba, Cuba	45	20°01'N	75°49'W
Santiago del Estero, Arg.	11	28°00'S	63°30'W
Santiago de los Caballeros, Dom. Rep.	50	19°27'N	70°42'W
Santiago Larre, Arg.	11	35°34'S	59°10'W
Sant Julia, And.	5	42°28'N	1°30'E
Santo, Vanuatu	182	15°32'S	167°08'E
Santo Antão, C.V.	34	17°05'N	25°10'W
Santo António, S. Tom./P.	146	1°39'N	7°26'E
Santo Antônio do Içá, Braz.	24	3°05'S	67°57'W
Santo Domingo, Dom. Rep.	50	18°28'N	69°54'W
Santo Domingo de los Colorados, Ec.	51	0°15'S	79°09'W
Santo Filomena, Braz.	24	9°07'S	45°56'W
Santos, Braz.	24	23°57'S	46°20'W
Santo Tomás, Peru	135	14°29'S	72°06'W
Santo Tomé, Arg.	11	31°40'S	60°46'W
San Vicente, El Sal.	53	13°38'N	88°48'W
San Vicente, Mex.	113	31°20'N	116°15'W
San Vicente de Baracaldo, Spain	154	43°18'N	2°59'W
San Vicente del Caguán, Col.	42	2°07'N	74°46'W
São Carlos, Braz.	24	22°01'S	47°54'W
São Francisco, Braz.	24	10°30'S	36°24'W
São João da Madeira, Port.	139	40°54'N	8°30'W

Name	Page	Lat.	Long.
São José do Rio Prêto, Braz.	24	20°48'S	49°23'W
São Luís, Braz.	24	2°31'S	44°16'W
São Manuel, Braz.	24	7°21'S	58°03'W
São Miguel, Port.	139	37°47'N	25°30'W
Saone, Fr.	58	45°44'N	4°50'E
São Nicolau, C.V.	34	16°35'N	24°15'W
São Paulo, Braz.	24	23°32'S	46°37'W
São Paulo, Braz.	24	22°00'S	49°00'W
São Rafael, Braz.	24	5°47'S	36°55'W
São Roque, Cape, Braz.	24	5°29'S	35°16'W
São Sebastião, Point, Moz.	118	22°07'S	35°30'E
São Tiago, C.V.	34	15°05'N	23°40'W
São Tomé, S. Tom./P.	146	0°20'N	6°44'E
São Tomé, S. Tom./P.	146	0°12'N	6°39'E
Sao Tome and Principe, Afr.	146	1°00'N	7°00'E
São Tomé Peak, S. Tom./P.	146	0°16'N	6°33'E
Saoura Wadi, Alg.	4	29°00'N	0°55'W
São Vicente, C.V.	34	16°50'N	25°00'W
Sapele, Nig.	127	5°54'N	5°41'E
Sapitwa, Mwi.	106	15°57'S	35°36'E
Sapporo, Japan	93	43°03'N	141°21'E
Saquena, Peru	135	4°40'S	73°31'W
Saragossa, Spain	154	41°38'N	0°53'W
Saraguro, Ec.	51	3°36'S	79°13'W
Sarajevo, Yugo.	189	43°52'N	18°25'E
Saramacca, Sur.	157	5°55'N	55°53'W
Sarandë, Alb.	3	39°52'N	20°00'E
Sarandí del Yi, Ur.	181	33°21'S	55°38'W
Sara Peak, Nig.	127	9°41'N	9°17'E
Saratov, U.S.S.R.	172	51°34'N	46°02'E
Saravan, Laos	100	15°43'N	106°25'E
Sarawak, Malay.	107	2°30'N	113°30'E
Sardinia, Italy	88	40°00'N	9°00'E
Sarektjåkkå, Swe.	159	67°25'N	17°46'E
Sarh, Chad	36	9°09'N	18°23'E
Sari, Iran	82	36°34'N	53°04'E
Sariwon, Kor., N.	98	38°31'N	125°44'E
Sark, Guernsey	36	49°26'N	2°21'W
Sarmiento, Arg.	11	45°36'S	69°05'W
Saronikós Bay, Grc.	67	37°54'N	23°12'E
Sarstoon, N.A.	20	15°53'N	88°55'W
Sárviz, Hung.	76	46°24'N	18°41'E
Sasamungga, Sol. Is.	151	7°02'S	156°47'E
Sasebo, Japan	93	33°10'N	129°43'E
Saskatchewan, Can.	32	54°00'N	105°00'W
Saskatchewan, Can.	32	53°12'N	99°16'W
Saskatoon, Sk., Can.	32	52°07'N	106°38'W
Sassandra, I.C.	90	4°58'N	6°05'W
Sassandra, I.C.	90	4°58'N	6°05'W
Sassari, Italy	88	40°44'N	8°33'E
Sataua, W. Sam.	187	13°28'S	172°40'W
Satkania, Bngl.	17	22°04'N	92°03'E
Satpura Range, India	79	22°00'N	78°00'E
Satsunan Islands, Japan	93	29°00'N	130°00'E
Satu Mare, Rom.	142	47°48'N	22°53'E
Sauðárkrókur, Ice.	77	65°46'N	19°41'W
Saudi Arabia, Asia	147	25°00'N	45°00'E
Saül, Fr. Gu.	60	3°37'N	53°12'W
Sault Sainte Marie, On., Can.	32	46°31'N	84°20'W
Saumâtre, Lake, Haiti	73	18°35'N	72°00'W
Saurimo, Ang.	6	9°39'S	20°24'E
Sauteurs, Gren.	68	12°14'N	61°38'W
Sava, Yugo.	189	44°50'N	20°26'E
Savai'i, W. Sam.	187	13°35'S	172°25'W
Savalou, Benin	20	7°56'N	1°58'E
Savannakhet, Laos	100	16°33'N	104°45'E
Savanna-la-Mar, Jam.	91	18°13'N	78°08'W
Save (Sabi), Afr.	118	21°00'S	35°02'E
Savitaipale, Fin.	57	61°12'N	27°42'E
Savona, Italy	88	44°17'N	8°30'E
Savusavu, Fiji	56	16°16'S	179°21'E
Savu Sea, Indon.	81	9°40'S	122°00'E
Sawwan, al-, Jord.	94	30°45'N	37°15'E
Sayan Mountains, Asia	172	52°45'N	96°00'E
Scafell Pikes, Eng., U.K.	175	54°27'N	3°12'W
Scarboro, Barb.	18	13°04'N	59°33'W
Scarborough, Trin.	166	11°11'N	60°44'W
Scarborough, Eng., U.K.	175	54°17'N	0°24'W
Schaan, Liech.	104	47°10'N	9°31'E
Schaerbeek, Bel.	19	50°51'N	4°23'E
Schaffhausen, Switz.	160	47°42'N	8°38'E
Schefferville, P.Q., Can.	32	54°48'N	66°50'W
Schelde, Eur.	19	51°22'N	4°15'E
Schiedam, Neth.	122	51°55'N	4°24'E
Schleswig, Ger., W.	64	54°31'N	9°33'E
Schönebeck, Ger., E.	64	52°01'N	11°44'E
Schouwen, Neth.	122	51°43'N	3°50'E
Schwäbische Alb, Ger., W.	64	48°25'N	9°30'E
Schwechat, Aus.	15	48°08'N	16°29'E
Schwedt, Ger., E.	64	53°03'N	14°17'E
Schweinfurt, Ger., W.	64	50°03'N	10°14'E
Schwerin, Ger., E.	64	53°38'N	11°25'E
Schwyz, Switz.	160	47°02'N	8°40'E
Sciacca, Italy	88	37°30'N	13°06'E
Scilly, Isles of, Eng., U.K.	175	49°55'N	6°20'W
Scotland, U.K.	175	57°00'N	4°00'W
Scranton, Pa., U.S.	178	41°24'N	75°39'W
Scunthorpe, Eng., U.K.	175	53°36'N	0°38'W
Scutari, Lake, Eur.	3	42°12'N	19°18'E
Seatoun, N.Z.	124	41°19'S	174°50'E
Seattle, Wa., U.S.	178	47°36'N	122°19'W
Seaward Roads, Mid. Is.	114	28°13'N	177°25'W
Sebastián Vizcaino Bay, Mex.	113	28°00'N	114°30'W
Sebes Körös, Eur.	76	46°55'N	20°59'E
Sebou, Wadi, Mor.	117	34°15'N	6°40'W
Sechura Bay, Peru	135	5°42'S	81°00'W
Sedroth, Isr.	86	31°31'N	34°35'E
Ségou, Mali	108	13°27'N	6°16'W
Segovia, Spain	154	40°57'N	4°07'W
Séguéla, I.C.	90	7°57'N	6°40'W
Segura, Sierra de, Spain	154	38°00'N	2°43'W
Seinäjoki, Fin.	57	62°47'N	22°50'E
Seine, Fr.	58	49°26'N	0°26'E
Seine, Bay of the, Fr.	58	49°30'N	0°30'W
Sekondi-Takoradi, Ghana	65	4°55'N	1°43'W
Selenge, Asia	115	52°16'N	106°16'E

Name	Page	Lat.	Long.
Selvas, Braz.	24	5°00'S	68°00'W
Semara, W. Sah.	186	26°44'N	11°41'W
Semarang, Indon.	81	6°58'S	110°25'E
Semeru, Mount, Indon.	81	8°06'S	112°55'E
Semipalatinsk, U.S.S.R.	172	50°28'N	80°13'E
Semnan, Iran	82	35°33'N	53°24'E
Semois, Eur.	19	49°53'N	4°45'E
Sen, Kam.	95	12°32'N	104°28'E
Sena, Bol.	22	11°32'S	67°11'W
Senanayake Samudra Lake, Sri L.	155	7°11'N	81°29'E
Sendai, Japan	93	38°15'N	140°53'E
Senegal, Afr.	148	14°00'N	14°00'W
Senegal, Afr.	148	15°48'N	16°32'W
Senja, Nor.	129	69°20'N	17°30'E
Senta, Yugo.	189	45°56'N	20°04'E
Seoul, Kor., S.	98	37°33'N	126°58'E
Sepik, Pap. N. Gui.	133	3°51'S	144°34'E
Sept-Îles, P.Q., Can.	32	50°12'N	66°23'W
Seraing, Bel.	19	50°36'N	5°29'E
Seram Sea, Indon.	81	2°30'S	128°00'E
Serang, Indon.	81	6°07'S	106°09'E
Serangoon, Sing.	150	1°22'N	103°54'E
Serbia, Yugo.	189	44°00'N	21°00'E
Serembam, Malay.	107	2°43'N	101°56'E
Serengeti Plain, Tan.	163	2°50'S	35°00'E
Sergipe, Braz.	24	10°30'S	37°30'W
Seria, Bru.	26	4°39'N	114°23'E
Serowe, Bots.	23	22°25'S	26°44'E
Serpents Mouth	166	10°00'N	62°00'W
Sérrai, Grc.	67	41°05'N	23°32'E
Serravalle, S. Mar.	146	43°57'N	12°30'E
Sese Islands, Ug.	170	0°20'S	32°20'E
Sète, Fr.	58	43°24'N	3°41'E
Sétif, Alg.	4	36°09'N	5°26'E
Settat, Mor.	117	33°04'N	7°37'W
Setúbal, Port.	139	38°32'N	8°54'W
Setúbal, Bay of, Port.	139	38°27'N	8°53'W
Sevastopol, U.S.S.R.	172	44°36'N	33°32'E
Severnaya Zemlya, U.S.S.R.	172	79°30'N	98°00'E
Seville, Spain	154	37°23'N	5°59'W
Sewa, S.L.	149	7°18'N	12°08'W
Seychelles, Afr.	149	4°35'S	55°40'E
Seychellois, Mount, Sey.	149	4°39'S	55°26'E
Seydisfjördur, Ice.	77	65°16'N	14°00'W
Sfax, Tun.	167	34°44'N	10°46'E
's Gravenhage, see The Hague, Neth.	122	52°06'N	4°18'E
Shabeelle, Webi, Afr.	151	0°01'S	42°45'E
Shache, China	38	38°25'N	77°16'E
Shackleton Ice Shelf, Ant.	8	66°00'S	100°00'E
Shagamu, Nig.	127	6°51'N	3°39'E
Shaib al-Banat, Mount, Egypt	52	26°59'N	33°29'E
Shaki, Nig.	127	8°39'N	3°25'E
Shandi, Sudan	156	16°42'N	33°26'E
Shandong Peninsula, China	38	37°00'N	121°00'E
Shanghai, China	38	31°14'N	121°28'E
Shannon, Ire.	84	52°36'N	9°41'W
Shan Plateau, Burma	29	21°30'N	98°30'E
Shantou, China	38	23°23'N	116°41'E
Shaoguan, China	38	24°50'N	113°37'E
Shaoxing, China	38	30°00'N	120°35'E
Shaoyang, China	38	27°06'N	111°25'E
Sharjah, U.A.E.	174	25°22'N	55°23'E
Shark Bay, Austl.	14	25°30'S	113°30'E
Shebele, Afr.	54	5°00'N	45°03'E
Sheberghan, Afg.	2	36°41'N	65°45'E
Sheffield, Eng., U.K.	175	53°23'N	1°30'W
Shelekhov, Gulf of, U.S.S.R.	172	60°00'N	158°00'E
Shenyang, China	38	41°48'N	123°27'E
Shepparton, Austl.	14	36°23'S	145°25'E
Sherbro Bay, S.L.	149	7°40'N	12°45'W
Sherbro Island, S.L.	149	7°45'N	12°55'W
's-Hertogenbosch, Neth.	122	51°41'N	5°19'E
Shetland Islands, Scot., U.K.	175	60°30'N	1°30'W
Shijak, Alb.	3	41°21'N	19°34'E
Shijiazhuang, China	38	38°03'N	114°28'E
Shikarpur, Pak.	131	27°57'N	68°38'E
Shikoku, Japan	93	33°45'N	133°30'E
Shilka, U.S.S.R.	172	53°22'N	121°32'E
Shillong, India	79	25°34'N	91°53'E
Shimonoseki, Japan	93	33°57'N	130°57'E
Shinkolobwe, Zaire	190	11°02'S	26°35'E
Shiraz, Iran	82	29°36'N	52°32'E
Shire, Afr.	106	17°10'S	35°20'E
Shir Mountain, Iran	82	31°37'N	54°04'E
Shizuoka, Japan	93	34°58'N	138°23'E
Shkodër, Alb.	3	42°05'N	19°30'E
Shkumbin, Alb.	3	41°01'N	19°26'E
Sholapur, India	79	17°41'N	75°55'E
Shreveport, La., U.S.	178	32°30'N	93°44'W
Shrewsbury, Eng., U.K.	175	52°43'N	2°45'W
Shumen, Bul.	27	43°16'N	26°55'E
Shuqra, Yem., P.D.R.	188	13°21'N	45°42'E
Shushtar, Iran	82	32°03'N	48°51'E
Shwebo, Burma	29	22°34'N	95°42'E
Sialkot, Pak.	131	32°30'N	74°31'E
Šibenik, Yugo.	189	43°44'N	15°54'E
Siberia, U.S.S.R.	172	65°00'N	110°00'E
Sibiu, Rom.	142	45°48'N	24°09'E
Sibu, Malay.	107	2°18'N	111°49'E
Sibuyan Sea, Phil.	136	12°50'N	122°40'E
Sicié, Cape, Fr.	58	43°03'N	5°51'E
Sicily, Italy	88	37°30'N	14°00'E
Sicily, Strait of, Eur.	88	37°20'N	11°20'E
Sico, Hond.	74	15°58'N	84°58'W
Sicuani, Peru	135	14°16'S	71°13'W
Sidi bel Abbès, Alg.	4	35°13'N	0°10'W
Sidon, Leb.	101	33°33'N	35°22'E
Sidra, Gulf of, Libya	103	31°30'N	18°00'E
Siedlce, Pol.	138	52°11'N	22°16'E
Siegen, Ger., W.	64	50°52'N	8°02'E
Siem Reap, Kam.	95	13°22'N	103°51'E
Siena, Italy	88	43°19'N	11°21'E
Sierra Colorada, Arg.	11	40°35'S	67°48'W
Sierra de Agua, Belize	20	17°32'N	88°54'W
Sierra Leone, Afr.	149	8°30'N	11°30'W
Sierre, Switz.	160	46°18'N	7°32'E
Sighetul Marmaţiei, Rom.	142	47°56'N	23°54'E
Sighişoara, Rom.	142	46°13'N	24°48'E
Siglufjördur, Ice.	77	66°10'N	18°56'W
Sigsig, Ec.	51	3°01'S	78°45'W
Siguiri, Gui.	71	11°25'N	9°10'W
Sikasso, Mali	108	11°19'N	5°40'W
Sikhote-Alin Mountains, U.S.S.R.	172	48°00'N	138°00'E
Silhouette, Sey.	149	4°29'S	55°14'E
Silistra, Bul.	27	44°07'N	27°16'E
Siljan, Swe.	159	60°50'N	14°45'E
Silkeborg, Den.	48	56°10'N	9°34'E
Silvassa, India	79	20°17'N	73°00'E
Simiti, Col.	42	7°58'N	73°57'W
Simla, India	79	31°06'N	77°10'E
Simplon Pass, Switz.	160	46°15'N	8°02'E
Simpson Desert, Austl.	14	25°00'S	137°00'E
Sinai, Mount, Egypt	52	28°32'N	33°59'E
Sinai Peninsula, Egypt	52	29°30'N	34°00'E
Sinajana, Guam	69	13°28'N	144°45'E
Sincelejo, Col.	42	9°18'N	75°24'W
Sines, Cape, Port.	139	37°57'N	8°53'W
Singapore, Sing.	150	1°17'N	103°51'E
Singapore, Asia	150	1°22'N	103°48'E
Singaraja, Indon.	81	8°07'S	115°06'E
Singatoka, Fiji	56	18°08'S	177°30'E
Singen, Ger., W.	64	47°46'N	8°50'E
Sinnamary, Fr. Gu.	60	5°23'N	52°57'W
Sinnamary, Fr. Gu.	60	5°27'N	53°00'W
Sinnuris, Egypt	52	29°25'N	30°52'E
Sint-Amandsberg, Bel.	19	51°04'N	3°45'E
Sint-Gilles, Bel.	19	50°49'N	4°20'E
Sint Nicolaas, Aruba	12	12°27'N	69°52'W
Sint-Niklaas, Bel.	19	51°10'N	4°08'E
Sint-Truiden, Bel.	19	50°48'N	5°12'E
Sinuiju, Kor., N.	98	40°05'N	124°24'E
Sion, Switz.	160	46°14'N	7°21'E
Sion Hill, Barb.	18	13°05'N	59°30'W
Siparia, Trin.	166	10°08'N	61°30'W
Siping, China	38	43°12'N	124°20'E
Siracuas, Para.	134	21°03'S	61°46'W
Sirajganj, Bngl.	17	24°27'N	89°43'E
Siret, Eur.	142	45°24'N	28°01'E
Sir Francis Drake Channel, V.I., Br.	185	18°25'N	64°30'W
Sisak, Yugo.	189	45°29'N	16°23'E
Sistine Chapel, Vat.	182	41°54'N	12°27'E
Sitra, Bahr.	16	26°09'N	50°38'E
Sittard, Neth.	122	51°00'N	5°53'E
Sittwe, Burma	29	20°09'N	92°54'E
Situbondo, Indon.	81	7°42'S	114°00'E
Sivas, Tur.	168	39°45'N	37°02'E
Sixth Cataract, Sudan	156	16°20'N	32°42'E
Sjællands Point, Den.	48	55°58'N	11°22'E
Skagen, Den.	48	57°44'N	10°36'E
Skagerrak, Eur.	129	57°45'N	9°00'E
Skalka, Swe.	159	66°50'N	18°46'E
Skeldon, Guy.	72	5°53'N	57°08'W
Skeleton Coast, Nmb.	119	21°00'S	13°00'E
Skellefteå, Swe.	159	64°46'N	20°57'E
Skellefteå, Swe.	159	64°42'N	21°06'E
Skien, Nor.	129	59°12'N	9°36'E
Skikda, Alg.	4	36°50'N	6°58'E
Skive, Den.	48	56°34'N	9°02'E
Skopje, Yugo.	189	41°59'N	21°26'E
Skövde, Swe.	159	58°24'N	13°50'E
Skye, Scot., U.K.	175	57°15'N	6°10'W
Slagelse, Den.	48	55°24'N	11°22'E
Slamet, Mount, Indon.	81	7°14'S	109°12'E
Slatina, Rom.	142	44°26'N	24°22'E
Slave Coast, Afr.	65	5°30'N	1°00'E
Slavonski Brod, Yugo.	189	45°10'N	18°01'E
Sliedrecht, Neth.	122	51°49'N	4°45'E
Sliema, Malta	109	35°55'N	14°30'E
Sligo, Ire.	84	54°17'N	8°28'W
Sliven, Bul.	27	42°40'N	26°19'E
Slovenia, Yugo.	189	46°15'N	15°10'E
Slovenské Mountains, Czech.	47	48°45'N	20°00'E
Słupsk, Pol.	138	54°28'N	17°01'E
Slyne Head, Ire.	84	53°24'N	10°13'W
Smålands Sound, Den.	48	55°05'N	11°20'E
Smederevo, Yugo.	189	44°40'N	20°56'E
Smolensk, U.S.S.R.	172	54°47'N	32°03'E
Snæfellness, Ice.	77	64°50'N	23°00'W
Snake, U.S.	178	46°12'N	119°02'W
Sneek, Neth.	122	53°02'N	5°40'E
Sniardwy, Lake, Pol.	138	53°46'N	21°44'E
Snøtinden, Nor.	129	66°38'N	14°00'E
Snowdon, Wales, U.K.	175	53°04'N	4°05'W
Snowy Mountains, Austl.	14	36°30'S	148°20'E
So, Benin	20	6°28'N	2°25'E
Sobaek Mountains, Kor., S.	98	36°00'N	128°00'E
Sobat, Sudan	156	9°22'N	31°33'E
Sobral, Braz.	24	3°42'S	40°21'W
Socompa Pass, S.A.	37	24°27'S	68°18'W
Socotra, Yem., P.D.R.	188	12°30'N	54°00'E
Söderhamn, Swe.	159	61°18'N	17°03'E
Södertälje, Swe.	159	59°12'N	17°37'E
Soest, Neth.	122	52°09'N	5°18'E
Sofia, Bul.	27	42°41'N	23°19'E
Sogamoso, Col.	42	5°43'N	72°56'W
Sogne Fjord, Nor.	129	61°06'N	5°10'E
Soke, Tur.	168	37°45'N	27°24'E
Sokodé, Togo	165	8°59'N	1°08'E
Sokoto, Nig.	127	13°04'N	5°16'E
Sokoto, Nig.	127	11°20'N	4°10'E
Sol, Costa del, Spain	154	36°30'N	4°30'W
Solbad Hall, Aus.	15	47°17'N	11°31'E
Solomon Islands, Oc.	151	8°00'S	159°00'E
Solomon Sea, Oc.	133	8°00'S	153°00'E
Solothurn, Switz.	160	47°13'N	7°32'E
Somalia, Afr.	151	10°00'N	49°00'E
Sombor, Yugo.	189	45°46'N	19°07'E
Somerset Island, Ber.	21	32°17'N	64°52'W
Somerset Island, N.T., Can.	32	73°15'N	93°30'W
Someş (Szamos), Eur.	142	48°07'N	22°22'E
Somme, Fr.	58	50°11'N	1°39'E
Sommen, Swe.	159	58°01'N	15°15'E
Soná, Pan.	132	8°01'N	81°19'W
Sønderborg, Den.	48	54°55'N	9°47'E
Songkhla, Thai.	164	7°12'N	100°36'E
Sonmiani Bay, Pak.	131	25°15'N	66°30'E
Sonora, Mex.	113	28°48'N	111°33'W
Sonsón, Col.	42	5°42'N	75°18'W
Sonsonate, El Sal.	53	13°43'N	89°44'W
Son Tay, Viet.	184	21°08'N	105°30'E
Sopachuy, Bol.	22	19°29'S	64°31'W
Sopot, Pol.	138	54°28'N	18°34'E
Sopron, Hung.	76	47°41'N	16°36'E
Soria, Spain	154	41°46'N	2°28'W
Sør Island, Nor.	129	70°36'N	22°46'E
Soroti, Ug.	170	1°43'N	33°37'E
Sorubi, Afg.	2	34°36'N	69°43'E
Soufrière, St. Luc.	144	13°52'N	61°04'W
Sousel, Braz.	24	2°39'S	51°55'W
Sousse, Tun.	167	35°49'N	10°38'E
South Africa, Afr.	152	30°00'S	26°00'E
Southampton, Eng., U.K.	175	50°55'N	1°25'W
Southampton Island, N.T., Can.	32	64°20'N	84°40'W
South Australia, Austl.	14	30°00'S	135°00'E
South Canal, Haiti	73	18°40'N	73°05'W
South Carolina, U.S.	178	34°00'N	81°00'W
South Comino Channel, Malta	109	36°00'N	14°21'E
South Dakota, U.S.	178	44°15'N	100°00'W
South East Cape, Austl.	14	43°39'S	146°50'E
Southend-on-Sea, Eng., U.K.	175	51°33'N	0°43'E
Southern Alps, N.Z.	124	43°30'S	170°30'E
Southern Sierra Madre, Mex.	113	17°00'N	100°00'W
Southern Uplands, Scot., U.K.	175	55°30'N	3°30'W
South Flevoland, Neth.	122	52°22'N	5°20'E
South Island, N.Z.	124	43°00'S	171°00'E
South Korea, Asia	98	36°30'N	128°00'E
South Magnetic Pole, Ant.	8	66°40'S	140°10'E
South Massif, Haiti	73	18°25'N	73°55'W
South Orkney Islands, B.A.T.	8	60°35'S	45°30'W
South Pole, Ant.	8	90°00'S	0°00'
Southport, Austl.	14	27°58'S	153°25'E
Southport, Eng., U.K.	175	53°39'N	3°01'W
South Shetland Islands, B.A.T.	8	62°00'S	58°00'W
South Shields, Eng., U.K.	175	55°00'N	1°25'W
South Taranaki Bight, N.Z.	124	39°40'S	174°10'E
South Uist, Scot., U.K.	175	57°15'N	7°24'W
Southwest Cape, N.Z.	124	47°17'S	167°28'E
Soyapango, El Sal.	53	13°42'N	89°09'W
Soya Strait, Asia	172	45°45'N	142°00'E
Spain, Eur.	154	40°00'N	4°00'W
Spanish Point, Ber.	21	32°18'N	64°48'W
Spanish Town, Jam.	91	17°59'N	76°57'W
Speightstown, Barb.	18	13°15'N	59°39'W
Spencer Gulf, Austl.	14	34°00'S	137°00'E
Speyer, Ger., W.	64	49°19'N	8°26'E
Spitsbergen, see Svalbard, Eur.	129	78°00'N	20°00'E
Split, Yugo.	189	43°31'N	16°27'E
Spokane, Wa., U.S.	178	47°39'N	117°25'W
Spoleto, Italy	88	42°44'N	12°44'E
Spree, Eur.	64	52°32'N	13°13'E
Springfield, Il., U.S.	178	39°48'N	89°38'W
Spring Garden, Guy.	72	6°59'N	58°31'W
Spring Hall, Barb.	18	13°19'N	59°37'W
Springs, S. Afr.	152	26°13'S	28°25'E
Sragen, Indon.	81	7°26'S	111°02'E
Srbobran, Yugo.	189	45°33'N	19°48'E
Sremska Mitrovica, Yugo.	189	44°58'N	19°37'E
Sreng, Kam.	95	13°21'N	103°27'E
Srepok, Kam.	95	13°33'N	106°16'E
Sri Lanka, Asia	155	7°00'N	81°00'E
Sri Lanka, Sri L.	155	7°00'N	81°00'E
Srinagar, India	79	34°05'N	74°49'E
Stade, Ger., W.	64	53°36'N	9°28'E
Stafford, Eng., U.K.	175	52°48'N	2°07'W
Stanavoi Range, U.S.S.R.	172	56°20'N	126°00'E
Stanke Dimitrov, Bul.	27	42°16'N	23°07'E
Stanley, Falk. Is.	55	51°42'S	57°41'W
Stanley Falls, Zaire	190	0°30'N	25°12'E
Stann Creek, Belize	20	16°58'N	88°13'W
Starachowice, Pol.	138	51°03'N	21°04'E
Stara Pazova, Yugo.	189	44°59'N	20°10'E
Stara Zagora, Bul.	27	42°25'N	25°38'E
Stargard Szczeciński, Pol.	138	53°20'N	15°02'E
Starogard Gdański, Pol.	138	53°59'N	18°33'E
Stavanger, Nor.	129	58°58'N	5°45'E
Stavropol, U.S.S.R.	172	45°02'N	41°59'E
Steep Point, Austl.	14	26°08'S	113°08'E
Stefanie, Lake, Afr.	54	4°40'N	36°50'E
Steg, Switz.	160	47°21'N	8°56'E
Steinkjer, Nor.	129	64°01'N	11°30'E
Stendal, Ger., E.	64	52°36'N	11°51'E
Stevns Bluff, Den.	48	55°18'N	12°27'E
Stewart Island, N.Z.	124	47°00'S	167°50'E
Steyr, Aus.	15	48°03'N	14°25'E
Štip, Yugo.	189	41°44'N	22°12'E
Stirling, Austl.	14	31°54'S	115°47'E
Stirling, Scot., U.K.	175	56°07'N	3°57'W
Stockerau, Aus.	15	48°23'N	16°13'E
Stockholm, Swe.	159	59°20'N	18°03'E
Stoke-on-Trent, Eng., U.K.	175	53°00'N	2°10'W
Stokes Valley, N.Z.	124	41°11'S	174°58'E
Stoney Tunguska, U.S.S.R.	172	61°36'N	90°18'E
Storå, Den.	48	56°19'N	8°19'E
Storavan, Swe.	159	65°40'N	18°15'E
Stornoway, Scot., U.K.	175	58°12'N	6°23'W
Storsjön, Swe.	159	63°12'N	14°18'E
Stralsund, Ger., E.	64	54°19'N	13°05'E
Strangford Lake, N. Ire., U.K.	84	54°30'N	5°36'W
Strasbourg, Fr.	58	48°35'N	7°45'E
Straubing, Ger., W.	64	48°53'N	12°34'E
Streymoy, Faer. Is.	55	62°08'N	7°00'W
Stromboli Island, Italy	88	38°48'N	15°13'E
Struer, Den.	48	56°29'N	8°37'E
Struga, Yugo.	189	41°11'N	20°40'E
Struma, Eur.	67	40°47'N	23°51'E
Strumica, Yugo.	189	41°26'N	22°38'E
Stung Treng, Kam.	95	13°31'N	105°58'E
Stuttgart, Ger., W.	64	48°46'N	9°11'E
Subang, Indon.	81	6°34'S	107°45'E
Subotica, Yugo.	189	46°06'N	19°39'E
Suceava, Rom.	142	47°39'N	26°19'E
Súchil, Mex.	113	23°38'N	103°55'W
Suchitoto, El Sal.	53	13°56'N	89°02'W
Sucre, Bol.	22	19°02'S	65°17'W
Sucre, Ec.	51	1°16'S	80°26'W
Sucúa, Ec.	51	2°28'S	78°10'W
Sudan, Afr.	156	15°00'N	30°00'E
Sudbury, On., Can.	32	46°30'N	81°00'W
Suddie, Guy.	72	7°07'N	58°29'W
Sudeten Mountains, Eur.	47	50°30'N	16°00'E
Sud-Ouest, Point, Mrts.	111	20°28'S	57°47'E
Suðuroy, Faer. Is.	55	61°32'N	6°50'W
Suez, Egypt	52	29°58'N	32°33'E
Suez, Gulf of, Egypt	52	29°00'N	32°50'E
Suez Canal, Egypt	52	29°55'N	32°33'E
Suhl, Ger., E.	64	50°37'N	10°41'E
Suir, Ire.	84	52°15'N	7°00'W
Sukabumi, Indon.	81	6°55'S	106°56'E
Sukkur, Pak.	131	27°42'N	68°52'E
Sulaiman Range, Pak.	131	30°30'N	70°10'E
Sula Islands, Indon.	81	1°52'S	125°22'E
Sulawesi, Indon.	81	2°00'S	121°00'E
Sulitelma, Eur.	129	67°08'N	16°24'E
Sullana, Peru	135	4°53'S	80°41'W
Sulmona, Italy	88	42°03'N	13°55'E
Sulu, Pap. N. Gui.	133	5°25'S	151°00'E
Sulu Archipelago, Phil.	136	6°00'N	121°00'E
Sulu Sea, Asia	136	8°00'N	120°00'E
Sumatra, Indon.	81	1°00'S	103°00'E
Sumba, Faer. Is.	55	61°24'N	6°42'W
Sumedang, Indon.	81	6°52'S	107°55'E
Sumenep, Indon.	81	7°01'S	113°52'E
Sunchon, Kor., S.	98	34°57'N	127°28'E
Sundarbans, Asia	17	22°00'N	89°00'E
Sunda Strait, Indon.	81	6°00'S	105°45'E
Sunderland, Eng., U.K.	175	54°55'N	1°23'W
Sundsvall, Swe.	159	62°23'N	17°18'E
Sungari, China	38	47°44'N	132°32'E
Sun Kosi, Asia	120	26°55'N	87°09'E
Sunyani, Ghana	65	7°20'N	2°20'W
Superior, Lake, N.A.	178	48°00'N	88°00'W
Surabaya, Indon.	81	7°15'S	112°45'E
Surakarta, Indon.	81	7°35'S	110°50'E
Surat, India	79	21°10'N	72°50'E
Surat Thani, Thai.	164	9°08'N	99°19'E
Sûre, Eur.	104	49°44'N	6°31'E
Suriname, S.A.	157	4°00'N	56°00'W
Surt, Libya	103	31°12'N	16°35'E
Surtsey, Ice.	77	63°16'N	20°32'W
Surud Ad, Som.	151	10°41'N	47°18'E
Susques, Arg.	11	23°25'S	66°29'W
Susubona, Sol. Is.	151	8°18'S	159°27'E
Sutherland Falls, N.Z.	124	44°48'S	167°44'E
Suva, Fiji	56	18°08'S	178°25'E
Suvadiva Atoll, Mald.	107	0°30'N	73°15'E
Suwon, Kor., S.	98	37°17'N	127°01'E
Suyo, Peru	135	4°30'S	80°00'W
Svalbard (Spitsbergen), Eur.	129	78°00'N	20°00'E
Svay Rieng, Kam.	95	11°05'N	105°48'E
Svendborg, Den.	48	55°03'N	10°37'E
Sverdlovsk, U.S.S.R.	172	48°05'N	39°40'E
Svetozarevo, Yugo.	189	43°58'N	21°16'E
Svitava, Czech.	47	49°10'N	16°38'E
Swakopmund, Nmb.	119	22°41'S	14°34'E
Swansea, Wales, U.K.	175	51°38'N	3°57'W
Swatow, see Shantou, China	38	23°23'N	116°41'E
Swaziland, Afr.	158	26°30'S	31°30'E
Sweden, Eur.	159	62°00'N	15°00'E
Świdnica, Pol.	138	50°51'N	16°29'E
Świętokrzyskie Mountains, Pol.	138	50°55'N	21°00'E
Swift Current, Sk., Can.	32	50°17'N	107°50'W
Swilly, Lake, Ire.	84	55°10'N	7°38'W
Swindon, Eng., U.K.	175	51°34'N	1°47'W
Świnoujście, Pol.	138	53°53'N	14°14'E
Switzerland, Eur.	160	47°00'N	8°00'E
Sydney, Austl.	14	33°52'S	151°13'E
Sydney, N.S., Can.	32	46°09'N	60°11'W
Sydney Bay, Norf. I.	128	29°04'S	167°57'E
Sylhet, Bngl.	17	24°54'N	91°52'E
Sylt, Ger., W.	64	54°54'N	8°20'E
Syracuse, Italy	88	37°04'N	15°17'E
Syracuse, N.Y., U.S.	178	43°02'N	76°08'W
Syr Darya, U.S.S.R.	172	46°03'N	61°00'E
Syria, Asia	161	35°00'N	38°00'E
Syrian Desert, Asia	83	32°00'N	40°00'E
Szamos (Someş), Eur.	76	48°07'N	22°22'E
Szczecin, Pol.	138	53°24'N	14°32'E
Szczecinek, Pol.	138	53°43'N	16°42'E
Szeged, Hung.	76	46°15'N	20°09'E
Székesfehérvár, Hung.	76	47°12'N	18°25'E
Szolnok, Hung.	76	47°10'N	20°12'E
Szombathely, Hung.	76	47°14'N	16°38'E

T

Name	Page	Lat.	Long.
Tabacunda, Ec.	51	0°03'N	78°12'W
Tabasara Mountains, Pan.	132	8°33'N	81°40'W
Table Mountain, S. Afr.	152	33°57'S	18°25'E
Tabligbo, Togo	165	6°35'N	1°30'E
Tabor, Mount, Isr.	86	32°41'N	35°23'E
Tabora, Tan.	163	5°01'S	32°48'E
Tabou, I.C.	90	4°25'N	7°21'W
Tabriz, Iran	82	38°05'N	46°18'E
Tacloban, Phil.	136	11°15'N	125°00'E
Tacna, Peru	135	18°01'S	70°15'W
Tacuarembó, Ur.	181	31°44'S	55°59'W
Tademait Plateau, Alg.	4	28°30'N	2°00'E
Tadjoura, Gulf of, Dji.	49	11°42'N	43°00'E
Taebaek Mountains, Asia	98	37°40'N	128°50'E
Taedong, Kor., N.	98	38°42'N	125°15'E
Taegu, Kor., S.	98	35°52'N	128°35'E
Taejon, Kor., S.	98	36°20'N	127°26'E
Taga, W. Sam.	187	13°46'S	172°28'W
Tagus, Eur.	154	38°40'N	9°24'W
Tahan Mountain, Malay.	107	4°38'N	102°14'E
Tahat, Alg.	4	23°18'N	5°47'E
Tahiti, Fr. Poly.	60	17°37'S	149°27'W
Tahoua, Niger	126	14°54'N	5°16'E
Tahta, Egypt	52	26°46'N	31°30'E
T'ai-nan, Tai.	162	23°00'N	120°11'E
Taipa, Macao	105	22°09'N	113°33'E
Taipei, Tai.	162	25°03'N	121°30'E
Taita Hills, Kenya	96	3°25'S	38°20'E
Taiwan, Asia	162	23°30'N	121°00'E
Taiwan Strait, Asia	162	24°00'N	119°00'E
Taiyuan, China	38	37°55'N	112°30'E
Taizz, Yemen	187	13°38'N	44°04'E
Tajrish, Iran	82	35°48'N	51°25'E
Tajumulco Volcano, Guat.	70	15°02'N	91°55'W
Takamatsu, Japan	93	34°20'N	134°03'E
Takapuna, N.Z.	124	36°47'S	174°47'E
Takeo, Kam.	95	10°59'N	104°47'E
Takla Makan Desert, China	38	39°00'N	83°00'E
Takutu, S.A.	72	3°27'N	60°06'W
Talagante, Chile	37	33°40'S	70°56'W
Talamanca Cordillera, C.R.	44	9°30'N	83°40'W
Talara, Peru	135	4°34'S	81°17'W
Talasea, Pap. N. Gui.	133	5°20'S	150°05'E
Talavera de la Reina, Spain	154	39°57'N	4°50'W
Talca, Chile	37	35°26'S	71°40'W
Talcahuano, Chile	37	36°43'S	73°07'W
Tall Afar, Iraq	83	36°22'N	42°27'E
Tallahassee, Fl., U.S.	178	30°26'N	84°16'W
Tallinn, U.S.S.R.	172	59°25'N	24°45'E
Talo, Eth.	54	10°44'N	37°55'E
Taloqan, Afg.	2	36°44'N	69°33'E
Tamakautonga, Niue	128	19°05'S	169°55'W
Tamale, Ghana	65	9°25'N	0°50'W
Tame, Col.	42	6°28'N	71°44'W
Tamiahua, Mex.	113	21°16'N	97°27'W
Tamiahua Lagoon, Mex.	113	21°35'N	97°35'W
Tamil Nadu, India	79	11°00'N	78°15'E
Tampa, Fl., U.S.	178	27°56'N	82°27'W
Tampere, Fin.	57	61°30'N	23°45'E
Tampico, Mex.	113	22°13'N	97°51'W
Tamshiyacu, Peru	135	4°05'S	72°58'W
Tamuning, Guam	69	13°29'N	144°46'E
Tamworth, Austl.	14	31°05'S	150°55'E
Tana, Kenya	96	2°32'S	40°31'E
Tana, Lake, Eth.	54	12°00'N	37°20'E
Tananarive, see Antananarivo, Madag.	105	18°55'S	47°31'E
Tanapag, N. Mar. Is.	128	15°14'N	145°45'E
Tanchon, Kor., N.	98	40°27'N	128°54'E
Tandil, Arg.	11	37°19'S	59°09'W
Tando Adam, Pak.	131	25°46'N	68°40'E
Tanega Island, Japan	93	30°40'N	131°00'E
Tanga, Tan.	163	5°04'S	39°06'E
Tangail, Bngl.	17	24°15'N	89°55'E
Tanganyika, Lake, Afr.	190	6°00'S	29°30'E
Tangarare, Sol. Is.	151	9°35'S	159°39'E
Tangerang, Indon.	81	6°11'S	106°37'E
Tangier, Mor.	117	35°48'N	5°45'W
Tangshan, China	38	39°38'N	118°11'E
Tanjungkarang, Indon.	81	5°25'S	105°16'E
Tano, Afr.	65	5°07'N	2°56'W
Tanta, Egypt	52	30°47'N	31°00'E
Tanzania, Afr.	163	6°00'S	35°00'E
Tapachula, Mex.	113	14°54'N	92°17'W
Tapaga, Cape, W. Sam.	187	14°01'S	171°23'W
Tapajós, Braz.	24	2°24'S	54°41'W
Tapalquén, Arg.	11	36°21'S	60°01'W
Tapanahoni, Sur.	157	4°22'N	54°27'W
Taperas, Bol.	22	17°54'S	60°23'W
Taranto, Italy	88	40°28'N	17°15'E
Taranto, Gulf of, Italy	88	40°10'N	17°20'E
Tarapoto, Peru	135	6°30'S	76°20'W
Taraqua, Braz.	24	0°06'N	68°28'W
Tarata, Bol.	22	17°37'S	66°01'W
Tarawa, Kir.	97	1°25'N	173°00'E
Tarica, Nic.	125	12°56'N	84°41'W
Tarija, Bol.	22	21°31'S	64°45'W
Tarim, China	38	41°05'N	86°40'E
Tarim Basin, China	38	39°00'N	83°00'E
Tarkwa, Ghana	65	5°19'N	1°59'W
Tarma, Peru	135	11°25'S	75°42'W
Tarn, Fr.	58	44°05'N	1°06'E
Tarna, Hung.	76	47°31'N	19°59'E
Tarnów, Pol.	138	50°01'N	21°00'E
Tarqui, Peru	135	1°35'S	75°15'W
Tarragona, Spain	154	41°07'N	1°15'E
Tarsus, Tur.	168	36°55'N	34°53'E
Tartagal, Arg.	11	28°40'S	59°52'W
Tashkent, U.S.S.R.	172	41°20'N	69°18'E
Tasikmalaya, Indon.	81	7°20'S	108°12'E
Tåsinge, Den.	48	55°00'N	10°36'E
Tasman, Mount, N.Z.	124	43°34'S	170°09'E
Tasman Bay, N.Z.	124	41°00'S	173°20'E
Tasmania, Austl.	14	43°00'S	147°00'E
Tatabánya, Hung.	76	47°34'N	18°26'E
Tatar Strait, U.S.S.R.	172	50°00'N	141°15'E
Tatry Mountains, Eur.	47	49°12'N	20°05'E
Tau, Am. Sam.	5	14°14'S	169°32'W
Tauern Mountains, Aus.	15	47°10'N	12°30'E
Taumaturgo, Braz.	24	8°57'S	72°48'W
Taungdwingyi, Burma	29	20°01'N	95°33'E
Taunggyi, Burma	29	20°47'N	97°02'E
Taunton, Eng., U.K.	175	51°01'N	3°06'W
Taupo, Lake, N.Z.	124	38°49'S	175°55'E
Tauranga, N.Z.	124	37°42'S	176°10'E
Taurus Mountains, Tur.	168	37°00'N	33°00'E
Taveuni, Fiji	56	16°51'S	179°58'E
Tavoy, Burma	29	14°05'N	98°12'E
Tavua, Fiji	56	17°27'S	177°51'E
Tawa, N.Z.	124	41°10'S	174°51'E
Taymyr Lake, U.S.S.R.	172	74°30'N	102°30'E